Understanding Interpersonal Communication

Understanding Interpersonal Communication

SEVENTH EDITION

Richard L. Weaver II

Bowling Green State University

 HarperCollins *CollegePublishers*

To Robert G. Gunderson and Edgar E. Willis—teachers who have contributed to my growth and development

Acquisitions Editors: *Cynthia Biron/Deirdre Cavanaugh*
Developmental Editor: *Elaine Silverstein*
Project Coordination and Text Design: *Ruttle, Shaw & Wetherill, Inc.*
Cover Designer: *Kay Petronio*
Cover Photographs: *Ron Chapple/FPG International; Mark Harmel/ FPG International; and Jim Whitmer/FPG International*
Photo Researcher: *Diane Kraut*
Electronic Production Manager: *Christine Pearson*
Manufacturing Manager: *Helene G. Landers*
Electronic Page Makeup: *Ruttle, Shaw & Wetherill, Inc.*
Printer and Binder: *R.R. Donnelley & Sons Company*
Cover Printer: *The Lehigh Press, Inc.*

For permission to use copyright material, grateful acknowledgment is made to the copyright holders on p. 521, which is hereby made part of this copyright page.

UNDERSTANDING INTERPERSONAL COMMUNICATION, SEVENTH EDITION

Library of Congress Cataloging-in-Publication Data
Weaver, Richard L., [date–   ]
    Understanding interpersonal communication / Richard L. Weaver II.
      p.   cm.
    Includes bibliographical references (p.   ) and index.
    ISBN 0-673-99581-X
    1. Interpersonal communication. I. Title.
  BF637.C45W35   1996
  158'.2—dc20   95-35466
                                                          CIP

      97 98   9 8 7 6 5 4 3

BRIEF CONTENTS

DETAILED CONTENTS

4 ▶ *Responding to Others: Listening and Feedback*   *118*

7 ▶ *Gender Communication: Understanding the Other Sex*   *244*

8 ▶ *Influencing Others: Interpersonal Persuasion*   *271*

14 ▶ *Experiencing Growth and Change: Communicating with Family*   *494*

PREFACE

▼ The seventh edition of *Understanding Interpersonal Communication*, like the previous editions, is intended to help students understand interpersonal communication and improve their skills in this area. The concepts, principles, and theories of human interaction not only must be learned but also must be made relevant to one's life. Thus, this book, even more than previous editions, emphasizes the practical skills needed to improve communication with others—indeed, the practical skills that evolve naturally from the concepts, principles, and theories discussed.

▲▲▲ *Approach and Focus*

The dual emphasis on concepts and skills underlies both the overall approach of the book and the organization within chapters. Chapters begin with an explanation of concepts and conclude with a discussion of skills. As I was preparing this edition, it became clear that the book was expanding rapidly and some material needed substantial trimming. Cutting material is always difficult, since certain information becomes a favorite for instructors and eliminating it is like losing a prized possession. But decisions had to be made: more on that in "Changes in the Seventh Edition."

I have tried to write a teachable book that covers essential content and a readable book that interests students. To these ends, the chapters are organized in a consistent manner that follows the way the course is often taught. There have been no changes in the overall order in this new edition.

In addition, each chapter is self-contained to permit maximum flexibility. Instructors can use the chapters in any order. I have tried for prose that is jargon-free and have buttressed the text with numerous pertinent examples to hold attention, spur interest, and maintain relevancy.

▲▲▲ *Pedagogical Features*

In addition to the dual emphasis on concepts and skills, this text has numerous pedagogical features—more in this edition than in the last:

- *Chapter objectives* are listed at the beginning of each chapter. Clear and specific, they represent the most significant concepts in the chapter.
- *Key terms* are printed in boldface in the text, and the definition follows immediately after the term is mentioned.
- *Key terms* also are listed at the end of each chapter in the order they occur in the chapter.
- *"Consider This"* readings are all new to this edition. They focus specifically on one of four aspects of interpersonal communication: multicultural issues, gender concerns, workplace examples, or ethical questions. An icon indicates the specific emphasis of each "Consider This" reading.
- *Critical thinking* skills are emphasized. Each "Consider This" box contains provocative questions to stimulate reader involvement in the reading.
- *"Try This"* features, which appear throughout the text, encourage students to try new behaviors and practice new skills. Many of the most popular "Try This" features have been retained from earlier editions.
- *Skill Building* sections conclude every chapter. The sections provide students with specific methods for changing their behavior with respect to the content of each chapter.
- *Chapter Summaries* allow students to recap briefly the chief points from each chapter.
- *Further Reading* suggestions at the end of each chapter are annotated and include both popular and scholarly sources. Substantially updated, these suggestions represent reader-oriented sources for extending the material of each chapter.
- *Diagrams and models* illustrate the textual material to make the concepts, principles, and theories easier to grasp.
- *Photographs with captions* add interest and visual reinforcement to the text and provide a source for additional discussion questions.
- *Relevant examples* begin each chapter. The examples provide a fresh way to introduce the ideas and immediately engage the interest and attention of readers.

▲▲▲ Changes in the Seventh Edition

Substantial changes mark this edition. Two additions are of special interest. The first is a new chapter, "Gender Communication: Understanding the Other Sex." This chapter underscores the importance of studying gender differences, recognizes some of the major gender differences, alerts readers to likely reactions to gender talk, explains why caution in applying generalizations about gender differences is necessary, and offers skills important in improving gender sensitivity.

The second substantial change is the new section on verbal aggression in the chapter, "Creating Messages: Verbal Communication." This section discusses why verbal aggression is destructive, what verbally aggressive messages are, why verbal aggression occurs, why it continues, why some people think there are good reasons for it, and how it can be prevented or kept from escalating.

Now, let's look at the new material chapter by chapter:

- The *Prologue* focuses on "Communication Competency: What It Is and How to Achieve It." The elements of communication competence are explained in detail, and a "Communication Competence Evaluation Form" is provided to make the concepts clear and specific.
- *Chapter 1*, "Speaking Interpersonally: Elements and Characteristics" combines Chapters 1 and 2 from the sixth edition. The goal was to bring similar information together in one place and reduce the amount of introductory information to heighten interest and increase attention.
- *Chapter 2*, "Creating Meaning: Perception," begins with three dramatic new examples and includes all new "Consider This" sections. In addition, the chapter provides a closer relationship between perception and effective interpersonal communication.
- *Chapter 3*, "Getting in Touch: The Self and Self-Disclosure," draws together in one place information from two chapters in the sixth edition. The new, more tightly organized chapter begins with three new examples and draws a closer relationship between self-concept and effective communication.
- *Chapter 4*, "Responding to Others: Listening and Feedback," also draws together in one place information from separate chapters on listening and feedback in the sixth edition. In addition to the new examples that introduce both sections, and the new "Consider This" readings, there are separate skills sections for improving both listening and feedback.
- *Chapter 5*, "Creating Messages: Verbal Communication," includes new opening examples, new "Consider This" boxes, and a new section, "Verbal Aggression."
- *Chapter 6*, "Communicating Without Words: Nonverbal Characteristics, Functions, Forms, and Types," combines two chapters on nonverbal communication from the sixth edition. There are new opening examples, a new "Try This" box containing 14 specific skills that can be applied when the student faces an intercultural communication situation, and all new "Consider This" information.
- *Chapter 7*, "Gender Communication: Understanding the Other Sex," is entirely new. The chapter attempts to make this study of gender interesting and provocative.

- *Chapters 8 to 14* include all new opening examples—three per chapter—all new "Consider This" material designed to focus reader attention on important related information, new skill-building sections in each chapter, new summaries at the end of each chapter, and new "Further Reading" selections. The former Chapter 18, "Communicating on the Job: Promoting Success in the Workplace," has been eliminated from the seventh edition.

▲▲▲ Supplements

Available with the seventh edition of *Understanding Interpersonal Communication* are the following materials:

- An expanded *Instructor's Manual* written by the author;
- A test bank, available in both the *Instructor's Manual* and in TestMaster-IBM, the HarperCollins computer software program;
- Grades-IBM, the HarperCollins grade-keeping computer program;
- HarperCollins Interpersonal Communication Video Library (available to qualified adopters).

▲▲▲ Acknowledgments

This edition, like those before it, reflects the contributions of many people. I am especially grateful for the suggestions provided by the manuscript reviewers for each edition.

For their reviews of the seventh edition manuscript, I would like to thank Judith Anderson, University of Rhode Island; Sara L. Cornette, University of Richmond; Arni Dunathan, Bay de Noc Community College; Reece Elliott, Austin Peay State University; Jerry L. Ferguson, South Dakota State University; Annette Joseph, Bronx Community College/CUNY; and Donna H. Martin, Danville Area Community College. For your comments and suggestions, I am most grateful.

At HarperCollins, I worked with Cynthia Biron, Elaine Silverstein, Betty Slack, Peter Glovin, and Diane Kraut. All writing benefits from knowledgeable, experienced, well-intentioned input. I am pleased by the support, guidance, and care.

Special thanks, as usual, go to Howard W. Cotrell, Associate Professor, and formerly Assistant Director for Instructional Development in Instructional Media Services, at Bowling Green. Howard has retired from the Instructional Media Services center and now has a courtesy appointment in the Department of Interpersonal Communication. As a co-facilitator in some of my courses, a colleague, and a friend for close to 20 years, he has generously contributed of his ideas, research, interests, and polishing to what is written here and elsewhere. I thank him for a warm, rich, challenging, and rewarding association.

My thanks go also to the faculty of the Department of Interpersonal Communication (IPC) at Bowling Green: John Makay, Chair; Julie Burke; Don Enholm; Al Gonzalez; Tina Harris; Ray Tucker; and Jim Wilcox. It is a pleasure to work with such a cooperative, supportive, and outstanding group of people who make it a joy to go to work on a regular basis.

I also want to thank my children: Scott, Jacquie, Anthony, and Joanna. And thanks to my extended family as well. To Dave Smeltzer and Jeff Limes, thank you. All of you have been an important influence on my writing.

Finally, and most importantly, thanks to my wife, Andrea. Throughout all the editions of this book, she has provided examples, support, and love. These editions have emanated from a positive, supportive, and loving interpersonal family climate that has continued to offer rich material from which to draw and rich rewards for participation. There is no way this book could have reached its seventh edition without the aid and assistance of my wonderful wife and family. I am fortunate, and I know and appreciate it.

Dick Weaver

Understanding Interpersonal Communication

PROLOGUE
Communication Competency: What It Is and How to Achieve It

Have you ever known someone who amazes you by how adept and successful he or she is in dealing with other people? Bethany was like this. She could easily begin conversations with people she had never known before. She just seemed to know what to say, what questions to ask, or what answers to provide in interviews. It was as if she had a sixth sense about what was appropriate or what would work. She would not just sit by and watch a small-group discussion dissolve or disintegrate because no one was willing to say anything; she pitched in, attempted to organize the procedure, offered suggestions and advice, and began to participate actively to fill the void. If you had to put a label on Bethany or other people like her, you might call them competent communicators.

Jeffrey, unlike Bethany, found talking with others difficult and awkward. If he was given a choice between having a conversation and playing a video game, the video game would win hands down. Jeffrey learned from his father never to admit that he was wrong, so he protected his public image carefully by speaking only when he was sure he was right, and by never expressing his opinions. If he had opinions, he simply kept them to himself. During his childhood, Jeffrey seldom, if ever, saw his parents express their feelings for each other. Just as he kept his opinions to himself, he learned not to express his feelings either. In the few relationships he had, his partners became frustrated, and in one case angry, because they never knew where they stood or what he thought about them, the relationship, or anything. Jeffrey was an example of the noncommunicator. Also, Jeffrey hated criticism of any kind. Because he put so much time and energy into his thoughts, Jeffrey did not like being found wrong. He accepted critical comments from no one except his teachers, and even then he resisted their comments as if to say, "Who do they think they are?" Jeffrey found it safest not to step out from the crowd. He avoided classes that involved oral communication. In his classes, he sat in the back toward the side; in a crowd he tried to blend in, not stick out; he never volunteered to speak, never countered the group's ideas in any way. He had few friends. Few people became close to Jeffrey or got to know him well. From all external appearances, he was not a competent communicator.

Although Bethany and Jeffrey are at the extremes, many people reveal portions of their behavior—seldom one or the other. People like Bethany are likely to be just as rare as the Jeffreys of the world, although people like Bethany, from everything we know about communication, are likely to have more friends and be able to function better personally than people like Jeffrey. Most of us, as noted, probably fall somewhere in between. You might wonder what is wrong with being an incompetent communicator. Maybe nothing is really wrong with it. However, in their book *Interpersonal Communication Competence* (1984), Spitzberg and Cupach link communication incompetence to mental illness, depression, anxiety, shyness, loneliness, developmental disorders, academic problems, sexual offenses, and drug abuse.[1]

Just from examining the links between communication incompetence and the problems noted above, perhaps you can see communication competence as a useful goal. But what is communication competence? A competent communicator is one who is suitable, fit, and sufficient for the purpose. The purpose of this prologue is to outline some of the goals communicators should strive for. Reading them here can provide you with some ideas that can serve to guide or direct your future behavior. Perhaps just as importantly, these ideas can offer a superstructure—like the frame of a building. The way the building is finished, or all the decisions that make one building distinctive from another, will depend on the skills developed in each of the following chapters. This prologue provides the big picture: the skeleton or superstructure upon which the distinctions of personal style and taste will be placed.

Why should you be concerned about what other people consider competent communication? The most important reason is that competent communication is a proven aid to success in a wide range of social and occupational situations.[2] **Communication competence** has been defined as "a process through which interpersonal impressions are shaped and satisfactory outcomes are derived from an interaction."[3] This definition shows how closely competence is aligned with success.

If you want to attain success in a wide range of social and occupational situations, what characteristics will you need? Six characteristics are associated with communication competence: adaptability, conversational involvement, conversational management, empathy, effectiveness, and appropriateness.[4] See the following "Try This" for a condensation of the information in the following section.

▲▲▲ *Adaptability*

Adaptability is the ability to change behaviors and goals to meet the needs of interactions.[5] It is the most commonly cited standard for judging communication competence. As noted in "Try This," on page 5, it is composed of six factors.

Social experience involves participation in various social interactions. For example, Leon was from Puerto Rico, but because he had been on the mainland for several years, and because he had negotiated with automobile sales personnel several times, he had developed and refined his skills. Now, Leon could select the most optimal communication behaviors to get the best car deal. Kara had always found funerals very difficult, but after her grandfather's death and after attending two separate funerals of her high school girlfriend's, she felt somewhat more comfortable at funerals.

Social composure has to do with keeping calm. More than anything else, this relates to perceiving situations accurately. Lee, for example, could have become upset after standing in line for over an hour for a concert ticket. However, after observing the frustration of the ticket seller because of a lack of help, a slow computer, and poorly labeled tickets, Lee remained calm.

Social confirmation refers to acknowledgment of the other person's self-presentation efforts. That is, recognizing and understanding others' reasons for doing and saying things helps you adapt. For example, when Mario realized that Adela was upset and acting depressed because she had just heard that a friend had been in a serious car accident, Mario decided not to tell her that he wanted to end their relationship.

Appropriate disclosure means being sensitive to the amount and type of information presented to someone else. Stephanie had just met Leonard. She had just come out of a destructive relationship in which there had been considerable abuse, and she had recently experienced a flashback to that abusive situation. But Stephanie, on her second date with Leonard, chose not to share that information at this time—not that she wouldn't at some later point. She just thought it was too early now.

Articulation is the ability to express ideas through language. Having a range of verbal skills helps you express your ideas to different people. Vance taught fifth-graders. His discussion of love with them was quite different from the one he had with Angela, his girlfriend. And that discussion was different from how he explained his love for Angela to his mother, and then to his best friend, Ralph, and then to Angela's parents.

Humor is the quality that makes things seem funny or amusing. Humor assists you in adapting to social situations. For example, Amy always seemed to make dull interactions brighter. By using humor, Brent was able to ease tensions between people. And Joetta alleviated embarrassment by using wit.

▲▲▲ *Conversational Involvement*

Being involved in conversations is critical to communication competence.[6] This requires more than just a cognitive (knowledge) commitment. For example, a cognitive commitment might be revealed when Henry sits in a lecture hall with his eyes closed but trying to understand the philosophical complexity of the ideas offered by the lecturer—weighing and considering the material as it is presented, but revealing no external signs of involvement. Communication competence includes a behav-

TRY THIS

Communication Competence Evaluation Form

Instructions: Use this form to assess communication competence. The criteria beneath each of the major characteristics should give you the data necessary to assess the major characteristic. Circle the numerical score that in your judgment best represents you or the other person's performance: 7 = outstanding (superb); 6 = excellent; 5 = very good; 4 = average (good); 3 = fair; 2 = poor; 1 = *very* minimal; 0 = no ability demonstrated.

                                                              Rating
1. Adaptability (or flexibility)   7 6 5 4 3 2 1 0

    _____ Social experience   _____ Appropriate disclosure
    _____ Social composure   _____ Articulation
    _____ Social confirmation   _____ Humor

2. Conversational involvement   7 6 5 4 3 2 1 0

    _____ Responsiveness   _____ Attentiveness
    _____ Perceptiveness

3. Conversational management   7 6 5 4 3 2 1 0

    _____ Who controls the conversation?
    _____ Is there an ebb and flow to the communication? (Turn taking, yielding, topic shifts, topic extensions, asking questions, intonation, nodding, interrupting)
    _____ How smoothly does the ebb and flow of the conversation occur?

4. Empathy   7 6 5 4 3 2 1 0

    _____ Were the person's personal attitudes set aside?
    _____ Did he or she adopt the perspective of the other person?
    _____ Did he or she feel the emotions that the other person was feeling?

5. Effectiveness   7 6 5 4 3 2 1 0

    _____ Achieved the objectives he or she had for conversation.

6. Appropriateness   7 6 5 4 3 2 1 0

    _____ Upheld the expectations for a given situation.

                                TOTAL POINTS _____

Additional Comments:

_____

_____

_____

_____

ioral involvement as well. When Lynn Ann was listening to DeWayne describe a math problem, she demonstrated her **conversational involvement** through head nods, vocal cues such as "uhh-huh," "right," and "I understand," and smiling in agreement with his explanations and descriptions.

As noted on the evaluation form in the "Try This," the three criteria by which conversational involvement is assessed are *responsiveness, perceptiveness,* and *attentiveness.*

Responsiveness means knowing what to say or not say, being aware of what your role is, and feeling part of the interaction. For example, when Adam and Jessica decided to talk to a department chairperson about the teaching style of an instructor in the department, Adam was careful not to intrude on Jessica's comments. Both knew that they were students, and they were careful not to be mean or disrespectful. Both felt that they were an intimate and important part of the interaction with the chairperson.

Perceptiveness means being aware of how others perceive you and how others respond to you, and being observant of others. In the example just given, Adam and Jessica knew by her behavior that the chairperson respected and appreciated their remarks. She was friendly, courteous, kind, and respectful of their ideas. They knew, too, by her sincerity and willingness to listen, that she took them seriously. When they left her office, Adam and Jessica talked about how the chairperson had responded to them. Not surprisingly, their perceptions agreed.

Attentiveness means listening carefully to others, focusing on the conversation, and not being preoccupied with your own thoughts. Curtis Bennett was a well-liked undergraduate adviser. According to students, this was because of his willingness to listen to advisees, his ability to focus on them when he was talking with them, and the rarity with which he used himself or his life as a reference point for his conversations. One student described Dr. Bennett as "an adviser who cares deeply about his students and wants the best for each of them."

▲▲▲ Conversational Management

Conversational management is how communicators regulate their interactions.[7] Competent communication doesn't involve just adaptation; it involves management and control as well. Several questions are at the heart of management. First, who controls the interaction? Who determines the topics discussed? Who determines when they should change? Second, is there an ebb and flow to the communication? Ebb and flow is revealed by turn-taking, yielding, topic shifts, topic extensions, asking questions, intonation, nodding, and interrupting.[8] Third, how smoothly does the ebb and flow of the conversation occur? That is, how do communicators alternate at speaking?

Those who manage their interactions are interested in maintaining some control over their communication. For example, they see the relationship between communication and rewards (getting what they want). They monitor their communication in relation to their goals. In addition, as they gain new information about how other people respond to what they say and do, they adjust their communication. At the same time, interaction managers are respectful of others, allow room for their expressive behavior, and enable them to achieve their goals, too, where possible.

Sometimes interaction management is easy: conversing is comfortable, interruptions feel natural, there are few awkward pauses, and the indications of when to speak are clear.[9] Sometimes it is difficult: conversing is uncomfortable, there are unnatural interruptions and numerous awkward pauses, and you find yourself stepping on the other's lines.

▲▲▲ Empathy

Empathy refers to the ability to show others that you understand their situation and that you share their emotional reactions to a situation.[10] Empathy is not the same as sympathy. Sympathy involves feeling sorry for others and wanting to help them. Empathy may not lead to a desire to help. There are three parts to the empathic process: (1) putting aside your own attitudes, (2) adopting the perspective of the other person, and (3) feeling the emotion the other person feels.

▲▲▲ Effectiveness

Effectiveness means achieving the objectives you have for your conversations. Can this be done without jeopardizing other important secondary goals? For example, Sheila wanted to achieve her objective of having Ramon spend more time with her; but she did not want to jeopardize an important secondary goal of keeping the relationship together. Cheryl wanted to inquire about her son's recent activities, but she did not want to sound so inquisitive or nosy that he would not choose to come home for the holidays. Erin wanted to ask for a salary increase, but she did not want to sacrifice her supervisors' perception of her as a loyal, responsible employee.

Certain communication behaviors can help you achieve effectiveness more efficiently or more readily than others. For example, conflict management strategies in which one partner asserts his or her desires specifically and concretely would be one such behavior. Revealing persistence in compliance-gaining situations would be a second. Achieving a persuasive goal, directly or indirectly, might be a third. Succeeding in forming a friendship with a desired partner could be a fourth.

▲▲▲ *Appropriateness*

Appropriateness refers to upholding the expectations for a given situation.[11] Some researchers believe that the two most important criteria are appropriateness and effectiveness. It is not difficult to understand their relationship. Think, for example, about the possibility of being appropriate but ineffective. A student could argue with an instructor about the evaluation received on a project. The student could be respectful, courteous, and kind in the communication—all appropriate behaviors. However, the student could also be ineffective in obtaining a reevaluation or reconsideration.

In another instance, a communicator could be effective but inappropriate. Cory, for example, was having a heated conflict with her friend Mary Christine. Cory was mad at Mary Christine because she continually flirted with her boyfriend, Shane. Finally, she got Mary Christine to back down and say she would never flirt with Shane again, but to do this, Cory became loud, angry, and incessant in her demands. By sheer force and by overpowering Mary Christine, she won the battle of effectiveness, but she lost the war of appropriate behavior.

These six characteristics provide you with a fairly broad guide to your progress as you begin to study interpersonal communication in more detail. If you picture these characteristics as the broad, overall goals to be achieved, you will find the skills mentioned in each of the chapters to be specific ways for achieving or moving closer to these broader goals and for establishing a solid and interpersonally competent foundation.

Many factors influence your communication competence. There will always be instances in which you are extremely competent and others in which you experience little competence. Thus, the situation may be a factor. Also, you may feel more competent discussing certain topics or issues, and awkward or uncomfortable discussing other topics or issues. Thus, the topic or issue may be a factor. Perhaps the most important factor, however, is likely to be the other person: your communication partner. In interpersonal communication, two people are involved in constructing goals and plans, two have various motivations and desires, two are offering a public presentation of who they are, two are defining relational desires, and two have specific objectives.[12] The more experience you have, the more skills you have. The more poise and confidence you have, the more likely it is that you will be able to deal with the factors likely to directly affect your communication competence. With this foundation as a starting point, it is more likely that you will be successful. Success comes as a result of having a solid knowledge base, formulating clear goals, having an arsenal of relevant skills, and being able to put those skills into practice in an appropriate and effective manner.

► **NOTES**

1. B. H. Spitzberg and W. R. Cupach. *Interpersonal Communication Competence* (Newbury Park, CA: Sage Publications, 1984).
2. W. H. Fitts, *Interpersonal Competence: The Wheel Model.* Studies on the self-concept and rehabilitation: Research Monograph 2. Dede Wallace Center (Nashville, TN: Author, 1970); B. D. Ruben, "Assessing Communication Competency for Intercultural Adaptation," *Group and Organizational Studies* 1:3 (1976):334–354; P. Trower, B. Bryant, and M. Argyle, *Social Skills and Mental Health* (Philadelphia: University of Pennsylvania Press, 1978).
3. Brian H. Spitzberg and Michael L. Hect, "A Component Model of Relational Competence," *Human Communication Research* 10 (Summer 1984): 575–599. The definition is provided on page 576.
4. I am indebted to Daniel J. Canary and Michael J. Cody, *Interpersonal Communication: A Goals-Based Approach* (New York: St. Martin's Press, 1994), for their condensation of this material. See pages 382–385.
5. Robert L. Duran, "Communicative Adaptability: A Measure of Social Communicative Competence," *Communication Quarterly* 31 (Fall 1983): 320–326.
6. Donald J. Cegala, "Affective and Cognitive Manifestations of Interaction Involvement During Unstructured and Competitive Interactions," *Communication Monographs* 51 (December 1984): 320–338. And Donald J. Cegala, *Conversational Involvement: Ten Years Later.* Paper presented at the Speech Communication Association Convention, Atlanta, Georgia, October 31, 1991.
7. J. M. Wiemann and P. Backlund, "Current Theory and Research in Communicative Competence," *Review of Educational Research* 50 (1980): 185–199.
8. Brian H. Spitzberg and W. R. Cupach, *Interpersonal Communication Competence* (Newbury Park, CA: Sage, 1984), 138.
9. H. Arkowitz, E. Lichtenstein, K. McGovern, and P. Hines, "The Behavioral Assessment of Social Competence in Males," *Behavior Therapy* 6 (1975): 3–13; D. H. Barlow, G. G. Able, B. B. Blanchard, A. R. Bristow, and L. D. Young, *Behavior Therapy* 8 (1977): 229–239; M. L. McLaughlin and M. J. Cody, "Awkward Silences: Behavioral Antecedents and Consequences of the Conversational Lapse," *Human Communication Research* 8 (1982): 299–316; J. M. Wiemann, "Explication and Test of a Model of Communicative Competence," *Human Communication Research* 3 (1977): 195–213.
10. G. A. Gladstein, "Understanding Empathy: Integrating Counseling, Developmental, and Social Psychology Perspectives," *Journal of Counseling Psychology* 30 (1986): 467–482.
11. Spitzberg and Cupach, 100.
12. See Canary and Cody, *Interpersonal Communication: A Goals-Based Approach,* 387.

1

CHAPTER OBJECTIVES

After reading this chapter, you should be able to

- ▲ See how interpersonal communication fits in with other types of communication.
- ▲ Recognize the importance of the three elements involved in any communication situation: people, messages, and effects.
- ▲ Distinguish between mental, physical, and emotional effects.
- ▲ Acknowledge feedback as an ongoing feature of communication situations.
- ▲ Realize the importance of face-to-face communication.
- ▲ Understand the role that intention plays in communication.
- ▲ Distinguish between psychological, physical, social, cultural, and temporal contexts.
- ▲ Recognize both the content and the relationship dimensions of interpersonal communication.
- ▲ Acknowledge the three general responses within the relationship dimension: conform, reject, and disconfirm.
- ▲ Distinguish between source-generated, receiver-generated, and environmental noise.
- ▲ Understand the importance of knowing that interpersonal communication is a process, is circular, is complex, is irreversible and unrepeatable, and is transactional.
- ▲ Use the general skills that relate to interpersonal communication.

▼ Think for a moment of all the **interpersonal communication** that goes on in your life. You talk with your parents and relatives, your brothers and sisters, and your friends and roommates. You talk, too, with your classmates, teachers, and librarians. You may have a relationship partner with whom you do a great deal of talking. At your workplace, you talk with your employer, supervisor, and co-workers. When you purchase something, you communicate with the salesperson, maybe with the manager, and sometimes even with the owner. You may have to make an appointment, and then communicate with a doctor, dentist, lawyer, or other professional. Then, too, you may simply have to give directions to, or provide information for, total strangers. You are an interpersonal communicator whether or not you like it or want to be one. Communication is a matter of life and in some cases survival, as when you learn from someone to avoid a potentially dangerous situation.

Because of your background and experience, you are probably quite a good communicator. At least, you are usually able to share ideas when you need to, and you can get information that is important to you. You might wonder, then, why you should read a textbook or take a class in interpersonal communication. The answer is this: Just because you communicate a lot does not necessarily mean that you do it as well as you can. Everyone can improve. The better you understand the elements of interpersonal communication and the specific ways people can change for the better, the more likely you are to improve.

Research provides some motivation for you to improve your communication skills. For example, Scott D. Johnson, a researcher who conducted a study entitled "A National Assessment of Secondary-School Principals' Perceptions of Teaching-Effectiveness Criteria," discovered that communication-related items "were rated as the most important criteria used by principals in the hiring of teachers."[1] Communication-related items included interpersonal communication, poise, enthusiasm, and listening skills. He also found that these same items played a major role in principals' judgment of the classroom effectiveness of teachers.

Johnson's study revealed the importance of communication in education. Curtis, Winsor, and Stephens, several years earlier, revealed the importance of communication in business.[2] They discovered that oral communication, listening ability, and enthusiasm are the three factors most important in helping graduating college students obtain employment; that interpersonal and human relations skills are the most important skills for successful job performance; and that working well with others one-to-one is the most important skill in an ideal management profile. In addition, they discovered that **interpersonal communication courses are considered second in importance to written communication courses for entry-level managers.** These are important findings.

The discoveries of Johnson and of Curtis, Winsor, and Stephens, echo those of Sypher and Zorn, who investigated upward mobility in business organizations. They discovered that "communication abilities are strong predictors of individual success in organizations."[3] There is little doubt about the contribution that effective interpersonal communication can make to your life.

Look at this class you are about to embark on as a new opportunity to grow, develop, and change. One purpose of the class will be to label and organize your behavior. Another will be to raise your awareness of the behaviors that surround you everyday. Some of the material may be familiar to you already, but if you assume that because something is familiar there is nothing more to learn, you will be creating an artificial barrier to your growth, development, and change.

In this chapter some of the elements and characteristics of the interpersonal communication process will be discussed. At the end of the chapter there will be some general suggestions on how you can improve your skills in interpersonal communication. These will help in a broad manner at this time; later chapters will offer you more refined skills to help you in certain specific areas.

Before we begin the discussion of interpersonal communication, it might be useful to see how it fits in with the other types of communication. Table 1.1 shows one way of categorizing these types with respect to participants and processes.

One type is not necessarily better than another, nor does one type necessarily take the place of another. It is possible for several types to occur simultaneously, as when two people talk (interpersonal communication) in a meeting **(small-group communication)** that is being televised **(mass communication)** to a wide audience. Interpersonal communication occurs in **organizational communication,** and mass communication can be a form of **public communication.** Interpersonal communication is likely to be the most familiar type, since normally you engage in it most often. And since you do engage in it most often, why not accept this challenge to make each experience more effective than the last—or, as a minimum, the best effort you have to offer?

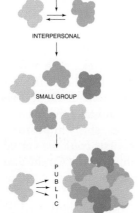

SELF

INTERPERSONAL

SMALL GROUP

P
U
B
L
I
C

Table 1.1
Types of communication.

TYPE	PARTICIPANTS	PROCESS
Intrapersonal	One person	Communication occurs within one person.
Interpersonal	Two people	Communication occurs on a one-to-one basis.
Small-group	Three or more people (five is ideal)	Communication occurs when a small number of people meet for a common purpose.
Organizational	Within and between organizations	People work together within a system of rules, norms, and routines to accomplish independent, goal-oriented activities.
Public	One person and an audience	A person sends a message to an audience for a specified reason.
Mass	Many people	Messages are transmitted to a mass audience through television, film, or some other medium.

It should be clear in this table that all categories are *not* necessarily mutually exclusive. They can interpenetrate—that is, interpersonal communication can occur in (penetrate) a small-group or a mass situation just as a small-group or a public speaker may occur in (penetrate) a mass situation.

▲▲▲ *Elements of an Interpersonal Communication Situation*

Figure 1.1 shows the skeleton of the communication process. It depicts in the most basic form the three elements necessarily involved in any communication situation. These elements are *people, messages,* and *effects.* Throughout this chapter you will build (put flesh) on this skeleton.

People

The fact that interpersonal communication involves people may seem too obvious to mention, but by saying that it involves people you rule out the communication you have with your pets, with your car (especially when it is running poorly), with your plants, or with any other objects of affection. Such communication may be important and healthy, but it is not "interpersonal" as the term will be used in this book.

At any point in an interpersonal communication situation, the people involved are both senders and receivers simultaneously. Notice the arrows in Figure 1.1. They have arrowheads on both ends. Messages are sent and received at the same time. Although I may be telling you how to get downtown, as I survey your face during the telling, I can determine whether you understand, whether I need to repeat something, or whether you are lost altogether.

Messages

The content may be verbal and/or nonverbal. Both kinds of messages are equally valid as communications. My directions, in the example above, are verbal. But your face provides important content that helps me get you downtown. You give me **feedback,** because your nonverbal cues tell me how my message is being received. These cues could take the form of head nodding, eye squinting, large and small gestures, shifts in posture, and many other gestures as well. The feedback, of course, could be verbal too: "I'm sorry, I just don't understand," you might say, or "Could you repeat that last part, please?" Because of the interplay of verbal and nonverbal content, messages can be complex.

When you think of messages, however, you usually think first of words, or verbal communication. It is important to remember that words mean different things to different people. Words are personal. Words depend for their meaning on the experiences, reaction, feelings, contexts, and ideas of the people using them. All words have these kinds of associations. It is vital to be aware always of other people's reactions to the words we use.

Effects

Notice that in Figure 1.1 the "message" arrow penetrates the heads; this is to show that the message is having an effect. An effect may be a mental, physical, or emotional response to a message. You may say something that causes another person to reconsider his or her position on a subject: a **mental effect.** You may say something that causes someone to break out in a sweat, run away, or fight: a **physical effect.** Closely tied to physical effects are emotional ones. Our message may cause the other person to feel angry, affectionate, or joyous: an **emotional effect.** The "Try This" on page 16 asks you to categorize comments based on the effect they have on you.

A message that has no effect serves no useful purpose in interpersonal communication. However, you must remember that all effects may not be readily observable. A person might respond to a message with silence. Silence is an effect. It could be based on a mental, physical, or emotional response, and it could have any one of several meanings. Also, the communication process may be completed even though the sender is unaware that the message has had an effect. For example, what about advice you give in passing to someone you may never see again? You shout from your car window after a close call, "Next time, watch where you're going!"—and the other driver, unknown to you, begins driving more cautiously and responsibly as a result of your utterance. You may not be aware that the message has had an effect, and yet, clearly, interpersonal communication *has* taken place. This situation admittedly is a bit unusual, as interpersonal communication usually involves *direct* feedback.

Another response that may appear to show no effect is boredom or apathy. But just because people do not care about what you are saying does not mean that your message has had no effect. They have chosen not to care, or they have perceived selectively. Just the same, you have produced an effect. No response *is* a response. Sometimes, too, an effect occurs only after some time has elapsed—a delayed effect. Some effects that take a long time to appear are more significant because they have been thought out more completely. The point is that for communication to take

Figure 1.1
The skeleton of the communication process.

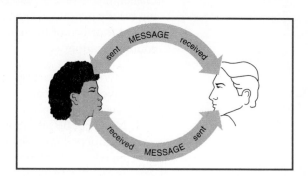

TRY THIS

Pretend that someone has made each of the following comments to you. This person is someone you know but do not consider a close friend. Categorize the comments according to the effect they might have on you. Is the effect mental, physical, or emotional?

1. "Have you ever considered changing your major?"
2. "Why don't you grow up?"
3. "You know, you really have a lot of friends."
4. "You're always complaining."
5. "What do you like best about this class?"
6. "For somebody taking interpersonal communication you sure don't know much about it."
7. "Are you really cut out for college?"
8. "You can give advice, but you can't take it."

Effects differ. Just because these comments have certain effects on you does not mean they would have the same effect on others. A lot depends on who makes the comments, and in what context. Can you think of other factors that might determine how you would react to them?

place, every message must produce some effect, even if that effect is not immediately apparent.

▲▲▲ *Characteristics of Interpersonal Communication*

Communication is the process of transmitting and interpreting messages. Having briefly examined the basic elements of interpersonal communication, look at fourteen of the features of the interpersonal process. Interpersonal communication

1. Involves at least two people.
2. Involves feedback.
3. Need not be face-to-face.
4. Need not be intentional.
5. Produces some effect.
6. Need not involve words.
7. Is affected by context.

How many of the characteristics of interpersonal communication are revealed in this father-and-son interaction?

8. Contains information and defines relationships.
9. Is affected by noise.
10. Is a process.
11. Is circular.
12. Is complex.
13. Is irreversible and unrepeatable.
14. Is transactional.

Interpersonal Communication Involves at Least Two People

To say that interpersonal communication involves at least two people rules out the kind of communication we have within ourselves. As noted in Table 1.1, **intrapersonal communication** is the name given to internal messages. In Chapter 3, you'll look at intrapersonal communication as a way you have for getting in touch with yourself. The self is the starting point for all messages you exchange with others. Because of its relationship to interpersonal communication, it must be examined.

For these purposes, think of interpersonal communication as involving no more than two people—a **dyad.** Two is not an arbitrary number. Three—the **triad**—can be considered the smallest of small groups. In the most comprehensive treatment of the nature of triads, Theodore Caplow suggests that "the most significant property of the triad is its tendency to divide a coalition of two members against the third."[4] William Wilmot concludes that "when three people are in a face-to-face transaction, the transaction *at any time* is composed of a primary dyad plus one."[5]

When we define interpersonal communication in terms of the number of people involved, we must remember that interpersonal communication may actually occur between two people who are part of a larger group. Sometimes within a group of people, splinter groups of two or three participants are formed. As groups increase in size, this becomes more likely. When two people in a larger group argue over a point, they are definitely engaged in interpersonal communication. We've all been in discussion groups where two members dominated the conversation until the discussion became simply an exchange of ideas between those two people. This kind of interpersonal communication often occurs in a group setting.

Interpersonal Communication Involves Feedback

Feedback, as noted previously, tells communicators how their message is being received. As in the earlier example, in which I give you directions, it is easy to think of feedback as an ongoing feature of every communication. Feedback does not need to emanate from a receiver of a message alone. For example, I could give you a direction and you could shake your head in disagreement, and while continuing to tell you how to get downtown, I could nod my head "Yes" to provide feedback to your shaking of the head. Think of an argument in which you are getting negative feedback from the other person, but you continue to talk louder and louder to try to counter the negative feedback. The loudness in this case is feedback to say, "Let me finish what I'm saying." In these cases, the feedback is coming from the message source as well as from the message receiver, and it shows how feedback is an ongoing feature of communication situations.

Interpersonal Communication Need Not Be Face-to-Face

Sitting on a bus, you may be affected by a noisy conversation between two people sitting in front of you (even though it does not involve you) and as a result choose to move to another seat. Notice that both transmitting and interpreting are taking place. You may speak to a person on the telephone; you may pass nonverbal messages to a friend across the room by using facial expressions or gestures; you could even be in another room and pass messages to another person by tapping on the wall. You need not be in a face-to-face situation to participate in interpersonal communication.

Although interpersonal communication need not be face-to-face, communication without face-to-face interaction is by no means ideal. Losing direct contact means losing a major factor in feedback. Also, a significant vehicle for conveying emotions is lost. Think about it. When you want to improve the quality of a relationship, how do you communicate this desire without words? Eye contact, head nods, and smiles are often major factors. Eliminating direct contact in interpersonal communication almost has the effect of taking the personal out of interpersonal communication.

In face-to-face situations, you receive more information because you can see more of the other person. Communication is likely to be more effective during a face-to-face encounter because you're more apt to catch the other's subtleties, special inflections, and emphases. You can perceive moods more accurately when you are face-to-face with the other person, and consequently you have a better chance of getting the whole message.

Interpersonal Communication Need Not Be Intentional

Interpersonal communication is not necessarily deliberate. For example, you might find out through a slip of the tongue that someone has lied to you. You might discover that someone is very nervous around you by the person's constant shifting of weight from one foot to another, continual fumbling over words, or other nervous reactions. You might decide that you do not want to be around a person at all because of a certain abrasiveness or disagreeable manner. The person probably didn't intentionally communicate these things, but they are messages because they are signals that affect you. Transmitting and interpreting are taking place.

Interpersonal Communication Produces Some Effect

To be truly considered interpersonal communication, a message must produce some effect. As mentioned earlier, this effect need not be immediately apparent, but it must occur. If you walk along the sidewalk toward a person you don't know, wearing your broadest, warmest, I-want-to-get-to-know-you-better smile, and the other person doesn't see you and walks on by, no interpersonal communication has taken place. A similar situation occurs if you are talking to someone while that person is listening to music on stereo headphones or using a hair dryer and doesn't hear you. These are not interpersonal communications if the messages are not received and have no effect.

Interpersonal Communication Need Not Involve Words

Though I've already mentioned some of the ways we can communicate without words, this characteristic needs emphasis because nonverbal communication is so important. Picture two people secretly in love with each other who are standing on opposite sides of the room at a party. A quick glance between them can reaffirm their whole relationship and love for each other. Often a look or a touch can convey far more than words.

Nonverbal messages are a powerful and significant form of interpersonal communication.

A unique aspect of interpersonal communication is its potential to involve several senses. People who are engaged in interpersonal communication generally stand or sit close to one another so they can touch and smell as well as see and hear. The message is intensified because far more stimuli of a personal nature are available to observers.

Interpersonal Communication Is Affected by the Context

Human communication does not occur in a vacuum. It *always* takes place in a series of interacting contexts, and these contexts *always* influence the kind of communication that occurs. Context simply refers to the environment in which communication takes place. Contexts include the *psychological, physical, social, cultural,* and *temporal.* What I have done in Figure 1.2 is to take the skeleton of the communication process from Figure 1.1 and place it in the center of these contexts.

When examining contexts, you are looking at the who, what, when, where, and how of interpersonal communication. These are all important variables. How they interact with each other is also important.[6] Unfortunately, it is impossible to be aware of *all* possible contextual elements, much less the way they affect each other.

Notice how much communication can take place without words. How many senses are likely to be in play by these two people in interaction?

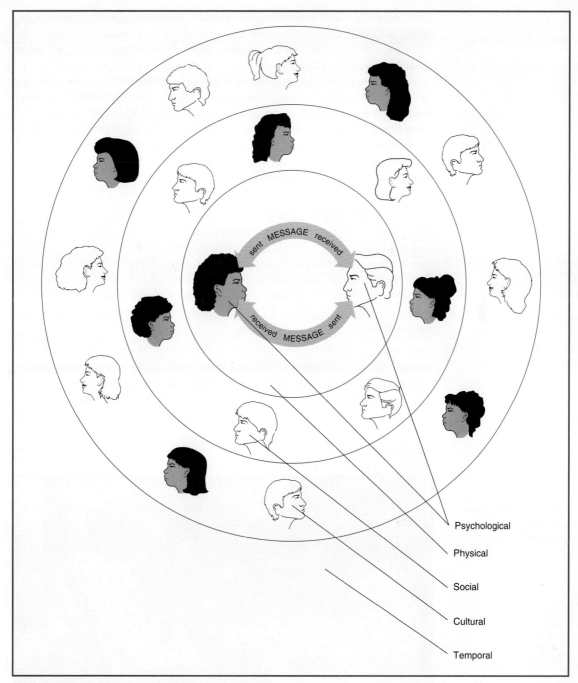

Figure 1.2
*Contexts. All of these contexts affect the communication you engage in with others.
Not only does each context have an effect, but there is an interaction effect as well,
as each context influences the others.*

Psychological The **psychological context** consists of aspects that occur in the minds of the participants. Because of the moods or attitudes of the communicators, contexts can be serious or humorous, formal, or informal, friendly or unfriendly.

The psychological context is especially important because you are the creators of the meaning. You create meaning based on what you have learned from our culture and our society. You add to, subtract from, and sometimes distort the information you receive through our senses. Then *your* values, past experiences, needs, cognitive styles (the way you think), and your perceptions of ourselves, other people, and situations help you attach meaning to that information.

Physical The **physical context** is the tangible, concrete environment, part of which is the physical presence and attractiveness of the communicators. Another part of this context is the location. Whether a conversation occurs in a hallway, classroom, theater, church, or bar will exert some influence on both the content and form of the messages sent. Employers sometimes take employees to a nice restaurant to deliver bad news; the ambience of the restaurant tends to soften the effect of harsh or hostile news.

Social The **social context** encompasses your relationships with others. Status relationships between the participants are included at this level. Communication is affected by whether you are talking with a peer or a superior, a parent or a child. The groups, organizations, or clubs to which

Can you identify characteristics of all the contexts from this interpersonal communication situation?

you belong will influence your communication—as discussed previously under sociological rules. Rules, roles (functions you fulfill in relation to others), norms (standards, patterns, or models that have been established for behavior), and games (individual sequences that follow definite patterns) are important factors. There is a close relationship between them; sometimes *rule* and *norms* are used synonymously because standards or patterns can become rules, just as a game can become a norm or rule for behavior.

Cultural　At a still more general level is the **cultural context.** It may be difficult to perceive the influence of this context unless one has experienced other cultures. Traditions, taboos, habits, and customs have powerful influences on the character and personality of people of all cultures; however, many people are ignorant of these influences. Our soldiers experienced differences when they visited the Persian Gulf. Some of the restrictions they encountered included prohibitions on the use of alcohol, on what women were allowed to wear, and on dancing. When in a culture not your own, you may be unaware of what you are communicating by what you consider to be normal behavior. Cultural influences, however, still get filtered through personal, psychological filters.

Temporal　The **temporal context** is the time at which the communication takes place. The time of the day, day of the week, week of the month, and so on may have an influence. The time in history may also be important.

TRY THIS

Think about the last communication you shared with the person you consider your closest friend. What contextual variables affected your communication? How many can you remember? Try to be specific. Here are several variables that may have affected it:

▲ time of day	▲ weather	▲ touch
▲ noise or distractions	▲ smells	▲ location
▲ how you met (at this time)	▲ what you talked about	▲ other people
▲ furniture	▲ what you wore	present

Explain the significance of each variable and how it affected your communication.

Some people are "morning" people, others "night" people. This could affect the content or form of the communication they carry on at particular hours of the day. A communication researcher often assesses the importance, impact, or insightfulness of communications in light of the time they took place.

These five contexts interact with each other; they influence each other and are influenced by all the other contexts. It is impossible to isolate these contexts or to plot all the possible interactions between them. What is possible and useful, however, is to become aware of the presence of contexts and to note their potential impact. When we look for the causes of certain behaviors, often more is going on than may be apparent at first. Planning for effective communication can be done only with careful consideration of contexts.

CONSIDER THIS

One goal of this book is to encourage intercultural sensitivity. Several of these boxes, which relate to intercultural topics and issues, will appear throughout the book. This one is the first. It is important to keep in mind the implications of the textbook material for diverse audiences. Read the following excerpt, and then answer the questions that follow it.

> Most of us have relatively little contact with people from other cultures and/or ethnic groups. Interacting with people who are different is a novel experience for most of us. The amount of contact we have with people who are different, however, is going to change in the near future. Recent estimates suggest that the work force in the United States is changing from white, male-dominated to a majority of women, immigrants, and nonwhite ethnics. While organizational cultures influence the way we behave in the workplace, they do not erase the effect of cultural and ethnic background on our behavior and work.*

Questions
1. What are the advantages of a diverse work force?
2. How would you go about interacting with people who are different?
3. Why are misunderstandings in intercultural or interethnic encounters likely to occur? What are some of the ways to anticipate and then avoid misunderstandings?

*From William B. Gudykunst, *Bridging Differences: Effective Intergroup Communication* (Newbury Park, CA: Sage, 1991), 1.

▲▲▲ Interpersonal Communication Contains Information and Defines Relationships

Imagine initiating a conversation with a woman by asking, "How about joining me for a cup of coffee?" The *informational* part of this message, or **content dimension**, refers to what you expect of her—namely, that you want her to join you for coffee. The *relationship* aspect of the message, or **relationship dimension**, is the meaning behind the words that says something about your relationship to her.

The relationship dimension tells her how to deal with the message. She recognizes, for example, that this is not a command but a friendly invitation that implies no status difference between the two of you. What if she made the same suggestion to you and she happened to be one of your teachers? The relationship aspect of the message would be quite different. Suppose she commanded, "Come, have a cup of coffee with me!" The relationship implied here is one of unequal status, known as a *complementary* relationship. When the status is equal, the relationship can be labeled *symmetrical*.

It isn't merely a question of equal versus unequal status that defines relationships. It is the kinds of behaviors being exchanged. For example, Jason might talk to his boss in a manner that suggests he is one up on the boss, and the boss might accept this definition of their relationship. Accordingly, even though their respective statuses may suggest one type of relationship, the way in which they actually communicate defines another. The *behavior* defines the relationship. That is what makes the communicative perspective of relationships more compelling than a primarily sociological or psychological perspective. Also, relationships between people change from complementary to symmetrical and back again, depending on the content of the message or the situation.

The messages, "Please, won't you come and have coffee with me?" and "You are going to have coffee with me!" contain the same information but imply a different relationship. The message "Could I please see your notes from yesterday's lecture?" has essentially the same relationship level as "Please, won't you come and have coffee with me?" but the content is very different. When we have an ongoing relationship with someone, we tend to operate on the same relationship level for all our communication, no matter what information we're exchanging. This relationship level changes only when one of us perceives a change in status in relation to the other.

When you speak to another person you reveal something about how you see the relationship between yourself and that person, not necessarily how the relationship *should* be. In the simple opening comment "How about joining me for a cup of coffee?" you have offered the woman a definition of yourself that implies you are her equal—that you have a symmetrical relationship. She can make any of three general responses:

1. She may **confirm** your definition of self. She might say, "I'd love to," and verify the equality.
2. She may **reject** your view of self by saying, "I'm really not interested." This response implies that her view of the relationship is not the same as yours.
3. She may **disconfirm** by ignoring you—denying your right to definition of self. By ignoring your questions, she could be saying she thinks you have no claim to a relationship at all.

True, these responses are extreme. There are many intermediate kinds of responses the woman could make. She could say no without rejecting your view of self by adding, "Could I take a rain check on it?" But clearly, the kind of response she makes has significant implications for the definition of self and the relationship that you have offered. Notice that you can control the relationship dimension by *how* you say something.

Problems in communication occur most often in the relationship dimension rather than in the content dimension. The *content* dimension involves the *information* conveyed through word symbols. The *relationship* dimension involves the *feelings* conveyed through nonverbal symbols. This distinction between the content and relationship dimensions is simplified here for the purposes of discussion. The distinction is *not* to suggest that people do not discuss relationship issues or express feelings using words, or that specific gestures cannot have clear content-oriented meanings. Obviously, there are crossovers between these dimensions.

Interpersonal Communication Is Affected by Noise

In every communication situation, noise is a factor. The purpose of communication is to try to make certain that the message you create in your brain is exactly re-created in the brain of the receiver. But this seldom, if ever, happens. There are many reasons for this, all of which can be labeled **noise.** Noise is *any interference in the source, receiver, or environment that reduces the exactness of the message.* Noise exists because we have no way to directly link one brain with another.

Source-generated noise results from several different behaviors. Linguistic problems, for example, can cause noise. A speaker may use faulty grammar, improper sentence construction, incorrect word choices, or mispronunciation. When a speaker has an unusual vocal quality, or uses inappropriate pitch or emphasis, or speaks too loudly, too slowly, too fast, or with an unusual rhythm, noise problems can occur. Additional problems may be caused by incongruence (lack of agreement) between the words and the speaker's gestures or facial expressions. Extraverbal behaviors such as incongruent or inappropriate gestures and expressions are a third category of source-generated noise.

Receiver-generated noise also results from different factors. Think, for example, about all the various elements *you* bring to any communication situation: your background and experience, your skills and abilities, your thoughts and feelings. And think how these affect the way you listen to, understand, and integrate what *anyone* says to you. What are your own experiences in communicating? Are you a skilled communicator? How do you feel about the other person's communication? What about your reactions to the other person? The level of respect—or distrust—can directly affect your response to the message.

Another important area of receiver-generated noise has to do with feelings about the other's subject matter. What are your own experiences, abilities, or feelings on this topic? Do you have fixed ideas on it, and are your feelings strong? If so, it could be that your mind is somewhat closed to ideas on this subject.

A final area of receiver-generated noise concerns emotional reactions to specific words that are said or things that are done. Some people, for example, stop listening when a speaker uses vulgar language or an obscene gesture. Listening ceases for some when labels that evoke stereotypical (negative) responses, such as *dago, polack, women's libber,* or *male chauvinist pig,* are used to describe people.

Environmental noise is that which occurs between the source and the receiver. The noise is *acoustic* if it consists of sounds other than those generated by the source or receiver that either block out the message or make hearing difficult. Think, for example, how hard it is to understand conversation at a loud party. Sometimes a message is heard, but heard incorrectly, because of acoustic noise.

Another area of environmental noise is *visual* noise. A lecturer was talking in a large lecture hall when a student came in late at the back of the hall and walked to the very front row of seats before sitting down. All eyes followed the student down the aisle and into the first row—visual noise blocked the lecturer's message. Have you ever been distracted by something occurring outside the classroom window while a student was giving a speech or a report? Environmental factors can disrupt communication and make the process more difficult.

Interpersonal Communication Is a Process

The statement that communication is a process means that each communication situation is part of an ongoing series of actions. The events and relationships are dynamic, ever changing, and continuous.[7] To fully understand any single communication, you really need to know all that has come before. Our communication experiences are cumulative—each is a result of what has preceded it. And each experience affects all the ones still to come. For example, as you talk with another person, you may discover an attitude of prejudice that you hadn't known about. That new information will change the way you communicate with that person in the future. The present conversation is a point of development for all future conversations with that person. Thus, this event is not static; it is moving.

It is in a state of flux. The components of the process interact, each affecting all the others.[8]

Think about the kind of conversation you would have if you, at your present age, could talk to the person you were at 16, at 13, and at 8. Each "you" would be a completely developed person *for that age,* yet each would be merely a developmental point for the "you" to follow. Communication builds on itself. The process goes on as long as we are alive.

Interpersonal Communication Is Circular

To view each of your interpersonal communication situations as circular means that you are concerned not only with the effect of your initial message on someone else, but also with the effect of his or her response on you. You then respond based on this new message. This process is important to grasp. (See Figure 1.3.) Though it may sound as if you and the other person are going in circles, you are not. Both of you are constantly changing and making corrections in your thinking as you interact.

Although a minimum number of stimuli and responses are depicted in Figure 1.3, this figure reveals the cyclical nature of communication triggered by the first stimulus. For example, if your initial stimulus is "How was the party last night?" I might reply, "Dull!" You might inquire, "Oh,

Figure 1.3
Communication is circular.

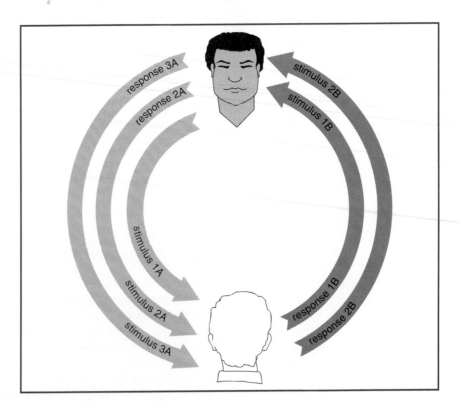

how come?" and I would answer, "Nothing happened." You might follow with "What do you mean?" and so on. The conversation builds on itself. Each remark makes sense only in terms of what preceded it. Remember that in real conversations, many stimuli can occur and be considered at once. Each person may, at any time, provide a new stimulus that can start off its own chain reaction.

Interpersonal Communication Is Complex

Some factors that contribute to the complexity of communication have already been noted. For example, refer back to the discussion of cultural, social, relational, and psychological rules. Communication also is complex because of the tremendous number of variables involved. In every interpersonal communication you share with another person, at least six "people" are involved:

1. The person you think you are.
2. The person your partner thinks you are.
3. The person you believe your partner thinks you are.
4. The person your partner thinks he or she is.
5. The person you think your partner is.
6. The person your partner believes you think he or she is.[9]

With just four constants, mathematicians must cope with approximately fifty possible relations. When you consider the number of variables involved in each interpersonal situation, you begin to appreciate the "terribly involved, and therefore fascinating puzzle" that is known as human communication.[10] Even the most apparently simple interpersonal encounter is actually quite complicated.

Notice how many variables are operating in the relationship shown in Figure 1.4 when the six "people" are described. When you talk with others, what you say depends on how you perceive each of the variables, just as what others say to you depends on the variables they perceive. The

TRY THIS

Pretend you are doing poorly in a course and decide to go in to see the instructor who knows you are not doing well. Briefly describe the six "people" who may be revealed at the beginning of your discussion with your instructor.

more honestly you talk, the more you can be sure that the variables you perceive are accurate. If the two people in Figure 1.4 take the time to get to know each other, he may discover she's not as self-confident as she first appeared to be, and she may find that his "enthusiasm" is nothing more than undirected nervous energy. She may start to appreciate his sincerity or ambitiousness instead, if those traits seem to apply to him. If your perceptions are not accurate, you correct them. Thus, as open communication proceeds, it becomes better and better because

1. It becomes grounded on perceptions that are more accurate—perceptions that are tested through actual interaction.
2. It becomes better adapted to the person you're talking to because you have a better idea of where he or she is coming from.
3. It becomes less open to chance. You need to do less guessing about the other person and less guessing about the nature of the message.
4. There is less chance for breakdowns to occur. Breakdowns often involve simple misperceptions and misinterpretations. These can never be avoided completely. But big breakdowns based on gross error become less likely. You know better who and what you are dealing with.

Communication is complex. There is no way to control all the variables involved, but the more accurate your perceptions are, the better chance you will have of minimizing the complexity of the communication.

Figure 1.4
There are at least six "people" involved in every interpersonal communication.

Interpersonal Communication Is Irreversible and Unrepeatable

Each interpersonal experience is totally unique. It can never occur again in just the same way under any circumstances. Sometimes you wish you *could* take back things you've said. Have you ever said, in the heat of an argument, "You're hopeless! You'll never amount to anything!" or something equally cruel? You can't ever take the sting out of a remark like that, no matter what you say or how you apologize later. The remark cannot be taken back.

It is impossible to re-create a communication situation because the knowledge, feelings, and impressions a person brings to an experience change with time, even within a matter of seconds. Saying "I love you" because you want to in a particular situation is quite different from repeating it because you are asked to, even if the words are the same both times. The communication can never be precisely repeated, no matter how many times you say the very same words, because both people are different as a result of the words having been said in the first place.

Despite thorough organization and planning, most of what occurs interpersonally is spontaneous—open to chance. Have you ever tried to repeat a funny story or describe a hilarious incident only to have your listeners say, "What's so funny about that?" You end up saying, "I guess you had to be there." It is impossible to reconstruct past communication experiences. Even when you come close, new and different factors over which you have no control arise to change the situation and the communication.

Interpersonal Communication Is Transactional[11]

Your whole being is involved in communication, not just your body or mind, reason or emotion. Just as every message you send reveals, in a way, where you are and how you have developed right up to that point, so you should look at the messages you receive from others as revealing the same things about them. From the various cues that others give, you construct a total picture of them. Whether or not the image is accurate does not matter as much as the fact that it is *your* configuration and you use it when you respond to them.[12]

Every time you communicate, you define those with whom you communicate just as you unconsciously offer others cues that help them define you. Anything that evokes meaning for others becomes part of your self-definition, whether it be appearance, voice, touch, distance, eye contact, or word choice. You define others and reveal cues for others to define you *every* time you communicate; there are no exceptions.[13]

Transactional communication—or communication as transaction—is the term used to refer to this process.[14] It emphasizes that who people are with reference to others is a result of the communication events—transactions—in which they are involved. Thus, part of what is going on when you communicate with others is this mutual process of defining.[15] You may wonder why this viewpoint is important. There are several reasons, but the main one is that this view takes into consideration all the preceding characteristics and principles:

1. Communication is *not* linear. From the arrows in the models offered thus far, it appears that interpersonal communication involves looking at one person's choices and then observing the behavior of the other person in response. Although some cause and effect, action and reaction, occurs, the whole process is far more complex than a model can represent.

When you view communication as linear—either one-way (from communicator to receiver) or two-way (simple cause and effect)—you miss the important dynamics of what occurs between the participants. A transactional viewpoint focuses on the dynamics that occur between communicators.

2. Communication is *not* easily observed. The definitions that communicators construct are likely to be complex images based on many interacting cues. These images are unique psychological experiences, almost totally private, and dependent on complex processes of drawing conclusions—that is, putting seemingly unrelated cues together to make sense of them.

When you take a transactional viewpoint, you recognize that communication is a psychological event and thus not easily observed. It involves the minds and behaviors of those involved. All parts of the communication event derive their definition—their very existence and nature—from having been part of the event and perceived by any of the participants.

3. Communication is *not* just people. It is people *meeting*. When you think of a transaction, think of people communicating *with* each other. To look at one person or the other—with no reference to who the others are—is not transactional. You must focus on the meeting between people because who the communicators are at any given moment in a transaction is a result of—or is defined by—both the context and whom they are communicating with and their relationship with those others at any given moment. It is that unique involvement and interaction of the communicators' identities with each other and with the context that gives the transactional viewpoint its distinctiveness and importance.

4. Communication is *not* a result of single forces. You may think you know why other people acted as they did, yet in many cases, the underlying reason was not the sole reason or even the principal one. Just as your definitions of others result from numerous cues, your behavior results from a larger number of causes. To view communication as a transaction is to suggest that it involves the total personality. What happens in any one instance is likely to be a result of multiple forces, factors, or causes.

5. Communication is *not* just what is going on *now*. All communications have a past, present, and future. This underscores the process na-

ture of communication. Every communication is part of an ongoing series of actions. What I think of you right now (present) is likely to be affected by the fight we had last night (past) and is likely to affect my willingness to be open and friendly to you at the party tonight (future). Even if a relationship has no immediate history, it is dependent on all the past relationships you have had. Thus, your experiences provide a past, help determine the present, and often forecast the future.

6. Communication is *not* dependent just on who you are. Who you really are is a very private matter! What you share with others are aspects of your public selves—the roles you play in relation to others. Some of those roles are established by society, some by individual relationships, and some by whim and fancy (moods). Compare the way you behave in the presence of your father with the way you behave in the presence of your best friend. Have you ever noticed that when you are with a person of the opposite sex and a group of his or her friends join you, the behavior of this person often changes—sometimes dramatically? Your behavior is based not just on who you are but also on whom you are with.

The transactional viewpoint is essential to a clear understanding of interpersonal communication. It suggests that when you engage another person through communication, you create a relationship that is totally unique, difficult to observe or describe because of its many facets, and, although changeable, likely to endure (and affect future encounters) forever. Relationships seldom cease to exist. They may change in how they are defined, but they do not end.[16] (See Figure 1.5.)

Building Interpersonal Communication Skills

The overall goal of this book is to help you understand interpersonal communication and become a more effective sender and receiver of interpersonal messages. Here are some general skills that relate to interpersonal communication as a whole. Developing these skills will make it easier to master the others discussed throughout the book. They are practical and can be started at once.

Broaden your experience You should actively search out new relationships and not shy away from potential encounters just because they appear to be unlike what you've dealt with before. Interpersonal communication must occur between people—between you and someone else—and often this means reaching out for new relationships.

You can take steps toward forming new associations rather than waiting to let them simply happen to you. Growth will not necessarily be immediate, but there is no doubt you will open up to many new kinds of

Figure 1.5
The transactional nature of communication. The amoebalike shape around each person represents both the involvement of the total personality in the communication and the changeable nature of the images projected to the other person. It is the meeting of the communicators as a whole as well as unique interaction of their identities that makes the transactional viewpoint distinctive.

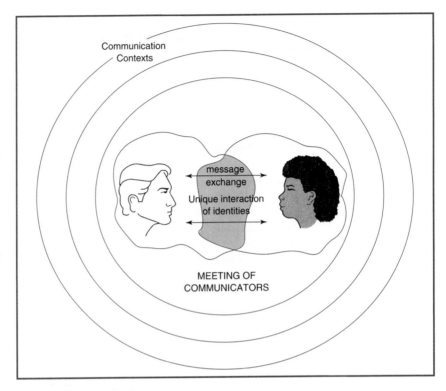

experiences. Willingness to reach out requires risk, but exciting relationships are often built on just that kind of risk.

▲ Plan to attend more activities (parties, athletic events, lectures, socials, movies, and so on).
▲ Plan to meet more people. Break out of your small group of friends and acquaintances. Make contact with at least one new person a day.
▲ Eat breakfast, lunch, or dinner with new people. Sit in a different place.
▲ Join a new club, organization, or program. Look for new ways to use your talents and abilities.

Realize that growth takes time Satisfying relationships don't develop overnight. Like getting to know yourself, really getting to know another person takes time. Give it time. If you know someone in one way only—in the college context, for example—and would like to know more about that person, try interacting in different social settings, talking about different things, and sharing reactions to the new things the two of you have experienced together.

CONSIDER THIS

Another goal of this book (in addition to encouraging intercultural sensitivity) is to provide some ethical framework for interpersonal communication. Read the following ten ethical guidelines, and then answer the questions that follow.

1. Strive to create and maintain an atmosphere of openness, freedom, and responsibility.
2. Reveal an appreciation for individual differences and uniqueness.
3. Seek both sincerity and honesty in your attitudes toward communication.
4. Treat others as human beings who are unique, have feelings, and have inherent worth (as opposed to treating others as objects).
5. Strive for accuracy in your communication with others.
6. Eliminate intentional deception, ambiguity, and obscurity from your communication.
7. Reveal candidness and frankness as you share your personal beliefs and feelings with others.
8. Make every possible attempt to understand the perceptual world of others.
9. Help others make free choices based on accurate bases for those choices.
10. Strive to communicate with others as you would want others to communicate with you.*

Questions
1. Do any of these ethical guidelines present problems or raise questions for you?
2. Are all these guidelines things you normally do anyway, or do some of them offer new approaches or guides?
3. Do you think it is reasonable to be concerned with ethics every time you are involved in interpersonal communication, or is this an unreasonable request?

*From Richard L. Johannesen, *Ethics in Human Communication,* 3d ed. (Prospect Heights, IL: Waveland Press, Inc., 1990). See especially Chapter 8, "Interpersonal Communication and Small Group Discussion," pages 139–149.

People are often quite different in the context of their own families than they are in the context of college. You may discover a new side of a person by observing him or her in a setting other than the one you're accustomed to. Traveling, shopping, eating, or simply spending time with a person can be very revealing if the two of you usually don't do these things together. Only through time can you become familiar enough with the feelings and motivations of another to really understand the person. The key to relationship building at this stage is simply patience.

▲ Ask new acquaintances to do things with you.
▲ Don't push yourself on other people.
▲ Allow relationships to develop—slowly.
▲ Begin to spend time with other people.
▲ Practice being a social animal—feeling the energy that other people transmit, and all their unique qualities.
▲ Decide what you need from other people and what you can give them.
▲ Let other people know you are ready and open to sharing.

Use existing relationships in new ways You might try using existing relationships as a testing ground for the information you'll be picking up about interpersonal communication. Try things out with a friend. Practice new patterns of sending and receiving messages. Create hypothetical situations similar to some of those described in this chapter, and develop other ways of coping with these situations. Allow "communication" to be the subject for conversations and discussions. (Don't give up if this feels strange at first!) Talk about the communication principles discussed in this chapter. Be specific about how to improve skills.

▲ Begin to talk about your behavior. Share your impressions, and be responsive to those of your friends and acquaintances. (Remember that as you encourage feedback, you are likely to get as much negative as positive feedback.)
▲ Do not refute comments or defend your behavior. It is important to get honest reactions; defensiveness may encourage dishonesty.
▲ Experiment with things you are learning about communication. Do some of the "Try This" activities suggested in this book with your friends. It is better to experiment first, in a warm, trusting environment, before taking new behaviors beyond the confines of such security and protectiveness.
▲ Engage in *metacommunication:* talking about the communication you engage in. Is it effective? Offensive? Can it be strengthened or improved? What can you do better?

Develop openness Developing skill in any area begins with an awareness that something can and should be done. You need to be open to

What interpersonal skills would you put to use if you found yourself in a situation like this? Pretend that you have just encountered this person. What special skills are necessary when you talk with a stranger in a new location?

change. You can start by simply trying to become more aware of the kinds of things you do, the feelings you have toward yourself and others, the way you view life and what you want your place in it to be. You should learn to monitor your own behavior and feelings as objectively as possible, becoming more open and responsive to your internal experiences.

Openness also means being receptive to all that goes on around you. As you open up to your environment, you will begin to be more sensitive to the small details of things that you may once have overlooked. This sensitivity will increase your ability to re-create situations in your mind and to better analyze and dissect their parts. Your new behavior may be more carefully considered than before in light of your past successes and failures. This is growth, change, development—maturity. A lot of people would discover a great deal more if only they would pause and look and feel and care just a bit more than they do.[17]

▲ Be prepared to find things about yourself that need changing.

▲ Realize that you are not perfect: there *is* room for improvement.

▲ Be ready to take action wherever necessary. As you open yourself to discovery, be conscious of those things about which something can be done. Commit yourself to those areas.

▲ Keep your sights on progress—moving forward in a positive direction. Do not be overly concerned with failures, and do not try to anticipate the future; deal with what can be done *now*—in the present.

Improve the exactness of your communication We all need to improve the exactness of our communication. It's a great help to be able to convey to others just what you mean to convey and to receive from them just what they mean to send to you. This quality has been labeled **fidelity.** Improving the exactness of your communication is a skill. If you're aware of the need for fidelity, you will become more sensitive to those situations in which some of the fidelity is lost. You will be better able to detect when meaning is becoming distorted. And, it is hoped, you'll be able to take steps to correct the situation.

▲ Think about what you intend to say before opening your mouth. Plan it out almost completely.

▲ Think about ways you can elaborate on or enumerate the things you have to say. Practice the art of skillful repetition; how many different ways can you say the same things?

▲ Be responsive to the feedback you get, and use it to alter your message as necessary. Plan to make changes in your message to ensure that the other person will hear what you intend him or her to hear.

Make a contract with yourself Vague, general plans for improvement or change generally do not work. What is needed is an explicit contract that identifies the objectives and enumerates specific measures you can use to achieve them.[18] In this way, progress can be charted.

▲ What changes do you want to make? Be realistic about this. You may want to divide your goal into smaller, more manageable parts. For example, if one of your goals is to make more friends, your first step might be to say hello to four new people each week.

▲ How will you monitor your progress? Charts and journals may help you keep track. You might also ask your friends to monitor your behavior.

▲ What rewards will you get for fulfilling each part of your contract? For every new person you say hello to, you might reward yourself with a new magazine or a milkshake. For accomplishing a major step, use a movie or a meal out as a reward. Minor accomplishments deserve small rewards; major ones deserve important rewards. Reinforcement is essential for making the contract work. It helps you meet your own desired standards of performance. Don't be stingy. Self-approval will help you continue the contract.

▲ How will you know when you have completed the contract? At the end of two weeks you will have said hello to eight new people, and you will be ready to move on to the next step in making friends. Set daily or weekly goals.

▲ What will you do if you fail to meet the contract? Appropriate punishments can be just as effective as appropriate rewards, provided they are realistic and established in advance of the contract period.

But plan to make them stick. Some possibilities are these: cleaning out your desk drawers, writing a thank-you note that you've been putting off for months, sorting out that pile of magazines and papers on the floor of your closet.

It is a good idea to put your contract in writing. This makes it more official and increases your likelihood of honoring it. With concentration and practice, many of the goals you set for yourself will soon become second nature to you. You can form a contract around many or all of the skills and activities in this book.

▶ ## SUMMARY

Interpersonal communication skills are important for teachers as well as for businesspeople. They are important not only in the hiring process but also for judging effectiveness on the job. Thus, in both cases, effective skills are strong predictors of success.

The elements of people, message, and effects were discussed in the first section. People are senders and receivers simultaneously. Messages may be verbal and/or nonverbal. Effects can be mental, physical, or emotional. Messages that have no effect serve no useful purpose.

Fourteen characteristics of interpersonal communication were discussed. It involves at least two people, involves feedback, need not be face-to-face, need not be intentional, and produces some effect. In addition, it need not involve words, is affected by context, contains information and defines relationships, and is affected by noise. Finally, interpersonal communication is a process, is circular, is complex, is irreversible and unrepeatable, and is transactional.

That interpersonal communication is transactional emphasizes that who people are with reference to others is a result of communication events or transactions. This viewpoint is important because it underscores the principles that communication is not linear, is not easily observed, is not just people, is not the result of single forces, is not just what is going on now, and is not dependent just on who you are. The transactional viewpoint is essential to a clear understanding of interpersonal communication.

The skills discussed in this chapter are broad; they relate to interpersonal communication as a whole. Although broad, they are practical. Suggestions include broadening your experience, realizing that growth takes time, using existing relationships in new ways, developing openness, improving the exactness of your communication, and making a contract with yourself.

Beginning in Chapter 2, "Creating Meaning: Perception," the discussion will become more specific. Also, the skills suggested in Chapter 2 and thereafter will tend to be more specific.

▶ ## KEY TERMS

intrapersonal communication
small-group communication
mass communication
organizational communication
public communication
feedback
mental effect
physical effect
emotional effect

interpersonal communication
dyad
triad
psychological context
physical context
social context
cultural context
temporal context

content dimension
relationship dimension
confirm
reject
disconfirm
noise
transactional communication
fidelity

▶ ## NOTES

1. Scott D. Johnson, "A National Assessment of Secondary-School Principals' Perceptions of Teaching-Effectiveness Criteria," *Communication Education* 43 (January 1994), 1–16. See especially page 13.
2. Dan B. Curtis, Jerry L. Winsor, and Ronald D. Stephens, "National Preferences in Business and Communication," *Communication Education* 38 (January 1989): 6–14.
3. Beverly Davenport Sypher and Theodore E. Zorn, Jr., "Communication-Related Abilities and Upward Mobility: A Longitudinal Investigation," *Human Communication Research* 12 (Spring 1986): 428.
4. Theodore Caplow, *Two Against One: Coalitions in Triads* (Englewood Cliffs, NJ: Prentice-Hall, 1968), as cited in William D. Wilmot, *Dyadic Communication*, 3d ed. (New York: Random House, 1987), p. 23.
5. William W. Wilmot, *Dyadic Communication*, 2d ed. (Reading, MA: Addison-Wesley Publishing Co., 1979), p. 23.
6. See Harold D. Lasswell, "The Structure and Function of Communication in Society," in L. Bryson, ed., *The Communication of Ideas* (New York: Harper & Row, 1948), 37.
7. David K. Berlo, *The Process of Communication* (New York: Holt, Rinehart and Winston, 1960), 24.
8. Berlo, 24.
9. Dean C. Barnlund, "Toward a Meaning-Centered Philosophy of Communication," *Journal of Communication* 12 (1962): 202.
10. Barnlund, 202.

11. John Stewart, "An Interpersonal Approach to the Basic Course," *The Speech Teacher* 21 (1972): 10.
12. Dean C. Barnlund, "Communication: The Context of Change," in Carl E. Larson and Frank E. X. Dance, eds., *Perspectives on Communication* (Milwaukee: The Speech Communication Center of the University of Wisconsin, 1968), 27.
13. John Stewart, "Interpersonal Communication: Contact Between Persons," in John Stewart, ed., *Bridges Not Walls: A Book About Interpersonal Communication,* 5th ed. (New York: McGraw-HIll, 1990), 22–24.
14. Stewart, "An Interpersonal Approach," 10.
15. Stewart, "Interpersonal Communication: Contact Between Persons," 22–24.
16. Stewart, "Interpersonal Communication: Contact Between Persons," 26–27.
17. Arthur Gordon, *A Touch of Wonder* (Old Tappan, NJ: Spire Books, 1976), 11.
18. Philip B. Zimbardo, *Shyness* (New York: Jove Publications, 1977), 229–230.

▶ ## FURTHER READING

Ruth Anne Clark, *Studying Interpersonal Communication: The Research Experience* (Newbury Park, CA: Sage Publications, 1991). In a chapter that emphasizes awareness, this is an excellent source because Clark begins by introducing the nature of communication research. She then explains evaluation of the research question, internal and external validity, the independent variable, treatment of subjects, evaluation and types of dependent measures, data sets, generalizing, the relationship between variables, and reporting studies. This is a clear introduction designed for undergraduates.

Gordon L. Dahnke and Glen W. Clatterbuck, eds., *Human Communication: Theory and Research* (Belmont, CA: Wadsworth Publishing Co., 1990). This multi-authored text provides a broad survey of recent developments in speech communication from an empirical research perspective. The editors integrate prevailing principles, current theory, and related research within specific content areas. They begin with a history of human communication inquiry, then in four parts discuss channels, contexts, persuasive functions, and methods of inquiry. Each chapter is written by a well-known scholar/empiricist in the field.

Steve Duck, *Human Relationships,* 2nd ed. (Newbury Park, CA: Sage Publications, 1992). In this 278-page paperback, Duck begins with interpersonal communication and goes on to emotion and the growth of personal relationships, influencing strangers, and social relationships in childhood. Duck examines the development of courtship, sexual decision making in dating, and the family. He discusses problems in relationships and how to put them right, deals with gossip and persuasion, and applies research on relationships to the psychology of health and to behavior in the courtroom.

Em Griffin, *A First Look at Communication Theory* (New York: McGraw-Hill, 1991). Griffin has written a text for students who have no background in communication theory. He makes 31 specific theories interesting and understandable. Indeed, he offers a shopping list of theories—a wide range that reflects the diversity of the discipline. One useful feature is the extended example used in each chapter to illustrate the theory described. Another is that technical language has been translated into familiar words and terms. A useful, interesting book.

Dominic A. Infante, Andrew S. Rancer, and Deanna F. Womack, *Building Communication Theory* (Prospect Heights, IL: Waveland Press, Inc., 1990). The authors begin with an introduction to studying communication, points of view about theory, and an explanation of covering laws, rules, and systems perspectives. In the section on major approaches, they discuss trait, persuasion, and verbal and nonverbal behavior approaches. Finally, they look at interpersonal, organizational and group, mass media, and intercultural contexts. Their appendix explains communication research methods. There is a great deal of information here.

Stephen W. Littlejohn, *Theories of Human Communication*, 4th ed. (Belmont, CA: Wadsworth Publishing Co., 1992) Littlejohn presents the best available textbook for examining the present state of the art in communication theory. He discusses the nature of theory and inquiry in communication and includes a summary of general and contextual theories of communication. This book is valuable not only for its chapter on communication in relationships (Chapter 12) but because it offers students a look at the whole range of theory and inquiry of which interpersonal communication is just one part. Readable, thorough, and well-researched, this book is designed for the serious student of speech communication.

Barbara M. Montgomery and Steve Duck, eds., *Studying Interpersonal Interaction* (New York: The Guilford Press, 1991). The editors offer a comprehensive, critical examination of current research methods used to study human social behavior in interpersonal settings. A few of the 18 topics addressed include optional metaphors, multiple perspectives, levels of analysis, accounts and narratives, diaries and logs, self-reports, discourse, behavioral observation, experimentation, content analysis, categorical data, and longitudinal analysis. For the serious student, this is an excellent introduction to the many methods used in studying interpersonal interaction.

Don Stacks, Mark Hickson III, and Sidney R. Hill, Jr., *Introduction to Communication Theory* (Fort Worth, TX: Holt, Rinehart and Winston, 1991). The authors include six sections: introduction to communication theory, the materials of communication theory, framing the edifice (rhetorical perspectives on communication), building the edifice for the individual (psychological approaches), building the edifice for society (sociological approaches), and integrating and living with the edifice. This book is designed for the first course in communication theory.

Creating Meaning: Perception

CHAPTER OBJECTIVES

After reading this chapter, you should be able to

- ▲ Define perception.
- ▲ Explain the perception sieve and how meaning is created.
- ▲ Identify the six implications of the perception-sieve analogy.
- ▲ Explain the process of receiving information.
- ▲ Explain the process of construction.
- ▲ Distinguish between selecting, organizing, and interpreting information.
- ▲ Explain the steps of enlarging, simplifying, and closing.
- ▲ Understand and provide an example of each of the three major barriers to accurate perception: stereotyping, proximity, and role.
- ▲ Explain the advantages and disadvantages of stereotyping.
- ▲ Distinguish between physical and psychological proximity.
- ▲ Practice the skills for improving perception.

▼ Javier was driving home from school. He was angry. He had just had a fight with his girlfriend, Rosalie, over what he thought was a silly matter. Javier and Rosalie had both witnessed an automobile accident. They were waiting at a stoplight when a car came from their right and hit a car that was turning left in front of them. The police interviewed both Javier and Rosalie, but their stories were different. Javier claimed the driver in front of them had not looked right before turning left and was at fault. Rosalie said she saw the driver look right but that the other driver was driving recklessly and too fast. Javier said there was nothing wrong with the driving of the car coming from their right.

Unfortunately, the driver turning left was a woman, and the driver coming from their right was a man, so Rosalie accused Javier of being sexist—of siding with the man just because he was a man. Javier and Rosalie were still angry with each other because they couldn't agree on the details of the accident both had witnessed and because of the arguments that resulted from their disagreement.

Leanne had just joined the future business executive's club (FBEC) at her university. When she mentioned this to her friends, they told her the club was run by a bunch of students who thought they were too good for everyone else. Since Leanne had just joined, she decided to look into this possibility and gather evidence for herself. At one meeting, she noticed that only certain people were called on and that not everyone was given an opportunity to speak. Another time, she saw a group of FBEC members meeting with a faculty member in the cafeteria, and she knew she had not heard about the meeting or been invited to it. After a meeting where officers were elected, and the nominations were never opened to nominations from the floor, Leanne decided to confront the president of FBEC about what she had observed.

The president had a clear and reasonable explanation for each item Leanne mentioned. She said that at the meeting when some people were not called on, the FBEC had to vacate the meeting room after only a short meeting. Therefore, she inadvertently overlooked some people in her haste to complete the agenda. She apologized. About the meeting with the faculty member, she said it was spontaneous and co-incidental and had not been planned beforehand. And with respect to the election of officers, the actual election, she said, was pro forma (for the sake of form). Candidates were required to submit their own nomi-nations with reasons to justify their nomination, and these candidates had all been interviewed by the current officers and the faculty adviser before the election meeting. The meeting was simply to agree to the slate that had previously been approved. Leanne apologized for judg-ing so hastily.

Javier, Rosalie, and Leanne are not unlike you when it comes to per-ception. You view the world from your own unique position in it. Whether Javier's view of the automobile accident was influenced by who was driving the cars will never be known. Perhaps Rosalie's view was also influenced by who was driving. What is known, however, is that whether or not their perceptions were influenced by the sex of the dri-vers, their views of the accident were very likely to be different because people are different.

In Leanne's case, her perception of a situation was directly affected by what she had been told by her friends. She probably would not have perceived these three situations in the same way without her friends' in-formation. Whether the situation was true as her friends had said or true as the president explained may be determined by Leanne at some future point—with more information and experience in the FBEC. Leanne was sensitive to her friends' point of view, but she was also willing to allow the president's explanations to hold true for now, because she had very little evidence otherwise.

This chapter is about **perception**: how we create meaning. It is di-vided into three parts: (1) reception [taking in information through your senses], (2) construction [constructing experiences according to the orga-nization of categories you possess], and (3) skills. The first part will cover how we select, organize, and interpret information. The second will cover some factors that affect construction—such as our tendency to label things, physical and psychological distance, and the restrictive roles we sometimes play. Finally, the last part will discuss how you can improve your skills in perception so that genuine, effective interaction is more likely to occur.

CONSIDER THIS

I want to begin this chapter by once again offering a broader, cultural point of view. Here, Edward T. Hall, a cultural anthropologist, talks about the elements that go into the programming of human beings.

> The rules governing what one perceives and [what one] is blind to in the course of living are not simple; at least five sets of disparate (distinct or different) categories of events must be taken into account. These are: the subject or activity, the situation, one's status in a social system, past experience, and culture. The patterns governing juggling these five dimensions are learned early in life and are mostly taken for granted.*

Questions

1. Using the example of Javier and Rosalie at the beginning of this chapter (page 45), what do you think the five categories might be for each person?
2. Is it clear from the categories Hall presents why perceptions from different people, even of the same event, will always be different?
3. Can you cite an example from your own experience in which differences in each of the categories affected differences in the perception of a common event?

*From Edward T. Hall, *Beyond Culture* (Garden City, NY: Doubleday & Company, 1976), 85–103, as reprinted in Larry A. Samovar and Richard E. Porter, *Intercultural Communication: A Reader,* 6th ed. (Belmont, CA: Wadsworth Publishing Company, 1991), 47.

▲▲▲ *What You Receive Is What You Get: The Reception of Stimuli*

Perception is the process of gathering information and giving it meaning
You see a movie, and you give meaning to it: "It's one of the best I've seen." You come away from a class after the third week, and you give meaning to it: "It finally makes sense." You gather information from what your senses see, hear, touch, taste, and smell, and you give meaning to that information. Although the information may come to us in a variety of forms, it is all processed, or *perceived*, in the mind.

Communication and perception are so closely related that you can't really mention one without the other. Look, for example, at the obvious relationship between the two when Leanne joined the FBEC. Her friends' communication with her had a direct and important effect on what she perceived during her first experiences in the FBEC. What she perceived, too, had a direct and important effect on the communication she had with the president of the FBEC. To understand interpersonal communication you need some understanding of perception, for it is through perception that you become aware of your surroundings, give meaning to our world, and come to know yourself and others. Most of the time, you engage in the process without paying attention to what you are doing. You rarely think of *how* it is occurring or how you could improve it. Perception is a complex activity, but by understanding the process, you can improve your chances for more effective interpersonal communication. You can not only expand the perimeters of your own personal world but try to improve the accuracy of your perceptions as well.

TRY THIS

For just a moment now, exercise your imagination. Listen to the messages being sent from the following environments. What are your perceptions in each case?

1. You see a slum with trash spilling out on the sidewalk. A child is looking down at the concrete from steps going into an apartment. What do you hear?
2. You are in a gray, bleak, and barren ward in a state mental hospital with people sitting on benches. Their drab appearance is heightened by faded, ill-fitting clothes, and there's a smell that is only too common in such a ward. How would you feel in that environment?
3. There is a beautiful, royal-blue ocean with whitecaps breaking against a sparkling, sandy beach. The beach is outlined by palm trees and a few fluffy white clouds. How do you feel about that message?
4. A warm fire is crackling in the fireplace. The lights are dimly lit, and outside the picture window, snow is falling quietly. Soft music is playing in the background, and you are there with the person with whom you want to share that environment? What are your feelings now?

Paraphrased from Ken Olson, *Can You Wait Till Friday?* (Phoenix: O'Sullivan Woodside, 1975), pp. 53–54. Used by permission of the author.

▲▲▲ *The Perception Sieve: How You Create Meaning*

The **perception sieve** is simply one way of illustrating our unique perceptual filtering system. Just as a sieve allows particles of certain sizes to pass through its perforated openings, our perception system does the same. In the case of the perception sieve, however, you will need to visualize a sieve with holes of different shapes and sizes. (See Figure 2.1.) Each hole in the sieve represents a category you understand or have had some experience with. Here, you'll look at development, size and shape, and blockage.

Development   Your perceptual categories develop as you grow. Your interests, experiences, and knowledge create them. Your culture, parents, religion, education, and peers are probably the strongest influences on how you perceive the world. As your interests change, you drop old categories and form new ones. As a child of six, you may have wanted to be a firefighter or law-enforcement officer; as an adolescent you may have wanted to be a veterinarian or teacher; as a college student you may want to be a doctor or lawyer; after college you may choose to be an electronics technician or computer programmer.

Size and shape   The largest categories are those areas you're most familiar with or have given preference to, like special needs and interests. When you go into a bookstore, for example, you might look only for books on the "New Fiction" shelf. A fellow thinking about preparing his fiancee a gourmet dinner might just be interested in cookbooks. Someone else might be drawn to the section labeled "Sports" or "Business" or "Psychology and Self-Help"—special needs and interests.

Notice, too, that the sieve holes are irregular in size and shape. If information comes to you that does not exactly fit one of your present categories, you may distort that information so that it does fit. For example, Bridget distorted information she heard about William. When Bridget overheard Rhonda talking about him, she distinctly heard her say all good things. In a later conversation, she learned that the words she heard—"hard working," "smile," and "patient"—were actually "works too hard," "vile," and "impatient." Realizing this totally changed her perception.

Blockage   One function of your perception filtering process is to protect you from information you dislike or disagree with. You do not let that information through, or you adjust it as necessary, as in the example of Bridget. In addition to adjusting the shape, you might totally block out negative information. For example, if you hear some unflattering remarks about your roommate but one favorable comment, like "You must admit she has a sense of humor," you might hear only the compliment and filter out all the other comments. You tend to hear what you want to hear.

But notice that certain holes in Figure 2.1 are black. There are some areas in which you make a determined effort *not* to gain any more information. You may no longer want to hear more rumors about a friend. You may no longer want to read science fiction. You may no longer want to taste any drinks containing rum and coconut milk. These are experiences you choose to close yourself off from, so you block them totally.·

Implications

The perception sieve analogy has six implications: (1) *uniqueness,* (2) *activity,* (3) *change,* (4) *rigidity,* (5) *acceptance,* and (6) *meaning.*

Uniqueness Every person has a unique perceptual filtering system, although there is some cultural overlap. For example, if you are a white, middle-class, urban, eighteen-year-old, your perceptions are likely to resemble those of other white, middle-class, urban, eighteen-year-olds more than those of any other group in society because of your socialization. But your own perceptions still won't be exactly like those of any

Figure 2.1
The perception sieve.

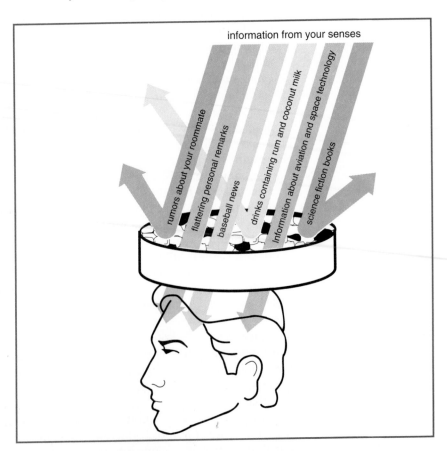

CONSIDER THIS

Perception and communication have an ethical component. Since communication is one way you have of negotiating your perceptions—what actually takes place—you need to be concerned about the people involved. Richard L. Johannesen, a writer on ethics, defined *dialogue* as "a genuine concern for the welfare and fulfillment of the other and a conscious choicemaking in response to the demands of specified situations." One of the characteristics of dialogue was a spirit of mutual equality:

> Although society may rank participants in dialogue as of unequal status or accomplishment, and although the roles appropriate to each partner may differ, participants themselves view each other as persons rather than as objects, as things, to be exploited or manipulated for selfish satisfaction. The exercise of power or superiority is avoided. Participants do not impose their opinion, cause, or will. In dialogic communication, agreement of the listener with the speaker's aim is secondary to independent, self-deciding participation. Participants aid each other in making responsible decisions regardless of whether the decision be favorable or unfavorable to the particular view presented.*

Questions

1. Do you think it is realistic that human beings can interact with each other on an ongoing basis in a spirit of mutual equality?
2. What are the normal, everyday, regularly occurring barriers to talking with others in a spirit of mutual equality?
3. What kinds of changes would you make in your interpersonal communication with others if you adopted the philosophy or the approach contained in the material quoted here? Could you do it?
4. With this point of view, are your perceptions of things likely to change along with changes in your ways of behavior? Why or why not?

*From Richard L. Johannesen, *Ethics in Human Communication,* 3rd ed. (Prospect Heights, IL: Waveland Press, Inc., 1990), 61, 63.

other person. Each individual's perceptual sieve depends on numerous elements that either broaden or limit the size of the categories.

Your physiological makeup affects how much information you are able to gather. The number of visual stimuli you take in is limited, for example, by how well your eyes work. And although the number of stimuli you ordinarily sense is impressive, it is small compared with the maximum amount of which you are capable. You probably are physiologically able to distinguish 7,500,000 different colors.[1] Your ears can pick up sounds ranging from 20 to 20,000 vibration cycles per second. You can distinguish between 5,000 different smells and 10,000 different tastes. Even your sense of touch is more sensitive than you may have thought. Your fingers can feel the separations between objects as little as 3 to 8 millimeters apart.[2] Your body is an extremely sensitive instrument for taking in sensory information.

The kind of information you perceive is strongly affected by your expectations, attitudes, values, interests, emotions, needs, language, experience, and knowledge. It is important to realize that the new information you pick up depends on the perceptual categories you have available, and that each of your systems is unique. Although several of your categories may be similar to someone else's, you must never assume that all of yours are like all of his or hers or even that *any* are identical.

Activity Perception is not a passive process; it requires activity. Your perceptions are your own, and you have some control over them; you do not have total control because of the rules governing what one perceives, as pointed out by Edward T. Hall in the first "Consider This" in this chapter.

Because you have most of the control, however, you do not record everything your senses take in. Perception is selective. You block out some sights, sounds, and smells. For the most part, you actively apply your perceptual filter to incoming stimuli. Your perceptual system gives you a way of dealing with outside reality in terms of inside reality—your own thoughts, feelings, and attitudes.

Change Although your perceptions may be well established, they can and do change. The more open you are to new experiences, the more likely it is that your perceptions will change. If you aren't willing to try new things, you may not allow information through that does not correspond with the categories you have consciously or unconsciously established. You may adapt some of the categories to keep up with the times but remain generally rather inflexible. That is why change is so difficult for people.

Rigidity For the most part, categories are stable, behavior is inflexible, and change is difficult. You can become less rigid if you realize you have a lot of room for new information and if you are willing to take in information unrelated to what you already know. You might develop conditional categories for information you consider risky and for information you're not yet sure what you're going to do with. You will have a hard time with information totally unrelated to your present knowledge and

Because our perceptual filtering system won't be exactly like any other person's, the differences can create problems.

experience because you have no familiar way of processing it. But knowing that you do have room for new experiences if you'll only let them in is a good start toward flexibility. And sometimes just realizing how little you know is an education in itself.

Acceptance Another implication of the perception sieve analogy is that you do not accept stimuli just as they are presented. You hear your instructor talking; what is actually being said may not be what you hear. If you do not understand an assignment, you might make the instructor's statements come as close as possible to an assignment you had in the past. Because you need a level of acceptance, you place what you take in against what you already know. The more you adapt stimuli to fit with what you know, the less likely it is that your views will reflect what actually occurred, and the more likely they are to be acceptable to you.

Meaning Whatever meaning you are left with is based on *how* you process the information rather than on what actually happened. When a friend says she sat through a doubleheader on a 90-degree day, what that experience means to you is a result of all your attitudes and feelings

Figure 2.2
Your perceptions are
based on your own
attitudes and
perceptions.

about baseball and hot weather. The experience might have meant something quite different to her. (See Figure 2.2.).

Your interpretation of something is just that: an interpretation. Objects, events, and words do not have inherent meanings. Their meanings are in you and in the way you evaluate them. When you talk with someone else, you make up what that person says, just as when you see an object, you make up what that object looks like. Your perceptual sieve, or filtering system, determines how you view the world. The world exists for you as you perceive it. You cannot "tell it like it is"; you can only tell it as you perceive it.

Understanding this is a big step toward more effective interpersonal communication. It will help you become more sensitive to reactions and to experiences, both your own and others', as personal interpretations of events. It's useful to think in terms of how and why you respond to something rather than in terms of the "something" as an experience in itself. *Experiences have meaning only as you respond to them. This is the transactional view of communication.*

Visual Perception: Coping with Ambiguity

There are some famous drawings that psychologists show their students. Two of these are reproduced in Figure 2.3A. Look at the drawing on the left. Do you see an old witch or a pretty young woman? If you look at the

Figure 2.3A

drawing long enough, can you see the other image? (If you have trouble
seeing both images in the left-hand figure, look at Figure 2.3B below.)
What do you see in the drawing at the right above? A vase—or two men
facing each other nose to nose? When you see one image in these drawings, you cannot see the other.

Writer Sydney J. Harris has suggested that there is a broader lesson
in perception to be learned from looking at these pictures. "What we call
our view of life," Harris writes, "is a shifting image, not a continuous reality. Our lives are ambiguous patterns made up of different strands, and
at different times we choose one pattern to look at rather than another—
but neither is more real than the other." Harris continues:

Figure 2.3B

> *Maintaining one's sanity and sense of balance depends in large part upon acceptance of ambiguity, in recognizing that this is part of the human condition. . . . Reality is not one picture, but two. We cannot see them together, but they are both there. Accepting this fact, and holding them in equilibrium, is more than half the art of coping with ambiguity.[3]*

Since we can never see both images at once, it is important to reserve final judgments and evaluations, remembering that *every* situation is part witch and part pretty young woman, part vase and part angry men.

If you wonder how much of perception is a matter of reception and how much must be constructed, the answer is clear. The more information available in the environment—that is, the more stimuli presented to your sense organs for reception—the less perception has to be constructed. This is discussed under the "Organizing" step of the construction process because it has to do with enlarging upon and closing in the data you receive.

▲▲▲ *The Perceiver: The Process of Construction*

To develop the concept of perception in greater detail, let's think in terms of construction. The main point of construction is that events do not just present themselves to people; people construct experiences according to the organization of categories they already possess in their minds. Those with a small number of categories reveal **cognitive simplicity** (cognition is the faculty of knowing). Such simplicity leads to stereotyping and nondifferentiation in their perceptions. Those with a large number of categories reveal **cognitive complexity,** which allows a more subtle and sensitive discrimination between perceptions.[4] Reading, traveling, experiencing, and learning contribute positively to our number of available categories.

For the purposes of discussion, let's divide construction into the three steps of *selecting, organizing,* and *interpreting* information. These steps occur simultaneously and often instantaneously. The construction process is complicated by the fact that each step depends upon and is affected by countless factors occurring within us and within our environment.

Selecting: Choosing the Pieces of the Puzzle

You perceive selectively. That is, you limit the quantity of stimuli to which you attach meaning. You are selective simply because you are exposed to too many stimuli each day to be able to deal with all of them. Notice, for example, how **selecting** works in reference to advertising messages:

> . . . *the average American adult is assaulted by a minimum of 560 advertising messages each day. Of the 560 to which he is exposed, however, he only notices seventy-six. In effect, he blocks out 484 advertising messages a day to preserve his attention for other matters.[5]*

You usually choose to focus on those messages you agree with or that are most meaningful to you. During an election campaign, you tend to recall acceptable comments made by the candidate you support and unacceptable comments made by the other person. And you tend to ascribe statements with which you agree to the person you support.[6]

You select what you will perceive on the basis of your experiences. The next time you go to a party, pay attention to what seems most important to the people there. One person may observe the "performance" of the host and hostess. Another person might be totally absorbed with what people are wearing. Only the handsome men might catch one person's eye, while somebody else is aware of the all the vivacious women present. The pretzels and cheese dip might be center of attention for some people.

Each person chooses what is most meaningful on the basis of his or her experiences. One person may have been brought up to believe that gracious hospitality is an essential element at a party. Another person may have parents who attach great importance to clothes. You will usually select for perception stimuli related to matters you've already given some thought to or had memorable experiences with. The act of selecting stimuli is the first step in the perceptual process. Once you select and receive certain stimuli, what do you do with that information?

TRY THIS

The next time you read a newspaper, be aware of what you decide to read and what you decide not to read. Answer the following questions with respect to your behavior:

1. What section of the newspaper did you turn to first? Why?
2. In what order did you read the remaining sections? Do you know why you chose this order?
3. What sections or articles did you choose not to read at all? Were the reasons the same as in numbers 1 and 2 above?
4. Have you perceived changes in the articles you are interested in reading over the past few months? Over the past few years? Do you expect further changes to occur? Can you predict what they will be?
5. What forces operate in your life that influence you to read certain sections or articles and not others? That is, why are you interested in certain topics and not others?
6. Are there changes in your behavior when you are monitoring or observing what you are doing?

Organizing: Putting the Pieces Together

Because information comes to you in a random, unstructured manner, you must do something with it to make sense of it. You must determine relationships: how the new information relates to other information you are receiving and to information you already have. To get an idea of how you need to organize cues, stop reading and look at this page and the marks on it as if there were no structure to it. Look at the room you are sitting in right now as if it contained no structure—as if you didn't know that chairs were for sitting on, floors for walking on, lamps for providing light. How about the view from the nearest window? Can you look at nature as if there were no structure? The world, for you to understand it, requires **organization,** and you organize it by perceiving relationships.

If you see a swallow flying by, you know from experience that it is not the only bird in the world. You know there are many swallows like it and many other birds unlike it. You know that birds eat insects or seeds for food, and that birds can be, in turn, eaten by larger forms of life. You know that birds are warm blooded as you are, and feathered as you are not. They walk as you do and fly as you do not. You organize your information about birds by noting relationships between this particular bird and all the other birds in your experience. You organize information more or less consciously, in more or less detail, with all incoming stimuli. Think of the organizing process as involving three steps—**enlarging, simplifying,** and **closing**—that occur simultaneously and instantaneously.

Enlarging   The information your senses receive is in small pieces. Think of words as tiny pieces of information. In any communication situation, *you try to put the words you hear into a larger context so that you can understand them better. This is called* **enlarging,** *looking for a frame of reference for the message.* Start by observing the whole nonverbal picture—the facial expressions, gestures, and body movements of the person sending the message—and placing the words into that picture. The fewer the pieces received, the more enlarging must be done.

Put yourself in a situation where a friend you are waiting for emerges from a classroom banging the door and stamping his feet. These cues, although small, provide the big picture for you. You "enlarge" by framing your friend's behavior as an emotional outburst, and this enlargement allows you to understand your friend's words when he says, "I *hate* that class; I just hate it! I'm never going back in there again." Framing is a process of enlarging because it provides the order or system for what is within the frame. If, later the same day, your friend becomes very short with another friend of yours, you might say, "Oh, Chris is still mad about that history class this morning." Framing suggests the mood into which other behaviors can be classified. In addition to mood, it could be humor, mental constitution, temper, or disposition. When you say that someone is in an unhappy frame of mind, you have organized the perception by enlargement.

Simplifying   Just as you search for a relationship between pieces of information and a larger framework into which you can place those pieces, you also look for ways to **simplify** complex or confusing stimuli. Complex stimuli are those that you have difficulty understanding. *You simplify complex stimuli by finding patterns, an order that will help you make sense of the message.*

For example, if you drive into a gas station to get directions, you might hear the attendant say something like this: "You go up here to your first stop light and turn left on Broadview. At your next light turn right. Then just after you pass Wiley High School, turn right; and the street you are looking for will be your next left." As a simplifying response you might reply, "So it's a left, two rights, and a left." You look for order in the stimuli that will help you remember the essential information.

You do the same thing when you hear a teacher explaining an assignment or when you are taking notes in a lecture. You do not need, and don't have time to record, all the teacher says. You simplify the message so as to have the essentials when it is time to complete the assignment or to study your notes for a test.

Given a relatively complex perception, you simplify it into some recognizable form. Look at Figure 2.4. You may simplify the five-sided figure in "A" by seeing it as a house, a triangle on top of a square, or an envelope. In "B" you may see a triangle resting on two rectangles (or posts) or even a covered bridge.

Stereotyping and proximity, which will be discussed shortly, are also ways of simplifying complex perceptions. You need to be able to make perceptions plain and easy to digest.

Closing   *The process of filling in gaps between pieces of information is called* **closing.** Although you think in unified wholes, you get information in scraps; thus, you must put it together yourself to make it complete rather than fragmented. For example, in Figure 2.5 you tend to see a triangle, a

Figure 2.4

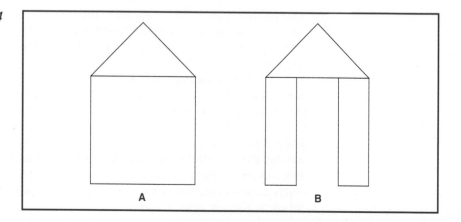

A   B

Figure 2.5
People tend to think in unified wholes.

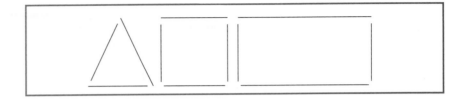

square, and a rectangle rather than a series of unconnected, unorganized lines.

You probably engage in closing (or closure) more often than you realize. For example, how often have you completed a sentence for the person you were talking to? The more you get to know people, the better you know how they think, and the more often you will think ahead and close their thoughts. Very close friends can say a great deal to each other with few words; without realizing it, they may depend on closure for their messages to get through. Another example of closing is when you overhear others talking but are able to pick up only fragments of their conversation. From the fragments you fill in the rest of the conversation. Have you ever sat in a bus station or airport and made up stories about the people you observed around you? From a minimum of cues you can put together a fairly complete story, making sense of the available information by closure. Though it may make sense to you, it may not be correct.

Interpreting: Giving the Puzzle Meaning

Not only do you select and organize information, you also interpret it. That is, you assign some meaning to information, making evaluations and drawing conclusions about it so that you can better predict future events and thereby minimize surprise.[7] Most of the **interpreting** you do takes either of two forms: **identification** or **evaluation.** Again, these processes occur rapidly and often simultaneously.

Stop reading for a minute and just listen. Can you label every sound you hear? Most of the sounds that go on are common ones and easily identifiable. Sometimes, however, there is a strange one—a scream, a bang, or a sound you've never heard before. After you identify the source of the noise, you evaluate it. Was it startling? Disruptive? Harmful? In identifying information, but more significantly in evaluating it, you bring to bear all of your experiences and knowledge. The interpretation of information is a subjective judgment; it is a product of your own creation, and it may or may not be valid.

You should realize that in interpreting the information you receive from your senses, you seldom stop with apparent, observable cues. You almost always infer other characteristics. A person's attitudes, values, beliefs, motives, personality traits, interests, and background are not directly observable. Although identification can be fairly reliable, interpretation is usually open to some question. You need to remember that if appearances are deceiving and untrustworthy, then your own inferences are even more tenuous. They may be little more than guesses.

▲▲▲ *Barriers to Accurate Perception*

Although the perceiver has been the main focus of this chapter so far, there are other factors that directly influence perception. In a sense, these factors—*stereotyping, proximity,* and *role*[8]—are restricting forces. Understanding them will help you detect, analyze, and cope with them as you engage in interpersonal communication.

Stereotyping, proximity, and role are only three barriers to accurate perception. There are many. Self-concept, to be discussed in the next chapter, is a major factor. Closely related is your health or the physical problems you have. The accuracy of your own five senses may serve as a barrier, just as your opinions, attitudes, beliefs, and values may. A list of various other barriers should indicate how likely it is that perceptions may be inaccurate: first impressions, a tendency to favor the negative, and culture as well as the time of day, month, or year. Your communication ability, along with your sensitivity to words and nonverbal cues, will make a difference, too. These are not the only potential barriers, but they will give an idea of some of the forces at work.

Stereotyping: Labels Are Restricting

Stereotyping *is the process of assigning fixed labels or categories to things and people you encounter or, in the reverse of this process, placing things and people you encounter into fixed categories you have already established.* When you stereotype a person, you assume certain things to be true about the individual because that person reminds you of someone else about whom those things may really have been true—at least, you *think* they were true. You assume that the pattern that applies to one person applies to another, even though the two people may actually have little in common. When Xinhong, for example, met Yuanyue, he assumed upon first meeting that Yuanyue believed, thought, and acted in the same way as he. In this section on stereotyping we will discuss three aspects: (1) *everyone does it,* (2) *physical appearance,* and (3) *major weaknesses.*

Everyone does it Stereotyping simplifies the task of making judgments about things and people. It is a commonly used device; all human beings employ it to deal with the tremendous flow of events around them.[9] The degree to which everyone does it varies with the individual. Sometimes it is determined by the groups to which an individual belongs—for example, college freshmen. A study was done in which college freshmen, male and female, looked at photographs of men with different amounts of facial hair. The students were to rate the men in the photos on masculinity.

The results? The more hair the man had on his face, the more likely students were to see him as "masculine, mature, good-looking, dominant, self-confident, courageous, liberal, nonconforming, industrious, and older."[10] The students didn't know anything about these men except what they looked like; they formed their judgments on the basis of a stereotype.

Xinhong, for example, knew that Yuanyue was an active member of the International Students' Union. This contributed to his assumption that Yuanyue believed, thought, and acted in the same way as he did.

Physical appearance   You can usually tell fairly quickly just by looking at another person whether or not you would like to strike up a relationship. How? From the person's physical appearance. That appearance provides just enough cues to enable you to stereotype him or her. Xinhong, for example, used Yuanyue's physical appearance to determine her initial attractiveness.

Unfortunately, you probably tend to give physical appearance a disproportionate emphasis as you communicate with another person. An attractive appearance creates a "halo effect"; this appeal influences all other impressions a person makes on you. For example, research on criminal trials showed that defendants received a harsher sentence if either the victim was attractive or the defendant was unattractive.[11] It has been shown, too, that an attractive female has a better chance of changing the attitudes of males than an unattractive one.[12] This is probably not news to anyone. Studies have proved that attractive people, regardless of their sex, are perceived as having higher credibility.[13] How fair is this? Can you think of any situations in which such stereotyping is justified?

Major weaknesses   There are two major weaknesses. First, stereotyping distorts your perceptions because it doesn't account for unique qualities. Second, it assumes that things don't change. Stereotyping places people into categories much as mail is pigeonholed according to route. She is a blonde, therefore she must "have more fun" (a category); he has a full beard and glasses, thus he must be an "intellectual" (a category); he plays football, thus he must be a "jock" (a category). You do this with individuals, events, ideas—anything. To each category you attach an extensive set of corresponding labels or stereotypes. But as you respond to those labels, you lose a great deal of information, and therefore your perceptions are distorted.

Take the man who plays football, for example. If you assign him the label of "jock," you may jump to the conclusion that he is insensitive, not very bright, and a male chauvinist. The man may or may not be any of these things. The point is that you don't know anything about him for certain except that he plays football.

Many of your stereotypes are so conditioned that it is hard for you to see that you have them, much less to get rid of them. Stereotyping

*From just what you ob-
serve in this picture and
nothing else, how would
you characterize the fel-
low with the handker-
chief on his head? Atti-
tudes, values, needs,
interests, and beliefs?
Communication style?*

doesn't take into account the unique qualities of individuals. For example, Xinhong did not know that Yuanyue's parents had come to this country before she was born. He did not know that Yuanyue was and always
had been a United States citizen and that she thought and acted like an
American and not like an international student.

The second weakness of stereotyping is that it implies, by its use,
that all people, events, ideas, and things are static and unchanging, when
in reality they are ever changing. Nobody is witty or bright all the time.
Everyone has good and bad moments. Yet, you tend to attribute static
qualities and respond to others as if those qualities were appropriate *all
the time*. Think carefully about the last time you made a comment like
"Emily is really the life of *any* party" or "Twila *always* looks so nice." We
use statements like these because they are the best predictors we have of

how a person "should" act, if everything we know about the person is right.[14]

Xinhong could not believe that Yuanyue had no cultural identification other than that of the United States. His identification with her was through the International Students' Union, even though she had carefully explained that she was there with a friend and would not have been there otherwise. It was difficult for Xinhong to change his impression because he had never met another person of Yuanyue's background or feelings. His first impression was static and unchanging—even though it was wrong.

Proximity: Distance Distorts

Proximity *is simply nearness in place, time, or relationship.* It can strongly affect the way we perceive. There are two types of proximity: *physical* and *psychological.*

An example of how physical proximity can influence perception is the experience of sitting near the back of a lecture hall on the first day of class and deciding that your new instructor is quite young. When you go down after class to ask a question, the hair that looked blond from a distance turns out to be gray, and the skin that looked smooth is crossed by age lines. Middle twenties turns out to be late forties. Everyone makes judgments that later prove to be inaccurate because they were either too close or too far from the objective to perceive it accurately.

Psychological proximity may have several effects on your communication. One is that the extent to which your own attitudes are similar to someone else's may determine how well you understand him or her. You must know some people you feel you always have to explain yourself to. You don't have psychological proximity with them—you just don't seem to understand each other. Then there are people with whom you "click." With such people you rarely have to say, "I *meant* that! I was serious," or "I was only kidding." They know without your telling them. Don't you feel you understand this other person? With this person you have achieved psychological proximity.

The second effect is that when you are attitudinally similar to someone, you evaluate this person more positively than if you are not. You probably like teachers you perceive as having tastes similar to yours—teachers who make a comment you might have made or wear a parka like yours. A research study demonstrated that when teachers are attitudinally similar to their students, the students give them higher ratings on such characteristics as open-mindedness, personal attractiveness, and teaching skills. Attitudinally dissimilar teachers are rated lower.[15]

A third effect of psychological proximity involves your readiness to respond in a specific way. For example, if you witness an automobile accident along with some other people, viewpoints may differ although

CONSIDER THIS

As you read the following excerpt, consider this question: How would the characteristics described affect perceptions?

> To a man, paying attention means knowing the physical information in the room. To a woman, paying attention (being aware) means being sensitive to the subjective environment (the senses, the emotional relationships in the room). Men use women's lack of attention to physical detail as proof that they are not as "intelligent" or "conscious" as men, and therefore not as reliable. Women use men's lack of attention to the subjective environment as proof that men are inconsiderate of others, insensitive to what is *really* going on, and therefore not as compassionate or as loving as women are.
>
> It appears to men as if women are deliberately behaving in ways that always keep men on edge. When men apply male standards or modes of behavior to women, they appear scattered, flighty, and disrespectful of men's physical reality. When women apply female standards to men, they appear stubborn, inflexible, and humorless.*

Questions

1. To what extent are the characteristics described merely stereotypes?
2. If these stereotypes are true—if men are aware of physical information and women are sensitive to the subjective environment—how would that affect their (men's and women's) perception of things? What would they look at?
3. If the stereotypes are true, how would that affect men's perception of women and women's perception of men? Can you cite examples from your own experience that people's perceptions conform to these observations?

*From Joe Tannenbaum, *Male & Female Realities: Understanding the Opposite Sex.* Costa Mesa, CA: Tannenbaum Associates, 1990, p. 85.

physical proximity is the same for all of you. A police officer might look at the accident from the point of view of what driving violations took place. A doctor might be most concerned about the injuries sustained by the people involved. A highway worker might notice broken curbs or uprooted sewers. Each person would bring his or her own experiences or psychological set to the accident. Each would be psychologically near to a

HI AND LOIS © 1984 reprinted with special permission of King Features Syndicate, Inc.

Perception here depends on size alone. Think about how many other factors can determine how you see what you see and the conclusions you draw based on what you see.

different aspect of the accident. The testimony of each would be necessary to learn all the important details of the accident. What you bring to such an event often influences your perceptions of it more than the actual facts of the event.

Role: A Limiting Point of View

The roles we play affect our perceptions strongly. In relation to your parents, your role is that of a son or daughter. In a classroom, your role is that of student. *A* **role** *is the stance you take or are assigned in a particular situation; the role you play affects your expectations, needs, attitudes, and beliefs about that situation; it restricts how you perceive that situation.* There are job roles, family roles, sex roles, friendship roles, and many others.

Individuals play roles defined by their culture, upbringing, and how they personally see those roles. You are familiar with the sex roles that have come to be traditional in our society. Think of how your perceptions are affected by the degree to which you accept these traditional roles. A strong-minded man may be perceived as assertive and a natural leader, while an equally strong-minded woman is perceived as pushy and overbearing. How often are male children dressed in pink? Your acceptance of traditional sex roles has a direct effect on your perception of the color pink as appropriate or inappropriate in certain situations. A woman wearing an apron at the kitchen sink is a natural and acceptable sight; you have been conditioned to squirm or laugh when you see a man in that same apron at that same sink. Your perceptions are affected.

You have learned to expect to hear a woman's voice in certain situations, a man's in others. Think of telephone operators, airplane pilots, and doctors' receptionists. Listen hard to television commercials. In how many of them is the voice-over provided by a man—even in advertising of products intended for use by women? Advertisers are banking on the fact that potential consumers will listen to a persuasive man's voice more

In what ways did the roles that you played in your family limit your point of view? What were the factors that determined the kinds of roles you played in your family?

TRY THIS

What is the first image that comes into your mind when you think of the following people?

1. A gas-station mechanic.
2. Someone who walks with a cane and lives in a rest home.
3. A rock musician.
4. A hairdresser.
5. Someone who sells vacuum cleaners door to door.
6. Someone who has five children and is on welfare.
7. A rapist.
8. A business executive for a large corporation.
9. A nurse.
10. Someone who is in the army.

What sex did you think of for each of these people? What age? What ethnic background? What stereotypes are you aware of holding? What do your stereotypes simplify for you? What do they complicate?

closely than to a woman's. They know society has trained us to perceive men's voices as more reliable and more authoritative. How many other instances can you think of in which acceptance of traditional sex roles affects perception in a directly observable way?

Certain roles carry higher prestige or credibility than others. What you see as another person's role will affect your perceptions of that person in certain situations. The role of professor, for example, might carry higher credibility and prestige in a faculty meeting on curriculum than the role of student. On the other hand, any student would probably be better able than a professor to discuss the availability of drugs on campus. In this case, the role of student is perceived as conferring more reliable information. If you see a person in a certain position fulfilling the duties and responsibilities of that job and serving your own best interests, then you are likely to overlook what you see as that person's shortcomings. Your perceptions are affected by the fact that the responsibilities of the position are being satisfied. Other considerations matter less to you in this situation.

Building Perception Skills

Because of the broad range of factors affecting perception and because of the number of ways these factors interact, there are no universal rules that will guarantee improved, accurate perception. But there are several guidelines that might help. Some seem obvious and easy to put into practice; others may require more time to develop and use. All will contribute to the improvement of your perceptual skills. You should find some that are especially pertinent and track your progress with them. Since your perception influences and directs your reactions to others, improvement becomes crucial to improving your interpersonal communication.

Don't jump to conclusions   One error you may tend to make that affects the accuracy of your perceptions is generalizing or drawing conclusions based on weak evidence. Just because you see something happen once, you may automatically assume it happens that way regularly.

You may see a bus stopping at a new location and assume that a new route has been established to include that location. You may see a person go into a bar and assume the person drinks heavily. Your perception will improve if you temper your thoughts and comments with conditional statements like "*I wonder if* the bus route has been changed to include . . ." or "*Maybe* he drinks heavily because I saw him. . . . " Even better, stick strictly to the simplest facts: "I saw the bus stop at a new location today" or "I saw Ralph going into a bar downtown." If you are not reporting first-hand information, you should identify your source to indicate the poten-

CONSIDER THIS

As you begin to read the final section of this chapter, "Building Perception Skills," the suggestions will encourage you to try some new things. You might wonder, what is the relationship between behavior (doing some new things) and perception? Edward T. Hall, the cultural anthropologist cited earlier, gives us a clue:

> I learned to have great respect for the army and for how it could take raw civilians and turn them into soldiers in a matter of months. It was a while, however, before I was able to loosen the grip that diffidence [distrust] had on me and to overcome my dislike of being yelled at. Much to my surprise, in the end the total experience made me over. I was given a whole new life. How do I explain it? *The army made me behave in new and different ways* and, as I later learned from the transactional psychologists, when you change behavior you change perceptions!*

Questions

1. Notice Hall's changes in perception regarding the army. Why do you think he said, "I *learned* to have great respect"?
2. Have you experienced or heard of situations like the one Hall describes, in which people have been "made over"? "Given a whole new life"? When? Where? How?
3. Can you see how making yourself behave in new and different ways can have an effect on your perceptions? Has this ever happened to you?

*From Edward T. Hall, *An Anthropology of Everyday Life: An Autobiography.* New York: Anchor Books (Doubleday), 1992, p. 148.

tial believability of the observation. That is, if you have heard information from someone else or read it somewhere, you should label what you report: *"Bill says* he saw Jane and Dave together downtown" or *"I read in the paper* that. . . . " This allows those who hear your information to gauge its believability without having your judgment interfere with it.

But often the problem is not in the labeling. Sometimes you believe your own judgments despite weak evidence. You convince yourself by phrasing the idea in a certain way, stating it to someone else, or repeating it. If you can learn to restrain yourself—suspend judgment—until you receive more evidence, you will improve the accuracy of your perceptions.

Maintaining a balance between openness and skepticism is difficult in our society. Forced to produce, make decisions, act, and respond quickly, you no doubt find it hard to stand back and judge the worth of the information you hear daily. The point is not to doubt the validity of everything you hear; the point is to place new evidence into the context of other evidence you already have before drawing conclusions. If no other evidence exists, it is wiser to continue to doubt than to make inferences. If a conclusion is necessary, the cautious skeptic will label the conclusion as a conditional one. You can never anticipate the decisions other people may make based on what you have told them; all you can do is be responsible in reporting what you actually do know. There are other ways, too, in which you can avoid jumping to conclusions. Some of these follow:

▲ Broaden your personal experience. The more experience you have, the better the frame of reference into which new information can be placed.
▲ Try to find out what other yardsticks can be used to measure the phenomena. Do not depend solely on your own yardsticks.
   —Are you depending on what others have told you?
   —Are you focusing primarily on the situation?
   —Are you looking simply at role relationships?
▲ Encourage communication. The more people talk, the more likely it is that new evidence and impressions will emerge.
▲ Encourage others to define the language they use. Even when two people hear the same cluster of cues and receive similar impressions, the language they use to express those impressions may be so different that one might suspect different perceptions.
▲ Be on guard for selective perception. Try to deal with contradictory information rather than overlook or deny it.
▲ Try to assume the role of detached observer: a third person who can be objective about what is being observed.

Give it time Physical togetherness helps increase the accuracy of our perceptions. You have surely had the experience of being impressed by a person from a distance, only to change your impression radically upon closer contact. The same phenomenon occurs after you know people better or work with them.[16] Accurate perceptions of another person do not occur instantaneously like the picture on a solid-state television set. They require both time and spatial closeness. Give yourself time to be with someone. Even so, long-term, face-to-face, physical togetherness only provides the opportunity to understand how another person interprets the world; it does not guarantee that you will understand it.

▲ Try to reserve judgment. Saying "I need time to think this over" is an easy way to admit this need and make it known to others.
▲ Be patient. Slow down a little. Let time and experience have an effect. It is amazing how much information can be acquired simply by

waiting. Your mind has an opportunity to sift through the relevant material.

▲ Study the situation. Learn all you can about it. Find out what you need to know to make a decision or identify an impression.

▲ Use your intelligence to help articulate the impression or perception you wish to convey. Try to reconstruct the cue as accurately as possible and rephrase, in your mind, the response to it until you feel it is accurate.

▲ Do not use lack of time as an excuse for not responding or for doing nothing.

Make yourself available   It's important to be available to most other people, both physically and psychologically.[17] This means trying to get on another's "wavelength" or "into another person's head." An old Sioux prayer stated it this way: "O Great Spirit! Let me not judge another man without first walking a mile in his moccasins." So often in this hurry-up, get-things-done society, people do not spend much time really making themselves available to others. Physical togetherness does not necessarily mean psychological availability.

Psychological availability requires an active commitment to openness on our part. You have to make time for other people—time not only to share but also to be aware. To improve the accuracy of your perceptions, you must be willing to go beyond cliché-level exchanges that require little time and demand no commitment.

One cautionary note is in order. Availability is not appropriate in every interpersonal-communication setting. Knowing when and where you should make yourself available to others or strive for peak communication is part of interpersonal competence.

▲ Strive for "peak communication" based on absolute openness and honesty.[18]

▲ Whenever possible, move toward complete emotional and personal connections with others. This connection may not be a permanent experience, but a time when you feel almost perfect and mutual empathy.

▲ Be willing to share your reactions with others. Enjoy sharing in their reactions as well, whether the occasion is one of happiness or grief.

Make a commitment   Any self-improvement requires active commitment, but it is especially important if you honestly try to increase your perception. If you want your perceptions to be accurate, you must make a conscious effort to seek out as much information as possible on any given topic or question before you make a judgment or form an opinion. The more information you have, the more likely it is that your perceptions will be accurate.[19] You should make a real effort to search for possibilities, asking "What if . . . ?" and "What about . . . ?" and "What else . . . ?" at every turn. You cannot hope to have reliable perceptions if you are indifferent and passive about acquiring information.

- ▲ Nothing happens unless you want it to. Change your attitude. Decide that change is good.
- ▲ Begin now to want to seek new information, knowledge, and experience. Decide what change is beneficial. There are personal benefits to be gained. The more information you have, the more accurate your perceptions are likely to be.
- ▲ Life can go by, and you may take little part in what happens. On the other hand, you can be a responding, actively immersed participant.
- ▲ Remember that the "commitment" is a frame of mind—an attitude—and it can be changed. Notice the people who are having fun, who are getting so much out of life. What do they have? Check it out. Think about it. You only go around once.

Establish the proper climate   Your perception will improve if you establish a climate conducive to communication. This means maintaining an atmosphere in which self-disclosure is likely to occur. Where open communication can be sustained, the likelihood of accurate perception will increase simply because people will trust each other enough to exchange honest messages. Of course, your behavior should be responsive to the realities of the multiple types of relationships you must manage, but the more you know about the needs and feelings of other people, the more likely it is that your actions toward them will be appropriate and your prediction of future interactions will be accurate. You must establish an environment in which truth is free to surface, so that your perceptions may be based on that truth. Face-to-face encounters in which visual and vocal ingredients are both part of the interaction help you gain the information you need.

Part of creating a proper climate also means recognizing that each person is unique—that is, recognizing that your view of the world is entirely your own. The world does not revolve around you, and if you see that everyone does not share your perceptions of the world, you will have at least acknowledged the need for a proper climate.

- ▲ Don't manipulate, dominate, and try to run other people's lives.
- ▲ Be authentic. Be yourself, honestly, in your relationship with others.
- ▲ Avoid pretense, defenses, and duplicity (being different at different times in relation to the same thing).
- ▲ Don't "play it cool."
- ▲ Never use your behavior as a gambit to disarm others—to get them to reveal themselves before you reveal yourself to them.[20]

Be willing to adjust   Perception involves a perceiver and a context within which the process occurs. These components are so interwoven that they cannot be analyzed apart from each other. Changes in any one affect all others. The most you can do is to recognize that as these components vary, so must your perceptions. The flawless friend of two weeks ago may now be seen as disloyal and hurtful. The arrogant and unfair teacher of yesterday may be the friendly and helpful teacher of today. To be unwilling to change your perceptions, and to be righteous in your inflexibility, can only cause you perceptual problems. What you need is **perceptual sensitivity:** *full recognition that your perceptions will change as your interests and experiences change.* You cannot expect today's perceptions to be accurate if you base them on yesterday's attitudes.

▲ Take a hard look at your openness. Can you open up to something new? Or do you rigidly adhere to your perceptions of what is expected of you?

▲ Take a hard look at your prejudices. Can you change your impressions of people, ideas, or activities?

▲ Take a hard look at your life. Are you living according to a rigid, well-defined plan that allows no deviation? There is certainty and security in such a life—but little excitement and growth. Change brings both.[21]

TRY THIS

Extend the normal limits of your senses. Try to answer the following questions:

1. What color is today?
2. What color is the smell of your favorite perfume?
3. How high is the sky? What does the sky sound like?
4. What does your favorite day taste like?
5. What color is a hug?
6. What does a favorite song or work of music smell like? How would you describe its shape?
7. What does yellow taste like?
8. What color is the sound of a parade?
9. How would you describe the texture of your own name?
10. What would your eyes feel like if they could shake hands?
11. What does your favorite season sound and smell like?
12. What is your favorite sense?
13. What smell describes your self-concept?
14. What color is love?
15. Write whatever enters your head (in two or three sentences).*

*From Genelle Austin-Lett and Jan Sprague, *Talk to Yourself.* Copyright © 1976 by Houghton Mifflin Co. Used with permission.

Your own interpersonal communications will be a great deal more effective when you realize the role that perception plays. In your own unique way, you are responsible for your method of arriving at the meaning of all things through the processes of **reception** and **construction.** Reception involves taking in information through your senses. Construction involves constructing experiences according to the organization of categories you possess.

Construction is a major element of the perceptual process, and it reinforces and underscores the idea of transactional communication developed in the first chapter. The point is that from the cues you receive from others or from the environment, you construct pictures that constitute your reality. No one gives you meaning, and no one can control the meanings you determine for yourself. It is you who create meaning out of your own experiences.

▶ SUMMARY

This chapter forms an important foundation for successful interpersonal communication because it concerns how you take in and process information. Perception was defined as the process of gathering information and giving it meaning.

The perception-sieve analogy was presented as a way to illustrate your unique perceptual-filtering system. You looked at the development of the sieve, the size and shape of the holes in the sieve, and the blockage that occurs when you want protection from information you dislike or disagree with. Six implications of the perception-sieve analogy were discussed: uniqueness, passivity, change, rigidity, acceptance, and meaning.

The section on visual perception was designed to offer valuable lessons—for example, the importance of reserving final judgments and evaluations. Another lesson was that every situation is made up of different parts and ambiguous patterns. No one has all the answers or can see all the parts and patterns. It is important to remain flexible, adaptable, and willing to change.

In the section on construction, the steps of selecting, organizing, and interpreting information were discussed. Selecting involves choosing the pieces of the puzzle, since you perceive selectively. Organizing involves putting the pieces of the puzzle together, since information comes to you in a random, unstructured manner. Organizing involves enlarging, simplifying, and closing. Interpreting involves giving the puzzle meaning, since you need to make evaluations and draw conclusions about it. The forms of identification and evaluation were discussed.

In the section on barriers to accurate perception, the three barriers of stereotyping, proximity, and roles were presented. Regarding stereotypes, we discussed the fact that everyone does it, the role that physical appearance plays, and the major weaknesses of the process. In the section on proximity, we discussed both physical and psychological proximity. Regarding roles, we looked at culture, gender, and credibility.

Six skills were offered for improving perception: don't jump to conclusions, give it time, make yourself available, make a commitment, establish the proper climate, and be willing to adjust.

The more accurate your perceptions, the more likely you are to communicate effectively with others. That is what Tanenbaum was illustrating in the "Consider This" regarding male and female differences. When you begin to understand perception and how it affects the information you acquire, the judgments you make, and the conclusions you draw, you begin to communicate with others in a different manner.

By acquiring more information, you increase the number of ways you can respond to other people, and you strengthen your ability to grow in a positive direction. And since your first step in communicating with others involves forming some impression of them (perceiving them), how well you form those impressions becomes crucial to interpersonal success and personal happiness.

▶ ## KEY TERMS

perception	simplifying	proximity
perception sieve	closing	role
cognitive simplicity	interpreting	psychological availability
cognitive complexity	identification	perceptual sensitivity
selecting	evaluation	reception
organizing	stereotyping	construction
enlarging		

▶ ## NOTES

1. Frank A. Geldard, *The Human Senses* (New York: John Wiley & Sons, 1953), 53.
2. Donald R. Gordon, *The New Literacy* (Toronto: University of Toronto Press, 1971), 25–47.
3. Sydney J. Harris, *Pieces of Eight* (Boston: Houghton Mifflin Co., 1982), 159–160.
4. Stephen W. Littlejohn, *Theories of Human Communication*, 4th ed. (Belmont, CA: Wadsworth Publishing Co., 1990), 120.

5. Alvin Toffler, *Future Shock* (New York: Random House, 1970).

6. Hans Sebald, "Limitations of Communication: Mechanisms of Image Maintenance in Form of Selective Perception, Selective Memory and Selective Distortion," *Journal of Communication* 12 (1962): 142–149.

7. J. S. Bruner, "Social Psychology and Perception," in E. Maccoby, T. M. Newcomb, E. L. Hartley, eds., *Readings in Social Psychology* (New York: Holt, Rinehart and Winston, 1958), 85–94.

8. Richard C. Huseman, James M. Lahiff, and John D. Hartfield, *Interpersonal Communication in Organizations: A Perceptual Approach* (Boston: Holbrook Press, 1976), 28–32.

9. George J. McCall and J. L. Simmons, *Identities and Interaction: An Examination of Human Association in Everyday Life* (New York: Free Press, 1966), 114.

10. Robert J. Pellegrini, "Impressions of the Male Personality as a Function of Beardedness," *Psychology* 10 (February 1973): 29–33.

11. D. Lancy and E. Aronson, "The Influence of the Character of the Criminal and His Victim on the Decisions of Simulated Jurors," *Journal of Experimental Social Psychology* 5 (1969): 141–152.

12. J. Mills and E. Aronson, "Opinion Change as a Function of the Communicator's Attractiveness and Desire to Influence," *Journal of Personality and Social Psychology* 1 (1965): 73–77.

13. R. N. Widgery and B. Webster, "The Effects of Physical Attractiveness upon Perceived Initial Credibility," *Michigan Speech Journal* 4 (1969): 9–15.

14. McCall and Simmons, p. 115.

15. Katherine C. Good and Lawrence R. Good, "Attitude Similarity and Attraction to an Instructor," *Psychological Reports* 33 (August 1973): 335–337.

16. J. W. Shepherd discusses how people's conceptions of each other change as a result of working together. See J. W. Shepherd, "The Effects of Valuations in Evaluations of Traits on the Relation Between Stimulus Affect and Cognitive Complexity," *Journal of Social Psychology* 88 (December 1972): 233–239.

17. For more on psychological availability, see John Stewart and Gary D'Angelo, *Together: Communicating Interpersonally*, 2d ed. (Reading, MA: Addison-Wesley Publishing Co., 1980), 110–112.

18. John Powell, *Why Am I Afraid to Tell You Who I Am?* (Allen, TX: Argus Communications, 1969), 61–62.

19. See Frederick W. Obitz and L. Jerome Oziel, "Varied Information Levels and Accuracy of Person Perception," *Psychological Reports* 31 (October 1972): 571–576.

20. Sidney M. Jourard, *The Transparent Self* (New York: D. Van Nostrand Co., 1971), 133.

21. Wayne W. Dyer, *Your Erroneous Zones* (New York: Avon Books, 1976), 126–131.

► FURTHER READING

Mary Catherine Bateson, *Peripheral Visions: Learning Along the Way* (New York: HarperCollins Publishers, 1994). Bateson takes readers on fascinating journeys to a Persian garden, a Philippine village, and the Sinai desert, and on a tour bus full of Tibetan monks. She encourages readers to interact with other people without knowing the rules, to improvise in uncertain situations, and to grow in new ways. She helps them discover new meanings—some that can be seen only through peripheral vision.

Mihaly Csikszentmihalyi, *The Evolving Self: A Psychology for the Third Millennium* (New York: Harper Perennial, 1993). What does it take to understand and overcome our evolutionary heritage with the purpose of re-creating ourselves and the world we live in? How can people begin to think about what lies ahead and how they can influence it? This is a powerful book that capitalizes and extends the ideas of his best-selling book, *Flow: The Psychology of Optimal Experience.*

David G. Myers, *The Pursuit of Happiness* (New York: Avon Books, 1992). Myers, a social psychologist, reviewed thousands of scientific studies related to happiness. This is not a self-help book about achieving happiness; it is a serious examination of what is known about human happiness. Myers offers readers a mind-expanding, purpose-filled approach to life. In addition, he stimulates readers to seek for deeper meaning through faith, hope, and joy. Notes and bibliography occupy almost a third of this book.

Gloria Steinem, *Revolution from Within: A Book of Self-Esteem* (Boston: Little, Brown and Company, 1993). This is really much more than a book on self-esteem. Steinem helps readers see across the boundaries of race, class, age, sexuality, and ability; that's why it is included here. She discusses the importance of un-learning and the need for re-learning, and she offers a realistic proposal for the future. With parables and personal experiences, Steinem causes readers to look inward and look outward as well. An engaging book.

Kathleen Wall and Gary Ferguson, *Lights of Passage: Rituals and Rites of Passage for the Problems and Pleasures of Modern Life* (San Francisco: Harper San Francisco, 1994). Wall and Ferguson provide us with a new way to examine our lives and a practical guide to reinventing rituals and ceremonies that allow us to let go of old patterns and discover new ones. This is a book of tools for dealing with life's challenges in work and career, intimate relationships, families, friendship and more. The authors offer a delightful, fresh perspective.

Jeffrey E. Young and Janet S. Klosko, *Reinventing Your Life: How to Break Free from Negative Life Patterns and Feel Good Again* (New York: A

Plume Book [Published by the Penguin Group], 1993). Many of our perceptions result from the rules that have governed us. Young and Klosko call these "lifetraps." They discuss eleven of them, such as "I can't make it on my own" and "I feel like such a failure." They provide practical advice for how to change these lifetraps and offer a philosophy of change in the final chapter.

3

Getting in Touch: The Self and Self-Disclosure

► CHAPTER OBJECTIVES

After reading this chapter, you should be able to

- ▲ Understand the relationship between self-concept and effective communication.
- ▲ Recognize the self-concept as the starting point for all interpersonal communication.
- ▲ Understand the role of self-awareness as the sum total of all of your perceptions of yourself.
- ▲ Know how difficult self-acceptance is to achieve and some of the things that stand in the way of self-acceptance.
- ▲ Realize the relationship of the real self to the ideal self and how self-esteem is tied to this relationship.
- ▲ Build your self-esteem.
- ▲ Understand the process of self-actualizing.
- ▲ Identify the characteristics of the self-actualizing person.
- ▲ Relate self-actualizing to effective interpersonal communication.
- ▲ Make what you have count by finding qualities you can emphasize and by acting on your likes and strengths.
- ▲ Identify why self-talk is important.
- ▲ Understand how self-talk affects behavior.
- ▲ Know how self-talk can be used.
- ▲ Use self-talk when it is appropriate.
- ▲ Understand the roles that internal dialogue, imagined interactions, and the internal advisor play in self-talk.
- ▲ Understand the role of self-disclosure in interpersonal communication.
- ▲ Know what happens in self-disclosure.
- ▲ Understand why people are afraid to self-disclose.
- ▲ Recognize the value of moderation in self-disclosure.
- ▲ Improve your skills in self-disclosure.

▼ Hanna had been dating Kelsey for six months, and she was insanely jealous. She did not want to let Kelsey out of her sight. She did not want him to even look at other women, thinking he might leave her in a second if he found anyone better—or available. Hanna was obsessed. Even her talks with Kelsey were designed to find out where he had been, what he had been doing, and who he was with. Hanna was consumed with worries over Kelsey because of her own weak self-esteem. She felt she could not measure up to any other woman. Even Kelsey's pledges of love, faithfulness, and the need for trust fell on deaf ears.

Miguel looked in the mirror when he got home from work. "What a big, fat slob I am,"Miguel thought. He had been turned down for a job promotion the week before, had just had a relationship break up over the weekend, and while driving home from work the evening before, had had a fender-bender, which had disabled his car. He hated having to take the bus. Miguel wanted to call his friends, but he just did not feel like communicating with anyone. His self-esteem was at an all-time low.

Victoria had just been elected president of her sorority. It was a position she had worked for for two years. She had gotten to know all of the girls in her house personally. She had participated in all sorority events and activities, volunteered for a variety of house positions, and kept her grades up as well. After the election, one of Vicki's sorority sisters told her that she was elected to the presidency because some girls thought she was a model sister. Vicki loved her new position because it gave her a chance to meet and talk with girls from all the other sororities.

In all three cases, notice the close relationship between self-concept and communication. Hanna's low self-concept not only controlled her thoughts but controlled the kind of conversations she and Kelsey had as well. Miguel's low self-concept actually made him not want to talk with his friends. By contrast, Vicki's positive self-concept helped her achieve the presidency of her sorority, and it helped her look forward to further opportunities to talk.

To be in touch with others, we must first be in touch with ourselves. In brief sections, this chapter will first examine the relationship between self-concept and effective communication. Then the components of self-concept—self-awareness, self-acceptance, self-esteem, self-actualizing, self-talk, and self-disclosure—will be discussed.

▲▲▲ *Self-Concept and Effective Communication*

Our **self-concept** *is how we define ourselves.* It consists of two components: a personal identity and a social identity.[1] The personal part includes those aspects of our self that make us a unique individual. Twila, for example, sees herself as a caring, nurturing, involved person who wants to improve relations between people from different racial and ethnic groups. Her personal identity came about from her own unique experiences, which included travel abroad, extensive reading about international issues and concerns, work in a ghetto recreational program, and active involvement in Planned Parenthood.

Unlike personal identities, social identities are derived from our shared membership in social groups.[2] David, for example, felt strongly about his Polish background, and his family had always observed Polish holidays and other cultural traditions. In addition, David's grandfather and father had both been in the U. S. Marine Corps. David joined the U. S. Marine Corps right out of high school and retired from the Corps as a master gunnery sergeant. Later he served as a marine recruiter.

David was an active member of the National Rifle Association and was a dedicated hunter. He would take at least one hunting trip with his Polish ex-marine "fightin' buddies" every year—to northern lower Michigan for deer, to Canada for moose, or to Montana for elk. He and his family led a structured military life. Because of his social identity, David spoke out on many issues that concerned him deeply. He was against abortion, against military base closings, and against gun-control legislation.

David's group memberships influenced even his most intimate forms of communication. David defined himself as blatantly heterosexual, and his strong concern about heterosexuality strongly influenced the partner he selected and the way he communicated with her. David was not one to keep his emotions to himself. He spoke out strongly against homosexuality and bisexuality as well.

It should be clear from the examples of both Twila and David that personal and social identities influence everyone's communication behavior, and it is difficult to determine which one predominates in particular situations. When your identifications—personal or social—are strong, there is an increased chance that misunderstandings will occur.[3] This is simply because you tend to interpret others' behavior based on your own.

Two skills will help you overcome the potential for communication misunderstandings when your personal and social identities are strong:

1. Recognize that you share a common identity with everyone: simply being human.[4]
2. Acknowledge the differences between you and others, and try to understand them and how they influence your communication.[5]

▲▲▲ Your Self-Concept

The starting point for all your interpersonal communication is your concept of self. Who are you, and how did you get to be this way?

Who Are You?

Your ideas of yourself, or how you define yourself, as noted previously, is called your *self-concept*. It is directly related to how you behave. Let's look at an example. If you had to use one word to characterize yourself, what would that word be? Shy? Enthusiastic? Loving? Confident? Your characterization of yourself will probably involve more than one word. You may think of yourself as interesting and friendly once people get to know you; you may think you are intelligent, attractive, and generally concerned about other people and what happens in the world. The words you select make up your self-concept.

How do these words relate to how you behave? Let's say that you have always had the knack for making new friends. Thus, you have come to think of yourself as friendly and outgoing. If you think of yourself as friendly and outgoing, this can actually make meeting other people and making new friends easier. *Your behavior reflects the opinion you have of yourself.*

Your success in college and in life may depend more on *how* you feel about yourself and your abilities than on your actual talents. And your self-concept will affect your skill in dealing with other people. You can see how your communications with people could go haywire if you think of yourself as a friendly, warm person, but the people around you see you as a loud, offensive boor. What you consider a concerned inquiry into a friend's health could be perceived by that person as nosy, prying into something that is none of your business. Interpersonal communication, to be effective, depends upon a realistic perception of self.[6]

How Did You Get to Be This Way?

The background for, development of, and influences on your self-concept are numerous. What makes it even more difficult to discover the roots of your self-concept is that all of the factors interact with one another in unpredictable ways. And even the ways you respond to various influences differ. Different people are born with different patterns of reaction. My wife and I have noticed, for example, that one of our four children has been independent and self-determined from birth, another has been timid and shy, a third has been affectionate and dependent, and a fourth has been extroverted and assertive. All were raised in the same environment, yet all grew up differently—different from birth. Children are not blank slates to be written on by family and fate. Imagine the possible effect on a child when parents who wanted a docile "doll" receive a tough kid!

There is no doubt that parents serve as a shaping force in a child's upbringing. Their influence can be direct and specific. Consider how much you may have been influenced by the family you were born into, the religion they followed, the ethnic culture they supported, the socioeconomic group with which they identified, and the national society of which they were a part.

Direct and specific influence also includes the respect you were shown. How did your parents treat your actions, feelings, and statements? Did your parents act as if you were worthwhile and valued? The respect they showed you probably had a major influence on your self-concept—an influence with a lasting effect as well.

What are some of the influences that had a direct effect on the development of your self-concept? Given an opportunity to make some changes in those influences, what changes might you make?

Another direct and specific influence was the standards your parents set for you. Did your parents ever say, "You should be a professional" or "You should be a parent" or "You are good for nothing?" These early goals—or nongoals—became part of your self-concept. What's more, they created the potential for fulfillment, disappointment, or failure. Think, for example, of the child who never reaches an assigned goal and feels like a failure despite other worthwhile achievements. Or, what about the child who achieves the goal and discovers he or she is not comfortable with it?

Self-concept can be formed, too, in the struggle against parents. Excessive parental pressure can cause grief. Some parents don't want their kids to grow up. Some expect perfection or skill beyond the realm of reality. Some want their kids to follow exactly in their footsteps. One student developed ulcers because he could not produce the grades his father desired.

Some people, on the other hand, received no direct guidance. They never had anything to struggle against! Lack of parental direction can lead to an unclear self-concept. Without such direction, some people have problems meeting their needs and being self-assertive. Frequently, these people work for the benefit of others and fail to pay sufficient attention to the kind of person they are and what is best for them. Sometimes it is useful for children to have parents who make suggestions and propose goals.

I am not trying to suggest that parents are the only influence on our self-concept. That is far from true. People whom you admired as you grew up influenced you; so did your friends, the parents of your friends, religious leaders and teachers, schoolteachers, and even the environment in which you grew up. Molding of self-concepts can result from contact with classmates, lovers, spouses, and even media personalities. Cathcart and Gumpert, writers in the area of self-development, claim that self-concept is dependent in large part on the media.[7] Motion pictures and television, they say, play a significant part in the role-taking function that is necessary to maintaining a self-image.

Although their position on the influence of the media is speculative, Cathcart and Gumpert offer food for thought as you try to determine how you got to be the way you are. The statistics regarding how much time the television set is on in the average home, and the informal surveys I have taken in my interpersonal communication classes regarding how much college students of *both* sexes watch soap operas, lead me to believe that the media can play a major role in self-development.

In discovering where self-concepts came from, it probably makes sense to look less at specific experiences and more at the conclusions you drew from those experiences. People get different information from the same stimulus. This is why a "lecture" from a father could serve as an instructional lesson for one child, a joke to another, a cause for rebellion in a third, and a "putdown" or reprimand to a fourth.

From this discussion, then, it becomes clear that your self-concept is a picture of yourself based on earlier experiences. It has been shaped by how people have treated you and what they have expected of you as well as by your own emotional reactions to and conclusions from these and other experiences.

Now, think back to the word or words you used to describe yourself a moment ago. Chances are that you arrived at that self-concept ("I'm popular") by the reactions other people have to you ("Glad to see you!"). But then you had to think about those reactions and decide what they meant to you ("They like to have me around. They appreciate my sense of humor."). In other words, your self-concept is created through both interpersonal and intrapersonal communication. Much of this occurs without your being really conscious of it. There are six processes we all more or less unconsciously engage in as we build our self-concepts. By becoming more aware of the processes and by working at them, you will gradually be more in touch with your true self. Those processes are (1) *self-awareness*, (2) *self-acceptance*, (3) *self-esteem*, (4) *self-actualizing*, (5) *self-talk*, and (6) *self-disclosure*.

CONSIDER THIS

Mary Catherine Bateson, a professor of anthropology and English, writes about the development of self in the Western mode as opposed to where she was when she wrote this: Tehran, Iran. Read her insight, then answer the questions that follow.

> Within the framework of Western assumptions, we begin to know a little about how the self is differentiated from others, how it takes shape for males and females, the kind of resilience associated with it. A wide range of pathologies have been associated with flawed attitudes toward the self: lack of self-esteem on the one hand and narcissism [self-love] on the other. Physical violence and sexual abuse deform the sense of self, or split it into multiples. So do insult and bigotry. So does invisibility or the realization that in a given context one is inaudible. We think of the self as a central continuity, yet recognizing that the self is not identical through time is a first step in celebrating it as fluid and variable, shaped and reshaped by learning.*

Questions

1. Do you know of differences between cultures in the way the self gets shaped?
2. In American culture, are there clear differences between the ways the self takes shape for males and females?
3. Can you cite, from your own life, examples that show how your self has been shaped and reshaped by learning?

*From Mary Catherine Bateson, *Peripheral Visions: Learning Along the Way* (New York: HarperCollins, 1994), p. 64.

▲▲▲ *Self-Awareness*

You have some understanding of yourself—how attractive, intelligent, influential, and successful you are. Understandings such as these constitute your **self-awareness.** *Self-awareness involves the sum total of all of your perceptions of yourself.* You derive these perceptions from experiences and interactions with others. (See Figure 3.1.) Not all your beliefs about yourself are realistic—some are beliefs about what you would *like* to be rather than what you are.

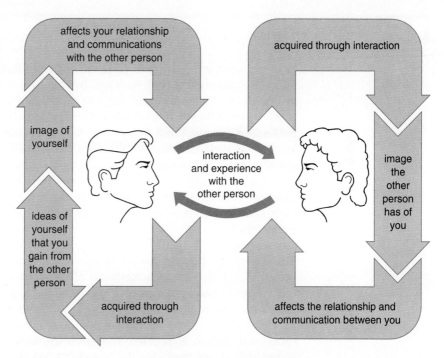

Figure 3.1
You derive information about yourself from your interactions with others.

For example, if you would like to be chosen as the leader of a certain organization, you may behave in a way you feel will get you the leadership role. What you would *like* to be—a leader—makes you more careful about your clothes, your speech, your associates. Both the roles you play and, perhaps, the roles you would like to play are important ingredients in your identity.

As another example, a woman who thinks of herself as fragile, elegant, and sophisticated may avoid anything that does not match her self-concept. She may avoid activities that require physical effort, like a touch football game or backpacking. Getting dirty or hurting herself wouldn't fit her self-image. Activities more satisfactory to her might be going to the theater, belonging to social organizations, or playing bridge.

Different experiences have different impacts on her self-image. She can accept experiences consistent with her values more easily; she will probably reject those that don't fit well. Everyone does this. You may rationalize some experiences to fit your needs if they are inconsistent with your perceptions of yourself. For example, if at a meeting the woman is asked to do something she considers inappropriate, like sitting on the floor, she may do it because she needs to be accepted by the members of this group. She may rationalize the activity as one that is novel or amusing—even though it is inconsistent with her self-image.

▲▲▲ *Self-Acceptance*

You begin by being aware of yourself, but you must also be satisfied with yourself. You must accept yourself. By this I do not mean you are smug or uncritical of negative qualities, but rather that you see your shortcomings for what they are, making neither too much nor too little of them. **Self-acceptance** *is seeing how your positive and negative qualities are equally valid, equally you, equally normal to have.* It means *building on those qualities you're satisfied with and working to change the ones you're not happy with.*

Like self-awareness, self-acceptance doesn't come easily. It isn't easy to accept yourself when you are constantly being measured by other people's standards. There are the standards of your parents ("Your friend Karen has been accepted by both Harvard and Yale. Have you heard from any schools yet?"); your teachers ("If you don't love *Moby Dick* you might just as well give up on American literature because you'll never understand it."); and even of advertisers ("Use Whammo lemon-herbal-avocado shampoo and get out there and have fun like you're supposed to."). If you are unsure of yourself and doubtful about how acceptable you are to others, if you cannot accept yourself much of the time, your communication will suffer. Accepting your feelings, beliefs, goals, and relationships with others provides the base for a healthy, integrated self. What are some of the things that stand in the way of your self-acceptance?

Living Up to an Image

If you are always trying to live up to the image of a perfect or straight-A student that your parents expect, you may have difficulty with your self-concept. Whenever someone else tries to impose an image on you, it may be an unrealistic one or one that demands qualities that simply are not important to you. In much the same way, setting your own goals too high may cause you to have a negative self-concept if you can't achieve fulfillment or satisfaction.

Teachers sometimes have a habit of setting students' goals for them. Have you ever been told, "You know, you're not working up to your potential?" With little or no positive reward, or with little or no definition about specific expectations, students often feel frustrated, confused, or depressed, which may result in low self-esteem. Parents, teachers, employers, and friends all seem to have goals for you—standards they want you to meet or think you should meet. Trying to live up to someone else's goals or image of you will make self-acceptance more difficult.

Living with Constant Change

In addition to having to cope with the high expectations of others, you also live in a society where a great deal of rapid technological and social change is occurring. This makes self-acceptance difficult. How do you relate to conditions that are always changing? How can you accept yourself when your own standards—and society's—change constantly?

Rapid change affects the level of self-acceptance you are able to achieve. Change in the environment affects the work you do. Are you preparing for an occupation that will be obsolete ten years from now? Change will affect your friendships. What kind of permanent relationship can you establish with someone you may never see again after two or three years? Change will affect your family. Will the ties in the family you form be the same as those in the family in which you were raised? What are the forces that cause a splintering of the family? Change will affect your religion. Do you want rigid dogma or a philosophy that is adaptable to you and to a changing world? Change affects your sexual relationships. How much stability do you want or need in your intimate associations? With all these changes, it's easy to become disoriented. How can you accept or measure the person you are when the measuring rod is different from one day to the next?

If these pressures and influences worry or upset you or make you uncertain, then you are normal. The adjustments you need to make to cope with the pressures of life change your life and your concept of who you are. Self-acceptance will always be a problem when you are not certain of who you are. But actively working to accept yourself is an important step toward healthy interpersonal communication.

▲▲▲ *Self-Esteem*

Self-acceptance and self-esteem are directly related. If you construct your self-concept mainly from your interaction with the people and world around you, and if those people and that world are constantly changing, then it is easy to see how difficult it is to get in touch with yourself and feel confident in accepting it. It is important to recognize the significance of change and its effect on your self-concept.

The more realistic your self-concept is, the more value it will have for you. To make it realistic means to consider the expectations that others have of you, to answer or at least confront the most important personal questions you face, and to fit your self-concept with your current environment, not the world you grew up in. The expectations others have of you, the questions you must answer, and the demands of your environment are continually shifting, and if your responses do not change accordingly, you may develop an unrealistic picture of the world and of your relationship to it.

The part of your self-concept that evaluates your self is **self-esteem.** The closer your real self is to your ideal self, the higher your level of self-esteem. Your real self is the self you reveal as you function in daily life; your ideal self is the self you want to be. The greater the distance between ideal and real, the lower the self-esteem. This is nothing new—you know

TRY THIS

Work toward independence in your life. That is, make a habit of setting and working toward your own standards. Some things you can do to establish adaptability—and independence at the same time—are these:

1. Be more independent. Listen when others tell you, "You can do it. You know what to do."
2. Act rather than react. When you make a decision, carry it out. Do not make excuses or rationalize about why you could not do it.
3. Rather than say, "I have to . . . ," say, "I've decided to. . . . " Take responsibility for your life.
4. Set your own standards. Stop looking over your shoulder for other significant standard setters.
5. Listen to praise and compliments. People are telling you that you are capable.
6. Learn to say "no" and really mean it.
7. Take chances. Test what happens when you let your desires be known.
8. Explore freedom—freedom to be yourself, to love, and to be loved on your own merits.

From Dr. Gregory Young, *Your Personality and How to Live with It*. Reprinted by permission of Dr. Gregory Young.

you're much prouder of yourself when you act according to your best impulses than when your hopes lie in one direction and your behavior in another. (See Figure 3.2.)

How closely do you measure up to the standards you've set for yourself as ideal? The closer you come, the more likely you are to respect yourself.[8] Self-confidence, self-respect, self-esteem—those words all have the same general meaning. If your self-esteem is high, your behavior will reflect that.

What happens if your self-esteem turns out to be low? A related question could be, how can I increase my self-esteem—although it is already quite good—beyond what it is now? First you must realize that self-esteem *is* shaped and molded. That is, you *do* have control over it. You can increase your liking for yourself. When you experience yourself positively, you have high self-esteem. Second, the primary difference between those with low self-esteem and those with high self-esteem is attitude. What can you do to improve your attitude toward yourself?

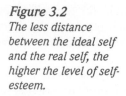

Figure 3.2
The less distance between the ideal self and the real self, the higher the level of self-esteem.

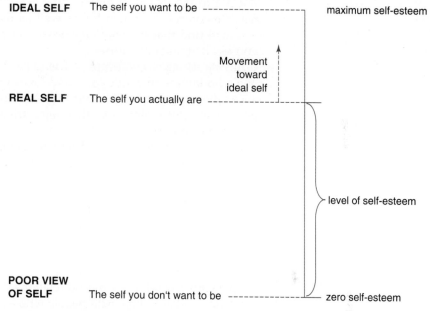

Building Self-Esteem

▲ Accept yourself totally and unconditionally, even if there is a distance between your ideal self and your real self, for that is the human condition. Start now! Since *you* control this, *you* can start by believing that you are worthy and that you are someone to be valued.

▲ Begin making positive affirmations about yourself. Stop cutting yourself down. When you feed positive thoughts and evaluations about yourself into your mind, you will begin to believe those things. Positive evaluations are something your self-esteem can grow on. This does not mean that you ignore criticisms from others but simply that you break the habit of devaluing yourself. Begin with "I appreciate and approve of myself."

▲ Go to work on the things that you need to, and can, change. Don't allow yourself to become hooked on "That's the way I am, I can't change!" Such a statement discourages further effort at self-understanding. The case is *not* closed. "That's the way I am" is likely to be an old decision, made without adequate data. A new decision is needed.

▲ Adopt a positive mental attitude and seek out positive people. It is possible to act your way into thinking positively. When you discover people with a positive attitude and spend your time with them, you will quickly discover that others do affect your outlook. Spend time with those from whom you can draw strength.

▲ Be self-reliant and helpful to others. You need not be one *or* the other. Self-reliance means learning to stand on your own two feet—

but not to the extent of saying, "It's every man for himself." You need to control your own life as well as reach out to help others. You will find that this interdependence of control and help makes you feel better about yourself.

▲ Cultivate strong relationships. A friend has been described as someone who knows all about you—and loves you anyway. Friends rejoice when you are happy, and they stick by you when the going gets tough. But realize, too, that some friends do not want to see change in you! They like what is predictable and known—the *old* you. Thus, sometimes your desire to change can best be accomplished by discussing it first with your current friends, so they know what's going on. The other alternative is to seek new supportive friends. We all need friends with whom we can share our misery as well as our victories. But we draw strength best from those who help us build our own self-esteem. One person said, "My friends didn't believe that I could become a successful writer. So I did something about it. I went out and found some new friends."

People with low self-esteem need relationships that will bolster their self-confidence—relationships with people who expect the best from them and will urge them to become all they can be. Does that apply just to people with low self-esteem? Don't we all need these kinds of relationships?

Self-acceptance is a difficult process, but it need not be painful. It's valuable to become conscious of and sensitive to the pressures that stand in the way of self-acceptance. Acquiring such sensitivity is an important first step, but it is important, too, to understand that learning to accept yourself is an ongoing, lifelong process. It involves continuous awareness and evaluation of yourself. The best way to cope with the changes that occur is through communication. *Communication is an important tool that allows us to relieve pressures, reduce strains, and gain answers.*

There is no "perfect" self; there is no "perfect" other. To pursue perfection in either can result in frustration and disappointment. It can result in people searching their whole lives and developing a reluctance to commit themselves to *any* less-than-perfect image of themselves or to relationships that appear to promise less-than-perfect results. Communication provides the buffer between perfection and reality. It allows you to discuss and negotiate realistic goals and expectations. You must be flexible, adaptable, and willing to change if you are to find happiness and a sense of well-being.

▲▲▲ *Self-Actualizing*

Self-awareness, self-acceptance, and positive self-esteem are necessary prerequisites for self-actualizing—an important idea in interpersonal communication. To actualize means simply *to make something (in this case, the self) actual, to develop it fully.* **Self-actualizing** involves growth that is motivated from within. It means willingness to pursue your ideal self on your own—to grow and change because *you* think it is important. I have used the term self-actualizing rather than self-actualization because it is a process: a never-ending process of movement and growth.

CONSIDER THIS

Carolynn Hillman, a psychoanalyst and psychotherapist, writes here about women and self-esteem.

> Women are especially vulnerable to feeling inadequate and depending on the approval of others for our sense of self-worth. Society, rather than valuing us as full human beings and empowering us, socializes us to focus on attracting, giving to, and pleasing others. We are "good girls" if we do as we're told, keep our voices down, willingly help out, and mind our manners. Advertisements and the media constantly barrage us with the message that we are to be beautiful and desirable, that our purpose in life is to snare and keep a man, and that failure to do so or the choice of other options means we are deficient and inadequate. Codependency, a problem that has received a lot of attention in recent years, involves getting your sense of self-worth from the approval of others, rather than generating it from within yourself—but this is precisely what women are taught to do. It is therefore not surprising that so many of us have limited or fragile self-esteem.*

Questions

1. Is codependency wrong? Is it insufficient? Is it out of synchronization with today's values?
2. How can women with limited or fragile self-esteem learn to value themselves?
3. Is a similar socialization likely to happen to men in the United States? Are there any parallels in Hillman's description to the way men are socialized?
4. Is there a possibility that our culture can or will change in the influence it has on women? Men? How would such changes come about, and what are they likely to be?

*From Carolynn Hillman, *Recovery of Your Self-Esteem: A Guide for Women* (New York: Simon & Schuster [A Fireside Book], 1992), p. 18.

The self-actualizing person is one who has taken steps to make things happen. Such people know their potential and actively strive to realize it. Victoria, who was elected president of her sorority, as discussed on page 81, is a good example. The question is, of course, how do you know what your potential is? The preceding discussions on self-awareness, self-acceptance, and self-esteem should give you some clues. What it amounts to, again, is being completely honest about your real self, your real abilities. The real self is not a fantasized version—positive *or* negative—of yourself, but a real picture of the you that other people see, the you that functions in the real world, the you that has been proved by experience to be your true self.

People who have a good idea of their potential are likely to act in ways they know are right for them, to establish and maintain personal standards, to become open to new experiences, and to trust themselves. That is, they have fairly assessed their own personal characteristics and have come to accept and believe in the self they discover. And, most important, such people are able to act on that belief. They tend to realize the importance of change in their lives, and they are willing to be forever in the process of "becoming."[9]

How might the behavior of a self-actualizing student be different from that of one who is not self-actualizing? Such a student is aware and accepting of his or her self. If this person consistently gets A's and B's, it is likely to be more out of a belief in the value of learning than out of a desire to play the role of perfect student for parents, peers, or professors. Such a student will work chemistry problems and write English papers without constant reinforcement or prodding or praise from other people. This student does not panic when a course in economics turns out to be tougher than expected, or when he or she receives a grade lower than hoped for. The self-actualizing student interacts on an equal basis with the people he or she lives with and socializes with. This person might really enjoy belonging to a choir, working on the yearbook, and being on an athletic team all at the same time, getting satisfaction from each activity. Such a student enjoys searching, seeking, and pursuing. This person might decide that after graduation he or she will live in California and work for a film-production company, selecting college courses accordingly, and at the same time remaining open to the possibility of living somewhere else and doing some other kind of work.[10]

You probably already know some people who seem to have it all together, the kind of people who know who they are and act on that knowledge. You may even know some for whom the whole process is pretty much unconscious, people who may have never even heard or considered the term *self-actualizing*.

There are certain characteristics that identify the self-actualizing person. If you are self-actualizing, you

1. Like yourself. You appreciate and try to capitalize on your own strengths and abilities.

What characteristics of the seated woman on the right facing the camera can you detect that would indicate she is likely to be self-actualized? Can you make judgments of a person's level of self-actualization from a picture alone?

2. **Trust yourself.** You are willing to make decisions for yourself, and you trust that those decisions will serve your own (and others') best interests.
3. **Are flexible.** Flexibility is the willingness to broaden your own interests by experiencing as much as possible. It is also the willingness to change when you see that certain decisions or alternatives don't work anymore.

An additional note of balance is needed. The assumption of constant growth of self and of one's relationships with others is implicit in the in-

TRY THIS

Have you ever recorded some of your personal goals so that you have a specific set of guidelines, a direction in which you want to move? Write down five of your most important personal goals—goals *you* want to achieve and goals *you* want to accomplish. Be as idealistic as you like. How do you want to accomplish these goals? For each of them, write three activities you can do that will help you reach them. Be as concrete and practical as you can. Setting goals is one thing; working toward them is another. Are your methods realistic?

formation in this section. But not every person is destined to become a self-actualizing person. No doubt you have observed stable and perhaps fulfilling relationships that, given their specific contexts, are stagnant. Once again—just as in our quest for an "ideal" self—the expectation of constant growth can, for some, lead to frustration and disappointment. It is important to maintain realistic goals and expectations.

Making What You Have Count

The phase of personal development called self-actualizing is important to an understanding of interpersonal communication because the self-actualizing person is usually more capable of using interpersonal communication skills in an effective, healthy way. As I have said, the self is at the heart of intrapersonal communication, and it is also at the heart of interpersonal communication. How well you'll be able to apply the concepts treated in the following chapters of this book depends on how realistic and well defined your self-concept is. It will be to your benefit if you know yourself well and are able to act on what you know.

What do you think about Lucy's description of the self-actualizing person? Is her description accurate?

PEANUTS reprinted by permission of United Feature Syndicate, Inc.

TRY THIS

Develop a skill or become proficient at something that you can share with others in a social setting. Develop some attribute that others will enjoy, profit from, be entertained by, or be wiser for.

Some of the following suggestions might be helpful to you in your quest:

1. Learn to play an instrument (guitar, harmonica, or piano).
2. Learn to tell jokes well.
3. Learn to do magic tricks.
4. Learn ballroom dancing well.
5. Get involved in body building or weight training.
6. Specialize in some particular world issue of importance (overpopulation, hunger, ecology, the decline of heroes in our culture, etc.).
7. Develop proficiency in art, literature, photography, music, dance, or theater.

The purpose of this exercise is to become a more social being. To succeed in social situations is positive reinforcement for further development of one's self—further self-actualizing.

From Philip Zimbardo, *Shyness,* © 1990, Addison-Wesley Publishing Co., Inc., Reading, MA. Reprinted with permission of the publisher.

Most of us are painfully aware of our shortcomings and failures. We can learn to be equally *realistically* aware of our strengths. To do this, first find qualities you already possess that you can emphasize. These can be very simple qualities. You might begin with statements like these: I am a good tennis player. I can make people laugh. I like animals. Make what you already have a starting place upon which you can build.

Then think about how often you act on your own likes and strengths. Do you play tennis often? Do you always wait for someone else to ask you to play? Try initiating a game with someone the next time *you* feel like playing. Do all your friends think you have a good sense of humor, or is your humor something you reserve for a few select people? Maybe you're holding back without knowing it. Do you own a pet? If you do, find out as much as you can about how to care for it. If you don't or can't have a pet, join an animal welfare society. Make a small donation to a zoo. Pursue your own interests! It makes sense. It can lead you to new, deeper interests and relationships. And it's the beginning of self-actualizing.

▲▲▲ *Self-Talk*

Self-talk is perhaps the best-known intrapersonal technique. **Intrapersonal communication,** as noted in Chapter 1, *involves all of the talk that occurs within us.* Also, it involves the processing of messages that occur within us. It is, indeed, the talk that often precedes most interpersonal communication. That is why it should be of concern to readers of this book, but it is not the only reason for concern.

In this section, the following questions will be answered: Why is it important? How does it affect behavior? How can it be used? When can it be used?

Why is it important? Speech is central to human communication *and* to self development. Self-talk is one way we have for getting in touch with the self. It is important for many reasons. It is personal and direct; people can use it on their own without direction. It is creative; often it frees the imagination, unleashes intuition, and allows people to explore their minds. It is motivational; self-talk can provide the force or influence to get people through difficult times. Also, it gives people time; people often need time to plan and prepare what will take place interpersonally.

How does it affect behavior? Modaff and Hopper, writing about why speech is basic, claim that "speech is a good behavior-regulator. If you want to do something well, tell yourself how. It is often best," they add, "if you tell yourself out loud."[11] Whether the talk is external, as Modaff and Hopper suggest, or internal, as it is most likely to occur, it is clearly a valuable technique.

Self-talk allows people to give *themselves* directions, thoughts, and images that will help guide their action. The idea here is that the words, phrases, and images people create help form a program or **script** for them to follow. *A script is rule-governed behavior.* In this case, you create the script you follow, much as you plan a route on a map. With no route, traveling can be haphazard. With no program, action can become random, spontaneous, or thoughtless—or there may be no action at all.

The programming helps people create beliefs, and the beliefs help determine attitudes. Attitudes create feelings, and the feelings determine people's actions. It is people's actions that create success or failure. So self-talk is simply what gets people moving. It may encourage them to think differently, change the way they look at problems, anticipate potential problems or situations, think through or plan actions, or cause them to seek more information. Whatever the result, it makes good sense.

How can it be used? The use of self-talk requires repetition, practice, and listening on the part of users. Scripts need to be repeated in much the same way you learn the words to music or television advertisements. When repeated, they are more likely to be remembered and thus to have impact. Repetition can occur the first thing in the morning; when you are driving the car; during exercise, meditation, or relaxation; or before you go to sleep at night. Scripts need to be listened to.

It is important to understand what is going on here. These messages, or scripts, are designed to direct behavior—often behavior that needs to be moved or changed—in new directions. The directions taken by behavior without these new messages are often governed by habits; thus, self-talk is often used to change habits—to introduce new behaviors. Baskin and Aronoff have written about what happens when you try to introduce new behaviors:

> *The attempt to introduce a new set of behaviors into an organization [or organism] is analogous to the attempt to transplant a new organ into a human being. Even when the new heart or kidney might prolong or save a person's life, the body tries to reject the organ. To the body, which has been genetically programmed to reject foreign cells, the new organ is just another intruder. That process, which usually protects the organism, in this case may prevent its survival.*[12]

The point is that changing habits is not easy. Because you are often dealing with entrenched habits—behaviors you have depended upon for many years—repetition, practice, and listening become important in the process of directing your behavior.

When can it be used? There are numerous possibilities for creating self-talk. Before a particularly challenging assignment, for example, self-talk (also called affirmations) could be programmed. Put yourself into these situations, and assume the "I" refers to you: "I have courage. I will meet this challenge with confidence knowing that I have the energy to endure and the determination to succeed." When people get down on themselves, depressed, or tired, the self-talk could read: "I build my enthusiasm by keeping my interest level high. The more interested I become in what I do, the more enthusiasm I have. The more enthusiasm I have, the more energy I create."

There are as many opportunities to use self-talk as there are situations to be faced. When a project requires organization: "I organize my thoughts. I assess the situation. I look for alternatives and different approaches. I select the proper course of action. I make the right decision. I record my thoughts and actions." For an oral report before a class: "In every opportunity I have to communicate with others, I am decisive, direct, warmly received—and effective." The goal here is to be suggestive, not to put words in people's mouths. The best self-talk is likely to be that which best fits the person creating it, the purpose for which it is intended, and the moment or situation it is designed to address.

There are two other ways in which people can develop and use self-talk. The first is through *internal dialogue* or *imagined interactions*. The second is through using an *internal advisor*. These methods are mentioned simply as catalysts for putting the technique into practice.

Internal dialogue **Internal dialogue,** or **imagined interactions,** occur when people create other characters with whom they internally converse; they imagine themselves talking to others. For example, people could create situations internally before they occur: a conflict with a parent, spouse, or relationship partner; a job or an appraisal interview; a confrontation with a friend or teacher; a situation in which one is asking for a raise or promotion. In these situations—especially where the potential for stress or loss of face is high—people can internally play out a variety of scenes to better prepare them for what might happen.

In their article on imagined interactions, Honeycutt, Zagacki, and Edwards say that they occur daily. "Most involve," they write, "actors in conversation with significant others, such as family members, close friends, intimates, or work partners."[13] The unique thing about internal dialogue is that it has been shown that people can envision participation in the discourse, they can anticipate responses, and they can even assume others' roles. These researchers suggest "that imagined interactions *can* help individuals predict a future event" [italics mine].[14]

Internal advisor Finally, the **internal advisor** is one more dimension or aspect of self-talk. Perhaps you have experienced one of your high-school or college teachers giving you advice and counsel long after you actually had the teacher for a course. This could be labeled residual (what remains *after* you or the teacher has been removed from the actual situation) mentoring. Sometimes the internal advisor experience can be like Freud's superego (the conscience of the unconscious)—the part of your psyche that *controls,* at an unconscious level, the impulses of the id (the source of instinctive energy and impulsive thinking). Sometimes, too, *it is an internal voice that guides and directs you.* It could be a father, mother, teacher, or even a member of the clergy. Sometimes, too, it can be your own subconscious helping you select proper choices, make correct decisions, or resolve problems in everyone's best interests.

CONSIDER THIS

Some people may still believe that using self-talk is weird or is only for people who are not in full command of their senses. Here, the anthropologist Edward T. Hall talks about his use of self-talk:

> Living without extended family and connections, young, restless, ambitious, wanting to make something of myself, full of energy, socially unskillful, lonely, perched on the bare fringes of life with a brain that wouldn't stop, there were times when it seemed as though I was facing impossible odds and would end up as nothing but a marginal misfit. What kept me going was that underneath, there was a tiny voice that kept saying if I could stick it out, things would eventually improve. That was the voice of the self, or to some, the soul.*

Questions

1. Can you identify with any of the feelings Hall expressed in this passage? Have you ever felt as he did here?
2. Would you call his "tiny voice" self-talk?
3. What has kept you going in times like these? Does your "voice of the self" ever give you messages? What does it say to you?

*From Edward T. Hall, *An Anthropology of Everyday Life: An Autobiography* (New York: Doubleday [Anchor Books], 1992), p. 144.

▲▲▲ Self-Disclosure

Think of the last interpersonal communication you had with someone in which you exchanged ideas and information freely and came away feeling the relationship had been strengthened, or at least better defined. What are the ingredients that cause one encounter to be memorable and another to be meaningless and forgotten? Perhaps one ingredient was the amount of self-disclosing that occurred. **Self-disclosure** means *deliberately disclosing or revealing information about yourself, telling what you know about yourself not normally known to others*. Isn't it true that when somebody reveals private, personal information you could acquire from no other source except him or her, the quality of communication increases?

Sharing experiences can have deep meaning. If a high-disclosure message was just shared by the woman on the left, what might be the next words from the woman on the right?

What probably made your encounter significant was that both of you shared information. It did not come from just one of you. In addition, the information probably concerned your feelings about each other, the social situation, or about other people in your social situation. For example, maybe you said, "I feel great just knowing you" or "I'm glad I could do this with you" or "Can you imagine what Erich would say if he could see us now?" You were revealing personal feelings that resulted from your interaction with the other person. These are potentially high-disclosure messages; that is, they say something particular about the circumstances of your relationship. Such messages need not be intimate (the term *intimate* does not always mean sexual intimacy) exchanges, but they can be. They can also be quite simple. But they do depend for their complete meaning on your having shared certain experiences with the other person.

Potentially low-disclosure messages might concern situations that the two of you do not share. For example, to mention the name of a book you have just read, or the fact that you did not like the eggs you had for breakfast, or that your roommate has a cold is to share low-disclosure messages. They may, however, pave the way for high-disclosure messages. Self-disclosing is important because you need to know yourself in order to do it, and because by disclosing yourself you come to define your feelings toward yourself more clearly.[15]

It's likely that the last significant interaction you thought of involved a friend. It is in such close relationships that most self-disclosure occurs because revealing yourself involves risk, and we are not as likely to take a risk with a new acquaintance. We usually do not want to share feelings with a person we have not yet learned to trust. It's interesting, however, that we cannot create trust in a relationship, and thus diminish the amount of risk in that relationship, without self-disclosure. And the more we trust another person, the more likely it is that we will self-disclose. Self-disclosure creates trust, and trust encourages self-disclosure. As in so much of what we talk about in interpersonal communication, a positive interacting cycle creates growth.

What Happens in Self-Disclosure?

Before looking for any further explanation of self-disclosure, consider some of the benefits to be gained. What happens when you self-disclose? One of the first things you might notice happening is *increasing accuracy in communication.* Because self-disclosure involves the expression of personal feelings, you not only pass along information ("Your philodendron died while you were gone.") but also say how you feel about delivering that message ("I'm sorry to have to tell you your philodendron died while you were gone. I know how diligently you cared for it."). Otherwise, the other person would have to guess how you feel from your behavior. Feelings are often interpreted from behavior, and you hope that others interpret your feelings correctly. But as you know from experience, other people do not always guess correctly how you feel unless you tell them. The first benefit of self-disclosure, then, is that it ensures a certain level of accuracy in communication.

Another benefit of self-disclosure has to do with *getting to know others better.* Interpersonal relationships are built upon self-disclosure. If you want to deepen your friendships, discover more about how others think and feel, and increase the intensity of your associations, self-disclosure provides one means. Think of the person you consider your closest friend. Chances are that more mutual self-disclosure has taken place with this person than with anyone else you know.

Self-disclosure also is a way of *increasing your number of contacts and enlarging your group of friends.* Getting to know a larger number of people can add knowledge, interest, and a degree of excitement to your present life. It might provide opportunities for you to experiment—to try out new attitudes, to experience new behaviors, and to encounter new relationships. It is not necessarily dishonest in your interpersonal encounters to be one thing to one person and something a little different to another. You have many sides. You are not composed of a single set of attitudes, behaviors, or relationships, but often routine, habits, or laziness can prevent you from sharing certain aspects of yourself. In every situation, the self you reveal should be an honest one, but it need not always be the same one exposed to everyone, and it certainly can change.

Perhaps the most important personal benefit to result from self-disclosure is *gaining increased personal insight*. Self-disclosure opens the window through which you see yourself. This is not to suggest that you will discover, nurture, or gain insight into a single "real" you. There are several (perhaps many) selves, all equally valid. The "ideal" or "real" self is neither achievable nor desirable. But through self-disclosure you are more likely to discover attributes, uniquenesses, and peculiarities that you may not have been aware of. Exposing these new facets is part of gaining increased personal insight.

What Are You Afraid Of?

Why are you afraid to reveal yourself to others? Why is it easier to hold back than to express your real being? In *Why Am I Afraid to Tell You Who I Am?* John Powell suggests that each of us thinks, "If I tell you who I am, you may not like who I am, and it is all that I have."[16] You fear rejection. You fear discovering that you might not be totally acceptable to others or that you are unworthy. Another reason is that you feel you may not get reinforcement. What if I open myself to you and you offer no support or positive feedback? Even the possibility of some slight negative reaction is scary. Or you may be afraid of hurting another person or making him or her angry. You may have wanted for a long time to tell someone that if she continues to treat her boyfriend callously she will lose him. Your fear of angering her may have kept you from telling her.

Researchers have found that whether or not people disclose themselves to others depends on several different factors:[17]

▲ The nature of the other person or people.
▲ The relationship between the discloser and the recipient.
▲ The kind of information to be disclosed.
▲ The degree of liking that exists between the people (particularly for women).
▲ The degree of trust that exists between the people (particularly for men).
▲ The perceived appropriateness (particularly on the part of recipients of disclosure).
▲ The degree of self-esteem on the part of both discloser and recipient.
▲ The willingness to risk.

Studies also indicate that the primary reason people avoid self-disclosure is a feeling that if they disclose themselves they might project an image they do not want to project. Research shows, further, that beyond protecting their image, males and females avoid self-disclosure for different reasons. Males, for example, do not want to give information that might make them appear inconsistent. They also do not want to lose control over other people, nor do they want to threaten their relationships with others. For males, the predominant concern is to maintain control.[18]

For females, research shows that they do not want to give other people information that might be used against them. Also, females feel that self-disclosure is a sign of emotional disturbance. Further, they do not want to hurt a relationship. Their object, according to the research, is to avoid personal hurt and problems with a relationship that might result from self-disclosure.[19]

You may avoid self-disclosure if you believe that no one else is interested in your thoughts, feelings, or view of the world.[20] Or you simply may not know how to self-disclose constructively. Since this disclosure is the primary channel for gaining information about yourself, some of the basic skills for successful, constructive self-disclosure will be outlined next.

Self-Disclosure: Everything in Moderation

When you become aware of some of the research findings about self-disclosure—it increases with relational intimacy, it increases when rewarded, it increases with the need to reduce uncertainty in relationships, it tends to be reciprocal, attraction is related to positive disclosure, and it is more likely to occur in moderately intimate relationships[21]—your first inclination might be to put your self-disclosure processes and utterances into high gear and proceed, self-disclosing at all costs and with all rapidity. Caution is advised—the purpose of this brief section.

Shirley J. Gilbert, a researcher in this area, discovered that satisfaction and disclosure have a curvilinear (consisting of a curved line) relationship; that is, *relational satisfaction is likely to be greatest at moderate levels of disclosure.* (See Figure 3.3.)

What is interesting about Gilbert's study, which seems to be supported by other researchers, is that we have, up to this point, believed that a linear relationship was ideal between satisfaction and disclosure. Look at Figure 3.3. A linear relationship (the straight line that becomes dotted) suggests that the greater the disclosure, the higher the satisfaction in the relationship. Gilbert suggests this is only likely to be true when both partners have healthy self-concepts, both are willing to take relational risks, and both are committed to unconditional positive regard in the relationship.

Gilbert suggests that there is more going on in relationships. "There are interpersonal price tags attached to intimate relationships," she says.[22] Relationships are composed of feelings (satisfaction) and commitment (willingness to risk), it is true. But relationships also can be charac-

Figure 3.3
Linear and curvilinear patterns in self-disclosure. Adapted from Shirley J. Gilbert, "Empirical and Theoretical Extensions of Self-Disclosure," 197–216, ed. Gerald R. Miller. Copyright © 1976 Sage Publications, Inc., with permission.

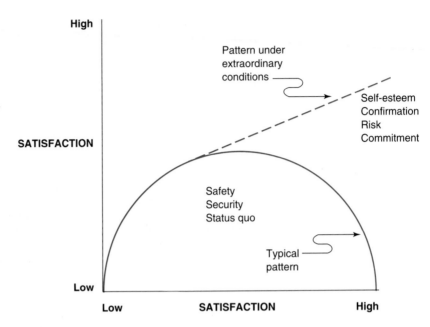

terized by the verbal and nonverbal *depth* of exchange and by the *depth* of acceptance and confirmation.

What this means—putting it all together—is that not all relationships are the same. More and more disclosure does not guarantee more satisfaction, greater intimacy, or a stronger relationship. This depends on the partners. But if you look at the components, (1) healthy self-concepts, (2) willingness to risk, (3) unconditional positive regard, (4) verbal and nonverbal depth, and (5) depth of acceptance and confirmation, as well as the price partners are willing to pay (the interpersonal price tags) to reveal and express these in open, honest, and unreserved ways with each other, you can see the value of Gilbert's curvilinear relationship. Relationships are likely to thrive when self-disclosure is moderated and controlled. We're not saying that it isn't healthy; we're not saying that it isn't beneficial; we're not saying that it should not be practiced. We're simply cautioning that more is not necessarily better. We're simply saying *everything in moderation.*

Building Self-Disclosure Skills

Before the skills that will improve self-disclosure are discussed, several comments need to be made. First, as already noted, a high degree of self-disclosure is *not* always preferred. That is, some research suggests that some people prefer others who are low disclosers.[23] This research highlights the importance of "testing the waters" before engaging in disclosure, especially if your goal is to impress the recipient. Testing might include starting with some low-risk, low-disclosure messages. Testing might also include patience—just waiting until the relationship develops a bit before engaging in disclosure.

Second, there are norms that govern self-disclosure. According to Gilbert, these norms "exert powerful influences to regulate times when it is socially acceptable and rewarding to divulge personal information about oneself to another."[24] Research done by P. M. Blau shows that in an initial encounter, disclosing negative aspects of oneself is considered inappropriate.[25] C. Arthur Vanlear warns that it is socially inappropriate and interpersonally inept to offer private, personal disclosures too early in a relationship.[26] Such norms are likely to vary from situation to situation.

Third, research suggests that the disclosure must be perceived as a social reward in order to produce a positive effect. Think about it: this other person chose *you* to disclose with; this makes you special. Think about how you would feel if you discovered that this discloser had shared this same information with others. *You* are no longer special! Perhaps you would feel betrayed. The social reward has been removed.

Finally, self-disclosure with another guarantees nothing. If you engage in it with the intention of establishing openness, closeness, friendship, or intimacy, you may be disappointed. Although it may be an index of the depth of your communication with another, there are no guaranteed outcomes.

This information is *not* designed to discourage you from self-disclosing; rather, it is to guide you in situations where self-disclosure is appropriate. My advice on self-disclosing in ambiguous situations is this: (1) do it cautiously, watching for *any* kind of response and (2) go slowly. Taking it slow and easy helps reduce some of the risk involved. Remember, there is a great deal of evidence to support the conclusion that self-disclosure is a critical ingredient in the development of relationships.[27]

Improvement in self-disclosure generally begins with attitudes. With the proper attitude, our skills in self-disclosure will improve.

Commit yourself to growth   If you have no desire to grow or change, and no commitment to improve your relationship with another person, you are not likely to self-disclose. You have to care about another person before taking the risk necessary to build a trusting relationship. The fact that you acknowledge the value of a relationship shows the other person your level of commitment and makes the self-disclosure even more useful.

It takes courage to let another person know he or she means something special to you. To say "It has been fun talking to you" sounds superficial, but it may be enough to trigger further interaction. So, feeling a commitment to a relationship is part of it, but you also need to disclose that commitment to the other person. How often do you tell other people that you need them or appreciate them?

TRY THIS

Write down some of your positive traits, characteristics, abilities, and accomplishments. What is there about yourself that you would like to emphasize? For example:

> Are you in good health?
> Are you comfortable meeting new people?
> Are you good at math problems and puzzles?
> Do you have a good memory?

List as many things as you can think of—they don't have to be earthshaking skills or accomplishments. Then, for each skill, write down the last time you can think of when you acted on that preference or ability. If it's been so long that you can't remember, list concrete steps you can take to revive that particular skill. This can be as simple as talking to someone, writing away for information, looking up something in the library, or joining a club or musical group. As you discover new preferences and skills, add to your list.

▲ Cultivate the ability to see—and enjoy—people as individuals. Look for the qualities in others that make them unique.
▲ Learn to enjoy life more. Take time to savor the things you do. Get involved in the world around you. Look for good experiences, expect them to happen, celebrate them when they do.
▲ Avoid cynicism. Cynics feel that everyone is out for his or her own personal gain. No one is genuine or generous; everyone wants to get something from others—this is the cynic's view. Allow yourself to act as if you expect the best from others.
▲ Try to be more positive. Do not blame others for your troubles or trace your unwise choices to their advice or example. Take responsibility for your behavior, ideas, and decisions.

Build trust Trust grows when you begin to risk with others and confirm them as human beings. For example, if you disclose a thought, feeling, or reaction to someone else, and he or she responds with acceptance, support, and cooperation, a risk has been taken and confirmation has followed. **Trust** *is simply your reliance on the character, ability, strength, or truth of others—you place your confidence in them.* To build trust you must

▲ Openly accept others. To demonstrate this, you must reveal favorable responses to them.

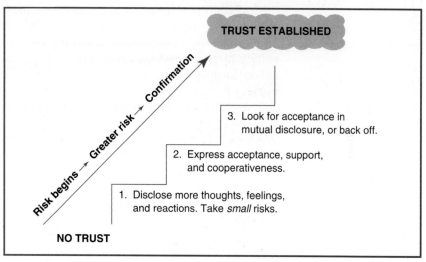

Figure 3.4
Building trust is a three-step process

- ▲ Demonstrate support and concern. Avoid making fun of others.
- ▲ Show respect. Let others know how you regard them or admire them. Help them to understand how worthy they are of esteem.
- ▲ Be understanding. Evaluative responses convey rejection as readily as moralizing responses or silence (no response at all). To react to others with rejection, ridicule, or disrespect destroys trust.
- ▲ Reciprocate the self-disclosure of others. To be closed or unresponsive is a sign of rejection. Responding with an adequate (near-equal) amount of self-disclosure of your own keeps others from feeling overexposed or vulnerable.
- ▲ Reveal your thoughts, feelings, and reactions if the other person has indicated considerable acceptance, support, and cooperativeness.
- ▲ Express warmth. Say it. Act it out. Smile. Use nonverbal behavior to express your sensations, feelings, and intentions. Eye contact, a touch, or a wink might express warmth. Verbal responses also work: saying, "I feel very good right now" or "I like you" are two possibilities.
- ▲ Communicate accurate understanding. Restate the content, feelings, or meaning of others' disclosure in your own words.
- ▲ Indicate cooperative intentions. Show that you are willing to work with others toward a common goal—getting to know them better, deepening a relationship, finding out what something means (together). (See Figure 3.4.)

Share your feelings Beyond sharing with another person what you consider the value of the relationship, it helps if you both agree to share feelings and awarenesses. This sharing often occurs naturally when the relationship is already comfortable and mutually supportive. Other times it might help if you simply make a comment like "I hope we can be honest with each other. I know I'm going to try." Self-disclosure operates best in a situation where both people know the value of sharing. Each should be willing to share feelings about the other person's actions, being careful not to confuse honest communication with thoughtfulness or cruel remarks.

We all need some reinforcement in our communications. Have you ever come out of a movie really excited and wanting to share your enthusiasm, only to have your companions say nothing at all? You don't know if they agree with you or don't agree with you or are simply thinking about something else! Sharing is a two-way process. Without give *and* take, one person might stop giving anything at all. To be ready and willing to share means that each partner views the relationship from nearly the same viewpoint, lessening the feeling of risk.

▲ Cultivate the ability to empathize—the ability to feel and to care about other people's experiences. Not only does this make your own life richer, it connects your life to that of others and makes you more likable as well. To develop empathy, study your own experiences. Remember the way you felt—or imagine the way you might feel—in similar situations. Relate your feelings—or probable feelings—to the other person.

▲ Encourage other people to talk about their feelings and their lives. Try to remember what they say and to get a sense of what their experiences feel like.

▲ Be ready to confront people when you disagree with them about a matter that is important to you. This helps give you purpose and identity. It also lets others know you are capable of strong beliefs and feelings.

▲ Cheer for your friends. Can you rejoice at other people's successes? Not being able to—because of envy or fear—makes you less a friend and less confident and secure in your own life.

Take a chance You must be willing to take chances in self-disclosure. There is no guarantee that you will not get hurt or that you will not be rejected. If a relationship is important, it is worth risking being honest so that both people can learn and grow. You may become angry or defensive at something the other person says, but if you aren't willing to express your real feelings, the result is superficiality and facade building.

If it bothers you that a friend always dominates conversations by griping about her parents, you might say, "Let's make any discussion of parents off limits for tonight." This takes some courage, but it allows your real feelings to show. And your friend may not even have been aware that she was dominating the conversation. It's worth taking the chance of telling her how you feel as long as you have her best interests at heart and care about preserving an honest relationship with her. The habit of honesty in all matters, no matter how small, makes it easier to be honest in more difficult, personal areas. For example, to tell a friend that he seems to be feeling sorry for himself takes a lot of courage. But taking such a chance is often worth the risk. The other person may value you even more because of your honesty.

▲ Don't suppress strong emotions—especially anger. If, for example, you feel you have more than fulfilled the instructor's requirements for a project or paper and yet you receive a low grade, tell the teacher that you are annoyed. Don't just let it go by saying, "It's no big thing." It *is* a big thing. Resigning yourself to mistreatment makes you believe that you *deserve* mistreatment.

▲ Meet all the challenges you possibly can. Decide for yourself—honestly—what you can and cannot do with respect to each one. Even if you know others will excuse you, do not excuse yourself from challenges you *can* meet with an effort.

▲ Act ethically toward others. How you treat others *does* matter—even in small things. Remember to thank people for small favors as well as great ones.

▲ Force yourself to do things you've never done before—talk to people you've never spoken to, engage in activities you haven't tried. Taking chances in some areas of your life makes it more likely that you will take chances in other areas.

▲ Snatch at all fleeting moments of intense feeling. Avoid the repetitive and automatic. Look for opportunities to inject freshness and emotionality into your experiences and your relationships.

Don't manipulate The best self-disclosure occurs when neither person tries to change or manipulate the other. Despite the intense emotions that may surface, conversation should never turn to who is at fault but rather focus on making the relationship more satisfying and productive for both parties. For example, if your friend seems to be indulging in self-pity, it would be more helpful to point this out than to tell him or her to stop it. Stopping or not stopping is your friend's choice to make. Any change that occurs in a relationship should result from one person acting freely in response to information provided or acquired. This nonmanipulative atmosphere is created when you truly care for and accept the other person.

▲ Do not tell other people how they feel: "I'm sure you don't like this." "I know how uncomfortable Sue makes you feel, so I won't invite her." People's feelings change. Ask others how they feel, but don't tell them.

▲ Do not tell other people what they should do: "You should never be angry." "You should control your temper." Let the other person decide what is or is not appropriate behavior.

▲ Do not always try to be the powerful one in your relationships. You may be forceful, but not dominating. Listen, and be aware of your own weaknesses.

▲ Don't be passive and let others control your life. Do not feign helplessness and stupidity. Learn to be willing to express your own convictions strongly.

Watch your timing Whenever possible, express your feelings and reactions at the time you actually feel them. Both parties must realize what behavior caused a particular reaction. Parents usually find that a reprimand means more to a small child if they say "No!" just as the child is about to do something wrong than if the incident goes undiscovered for an hour and the "No!" comes too late. This is true for adult interactions, too. Even disturbing reactions should be discussed at once. Sometimes feelings are accumulated and then dropped on the other person; this hinders healthy self-disclosure. Of course there are times when immediate expression of your reaction may be inappropriate. For example, you would not want to share highly personal reactions with a friend in a crowded elevator. It's generally better to wait until no one else is around.

▲ When someone asks you how you feel about something, answer as quickly as possible. Don't censor your response. You have the right to any reaction you feel. A quick answer is often more authentic and accurate than a delayed one.

▲ Make your comments to the people you think are affecting you and to no one else.

▲ Do not object to another person's behavior in front of others. Objections often are interpreted as personal attacks. Unless waiting would be costly, waiting until you are alone reveals your concern for fairness to the other person and your consideration for his or her feelings.

▲ Avoid comparisons. Nobody likes being described as inferior to someone else. Comparisons may predispose others not to listen to what you have to say.

▲ Make your comments as soon as you can. Speaking up becomes more difficult the longer you postpone it. Also, if the comments are tied to a strong emotional reaction, like anger, waiting allows the reaction to build with the possibility that irrelevant comments will be added. If you comment on things that happened a long time ago, you will look as if you have been holding a grudge.

▲ Try to make only one comment at a time. Too many comments—especially criticisms—might demoralize the other person and may obscure and detract from the major point.

Clarify, clarify If you're not sure you understand what another person means, you should try restating his or her comments. If you offer a paraphrase of the other person's remarks before supplying your own response, there's less chance of your misunderstanding each other. (Ralph: "I'm sick of taking this bus with you every day." Mike: "I hear you saying you're sick of riding to work with me. Is that right?" Ralph: "No, I just meant I'm sick of this bus. I wish we had a car.") Make sure the other person understands your comments in the way you mean them.

As you respond to another person, you can try to eliminate any kind of personal judgments ("Don't you ever listen?"), name-calling ("You really are a hypocrite!"), accusations ("You love walking all over people, don't you?"), commands or orders ("Stop running his life!"), or sarcasm ("You really want to get to the top," when the other person just flunked an exam). Instead, talk about things the other person did—actual, accurate descriptions of the action that took place. You can try to describe your own feelings, letting the other person see them as temporary rather than absolute. Instead of saying "I hate sitting next to you in class," you might try "I can't stand it when you crack your knuckles."

According to research, the clearest self-disclosure messages are

▲ Mutually relevant. That is, they are based on the immediate situation—the here and now, not something that is past or unrelated to the present situation.
▲ Personally owned. To say "I feel" is much more exact than the more general "People feel."
▲ Source specific. Say "I feel anxiety toward you, Daniel" rather than "I feel anxious around people."
▲ Based on a clear causal connection with your feeling or perception. Try to use the word *because* rather than omitting a reason or alluding to the cause indirectly by saying something like "There may be a reason."
▲ Behavior specific. Rather than saying that someone is irresponsible or can't be counted on, it is better to say, "You were late for our appointment."

► ## SUMMARY

People's self-concept is directly related to interpersonal communication. People with a weak self-concept, for example, reveal this weakness to others through their weak or ineffective behaviors. Also, people with a weak self-concept tend to distort the perceptions they receive from others. The information they receive may be negative and nonsupportive. This creates inaccurate, negative, or weak communication because communication based on poor information relies on hunches, feelings, and impulses without regard for facts. Often these people act impulsively rather than gathering the facts before making decisions. This creates confusion and problems.

Because of the negative reactions such communication attracts, further problems with self-concept result, and an ongoing, negative, spiral of frustration, suspicion, and doubt is produced. Is more proof of the relationship between self-concept and communication needed?

In this chapter we looked at the relationship between self-concept and effective communication. After discussing both personal and social identity, we noted that the two skills that will help us overcome misunderstandings involve recognizing we share a common identity with everyone, and acknowledging our differences and trying to understand how they influence our communication.

In the section on self-concept we looked at who you are and how you got to be this way. In the section on self-awareness we noted that self-awareness involves the sum total of all your perceptions of yourself—but we cautioned that not all your beliefs about yourself are realistic.

Under self-acceptance, we stated that it involves seeing how your positive and negative qualities are equally valid, equally you, equally normal to have. The two major things that stand in the way of self-acceptance are living up to an image and living with constant change. Actively working to accept yourself is an important step toward healthy interpersonal communication.

The part of your self-concept that evaluates your self is self-esteem. We looked at the relationship between the ideal and the real self, offered six suggestions for building self-esteem, and noted that communication is the tool that allows you to relieve pressures, reduce strains, and gain answers.

Self-actualizing was defined as growth that is motivated from within. In this section, the three main characteristics of self-actualized people were offered, how self-actualizing is related to interpersonal communication was noted, and then the two ways people have for becoming realistically aware of their strengths were discussed.

In the section on self-talk, defined as all the talk that occurs within us, four questions were answered: Why is it important? How does it affect behavior? How can it be used? When can it be used? In the final paragraphs, internal dialogue, imagined interactions, and the internal advisor were mentioned as other ways people can develop and use self-talk.

In the final section on self-disclosure, four important comments preceded the discussions: (1) high disclosure is not always preferred, (2) norms govern disclosure, (3) disclosure must be perceived as a social reward, and (4) there are no guarantees. We then looked at what happens in self-disclosure, what you may be afraid of, the need for moderation, and how to improve skills.

Your success in college and indeed in life will depend on *how* you feel about yourself and your abilities. Your self-concept is a product of intrapersonal and interpersonal communication. What you think about yourself affects your behavior toward others. What other people say about you and to you constitutes the information you use in thinking about and talking to yourself. Thus, intrapersonal communication and interpersonal communication are intricately entwined. We see this especially in the process of self-talk and self-disclosure. Talking to yourself and disclosing yourself are keys to discovering yourself. Self-talk and self-disclosure are important methods of acquiring information. Other practical methods of acquiring new information are listening and feedback. These subjects are discussed in the next chapter.

▶ ## KEY TERMS

self-concept
self-awareness
self-acceptance
self-esteem
self-actualizing

self-talk
intrapersonal communication
script
internal dialogue

imagined interactions
internal advisor
self-disclosure
trust

▶ ## NOTES

1. See William B. Gudykunst, *Bridging Differences: Effective Intergroup Communication.* (Newbury Park, CA: Sage Publications, 1991), 20.
2. Gudykunst, 20.
3. Gudykunst, 21.
4. Gudykunst, 22.
5. Gudykunst, 22.
6. David Washburn, "Intrapersonal Communication in a Jungian Perspective," *Journal of Communication* 14 (1964): 131–135.
7. Robert Cathcart and Gary Gumpert, "I Am a Camera: The Mediated Self," *Communication Quarterly* 34 (1986): 89–102.
8. Nathaniel Branden, *The Psychology of Self-Esteem* (Los Angeles: Nash, 1969), 103.
9. Earl C. Kelly, *Perceiving, Behaving, Becoming: A New Focus on Education*, 1962 Yearbook (Washington, DC: Association for Supervision and Curriculum Development, 1962), 9–20.
10. From Don E. Hamachek, *Encounters with the Self.* Copyright © 1971 by Holt, Rinehart and Winston, New York. Adapted by permission of Holt, Rinehart and Winston.
11. John Modaff and Robert Hopper, "Why Speech Is 'Basic,'" *Communication Education* 33 (1984): 37–42.
12. O. W. Baskin and C. E. Aronoff, *Interpersonal Communication in Organizations* (Santa Monica, CA: Goodyear Publishing Company, 1980), 137.
13. James M. Honeycutt, Kenneth S. Zagacki, and Renee Edwards, "Intrapersonal Communication, Social Cognition, and Imagined Interactions," in *Intrapersonal Communication Processes*, ed. Charles Roberts, Renee Edwards, and Larry Barker (Scottsdale, AZ: Gorsuch Scarisbrick, Publishers, 1989), 166–184.

14. Honeycutt, Zagacki, and Edwards, 169.
15. Sidney M. Jourard, *The Transparent Self* (New York: D. Van Nostrand Co., 1971), 6.
16. John Powell, *Why Am I Afraid to Tell You Who I Am?* (Chicago: Argus Communications, 1969), 27.
17. Shirley J. Gilbert, "Empirical and Theoretical Extensions of Self-Disclosure," in *Explorations in Interpersonal Communication,* ed. Gerald R. Miller (Beverly Hills, CA: Sage Publications, 1976), 200. This is Volume V in the Sage annual review of communication research. For a review of the literature on self-disclosure, see P. W. Cozby, "Self-Disclosure: A Literature Review," *Psychological Bulletin* 79 (1973): 73–91.
18. Lawrence B. Rosenfeld, "Self-Disclosure Avoidance: Why I Am Afraid to Tell You Who I Am," *Communication Monographs* 46 (1979): 72–73.
19. Rosenfeld, 73.
20. Jourard, 193.
21. From Gilbert, 200–201.
22. Gilbert, 212–213.
23. S. A. Culbert, "Trainer Self-Disclosure and Member Growth in T-Groups," *Journal of Applied Behavioral Science* 4 (1968): 47–73; R. G. Weigel, N. Dinges, R. Dyer, and A. A. Straumfjord, "Perceived Self-Disclosure, Mental Health, and Who Is Liked in Group Treatment," *Journal of Counseling Psychology* 19 (1972): 47–52.
24. Gilbert, 202.
25. P. M. Blau, *Exchange and Power in Social Life* (New York: John Wiley & Sons, 1964), 49.
26. C. Arthur Vanlear, Jr., "The Formation of Social Relationships: A Longitudinal Study of Social Penetration," *Human Communication Research* 13 (1987): 314.
27. J. Altman and D. A. Taylor, *Social Penetration: The Development and Dissolution of Interpersonal Relationships* (New York: Holt, Rinehart and Winston, 1973); C. R. Berger and R. J. Calabrese, "Some Explorations in Initial Interaction and Beyond: Toward a Developmental Theory of Interpersonal Communication," *Human Communication Research* 1 (1975): 99–112, as cited in Rebecca J. Cline and Karen E. Musolf, "Disclosure as Social Exchange: Anticipated Length of Relationship, Sex Roles, and Disclosure Intimacy," *The Western Journal of Speech Communication* 49 (1985): 43–56.

▶ FURTHER READING

Kathleen Adams, *Journal to the Self: Twenty-Two Paths to Personal Growth* (New York: Warner Books, 1990). Adams, a psychotherapist, suggests readers can open the door to self-understanding by writing, reading, and creating a journal of their lives. This work precedes by four years her book titled *Mightier Than the Sword: The Journal As a Path to Men's Self-Discovery* (New York: Warner, 1994). Both are practical, specific, and important.

Nathaniel Branden, *The Six Pillars of Self-Esteem* (New York: Bantam, 1994). First, Branden demonstrates why self-esteem is basic to psychological health, achievement, and positive relationships. Second, he introduces the six pillars—action-based practices for daily living. Finally, he applied self-esteem to the workplace, parenting, education, psychotherapy, and society.

Albert Ellis and Arthur Lange, *How to Keep People From Pushing Your Buttons* (New York: Carol Publishing Group [A Birch Lane Press Book], 1994). This book relates to this chapter's section on self-acceptance and living up to an image. The authors offer specific, realistic ways to keep people and events from pushing your buttons. Basically, this is a book about irrational thinking and how to change it.

Ronald Gross, *Peak Learning: A Master Course in Learning How to Learn* (New York: The Putnam Publishing Group [Jeremy P. Tarcher/Perigee Books], 1991). As noted in the first "Consider This" by Bateson, the self is shaped and reshaped by learning. Gross will change readers' ideas of learning. He offers a learning style that is fast, efficient, thorough, productive, and enjoyable. Through explanations, examples, and exercises, Gross encourages lifelong learning.

Carolynn Hillman, *Self-Esteem: A Guide for Women* (New York: Simon & Schuster [A Fireside Book], 1992). Hillman, a psychoanalyst and psychotherapist for 24 years, provides warm, encouraging, nurturing advice for anyone with self-esteem problems. Her ten steps to liking the person you are are practical and specific. Full of examples and good advice.

William W. Hewitt, *The Art of Self Talk* (St. Paul, MN: Llewellyn Publications, 1993). This book is about using the spoken word as a powerful tool for enriching every area of your life. This is a simple book, written in an easy style, with clear specific examples and solid armchair advice. Hewitt's selection of scenarios is useful and easy to identify with.

Matthew McKay and Patrick Fanning, *Self-Esteem,* 2d ed. (Oakland, CA: New Harbinger Publications, 1992). Using explanation, examples, and exercises, McKay and Fanning show readers how to talk back to their self-critical voices, foster compassion for themselves and others, handle mistakes and respond to criticism, ask for what they want, and raise children with high self-esteem. Theirs are not simplistic solutions; rather, they offer a systematic approach to self-esteem development.

4

Responding to Others: Listening and Feedback

CHAPTER OBJECTIVES

After reading this chapter, you should be able to

▲ Explain the importance of listening.
▲ Describe the difference between empathic and deliberative listening.
▲ List and explain the four steps in the listening process.
▲ Identify the four influences that affect listening.
▲ Explain why you do not always listen empathically.
▲ List the factors in and related barriers to effective listening.
▲ Describe the results of effective listening.
▲ Explain six ways to improve listening skills.
▲ Explain the importance of feedback.
▲ Describe the three parts of the process of feedback.
▲ Explain what the heart of the feedback process is and why.
▲ Describe internal feedback and explain its importance.
▲ List and describe the six styles of feedback.
▲ Identify which of the six styles of feedback is likely to be most effective and why.
▲ Describe each of the six ways of improving feedback skills.
▲ Develop and use owned messages.

Rita: Well, what do you think?
Brent: What do you mean, What do I think?
Rita: I mean, do you think we should go?
Brent: Go where?
Rita: Go to the party.
Brent: What party?
Rita: The party we were just invited to. Weren't you listening?
Brent: I *was* listening, but I didn't hear anything about a party. When is it?
Rita: It's Saturday night . . . just like Morella said.
Brent: Where is it?
Rita: Morella said it was going to be at Jamal's.
Brent: Who'll be going?
Rita: Didn't you hear anything? Morella said everyone is going.
Brent: What's it for?
Rita: You weren't listening at all. Morella said it was going to be a surprise birthday party for JoLynn—so please don't mention this to her.
Brent: Oh, I won't. It sounds like fun. Let's go.
Rita: All right, but now we have to call Morella and tell her we will be going. She wanted to know right away.

▼ Sushila had just been given the reporting job of her career. Sushila worked for the city newspaper, and she knew this could be a big story. The city was contemplating building a new high school, and Sushila was assigned to cover the story from all angles. She had taken careful notes about the parameters of her responsibility just as her chief editor had outlined them for her. Before Sushila began her work, she wrote out carefully on her computer her responsibilities. Because of the importance of this story, she made an appointment with the chief editor just to check her own perceptions and to go over with him some of her preliminary thinking. This was too important a situation to fumble, stumble, or fall, and Sushila's goal was to get it right the first time. Also, because others on the city beat had written related stories, she not only had pulled those stories up on her computer and read them but had interviewed those writers as well. Sushila listened well, took notes, reviewed her notes, and only then set out to capture her story.

Jason was working on his speech assignment at the library when his friend from class, Valerie, came over to talk with him. Valerie asked if he had found all his sources, and Jason asked her what she meant. "You're supposed to have a minimum of five sources," Valerie said.

"I didn't know there was a minimum," Jason said.

"Yes, Mrs. Ortiz said five was a minimum," Valerie added, "and she said three of those five had to be within the last six months."

"Are you sure?" Jason asked.

"Yes, I'm sure. I have the whole assignment written in my notebook if you want to read it. It's just over there," Valerie said pointing to a table near the door.

"Oh, I take your word for it. But maybe if you read your notes to me, I could make sure I have the rest of the assignment correct," Jason added.

Notice the role that listening played in all these situations. It was clear that Brent's mind was somewhere else when he and Rita were talking with Morella. Sushila listened extremely well and even checked on her own listening skills to make certain she had gotten her assignment correctly. Jason had not listened well when Mrs. Ortiz gave out the speech assignment for his class; Valerie had not only listened but taken notes as well.

▲▲▲ Listening

Do I listen well? Chances are this is a question you never ask yourself. After all, listening is something you have done all your life with no special training. You take it for granted. Everything in this book about successful interpersonal communication describes it as a circular give-and-take situation in which you really tune in to the other person. An essential part of that give-and-take is listening. This does not mean simply putting on a "listening" expression and nodding and grunting agreement now and then while mentally planning your evening; it means listening with full and active attention—listening empathically, as though you are in the other person's place. You can never take this kind of listening for granted. It requires skill and constant practice, but the reward is greatly improved communication.

This chapter is about the importance of listening empathically and giving appropriate feedback. I'll first discuss the importance of listening and describe the difference between empathic and deliberative listening. The process of listening will then be explained. In the next section I identify the factors that influence listening. And since empathic listening is so central to effective interpersonal communication, I include a section on some of the barriers to empathic listening. A brief discussion of the results of effective listening and improving skills in listening concludes the section on listening. In the section on feedback, importance will be discussed first, styles of feedback second, and improving skills in feedback last. The final section on skills includes important information on using owned messages.

The Importance of Listening

When you think of yourself in communication situations, you usually think more about getting your ideas to others than about receiving ideas from them. This is normal. You've come to think the word *communication* means a process that flows out from you rather than one in which you are the receiver. But communicating orally involves far more than just talking to another person. It involves sharing ideas, trying to exchange meaning with each other as perfectly as possible. In most interpersonal situations, you spend just as much time listening and responding to the other person as you do talking. Considering all the communication activities of a normal day—speaking, listening, reading, writing—you spend, on the average, more time listening than in any of the other activities. (See Figure 4.1.[1]) In your daily life, listening is the most important form of verbal communication response.[2] A number of authors, too, suggest that listening is important in the organizational setting.[3] Steil et al., suggest that executives spend 63 percent of their day listening, while workers spend just over 30 percent of their communication time listening.[4]

You probably take listening for granted until someone does not listen to you. You *do* get a great deal of experience in it. Think of all the things and people you listen to in an ordinary day: a clock radio to wake up by, family or friends at meals, teachers and other students in classes, piped-in music in stores, radios and tape players in cars, television and stereo at home.

Figure 4.1
Percentage of time used in various communication skills.

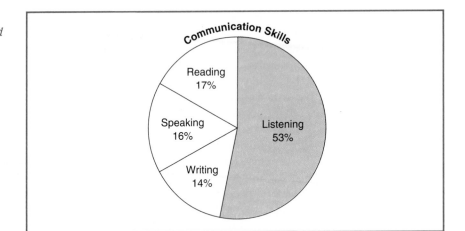

Because you spend so much of every day listening, you may think it takes little effort. Not true. Listening is not the same as hearing. Hearing is done with the ears and, unless your hearing is impaired, goes on virtually all the time. You have no mechanism in your body that lets you shut your ears as you shut your eyes. If you want to improve your listening you need to monitor your own listening habits and then actively work to improve them. The kind of practice you get is important if you really want to get rid of bad habits.

The kind of listening needed here is empathic listening. You cannot and need not listen empathically to every gas station attendant or bank teller with whom you exchange a few words during the course of a day.[5] There are situations that require only the simple exchange of information and small talk. But empathic listening is quite different.

Empathic listening *involves integrating physical, emotional, and intellectual inputs in a search for meaning and understanding.* It is an active, not a passive, process. You cannot just make sure that your ears are alert or open and let the rest come naturally. Because empathic listening involves both emotional and intellectual inputs, it does not just happen. You have to make it happen, and that's not easy. It takes energy and commitment. You have a lot going against you—there are many influences that combine to make you poor listeners. Some of them you can control, some you cannot.

Perhaps it will be easier to understand the nature and function of empathic listening if you contrast it to **deliberative listening.**[6] *When you make a definite, "deliberate" attempt to hear information, analyze it, recall it at a later time, and draw conclusions from it, you are listening deliberately.* This is the way most of you listen because this is the way you have been trained. This type of listening is appropriate in a lecture-based education system where the first priority is to critically analyze the speaker's content.

In empathic listening the objective is also understanding, but the first priority is different. Because empathic listening is transactional, the listener's first priority is to understand the speaker. Empathic listening

? CONSIDER THIS

There is no doubt that effective listening makes a difference in the work world. Read the following conclusion from the study by Sypher, Bostrom, and Seibert on listening, then answer the questions that follow:

> Listening is related to other communication abilities and to success at work. Better listeners held higher level positions and were promoted more often than those with less developed listening abilities. Short-term listening . . . appeared to have the greatest effect on level and mobility.*

Questions

1. Does the relationship between effective listening and success in the workplace make sense to you, or do you think the importance of effective listening has been exaggerated?
2. If this conclusion is true, what program might you follow to increase your listening skills?
3. Do you think there is a relationship between level of education and ability to listen?

*From Beverly Davenport Sypher, Robert N. Bostrom, and Joy Hart Seibert, "Listening, Communication Abilities, and Success at Work," *The Journal of Business Communication* 26 (Fall 1989): 301. Reprinted with permission of Beverly Davenport Sypher.

PEANUTS reprinted by permission of United Feature Syndicate, Inc.

Is there ever a conversational situation where listening is not necessary? Not important? Are there some situatons where listening is very important? When?

means listening to the whole person. You listen to what is being communicated not just by the words but by the other person's facial expressions, tone of voice, gestures, posture, and body motion. It is the integration of these functional units—their combination—that tells you what you want to know. You seek maximum understanding of the speaker's comments from his or her point of view. Deliberative listeners listen with a view to criticizing, summarizing, concluding, and agreeing or disagreeing.[7] To be an empathic listener, you must not limit your concentration and focus to words alone. That kind of listening restricts the amount of information available to you and inhibits your behavior because you base your behavior on insufficient information. That is why empathic listening—the most effective kind of listening—means responding to the **gestalt:** *the totality that is the other person.*

The Process of Listening

Hearing and listening are *not* the same. **Hearing** *is a physical process done with the ears alone.* Listening is not part of hearing. Hearing is part of listening, however. Listening includes the physical (hearing), the emotional (feelings), and the intellectual (thoughts). With this in mind, it will be easier to understand the four steps that follow. (See Figure 4.2.)

The process of listening is identical to the process of perceiving. The first step is **receiving.** *To receive is to get, accept, take, or acquire information.* You probably think of the ears as the primary receiver of information in listening, and yet you listen with your whole body to the whole (gestalt) that others present. Although you may think you are only hearing, your reaction to stimuli is likely to be based on a combination of variables, not just on what you hear. If I hear someone say, "Get out of there," I may not be prompted to move as quickly as when I simultaneously see that the phrase is being uttered by a 250-pound man with his fist raised and moving rapidly in my direction!

Figure 4.2

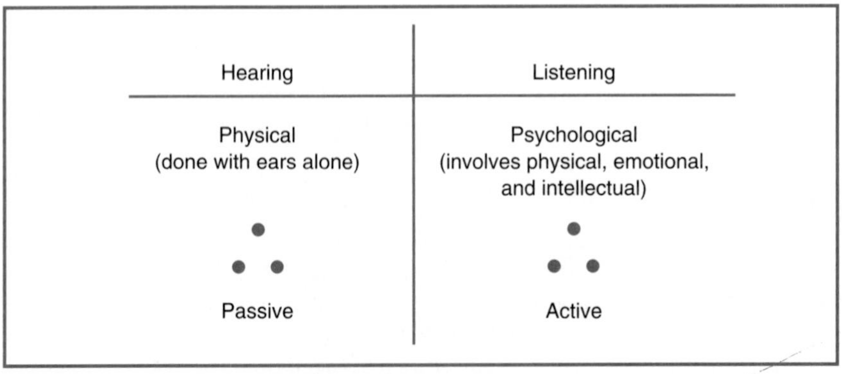

Hearing	Listening
Physical (done with ears alone)	Psychological (involves physical, emotional, and intellectual)
Passive	Active

When you attend to particular stimuli in listening, you are involved in **selecting**—listening selectively. You may even have to concentrate very hard to select just those cues you need or want. Think about how effectively—selectively—you listened at a party when the group of people standing behind you began discussing your best friend!

Once you have received the stimuli and selected them, you **organize** the information. *To do this, you must assign meaning to what you have perceived.* At this moment, your mind is actively carrying out an array of processes. Data are identified, registered, and analyzed. This is the time when you enlarge, simplify, and close the information you have received and selected. It is all part of this near-instantaneous process of getting material into order.

Just as in the perception process, the final step in listening is **interpreting.** *You relate the information received, selected, and organized to past experiences or future expectations.* To be able to respond as a result of your listening, you must interpret what you have taken in. If you do not understand it, you may interpret the data as "confusing." That could prompt the response "What do you mean by that?" or "Could you explain that to me?"

Because these steps occur spontaneously (when you have chosen to listen) and with amazing speed, they often overlap or occur out of sequence. For example, you might wonder how people can organize data without interpreting it first; no doubt these processes interact closely, just as the reception, selection, organization, and interpretation of data interact. The ears provide one input; your other four senses offer four others. Thus, listening is just part of the whole perceiving process.

What Influences Your Listening?

Being aware of the factors that affect listening not only will help you improve your own listening skills but also will help you become more considerate of people who listen to you. Knowing what factors operate increases your understanding of the entire communication process and can help explain why breakdowns and confusion sometimes result. Following are some of the factors that influence how well you listen.

Physiological Differences Affect What You Hear

Because listening is part of the perceiving process, its effectiveness is limited by the mechanics of the physical process of hearing—to be able to select from aural stimuli, you must first be able to hear them. People differ from each other **physiologically,** in *the makeup and responsiveness of their organs, tissues, and cells.* If you are hard-of-hearing, your listening will be affected simply because you won't have as many stimuli to choose from, to organize, and to interpret as someone who hears well.

You Process Words Faster Than They Can Be Spoken

The average person speaks at a rate of 125 to 150 words per minute. But as a listener, you can easily process 600 or more words per minute.[8] Though your mind can absorb words very rapidly, in your ordinary listening you are rarely challenged to process them as efficiently as you can. Even the most skilled speaker pauses and stumbles occasionally; even the most polished speech contains words that are not essential to the message. These hesitations and extraneous elements add up to many precious seconds of unused time *within* a message. What do you, as a listener, do with this time? You let your mind wander, mostly. Unless you purposefully make use of that time to concentrate on the speaker's message, you are easily distracted.

Effective Listening Requires Active Commitment

If you believe that listening is a passive process in which you simply monitor what you hear, you may misinterpret information or overlook important cues. You'll hear only what you want to hear or what grabs your attention. Productive listening involves real work. It takes emotional and intellectual commitment. It's possible that TV-watching habits contribute to your tendency to listen passively. For example, often you simply hear the TV in the background while your thoughts are elsewhere; this is especially true during commercial breaks. You don't have to respond to commercials; you just let them happen. But in interpersonal communication, if you listen halfheartedly and passively, you get only part of the message.

Those Hidden Messages . . .

Effective listening means listening with a third ear. By this I mean trying to listen for the meanings behind the words and not just to the words alone. The way words are spoken—loud, soft, fast, slow, strong, hesitating—is very important. There are messages buried in all the cues that surround words.[9] If a mother says, "Come *in* now" in a soft, gentle voice, it may mean the kids have a few more minutes. If she says, "Come in NOW," there is no question about the meaning of the command. To listen effectively, you have to pay attention to facial expressions and eye contact, gestures and body movement, posture and dress, as well as to the quality of the other person's voice, vocabulary, rhythm, rate, tone, and volume. These nonverbal cues are a vital part of any message. Listening with your third ear helps you understand the whole message.

CONSIDER THIS

Did you know that your gender can influence your listening? Men and women listen differently. Read this segment, based on the work of Deborah Tannen, professor of linguistics at Georgetown University, and answer the questions that follow:

> Men and women seem to have very different styles [of listening] with men again focusing on the content of what is said and women on the relationship between the interactants. For example, during situations where someone is disclosing a personal problem or issue, men seem to listen for solutions and to give advice to "solve the problem." This may or may not be what the speaker wants. Women, on the other hand, tend to listen to reflect understanding and support for the other person. As you might guess, this behavior makes both sexes feel more understood. This basic difference also leads to a difference in the amount of effort each sex puts into listening. Men tend to tune out things they can't solve right away or wonder why they should even listen if there isn't a problem to solve. Women tend to become more involved and connected to the speaker and see listening as something important to do for the other person.*

Questions
1. Do you think these differences are real or exaggerated?
2. What effect are these differences likely to have on a conversation? In an intimate relationship?
3. If you were responsible for trying to create understanding in the other sex of your own listening style, what would you do? How would you go about it?

*From Diana K. Ivy and Phil Backlund, *Exploring GenderSpeak: Personal Effectiveness in Gender Communication* (New York: McGraw-Hill, 1994), p. 224.

The ability to expand on the obvious—to listen beyond words—allows you to really "see into" another person. People who seek help and sympathy bear two messages—the one they speak and the one beneath the surface. To help them you need to "see through" what they say. You may know a person to whom everyone goes with problems, a person other people seek out for counsel or just to share ideas. This person is probably an effective listener, someone who listens with the third ear.

Effective Listening Requires Empathy[10]

What is it that you derive from empathy? It helps you in two ways. First, it helps you understand another person from within. With empathy, you communicate on a deeper level and actually share the other person's feelings. This kind of communication often results in your acceptance of the other person and your entering into a relationship with him or her of appreciation and understanding. Second, it becomes a source of personal reassurance. Empathy often evokes sympathy. You are reassured when you feel others really understand your state of mind. You enjoy the satisfaction of being accepted and understood. When others fail to empathize you feel disappointed and rejected. You look for a feeling response just as others do, and when that is lacking, you often feel something is wrong with the relationship. Empathy, then, helps you achieve a correspondence of mood.

However similar human beings may be, there is something distinctive and unique about each. If you are to communicate effectively, your

Can you see how empathy helps people communicate on a deeper level?

goal must be to understand what is individual and distinctive in others. To achieve this goal, you need empathic methods.

Why Don't You Always Listen Empathically?

If it is so helpful, you might wonder why more people are not empathic listeners. Actually, there are three reasons—all of them directly interrelated. First, listening empathically is not easy. It is far more difficult than simply taking note of actual words spoken and responding to them literally. Second, empathic listening requires that you get outside yourself by trying to share in the meaning, spirit, and feelings of another person. You're not always willing to do this. Your ego gets tied up in your communication; you get involved in your own thoughts and problems. The next time you are involved in an interpersonal encounter, notice how hard it is to concentrate on what the other person is saying if you are preoccupied with your own next remark. Do you begin to plan what you are going to say before the other person even has a chance to stop talking? Instead of listening, you may find you are figuring out how to impress him or her with your next comment.[11]

The third reason you may not listen empathically is ingrained listening habits. You may listen too literally or too judgmentally by habit. You may habitually think of communication as a talking medium rather than a listening medium. The following sections discuss some other habits you may have that hinder effective listening.

Tuning out   Habit may cause you to tune out much of the talk you hear. This society is talk-oriented. You tune out to avoid listening, to protect yourself from the communication babble that sometimes seems to surround you. You may tune out for physical and emotional preservation as well. It is necessary to tune out some things. You must be selective or you would be inundated. But you cannot listen empathically if habit has caused you to avoid the very basics of the process—tuning *in!*

This does not mean you need to tune in to everything you hear. But good listeners do tend to discover interesting elements in almost all communications. They are able to cope with the bombardment of stimuli. Whereas poor listeners tend to find all topics uniformly dry and boring, effective listeners concentrate their attention well and learn efficiently through listening.

You can't expect to be fascinated by every subject. But if you too often find yourself bored by the communication in a certain situation—eating lunch with the same people every day, for example—you might ask yourself, "What were my reasons for going to lunch with these people in the first place? Do those reasons still hold?" Perhaps you started eating with these people because they are politically active and you wanted to discuss politics with them. If you still feel the same way, remembering the original motive can help you focus your listening in this group's communications. You may be able to pick out useful bits of information from conversations that would otherwise seem pointless.

Wanting to be entertained   Another habit that can affect your listening might be labeled the "Sesame Street Syndrome." You want to be entertained. You may mentally challenge a speaker: "Excite me or I won't listen." If you think ahead of time that the message you're going to hear will be dull, you're not likely to listen well. And if you expect to be bored, there's a good chance you will be. You generally prefer a lively, entertaining presentation to a straight, unembellished delivery. Think of the difference between receiving a message from a lively, enthusiastic, and involving speaker and receiving one from a dull, lifeless, detached speaker. You could think of these features (lively, enthusiastic, and involving) as being much like television shows—they are like program elements designed to grab and hold attention.

Avoiding the difficult   Another version of the "Sesame Street Syndrome" is that you tend to stay away from difficult listening. That is, given a choice, you are likely to avoid listening that requires mental exertion. Any kind of communication that deals with unfamiliar subjects can seem tough to follow, especially if the speaker moves quickly from one point to the next. If you're not used to a speaker's reasoning, you may give up on the message rather than try to follow his or her thought processes. Speakers are hard to follow when they try to explain difficult or complex ideas.

Criticizing the superficial   Think about a recent interpersonal encounter you had with people you did not know well. Can you remember what they looked like? What they were wearing? What they said? Often you let externals distract you from what the other person is saying.

TRY THIS

Next time you catch yourself being distracted by another person's clothes, mannerisms, or looks, *stop* and try to:

1. *Refocus* your attention on the message.
2. *Paraphrase* what is being said.
3. *Review* the important elements of what has been communicated.

The idea is to redirect your attention to the message and away from distracting elements.

CONSIDER THIS

Based on the work of Marsha Houston of Tulane University, here is a description of "white women's talk" by African American women and a description of "black women's talk" by a group of white women. Read these most frequent responses, then answer the questions that follow.

African American women described white women's talk as

▲ Friendly (with an air of phoniness)
▲ Arrogant
▲ Know-it-all
▲ Talking as if they think they're better than the average person
▲ Mainly dealing with trivia
▲ Talking proper about nothing
▲ Weak, "air-headish"
▲ Silly but educated
▲ Illustrating fragility; seemingly dependent and helpless
▲ Passive, submissive, delicate

White women described the talk of black women as

▲ Using black dialect
▲ Saying things like "young 'uns," "yous," "wif," and "wich you"
▲ Using jive terms*

Questions

1. Is it clear why African American women and white women hear different things when they talk with each other?
2. Can you detect a concentration on different aspects of talk when the two groups described the other's dialogue?
3. When there are cultural differences between speakers and listeners, how are stereotypes and misattributions likely to affect the conversations?
4. Can you see how these descriptions may help answer the question "Why don't we always listen empathically?" at least in some circumstances?

*From Alberto Gonzalez, Marsha Houston, and Victoria Chen, *Our Voices: Essays in Culture, Ethnicity, and Communication (An Intercultural Anthology)* (Los Angeles, CA: Roxbury Publishing Company, 1994), p. 135.

If you don't know someone well, you're more likely to be diverted by that person's lisp or hairstyle or purple sweater. You may find yourself criticizing some unimportant characteristic of the person instead of listening to what he or she is saying. Think of how you size up a person you meet for the first time. Do you notice his or her hairstyle? Smile? Clothing? These nonverbal cues are important, but they shouldn't distract you from really listening to what the person is saying.

Letting emotions take over   Finally, you may habitually either (1) block things out, (2) distort things, or (3) agree too readily to everything. When you hear things that don't fit in with your own beliefs, you often put up a mental block so you don't get frightened or angry. Sometimes you hear just what you want to hear. You may have a conviction so strong that you twist whatever you hear to conform. Some words (*mother, I love you*) may appeal to your emotions to such an extent that you agree with anything that follows. If you loved every minute you spent at Barnwood High School, meeting someone else from old Barnwood automatically produces a favorable emotional climate for the conversation.

Your emotions may be triggered by a single word or phrase that seems to leap out. Suppose you meet a woman at a party who says, "I just got back from Colorado." Some emotional reactions you may have are "I never get to go anywhere" or "Colorado is overrun by crazy outdoor types. I wouldn't go there if you paid me" or "Colorado! I love Colorado! Mountains! Fresh air! Good times!" Any of these thoughts will color how you hear the rest of what the woman says. Once you hear that trigger-word, *Colorado,* you listen to nothing else. Instead you plan a defense, rebuttal, supportive example, argument, or other way to involve your ego. Effective listening means controlling your emotional responses—trying to break old habits.

In a study on barriers to effective listening, Steven Golen found that out of 23 potentially important barriers, six factors stood out.[12] Because these are important, because these *can* make a difference in your life, and because your awareness of these factors is the first step toward overcoming them, they have been listed in a table so they can all be examined. (See Table 4.1.)

The two or three barriers that make up each factor are listed. They are self-explanatory. When students in a basic speech-communication mass-lecture were asked "How many of you have been in situations where any one of the top three factors affected you?" the results were nearly unanimous. These results suggested that the factors are real, personal, and pervasive (operating from situation to situation).

Results of Effective Listening

Animated, cooperative, and responsive listeners help the person they are talking to because their reactions produce an immediate effect. They can

Table 4.1
Factors and Barriers to Effective Listening

FACTOR	BARRIER
Laziness	Avoid listening if the subject is complex or difficult
	Avoid listening because it takes too much time
Closed-mindedness	Refuse to maintain a relaxing and agreeable environment
	Refuse to relate to and benefit from the speaker's ideas
Opinionatedness	Disagree or argue outwardly or inwardly with the speaker
	Become emotional or excited when the speaker's views differ from yours
Insincerity	Avoid eye contact while listening
	Pay attention only to the speaker's words rather than the speaker's feelings
Boredom	Lack interest in the speaker's subject
	Become impatient with the speaker
	Daydream or become preoccupied with something else when listening
Inattentiveness	Concentrate on the speaker's mannerisms or delivery rather than on the message
	Become distracted by noise from office equipment, telephone, other conversation, etc.

Adapted from Steven Golen, "A Factor Analysis of Barriers to Effective Listening," The Journal of Business Communication 27:32. Reprinted by permission of Steven Golen.

influence what the other person will say next. And the listener will benefit from the improved communication that results. (See Figure 4.3.)

Specifically, what are the rewards of effective listening? The first is that you will get a more stimulating and meaningful message—the other person may subconsciously adapt the message specifically to your knowledge and background. The more closely you listen to a person and indicate what you do and don't understand, the more likely you are to receive a message that makes sense. And you're more likely to remember it. By improving your listening habits you should be able to recall more than 50 percent of the information you hear, rather than forget it.[13]

For example, if you respond to a friend's description of a recent trip with partial or complete silence, your friend will probably cut the description short. But if you ask such questions as "Where did you go?" or "What did you do?" or "Was it fun?" or "Who did you see?" he or she

Figure 4.3
The cycle of improved communication through effective listening.

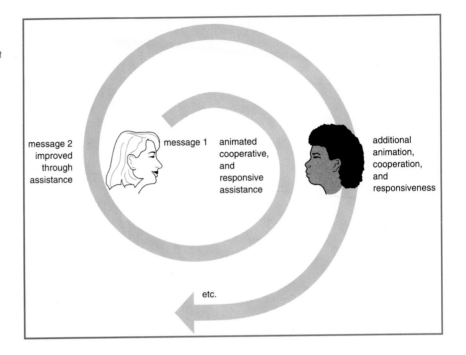

message 2 improved through assistance

message 1 animated cooperative, and responsive assistance

additional animation, cooperation, and responsiveness

etc.

will be more interested in providing the details. Your understanding of your friend's experience will be far more complete. Of course, you can purposely cut short a conversation by showing no interest or involvement. But you might miss out on a stimulating and meaningful message.

The second reward of effective listening is improvement in your own communication techniques. By paying closer attention to the communication of others and by observing their methods, you will be able to analyze your own efforts more completely.

For example, you may notice that a friend ends every other sentence with the words *you know*. If this interferes with your listening, you'll be more alert to certain phrases or words that you yourself overuse. Once you see how distracting such things are, you'll be more inclined to ask a friend to point out mannerisms you have that you are not aware of.

You may find that another reward of effective listening is an enlarged circle of friends. Good listeners are in great demand. People have an emotional need to be heard; the person who is willing to take the time to listen is often sought out.

Finally, in becoming an effective listener you are likely to become a more open and involved human being. The ultimate reward is more meaningful interpersonal relationships. Effective listening habits will increase your capacity to meet the demands of modern life. Good listening is one of the most important communication skills needed for human interaction.

Building Listening Skills

As I said earlier, improving listening skills requires time and energy. The suggestions that follow may seem to be based on ordinary common sense. Some may seem obvious. Even so, the most commonsensical ideas are often not put into practice. If you simply read these and do not incorporate them into your own listening behavior, they will serve little purpose. Perhaps these suggestions will also bring to mind other practical ideas you can put to use in listening settings.

Prepare to listen In many cases you do not listen well because you are not physically or mentally prepared. Your attention span is directly related to your physical and mental condition. This is obvious if you recall that listening involves an integration of physical, emotional, and intellectual elements. Think how impatient or short-tempered you become when you are mentally run down or physically tired. You stayed up all night studying for an exam, and now everyone around you pays for it! You do not want to listen to anyone!

Control or eliminate distractions Anticipating situations in which you might have to listen helps prepare you for the experience. There may be something you can do to improve the situation: turning off a television, closing a door, asking the other person to speak louder, or moving to a less distracting location. If you can't eliminate distractions, you'll have to concentrate with greater effort.

Anticipate the subject Whenever possible, think ahead about the topics or ideas that might be discussed. The more familiar you are with the subject matter, the more likely you are to learn, and the more interested you will be. Also, thinking ahead may prompt questions to ask. Becoming actively involved in interpersonal situations makes them more memorable and meaningful.

Anticipate the speaker Anticipating the speaker means adjusting in advance (or being prepared to adjust) to the other person. You cannot control how the speaker will look or talk, but you can make sure, in advance, that distracting appearance or faulty delivery does not dominate your attention. Your aim should be to try to find out what the other person is saying. You should try not to be bothered by peculiarities or eccentricities. If you are always ready to adjust, you will find it becomes a natural part of your behavior when you *must* adjust.

Create a need to listen You do not enjoy listening to some people as much as to others. You do not listen as well to some topics as to others. You often know in advance that you may not listen as well as you might in a certain situation. To try to counteract this situation, become a "selfish listener."[14] What can the speaker do for *you*? The key to being interested in another person or in a topic is making it relevant or useful to yourself.

Try to discover if the message has any personal benefits for you. Can it provide personal satisfaction? Does it stimulate new interests or insights? Good listeners are interested in what they are listening to, whereas poor listeners find all people and all topics dry and boring. True, some topics are dull, but people often decide this in advance and don't give the speaker a chance.

If the speaker or the material does not satisfy a need, ask yourself, "Why am I here?" Try to remember what caused you to be there and see if the motive is still active. You might also try to discover a reward—some immediate way to use the material that will make the experience personally profitable.

Monitor the way you listen   Even if you are prepared to listen and need to listen, your listening will not necessarily be effective. You need to check occasionally to make sure your thoughts are not wandering and you are keeping an open mind to the other person's ideas. Because of the difference between speaking and listening rates, you need to use wisely the spare time that results.

Concentrate on the message   To keep your mind on the message, try to review what the speaker has already said so that you can keep ideas together and remember them. Listen for the main ideas. Try to go "between" the words. Listen with your third ear. Listen for words that may have more than one meaning and discover, if possible, how the other person is using the word. Try to anticipate what the speaker will say next,

TRY THIS

As you are listening to someone or just after a conversation, ask yourself the following questions:

1. What did the other person do—as far as effective communication goes—that was particularly strong? What aspects of the other person's presentation were especially powerful or convincing?
2. What did the person do that was especially weak? What would you change in his or her presentation?

The purpose here is growth and change. Try to learn something from each communication experience that will help you improve your own communication patterns and behaviors.

and compare this with what he or she actually says. This keeps your mind focused on the message.[15] Concentrate on the message, not on the speaker's blue eyes or Hawaiian shirt.

Suspend judgment   Some words, phrases, or ideas evoke an automatic reaction. You may overreact to bad grammar, ethnic slurs, or vulgarity. You must learn not to get too excited about certain words until you have the whole context. Suspend judgment until you thoroughly understand where the speaker is coming from.

Think about those words you react strongly to. Why do they affect you like that? Sharing your reactions with others will often help you see that your reactions are entirely personal. Finally, try to reduce the intensity of your reaction by convincing yourself that the reaction is extreme and unnecessary, that the word does not merit such a reaction.[16] Your listening will always be affected when certain words touch your deepest prejudices or most profound values. Knowing that such reactions can occur is the first step toward overcoming them.

Empathize   Try to see the other person's ideas from his or her perspective. If Sam is telling you how angry he is with his brother, try to discover why he says what he does. Listen for his feelings, his views, and his arguments. You needn't agree with him. Sam's brother may be a friend of yours. But just because Sam's feelings differ from yours does not mean they aren't valid. Since you differ from Sam as a result of different past experiences, search for the message he is *really* trying to communicate. Look for elements he may have left out. What is he basing his evidence on? How did he come by his opinion? Through personal experience? Other people's observations? Guesswork? You should try to see the problem through Sam's eyes.

▲▲▲   Feedback

LeeAnn was giving her employee, Victor, some important information that involved procedures for dealing with a customer complaint. Knowing how important the information was, Victor nodded his head when he understood and asked questions to clarify things that could be confusing. His enthusiastic and confirming responses were so effective that on the spot, LeeAnn gave him two other similar complaints to take care of.

Max had been dating Sasha for just over six months. Now, they were having an ice-cream sundae and discussing their dinner and the movie they had just seen. Max had just asked Sasha if she liked the movie, and she said she thought it had an important message. He said, "The acting was good, too." They agreed it was one of the better movies they had seen.

It had been a terrific evening, and both Max and Sasha were in a good mood. Just after telling Max about the movie, Sasha talked about

CONSIDER THIS

Reasoned skepticism might be defined as "moderate doubt" or "thoughtful consideration." The question here is, What ethical responsibility do listeners have? Read the quote by Johannesen, a writer on ethics, and then answer the questions that follow.

> Reasoned skepticism includes a number of elements. It represents a balanced position between the undesirable extremes of being too open-minded, too gullible, on the one hand and being too closed-minded, too dogmatic, on the other. We are not simply thinking blotters "soaking up" ideas and arguments. Rather we should exercise our capacities actively to search for meaning, to analyze and synthesize, to interpret significance, and to judge soundness and worth. We do something to and with the information we receive; we process, interpret, and evaluate it. Also, we should inform ourselves about issues being discussed. We should tolerate, even seek out, divergent and controversial viewpoints, the better to assess what is being presented. We should not be so dogmatic, ego-involved, and defensive about our own views that we are unwilling to take into account (understand, evaluate, and perhaps even accept) the views and data presented by others.*

Questions

1. Have you ever thought of receivers having responsibilities? These responsibilities?
2. Would this kind of responsibility be the same in intimate relationships?
3. Are listeners responsible for encouraging nondeceptive, nonmanipulative communication?

*From Richard L. Johannesen, *Ethics in Human Communication*, 3d ed. (Prospect Heights, IL: Waveland Press, 1990), pp. 135–136.

what a great relationship they had. Because of Sasha's good mood, because of the pleasant circumstances, and because of the positive responses Max had received from Sasha throughout the evening, Max decided to ask her if she would be willing to make theirs an exclusive relationship—something Sasha had wanted for several weeks but had been unsure of Max's interest in.

In both of these situations, feedback was critical to what occurred. In the first example, it was clear to the employer that the employee was interested, concerned, and involved in trying to get correct information regarding dealing with customer complaints. In the second, Max's and Sasha's discussion of the movie depended on their mutual feedback. Feedback is critical to effective communication.

In this section, **feedback** will be discussed. The more you are aware of what goes on and what can go on in interpersonal communication situations, the more you can control what you do and the better you can predict the outcomes of such circumstances.

The Importance of Feedback

The benefits of good listening occur only when the cues you give back to a speaker allow that person to know how you receive the message, permitting the speaker to adjust the message as needed.[17] If you ever think that your feedback is insignificant and makes no difference, remember that in a two-person interpersonal situation, you are the *only* source of reaction for the other person. If you do not provide feedback, the other person can't know how well he or she is getting through. It's up to you to help the other person make the message as accurate as possible. How much feedback you give is also important.

In a landmark study, researchers investigated the role of feedback in message transmission in a classroom setting.[18] The students participating in the study were divided into four groups, each with an instructor. They were all to draw geometric patterns according to oral instructions given to them by the instructor. In one group the students could hear the directions but could not see the instructor; no feedback of any sort was permitted. In a second group, the students and the instructor could see each other but could not ask or answer questions. In a third group, the students could answer yes or no questions from the instructor. In a fourth group, students could ask any questions and get information—a free-feedback situation. The researchers discovered that as the amount of allowed feedback increased, it took students longer to complete their tasks, but they also drew their geometric figures more accurately. And they felt far more confident about their success in drawing the figures when free feedback was permitted. We can conclude from this that feedback in an interpersonal communication encounter takes extra time but results in more accurate message transmission and more confidence in the message transmission process.

The Process of Feedback

The important process known as *feedback* is not a simple, one-step process. First, it involves **monitoring** the impact or the influence of our messages on the other person. Second, it involves **evaluating** why the reaction or response occurred as it did. Third and finally, it involves **adjustment** or modification. The adjustment of our future messages reveals the process-oriented nature of communication and also the impact the re-

TRY THIS

In your next conversation with people, notice the feedback you receive as you talk:

1. How extensive is it?
2. What are the primary cues that provide the feedback (eyes, face, gestures, posture, body movement, tone of voice)?
3. Do different people use different kinds of feedback? Do they depend on different cues?
4. Does the amount of feedback differ between friends and strangers? Does it depend on the nature of the message or situation?
5. How much do you depend on the feedback you get from others?
6. Do you find yourself adjusting your message when you receive feedback? In what ways?

If nothing else, this exercise should encourage you to become more conscious of feedback in any communication situation. As you grow more sensitive to it, your messages can become more exact and specific.

ceiver has on the communication cycle. Feedback can provide reinforcement for the speaker if it shows that he or she is being clear, accepted, or understood.

Can you see how difficult this interpersonal communication would be without the feedback that is taking place?

The heart of this feedback process is the adjustment or corrective function. Feedback can be words ("Yes, I get it") or physical messages (a smile) or responses that show the other person that we are, indeed, sharing in the spirit of what he or she is saying. It can also show if we do *not* understand or agree. Just as we know, by the response we get, whether or not we are being listened to, the other person is in the same situation. We recognize that mutual understanding has or hasn't occurred through feedback. An atmosphere that promotes honest feedback is a necessary condition for understanding and for reinforcement.

In any communication setting, each participant is both a source of messages and a receiver of messages simultaneously. This means that you are at all times responding and being responded to. Feedback exists when each person affects the other—each is a cause and an effect.[19] Just as you cannot *not* communicate, you cannot *not* send some kind of feedback. You send messages even when you do not speak.

Receiving Feedback

Imagine yourself, for a moment, as only a source of messages; you gain no feedback to any message you send out. You say hello and nobody answers. You say, "It sure is a beautiful day" and nobody reinforces or ac-

TRY THIS

Next time you are in a conversation with someone, listen with the goal of finding out as much as you possibly can. Plan to ask the other person a series of probing questions to gain the necessary information. Some sample questions might be these:

1. How did you discover that?
2. What else happened?
3. Why do you suppose that is so?
4. What was the outcome?
5. Would you do the same again?
6. Do you think it could happen again?
7. What do you think you gained from this experience?

Do not interrupt the other person with your probes. Listen closely so that your questions will be relevant to what is being said. Maintain a positive, supportive spirit of inquiry.

Wouldn't it be fascinating if you had more time to do this on a regular basis? You would become not only a better listener but a more retentive learner as well.

knowledges what you've said. You have no way of knowing whether you were heard or understood. You have no way to gauge your effectiveness. It's understandable that someone in this hypothetical one-way-communication situation could become frustrated, feel unaccepted and unloved.[20] What's the use in talking if there is no one to respond? Receiving feedback is one of the best ways you have of modifying your behavior. Monitoring feedback is your way of assuring that the message you intended is as closely related as possible to the message received.

Think of some people with whom you enjoy communicating. Do these people provide you with honest feedback as you speak? Their feedback affects not only *how* you communicate with them but *why* you express yourself as you do and why you treat them as you do. The cues you receive may cause you to keep talking, restate your ideas, begin to stumble or stammer, or become silent. Whatever the case, you need feedback to gain insight into your own communication and to help you understand the communication behavior of others.

Giving Feedback

Just as you need to receive feedback, you also need to give it. Listening attentively and giving appropriate feedback show that you are attempting to cope successfully with your environment; you are an active participant, not a passive observer, able to act in direct response to a specific stimulus.[21] The feedback you give people can make them feel unique and worthwhile and heighten their sense of well-being—it's personally rewarding to know that your reactions matter.

Communication does not continue for long when the direction of flow is one-way. A person who receives no feedback, whose feelings are not encouraged and reinforced, will look somewhere else for support. Effective communication assumes a two-way flow of information.

Styles of Feedback

Feedback begins within you. **Internal feedback** takes place all the time as you communicate with others.[22] *It is all the messages you give yourself about the communication taking place.* As you speak, you anticipate certain responses from the other person. As you receive feedback from the other person, you adapt and correct your own message; the process of adapting and correcting depends on internal feedback.

Giving feedback to the other person also begins with your own internal feedback. If you want to give someone feedback as he or she speaks, you must first be very attentive to that person's communication. You can't give helpful feedback if you aren't listening effectively to start with. To be ready to respond appropriately you must be alert to the other person's overall message, trying hard to see where he or she is coming from so that your feedback is not insensitive or confusing.

Thomas Gordon, in *Parent Effectiveness Training*, suggests that there are twelve kinds of response styles for giving feedback.[23] Other authors list only five.[24] The following scheme describes six typical ways of responding—withdrawing, judging, analyzing, questioning, reassuring, and paraphrasing. Paraphrasing is the one that I feel leads to the most successful interaction.

Withdrawing The **withdrawing response** essentially *ignores what the other person has said.* "Just forget about it" or "Let's not talk about it now" are common examples of this style. Withdrawing can also take the form of distracting. For example, when a friend comes to you with a problem about one of her professors, you might ask her, "Say, how is your boyfriend? I haven't heard much about him lately." If that appears too obvious a change of subject, you might ease into the distraction with the question, "That's the professor you liked so much last week?"

Withdrawing responses are weak because they do not address the problem at hand. Responding in this way *can* spring from a sincere wish to take the other person's mind off a problem, but it is likely to come across as lack of concern, poor listening, or callousness on the part of the listener. With so many other possible responses available, withdrawing is not considered a positive method for successful interaction.

Judging The **judging response** *means giving advice or making a judgment.* It is one of the most common responses. It is very easy to give advice or make a judgment. By telling people that their idea or behavior is good or bad, appropriate or inappropriate, effective or ineffective, right or wrong, you imply that you know how they can solve their problem or how they ought to behave. Judging responses often begin with "If I were you, I would . . . ," "You know you should . . . ," or "The thing you might consider doing is. . . . "

One reason a judging response can hinder a relationship is that it can appear threatening. What is your immediate reaction when someone tells you that something you did, or an idea that you have, is wrong? You probably get defensive; defensiveness causes closed-mindedness, rejection, and resistance. You want to stop exploring, to change the subject, to retreat or escape. When people judge, they imply that their evaluation is superior to someone else's. Someone with a problem or with specific feelings about something that has happened does not want to feel inferior.

Further, judging responses are quick ways to deal with other's problems or feelings. They do not necessarily reveal genuine concern. If others perceive that you are trying to deal with them in a quick or easy way, rejection is likely to follow. Nobody wants to be brushed off.

Also, when you give advice often you encourage others not to take responsibility for their own problems. You provide an escape route—an "easy out." If others can ask for and get advice whenever they are face to face with problems, why should they bother to take responsibility for or solve their own problems? In addition, if you give advice they could blame you when your evaluation or suggestion does not work out. You set yourself up as a convenient scapegoat.

Finally, a judging response can limit communication. By making a judgment, the responder takes over the communication and cuts things off before real communication can take place. The judging responder may not seem to be really interested in hearing the whole story, and the person who receives the judgment may feel there is no point in continuing the discussion.

Analyzing If you rephrase your judging response so that it explains the other's action or dissects it, you are **analyzing**—and the situation is not greatly improved. "You know, the reason you are disturbed is . . . " or "Your situation is simply . . . " are likely to be analyzing responses. In these cases you end up trying to instruct others or to tell them what their problems or feelings mean. It is as if you have assumed the role of psychiatrist: "Your problem implies (or indicates) that. . . . " The difference between judging and analyzing responses is small. When analyzing others' problems you imply what they ought to think. You are supplying the motives, justifications, or rationale for their behavior—once again, giving them a convenient out.

The drawbacks, too, are similar to those for the judging response. Analyzing the behavior of others can make them defensive and less likely to reveal thoughts and feelings, thus preventing them from engaging in further interpretation or analysis. Although analyzing takes longer than judging, it still can seem to "brush others off" because with a single analysis, you may explain their behavior. It may encourage others *not* to take responsibility for their own problems; analyzing supplies answers that keep them from thinking through and trying to solve their own problems. Also, it can convey superiority: "I know more about what makes you tick than you do."

Questioning A **questioning response** may draw out other people. The purpose of questioning feedback is to get other people to discuss their feelings. A questioning response is a good beginning, because it gives us information about the nature of the situation and provides an emotional release for other persons at the same time. This response takes the form of a question: "What makes this situation so upsetting to you?" or "What do you suppose caused this to happen?"

In questioning, you don't want to be threatening or accusatory. Phrasing your questions carelessly can cause more problems than you solve. For example, you would probably not ask, "How did you ever get into this mess?" because that puts a value judgment on the experience and changes the response to a judging one. Questions like "Didn't you know that was wrong?" or "You really weren't thinking, were you?" are

CONSIDER THIS

Did you ever think ethics and ethical responsibility were related to providing feedback? Read this piece from Richard L. Johannesen, a writer on ethics, then answer the questions that follow.

> As active participants in the communication process, the feedback we provide to senders needs to be appropriate in a number of senses. Our response, in most situations, should be an honest and accurate reflection of our true comprehension, belief, feeling, or judgment. Otherwise communicators are denied the relevant and accurate information they need to make decisions. If we are participating in communication primarily for purposes other than seriously trying to understand and assess the information and arguments (perhaps to make friends, have fun, be socially congenial), we should reveal our intent to the other participants. It would seem ethically dubious to pretend acceptance of an argument with the actual intent of later condemning it on a more opportune occasion. Likewise it seems ethically dubious to lack understanding of an argument but to pretend to agree with it in order to mask our lack of comprehension.*

Questions

1. Have you ever thought about the important role receivers of messages have in the interpersonal communication process?
2. In what circumstances are receivers freed from providing honest and accurate reflections of their true comprehension, belief, feeling, or judgment?
3. How do receivers decide whether their feedback is appropriate for the subject, audience, or occasion?

*From Richard L. Jonannesen, *Ethics in Human Communication*, 3d ed. (Prospect Heights, IL: 1990), p. 136.

also judging. Again, you don't want to imply what that person should have done or ought to do.

In using the questioning response, communicators should avoid questions beginning with *why*. *Why* questions create defensiveness. When asked "Why did you do that?" your immediate impulse is to defend yourself. The question automatically indicates disapproval: "You shouldn't have done that." Criticism and advice tend to be threatening. *What*, *where*, *when*, *how*, and *who* questions are more helpful in opening others up. They encourage specificity, precision, and more self-disclosure.

Reassuring   If a friend comes to you upset, you probably want to reassure him or her that all is not lost. Pointing out alternative ways for perceiving the situation that he or she may not have thought of would **be reassuring.** Your response should be calming, to reduce the intensity of your friend's feeling. Initially, your reassurance may be no more specific than a look or a touch that says, "I'm on your side." A reassuring response may reveal agreement. Once a friend knows that you are empathic, you can discuss actions, alternatives, or other choices.

To provide reassurance you should first reduce the intensity of the feeling. A comment like "That is a serious situation, and I can see why you are upset . . . " is a good beginning. Reassurance means acknowledging the seriousness of the other person's feelings. It does not need to reveal agreement, but you don't want to argue or suggest that these emotions are inappropriate.

Although reassuring responses may be stronger than many of the preceding styles, they can come across negatively, too. If by tone of voice or phrasing you imply that others should not feel the way they do (e.g., "You *really* don't need to feel bad') once again you have turned your response into a judging one, and the weaknesses of the judging response become operative.

Paraphrasing   *Paraphrasing is rewording another's thought or meaning.* Your first comment to your friend could be "I can see you're very upset about this. It must mean a great deal to you." In **paraphrasing** the other person's remarks you show that you understand. Thus, paraphrasing can show that you care about correctly understanding your friend's situation. When you reinforce your remarks with nonverbal cues—eye contact, facial expressions of sincerity, touching, tone of voice—this response is very supportive.

You might ask, why paraphrase? Why restate in your own words what others have just said? First, paraphrasing helps make certain that you have understood what others are saying. In a sense, it gives you a second chance to make sure you are understanding them. Second, it can begin a clarifying process—drawing others out, gaining more information, and talking things out more extensively. Both talk and time allow communicators opportunities to gain clearer understanding of themselves and the implications of their feelings and thoughts. Third, paraphrasing can serve as a summarizing process—covering the main points of a situation more concisely, or trying to add things up—as others reflect and review. Fourth, it assures others that you did, indeed, hear what they said. You are alert, responsive, involved. And finally it shows others that

TRY THIS

To practice your response styles, think of one response of each kind for each of the following situations:

1. Your best friend tells you, "I just flunked my second exam in my psychology course. It's all over. I just don't care about anything anymore."
2. Your roommate says, "Someone stole my books and notebooks. I left them on a table in the cafeteria and when I came back they were gone."
3. A friend down the hall laments: "Oh, I can't stand it, I can't stand it any more! My roommate leaves the room in a mess, plays the stereo at full volume, and sleeps only during the day. It's driving me out of my mind and . . ."

you are trying to understand their thoughts and feelings. It helps legitimize your efforts as a concerned, caring person.

Building Feedback Skills

Effective feedback is as important as good listening. As a listener, you have a duty to respond, to complete the communication cycle. Although you can't avoid giving some feedback even if you don't say a word, there are ways you can improve your conscious feedback.

Be prepared to give feedback Feedback can be verbal, nonverbal, or both. Nonverbal feedback usually can say more about your sincerity than words alone. Your verbal feedback is more likely to be believed if you support it with appropriate gestures, direct eye contact, and possibly touching. Be certain that you are close enough to the other person—face to face if possible—for your feedback to be perceived. We will discuss nonverbal communication in more detail in a later chapter.

Although you must be prepared to give feedback, you shouldn't enter a situation with your specific reactions already planned. Spontaneity is important. The best feedback arises naturally as a result of an immediate and specific stimulus. But being prepared to give feedback does not

TRY THIS

The next time you are communicating interpersonally, do not respond to what the other person says until you do three things:

1. Wait until the other person *finishes* what he or she has to say.
2. Fully *paraphrase* what he or she has said.
3. Receive an *affirmative response* to the question, "Is that what you mean?" directly following your paraphrase.

Following an affirmative response, you may make any appropriate comment you wish to keep the conversation going. If the other person says your paraphrase was inaccurate, keep trying until you get it right.

Although in many situations you don't need to wait until the other person finishes talking before you respond, forcing yourself to wait will indicate how often you do *not* wait. Does this kind of communication seem awkward or labored to you? (Sometimes paraphrasing does seem labored; however, its values outweigh its weaknesses.) Do you think it is a good way to get at the other person's meaning?

preclude being spontaneous; it simply means that you are alert and sensitive to the need for feedback and are ready to give it.

Make your feedback prompt Your response to the other person should be clear and prompt. The more closely feedback is tied to the original message, the less ambiguous it will be. The longer the delay between message and feedback, the more likely you are to confuse the other person.

Make your feedback accurate Accuracy means making feedback specific to a single message and not general to the whole conversation. You probably know people who continually nod and smile the entire time you're talking to them. In addition to being distracting, this also appears insincere. It makes you want to ask, "All right, what exactly do you agree with? How will I know when you disagree?" Try to provide only necessary feedback.

React to the message, not the speaker Your accuracy in giving feedback also will improve if you remember to direct it to the message and not to the person communicating. In addition to being distracting, personal comments may create hostility or frustration and a breakdown in communication.

Oddly, both complimentary and critical feedback may be better received if you phrase your responses in a slightly impersonal way. If you wish to praise someone for playing a piano sonata well, saying, "I've never heard that piece done so beautifully. I really heard it in a new way" may make the performer less uncomfortable than "Sarah, you really did that well. I didn't know you were that good." Such personal comments can imply, however subtly, "That was good, for *you*" when what you mean is "That was good." Effective feedback is message-oriented.[25]

Monitor your own feedback If your feedback is not interpreted by the other person as you mean it, it serves no purpose. Check the effect you're making. You might have to repeat or clarify a feedback response. If Louise says, "I can never think of what to say to Alvin," and your response is "I know," it can either mean, "I know. I've noticed you never have anything to say" or it can mean "I know. Alvin is hard to talk to." You must monitor your feedback to make sure you're being understood. Like any message, feedback can be blocked or distorted.

Use owned messages An **owned message** (also known as an I-message, as coined by Thomas Gordon[26]) is "*an acknowledgment of subjectivity by a message-sender through the use of first-person-singular terms* (I, me, my, mine). 'Responsible' communicators are those who 'own' their thoughts and feelings by employing these pronouns."[27]

 Owned messages tend to provoke less interpersonal defensiveness than you-messages, and they are useful for conveying negative information. A simple example of owned and unowned messages will demonstrate the problem. To say "You make me mad" is an example of an unowned message (a you-message) and, as is obvious, has the potential for creating defensiveness in another person. To say "I'm feeling angry" is an

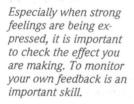

Especially when strong feelings are being expressed, it is important to check the effect you are making. To monitor your own feedback is an important skill.

example of owning a message and is less likely to create defensiveness. Clearly, you have a problem (potential defensiveness) when you use unowned messages; the solution is to use owned messages (owning your feelings).

To familiarize yourself with owned messages, do the next "Try This" that follows.

TRY THIS

Imagine yourself in a romantic relationship (i.e., steady dating, engagement, or marriage). Assume the relationship has been intact for at least six months and that it has been generally satisfying for both parties. The two of you are having dinner together. After some casual conversation about the day's events, your partner says the following:

I want to discuss something I'm unhappy about. I'm concerned that we may not be communicating as well as we could. For instance, when I was telling you about my job a few minutes ago, instead of responding to what I said, you started talking about your day at school. I felt hurt and unimportant because it seemed like you weren't listening to me. Then I realized I wasn't listening to you, either. I know your schoolwork means a lot to you, and I want to hear about it. I just would like some kind of response that lets me know I've been heard. I think it might help if we tried to comment about what the other person has said before changing the subject. I know that would mean a lot to me. What do you think?

To what extent do you feel *defensive* in response to this message from your partner? (PLEASE CIRCLE *ONE* NUMBER ON THE SCALE BELOW)

1	2	3	4	5

Not --- Very
Defensive   Defensive*

How would *you* respond to this message? In Proctor's study, more than 75 percent of the student respondents reported low levels of defensiveness (options 1 or 2), despite the message's relatively negative topic. Proctor concluded this was due, at least in part, to owned-message techniques used in the message.

*This is the owned negative message developed by Proctor. See R. F. Proctor II (1992). *An Exploratory Analysis of Responses to Owned Messages in Interpersonal Communication* (doctoral dissertation, Bowling Green State University, 1991). *Dissertation Abstracts International* 52, 3768A (University Microfilms No. 92–10, 466).

This "Try This" scenario was designed to be realistic for the undergraduates who served as research subjects for Proctor.

The strength of I-messages was summarized by Gordon. He said they can be called "responsibility messages" because those who send them are taking responsibility for their own inner condition (listening to *themselves*) and assuming responsibility for being open enough to share their assessment of themselves with others. In addition, they leave the responsibility for the other person's behavior with them.[28]

What does an I-message look like? Gordon suggests a behavior/feelings/effects formula for constructing I-messages. An example will illustrate its ease of construction:

1. A description by the one concerned of the other's unacceptable (disruptive) behavior.
2. The feelings of the one concerned in reaction to the other's unacceptable behavior.
3. An explanation of how the other's behavior interferes with the one concerned's ability to answer his or her own needs.

Example: "Jennifer, when you leave things everywhere (1) I get frustrated (2) because I cannot do what I have to do (3)."

Example: "Paul, when you take such long showers (1) I get annoyed (2) because there is no hot water left for me to take a shower, to do dishes, or to do the laundry (3)."

Example: "Susan, when you come home early in the morning (1) I get angry (2) because you wake me up from a deep sleep (3)."

Developing and using owned messages Some comments about using owned messages may assist you in proper development and use. First, try to avoid substituting the term "I feel" to describe your thoughts and

TRY THIS

Take a moment here to frame some I-messages of your own. Make certain all three parts are included: (1) behavior, (2) feelings, and (3) effects.

1. A roommate does not help wash dishes after meals.
2. A group member does not participate in committee activities.
3. A friend uses your car without asking permission.
4. A relationship partner does not offer her opinion on ideas discussed by you.
5. A close friend swears too much.

interpretations. For example, "I feel that you're not listening to me" does not describe a *feeling*. Rather, it describes a *thought*. Often, the phrase "I feel that" is a dead giveaway that someone is about to describe a thought, not a feeling. The term "I feel" should be restricted to use in the center part of Gordon's formula (behavior, feelings, and effects) only. For the sake of clarity and accuracy, "I feel" should be used to express affective (rather than cognitive) information.

In the above example, "I feel that you're not listening to me," the thought could be changed to a feeling in this way: "I feel hurt because I think you're not listening to me." This makes the sentence an accurate identification of both thoughts and feelings.

Second, try to avoid using the word "make" as in "your *behavior* (whatever is being described) makes me angry." Others do not make us like or dislike them. Believing that they do denies us the responsibility we have for our emotions. We are the ones who get angry or upset; it is a choice that we have, and it keeps the idea of owned messages in proper perspective. We own our feelings.

Third, avoid coercion. Jack Gibb believes a supportive communicator should *describe* rather than *evaluate* others' behavior. Gibb further maintains that asking—or even *implying*—that others must change their behavior will provoke defensiveness.[29] It may be impossible to avoid *implying* that you would like others to change their behavior, but certainly you can offer your observations without coercion. This is basic to Gordon's I-message technique: owning and describing *your* thoughts and feelings, then letting others choose how they will respond to your message. Notice how in the first "Try This" of this section, Proctor attempted to express negative sentiments without coercion in the constructed message.

Fourth, avoid exaggeration. In their book, Mader and Mader said that if the descriptions you offer tend toward exaggeration, they could end up being as intimidating and defense-provoking as evaluations. As an example, they state, "If you say 'I want to throw up every time you open your mouth,' the other person would probably not be much concerned with whether it was descriptive or evaluative."[30]

Fifth, use provisional language. Winer and Majors showed that provisional language is received less defensively than nonprovisional language. That is, if you say "might" or "seems" that would not be perceived as defensively as words like "must" or "have to." "It seems like every time you interrupt me I get confused because I can no longer remember what I was going to say," would be a better statement than "You have to stop interrupting me."[31]

Sixth, try to keep the comments positive and not negative. Not surprisingly, research shows that positive statements generate less defensiveness than negative statements.[32] Ideally, supportive climates reveal messages with content that is positive. But how do you convey negative information positively? Try to incorporate Gibb's components such as empathy, equality, and problem orientation into your communication. Look back at the first "Try This" message, and see if you can identify examples of these components (empathy, equality, and problem orientation) in the message there. Gibb's components are interactive; that is, they will work in combination with each other.

Seventh, avoid sarcasm. Although this was not part of Proctor's study, sarcasm needs to be avoided at all costs. It adds an element of manipulation, power, and bitterness that confounds, complicates, and compounds defensive climates. Sarcasm is sharp, often satirical, sometimes ironic; but whatever it is, it is designed to cut or give pain. Always, it is directed against another person—designed to enhance defensiveness, not appease it. An already defensive situation is no time to indulge in sarcasm.

Eighth, think through what you want to say and how you want to say it before saying it. In defensive situations, anything said is likely to be sensitive. Because of the defensiveness, people's senses are tuned to all verbal and nonverbal cues. What is said becomes as important as how it is said, if not more important. Choose in advance the phrasing that you think is best, and consider the tone of the approach as well.

Ninth, *combine* first person singular and plural pronouns. In this way, you will end up with phrasing that is both self-responsible (I-messages) and other-oriented (we-language). You will have captured the best of both "I" and "we" language. "I/we combinations," according to Proctor, "were consistently endorsed by interviewees."[33] For an example of this, go back to the "Try This" that includes the sample "owned message."

Winer and Majors also found that owned messages beginning with "I" generally are received less defensively than those using "me," "my," or "mine." First person plural pronouns like "we," "us," and "our" signify inclusion. They indicate the existence of dialogue (rather than debate); are nonthreatening, nonnarcissistic, other-oriented; and may be verbally immediate as well.[34] These are useful characteristics that should encourage the use of "we," "us," and "our."

Cautions about using owned messages   Three caveats (warnings) should be pointed out. These explanations are designed to prevent misinterpretation of Proctor's results and to encourage some adherence to the preceding guidelines. First, "owned messages clearly have the potential to generate *defensive* as well as *nondefensive* responses in interpersonal communication."[35] Although highly defensive responses are less likely than nondefensive or moderately defensive responses, it is difficult to claim that *any* owned message, however phrased, will result in a nondefensive climate or defuse a highly charged situation.

An owned message is neither a panacea nor a magic formula and does not always lead to interactional success. For verification, we need only to remember the influence of *how* a message is communicated, or *who* is doing the speaking or *where* this communication is taking place to understand the influence of factors other than phrasing alone.

Second, "interpersonal messages that are 'owned' by their senders will not always be *heard* as owned by their receivers."[36] Some of those in Proctor's research project read the constructed message that appears in the first "Try This" in this section and felt blamed and attacked. Some even focused on the "you" in the constructed message and not on the "I." Some substantiated their claims by inaccurately quoting their partners—even with a copy of the message in front of them. Ownership is a matter of perception.

Third, anything can be overused. The old proverb "Everything in moderation" applies here. When overused, owned messages may appear to be self-promoting rather than self-revealing.[37]

Any given behavior can be an asset or a liability, depending on the goal or situation. Interpersonal skills are competent when communicators employ them sensitively and sensibly according to the requirements of a particular social system. Using owned messages is a skill that is generally perceived to be competent across contexts. It can increase your sense of control and responsibility, and control and responsibility are issues that are basic and paramount to interpersonal competence.[38]

▶ ## SUMMARY

In responding to others, both effective listening and feedback are essential. In this chapter, listening was considered first. We looked at the importance of listening, and we noted that one of the main problems with effective listening is that most people take it for granted. This first part ended with a definition of both empathic and deliberative listening.

In the section on the process of listening, hearing and listening were contrasted. Also, the four steps of receiving, selecting, organizing, and interpreting (the same four steps of the process of perceiving) were reviewed. In the section on what influences your listening, the factors of physiological differences, rate of processing, active commitment, hidden messages, and empathy were discussed. In the section on why people don't listen empathically, we discussed tuning out, wanting to be entertained, avoiding the difficult, criticizing the superficial, and letting emotions take over. Table 4.1 is especially important for outlining the factors and barriers to effective listening.

In the section on results of effective listening, three rewards were mentioned. The first is getting a more stimulating and meaningful message. The second is improvement in our own communication techniques. And the third is an enlarged circle of friends. In the final section on listening, ways to improve listening skills were listed. These included preparing to listen, controlling or eliminating distractions, anticipating the subject, anticipating the speaker, creating a need to listen, and monitoring the way you listen by concentrating on the message, suspending judgment, and empathizing.

In the section on feedback, we discussed its importance first, the process second, and styles of feedback third. Under styles, withdrawing, judging, analyzing, questioning, reassuring, and paraphrasing were discussed. In the final section on improving skills in feedback, the suggestions included being prepared to give feedback, making your feedback prompt, making your feedback accurate, reacting to the message, not the speaker, monitoring your own feedback, and using owned messages. This final section on using owned messages included nine suggestions for developing and using owned messages and three cautions about their use.

The process of listening, and its related part, feedback, are considered the most difficult, challenging, and ineffective areas in interpersonal relations. You are involved in them more than any other communication activity, and yet they are likely to be the areas in which you perform most poorly. Perhaps that is because they are procedures you take for granted. Also, they are skills taught the least. It is an interesting paradox that the skills you use the least (reading and writing) are taught the most, and the skills you use the most (listening and feedback) are taught the least. That is why the suggestions for change and improvement in *this* chapter are especially important, deserve your attention, and need implementation.

▶ KEY TERMS

empathic listening	interpreting	withdrawing response
deliberative listening	physiologically	judging response
gestalt	feedback	analyzing response
hearing	monitoring	questioning response
receiving	evaluating	reassuring response
selecting	adjustment	paraphrasing response
organizing	internal feedback	owned messages

▶ NOTES

1. Adapted from Lyman K. Steil, Larry L. Barker, and Kittie W. Watson, *Effective Listening: Key to Your Success* (New York: Random House, 1983), 3. Copyright © 1983 Random House. Used by permission.
2. Andrew D. Wolvin and Carolyn Gwynn Coakley, *Listening* (Dubuque, IA: Wm. C. Brown Co., 1982), 4. See also R. O. Hirsch, *Listening: A Way to Process Information Aurally* (Scottsdale, AZ: Gorsuch

Scarisbrick, Publishers, 1979); Carl H. Weaver, *Human Listening: Processes and Behavior* (Indianapolis: Bobbs Merrill, 1972).

3. See Larry R. Smeltzer and Kittie W. Watson, "Listening: An Empirical Comparison of Discussion Length and Level of Incentive," *Central States Speech Communication Journal* 35 (1984): 166–170; Steil, Barker, and Watson, 1983; Wolvin and Coakley, 1982; Vincent DiSalvo, David C. Larsen, and William J. Seiler, "Communication Skills Needed by Persons in Business Organizations," *Communication Education* 25 (1976): 273–275; Vincent DiSalvo, "A Summary of Current Research Identifying Communication Skills in Various Organizational Contests," *Communication Education* 29 (1980): 283–290.

4. Steil, Barker, and Watson.

5. Charles M. Kelly, "Empathic Listening," in *Readings in Speech Communication,* ed. Richard L. Weaver II (Dubuque, IA: Kendall/Hunt, 1985), 33–39.

6. Kelly, 33–35.

7. Kelly, 34.

8. Wolvin and Coakley, 1982, 88.

9. G. Egan, *Encounter: Group Processes for Interpersonal Growth* (Belmont, CA: Brooks/Cole, 1970), 248.

10. Based on Robert L. Katz, *Empathy: Its Nature and Uses* (London: Collier-Macmillan Ltd., 1963), 7–8. Katz's development of the four phases of the empathic process follows the outline provided by Theodor Reik, *Listening with the Third Ear* (New York: Farrar, Straus & Co., 1979).

11. This phenomenon is called "EgoSpeak." Edmond G. Addeo and Robert E. Burger, *EgoSpeak* (New York: Bantam Books, 1973), xiii.

12. Steven Golen, "A Factor Analysis of Barriers to Effective Listening," *The Journal of Business Communication* 27 (Winter 1990): 25–36.

13. The retention rate of orally communicated messages is approximately 50 percent immediately after the message is communicated and only 25 percent two months later. Ralph G. Nichols, "Do We Know How to Listen?" in *Communication: Concepts and Process*, ed. Joseph A. DeVito (Englewood Cliffs, NJ: Prentice-Hall, 1971), 207–208.

14. Larry L. Barker, *Listening Behavior* (Englewood Cliffs, NJ: Prentice-Hall, 1971), 74.

15. Barker, 75–76.

16. Barker, 76–77.

17. Norbert Wiener, one of the first persons to be concerned with feedback, defined it as "the property of being able to adjust future conduct by past experience." Norbert Wiener, *Cybernetics* (New York: John Wiley & Sons, 1948), 33, and Norbert Wiener, *The Human Use of Human Beings: Cybernetics and Society* (Boston: Houghton Mifflin Co., 1950). Also see discussion of the monitoring function of feedback in

David K. Berlo, *The Process of Communication* (New York: Holt, Rinehart and Winston, 1960), 111.

18. Harold J. Leavitt and Ronald A. H. Mueller, "Some Effects of Feedback on Communication," in *Interpersonal Communication: Survey and Studies,* ed. Dean Barlund (Boston: Houghton Mifflin Co., 1968), 251–259.

19. Arnold Tustin, "Feedback," in *Communication and Culture,* ed. Alfred G. Smith (New York: Holt, Rinehart and Winston, 1966), 325.

20. Warren G. Bennis, et al., eds., *Interpersonal Dynamics: Essays and Readings on Human Interaction* (Homewood, IL: Dorsey Press, 1968), 214.

21. William C. Schutz, *The Interpersonal Underworld* (Palo Alto, CA: Science and Behavior Books, 1966), 13.

22. See Wendell Johnson, *Your Most Enchanted Listener* (New York: Harper & Row, 1956), 174.

23. See Thomas Gordon, *P.E.T.—Parent Effectiveness Training: The Tested New Way to Raise Responsible Children* (New York: New American Library, 1975), 41–44.

24. David W. Johnson, *Reaching Out: Interpersonal Effectiveness and Self-Actualization,* 2d ed. (Englewood Cliffs, NJ: Prentice-Hall, 1981), 150–155. These styles are also discussed in Thomas G. Banville, *How to Listen—How to Be Heard* (Chicago: Nelson-Hall, 1978), 166–177.

25. Larry L. Barker, *Listening Behavior* (Englewood Cliffs, NJ: Prentice-Hall, 1971), 124.

26. Gordon, *P.E.T.—Parent Effectiveness Training.*

27. Russell F. Proctor II, *An Exploratory Analysis of Responses to Owned Messages in Interpersonal Communication.* (Unpublished doctoral dissertation. Bowling Green State University, Bowling Green, OH, 1991), ii.

28. Thomas Gordon, *T.E.T.: Teacher Effectiveness Training* (New York: Wyden, 1974), 139.

29. Jack R. Gibb, "Defensive Communication," *Journal of Communication* 11 (1961), 144.

30. Thomas F. Mader and Diane C. Mader, *Understanding One Another: Communicating Interpersonally* (Dubuque: IA: Wm. C. Brown Co., 1990), 283.

31. Steven Winer and Randall E. Majors, "A Research Note on Supportive and Defensive Communication: An Empirical Study of Three Verbal Interpersonal Communication Variables," *Communication Quarterly 29* (Summer 1981): 166–172.

32. See Jack R. Gibb, E. E. Smith, and A. H. Roberts, "Effects of Positive and Negative Feedback Upon Defensive Behavior in Small Problem-Solving Groups," *American Psychologist,* 10 (1955): 355; also see Winer and Majors, 166–172.

33. Proctor, 1991, 88.

34. Winer and Majors, 166–172.

35. Proctor, 1991, 84.

36. Proctor, 1991, 84.

37. Anita L. Vangelisti, Mark L. Knapp, and John A. Daly, "Conversational Narcissism," *Communication Monographs* 57 (1990): 251–274.

38. Malcolm R. Parks, "Interpersonal Communication and the Quest for Personal Competence," in *Handbook of Interpersonal Communication*, ed. Mark L. Knapp and Gerald R. Miller (Beverly Hills, CA: Sage Publication, 1985), 171–201.

▶ ## FURTHER READING

Dan B. Curtis, Jerry L. Winsor, and Ronald D. Stephens, "National Preferences in Business and Communication Education," *Communication Education* 38 (January 1989): 6–14. The results of this research study are based on a survey questionnaire sent to a random sample of 1000 personnel managers across the United States. Communication activities occupy the top three positions in helping graduating college students obtain employment, in successful job performance and in an ideal management profile, and in three of the four top positions for courses of importance for entry-level management. The authors list listening ability as the second most important factor in helping graduating college students obtain employment and the fourth most important factor in an ideal management profile. Their review of previous research also is helpful to understanding the importance of communication-related skills in business.

Suzette Haden Elgin, *Staying Well With the Gentle Art of Verbal Self-Defense* (Englewood Cliffs, NJ: Prentice-Hall, 1990). Elgin shows readers how to apply their knowledge about the gentle art of verbal self-defense to work in everyday life. Although she does not focus on feedback directly, she helps readers understand how to reduce hostility and tension, replace negative thinking with positive thinking, and build both strong social support networks and a self-perception of someone in control. Elgin helps her readers become sensitive to the whole environment in which they operate. This information is useful in increasing one's ability at feedback and feedforward.

Scott D. Johnson, "A National Assessment of Secondary-School Principals' Perceptions of Teaching Effectiveness Criteria," *Communication Education* 43 (January 1994): 1–16. Johnson sent his survey to a sample of 1000 public, secondary-school principals across the United States and discovered that communication-related items (including interpersonal communication and listening skills) were rated as "the most important criteria used by principals in the hiring of teachers" (p. 13). Also, "communication skills seem to be at least as valuable as other pedagogical skills in a repertoire of skills and factors needed for effective classroom performance" (p. 13).

Dawna Markova, *The Art of the Possible: A Compassionate Approach to Understanding the Way People Think, Learn and Communicate* (Berkeley, CA: Conari Press, 1991). Although Markova will help readers in understanding themselves—which is a useful base for understanding others—she includes a chapter on "Partnering the Possible: Connecting With Others" that is designed to awaken readers' ability to bridge communication gaps with people in their lives. She focuses specifically on how to relate to different mental patterns—a practical base from which to practice feedback and feedforward.

Florence I. Wolff, Nadine C. Marsnik, William S. Tacey, and Ralph C. Nichols, *Perceptive Listening* (New York: Holt, Rinehart and Winston, 1983). This is a comprehensive textbook on listening. The authors combine an explanation of current theory about the listening process with numerous research-based principles designed to guide the reader toward improvement. They emphasize both economy and enjoyment. A useful, practical, readable approach.

Andrew D. Wolvin and Carolyn Gwynn Coakley, *Listening* (Dubuque, IA: Wm. C. Brown Co., 1982). After treating the need for and the process of listening, the authors give individual treatment to appreciative, discriminative, comprehensive, therapeutic, and critical listening. This is a thorough, well-researched, well-documented—but readable—textbook. Each chapter begins with concepts and skills and ends with activities and extensive notes.

5

► CHAPTER OBJECTIVES

After reading this chapter, you should be able to

- ▲ List and explain the three energy transformations that occur in the process of producing words.
- ▲ Describe the three-step process of abstracting and the reasons we do it.
- ▲ Explain how words function as symbols.
- ▲ Explain the concept "meanings are in people."
- ▲ Justify why the knowledge that "meanings are in people" is so essential.
- ▲ Understand what words can and cannot do.
- ▲ Define and provide examples of denotative and connotative meanings.
- ▲ Explain how levels of abstraction and the abstraction ladder relate to effective interpersonal communication.
- ▲ Describe the six essential characteristics of powerful talk.
- ▲ List and explain the characteristics that identify communicators as powerless.
- ▲ Understand the nature of verbal expression.
- ▲ Use several techniques for controlling verbal aggression.
- ▲ Explain the purpose of, key to, and results of fine-tuning your language behavior.
- ▲ Improve your skills in verbal communication.

▼ Timothy and Kerry Anne had just moved into the community. Soon after their arrival, they saw a speech by the town's mayor announced in the local paper, so they decided to attend. It turned out that the mayor was presenting a proposal for setting aside land for a new industrial park on the outskirts of town. Timothy listened closely to the speech, hearing the mayor talk about "new opportunities," "bringing more jobs," and "establishing a broader tax base" for the community. Kerry Anne, of course, heard the same speech, but she heard "the need for sewer and water hookups" (in a town already suffering from lack of water availability), "increased automobile and truck traffic," and "air pollution."

When Timothy and Kerry Ann talked together about the speech, Kerry Ann asked Tim what he thought the mayor meant by these "new opportunities." She asked him what he thought the mayor meant by "more jobs"—how many more jobs, and of what kind? Finally, she asked Tim what he thought the mayor meant by "a broader tax base"—how much "broader," and "so what?" Once Timothy and Kerry Ann had had a chance to talk, Timothy realized the language the mayor had used lacked specifics. Kerry Ann had listened closely to the mayor's language and had questioned his motives because he talked in generalities and offered few facts that citizens could use to make a decision on the value of the proposed industrial park.

In another example, Felicia and Rodney were discussing their relationship:

Felicia:	Do you think you are ready to make a serious commitment?
Rodney:	I thought we already had a serious commitment.
Felicia:	We aren't going out with anyone else, that's true, but we have no commitment.
Rodney:	What do you call that then?
Felicia:	Nothing really. We haven't even got a formal agreement not to date anyone else.
Rodney:	You mean to say that you think we have 'nothing really'?
Felicia:	No, I don't mean we have nothing. We have a very nice relationship. But I just think we've been seeing each other long enough now to have more of a serious commitment.
Rodney:	But I thought that was what we had. I feel pretty serious about you.
Felicia:	Pretty serious? Pretty serious? And you think we have a serious commitment because you 'feel pretty serious about me'? How would *you* like it if I told you that I feel 'pretty serious' about you? Don't you want more than that?
Rodney:	Nope. That's just fine for me. Pretty serious is just about right.
Felicia:	Well, it's not 'just fine' for me. If you are not ready to make a 'serious commitment' than maybe we should not continue seeing each other.
Rodney:	Come on, Felicia. You just want too much too fast. Let's not destroy what we already have. Just give it more time. All right?

Hideo was trying to decide whether or not to take a certain philosophy course. He asked one of his close friends, who said the teacher was "tough." Another friend said the course had a "heavy workload." A third friend observed that the instructor was "rigid and inflexible." Hideo decided to take the course anyway. It turned out the friend who said the teacher was "tough" was not a very hard worker and did not like teachers who had high expectations and pushed their students to excel. These traits appealed to Hideo. The "heavy workload" turned out to be a lot of library work, which Hideo not only enjoyed but found easy. "Rigid and inflexible" turned out to refer to the standards she expected for submitted papers, and since Hideo had written many papers in college, the expectations were consistent with what he expected and how he worked.

Isn't language fascinating? Timothy and Kerry Ann listened to the same speech, but because of the language each one heard, they came away with different impressions. Once Kerry Ann quizzed Timothy on the language he heard, he realized the speech was full of generalities and no facts. Rodney and Felicia never defined what was meant by "serious commitment." I don't think Rodney even wanted to hear what Felicia meant by it, because he was happy with the status quo. Notice, in their discussion, how they became sidetracked by language like "nothing really," "pretty serious," and "give it more time." Imagine Felicia's continuing unhappiness because Rodney was unwilling to make what she called a "serious commitment." Maybe if they had defined it, Rodney wouldn't find it so bad. He may have even agreed to "a serious commitment" if it just meant making a formal agreement to date each other exclusively or if it just meant giving her something of his own to indicate his seriousness.

In the final example, Hideo actually had a chance to find out what his friends meant by words like "tough," "heavy workload," and "rigid and inflexible." Isn't it interesting that your words have special meanings just for you? When you try to interpret the words of others you get into trouble simply because the way they use the words is not the same way you use the very same words. Whether in hearing a speech, talking together in a close relationship, or making decisions in your daily life, the words you use and the words you hear make a major difference in how you run your life.

Think about language and the transactional nature of communication. In any communication transaction you are involved in constructing a mental image of the other person, just as he or she is constructing a mental image of you. You base all future communication with each other on these mental images. Your use of language, and especially the way you view each other's use of language, will affect how you construct these mental images. The more closely you can make the other person's mental image of you conform to the one you have of yourself, the more effective your interpersonal communication will be. You use words to communicate ideas and describe feelings. You use them to reason and to transform experience into ideas and ideas into experience. Knowing how to use them well will increase your effectiveness in interpersonal communication.

In this chapter I will discuss language from the perspective of you, the language user. After brief sections on the process of producing words, and on the concept that meanings are in people, I will discuss what words can and cannot do. Since the problem of abstract language is major, I will spend more time talking about how you can modify your use of words for more precise meaning. I will explore powerful and powerless talk. Before suggesting specific things you can do to improve your language skills, I will discuss the need for fine-tuning your language behavior.

▲▲▲ *Language: The Process of Producing Words*

The process of producing words is a personal matter, just as the way you perceive is a personal matter. These processes help define the transactional nature of communication. That is, how you construct an image of the person with whom you are communicating depends on your perceptions of that person and also on the words you choose to use as you label and mentally describe that person. Through your perceptions and your choice of words, you create your own personal reality. Each of us does it differently because no two of us are alike.

The process of producing words goes on in your nervous system. It involves three types of energy transformations: (1) **sensory input**, (2) **filtering**, and (3) **symbolic output**, in that order.[1] (See Figure 5.1.) You can think of these in terms of the three processes of receiving, evaluating, and speaking. The first energy transformation occurs at the point of contact between your sensory receptors (sight, sound, smell, taste, or touch) and an outside event. This contact may be made by your senses unaided, that is, by the naked eye, the naked ear, or the naked nose. It may be made by

Figure 5.1
The process of producing words.

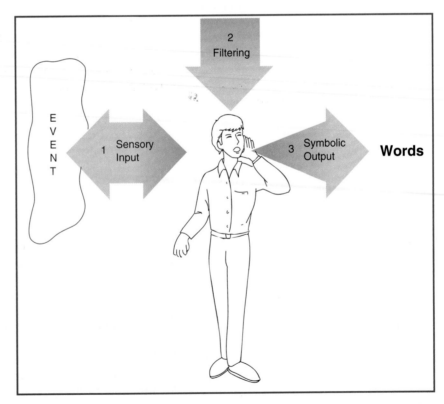

the senses aided, that is, by the eye aided by the lens or by the ear aided by the sound amplifier.

The second energy transformation is in your nervous system. Here, you filter the sensory input. Some of the ways that information can be filtered were mentioned in the discussion of the perception sieve in Chapter 2. At this point you join the sensory input with whatever is going on in the nervous system at the time and anything else that is available to you to help you select, organize, and evaluate that input. This is a preverbal state of affairs.

In the third transformation you manage to symbolize (put into symbols) this preverbal state of affairs. A **symbol** *is simply something that represents something else,* as the word *table* represents a real, physical table. You deliver this preverbal state of affairs in the form of a symbol. If language is the symbol system you're using, you use words.

But look what else is going on at each energy transformation point. Because you are affected by a broad barrage of stimuli, at each transformation point you must select details to pass on. You abstract (abridge or summarize) at each point so that fewer details are passed on than were taken in. **Abstracting** involves three processes: (1) **ignoring** many of the stimuli that might be perceived, (2) **focusing** on a limited number of stimuli, and (3) **combining** and **rearranging** what is perceived into a meaningful pattern.[2] The sensory input is an abstraction of the event. The preverbal state of affairs is an abstraction of the sensory input. The symbol is an abstraction of the preverbal state of affairs.

Why do you abstract? At the point of contact between your sensory receptors and the event, you abstract because that is the way your receptors are constructed. Your eyes react to only a small part of the light spectrum, just as your ears react to only a small part of the sound spectrum. In addition, there can be some impairment of the sensory functions which would cause greater abstraction.

There is another reason for abstracting, however. You have no choice! Even if you have all your sensory marbles and a powerful lens through which to view stimuli, your fate is that you sense the world only by the weak signal that comes to you through a tiny antenna atop a very small and insignificant tower. Of all the information that is available, you get but a small fraction. You can know our world only in part; thus, you come to know only an abstraction of it.

As if this first abstraction were not limited enough, you limit it further by filtering. How many filters you have, what kind they are, and how they are arranged vary from person to person. No two people have the same filtering system. You have mood filters, family filters, economic filters, doctrinal filters, ethnic filters, geographic filters—and the list goes on.

Take the mood filter, for example. Two people are watching a sunset. One has just learned that his mother is gravely ill. The other has just received a phone call from his girlfriend saying that she will marry him after all. Imagine the different perspectives each one will have on this sunset. The reports are likely to be dramatically different based on the mood filter alone.

When you reach the third transformation, where you symbolize the filtered preverbal state of affairs, you are dealing with a third-level abstraction. The sensory input was an abstract of the event, to begin with. The preverbal state of affairs was an abstract of that abstract. Now, symbolizing is a third level of abstracting.

Words as symbols Words are *symbols:* as previously stated, they *stand for something other than what they are.* Certainly, symbols are more than just words. Symbols can be numbers, letters, colors, shapes, figures—perhaps even sounds such as a horn, bell, or beep. No symbol exactly or completely duplicates that which is being symbolized. It takes the place of, or serves instead of, that other level of experience—that which is being symbolized. And so the word is not the thing. A word is an abstraction of the thing. Thus, words—your verbal output—are incomplete because they are abstractions. Symbols acquire meaning because you assign meaning to them. Symbols by themselves mean nothing until you say what they mean.

Have you ever tried to explain something to someone and realized that you could go on forever and still never completely describe it? You could talk about an experience all day, all week, all your life—and still find something that you hadn't already said about it. There is no one-to-one relationship between your words and what you use them to describe. A picture is said to be worth a thousand words. An experience may be worth a million!

Here is the point: When you talk, you are talking mainly about yourself. Because of filtering and abstracting, it is your background of experience, your ignorance or knowledge, your anxieties and exasperations, your likes and dislikes, and your purposes and interests that come into play. No matter what else you may be talking about, you also are talking about yourself. There is a good deal of you in whatever you say.

Not only are you giving others a highly personal account of reality, but your account is very incomplete as well. Physically, you are able to sense only part of what there is to sense. Perceptually, you are able to perceive only part of what there is to perceive. Verbally, you filter and symbolize the part that remains in a system both limited in scope and faulty in structure. Thus, it is essential to be aware that your use of language is always personal, partial, and tentative—and always subject to revision.

There are several essential skills implicit in these observations. When you realize how restricted and inhibited you are in your use of symbols, you can

▲ Make your observations as carefully as you can.
▲ Report your observations as carefully as you can.

▲ Discipline your generalizations as much as you can.
▲ Realize how much you don't know.
▲ Recognize that inner and outer space are different and are not to be confused.

When you recognize the problems you have with perception and the problems you have with language, it becomes clear that the transactional communication process—dependent for accuracy on both perception and language use—is fraught with problems: basically, inaccuracies and incompleteness. You must be cautious, tentative, and careful as you construct your images of those with whom you communicate.

▲▲▲ *Meanings Are in People*

Often the language you use in interpersonal communication is essential to your success. But no matter what words are selected for use, a principle that underlies all elements in this chapter needs to be understood. That is, **meanings are in people,** *not in the words.* It is the meanings people have for the words that need to concern you, not the words themselves.

Sometimes you think it is the word choices themselves that make the difference in communication, and there are situations, of course, where word choice *does* make a difference—as when you are being verbally abused or when someone uses profane or obscene language. But even *these* words do not take on their negative meanings (abuse, profanity, or obscenity) apart from the users. To think that words themselves have meanings tends to separate the words from their users. You have undoubtedly heard the quotation "I know you believe you understand what you think I said, but I'm not sure you realize that what you heard is not what I meant." One person's understanding is unlikely to be the same as another person's understanding, even though one person used words, and these may be the exact same words as those received.

You might wonder why this knowledge is so essential.

1. It underscores the concept that what you hear is not necessarily the message conveyed. Because words are selected and used does *not* mean they will be received and interpreted in the same way. Sources must be prepared for misinterpretations under *normal* conditions of interpersonal communication. This once again underscores the basic principle explained in Chapter 2, that every communication contains information and defines relationships. Receivers must be sensitive to these possibilities as well.

2. It emphasizes that meanings are negotiated. Since there is no such thing as two people having *exactly* the same meanings, the most that can be expected would be overlapping meanings. Often, it

takes communication (and negotiation) to realize how much overlap exists.

3. It highlights the intrapersonal nature of meaning. Meanings are intrapersonal experiences and, therefore, are unlikely to ever be *totally* revealed or uncovered. They exist in people's heads.

4. It suggests that the confusion, misunderstandings, and conflict that occur in interpersonal communication inevitably result from differences in meanings. This is normal and cannot be totally avoided, but it needs to be anticipated—and, when possible, dealt with effectively.

5. It reinforces the importance of awareness, understanding, tolerance, and sensitivity in interpersonal communication. With these aspects reinforced, you can help resolve the problems that result from the fact that meanings are in people:

   a. *Don't assume.* Because a word is used does *not* necessarily mean that it means what you think it means.

   b. *Ask questions.* To clarify meanings, you need to ask questions of the source. "How are *you* using this word?" "What does that word mean to *you*?"

   c. *Solicit feedback.* There may be no difference between asking questions and soliciting feedback; the purposes are identical. You need clarification. "Am I understanding you correctly?" "Is this what you mean?"

It is obvious as you read these points that they overlap. But the principle is important, and it has many potential applications as you strive for effective interpersonal communication. The overlap between the points becomes useful and instructive if it helps you to remember the principle that meanings are in people. It shows, for example, the essential role that intrapersonal communication plays in effective communication, whether from the sender's or receiver's perspective. It places emphasis on the *people* communicating and not just on what happens between the people (the words or the nonverbal communication). It underscores the importance of *two-way* communication as senders and receivers come together to discover meanings. Finally, it makes certain that communication is not taken at face value; there is far more going on in *any* communication situation than what first meets the eye. It is both a complex and a complicated activity.

▲▲▲ What Words Can and Cannot Do

If you see a series of stones lying across a stream, you know they will help you get to the other side. But your experience with such stones tells you that some of the stones may be loose or covered with slime and could

CONSIDER THIS

One of the most significant contributions to our understanding of language usage, especially between people of different cultures, is the Sapir-Whorf hypothesis. The essential learning that Benjamin Whorf provides, drawing upon the work of Edward Sapir, is that language is not only an instrument for expressing ideas but is a shaper of ideas as well. That is, Whorf believes that language plays a major role in actually molding the perceptual world of the user. Read his words, and then answer the questions that follow.

> We dissect nature along lines laid down by our native languages. The categories and types that we isolate from the world of phenomena we do not find there. On the contrary, the world is presented in a kaleidoscopic flux of impressions which has to be organized by our minds and this means largely by the linguistic systems in our mind.*

Questions

1. Can you generalize as Whorf does here about an entire culture? That is, can you say that people of any culture organize all the impressions they receive based largely on the linguistic systems in their minds?
2. Does it make sense to you that how you process any information you receive from your environment depends largely on the language you possess?
3. What implications does the Sapir-Whorf hypothesis have for the differences that occur between people who have acquired a large vocabulary and those who do not have a large vocabulary?
4. Do you agree with Whorf regarding the close and important relationship of language, mind, and the total culture of a speech community?
5. Does Whorf answer the question "Where does meaning lie?"

*From Benjamin L. Whorf, *Collected Papers on Metalinguistics* (Washington, DC: Department of State, Foreign Service Institute, 1952), p. 5.

cause you to slip. Like these stones, words can help you reach your goals, or they can cause you to stumble and fall. Here are some characteristics of language that affect your interpersonal communication.[3]

When you talk to people you often assume too quickly that you are being understood. If you tell people you are going to put on some music, you probably don't think about whether they are expecting to hear the kind of music you intend to play—you just turn it on. But think about the

Figure 5.2
One word may have
many different
interpretations.

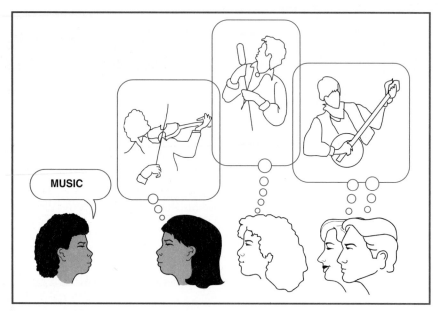

word *music* and how many different interpretations there are of it. (See Figure 5.2.)

You depend on context and on nonverbal cues to give you the meaning of words. If you say you are going to put on some music, your friends may be able to predict from knowing your taste and from nonverbal cues (your mood) what you might play. But they have a good chance of being wrong. In daily conversation you use about 2,000 words. Of those 2,000, the 500 you use most often have more than 14,000 dictionary definitions.[4] Think of the possibilities for confusion! The problem of figuring out what a person means by a certain word is compounded by the fact that even dictionary meanings change, and new words are constantly being added to the language.

Denotative meanings The **denotative meaning** *of a word is its dictionary definition*. Dictionaries provide alternatives; you still must choose from those alternatives. The choice of what is "appropriate" or "inappropriate" is left to the user.

Some words have relatively stable meanings. If several people were to define a particular word special to their discipline, they would probably use about the same definition—an agreed-upon interpretation. To lawyers, the word *estoppel* has one precise, *denotative* meaning. Doctors would probably agree upon the definition of *myocardial infarction*. People in many disciplines depend on certain words having precise, unchanging meanings in order to carry on their work. There is little likelihood of confusion with denotative meanings because there is a direct relationship between the word and what it describes. Connotative meanings, on the

Figure 5.3
Connotative meanings may depend a great deal on the perceiver's experience.

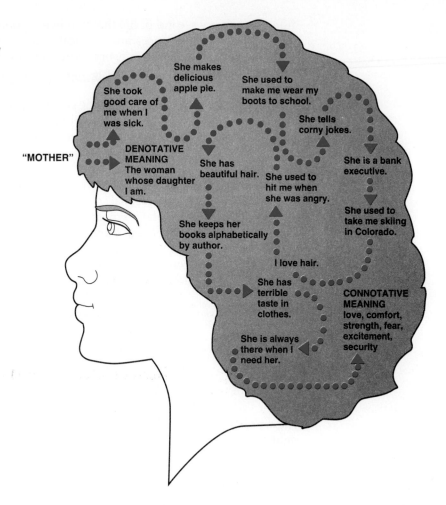

"MOTHER"

She took good care of me when I was sick.

She makes delicious apple pie.

She used to make me wear my boots to school.

She tells corny jokes.

DENOTATIVE MEANING
The woman whose daughter I am.

She has beautiful hair.

She used to hit me when she was angry.

She is a bank executive.

She keeps her books alphabetically by author.

She used to take me skiing in Colorado.

I love hair.

She has terrible taste in clothes.

CONNOTATIVE MEANING
love, comfort, strength, fear, excitement, security

She is always there when I need her.

other hand, depend a lot more than denotative meanings on subjective thought processes.[5] (See Figure 5.3.)

Connotative meanings   The **connotative meaning** of a word is the associations and overtones people bring to it. Dictionary definitions would probably not help your friends predict the kind of music you would play or what you mean by *music*. But their experience with you and with music will give them a clue as to what you mean. If *music* connotes the same thing to you and to your friends, there's less chance of misunderstanding.

When you hear a word, the thoughts and feelings you have about that word and about the person using it determine what that word ultimately means to you. This is the word's *connotative* meaning. Connotative meanings change with your experience. Just as you experience something different in every second of life that you live, so does everyone else. And no two of these experiences are identical! It's no wonder there are infinitely many connotations for every word you use. Figure 5.3 illustrates the process through which words may accumulate their connotative meanings.

If a word creates pretty much the same reaction in a majority of people, the word is said to have a general connotation. Actually, the more general the connotation of a word, the more likely that meaning is to become the dictionary meaning, because most people will agree on what that word represents. The more general the connotation of a word, the less likely people are to misunderstand it.

Problems in interpersonal communication increase as you use words with many connotative meanings. Because these meanings are so tied to the particular feelings, thoughts, and ideas of other people, you have a bigger chance of being misunderstood when you use them. On the other hand, richly connotative words give your language power. Note, for example, the differences between the following lists of words:

freedom	book
justice	piano
love	tree
liberty	teacher
music	fire

The words in the left column have many connotations; the words in the right column are more strictly denotative. "The teacher put the book on the piano" is an unambiguous statement. The sentence, "The love of freedom burns like a white flame in all of us" can be interpreted in numerous ways.

What does all this have to do with your use of words? First, you should recognize that words evoke sometimes unpredictable reactions in others. You should try to anticipate the reactions of others to your words as much as you can. For example, if you are talking to an art major you may cause confusion or even produce a hostile response if you use the psychology-major jargon you have picked up. If you anticipate this negative reaction, you'll leave the jargon in the psychology classroom.

Second, most words have both denotative and connotative meanings, and you should recognize that these meanings vary from person to person. People will react to words according to the meaning *they* give them. An effective communicator tries to recognize different reactions and to adapt to them. Remember, as you communicate, what we discussed previously: meanings do *not* reside in the words themselves. Meanings are in the minds of the people who use and hear the words. That is the essence of the transactional view of communication.

CONSIDER THIS

Dale Johnson, a chairman and chief executive officer, discusses language usage in business. Read his observations, and then answer the questions that follow.

> Executives tend to be comfortable with their nice, safe, stuffy business language!
>
> Bring a group of business people together in a room, and they chatter on about "boundaryless organizations," "dotted-line responsibilities," "reengineering," "matrix organizations," "multi-disciplinary teams," "bottom-line" this and "top-of-the-line" that.
>
> Oh, occasionally we sound lyrical—when we talk about "white knights," "golden parachutes," "queen bees," and "baby Bells." But it still doesn't mean anyone outside the corporate world knows what we're talking about.
>
> Like any other specialized group, people in business develop jargon, buzz phrases, and code words—this is insider language, and every group eventually develops it.*

Questions

1. Is what Johnson observes likely to happen in language used by doctors, engineers, prisoners, street gangs, or between family members or close friends?
2. Where does the problem with using jargon, buzz phrases, and code words occur?
3. How is it possible to help those who use jargon, buzz phrases, and code words when they talk with others, to understand how their words and messages fall on others' ears? In other words, what role do receivers have in helping senders become more effective communicators?

*From Dale Johnson, "With a Little Help from My Friends: Ten Ways for Company Communicators to Help a Chief Executive," *Vital Speeches of the Day* LX (August 15, 1994), pp. 666–667. (Dale Johnson is Chairman and Chief Executive Officer, SPX Corporation and Chairman, Motor Equipment Manufacturers' Association. The speech was delivered at the Automotive Public Relations Council, Detroit, Michigan, May 12, 1994.)

Coping with Levels of Abstraction

In this section, the words we use will be examined specifically. This is the third energy transformation, that of symbolic output. Words, you will recall, are an abstraction of the things they represent. Also, words vary in their **level of abstraction**.[6] (See Figure 5.4.)

The word *cow* means different things to different people. Think of experiences you have had with cows. It is considered a low level of ab-

Figure 5.4
S. I. Hayakawa's
Abstraction Ladder.

ABSTRACTION LADDER[7]
Start reading from the bottom UP

8. "wealth"

8. The word "wealth" is at an extremely high level of abstraction, omitting *almost* all reference to the characteristics of Bessie.

7. "asset"

7. When Bessie is referred to as an "asset," still more of her characteristics are left out.

6. "farm assets"

6. When Bessie is included among "farm assets," reference is made only to what she has in common with all the other salable items on the farm.

5. "livestock"

5. When Bessie is referred to as "livestock," only those characteristics she has in common with pigs, chickens, goats, etc., are referred to.

4. "cow"

4. The word "cow" stands for the characteristics we have abstracted as common to cow_1 cow_2 cow_3 ...cow_4. Characteristics peculiar to specific cows are left out.

3. "Bessie"

3. The word "Bessie" (cow_1) is the *name* we give to the object of perception of level 2. The name is *not* the object; it merely *stands for* the object and omits reference to many of the characteristics of the object.

2.

2. The cow we perceive is not the word, but the object of experience, that which our nervous system abstracts (selects) from the totality that constitutes the process-cow. Many of the characteristics of the process-cow are left out.

1. The cow known to science ultimately consists of atoms, electrons, and so on, according to present-day scientific inference. Characteristics (represented by circles) are infinite at this level and ever-changing. This is the *process* level.

straction when you perceive not the word *cow* but the cow itself as an object of your experiences. If you think of *Bessie,* a particular cow, the name of this cow stands for one cow and no other. Or you may think of cows in general—all the animals that have the characteristics common to cows. This is a higher level of abstraction. At a higher level yet, you might think of *cow* as part of the broader category of *livestock.* Going higher up the abstraction ladder, Bessie may be thought of as a *farm asset,* as an *asset,* or as *wealth.*

You can see how these references to the word *cow* have become more and more abstract. At each higher level of abstraction, more items could be included in the category. The more that can be included in a category, the less possible it is for someone to know exactly what you are talking about.

You may have been in conversations in which different levels of abstraction were at work without your being aware of it. You can see from the abstraction ladder how easy it would be, when dealing with something specific, to jump to a higher level and avoid answering or responding to the specific issue. If someone asked you, "What do you think of Kala as a boss?" you could say, "I like her way of handling employees," which would be answering at the same level of abstraction. But if you think such a commitment is risky, you might say, "Bosses in this company really seem to care about the people in their employ." By doing that, you move to a higher level of abstraction. If you say, "Bosses [meaning *all* bosses] really seem to care about those who work for them," you move to yet a higher level. Saying "Businesses sure have improved in the way they treat employees" is even more abstract. Educators and politicians often try to avoid difficult questions by escaping to a higher level of abstraction when pressed on specific issues. Rather than say something specific is bad, they might say "You're right; that can present problems."

As you escape to a higher level, you depend more on the connotative meanings of words than on the denotative meanings. Moving up the abstraction ladder causes the meanings of words to be less directly related to the thing they present and more dependent on the perceiver of the word. If you actively work to keep your language at a low level of abstraction, there's much less chance for ambiguity and misunderstanding.

Some teachers deal only in principles and theories and do not tie these abstractions to concrete reality. When you ask, "What does that have to do with me?" or "How can I apply that in my life?" you are asking to have the level of meaning brought down the abstraction ladder. You are asking for concrete particulars so that you can make sense out of the abstract principles.

Usually when you talk to people you go continually up and down the abstraction ladder. You adapt your words to the other's experiences. Knowing that certain words are more abstract than others will help you stay flexible. Words like *love* and *beauty* and *truth* are highly abstract and are open to the possibility of confusion and error.

Giving Power to Your Words [8]

Powerful talk is straightforward and to the point. It causes people to perceive communicators as having high power and dominance. **Powerless talk is tentative and uncertain, characterizing communicators as powerless and submissive.** It is important to understand these differences when you want your interpersonal communication to have impact. Powerful talk has been shown to benefit communicators in such widely varying situations as a job interview,[9] a courtroom witness box,[10] a small group,[11] and a crisis intervention dialogue.[12] One would expect powerful talk to make a difference whenever one wanted to reveal assertiveness, take a stand on an issue, or gain compliance (persuade others to do what you request). Because researchers have devoted their attention to defining the types and effects of powerless talk, more powerless forms have been identified. It is useful to know that communicators are often perceived as powerful or powerless solely on the basis of their language choices.[13] Thus, knowing which features to *avoid* will help you give power to your speech. According to recent speech communication research, the following characteristics type communicators as powerless.[14]

▲ **Hedges/qualifiers.** Hedges such as "kinda," "I think," and "I guess" qualify statements by detracting from their certainty and weakening their impact.

What additional meanings are likely to reside in these two people that are not in the words being shared? Put yourself in the place of one of these two people. What would be the meanings you might have?

▲ **Hesitation forms.** When communicators use "uh," "ah," "well," and "um" (all but "well" are called vocalized pauses), they are not being straightforward and direct.[15]

▲ **"You knows."** Heard often in informal conversation, this expression is often used for emphasis, and yet, similar to the hesitation forms, "you knows" contribute to perceptions of powerlessness.[16]

▲ **Tag questions.** Tag questions make declarative sentences less forceful. "Sure is cold in here, isn't it?" has less impact than "It sure is cold in here."[17]

▲ **Deictic phrases.** (Pronounced "dike-tick." *Deictic means pointing out or proving by showing.*) "Over here" and "over there" are deictic phrases. "That woman over there looks like a teacher of mine."[18] These expressions are rated as powerless because they have been linked to perceptions of low status in courtroom situations.[19]

▲ **Disclaimers.** Disclaimers are "introductory expressions that excuse, explain, or request understanding or forbearance."[20] "Don't get me wrong, but . . . " is one form and "I know this sounds crazy, but . . . " is another. Such phrases indicate uncertainty and lack of commitment to a position.[21]

Powerless talk may have direct, negative effects of which the communicator is completely unaware. It is important to recognize the features that characterize talk as powerless and to eliminate them from your communications because powerless communicators have lower credibility, appear less attractive, and may be less persuasive.[22]

Since meanings are in people's heads and *not* in words, you need to monitor your language so that the impressions others have of you are exactly the impressions *you* desire them to have. Powerless talk may be appropriate in some situations; however, if you are trying to have a positive impact, you need to be aware of your language usage. Awareness and monitoring are often the first steps toward control and increased effectiveness.

▲▲▲ *Verbal Aggression*[23]

Verbal aggression is message behavior that attacks a person's self-concept with the purpose of delivering psychological pain.[24] Dominic A. Infante, a researcher into verbal aggression for more than ten years, states that it is a highly destructive form of communication because it can lead to violent crimes, interpersonal violence, and negative superior–subordinate relationships.[25] In this brief section, verbal aggression will be examined, and then several strategies for controlling it will be offered.

CONSIDER THIS

Writers on power and its relation to language make a clear case for their intimate relationship. It is human communication that both activates and sustains power. Read the following excerpt from Richard L. Johannesen, a writer on ethics, and then answer the questions that follow.

> A governmental leader's abuse of language is one type of abuse of power. The techniques of communication used by governmental officials can have long-term cumulative effects on citizen habits of thought and decision-making in addition to the impact of specific policies sought by the officials. No matter the purpose they serve, the arguments, appeals, and language chosen gradually do shape a citizen's values, standards of judgment, language patterns, range of ethical tolerance, and level of trust.*

Questions
1. Do you have any examples of "a governmental leader's abuse of language?" What is the likelihood of such abuses occurring in a democracy?
2. What are the protective devices built into our society that help detect abuses of language by governmental leaders?
3. Have there been historical occurrences of long-term cumulative effects of communication used by governmental officials on citizens' values, standards of judgment, language patterns, range of ethical tolerance, and level of trust?

*From Richard L. Johannesen, "Haigspeak, Secretary of State Haig, and Communication Ethics," in Richard L. Johannessen, *Ethics in Human Communication*, 3rd ed. (Prospect Heights, IL: Waveland Press, 1990), p. 233.

Why Is Verbal Aggression Destructive?

The main reason verbal aggression is destructive is that it applies force to influence receivers. The force can appear to be physical, as when receivers feel the sensation of being punched. More often, however, the force is psychological—receivers feel humiliated, belittled, demeaned, or degraded. Verbal aggression may be accompanied by physical violence, and it usually includes nonverbal behavior such as eye behavior and gestures.

What verbally aggressive messages might be taking place in this situation? If one of these two people chose to stop the verbal aggression, what might she do?

Words and their accompanying nonverbal messages are more damaging than physical aggression. A punch that breaks a child's nose, for example, could result in less pain than a derogatory description of the child's nose by another child. The derogatory description could produce pain that persists for a lifetime, whereas by comparison, the pain from the physical break soon disappears. Lifetime pain may include feelings of inadequacy, depression, despair, hopelessness, embarrassment, and anger, to name a few.

With respect to interpersonal relationships, the destructiveness may be just as damaging. It may result in reduced trust, relationship deterioration, and relationship termination. In organizations, supervisors' verbally aggressive behavior has negative effects. Also, verbally aggressive subordinates are evaluated unfavorably by their supervisors.[26]

What Are Verbally Aggressive Messages?

Because of the wide range of potentially verbally aggressive messages, there is not enough space to consider each one. It should be clear, here, that some of them take on their negative and hostile connotations because of the sender, the context, or the intent. Some, too, are clearly negative and hostile at the outset (like any of those labeled "attack"), without context or intent. Some, like commands, may be perfectly normal and expected behaviors in specified contexts and with appropriate people, such as superiors or bosses. Teasing may be appropriate among friends. A list, however, will give you an idea of the potential pervasiveness of verbal aggression:

character attacks	nonverbal emblems
competence attacks	blame
background attacks	personality attacks
physical appearance attacks	commands
maledictions	global rejection
teasing	disconfirmation
swearing	negative comparison
ridicule	sexual harassment
threats	attacking the target's significant others[27]

Why Does Verbal Aggression Occur?

Why would people send messages they know will hurt receivers? There are likely to be as many answers to this question as there are verbally aggressive people, and the answers are unlikely to be simple and easy to explain. Some answers may focus on human nature, victimization, abnormal psychology, or even the influence of the mass media. Research has identified four basic causes of verbal aggression.[28] The first is *psychopathology*, which involves a transference whereby a person attacks others who remind him or her of an unresolved source of hurt. A young man, for example, attacks his new in-laws because of the hurt he suffered as a child at the hands of his own parents.

There are three other basic causes. *Disdain* means verbally expressed dislike for another person. Someone may have a clear dislike or utter disregard for another person. In *social learning*, a third basic cause of verbal aggression, a person experiences direct or vicarious rewards for verbally aggressive behavior. Society may condition people to be aggressive, to express anger, and to ventilate frustrations.[29] For example, a worker seeking a higher position spreads vicious, negative rumors about the person occupying the desired position to try to get that person fired, thus opening the position for himself.

A fourth basic cause may be *argumentative skill deficiencies*. People with such deficiencies attack others personally out of frustration with not being able to attack their positions effectively. For example, a person may lash out and verbally attack another's credibility ("Why you no-good, rotten, son-of-a- . . . ") because the other person had discovered the facts, and the facts could not be disputed.

Some additional causes of verbal aggression may exist.[30] Some people, for example, just want to be mean. Others may want to appear tough. Still others may be trying to be humorous, are just plain angry, may be imitating a TV character, or are just in a bad mood. Also, males are more likely than females to use verbal aggression,[31] because males in American culture have been conditioned to be more competitive, dominant, and assertive. The use of verbal aggression, therefore, is more in line with male than with female role behavior. However, females sometimes use verbal aggression as frequently as males, or even more often.[32]

Why Does Verbal Aggression Continue?

A basic reason why it continues, once initiated, is *reciprocity*. When verbal aggression occurs, the natural instinct is to return it or to increase its intensity. People may do this to save face or to discourage future attacks.[33] If verbal aggression is reciprocated, escalating tension is likely to follow, and it can result in explosive acts of physical aggression. Even if reciprocity does not take the interaction to a violent climax, the destructiveness that results may be more than what would have occurred if one party had not reciprocated.

Are There Any Good Reasons for Verbal Aggression?

Yes, but in all cases it is questionable. There may be three reasons why some may think it is valid. The first occurs when it is used to motivate positive behavioral change. For example, drill instructors in the military and athletic coaches use self-concept attacks extensively. But, an ethical question is, Should verbal aggression ever be used to motivate behavioral change?

A second reason why some people may think verbal aggression may be acceptable is that a situation is highly competitive. Examine, for example, the extent of "trash talk" or "in your face" behavior of professional athletes. You may see it in professional hockey, basketball, football, and boxing, to name several sports where it occurs. An ethical question is, Should this be considered unsportsmanlike conduct that deserves a penalty? Should this be a natural and expected part of such competition?

Finally, a third reason why some people may think verbal aggression may be acceptable is that it can be used as a substitute for physical aggression. "Would you rather have me bash your face in?" someone might say. As part of this reason, some people may use verbal aggression as catharsis—as a way to release pent-up emotions and feelings. Some evidence suggests that the more verbal aggression there is in a marriage, the more likely is the possibility of interspousal physical violence.[34] An ethical question might be, Is verbal aggression, whether intrapersonal or interpersonal, ever appropriate?

A wide variety of other destructive outcomes of verbal aggression have been researched. In family communication, children may be harmed by their parents' verbal aggression. Husbands of verbally aggressive wives are more depressed. Verbal aggression in marriages is negatively related to marital satisfaction. It may even lead to interspousal violence.

In other forums, verbal aggression may have a negative effect on a person's credibility.[35] The important conclusion to be drawn from all these effects is that verbal aggression has direct negative outcomes. It is a destructive form of communication and should be discouraged.

How Can Verbal Aggression Be Controlled?

This brief section will be divided into two parts: preventing verbal aggression from occurring, and neutralizing its effects and preventing escalation.

Preventing verbal aggression To prevent verbal aggression from occurring requires, first, an awareness of situations to avoid. For example, you should attempt to avoid situations in which no negotiation can occur, a high level of blame exists, hitting below the belt is standard procedure, manipulation is prevalent, personal rejection occurs, and force is common. Verbal aggression is less likely to occur in situations that are open, empathic, supportive, positive, and equal.

A second way to prevent verbal aggression is to offer direct forms of verbal and nonverbal support. For example, you can reaffirm an opponent's sense of competence, allow an opponent to speak without being interrupted, emphasize attitudes and values shared with the opponent, show an interest in an opponent's views, use a calm delivery, control the pace of the argument, and allow the opponent to save face.[36] If you create situations that are stimulating but pleasant, and low stress but without hostility, you are more likely to control the potential arousal of verbal aggression.

A third way to prevent verbal aggression is to avoid forming relationships with verbally aggressive individuals. Some people are more verbally aggressive than others. Not only does aggressiveness tend to be transmitted from one generation to another,[37] but longitudinal studies show that people are persistent in abusive patterns of behavior.[38] Women, for example, could be advised not to marry someone who verbally abuses them while dating, because the abuse is likely to continue in marriage and will probably get worse. It should be clear that this does not always occur. This advice is premised on the idea that accurate reading of people early in the acquaintance process is possible—but may not be.

Possible signs of verbal aggressiveness, however, may not be subtle or hard to detect. For example, how a person reacts to another automobile driver's aggressiveness may be an indicator. Another might be the way another person interacts with family members, friends, children, and even animals. One verbal aggressor, for example, treated animals with cruelty. In addition, does the person pick fights, use extreme (highly inflammatory) language, or become emotional over seemingly trivial matters?

A fourth way to keep verbal aggression from happening involves communication skills training. If you have experience in negotiation, practice using empathy, a background in problem solving, and skill in using assertive behavior—all important communication skills—it is more likely aggression can be controlled. Physical and verbal abuse is less likely to happen when the interactants are skillful communicators.[39] Skillful communication helps avoid frustration, and avoidance of frustration may prevent triggering anger and the resulting aggression.

Keeping verbal aggression from escalating Once verbal aggression is part of an interpersonal situation, how can it be neutralized? How can escalation be prevented? Three approaches have been discussed by Infante in his research.

To help keep verbal aggression from escalating, couples need training in *how to manage their anger.* This would include learning effective problem-solving skills. Margoline, a researcher in spousal abuse, offers a seven-phase method of treatment:

1. Identify cues that stimulate anger during interactions.
2. Develop tactics to interrupt anger patterns.
3. Create tactics for meeting to deal with the anger-provoking problem at a later date.
4. Strive to eliminate a behavior that provokes anger in the other person.
5. Modify faulty thoughts about the relationship.
6. Develop problem solving skills.
7. Improve the general positive tone of the relationship.[40]

The second way to neutralize verbal aggression or prevent escalation is to use *dismissal strategies.* Dismissal strategies include *misinformation:* a claim that the attack is based on incorrect information. Using *coercion,* you could claim that the information being used was obtained by force and therefore not true. In the strategy of *personal growth,* you claim that the characterization of yourself by your attacker no longer exists; you've changed. Using the *unconscious* strategy, you would agree with the unfavorable characterization by your attacker but claim that the matter is beyond your personal control, since your unconscious mind is responsible. In the *excuse* strategy, you claim that the behavior was not your fault. Using *ignorance,* you claim that the attacker doesn't know what he or she is talking about. In the *dark side* strategy, you claim that he or she is motivated by lesser human tendencies such as jealousy, enviousness, resentfulness, viciousness, or sadism. Using the strategy of *unacknowledged motives,* you would claim that the attacker has a hidden agenda.

A third and final way to neutralize or reduce the possibility of verbally aggressive escalation is to use an *argumentative approach*—direct refutational strategies. The first is to refute the claim. If a person said,

"You do not deserve what you got," then you engage in the four-step strategy of refutation offered by Infante:[41]

1. Summarize the argument to be refuted.
2. Give an overview of your objections.
3. Attack the evidence and/or the reasoning.
4. Summarize your refutation and explain how the refutation weakens your opponent's claim.[42]

This is not an argumentation textbook; however, Infante's approach has merit. When verbal aggression is treated as argument, often it is an easy argument for the victim to win. Typically, the aggression advanced by the opponent will be based on emotions, unsupportable data and opinions, illogical statements, and perhaps irrelevant information and ideas. Since verbal aggression is essentially irrational, when you employ the argumentative framework for rebuttal, the verbally aggressive message will not fit, and your opponent will have a difficult time refuting your approach.

There are other strategies that fit the argumentative approach. One effective one is an appeal to rationality. For example, you could say to your opponent, "Our discussion was very rational until the swearing. Neither of us values irrational behavior. Both of us need to try to be as rational as possible here." This approach avoids placing blame, avoids putting the other person under attack, and takes a "we" approach to the situation—which is safest here. The value of this approach is that it indicates an awareness by the victim that verbal aggression is something different and undesirable—and labels it this way.

A final strategy that may have to be used if the verbal aggression continues is *interaction termination*. Simply say, "I don't think we should continue this conversation if it is going to degenerate into name-calling and personal attacks." Make it clear to the opponent that certain behavior will not be tolerated. This can be effective, too, in preventing future occurrences.

▲▲▲ *Fine-Tuning Your Language Behavior*

You've looked at the process of producing words; you've looked at what words can and cannot do; you've looked at powerful and powerless talk; and you've looked at verbal aggression. It seems clear that using language effectively presents difficulties and challenges. The way you meet these difficulties and challenges is likely to determine others' impressions of you, and yet it is likely to be personal and unique as well. Although there are specific suggestions for building language skills in the next section, I first want to discuss a *framework* for implementing verbal skills. This *framework* involves *the need for and process of fine-tuning and making adjustments to your conversational partners.* Suzette Haden Elgin calls this process **syntonics,** an idea that gains its strength from its reliance on the transactional-communication perspective.

Syntonics, according to Elgin, is "*a system of putting human beings in tune with one another linguistically [through their language usage] so that they are able to communicate with maximum efficiency and effectiveness and satisfaction.*"[43] Indeed, this definition resembles one of the broadest definitions of rhetoric (the art or science of using words effectively) as the art by which communication is adapted to its end. Marie Hochmuth Nichols, a writer on rhetoric, sharpened this definition somewhat when she wrote that rhetoric is "a means of so ordering discourse as to produce an effect on the listener or reader." Kenneth Burke, one of our discipline's legends in rhetoric, defined it as "the use of language as a symbolic means of inducing cooperation in beings that by nature respond to symbols." Aristotle's definition of rhetoric focuses most sharply on the specific kind of verbal activity that Elgin is talking about: "the faculty of discovering all the available means of persuasion in any given situation."[44] The field of speech communication has a rich heritage of writers and researchers who have addressed the need for communicators to fine-tune their messages for particular listeners.

The key to fine tuning a message is **adjustment:** the willingness of both parties to make every effort to adjust to the other to maximize their communication. Obviously, this requires *both* effective listening and feedback—making adjustments based on the information we get and our reactions to that information.

One way to think of "adjustment" would be to think of a perfectly tuned situation. Pretend you want to tune the A string on your guitar to the A of a pitch pipe. You pluck the guitar string and listen; then you blow into the A slot of the pitch pipe and listen. You compare the two. If the pitch pipe sounds higher, you tighten the A string; if it sounds lower, you loosen the string. You continue this until you hear no difference between the two sounds. This is perfect tuning because you have an exact target to match. It is exact because it can be measured by scientific instruments. If the string vibrates at 440 cycles per second, it is correct.

The goal in the situation just described is to detect the match between the pitch pipe and the string. One task humans are good at is comparing things, detecting similarities and differences, and making adjustments until the two are perceived the same. But can we compare this situation with one in which the two items being compared are people using language? After all, language transactions

▲ cannot be measured scientifically
▲ do not follow orderly steps
▲ reveal little or no control over the responses of the other

▲ allow little or no control over the number of chances you have to speak

▲ give little or no control over the number of opportunities you have to observe the other's behavior

▲ do not guarantee predictable responses

▲ are a two-way process in which both people are adjusting to each other

But do not be deterred. People are *not* at the mercy of totally random, unstructured, unpredictable events and occurrences. You *can* detect a mismatch between your language behavior and that of another person. Rapport, symmetry, synchrony, agreement, harmony, and congruence—all synonyms for success—*can* be achieved.

The basic concept of fine-tuning involves an overall change in focus. When you listen to someone else, you often ask yourself, "What's in this for *me?*" "What am I going to say when he/she stops talking?" or "When will he/she give me a chance to say something?" This self-centered approach distracts you from concentrating on *what* the other person is saying. Fine-tuning requires understanding *what* the other person is saying. This can be accomplished in a two-fold approach: (1) you assume that what is being said is true, and (2) you try to imagine and discover what it is true of.[45] For example, if someone tells you he or she is not getting along with his or her relationship partner, you may not like the reality in which the statements are true, but nothing obliges you to live in that reality. This is simply a framework for getting yourself in tune with the signal provided by your listener's reactions.

Fine-tuning does *not* mean accepting or believing the content. It means trying to avoid a negative reaction to yourself as a communicator in order to avoid a negative reaction to your message.[46] This is why adjustment is so important. Think of it this way: if *we* are rejected, whatever we are saying becomes superfluous and meaningless.

Fine-tuning and adjustment provide both a framework and a goal. The framework is transactional communication: people communicating *with* each other. But fine-tuning is a goal as well, because a perfect match can never be achieved. The better the tuning that takes place, however, the more likely the communication will be efficient, effective, and satisfying. Keep the concept of fine-tuning in mind as you consider the following skills for improving your language use.

Building Language Skills

A word is simply a vehicle you use to produce a certain response in another person. If your words do not accomplish their mission, there is a breakdown in communication. There is no guarantee that your language will produce the responses you want even if you apply all the suggestions given here. Interpersonal communication can never be perfect. But learning language skills can help you move closer to the goal of effective, efficient communication. It will increase the chances for your success as communicators.

Make the message complete   Because there are so many ways for words to be misinterpreted, you must try to give listeners as much information as possible about your ideas, experiences, feelings, and perceptions. There should be enough information so the other person can understand your frame of reference. But don't go too far! Too much information can create a negative effect. You're very likely to bore or overwhelm your listener if you give more details than are necessary or manageable.

Your message will be more complete if you repeat the message with some variation; that is, if you add details to the original message that make it more accurate. If the listener does not "get it" one way, he or she will have another chance the second time with the added information. To simply restate a misunderstood word or phrase in precisely the same way does not serve the listener's purposes and perpetuates confusion. What you want to make sure of is that your message is as complete and "on the mark" as possible.

Talk the same language   If you can comfortably and naturally use words, including slang and jargon, that your listener understands, so much the better. If you adapt your language to the listener, very specifically, you show concern for him or her—an attempt at genuine communication to reach honest understanding. It is helpful to remember that fine-tuning is a two-way process of accommodation and adjustment. To litter your speech with fancy words, "cute" phrases, or inappropriate slang will do little to help create understanding (and can make you look ridiculous and phony).

There is nothing "wrong" with any word that you have in your vocabulary or that appears in any dictionary. *Words are wrong only if they are used inappropriately.* You might not talk to your roommate as you do to your parents; the language you use with your roommate may be inappropriate for your parents. You may have all kinds of names and profanities to describe a teacher who seems to be doing you in, but you use them with your friends or classmates, not with the teacher. It would serve a negative purpose to use abusive language with the teacher; it would be "wrong" in that context.

To use different language in different contexts and with different people is not necessarily deceptive or hypocritical. Some language may be appropriate for a casual party with a group of friends; other language is better suited for dinner with one's future mother-in-law. Hypocrisy and deceit *do* result from using language that is not our own—language that reflects character or beliefs and principles that we do not really possess. You are being hypocritical when you try to appear as you are not or

What are the two ways you have for adapting your language to listeners? Can you see how important this might be?

try to present a facade, when you are no longer adapting your language to the context in an honest manner. Falsely ripping apart a competitor's product to sell one's own is a blatant example; revealing the false weaknesses of another's partner so that he or she will drop the partner and give you a chance to date him or her may be closer to home. It is deceptive to manipulate others by using language that misrepresents who you really are.

Be flexible   Stereotyping paints an unrealistically black-or-white world because things either fit your categories or do not. If you say, "Teachers are too tough," meaning *all* teachers are too tough, you haven't allowed for variations among teachers. If you think in terms of what is unique to a person or a situation, your language will become more accurate and flexible.

You increase your **flexibility** if you avoid extreme language. If you say, "I am totally happy," you allow no room for increased happiness. Happiness is seldom total, just as success and failure most often occur in degrees. Saying "I am a complete failure" is a rigid, inflexible response.

True, some things *are* either-or, such as whether a person is employed or not, whether you are here or somewhere else, or whether or not there is another person in the room with you right now. You can describe these things in definite terms. But generally people tend to be too rigid rather than too flexible in their use of language. Rigidity makes adjustment difficult.

CONSIDER THIS

In learning a foreign language, why is it so difficult to use the learned language properly—talk the same language—with people from that foreign culture? Read the following explanation, and then answer the questions that follow.

> To be literate in Chinese, one must understand the implicit meaning and significance of the characters and Chinese history. Also, one must know the spoken pronunciation system in which there are four tones and a change of tone means a change of meaning. Understanding a restricted, high-context linguistic system [meaning a language system highly dependent on the context in which it is used] such as Chinese requires not only a functional knowledge in the culture and history but also a sensitivity to the specific social context in which a particular communication transaction occurs. Many Asian languages, for example, including Chinese, Japanese, and Korean, are sensitive to the social status of the addressee. These languages implicitly or explicitly indicate the other person's social position relative to the speaker.*

Questions

1. Is the necessity for having "a functional knowledge in the culture and history" of people true with respect to *any* foreign language?
2. Is it clear why misunderstandings between people of different cultures exist?
3. Gudykunst and Kim go on to say that "certain nouns, pronouns, and verbs can be used only when speaking to or of a superior; a second group of words having the same basal meanings can be used only when speaking to or of an equal; a third group can be used only when speaking to or of an inferior" (p. 156). Do you see why learning a foreign language means learning more than just the words? Is this true of learning American English?
4. Can we *ever* talk the same language as someone else?

*From William B. Gudykunst and Young Yun Kim, *Communicating With Strangers: An Approach to Intercultural Communication,* 2nd ed. (New York: McGraw-Hill, 1992), pp. 155–156.

It's a good idea to think in terms of *sometimes, possibly, normally,* and *now and then.* Such words as *always, never, all,* and *none* can cause problems. "Allness" language makes you tend to think in set, rigid patterns. And in doing so, not only do you fail to distinguish what is unique in each case, but you do not allow for change.

Get others involved   If you assume that your communication has a chance of being *un*successful and if you accept the fact that misunderstanding will occur, you will be more cautious in your use of words. It will help if you can get others to share in your frame of reference. It is very easy to overwhelm another person with a verbal barrage and not realize you have caused that person to withdraw or become defensive. Saying "Do you understand?" or "You *do* see what I mean?" can seem accusatory or severe. But asking "Am I making sense?" or, simply, "What do you think?" involves the listener and can help you find out whether you really have been understood.

Tie your impressions down   You have probably met people who are immune to new information. They continue to vote by party label, view all "baseball players" or "Harvard graduates" as exactly alike, and regard all "mothers" as sacred. You may have a friend like one of mine. Once, simply to be polite, I said something nice about a piece of music he was playing. Now, despite all my negative comments since then about that kind of music, he still plays it whenever I'm around. Can I convince him that I really don't like it at all? I finally *did* convince him. How? I brought some of my own music.

But how do *you* prevent yourself from getting in such intellectual blind alleys? Or, when you discover you are already in one, how do you get out? First, specifically what is the blind alley? It occurs when you refer to one particular situation as if it represents *all* such situations. S. I. Hayakawa gives examples such as "Business is business," "Boys will be boys," and "Republicans are Republicans" to show this kind of thinking.[47] How might this look in the context of college life?

"I don't think you need to go in to talk to Professor Jones. He won't remember that he said it anyway."

"Yeah, I suppose not. Just another absent-minded professor."

The final assertion. "Just another absent-minded professor," may look like a simple statement of fact, but it is not. It is a directive. In effect, it says, "Let us treat this transaction with complete disregard for Professor Jones's personal qualities as a human being." Statements like "Blondes have more fun," "Athletes are dumb," and "Used-car salespeople are fast-talking crooks" do the same thing. They are directives that tell us to classify a person in a given way so that we feel or act toward the person or event in the way suggested by the terms of the classification.

The simple technique for preventing such directives from having a harmful effect on our thinking is **indexing,** or **dating.** Korzybski suggested the idea of indexing.[48] He said we should add "index numbers" to our terms; for example, cow_1, cow_2, cow_3, . . . The terms of classification, like *cow*, tell us what the individuals of the class have in common; the index numbers remind us of the characteristics left out. The rule that follows is that cow_1 is not cow_2, boy_1 is not boy_2, and $professor_1$ is not $professor_2$.

Dates can be substituted for index numbers as a reminder that no word ever has exactly the same meaning twice. Then Professor $Jones_{1994}$ is not Professor $Jones_{1995}$, and Professor $Jones_{1995}$ is not Professor $Jones_{1996}$. The point of all this is to help you remember to consider the facts of each particular thing, person, or place. If you leap to conclusions you might later have cause to regret, just remember cow_1 is not cow_2, and cow_2 is not cow_3.[49]

Using words well is not simple. Trying to put your finger on the problems of using words is hard because so much depends on the users of the words and the contexts in which they are used, and you have to use words even to describe the problems of using words! There's no way around it. Even if you understood all about users and contexts, you wouldn't have all the answers, because things would change. Words, as you have seen, are flexible in meaning. Your effectiveness in using them depends upon understanding how they can vary depending on different communication contexts. In this chapter I have tried to make it clear that as humans we belong to a peculiarly symbol-making, symbol-using, symbol-misusing species.

▶ SUMMARY

Verbal communication has a major impact on interpersonal relationships. Verbalizing your feelings, and effectively articulating your ideas, can help you feel better about yourself, and it can strengthen your interpersonal interactions. The process of producing words involves three types of energy transformations: (1) sensory input, (2) filtering, and (3) symbolic output. As part of the explanation of the process, I answered the question, "Why do you abstract?" and I looked at words as symbols as well.

There are five specific reasons why the knowledge that meanings are in people is so important. These reasons underscore the importance of intrapersonal communication, discussed in Chapter 3. This knowledge places an emphasis on the people communicating and not just on the words. It reinforces the importance of two-way communication, and finally, it reveals the complex and complicated nature of communication.

In the section on what words can and cannot do, denotative and connotative meanings were discussed. This discussion helps us recognize that words sometimes evoke unpredictable reactions in others and that most words have both denotative and connotative meanings. It underscores that meanings are in people.

The remaining sections of the chapter treated coping with levels of abstraction, giving power to your words, verbal aggression, fine-tuning your language behavior, and building language skills. In the first, I discussed the abstraction ladder. In the second, I looked at the qualities of powerless communication: hedges/qualifiers, hesitation forms, "you knows," tag questions, deictic questions, and disclaimers. In the section on verbal aggression, I discussed why it is destructive, what are aggressive messages, why it occurs, and how it can be controlled. In the section on fine-tuning, I looked at syntonics—the process of getting in tune with others linguistically—and the key to fine-tuning messages, which is adjustment. Finally, for building skills, there were five suggestions: make the message complete, talk the same language, be flexible, get others involved, and tie your impressions down.

▶ KEY TERMS

sensory input
filtering
symbolic output
symbol
abstracting
ignoring
focusing
combining and rearranging
meanings are in people

denotative meanings
connotative meanings
levels of abstraction
abstraction ladder
powerful talk
powerless talk
hedges/qualifiers
hesitation forms
you knows

tag questions
deictic phrases
disclaimers
fine-tuning
syntonics
adjustment
flexibility
indexing
dating

▶ NOTES

1. Based on Wendell Johnson and Dorothy Moeller, *Living with Change: The Semantics of Coping* (New York: Harper & Row, 1972), 74–79.
2. John C. Condon, Jr., *Semantics and Communication*, 3d ed. (New York: Macmillan Publishing Company, 1985), 25.
3. For their ideas on characteristics of language, see Kim Giffin and Bobby R. Patton, *Fundamentals of Interpersonal Communication*, 2d ed. (New York: Harper & Row, 1976), 161–172.
4. Giffin and Patton, 161.
5. C. K. Ogden and I. A. Richards, *The Meaning of Meaning* (New York: Harcourt Brace Jovanovich, 1953).
6. For the discussion on levels of abstraction I am indebted to S. I. Hayakawa, *Language in Thought and Action*, 5th ed. (New York: Harcourt Brace Jovanovich, 1990), 99–111.

7. From S. I. Hayakawa, *Language in Thought and Action,* 5th ed., copyright © 1990 by Harcourt Brace Jovanovich, Inc. Reproduced by permission of the publisher. This "Abstraction Ladder" is based on a diagram originated by Alfred Korzybski to explain the process of abstracting. See Alfred Korzybski, *Science and Sanity: An Introduction to Non-Aristotelian Systems and General Semantics* (Lancaster, PA: Science Press Printing Co., 1933), especially Chapter 25.

8. For the discussion of powerful and powerless talk I am indebted to Craig E. Johnson, "An Introduction to Powerful and Powerless Talk in the Classroom," *Communication Education* 36 (April 1987): 167–172.

9. J. Bradac and A. Mulac, "A Molecular View of Powerful and Powerless Speech Styles: Attributional Consequences of Specific Language Features and Communicator Intentions," *Communication Monographs* 51 (1984): 307–319.

10. B. Erickson, E. Lind, A. Johnson, and W. M. O'Barr, "Speech Style and Impression Formation in a Court Setting: The Effects of 'Powerful' and 'Powerless' Speech," *Journal of Experimental Social Psychology* 14 (1978): 266–279; J. Conley, W. O'Barr, and E. A. Lind, "The Power of Language: Presentational Styles in the Courtroom," *Duke Law Journal* (1978): 1375–1399; E. A. Lind and W. O'Barr, "The Social Significance of Speech in the Courtroom," in H. Giles and R. St Clair, eds., *Language and Social Psychology* (College Park, MD: University of Maryland Press, 1979), 66–87; W. M. O'Barr, *Linguistic Evidence: Language, Power, and Strategy in the Courtroom* (New York: Academic Press, 1982).

11. P. H. Bradley, "The Folk-Linguistics of Women's Speech: An Empirical Examination," *Communication Monographs* 48 (1981): 73–90.

12. J. Bradac and A. Mulac, "Attributional Consequences of Powerful and Powerless Speech Styles in a Crisis-Intervention Context," *Journal of Language and Social Psychology* 3 (1984): 1–19.

13. Bradac and Mulac, "A Molecular View," 307–319.

14. These features are based on Johnson's review of the powerful-powerless talk literature. See Craig E. Johnson, "An Introduction," pp. 167–172.

15. Bradac and Mulac, "A Molecular View," 307–319; Erickson, Lind, Johnson, and O'Barr, 266–279; A. Siegman and B. Pope. "Effects of Question Specificity and Anxiety-Producing Messages on Verbal Fluency in the Initial Interview," *Journal of Personality and Social Psychology* 2 (1965): 522–530.

16. S. L. Ragan, "A Conversational Analysis of Alignment Talk in Job Interviews," in R. Bostron, ed., *Communication Yearbook 7* (Beverly Hills, CA: Sage Publishing, 1983), 502–516; C. Johnson, "Powerful and Powerless Forms of Talk, Status, Credibility, and Financial Awards" (doctoral dissertation, University of Denver). *Dissertation Abstracts International.* In publication.

17. See C. L. Berryman and J. R. Wilcox, "Attitudes Toward Male and Female Speech: Experiments of the Effects of Sex-Typical Language,"

Western Journal of Speech Communication 44 (1980): 50–59; N. Newcombe and D. B. Arnkoff, "Effects of Speech Style and Sex of Speaker on Person Perception," *Journal of Personality and Social Psychology* 37 (1979): 1293–1303; D. Siegler and R. Siegler, "Stereotypes of Males' and Females' Speech," *Psychological Reports* 39 (1976): 167–170.

18. Bradac and Mulac, "A Molecular View," 310; Erickson, Lind, Johnson, and O'Barr, 266–279.

19. Erickson, Lind, Johnson, and O'Barr, 266–279.

20. Bradley, 73–90; B. W. Eakins and R. G. Eakins, *Sex Differences in Human Communication* (Boston: Houghton Mifflin, 1978), 45; J. P. Hewitt and R. Stokes, "Disclaimers," *American Sociological Review* 40 (1975): 1–11; K. Warfel, "Gender Schemas and Perceptions of Speech Style," *Communication Monographs* 51 (1984): 253–267.

21. Warfel, 253–267; Bradley, 73–90.

22. C. Johnson, "An Introduction," 169.

23. I am indebted to Dominic A. Infante for the information in this section. See Dominic A. Infante, "Teaching Students to Understand and Control Verbal Aggression," *Communication Education,* 44 (1995): 51–63. Some of the language is exactly the same as Infante's. I have avoided using quotation marks for each quotation because they would intrude into the text and thus distract the reader.

24. D. A. Infante and C. J. Wigley, "Verbal Aggressiveness: An Interpersonal Model and Measure," *Communication Monographs* 53 (1986): 61–69.

25. See Dominic A. Infante, "Teaching Students to Understand" for the research citations that support these conclusions.

26. See D. A. Infante and W. I. Gorden, "Superiors' Argumentativeness and Verbal Aggressiveness as Predictors of Subordinates' Satisfaction," *Human Communication Research* 12 (1985): 117–125; D. A. Infante and W. I. Gorden, "Superior and Subordinate Communication Profiles: Implications for Independent-Mindedness and Upward Effectiveness," *Central States Speech Journal* 38 (1987): 73–80; D. A. Infante and W. I. Gorden, "Argumentativeness and Affirming Communicator Style as Predictors of Satisfaction/Dissatisfaction with Subordinates," *Communication Quarterly* 37 (1989): 81–90; D. A. Infante, and W. I. Gorden, "How Employees See the Boss: Test of an Argumentative and Affirming Model of Supervisors' Communicative Behavior," *Western Journal of Speech Communication* 55 (1991): 294–304.

27. See Dominic A. Infante, "Aggressiveness," in *Personal and Interpersonal Communication,* ed. J. C. McCroskey and J. A. Daly (Newbury Park, CA: Sage Publications, 1987): 157–192.

28. See D. A. Infante, J. D. Trebing, P. E. Shepherd, and D. E. Seeds, "The Relationship of Argumentativeness to Verbal Aggression," *The Southern Speech Communication Journal* 50 (1984): 67–77.

29. See Dominic A. Infante, "Arguing May Be Good for You," unpublished manuscript, Kent State University, 1983.

30. See D. A. Infante, B. L. Riddle, C. L. Horvath, and S. A. Tumlin, "Verbal Aggressiveness: Messages and Reasons," *Communication Quarterly* 40 (1992): 116–126.

31. See Infante, Trebing, Shepherd, and Seeds, 70. The authors cite Michael E. Roloff and Bradley S. Greenberg, "Sex Differences in Choice of Modes of Conflict Resolution in Real-Life and Television," *Communication Quarterly* 27 (1979): 3–12; A. Bennett Whaley, "Televised Violence and Related Variables as Predictors of Self-Reported Verbal Aggression," *Central States Speech Journal* 33 (1982): 490–497.

32. See D. A. Infante, "Motivation to Speak on a Controversial Topic: Value Expectancy, Sex Differences, and Implications," *Central States Speech Journal* 34 (1983): 96–103; cf. Michael Burgoon, James P. Dillard, and Noel E. Doran, "Friendly or Unfriendly Persuasion: The Effects of Violations of Expectations by Males and Females," *Human Communication Research* 10 (1983): 283–296.

33. See R. B. Felson, "Aggression as Impression Management," *Social Psychology* 41 (1978), 205–213; R. B. Felson, "Impression Management and the Escalation of Aggression and Violence," *Social Psychology Quarterly* 45 (1982): 245–254.

34. See M. A. Straus, "Leveling, Civility, and Violence in the Family," *Journal of Marriage and the Family* 36 (1974): 13–29.

35. For the research that supports all of these observations, please see Dominic A. Infante, "Teaching Students to Understand," 11.

36. See Infante, "Teaching Students," 13.

37. See. D. Kalmus, "The Intergenerational Transmission of Marital Aggression," *Journal of Marriage and the Family* 46 (1984): 11–19.

38. See K. D. O'Leary, J. Bargling, I. Arias, A. Rosenbaum, J. Malone, and A. Tyree, "Prevalence and Stability of Physical Aggression Between Spouses: A Longitudinal Analysis," *Journal of Consulting and Clinical Psychology* 57 (1989): 263–268.

39. See Infante, "Teaching Students," 15. Much evidence is supplied by Infante regarding abuse prevention programs based on communication skills that have been tested successfully with distressed and abusive couples.

40. See G. Margoline, "Conjoint Marital Therapy to Enhance Management and Reduce Spouse Abuse," *Journal of Family Therapy,* 7 (1979): 13–23.

41. See Infante, "Teaching Students," 20.

42. Because of the importance and potential effectiveness of this strategy, please see Infante's original explanation of this strategy: Dominic A. Infante, *Arguing Constructively.* (Prospect Heights, IL: Waveland Press, 1988).

43. Suzette Haden Elgin, *The Last Word on the Gentle Art of Verbal Self-Defense* (New York: Prentice Hall Press, 1987). See also Elgin, *Genderspeak: Men, Women, and the Gentle Art of Verbal Self-Defense* (New York: John Wiley & Sons, 1993), 91 and 286.

44. Edward P. J. Corbett, *Classical Rhetoric for the Modern Student* (New York: Oxford University Press, 1965), 6.

45. Elgin attributes this to George Miller. See "Giving Away Psychology in the 80's: George Miller Interviewed by Elizabeth Hall," *Psychology Today* 14 (January 1980): 46.

46. Elgin, p. 211.

47. See S. I. Hayakawa, *Language in Thought and Action,* p. 204.

48. Alfred Korzybski, *Science and Sanity: An Introduction to Non-Aristotelian Systems and General Semantics* (Lancaster, PA: Science Press Printing Co., 1933).

49. Hayakawa, p. 205.

▶ FURTHER READING

Michael Agar, *Language Shock: Understanding the Culture of Conversation* (New York: William Morrow, 1994). In this fascinating book, linguistic anthropologist Agar shows how people unconsciously bring their cultural differences to life through their everyday language. Agar shows readers how to find culture in language and how to pursue a different, richer point of view. Much insight here into the relationship of language, culture, and society. Exciting.

Elaine Chaika, *Language: The Social Mirror,* 3rd ed. (Boston, MA: Heinle & Heinle Publishers [A Division of Wadsworth, Inc.], 1994). In this excellent, engaging book, Chaika focuses on the ways in which language serves the needs of the individual and society. Some useful chapter topics include pragmatics, orality, dialect, speech communities, gender and language, and sociolinguistics and the professions. A well-researched textbook.

Suzette Haden Elgin, *The Gentle Art of Verbal Self-Defense* (1980), *More on the Gentle Art of Verbal Self-Defense* (1983), and *The Last Word on the Gentle Art of Verbal Self-Defense* (1987) (New York: Prentice Hall Press). The first book is an emergency first-aid manual that tells what to do when under verbal attack. The second extends the system developed in the first book beyond one-to-one interaction to other language situations. The third brings in a new set of verbal skills and offers ways to improve the entire language environment so that verbal abuse is abolished.

Patricia Evans, *The Verbally Abusive Relationship: How to Recognize it and How to Respond* (Holbrook, MA: Bob Adams, Inc., 1992). This is a useful, practical book that begins with a base for self-evaluation, then includes an examination of power, a look at the abusive relationship, a discussion of consequences of verbal abuse, characteristics and categories of abuse, how to ask for change, responding with impact, and, finally, chapters on recovery, looking back, and some of the underlying dynamics. Excellent examples.

S. I. Hayakawa and Alan R. Hayakawa, *Language in Thought and Action,* 5th ed. (San Diego, CA: Harcourt Brace Jovanovich, 1990). A classic book. Semantics is the study of human interaction through communication. The assumption of this book is that cooperation is preferable to conflict. The principles that Hayakawa explains relate to thinking, speaking, writing, and behavior. In this edition, all of the exercises have been placed in an "Appendix of Applications." These allow readers to explore the potential of language in action and thought. A readable book that provides a practical look at language.

Geneva Smitherman, *Black Talk: Words and Phrases from the Hood to Amen Corner* (Boston: Houghton Mifflin, 1994). This is an informal dictionary of terms and sayings of black speakers. Especially insightful is the author's 28-page introduction, which details the uniqueness of the AAE (African American Experience), patterns of AAE grammar and pronunciation, forces in nurturing AAE, dynamism and creativity in AAE, and historical perspective.

6

Communicating Without Words: Nonverbal Characteristics, Functions, Forms, and Types

▶ CHAPTER OBJECTIVES

After reading this chapter, you should be able to

- ▲ Frame a definition of nonverbal communication.
- ▲ Explain why our knowledge of nonverbal communication is incomplete.
- ▲ Describe how much nonverbal communication counts in the meaning of a social situation.
- ▲ Defend the importance of studying nonverbal communication.
- ▲ List and explain the six characteristics of nonverbal communication.
- ▲ List and explain the six functions of nonverbal communication.
- ▲ List and explain the five forms of nonverbal communication.
- ▲ Define and provide an example of each of the types of nonverbal cues.
- ▲ Understand the three cautions about reading the nonverbal cues of others.
- ▲ Improve your skills in nonverbal communication.

▼ Clarissa had a boss, Edwin, who talked in a monotone. When Edwin gave orders, emphasized ideas, or talked conversationally, all his talk was delivered at the same vocal level with no changes in pitch. As director of marketing, Clarissa was given three projects to work on by Edwin. They were given to her one after another, in a private conversation, in Edwin's office. Each project was likely to take a good deal of time. Clarissa often worked on several projects at the same time, but in this case, it was impossible for her to discover which project was most important, which deserved her immediate attention, or even which one Edwin felt would benefit the company most. Clarissa's difficulty in determining which project was most important occurred because she had difficulty sensing Edwin's vocal emphasis. Normally, Clarissa was interpersonally sensitive and easily able to determine priorities expressed by others—but not Edwin. As it turned out, a problem closely related to Clarissa's difficulty with his monotone was that Edwin was a boring conversationalist, a dull speaker, and an unenthusiastic supervisor, too.

Mario could not find out what his problem was, but it bothered him endlessly. Mario was 26 years old, a nontraditional college student just completing a degree in education, unmarried, and unsuccessful in relationships. Mario wanted a relationship, but his attempts at establishing relationships were unsuccessful. Noelle, Mario's last relationship partner, knew Mario's problems but never felt comfortable enough to let him know. Some of his problems were superficial; some were not. It wasn't really the superficial problems that pushed Noelle away but the serious ones. Mario broke nonverbal rules. For example, he would stand too close to others when he talked with them. Rather than look others in the eye, he would never make direct eye contact. Also, he talked too loud.

These characteristics embarrassed Noelle, but she tolerated them. But Noelle knew why Mario had difficulty meeting others. The more serious nonverbal problems, for Noelle, involved Mario's dress, cleanliness, and personal hygiene. Mario had no understanding of fashion or color and did not consider clothes to be important. He wore anything with anything else. Worse, however, he did not change his clothes regularly, and there always seemed to be an odor to them. Noelle thought his lack of clean clothes might be related to his unshaven appearance, teeth that looked stained, and greasy-looking hair. Perhaps Mario was better off single until his nonverbal concerns could be solved.

Leonardo was one of the most effective conversationalists Rosemary had ever heard. It wasn't necessarily what Leonardo said but how he said it that seemed to hold the attention of his listeners. When Leonardo was at a party, there was almost always a crowd around him. Why? Because he was so motivational and encouraging. He expressed his ideas with energy and conviction that were contagious. The flair and style with which he discussed and shared ideas made him not only well liked but sought after as well. Extroverted, poised, comfortable with others, well informed, and well liked, Leonardo had some of the most effective nonverbal communication Rosemary had ever witnessed, and he had numerous friends as well. Of all of the people she had come into contact with, Rosemary felt Leonardo was the most interpersonally effective.

There is no doubt about the importance and influence of nonverbal communication. Edwin's monotone not only influenced his interpersonal effectiveness but had a negative effect on all his communication. Mario's problems were more serious than Edwin's. Mario broke nonverbal rules considered by most to be important. Even those nonverbal rules—standing too close to others when talking with them, not giving direct eye contact, and talking too loud—are not nearly as important as improper dress, lack of cleanliness, and poor personal hygiene. Noelle was probably fortunate to have escaped that relationship early. Finally, a positive example: Leonardo, as observed by Rosemary, was a success because of his superior nonverbal ability.

In this chapter, a definition of nonverbal communication will be offered first. How much it counts will be discussed. In separate sections, then, some of its characteristics, functions, forms, and types will be examined. Finally, suggestions for improving skills in nonverbal communication are offered in the final section.

▲▲▲ *Definition*

Nonverbal communication *is any information or emotion communicated without using words—or nonlinguistically.* Nonverbal communication is important, as already demonstrated, because what you do often carries far more importance than what you say. The cliché that "a picture is worth a thousand words" suggests that the senses you use to pick up nonverbal cues are, indeed, different from those you use (and the information you gain from) words alone.

One of the reasons for this is that words, in general, trigger one set of senses (auditory—you hear them), while nonverbal communication may trigger several senses—visual, olfactory (smell), or gustatory (taste), to name a few. With several senses stimulated, it seems more likely that people will respond emotionally to nonverbal cues, while their reactions to the words alone are more likely to be rational. This same case can be made for right-brain and left-brain orientations. Nonverbal tends to be more right-brain or affective—emotional. Words tend to be more left-brain or cognitive—rational.

It should be clear, however, that our knowledge of nonverbal communication is *not* complete. The first treatment of nonverbal communication is found in the time of Aristotle, about 400 to 600 B.C.E., but contemporary nonverbal approaches can be traced to the work of Charles Darwin and his *The Expression of Emotions in Man and Animals*.[1] But, despite a large number of recent studies and approaches, we are still learning about the ways in which nonverbal communication affects people and about the differences between people in their ability both to convey nonverbal communication and to understand it. We are still learning, too, about the ways in which nonverbal communication matters in people's lives.

There are many reasons why our knowledge is incomplete. For example, in our society we tend to have a verbal orientation. In the thinking and training of children, successful communication often is linked with the effective use of words. This is one reason why research on nonverbal communication was slow to develop.

Other explanations exist as well. One is that different types of nonverbal communication are embedded in your daily behavior. You use them without being aware of them. This means, too, that you are less aware of nonverbal communication than verbal communication. You not only *use* nonverbal communication without being aware of it but make judgments based on nonverbal cues without being aware of the cues used. Edward Sapir, an anthropologist, captured this paradox as far back as 1949 when he said people could understand nonverbal communication because of "an elaborate and secret code that is written nowhere, known by none, and understood by all".[2] Research, study, and understanding have progressed considerably, of course, since 1949, but Sapir's point is still relevant. There is much yet to be known about nonverbal communication.

Another possible explanation of why our knowledge of nonverbal communication is incomplete involves methodological barriers—or how to study it. Think about it. Nonverbal communication is difficult to record, code, analyze, and reproduce. Even with the use of film and videotape, all the methodological problems have not been solved. And there is a related problem as well. Just think of the wide range of behaviors that are, in some way, nonverbal. Nonverbal cues interrelate much like the strands of a spider's web. It is the strands in relation to each other that give the final impression, no single strand standing by itself.

▲▲▲ How Much Does Nonverbal Communication Count?

It may be clear from the examples thus far that nonverbal communication is significant—it counts. But how much? Is it really important enough to research thoroughly, study closely, and understand completely (as completely as we can, of course)? In this section, how much nonverbal communication counts will be discussed. From this discussion, it should be clear that nonverbal communication supplies essential information for effective interpersonal communication. From this discussion, too, perhaps you will agree that it plays a central role in human behavior. All nonverbal researchers suggest that nonverbal factors are the *major* determinants of meaning in interpersonal contexts.

One researcher, Albert Mehrabian, a psychologist who focused on how liking is transmitted in messages, suggests that as much as 93 percent of the total impact of a message is due to nonverbal factors.[3] He estimates that in face-to-face interaction, the total message may be broken down like this:

38 percent of the meaning is VOCAL
55 percent of the meaning is FACIAL EXPRESSION
7 percent of the meaning is VERBAL

Although these figures may be a bit high, they underscore the impact of nonverbal communication. Ray Birdwhistell, an early researcher in the area, suggested that nonverbal communication accounts for at least 65 to

CONSIDER THIS

What are the ethical responsibilities of those using or receiving nonverbal communication? The answer is not clear, but the questions are numerous. Read the questions posed by Richard Johannesen, a writer on ethics, and then answer the questions that follow.

> Do the ethical standards commonly applied to verbal communication apply equally as appropriately to nonverbal elements in communication? Should there be a special ethic for nonverbal communication in place of, or in addition to, the ethical criteria for assessing human use of language? For instance, what ethical standards should govern eye contact, facial expression, tone of voice, or gestures? How should the ethics of silence be judged? In television news coverage or political advertisements, what ethical standards should govern editing out of material, camera angles, or lighting of a person's face as they stimulate accurate or inaccurate meanings and impressions in the viewer?*

Questions
1. Do the questions that Johannesen raises create any questions in your mind? What are they?
2. Do you think there are some universal kinds of ethical standards that every communicator should follow, no matter what kind of communication or interaction is taking place? Yes or No?
3. If you were in charge of developing ethical standards for all of communication, what would they be? How might they be enforced?

*From Richard L. Johannesen, *Ethics in Human Communication,* 3rd ed. (Prospect Heights, IL: Waveland Press, 1990), p. 127.

70 percent of what we communicate to one another.[4] What he actually said was that "probably no more than 30 to 35 percent of the social meaning of a conversation or an interaction is carried by the words."[5] His figures seem more reasonable; however, the point is that nonverbal communication counts a great deal.

The statistics are important, but nonverbal communication can be shown to count in other ways as well. There are at least five reasons why nonverbal communication counts so much in your life. These five reasons

Can you see the contribution nonverbal communication makes to your knowledge of another person's emotions and feelings? What do you think the emotions being expressed here mean?

relate to (1) emotions and feelings, (2) deception, distortion, and confusion, (3) high-quality communication, (4) highly efficient communication, and (5) suggestion.

Emotions and feelings Nonverbal communication is your richest source of knowledge about emotions and feelings. Feelings and emotions are more accurately exchanged by nonverbal means than by verbal means, and the nonverbal cues are reliable and stable indicators of the emotions and feelings being conveyed.

Deception, distortion, and confusion Nonverbal communication conveys meanings and intentions that are relatively free of deception, distortion, and confusion. Because most of your nonverbal communication is natural, comfortable, and automatic, it is rarely under your sustained, conscious control. Words are what you use to conceal, distort, confuse, and deceive.

High-quality communication Nonverbal communication is indispensable in attaining high-quality communication. In this capacity, nonverbal cues serve a paralinguistic function. **Paralanguage** *includes all the nonlanguage means of vocal expression, such as rate, pitch, and tone.* An example will clarify paralanguage. Just before going out, Maria asks you, "Well, how do I look?" In this situation, you know that Maria will be looking for all the possible cues to be able to interpret your response. If you say, "Maria, you look *great*!" which is a likely response, how you say that can reveal enthusiasm and support—or it can reveal that you feel Maria looks great if she is going to a circus and is the opening act! It is not *what* you say; it is *how* you say it. And the *how* is conveyed by paralanguage.

Highly efficient communication   Often, nonverbal communication represents a much more efficient means of communicating than verbal cues. Verbal discourse is highly inefficient. Standard qualities of verbal communication are redundancy, repetition, ambiguity, and abstraction. These qualities are important at times, but they assure that the communication will be inefficient.

To reveal high efficiency, think of the thumbs-up signal flashed by someone to represent victory, the signal "I love you" from a loved one across a crowded room, or the preplanned signal "It's time to leave" by a friend involved in a boring conversation. Nonverbal communication possesses much greater potential for efficiency than verbal communication.

Suggestion   Nonverbal communication represents the most suitable vehicle for suggestion. Often, you want to express your emotions *indirectly* rather than directly. Let's say you meet another person you would like to get to know better. And yet, because you do not know the other person, you would rather test the water. How do you do it? By flirting—or by making nonverbal suggestions of your intent. **Suggestion** *is the process whereby you imply what you mean but never commit it to words.* That way, if you are caught flirting, you can deny it. Words are more permanent; nonverbal communication is not. In this way you avoid negative psychological consequences. You protect your ego and self-image.

▲▲▲ Characteristics

Most nonverbal cues share certain characteristics in common. Here, six will be discussed. Nonverbal communication (1) is continuous, (2) is rich in meaning, (3) can be confusing, (4) conveys emotions, (5) is guided by norms and rules of appropriateness, and (6) is culture-bound.

Nonverbal Communication Is Continuous

Your words come out one at a time; your nonverbal cues come out continuously. As an example, let's say someone asked you a question. Regardless of how you responded, the person who asked you the question may look for clues to your reaction. Whether you speak or not, he or she may look closely at your face, body (movement or posture), and voice. These are the signals that are used as a foundation for understanding your response. The point is that you send *and* receive nonverbal messages in an uninterrupted, persistent flow. And while you are observing someone else's gestures and mannerisms, that person also may be observing yours.

Nonverbal Communication Is Rich in Meaning

Think of the last time you went to the doctor when you had certain symptoms but did not know what your illness was. You probably listened as the doctor mystified and perhaps terrified you by using polysyllabic technical terms to describe your disorder. But what did you do? You watched the doctor's face very carefully to see if you could detect how sick you really were. How did the doctor *say* the words? What kind of sounds like "Hmm-m-m" or "Aha!" could you detect? In such situations, you look for even the most minute nonverbal signs to interpret—especially when you cannot understand the verbal signs. There is even a field known as *iatrogenics,* which is, in part, "the study of how doctor-talk can intensify and even induce illness."[6]

Consider how the slightest sound or the most delicate movement can be fraught with meaning. Put these sounds and movements together into the larger context in which they occur, and you realize how rich nonverbal communication can be. A raised eyebrow, a sly smile, a touch of the hand can all say a lot in the right circumstances. Such nonverbal cues are especially useful when for some reason oral or written communication is inappropriate—during a concert or a lecture, perhaps, or even a movie. Nonverbal communication can be rich with meaning.

Nonverbal Communication Can Be Confusing

Although nonverbal communication may be rich with meaning, it can also be confusing. Certain cues may mean something entirely different from what you imagine. A man may be sitting on a sofa next to a woman with his legs crossed away from the woman. "Aha, obviously he has no interest in her since his legs are crossed away from her," the enthusiastic reader of nonverbal communication might think; "he is excluding her." Not necessarily. Some people *always* cross their legs right over left, no matter what. It's their habit, it's comfortable, and it doesn't mean a thing as far as nonverbal communication goes (except perhaps to show that they feel at ease in the situation). This may be a good place to point out the difference between behavior (that which occurs naturally and automatically) and communication (that which occurs with purpose and intent).

You can't assume that a woman with her arms folded in front of her is close-minded and rigid—she may simply feel cold! You must be careful in interpreting nonverbal cues. You do not always have enough information to make a judgment, and your guesses may be far from accurate.

Nonverbal Communication Conveys Emotions

When you think of it, objects and actions can generate more emotion than words because objects and actions are less abstract than words. Words usually exert a more intellectual appeal. To hear that someone cried or was injured is not nearly as powerful as seeing that person cry or get hurt. If you want to convey sincerity, your facial and bodily gestures can probably do it more effectively than your words, although words *reinforced* by nonverbal cues will convey the most unmistakable message.

Since nonverbal cues are so closely tied to the emotions, how well you understand nonverbal messages depends on how empathic you are. Everything I have said earlier about empathic listening applies here as well. The empathic, alert perceiver is very likely to understand (or at least be aware of) nonverbal cues. Understanding verbal expression requires more skill. Nonverbal expression, learned much earlier and often closely tied to universal human emotions, is sometimes easier to attach meaning to, even though that meaning may be less than perfectly accurate.

Nonverbal Communication Is Guided by Norms and Rules of Appropriateness

On some sidewalks in downtown Brisbane, Australia, there is a red brick division embedded in the cement that divides the sidewalks into halves. At one time in the state of Queensland, where Brisbane is, a law stated that pedestrians must keep to the left of the line or be fined. In Australia, walkers and drivers keep to the left, as they do in Britain. Most nonverbal communication is not governed by specific laws; however, the system of **norms and rules** that *tell us what is appropriate, expected, or permissible in social situations* may be just as specific as if it were law. The norms and rules, though, vary greatly from culture to culture.

You learn most of the norms and rules early from parental or family guidance. Some of them you learn from observing others. Some, too, you learn from errors and failures and subsequent punishment (negative reinforcement). You learn, for example, not to interrupt when someone else is talking, not to criticize another person in public, and not to use vulgar language around members of the opposite sex. You learn that touching another person is permissible under certain circumstances and not under others. You learn to maintain direct eye contact with certain people; reveal some eye contact, yet not too much, with others; and, when volunteers are asked for answers in class and you don't know the answer, avoid all eye contact with the instructor. Some instructors accept this nonverbal signal as a reason for calling on a student. (The signal is already well known.)

The point here is not to offer a list of norms and rules. It would be almost endless. The point, rather, is to indicate that most nonverbal behavior is governed by norms and rules. Unaware of the norms and rules, one can appear crude, rude, or ignorant. It's like inviting important people over for a meal and not knowing how to seat a proper table. The suggestions made in the next "Try This" can assist here. The suggestions work when norms and rules are not known. Many of these vary with the context and with the occasion. Effective communicators proceed slowly and with caution to help assure success. In setting a table, slowness and caution make no difference; one must simply learn how to do it correctly.

Nonverbal Communication Is Culture-Bound

Although this is the sixth and final characteristic of nonverbal communication, it is, perhaps, the most important of the six. Culture is essentially a nonverbal phenomenon.[7] That is, most aspects of our culture are learned through observation and imitation rather than through explicit verbal instruction. And, what is more, much of what we learn is communicated implicitly, without awareness. "Nonverbal behavior communicates the beliefs, attitudes, and values of cultures to others."[8] That is why most people are not aware of their own nonverbal behavior. It "is enacted mindlessly, spontaneously, and unconsciously."[9] But it is precisely because of this that often it is difficult to identify and master the nonverbal communication of another culture. It is the reason, too, why many people feel uncomfortable in other cultures. We just know that something doesn't fit right.[10]

It should be clear that cultural differences can be discovered with respect to every type of nonverbal behavior from appearance to gesture and movement, face and eye behavior, vocal behavior, space, touch, environment, scent, and time. With respect to appearance, what is attractive in one culture is not likely to be attractive in another. "If one does not look like they belong to the culture, they will not be listened to, will not be able to persuade others, and many times will not be able to successfully communicate with others. Anyone who does not fit the physical norm of the culture will have trouble communicating in that culture."[11] The clear conclusion is this: "Culture is one of the most enduring, powerful, and invisible shapers of our behavior."[12]

▲▲▲ Functions of Nonverbal Communication

It is easy to think that nonverbal communication has a life of its own, independent of the verbal communication often occurring at the same time. In most cases they are not functioning independently of each other; both are likely to be operating as you send and receive messages. Nonverbal communication serves six functions.[27]

TRY THIS

Here are fourteen specific skills you can apply next time you are facing an intercultural-communication situation.

1. *Prepare yourself.* If you know about your travels in advance, read books and brochures, arrange to meet people who have traveled there, take courses, and ask questions before you go.
2. *Develop self-awareness.* Become more sensitive to aspects of your own behavior that are often invisible and taken for granted. Expose and challenge your behavior through the study of other cultures and actual intercultural encounters.[13]
3. *Observe behaviors.* Much of intercultural sensitivity comes from observation.[14]
4. *Share interaction.* Engage people from other cultures in speaking, listening, and turn-taking.[15]
5. *Reserve judgment.* Be careful in the attributions made about the nonverbal communication of people from other cultures. Judgments often are wrong.[16] People cannot be read like books; thus, you should be nonjudgmental and avoid evaluative statements.[17]
6. *Communicate respect and positive regard.*[18] Such an attitude is likely to attract rather than repel others and may bring with it the opportunities to learn and appreciate. This reduces ethnocentrism and makes strangers from other cultures less threatening.[19]
7. *Display empathy.* Try to see things from others' viewpoints and cultural backgrounds.[20]
8. *Tolerate ambiguity.* Try to cope patiently with the cultural barriers imposed by both verbal and nonverbal communication.[21]
9. *Personalize your knowledge.* Understand that your own values, beliefs, attitudes, and experiences are all relative and culture-bound. They are not absolute.[22]
10. *Be flexible.* Understand how other people's roles, social stratifications, and communication practices are likely to affect their communication.[23]
11. *Maintain emotional control.* Because the nonverbal behaviors differ in other cultures, they may make us emotionally insecure. This may occur, especially, when others touch or bump us or try to stand to close to us.[24]

12. *Ask questions.* Most people are not offended when you ask questions. When people do things that puzzle you, ask them why they are acting in that manner. Or, if you think you acted incorrectly, ask people what seems appropriate or what you did wrong. Only by asking will you learn.[25]

13. *Take risks.* Most people are unwilling to try new foods, enjoy new sounds, or experience new environments. Be positive about cultural differences. Only when you are willing to take risks will you begin to appreciate more of what our world is all about.[26]

14. *Acknowledge errors.* Realize that you will make mistakes, violate rules, or break norms. Learn from them, try to avoid them in the future, and maintain a sense of humor at these times.

What is interesting about putting into use these fourteen skills is that they are often the same kinds of skills you need to adopt and use to approach anyone who is not like you.

1. **Redundancy:** *it may say the same thing as the words.* You may compliment a person by saying, "That was well done," and yet your touch of their shoulder, smile, and nod of the head may convey the same message. In a noisy restaurant you might shout out *two* orders of fries and hold up two fingers as well. In both cases, the nonverbal repetition increases the accuracy of the communication.

2. **Substitution:** *it may take the place of words.* There are definite and specific nonverbal cues used instead of words. The hitchhiking sign is one; the thumbs-up sign is another. At a movie theater, you might be asked how many tickets you want, and you raise four fingers. In high-context situations, like relationships, those signals discussed earlier that are used to say "I love you" or "It's time to leave" would be further examples.

But the signals can be more complex than this. For example, Albert Mehrabian suggests that pleasure-displeasure, arousal-nonarousal, and dominance-submissiveness are expressed through nonverbal communication.[28] Sometimes you do not realize that being happy, pleased, or satisfied is likely to reveal pleasure; activity and alertness are likely to reveal arousal; or control, influence, or importance may reveal dominance.

3. **Complementation:** *it may supplement or modify the words.* Nonverbal behaviors can add more details to the verbal message. In this case, however, the details are neither identical to, nor a replacement for, the verbal message. For example, when a person is terribly excited about an event that just took place, his or her rate of speaking may be rapid, gestures may be hurried and active, and facial expression may be animated and expressive. The nonverbal communication adds to the verbal explanation of the event and makes the explanation more vivid and interesting. Also, the nonverbal cues reveal how the communicator feels about the event.

4. Emphasis: *it may accentuate or punctuate the verbal message.* The voice is often used for this. You change your pitch or rate to emphasize a point. A speaker may strike the lectern with a clenched fist to reveal the importance of an idea. Notice how effectively many comedians use the long pause after a joke to let it sink in and gain the laugh.

5. Contradiction: *it may conflict with the verbal message.* For example, you say you are not nervous, yet your hands are cold and clammy and the paper you are holding is trembling. Of course, lie detector tests work off this concept. Or, you say that it doesn't make *any* difference to you at all, and yet you leave the room and slam the door after you. In these cases, the nonverbal behaviors are likely to override the verbal meaning. This is true because nonverbal behaviors, as explained previously, are less likely to be consciously controlled.

Nonverbal behaviors can create confusion, too, when they do not *seem* to agree with the words. This is especially true in the use of sarcasm. "Nice play, Robert!" when said in a sarcastic tone will be perceived negatively. But children are more likely to believe the words.[29] Perhaps it is because they have just begun to use the words; perhaps, it is simply naiveté. That is, they have not yet learned to detect sarcasm.

What are the ways you have of discovering cultural differences? Would cultural differences come into play in a group situation such as this?

CONSIDER THIS

Nonverbal communication has received attention with respect to political correctness. Some current signs used by 500,000 people to communicate with the deaf are being updated because they are considered stereotypical and insensitive (*not* politically correct). Read the following excerpt from *USA Today* and answer the questions that follow.

> The sign for Japanese was a twist of the little finger at the corner of the eye, denoting a slanted eye. But the new, multicultural-friendly sign, taken directly from Japanese Sign Language, is a hand signal to show the shape of the Japanese islands.
>
> Until recently, the sign for African-American was flattening the nose with the index finger. The new sign is also geographical, indicating a map of Africa.*

Questions

1. What is a communicator's responsibility with respect to political correctness? Should it be "Let the buyer (receiver) beware," or do communicators have a responsibility?

2. How far do you think political correctness should extend? Do you think the people of the world are becoming too sensitive?

3. The writer went on to note that the sign for *gay,* which used to be a limp wrist, has been changed to spelling out the word *gay* or placing the sign for the letter "g" on the chin. Does it become sexist to indicate whether or not a person is male or female?

4. Should political correctness in our country lead or follow that of other countries? In Japanese Sign Language, the sign for *foreigner* is the index finger making a circular motion around the eye, denoting "round eye."

*From Cathy Hainer, "A Sensitive Gesture from Sign Language," USA Today (August 23, 1994), p. 1D.

6. Regulation: *it may regulate the flow of verbal interaction.* What is it that tells you, during a conversation, when it is your turn to speak? Is it eye contact? Is it the other person's vocal pitch? Is it his or her gestures? You use many different nonverbal cues to tell others when to talk and when to be quiet. You use them, too, to maintain the smoothness of the conversation, to eliminate long pauses in conversations, to change topics, and even to end the conversation altogether. The point is, they serve a valuable function in regulating the flow of interaction.

▲▲▲ *Forms of Nonverbal Communication*

Nonverbal elements, as already noted, sometimes work separately from verbal communication; that is, you may receive a nonverbal message without any words whatsoever. But usually the nonverbal domain provides a framework for the words you use. If you think of nonverbal communication as including all forms of message transmission *not* represented by word symbols, you can divide it into five broad categories: emblems, illustrators, affect displays, regulators, and adaptors.[30]

In their early work in this area, Jurgen Ruesch and Weldon Kees outlined just three categories: sign, action, and object language.[31] **Sign language** *includes gestures used in the place of words, numbers, or punctuation.* When an athlete raises his index finger to show his team is "Number One," he is using sign language. **Action language** *includes all those nonverbal movements not intended as signs.* Your way of walking, sitting, or eating may serve your personal needs, but they also make statements to those who see them. **Object language** *includes both the intentional and unintentional display of material things.* Your hairstyle, glasses, and jewelry reveal things about you, as do the books you carry, the car you drive, or the clothes you wear.[32]

These early categories have been subsumed in a classification system developed by Ekman and Friesen (1969). The advantage of their classification system is that it permits further divisions and, thus, more accurate classification of nonverbal behavior. Also, it reflects the writing and research that has been done since Ruesch and Kees—much of it generated from the base they provided.

Emblems

Emblems are similar to Ruesch and Kees's sign language. They *have a direct verbal translation,* usually a word or a phrase.[33] Many of these are culture specific; that is, they are known or recognized by members of a particular culture or historical period only. Hand gestures indicating "A-OK" or "Victory" (popularized by Winston Churchill during World War II) are examples of emblems. Although most emblems are produced with the hands, a facial expression such as a nose-wrinkle that says "I'm disgusted" or "It stinks!" also qualifies as an emblem. Shaking the head might represent "No more!" or "No, thank you." Slouched posture could represent "I'm not interested" or "Count me out." Think of the emblems you use to indicate "Okay," "It's hot," "Tastes good," "Whoopee," "Gossip," or "I don't know."

Illustrators

Illustrators are similar to Ruesch and Kees's action language. *Illustrators are nonverbal cues directly tied to speech.* They serve to illustrate what is being said in words. Think of all the movements you use to accent, emphasize, or reinforce your conversations: gestures, bodily action, even emblems. Used in context, these emblems are illustrators because their primary intention is to reinforce (not substitute for) verbal communication. Yitong slammed his fist against the table when he said, "I think that is wrong!" Tazha paused, then said very slowly, "But Al, I just don't want a serious relationship at this time." Tim is one of those people who talks with his hands. Someone once said of him, "If you tied Tim's hands behind him, he'd fall silent."

Affect Displays

Affect displays *are all those nonverbal cues that reveal your affective—or feeling—state.* These are primarily facial cues since the main way we reveal our feelings to others is through facial expressions. Luiz's smile turned sour when he actually saw the grade he received on his exam. Tina knew her evening was going to be rough when she saw Jamal's face. Jamal had gone for a job interview earlier in the day, and Tina knew by looking at his face that it hadn't gone well. The students sensed it was going to be a long class period when their normally jovial instructor came into class looking serious and determined. However, you may reveal affect displays with other parts of the body, too. The face may give the first sign of sadness, but a drooping, slouched posture may confirm it.

Regulators

Regulators *are nonverbal cues that regulate the give-and-take of speaking and listening.* The most commonly used regulators are those that occur in normal conversations. These regulators are associated with turn-taking.[34] When you are talking to others, you use specific cues to let them know you want to talk, to keep them from talking, or to show them you are finished talking. Most of these are nonverbal cues such as head nods, eye behavior, and inflection. In talking with Ron, you find that he gets his comments into the conversation by raising his voice slightly. Gabrielle dips her head and looks directly at the other person when it's that person's time to talk. Ed raises his voice at the end of his last sentence when the other person is supposed to talk. Sheela uses rapid head nods to indicate "Hurry up." Marcus's head nods are slow and deliberate and emphasize others' points as they are presented, thus conveying, "I like what you're saying."

Adaptors

Adaptors *are objects manipulated for a purpose.* They are related to Ruesch and Kees's object language. When objects like pencils, cigarettes, and glasses are manipulated for a purpose, they become adaptors. Other objects we exert control over include our clothing, hairstyle, and, to a certain degree, our body shape. Darnell normally dresses very casually, but today he is wearing a three-piece suit, manipulating the clothing he is wearing to make a good impression on the company representatives who are conducting employment interviews. Anyone who knows Carmela knows that whenever she gets nervous or upset she lights a cigarette. Jim controls his mood by the way he dresses. On days when he feels down, he can improve his mood by dressing up, getting somewhat the same feeling a soldier or a police officer may get when he or she puts on a uniform.

But adaptors include more than the manipulation of objects. Ekman and Friesen have also identified self- and alter-directed adaptors. **Self-adaptors** *are manipulations of your own body by scratching, rubbing, pinching, picking, holding, squeezing, and touching.* **Alter-adaptors** *are giving and taking from others, attacking and protecting, establishing closeness and withdrawing.* Think, for example, of how you indicate to others that you disagree with an idea that has been mentioned, that you want to terminate a conversation, or that you are interested in pursuing a more intimate relationship.[35]

▲▲▲ Types of Nonverbal Cues

You now have a definition of nonverbal communication, you know how much nonverbal communication counts, you understand the characteristics most nonverbal cues share, and you know the functions and forms, now it is time to examine the types of nonverbal cues. In this section, spatial cues, visual cues, vocal cues, touch, time, and silence will be discussed.

Spatial Cues

Spatial cues are the distances we choose to stand or sit from others. Each of us carries with us something called informal space. We might think of this as a bubble; we occupy the center of the bubble. This bubble expands or contracts depending on varying conditions and circumstances such as these:

- ▲ Age and sex of those involved.
- ▲ Cultural and ethnic background of the participants.

CONSIDER THIS

There are clear gender differences in the area of nonverbal communication. Read this summary of some of these by Julia T. Wood, a writer on gender communication, and then answer the questions that follow.

> Men and women learn different styles of nonverbal interaction. Social definitions of women as deferential, decorative, and relationship-centered are reinforced through nonverbal communication that emphasizes their appearance, limits their space, and defines them as touchable. Views of men as independent, powerful, and in control are reflected in nonverbal behaviors that accord them larger territories and greater normative rights to invade others by entering their space and touching them. Consistent with how nonverbal communication defines men and women are differences in how they use it. While women tend to embody femininity by being soft-spoken, condensing space and yielding territory, and being facially responsive, men are likely to command space and volume, defend their turf, and adopt impassive facial expressions to keep feelings camouflaged.*

Questions
1. How do you think these different styles of nonverbal interaction are learned?
2. Have you discovered examples that would confirm aspects of Wood's summary, or does your experience disconfirm what she has written above?
3. Are these differences beneficial? In what ways? Detrimental? In what ways?
4. Why is it important to understand differences between genders in their nonverbal communication?

*From Julia T. Wood, *Gendered Lives: Communication, Gender, and Culture* (Belmont, CA: Wadsworth, 1994), p. 173.

▲ Topic or subject matter.
▲ Setting for the interaction.
▲ Physical characteristics of the participants (size or shape).
▲ Attitudinal and emotional orientation of partners.
▲ Characteristics of the interpersonal relationship (like friendship).
▲ Personality characteristics of those involved.[36]

In his book *The Silent Language,* Edward T. Hall, a cultural anthropologist, identifies the distances that people assume when they talk with others. He calls these distances intimate, personal, social, and public.[37] In many cases, the adjustments that occur in these distances result from some of the factors listed above.

Intimate distance   At an **intimate distance** (0 to 18 inches), you often use a soft or barely audible whisper to share intimate or confidential information. Physical contact becomes easy at this distance. This is the distance you use for physical comforting, lovemaking, and physical fighting, among other things.

Personal distance   Hall identified the range of 18 inches to 4 feet as **personal distance.** When you disclose yourself to someone, you are likely to do it within this distance. The topics you discuss at this range may be somewhat confidential and usually are personal and mutually involving. At personal distance you are still able to touch another if you want to. This is likely to be the distance between people conversing at a party, between classmates in a casual conversation, or within many work relationships. This distance assumes a well-established acquaintanceship. It is probably the most comfortable distance for free exchange of feedback.

Social distance   When you are talking at a normal level with another person, sharing concerns that are not of a personal nature, you usually use the **social distance** (4 to 12 feet). Many of your on-the-job conversations take place at this distance. Seating arrangements in living rooms may be based on "conversation groups" of chairs placed at a distance of 4 to 7

TRY THIS

Would you like to know the size of "bubble" that a friend of yours carries around as his or her personal space? The next time you are involved in a conversation with your friend, get into a position where you are directly facing each other and there is nothing behind him or her. Then, as you talk, *slowly* inch closer and closer. As you infringe on the "bubble," your friend may begin to move backward. As the movement just begins, notice the size of the personal space that your friend is protecting. To test your perception of the size of the "bubble," *slowly* move closer yet. What distance did you find most comfortable for a casual conversation?

*What is the distance be-
ing used by these two
women? Is it an appro-
priate distance for what
they are doing? Can you
imagine them using one
of the other distances for
transacting this busi-
ness?*

feet from each other. Hall calls 4 to 7 feet the close phase of social distance; from 7 to 12 feet is the far phase of social distance.

The greater the distance, the more formal the business or social discourse conducted is likely to be. Often, the desks of important people are
broad enough to hold visitors at a distance of 7 to 12 feet. Eye contact at
this distance becomes more important to the flow of communication;
without visual contact one party is likely to feel shut out and the conversation may come to a halt.

Public distance **Public distance** (12 feet and farther) is well outside the
range for close involvement with another person. It is impractical for interpersonal communication. You are limited to what you can see and hear
at that distance; topics for conversation are relatively impersonal and formal; and most of the communication that occurs is in the public-speaking
style, with subjects planned in advance and limited opportunities for
feedback.

Hall points out that his distances are based on his own observations
of middle-class people native to the northeastern United States and employed in business and professional occupations. You should be cautious
about extending his generalizations to other regional, social, vocational,
and ethnic groups.

The important point about intimate, personal, social, and public distance is that space communicates. Your sense of what distance is natural for you for a specific kind of interaction is deeply ingrained in you by our culture. You automatically make spatial adjustments and interpret spatial cues. Can you imagine, for example, talking to one of your professors at the intimate distance? What would your most intimate friend say if you maintained the social distance for an entire evening? Try talking to people you interact with daily at a public distance. Becoming aware of how you and other people use space will improve your communication.

Let's look briefly at some of the factors that may affect how close you sit or stand to someone. The distance is likely to be dependent on both social norms and the idiosyncratic (unique) patterns of those interacting.[38] You are likely to stand closer to a member of the opposite sex than to one of the same sex.[39] There may be distance shifts during an encounter, too, because of topic changes or beginnings and endings.[40] How pleasant, neutral, or unpleasant the topic being discussed is to the participants may also affect distance.[41]

When a topic is pleasant, people stand or sit closer together. Also, one research study indicates that close distances may decrease the amount of talking between the partners.[42] There is little doubt that social setting can make a great deal of difference in the spatial relationships, too. The amount of space available may be a factor, as well as the light, noise, and temperature. The physical characteristics of the people involved may cause changes in distance; for example, a short person and the captain of the basketball team will not have a very comfortable conversation if they stand too close to each other. Attitudinal and emotional orientations also have an important effect on distance. Wouldn't you choose to stand closer to someone you thought was friendly and farther from one you were told was unfriendly? When you see a group of people standing close together as they talk, you perceive them as being warmer, more empathic and understanding, and liking one another more.[43] It follows, then, that you interact more closely with friends than with acquaintances, and more closely with acquaintances than with strangers.[44] Closer distances are perceived, too, when people have a high self-concept and high affiliative needs (needs to associate with others), are low on authoritarianism, and are self-directed.[45]

Visual Cues

Greater visibility increases your potential for communicating because the more you see and the more you can be seen, the more information you can send and receive. Mehrabian found that the more you direct your face toward the person you're talking to, the more you convey a positive feeling to this person.[46] Another researcher has confirmed something most of you discovered long ago, that looking directly at a person, smiling, and leaning toward him or her conveys a feeling of warmth.[47]

Facial expression The face is probably the most expressive part of the human body. It can reveal complex and often confusing kinds of information. It commands attention because it is visible and omnipresent. It can move from signs of ecstasy to signs of despair in less than a second. Research results suggest that there are ten basic classes of meaning that can be communicated facially: happiness, surprise, fear, anger, sadness, disgust, contempt, interest, bewilderment, and determination.[48] Research also has shown that the face may communicate information other than the emotional state of the person—it may reveal the thought processes as well.[49] In addition, it has been shown that you are capable of facially conveying not just a single emotional state but multiple emotions at the same time.

The face can communicate more emotional meanings more accurately than any other factor in interpersonal communication. Dale G. Leathers has determined that the face

1. communicates *evaluative* judgments through pleasant and unpleasant expressions.
2. reveals level of *interest* or lack of interest in others and in the environment.
3. can exhibit level of *intensity* and thus show how involved you are in a situation.
4. communicates the amount of *control* you have over your own expressions.
5. shows whether or not you *understand* something.[51]

Because faces are so visible and so sensitive, you pay more attention to people's faces than to any other nonverbal feature. The face is an efficient and high-speed means of conveying meaning. Gestures, posture, and larger body movements require some time to change in response to a changing stimulus, whereas facial expressions can change instantly, sometimes even at a rate imperceptible to the human eye. As an instantaneous response mechanism, it is *the* most effective way to provide feedback to an ongoing message. This is the process of using the face as a regulator.

People seem to judge facial expression along these dimensions: pleasant/unpleasant, active/passive, and intense/controlled. It has also been shown that no single area of the face is best for revealing emotions. For any particular emotion, however, certain areas of the face may carry important information. For example, the nose-cheek-mouth area is crucial for conveying disgust, the eyes and eyelids for fear, the brows-forehead and eyes-eyelids for sadness, and the cheeks-mouth and brows-forehead for happiness. Surprise, it has been shown, can be seen in any of these areas.[52] The research has also confirmed that judgments of emotion from facial behavior are more accurate.[53]

Eye contact A great deal can be conveyed through the eyes. If you seek feedback from another person, you usually maintain strong eye contact. You can open and close communication channels with your eyes as well. Think of a conversation involving more than two people. When you are interested in a certain person's opinion, you will look him or her in the eye, opening the channel for communication. If you are having difficulty finding the right words to say, you may break eye contact. You not only signal your degree of involvement or arousal through eye contact but you use eye contact to check on how other people are responding. Have they completed a thought unit? Are they attentive? What are their reactions?

Eye contact may be hard to maintain if you are too close to someone. You can use your eyes to create anxiety in another person. Eye contact also can show whether you feel rewarded by what you see, whether you are in competition with another person, or whether you have something to hide. Your eye-contact habits may differ depending on the sex and status of the person you're talking to (we will discuss sex and status influences in a moment). In addition, if you are extroverted, your eye behavior is likely to be different than if you are introverted.[54]

Of all facial cues, eye contact is perhaps the single most important one. The fact that our culture has imposed so many rules regarding its use shows its significance. Think about your own patterns of eye contact. What rules do you follow? Until a certain age, children are rarely uncomfortable staring or being stared at. How long can you maintain eye contact with someone before it starts to feel awkward to you? It has been observed that as two people who do not wish to speak to each other approach, they will cast their eyes downward when they are about 8 feet apart so that they don't have to look at each other as they pass. Goffman calls this "dimming your lights."[55] Eye contact can have a major impact on both the quality and quantity of interpersonal communication.[56]

Eye contact often indicates the nature of the relationship between two people. One research study showed that eye contact is moderate when one is addressing a very high-status person, maximized when addressing a moderate high-status person, and only minimal when talking to a low-status person.[57] There are also predictable differences in eye contact when one person likes another or when there may be rewards involved.

Increased eye contact is also associated with increased liking between the people who are communicating. In an interview, for example, you are likely to make judgments about the interviewer's friendliness according to the amount of eye contact shown. The less eye contact, the less friendliness.[58] In a courtship relationship, more eye contact can be observed between those wishing to develop a more intimate relationship.[59] One research study suggests that intimacy is a function of the amount of eye gazing, physical proximity, intimacy of topic, and amount of smiling.[60] This model best relates to established relationships. It could also include body orientation, forms of address, tone of voice, facial ex-

TRY THIS

In your next conversation with others, keep track of your eye contact. Which of the following motives for eye contact are you most aware of using? Does it depend on the other person? Does it depend on what you are talking about? Does it depend on the context? What other factors about the communication situation affect the kind of eye contact you use?

▲ monitoring the feedback
▲ regulating the flow of the communication
▲ expressing your emotions
▲ communicating the nature of the interpersonal relationship

Do you usually combine these as you talk? Are they ever used independently of each other?

pression, or other factors.[61] All the factors interact; a change in one causes changes in the others.

The body The body reinforces facial communication. But gestures, postures, and other body movements can also communicate attitudes. They can reveal differences in status, and they can also indicate deception. With respect to attitudes, as noted previously, body movements also reveal feelings of liking between people.[62]

According to some investigators, a person who wants to be perceived as warm should shift his or her posture toward the other person, smile, maintain direct eye contact, and keep the hands still. People who are cold tend to look around, slump, drum their fingers, and generally refrain from smiling.

When a male or female in our society engages in courtship, he or she reveals this attitude, according to one researcher, through a category of behaviors. The first stage is **courtship readiness.** This stage is characterized by high muscle tone, reduced eye bagginess and jowl sag, lessening of slouch and shoulder hunching, and decreasing belly sag. The second stage is **preening behavior.** At this stage males and females will stroke their hair, rearrange makeup, glance in the mirror, rearrange clothes, leave buttons open, adjust suit coats, tug at socks, and readjust knots. The third stage involves **positional cues** such as sitting in a way that prevents third parties from joining the conversation, or moving arms, legs, or torsos to inhibit others from interfering. The final stage, labeled **actions of appeal,** includes flirtatious glancing, gaze holding, and moving the body in a sexually suggestive way.[63]

TRY THIS

Try an experiment. Assume various body postures. How do you feel when you assume each one? Does each position allow you to experience different emotions? Can you assume a body posture that makes you feel confident? Insecure? Elated? Depressed? Emotional change involves the body. When you assume a new attitude, the new attitude brings on new perceptions, new feelings, and new muscular patterns. There is a close link between the body and the mind.

Body movement can also reflect status differences between people. Mark Knapp, a researcher and writer on nonverbal communication, summarized Albert Mehrabian's findings on nonverbal indicators of status and power as follows:

> *High-status persons are associated with less eye gaze, postural relaxation, greater voice loudness, more frequent use of arms-akimbo [hand on hips], dress ornamentation with power symbols, greater territorial access, more expansive movements and postures, greater height, and more distance.*[64]

These characteristics are in contrast to the behaviors of the low-status person. Lower-status people communicating with higher-status people tend to be more formal, more rigid, and less adaptable.[65]

Personal appearance Even if you believe the cliché that beauty is only skin deep, you must recognize that not only does your personal appearance have a profound effect on your self-image, but also it affects your behavior and the behavior of people around you. Your physical appearance provides a basis for first and sometimes long-lasting impressions. It also affects who you talk to, date, or marry; how socially and sexually successful you will be; and even your potential for vocational success. This is unfair, but it's true.

The billion-dollar cosmetics industry testifies to the fact that people care about physical appearance and firmly believe it makes a difference. You apply all kinds of creams, lotions, and colorings to your skin. You may adorn your body with glasses, tinted contact lenses, ribbons, beards, hair ornaments, jewelry, and clothes. Body adornments are a big part of what Ruesch called object language.

Clothing is another communication medium over which you exert special control. Clothing reflects the way you choose to package yourself. Researchers have determined that clothes provide three different kinds of information about the wearer.[66]

CONSIDER THIS

According to Edward T. Hall, **interpersonal synchrony** *is the similar and harmonious rhythmic movement between two people on both the verbal and nonverbal levels.* You will demonstrate and witness interpersonal synchrony between mates and co-workers even across cultural boundaries. Read what Gudykunst and Ting-Toomey, writers on communicating with strangers, say about interpersonal synchrony, and then answer the questions that follow.

> Interpersonal synchrony or convergence is achieved when the nonverbal behavior between two individuals moves toward broadness, uniqueness, efficiency, flexibility, smoothness, personalness, and spontaneity, and when overt judgment is suspended. Interpersonal misalignment or divergence occurs when the nonverbal behavior between two individuals moves toward narrowness, stylized behavior, difficulty, rigidity, awkwardness, publicness, and hesitancy, and when overt judgment is given.*

Questions

1. Have you ever experienced interpersonal synchrony? Misalignment? Would your description be similar to the ones above?
2. What types of nonverbal behavior did you notice most revealing of or most involved in the synchrony or misalignment?
3. Can you see how synchrony or misalignment tends to be primarily a nonverbal phenomenon (as opposed to a verbal phenomenon)?
4. Is synchrony more or less likely to occur between people of different cultures? Different genders?

*From William B. Gudykunst and Stella Ting-Toomey, "Nonverbal Dimensions and Context-Regulation," in *Readings on Communicating With Strangers: An Approach to Intercultural Communication,* eds. William B. Gudykunst and Young Yun Kim, (pp. 273–297) (New York: McGraw-Hill, 1992), p. 281.

1. Clothes reveal something about the *emotions* you are experiencing. This works both ways: how you feel affects what you wear, and what you wear affects how you feel. You'll put on your most comfortable clothes in the morning if comfort is going to be your most important consideration that day. If you're going to speak as a student representative at a meeting of the board of regents of your college, chances are you'll

Have you ever noticed how your emotions are affected by what you are wearing? What would be the difference in the emotions of these two people based just on what they are wearing?

choose your clothes less for comfort and more for the feeling you hope to convey at the meeting—confidence or maturity or whatever. In these cases you are dressing for both how you feel and how you intend to feel later on. You've all had the experience of feeling inappropriately dressed, either too formally or too informally, on some occasions, and you know how your clothes affect how you feel about those occasions.

2. Clothes may disclose something about your *behavior*. If you have ever worn a uniform of any kind, you know how clothes can transform you and change your behavior. If you get dressed up for a job interview, you feel important; in your own mind, your actions also take on importance. Because this occurs in your mind, it is also very likely to affect your behavior. You will be more calculated, purposeful, and dynamic. You may stand erect rather than slouch. You may tend to lower your voice, slow your rate of speaking, and use fewer nonfluencies ("uh's" and "um's"). Just as dress affects you, you are also likely to judge other people's behavior by the way *they* dress. What expectations do you have for a person dressed as a police officer, judge, nurse, or priest?

3. Clothes function to *differentiate* you from other people. Twenty-year-old college students dress differently than do twenty-year-olds with jobs in the business world. Clothing also differs between age groups. For example, one group of researchers determined that a single man of 20–25 spends twice as much on clothes as a man of 45–50 and three times as much as a man of 65–70.[67] Clothing may also be used by people to raise themselves from a subordinate position, to raise self-esteem and apparent status.[68] Clothes serve to differentiate, too, between people who wish to be perceived as fashionable and those who don't care about fashion, between the formal and the informal, and between people with different social roles.

Personal appearance also relates to body type. That is, your particular body configuration (fat, thin, or athletic) affects the way you are perceived and responded to by others, and even what they expect of you. In research studies, body types have been labeled **endomorph** (fat), **ectomorph** (thin), and **mesomorph** (athletic). (See Figure 6.1.) People who were shown silhouette drawings of such body types in males were asked to respond on a variety of scales. Knapp summarizes the findings of these tests:

> *Their results show that (1) the endomorph was rated as fatter, older, shorter (silhouettes were the same height), more old-fashioned, less strong physically, less good-looking, more talkative, more warmhearted and sympathetic, more good-natured and agreeable, more dependent on others, and more trusting of others; (2) the mesomorph was rated as stronger, more masculine, better-looking, more adventurous, younger, taller, more mature in behavior, and more self-reliant; (3) the ectomorph was rated thinner, younger, more ambitious, taller, more suspicious of others, more tense and nervous, less masculine, more stubborn and inclined to be difficult, more pessimistic, and quieter.[69]*

Although space does not allow a complete presentation of research findings in all areas of personal appearance, it should be noted that some of the other cues that may affect interpersonal responses are height, body color, body odor, body hair, and other body-related cues (freckles, moles, acne, and beauty marks). Even your own perception of your personal appearance—your self-image—will affect your interpersonal communication. It is the basic kernel from which your communication behavior grows and flourishes.

Vocal Cues

Vocal cues *are all those attributes of sound that can convey meaning.* Sounds (not words) are considered nonverbal communication. This includes how loudly or quickly you speak, how much you hesitate, how many nonfluencies you use. These vocal cues can convey your emotional state.

As you well know, all you have to do to reveal anger is change the way you talk: you may talk louder, faster, and more articulately than usual. You may use your silences more pointedly. You can say exactly the

Figure 6.1
Characteristics associated with particular body configurations.[70]

1 ENDOMORPHIC	2 MESOMORPHIC	3 ECTOMORPHIC
dependent	dominant	detached
calm	cheerful	tense
relaxed	confident	anxious
complacent	energetic	reticent
contented	impetuous	self-conscious
sluggish	efficient	meticulous
placid	enthusiastic	reflective
leisurely	competitive	precise
cooperative	determined	thoughtful
affable	outgoing	considerate
tolerant	argumentative	shy
affected	talkative	awkward
warm	active	cool
forgiving	domineering	suspicious
sympathetic	courageous	introspective
soft-hearted	enterprising	serious
generous	adventurous	cautious
affectionate	reckless	tactful
kind	assertive	sensitive
sociable	optimistic	withdrawn
soft-tempered	hot-tempered	gentle-tempered

same thing in a fit of anger as in a state of delight and change your meaning by how you say it. You can say "I hate you" to sound angry, teasing, or cruel. Vocal cues are what is lost when your words are written down. The term often used to refer to this quality is paralanguage.[71] As noted before, it includes all the nonlanguage means of vocal expression, such as rate, pitch, and tone. It includes, therefore, what occurs beyond or in addition to the words you speak.

TRY THIS

Read the following sentence aloud seven times, each time emphasizing a different word in the sentence: I hit him in the eye yesterday.

Notice how the meaning changes as you change your emphasis. You can get seven more variations by reading the sentence as a question instead of a statement.

If you don't think paralanguage is very important, think of the impression made in a job interview by an applicant who mispronounces words or speaks too loudly or too fast or with too many hesitations. Such a person might find it hard to get employment in some prestigious business firms or to penetrate the upper strata of society. Although a person's social or business acceptance will probably never depend *only* on vocal cues, there are times when it helps to have correct pronunciation and articulation as part of your credentials.

It has been observed that if you use great variety in pitch (high or low), you are likely to be perceived as dynamic and extroverted. Males who vary their speaking rate are viewed as extroverted and animated. Interestingly, females demonstrating the same variety in rate are perceived as extroverted but also high-strung, inartistic, and uncooperative. If your voice is flat, you may be thought of as sluggish, cold, and withdrawn. A person with a nasal voice is often perceived as unattractive, lethargic, and foolish.[72] Whether these perceptions are accurate or not, it's useful for you to know how you are likely to be perceived if you speak a certain way.

Certain vocal characteristics are perceived as revealing interpersonal trust, confidence, and sincerity: when trust or confidence is in jeopardy, excessive pauses and hesitations tend to increase. Also, the number of nonfluencies you use—stuttering, repetitions, slips of the tongue, incoherencies—increases in situations where you are nervous or ill at ease.

It should be clear that vocal cues do not just refer to *how* something is said. Frequently they *are* what is being said. Vocal cues, then, can reflect attitudes, emotions, control, personality traits, background, or physical features.[73]

There are also vocal stereotypes that relate vocal characteristics to one's occupations, sociability, race, degree of introversion, and body type, among other characteristics.

Although different times, situations, and causes may result in different ways of expressing emotion, it is true that people use vocal cues to judge emotions and feelings. Your total reaction to others may be colored by your reaction to their vocal cues.

Touch

Touch *is the perception by a sense of feeling as that derived by the hand, finger, or other part of the body.* There are numerous positive effects of touch on people in our society. In a library, those touched when their library cards were returned evaluated the clerk and the library more favorably. Waitresses who touched diners received bigger tips, psychologists who touched students on the shoulder found greater compliance, therapists who touched clients facilitated the healing process,[74] and communicators who touched those persons they were trying to persuade were more successful than those who did not.[75] Touch is a critical aspect of human relationships.

TRY THIS

Next time you get a telephone call, make some judgments about what you heard. Which of the following vocal cues* did you perceive?

▲ breathiness　　　▲ throatiness
▲ thinness　　　　 ▲ orotundity
▲ flatness　　　　　▲ increased rate
▲ nasality　　　　　▲ increased pitch variety
▲ tenseness

Now determine which of the following feelings were being conveyed:

▲ affection　　　　▲ impatience
▲ anger　　　　　　▲ joy
▲ boredom　　　　 ▲ sadness
▲ cheerfulness　　　▲ satisfaction

Was there any relationship between vocal quality and the feeling being expressed? Could you find reasons or justifications for what you heard?

*For descriptions of these cues, see P. Heinberg, *Voice Training for Speaking and Reading Aloud* (New York: Ronald Press, 1964), pp. 152–181. Copyright © 1964 by John Wiley & Sons. Used by permission.

In your relationships with others, touch serves to reveal appreciation, give encouragement, express tenderness, show emotional support, convey security, and indicate sexual attraction. It should be clear, too, unfortunately, in a society that often automatically connects touch with sexual intent, "it is the type of touch, the timing of the touch, the location of the touch," and your ability in giving the touch that are the keys to success.[76]

There are people who could be labeled nontouchers. Because of a variety of experiences, admonitions (mild warnings), and models, they have learned not to touch. Studies on personality characteristics reveal that nontouchers "report more anxiety and tension in their lives, less satisfaction with their bodies, more suspicion of others," and tend to be "more socially withdrawn and more likely to be rigid or authoritarian in their beliefs."[77]

Because of the potential connection between touch and sexual intent and because of the existence of nontouchers, people must be careful in expressing themselves in this area. "Successful communicators," says Dale G. Leathers, a researcher on the subject, "will not only exhibit an awareness of what regions of the body may be touched in specific contexts but will also understand that the gender, race, age, status, and culture of the interactants dictate what type and how much touching is socially acceptable."[78]

Research has shown that 12 different meanings can be communicated by touch: support, appreciation, inclusion, sexual interest or attraction, affection, playful affection, playful aggression, compliance, gaining attention, announcing a response, greeting, and departure.[79] Because of this, effective communicators need to be sensitive to this vital nonverbal area in conveying their interpersonal attitudes.

Time

Time *is the period during which something exists, happens, or acts.* We all recognize the role that time plays in our life. We save it, spend it, make it, waste it, and divide it up. How to manage it effectively is important to anyone who wants to climb the corporate ladder. Time is important; there are no two ways about it. But we sometimes forget the role that it plays in social interaction. Notice, from the following comments, how it influences our perceptions of others:

"If he were responsible, he'd be on time."

"Notice that every time you talk to her, she looks at her watch to see how much time you're taking."

"Every time he opens his mouth, he just goes on and on and on."

"She is so insensitive; her timing is so bad. She should have known better than to say that at that time."

"We just never have time to be alone together."

"If you really loved me, you'd spend more time with me."

It is important to understand that time has both a physical and a psychological dimension, and how we perceive time depends on how these dimensions influence each other. An example will show this relationship. You all know that a lecture often takes a full class period. If that is 50 minutes, that is a physical reality. But how fast that 50 minutes goes by is a psychological phenomenon. It could depend on the relationship of the content to you; the use of examples and illustrations; the enthusiasm, clarity, and organization of the lecturer; the lecturer's voice qualities; the mood you are in when you hear the lecture; or the lecturer's involvement of the audience in the lecture material. The same relationship often occurs at parties. Two separate parties take the same amount of physical time; yet one flies by and is fun and exciting, while the other drags on and on and never seems to end.

Silence

Silence *is the absence of any sound or noise.* Considering the noise that has become an accepted and automatic part of existence in much of our society, silence may be perceived as an impossible dream, a wonderful trade

*How do you normally re-
spond to silence? When
someone is silent in a
conversation, how do
you interpret that si-
lence? What is the si-
lence demonstrated in
this photograph likely to
mean?*

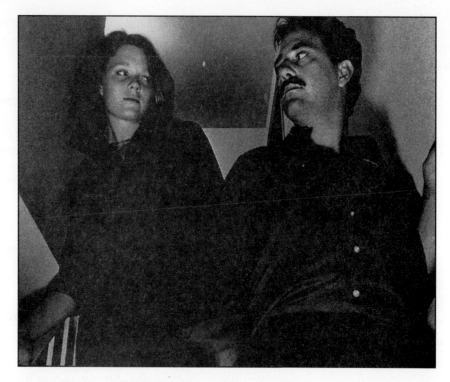

(to trade silence for the noise), or a necessary repose ("I need silence to do
my best work."). Often, silence is imposed, as in churches, libraries,
courtrooms, and hospitals. It may be imposed, too, for a shorter duration
at funerals, for prayer, during the playing of "Taps," or the singing of the
national anthem. Silence can be self-imposed, too, when you are studying, thinking, reading, trying to capture the sounds of nature, or enjoying
natural closeness with a relationship partner. In these cases silence occurs
because of respect, reverence, reflection, and romance.

Silence can mean anything that can be expressed verbally. Usually
its meaning derives from verbal exchanges, and because of the array of
verbal possibilities—past, present, and future—a list of meanings for silence is absurd. *Silence takes its meaning from "the communicators, subject
matter, time, place, culture, and the like."*[80]

In their work on silence, J. Vernon Jensen and Thomas J. Bruneau,
suggest at least five interpersonal functions that can be served by silence:

1. **Punctuation or accenting**—*when communicators draw attention to certain words or ideas.*
2. **Evaluating**—*when communicators provide judgments of others' behavior
or ideas, show favor or disfavor, or agree or disagree.*
3. **Revelation**—*when communicators make something known or hide something by being silent.*

4. **Expression of emotions**—*when communicators reveal disgust, sadness, fear, anger, or love by silence.*
5. **Mental activity**—*when communicators show thoughtfulness, reflection, or ignorance through silence.*[81]

Because often silence is so private and personal, it is difficult to discover the meaning of others' silences. But knowing the various interpersonal functions that can be served by silence will help you become more versatile and flexible. It gives you another technique or tool in your communication arsenal that can help you be more effective—a better communicative warrior (simply a person experienced or engaged in communication).

Building Nonverbal Communication Skills

As you try to improve your nonverbal communication skills there are three important ideas to keep in mind:

1. *Nonverbal communication always occurs in a context.* The meanings conveyed are intimately and directly tied to that context. If a man at a party stands with his hips thrust forward slightly, his legs apart, his thumbs locked in his belt, and his fingers pointing down toward his genitals, it may be considered a sexually provocative pose in that context.[82] If he stands the same way when he waits in line for a hamburger with his family, his pose probably does not carry the same message.

2. *No nonverbal cue should be viewed in isolation.* Cues must be observed as they interact with each other. In the instance just cited, it was not the man's posture alone that was suggestive, but that cue in combination with the position of his legs, thumbs, and fingers. Cues must be viewed in combination.

3. Although you can learn a great deal from observing nonverbal communication, *your conclusions should always be tentative rather than final.* Every individual is unique. There is always the possibility of actions occurring that are exceptions to any rule. You should view each behavior as existing at this time only, not assume it exists permanently or always.

Some people have mannerisms that are habitual and are not meant to convey any special meaning. You must be careful not to read too much into the behavior of people you don't know well and can only guess

CONSIDER THIS

Who would you suspect to be better in developing their observational skills in the area of nonverbal communication—men or women? Read the comments of Elgin, a writer on male-female communication, and then answer the questions that follow.

> The first step in developing observational skills for nonverbal communication is simply learning to PAY ATTENTION to the speaker's body and voice. Men in the AME [American Mainstream English] culture tend not to do this, and to be unaware that it matters; when they do pay attention they usually follow a rule that tells them to pay attention only to the speaker's face. Women do somewhat better, not because they have any built-in biological advantage, but because it is universally true that those having less power pay more attention to the body language of those having more power. (In the most primitive situations, this means being alert to the movements of the powerful person so that you will be able to get out of the way before the powerful person grabs or hits you.)*

Questions

1. Do you think it is true that those having less power pay more attention to the body language of those having more power?
2. Are there other reasons why women are likely to have better developed nonverbal observational skills than men?
3. What are likely to be the implications of women having better observational skills than men?

*From Suzette Haden Elgin, *Genderspeak: Men, Women, and the Gentle Art of Verbal Self-Defense* (New York: John Wiley & Sons, 1993), p. 66.

about. A person's eye may twitch when he or she is nervous; the twitch could be interpreted by a stranger as an enticing wink. You don't have to refrain from making *any* observations, but it is good to be cautious. Remember, whatever meaning you assign to what you see is a meaning that exists for *you*. Meaning is not in the nonverbal cues you observe; meaning is *in you*. Because it is in you, it will differ from the meaning assigned by other people.

Work on your self-awareness   The more you are able to express yourself clearly and accurately and the more in touch you are with your own feelings, the more likely you are to understand the nonverbal communication of others.[83] Your knowledge of yourself can be increased through self-disclosure and feedback. To open up, share, and request feedback from people you trust increases personal sensitivity. Opening channels for healthy, honest, open feedback can be of mutual benefit for you and for your friends. Your effectiveness in receiving nonverbal cues will be increased through self-awareness.

Monitor your own behavior   It's helpful to review your own communication experiences, whether positive or negative, to become aware of what you are doing. If you discover something you think might be important, you could solicit the help of friends to verify or deny your observations. You should think more about what you do. It is not easy to see yourself as others see you, but difficult or not, it is useful and worthwhile. It would be ideal if you could watch a videotape of your interactions with others over a period of twenty-four hours or so. Since this is not likely, what you *can* do is enlist the cooperation of close friends to help you identify your nonverbal cues that are disruptive to communication.

Experiment with your behaviors   There are two reasons for trying out different behavior: to improve communication and to break some of your routine, habitual ways of interacting. When you discover you have certain ineffective or distracting mannerisms, you should try to alter them in a meaningful way to increase your interpersonal effectiveness. If you force yourself to try new approaches, you'll increase the number of alternatives you have for behaving. You can "try on" new behaviors to see how they fit. This is part of the process of growing, changing, and becoming. If you find it very hard to break away from your usual routine, you can at least observe how other people handle themselves in similar circumstances to get a framework for monitoring your own behavior in the future.

Respond empathically   Your sensitivity to nonverbal communication will increase as you train yourself to be empathic. Try to understand how the other person feels. Try to get "the big picture." You should always imagine how you would feel if you experienced the same thing. If you are the twentieth applicant for a job to be interviewed on a certain day and you see a tired, expressionless face on the interviewer, you should try to understand how you would feel if you had just been through a day of interviews. Again, this means trying to see where the other person is coming from. It can explain a lot when you're trying to understand what a certain twitch or posture might signify. Your success in reading nonverbal messages will increase if you try to be *empathic*.

Look for patterns The behavior you observe in others is usually reflected in their whole body, not just in their face or hands. You can usually recognize trembling hands as a sign of nervousness, but nervousness may be shown in other ways as well. Nervous people may bite their lips, speak too quickly, squirm in their chairs, always be ready to leave, avoid direct eye contact, or play with paper clips while talking. Too often you draw conclusions from too little evidence. The face and the hands are obvious and easy to observe, but you must also notice posture, body movement, dress, and speech, and try to see patterns of behavior as they relate to different social settings.

Check your perceptions If you feel that someone's nonverbal behavior is influencing your reaction to that person, it may be wise to find out whether you have correctly understood the behavior. Just because people close their eyes does not mean they are not paying attention. Some people

TRY THIS

Watch parts of TV programs with the sound turned way down. Notice how skilled certain actors or entertainers are in enhancing their messages with nonverbal activity. Notice specifically if they:

▲ use exaggerated facial expressions
▲ touch other people in some way
▲ make special use of hand gestures
▲ use the space in which they are communicating (moving closer to or away from other people)
▲ seem to move naturally and comfortably, like "real" people

You may find that some performers you thought were quite skilled turn out to depend almost entirely on their verbal messages to make a point. In which kinds of programs did you find the performers most adept at nonverbal communication: comedy? drama? action programs? news presentations? commercials?

close their eyes to concentrate better on the message by blocking out distractions. If you are talking to Jennifer and she keeps looking beyond, you could ask, "Do you care about this?" or "Are you listening to me?" Something may be occurring behind you that you should see too!

Express your feelings   The cultural norm that says people should not openly express their feelings is powerfully restricting. How can you accurately read other people's nonverbal cues if they are feeling one thing and trying to show something else? All you can do is try to watch for congruency or noncongruency in the total communication. Some people smile constantly; a pleasant expression has become such a habit with them that they cannot clear their faces of pleasantness even when they are feeling frustration or despair. To understand a person's total message, you need to put together the whole communication puzzle—including all verbal and nonverbal elements—and notice which pieces fit together and which don't.

Likewise, you must strive for congruency in your own communication. If you concentrate on not hiding what you feel, it will be much easier to make your nonverbal messages congruent with your verbal messages. In fact, if you are being perfectly honest, you shouldn't have to worry about sending consistent signals—they will take care of themselves. You must discover the potential of your body; what messages does it want to send? Many of us tend to be too restrictive, too closed, and too inhibited in bodily expression. It's healthy to open the channels for sending honest messages.

People are often influenced more by nonverbal messages than by words. You tend to believe what you see and the tone of what you hear far more than the words you hear, and rightly so. People generally have more control over their verbal messages than over their nonverbal ones. True feelings, as revealed through nonverbal cues, are difficult to disguise. Becoming aware of your nonverbal communication habits will help you become more expressive. It will also increase your sensitivity to others.

▶ ## SUMMARY

This chapter began with a definition of nonverbal communication as any information or emotion communicated without using words—or nonlinguistically—and an explanation of why the knowledge of nonverbal communication is incomplete. Following a section on how much nonverbal communication counts, in which it was related to emotions and feelings, deception, distortion, and confusion, high-quality communication, highly efficient communication, and suggestion, the characteristics of nonverbal communication were discussed. Nonverbal communication is continuous, is rich in meaning, can be confusing, conveys emotions, is guided by norms and rules of appropriateness, and is culture-bound.

Nonverbal communication serves six functions: redundancy, substitution, complementation, emphasis, contradiction, and regulation. It is likely to appear in one of five forms: emblems, illustrators, affect displays, regulators, or adaptors. The types of nonverbal cues discussed included spatial cues, visual cues, vocal cues, touch, time, and silence.

In the final section, three cautions were offered regarding the reading of others' nonverbal cues. First, nonverbal communication always occurs in a context; second, no nonverbal cue should be viewed in isolation; and third, your conclusions should always be tentative rather than final. The seven suggestions for improving your nonverbal skills included working on your self-awareness, monitoring your own behavior, experimenting with your behaviors, responding empathically, looking for patterns, checking your perceptions, and expressing your feelings.

▶ ## KEY TERMS

nonverbal communication	illustrators	actions of appeal
paralanguage	affect displays	interpersonal synchrony
suggestion	regulators	endomorph
norms and rules	adaptors	mesomorph
redundancy	self-adaptors	ectomorph
substitution	alter-adaptors	vocal cues
complementation	spatial cues	touch
emphasis	intimate distance	time
contradiction	personal distance	silence
regulation	social distance	punctuation or accenting
sign language	public distance	evaluating
action language	courtship readiness	revelation
object language	preening behavior	expression of emotions
emblems	positional cues	mental activity

▶ ## NOTES

1. Charles Darwin, *The Expression of Emotions in Man and Animals* (New York: Greenwood, 1955).

2. Edward Sapir, "The Unconscious Patterning of Behavior in Society," in D. Mandelbaum, ed. *Selected Writings of Edward Sapir in Language, Culture, and Personality,* (Berkeley, CA: University of California Press, 1949), 556.

3. Albert Mehrabian, *Silent Messages: Implicit Communication of Emotions and Attitudes,* 2d ed. (Belmont, CA: Wadsworth Publishing Co., 1981), 77.

4. Ray L. Birdwhistell, *Kinesics and Context: Essays on Body Motion Communication* (Philadelphia: University of Pennsylvania Press, 1970), 158.

5. Birdwhistell, 158.

6. Neil Postman, *Crazy Talk, Stupid Talk: How We Defeat Ourselves by the Way We Talk—and What to Do About It* (New York: Delacorte Press, 1976), 228.

7. Peter A. Andersen, "Explaining Intercultural Differences in Nonverbal Communication," in Larry A. Samovar and Richard E. Porter, eds., *Intercultural Communication: A Reader,* 6th ed., 286. Copyright © 1991 by Wadsworth, Inc. Excerpts reprinted by permission of Wadsworth, Inc. and Professor Peter Anderson.

8. Virginia P. Richmond, James C. McCroskey, and Steven K. Payne, *Nonverbal Behavior in Interpersonal Relations* (Englewood Cliffs, NJ: Prentice-Hall, 1987), 263.

9. Peter A. Andersen, "Consciousness, Cognition, and Communication," *Western Journal of Speech Communication* 50 (1986): 87–101; Judee K. Burgoon, "Nonverbal Signals," in M. L. Knapp and G. R. Miller, eds., *Handbook of Interpersonal Communication,* (Newbury Park, CA: Sage Publications, 1985); and Larry A. Samovar and Richard E. Porter, "Nonverbal Interaction," in Larry A. Samovar and Richard E. Porter, eds., *Intercultural Communication: A Reader,* (Belmont, CA: Wadsworth Publishing Co., 1985).

10. William B. Gudykunst and Young Yun Kim, *Communicating with Strangers: An Approach to Intercultural Communication* (New York: Random House, 1992), 183.

11. Richmond, McCroskey, and Payne, 265.

12. Andersen, 1991, 288.

13. Andersen, 1991, 294.

14. Carley H. Dodd, *Dynamics of Intercultural Communication* (Dubuque, IA: Wm. C. Brown Co., 1982), 242.

15. Richmond, McCroskey, and Payne, 278.

16. Andersen, 1991, 294.

17. Richmond, McCroskey, and Payne, 278.

18. Richmond, McCroskey, and Payne, 278.

19. Andersen, 1991, 294.

20. Richmond, McCroskey, and Payne, 278.

21. Richmond, McCroskey, and Payne, 278.

22. Richmond, McCroskey, and Payne, 278.

23. Richmond, McCroskey, and Payne, 278.
24. Dodd, 242.
25. Dodd, 242–243.
26. Dodd, 243.
27. Judee K. Burgoon and Thomas Saine, *The Unspoken Dialogue: An Introduction to Nonverbal Communication* (Boston: Houghton Mifflin Co., 1978), 10–13.
28. Mehrabian, 44.
29. Daphne E. Bugental, Jacques W. Kaswan, Leonore R. Love, and Michael N. Fox, "Child Versus Adult Perception of Evaluative Messages in Verbal, Vocal, and Visual Channels," *Developmental Psychology* 2 (1970): 367–375.
30. Ekman and Friesen developed this system. See Paul Ekman and Wallace V. Friesen, "The Repertoire of Nonverbal Behavior: Categories, Origins, Usage, and Coding," *Semiotica* 1 (1969): 49–98. Also see updated reports of their research: Paul Ekman and Wallace V. Friesen, "Hand Movements," *Journal of Communication* 22 (1972): 353–74, and Paul Ekman and Wallace V. Friesen, "Nonverbal Behavior and Psychopathology," in *The Psychology of Depression: Contemporary Theory and Research,* eds. R. J. Friedman and M. M. Katz (Washington, DC: Winston & Sons, 1974).
31. See Jurgen Ruesch and Weldon Kees, *Nonverbal Communication: Notes on the Visual Perception of Human Relations* (Berkeley and Los Angeles: University of California Press, 1956), 189.
32. I am indebted to Mark L. Knapp for his "Perspectives on Classifying Nonverbal Behavior." See Mark L. Knapp, *Nonverbal Communication in Human Interaction,* 2nd ed. (New York: Holt, Rinehart and Winston, 1978), 12–18.
33. See Paul Ekman, "Movements with Precise Meanings," *Journal of Communication* 26 (1976): 14–26.
34. For more information on these regulators, see John M. Wiemann and Mark L. Knapp, "Turn-Taking in Conversations," *Journal of Communication* 25 (1975): 75–92.
35. Knapp, 12–18.
36. Mark L. Knapp and Judith A. Hall, *Nonverbal Communication in Human Interaction,* 3d ed. (Fort Worth: Holt, Rinehart and Winston, 1992), 160–167.
37. Edward T. Hall, *The Silent Language* (Greenwich, Conn.: Fawcett Publications, 1959), 163–164. He expands upon these classifications in his second book, *The Hidden Dimension* (Garden City, NY: Doubleday, 1966), 114–129.
38. K. Burgoon and S. B. Jones, "Toward a Theory of Personal Space Expectations and Their Violations," *Human Communication Research* 2 (1976): 131–146.
39. F. N. Willis, "Initial Speaking Distance as a Function of the Speaker's Relationship," *Psychonomic Science* 5 (1966): 221–222.

40. F. Erickson, "One Function of Proxemic Shifts in Face-to-Face Interaction," in *Organization of Behavior in Face-to-Face Interactions*, eds. A. Kendon, R. M. Harris, and M. R. Key (Chicago: Aldine, 1975), 175–187.

41. W. E. Leipold, "Psychological Distance in a Dyadic Interview" (Ph.D. dissertation, University of North Dakota, 1963); and K. B. Little, "Cultural Variations in Social Schemata," *Journal of Personality and Social Psychology* 10 (1968): 1–7.

42. R. Schulz and J. Barefoot, "Non-verbal Responses and Affiliative Conflict Theory," *British Journal of Social and Clinical Psychology* 13 (1974): 237–243.

43. M. Patterson, "Spatial Factors in Social Interaction," *Human Relations*, 21 (1968): 351–361.

44. Willis, 221–222.

45. For an excellent discussion of the factors that affect spatial distance, see Mark L. Knapp, *Essentials of Nonverbal Communication*, 2d ed. (New York: Holt, Rinehart and Winston, 1980), 81–87.

46. Albert Mehrabian, "Orientation Behaviors and Nonverbal Attitude Communication," *Journal of Communication* 17 (1967): 324–332.

47. Michael Reece and Robert N. Whitman, "Expressive Movements, Warmth, and Verbal Reinforcement," *Journal of Abnormal and Social Psychology* 64 (1962): 250.

48. P. Ekman, W. V. Friesen, and P. Ellsworth, *Emotion in the Human Face: Guidelines for Research and an Integration of the Findings* (Elmsford, NY: Pergamon Press, 1972), 57–65. These authors suggest eight categories. Dale G. Leathers adds the last two in *Nonverbal Communication Systems* (Boston: Allyn and Bacon, 1976), 24.

49. C. E. Izard, *The Faces of Emotion* (New York: Appleton-Century-Crofts, 1971), 216.

50. D. Ekman and W. V. Friesen, "The Repertoire of Nonverbal Behavior: Categories, Origins, Usage, and Coding," *Semiotica* 1 (1969): 49–98. Especially see p. 75.

51. Dale G. Leathers, *Successful Nonverbal Communication: Principles and Applications*, 2d ed. (New York: Macmillan Publishing Company, 1992), 32.

52. Knapp, 1980, 167.

53. Ekman, Friesen, and Ellsworth, 107.

54. Knapp, 1978, 305.

55. E. Goffman, *Behavior in Public Places* (New York: Free Press, 1963), 84.

56. See A. Kendon, "Some Functions of Gaze Direction in Social Interaction," *Acta Psychologica* 26 (1967): 46.

57. G. Hearn, "Leadership and the Spatial Factor in Small Groups," *Journal of Abnormal and Social Psychology* 54 (1957): 269–272. As cited in Knapp, 1980, 188–189.

58. M. Wiemann, "An Experimental Study of Visual Attention in Dyads: The Effects of Four Gaze Conditions on Evaluations by Applicants in

Employment Interviews," paper presented to the Speech Communication Association, Chicago, 1974.

59. Z. Rubin, "The Measurement of Romantic Love," *Journal of Personality and Social Psychology* 16 (1970): 265–273.

60. M. Argyle and J. Dean, "Eye Contact, Distance, and Affiliation," *Sociometry* 28 (1965): 269–304.

61. From Knapp, *Essentials*, 2d ed., 190. Reprinted by permission of CBS College Publishing. Permission also covers material cited in notes 64 and 70.

62. A. Mehrabian, *Nonverbal Communication* (Chicago: Aldine, 1972). This source includes a summary of his work. As cited in Knapp, 1980, 135.

63. A. E. Scheflen, "Quasi-Courtship Behavior in Psychotherapy," *Psychiatry* 28 (1965): 245–257. As cited in Knapp, 1980, 136–137.

64. Knapp, 1980, p. 138. See note 73.

65. Knapp, 1980, p. 138. See note 73.

66. Mary Kefgen and Phyllis Touchie-Specht, *Individuality in Clothing Selection and Personal Appearance: A Guide for the Consumer* (New York: Macmillan Publishing Company, 1971), 12–14.

67. F. Zweig, "Clothing Standards and Habits," in *Dress, Adornment and the Social Order*, eds. M. E. Roach and J. B. Eicher (New York: John Wiley & Sons, 1965), 164.

68. Schwartz, "Men's Clothing and the Negro," *Phylon* 24 (1963): 164.

69. Knapp, 1980, 106 (see note 73). From W. Wells and B. Siegel, "Stereotyped Somatypes," *Psychological Reports* 8 (1961): 77–78; and K. T. Strongman and C. J. Hart, "Stereotyped Reactions to Body Build," *Psychological Reports* 23 (1968): 1175–1178.

70. From J. B. Cortes and F. M. Gatti, "Physique and Self-Description of Temperament," *Journal of Consulting Psychology* 29 (1965): 432–439. Copyright © 1965 by the American Psychological Association. Adapted by permission of the publisher and author.

71. See George L. Trager, "Paralanguage: A First Approximation," *Studies in Linguistics* 13 (1958): 1–12.

72. D. W. Addington, "The Relationship of Certain Vocal Characteristics with Perceived Speaker Characteristics" (Ph.D. dissertation, University of Iowa, 1963), 157–158. Also see D. W. Addington, "The Relationship of Selected Vocal Characteristics to Personality Perception," *Speech Monographs* 35 (1968): 492–503.

73. See Addington, 1968, 492–503. As reported in Knapp, 1980, 208.

74. Mark L. Knapp and Judith A. Hall, *Nonverbal Communication in Human Interaction*, 3d ed. (Fort Worth, TX: Holt, Rinehart and Winston, 1992), 229–230.

75. Dale G. Leathers, *Successful Nonverbal Communication: Principles and Applications*, 2d ed. (New York: Macmillan Publishing Company, 1992), 132.

76. Knapp and Hall, 230.

77. Knapp and Hall, 234.

78. Leathers, 1992, 127.
79. Leathers, 1992, 135.
80. Knapp, 1978, 224.
81. Knapp, 1980, 224.
82. Julius Fast, *Body Language* (New York: Pocket Books, 1971), 85.
83. J. R. Davitz, *The Communication of Emotional Meaning* (New York: McGraw Hill, 1964).

▶ ## FURTHER READING

William B. Gudykunst and Young Yun Kim, *Communicating With Strangers: An Approach to Intercultural Communication*, 2d ed. (New York: Random House, 1992). In this very readable, interesting, and useful textbook, the authors use numerous examples supported by solid research from the fields of social psychology, sociology, cultural anthropology, sociolinguistics, and communication to draw their conclusions.

Edward T. Hall, *The Hidden Dimension* (New York: Anchor Books, 1969). In this book Hall focuses on people's use of space—that invisible bubble that constitutes personal territory. He demonstrates how the use of space can affect personal and business relations. This is a well-written, entertaining book full of examples and illustrations.

Edward T. Hall, *The Silent Language* (New York: Premier Books, 1959). Behind the mystery, confusion, and disorganization of life, there is order. Hall urges a reexamination of much that passes as ordinary, acceptable behavior.

Mark I. Hickson III and Don W. Stacks, *NVC—Nonverbal Communication: Studies and Applications*, 2d ed. (Dubuque, IA: Wm. C. Brown Co., 1989). The contribution of *this* textbook to this chapter is not simply that the authors focus on nonverbal communication; it is their emphasis on the sociological influence on nonverbal communication. The book results from almost 15 years of study and research and presents an excellent theoretical overview of the subject.

Mark L. Knapp and Judith A. Hall, *Nonverbal Communication In Human Interaction*, 3d ed. (Fort Worth: Holt, Rinehart and Winston, 1992). In this well-written, popular textbook, the authors have blended research from a wide variety of disciplines. They cover theory and research on environment, physical appearance, odor, space, territory, gesture, posture, touch, face, eye behavior, and voice, as well as chapters on acquiring and using nonverbal communication.

Dale G. Leathers, *Successful Nonverbal Communication: Principles and Applications*, 2d ed. (New York: Macmillan Publishing Company, 1992). Written for the introductory course in nonverbal communication,

Leathers's book demonstrates how knowledge of the informational potential of nonverbal cues can be used to communicate successfully in the real world. The real strength of this book is its emphasis on applications.

Patricia St. John, *Beyond Words: Unlocking the Secrets to Communicating* (New Hampshire: Stillpoint, 1994). This is a fascinating story about experiencing the joy and richness of communication—especially nonverbal communication—with those who appear different from us. St. John immerses readers in the inspiring world of dolphins and autistic children and introduces a world of heightened perceptions, subtle communication bridges, and universal forms of self-expression.

Larry A. Samovar and Richard E. Porter, eds., *Intercultural Communication: A Reader*, 6th ed. (Belmont, CA: Wadsworth Publishing Co., 1991). One of the most thorough, in-depth, and comprehensive examinations of intercultural communication written by experts in the field. They include five readings on nonverbal interaction.

7

Gender Communication: Understanding the Other Sex

► CHAPTER OBJECTIVES

After reading this chapter, you should be able to

- ▲ Understand the importance of studying gender differences.
- ▲ Recognize some of the major gender differences.
- ▲ Know what reactions to gender talk are likely to occur.
- ▲ Explain why it is necessary to be cautious in applying generalizations about gender differences.
- ▲ Recognize the skills necessary to improve gender sensitivity.

▼ Letitia and Reggie have been seeing each other for four months. They are having a quiet lunch together when the following dialogue occurs:

Letitia: I think we should talk about our relationship.

Reggie: What's wrong?

Letitia: There's nothing *wrong*. I just think we should talk.

Reggie: Okay. What do you want to know?

Letitia: I don't want to know anything, really. I just think we should talk.

Reggie: But if you don't want to know anything, then why should we talk?

Letitia: I think we should talk about our feelings for each other, our communication with each other, and even our future together.

Reggie: Whoa, you want to talk about heavy stuff. Okay, okay. What do you want to know?

Letitia: Well, let's start by talking about our feelings for each other.

Reggie: No problem. If we didn't have feelings for each other, we wouldn't still be hanging out together. How's that?

Letitia: That's great, Reg. But, I want to know if you love me. You know, you've never said it. . . .

In the following scenario, Barbara has a report to share with a group of people. Barbara's husband, Brian, begins this dialogue:

Brian: I just don't understand why you don't think it's important to make the report to the group.

Barbara:	It's not that I don't think it's important, because it is. It's just that I don't want to make it.
Brian:	Well, if you think it's important, then why don't you just make it?
Barbara:	You just don't understand.
Brian:	What do you mean, I don't understand? If I had a report that I thought was important, I would just stand up and give my report to the group.
Barbara:	That's easy for you to say. It has nothing to do with importance. I just don't feel comfortable speaking in front of people.
Brian:	You're scared?
Barbara:	I'm *not* scared. I just don't feel comfortable doing it.
Brian:	Admit it. You're just scared.

Zhen and his wife Avela have just arrived home from work. It is about 5:45 P.M. Zhen and Avela are what are sometimes referred to as a DINK family: double-income, no kids.

Avela:	Did you hear what Jamal and Molly did? They went to a family counselor.
Zhen:	No, I hadn't heard that. Our company has made the decision to open a branch office.
Avela:	Molly said she was the one who convinced Jamal to go.
Zhen:	I'm not surprised. They should have tried to work their problems out by themselves, first. I thought people only went to family counselors as a last resort. By the way, did your car work all right today?
Avela:	Yes. Would you want to have Jamal and Molly over for dinner this weekend?
Zhen:	You know, it's their problem, not ours.
Avela:	I'm not doing this to *solve* their problems. I'm doing this to be nice.
Zhen:	Okay, sure. Now I'm going to see if I can get my car running right.
Avela:	Molly said they would be free on Friday. Does that sound all right?
Zhen:	Yeah. Did you get the newspaper in?

Perhaps you think each of these scenarios is stereotypical. It is. And yet, each one points to several important aspects of gender differences in communication. They have been designed to show why the study of gender differences is important. In the first, Letitia wants to talk about the relationship and Reggie's feelings. Usually, when talk turns to the relationship, men immediately think something is wrong. Many men do not want to talk about relationships and feelings. Notice how Reggie wants to answer Letitia's questions and cut the conversation short; Letitia wants Reggie to open up and talk. Considering her interest in talking about their communication and their future together, it sounds as if Letitia thinks there may be a problem. If there is, it may simply be that Reggie has never let her know what he thinks of her or how he views the relationship. Letitia may simply want Reggie's love and affection, or perhaps some minimal show of concern. It sounds as though Reggie does not communicate the way he feels.

Brian and Barbara are dealing with a similar issue—feelings—as Letitia and Reggie, but an additional gender difference is introduced. With respect to feelings, Brian doesn't appear to be sensitive to Barbara's feelings about speaking in public. The gender difference is simply that males, in general, feel comfortable doing public speaking; women feel more comfortable doing private speaking.[1] Notice, however, that in this scenario Brian actually carries his lack of sensitivity to intimidation when he tries to force Barbara to admit that she is scared. People tend to judge others on the basis of their own beliefs, attitudes, values, and abilities.

Another gender difference was revealed in both the first and second scenarios. According to Joe Tanenbaum, in *Male and Female Realities: Understanding the Opposite Sex,* men express themselves with the purpose of resolution.[2] Notice, for example, how Reggie tries to resolve the issue of talking about his feelings. Notice, too, how Brian tries to resolve Barbara's problem about talking in public: just do it.

In the third scenario, Zhen and Avela demonstrate at least four gender differences. The first is talking at cross-purposes.[3] Avela wants to talk about Jamal and Molly because Jamal and Molly are having relationship problems, and Avela is concerned. Zhen responds only briefly to Avela's comments about Jamal and Molly and reveals more interest in a company decision, Avela's car, his car, and the newspaper. The second gender difference is Zhen's willingness to give advice: "They should have tried to work their problems out by themselves, first," or "You know, it's their problem, not ours." By making these statements, Zhen expresses his superiority—he knows what should be done. These statements could be interpreted as unfeeling and condescending; however, Avela chooses to ignore the first and quickly disallows the second.

The third gender difference is that Avela is speaking from her world of connections; she uses rapport-talk. She is close friends with Molly, and Molly's relationship with Jamal is important to her. Not only does it appear that Zhen is unconcerned about Jamal and Molly, but he is focusing on report-talk—reporting on a company decision, getting a report on Avela's car, reporting on his next job (his car), and getting a report on the whereabouts of the newspaper.[4]

A fourth gender difference involves Zhen's minimal response cues. Notice that with the exception of his comment about Jamal and Molly trying to work out their problems first, most of his responses to Avela are "Sure," or "Yeah." His responses could be interpreted by Avela as indicating lack of involvement. Perhaps here too, Avela has become accustomed to his low level of involvement.

In Zhen and Avela's scenario, both Zhen and Avela appear to be insensitive to each other's gender preferences. Of course, the scenario could be evaluated from the opposite perspective as well: they have grown comfortable and tolerant of each other, and cross-talk represents much of their communication with each other. Better some communication than none!

In this chapter the focus will be on gender differences in communication. **Gender Communication** *is communication between men and women*.[5] In the first section, the importance of studying gender differences will be explained. In the second section, some of the major differences will be discussed. The third section lists cautions about applying generalizations about gender differences. The final section offers specific ways for improving our sensitivity toward gender communication.

▲▲▲ *The Importance of Studying Gender Differences*

There are at least five reasons why studying gender differences is important: (1) confirmation, (2) understanding, (3) empathy, (4) improvement, and (5) universal sensitivity.

Confirmation Studying gender differences confirms something you may have suspected all along. You communicate differently than do members of the other sex. As I write this, John Gray's book *Men Are From Mars, Women Are From Venus: A Practical Guide for Improving Communication and Getting What You Want in Your Relationships* has been on the *New York Times* bestseller list for a long time. This confirms that many others are interested in gender differences as well. Deborah Tannen's *You Just Don't Understand: Women and Men in Conversation* was the previous *New York Times* bestseller on this issue and brought the topic to broad public awareness. Tannen did for gender differences what Julius Fast and his *Body Language* did for nonverbal communication.

Understanding Knowing that your language and that of most members of the other sex differ significantly is one more piece of information that helps you understand others. It's like having one more piece of the puzzle—the puzzle that makes up human interaction. Language is one means of sharing perceptions with others as well as giving them an impression of yourself. Thus, the language choices you make are likely to affect how

CONSIDER THIS

Gender communication can lead to ethical problems. Read the following excerpt by Lesley DiMare, a writer on rhetoric and women, and then answer the questions that follow.

Current research indicates that women, in their attempts to assume more than a biological role and to move from the private to the public sphere, encounter difficulties. In her book *Quiet Desperation,* Janice Halper points out that 'many men don't know how to interact with women in a way that isn't sexual' (1988). A study conducted by Fortune 500 supports this observation.[1] The sexual interaction can be attributed to society's conception of women as serving only biological functions—functions which are essentially sexual in nature and which encourage men to interact with them in a style and with a language inappropriate in the public sphere. Such interaction in the workplace causes frustration for both women and men. Women are prevented from effectively assuming dual roles, and men tend to communicate in a style which is both offensive and unproductive, and which may lead to accusations of sexual harassment and discrimination.[2]*

Questions

1. Do you see the ethical problems created by the view of women by men "as serving only biological functions"?
2. Do you have specific examples of the offensive communication style of men as noted in this excerpt?
3. If you were in charge of changing this male interaction mode—not knowing how to interact with women in a way that isn't sexual—what suggestions would you have?

[1]*"Working Woman* Survey Results: Sexual Harassment in the Fortune 500," *Working Woman,* December 1988, 72.

[2]*Working Woman,* 72.

*From Lesley DiMare, "Rhetoric and Women: The Private and the Public Spheres," in *Constructing and Reconstructing Gender: The Links Among Communication, Language, and Gender,* eds. Linda A. M. Perry, Lynn H. Turner, and Helen M. Sterk (pp. 45–50) (Albany, NY: State University of New York Press, 1992), p. 48.

other people perceive you and your world. Knowing that certain differences exist simply because you are male or female can add to your understanding of how and why people make the language choices they do.

Are there likely to be confirmation, understanding, and empathy in this interpersonal situation? What are the keys for making these assessments?

Empathy   Increased understanding is likely to bring increased empathy. If you know, for example, that friends or relationship partners are expressing themselves the way they are because that is the way many men or many women do, it is easier for you to be supportive and accepting rather than defensive and unaccepting. It is too bad, for example, that Brian did not reveal empathy for Barbara's feelings about speaking in public (see page 246). For him to express empathy might have enhanced their relationship. Often people are quick to criticize others who do not say or do things the way they do, just as Brian made fun of Barbara's feelings: "Admit it. You're just scared."

Improvement   With confirmation, greater understanding, and increased empathy, communication is likely to improve. There is no guarantee that communication will improve, of course. Reggie might be more willing to open up with Letitia and share some of his feelings, knowing that is what she wants (see page 246). Brian might have been more sensitive and less critical of Barbara's situation when she let him know, gently at first, that she did not want to speak in public. Zhen and Avela might have decided to take turns, first discussing Jamal and Molly's relationship situation, for example, and then discussing the topics Zhen wanted to discuss (see page 246).

Universal sensitivity There is a more universal reason, however, for looking at gender differences. As the "Consider This" boxes in each chapter have indicated, there are numerous problems in communication, whether they arise interculturally, because of gender, because of ethical concerns, or within the workplace. Acknowledging gender differences is not unlike acknowledging any other differences that occur between human beings. Encouraging and promoting sensitivity and concern between human beings, whoever they are, can only serve the important purpose of promoting peace and harmony in humankind throughout the world. What better goal is there?

As you read the sections that follow, notice how males and females tend to complement each other's behavior. That is, one gender often supplies a quality or feature the other does not. This can be a valuable feature in relationships. For example, my wife and I tend to approach situations, people, and events in different ways. Each of us offers a perspective that, taken with the other's, offers a more complete picture of what is under consideration. Using Tannen's distinguishing language features, my wife and I choose different words based on our different worlds, we differ in our preferences for public and private speaking, we are on opposite ends of the lecturing and listening continuum just as we are on the extreme

TRY THIS

Are there major differences in the kind of communication that exists when women talk with women than when they talk with the other sex? Or when men talk with men than when they talk with the other sex? What are some of these differences? Use some of these suggestions to guide your analysis:

- ▲ frequency of the interaction
- ▲ context in which the interaction occurs
- ▲ length of the interaction
- ▲ forms of communication used in the interaction
- ▲ characteristics of the communication
- ▲ functions of the communication
- ▲ differences in the interactions

ends of the report/rapport continuum and the high considerateness/ high involvement continuum as well.[6] Think about it: whether it is universally true or not, where did the cliche that "opposites attract" come from anyway?

▲▲▲ *Some Major Gender Differences*

Considering the number of contributors to this topic, judged merely from the books now available, this section alone could fill a book—perhaps several. Even if some of the descriptions that follow appear to be merely stereotypical, don't let that be of concern. The clear point, of which you will be reminded near the end of this chapter, is that all people are different. Because some members of a gender do something does not mean that all members of a gender do it. The point of this section is to emphasize or at least point out some of the differences. Please accept them in the context of understanding for the purposes of appreciation and sensitivity and not for the purposes of placing negative labels on behaviors or trying to legitimize negative behaviors by either sex.

It should be clear that when you were born, you were born into a society divided by gender and a social world that emphasizes masculinity and femininity. You could not escape it. Think about the pink or blue blankets in which you were wrapped. Think about the distinctive interactions parents had with their "cute" little girl or their "handsome" little boy. Think, too, about the gender differences in the language used with boys and girls, whether the language comes from parents, teachers, or peers. Even permissible "growing-up" activities were likely to be different—boys being given more freedoms and allowed to be rough and get dirty. Often, girls have more restrictions and may become "mommy's little helper." That is why it was easy for Deborah Tannen, in *You Just Don't Understand*, to make a clear case for "Different Words, Different Worlds"—the chapter she uses to begin her book.[7] It is important to note, however, that gender differences have as much to do with the biology of the brain as the way we are raised.[8]

From what has been said thus far, it should be clear that communication plays an essential role in shaping gender identity.[9] Interaction with others helps you define masculinity and femininity; outline peer, parent, and teacher expectations; and change you from a biologically determined male or female into one who recognizes and responds to gender differences.[10]

In this section the topics are limited to discussing gender differences with respect to (1) intimacy versus independence, (2) topics of interest, (3) lecturing versus listening, (4) leadership styles, (5) differences in language, (6) differences in nonverbal communication, and (7) reactions to gender talk.

Intimacy versus Independence

Women speak and hear a language of connection and **intimacy** whereas men speak and hear a language of status and **independence**.[11] John Gray, writing in *Men Are From Mars, Women Are From Venus,* claims that women are more interested in people and feelings and men are more interested in objects and things.[12] The "things" Gray refers to include whatever can help men express power by creating results, achieving goals, and doing things by themselves. This is how men prove their competence and strengthen their egos.

These characteristics, as it turns out, answer several related questions, for example, "Why don't men ever stop and ask for directions when they are lost?" Men take great pride in handling problems on their own. "Why involve others," they might think, "when I can do it myself?" Asking others for help when they can do it themselves is perceived as a sign of weakness. Also, there is a great deal of pride to be gained from having resolved the problem of how to get there. (They seldom admit to being lost.) That is why, when in dialogue (like the first two examples that opened this chapter) the men involved attempt to solve the problems their partners are facing. Women, on the other hand, enjoying intimacy or connection, spend a lot of time supporting, helping, and nurturing; thus, they see no problem in seeking others—especially when lost—who can offer these features.[13] Sharing and relating is natural, easy, and proper.

Other related questions can be answered with the "intimacy versus independence" base. Women often wonder why men become absorbed in sports; men often wonder why women become absorbed in soap operas or romance novels. It should be clear with respect to interests in sports and soap operas, however, that they do not split evenly along gender-based lines. Many females enjoy sports; many males enjoy soap operas. But this does not explain the predominant gender-based interests. Think about it. Men value power, competency, efficiency, and achievement.[14] These characteristics are clearly demonstrated on the athletic field. Women value love, communication, beauty, and relationships.[15] These characteristics are clearly demonstrated in soap operas and romance novels.

This is but one area where rules of communication collide. Women use talk to build and sustain connections with others. Men use talk to convey information and establish their independent status. These differences, obviously, give rise to many others. With just these two ideas as starting points, however, the number of misunderstandings that are likely to follow is not surprising.[16]

Topics of Interest

With the characteristics of intimacy versus independence established, you can expect that men and women see different things in the same situation. For example, witnessing an automobile accident, women might reveal immediate concern for the occupants, who they were, their relationships with each other, and how the families of those involved might be affected. Males may be interested in the same things, but their interests are likely to extend to the damage to the car, the way the accident occurred, how it could have been prevented, and even who was at fault. "Who was at fault" is the male characteristic related to resolving problems. Talking about the automobile accident to others, you would likely hear the man and the woman talking about entirely different features of the accident.

Just as their topics of interest are likely to be based on the kinds of things that interest them (intimacy versus independence, for example), they are likely to be based, too, on the backgrounds in which they grew up. Tannen claims that even when males and females grow up in the same neighborhood, on the same block, or in the same house, they grow up in different worlds. I have already referred to the influence of parents, peers, and teachers. Anthropologists Daniel Maltz and Ruth Borker have clearly shown that boys and girls have very different ways of talking with their friends. Their games are different, their language is different, and their experiences are different.[17] It takes little imagination, then, to extend these insights to suggest that the topics males and females are likely to be interested in will be different.

When the topics interesting to each gender are different, it takes little imagination, once again, to extend this observation to **cross-talk.** Remember, for example, the conversation of Zhen and Avela at the opening of the chapter (see page 246). Avela talked about the topics that interested her (relationships); Zhen talked of those that interested him (decisions, objects, and things). Males and females find different topics interesting.

Lecturing versus Listening

If you understand the differences explained in the first section on intimacy versus independence, then you have a solid basis for this distinction as well. This could be as simple as the Brian and Barbara example in the opening (see page 246), but it is likely to have far broader implications. Tannen suggests that men are more comfortable giving information and opinions and speaking in an authoritative way to groups. Women are more comfortable, Tannen says, in supporting others (intimacy).[18] The implications of this distinction are important.

Lecturers often are thought superior in status and expertise. They are cast in the role of teachers; listeners are cast in the role of students. These differences occur because of male-female interactional habits. Women want to build rapport; thus, they play down their expertise rather than display it. Men prefer the center-stage position and the related feelings of knowing more, gathering more facts, and disseminating factual information. Tannen also refers to this distinction as **rapport-talk**

If you accepted the "intimacy versus independence" idea, how could the communication in this scene be explained? Do you think this scene is typical or too stereotypical?

versus **report-talk.** Report-talk has to do with dealing with facts and factual information. This imbalance occurs because of differences between women's and men's habitual conversational styles.[19]

Leadership Styles

Like the other characteristic differences, when you understand the base (intimacy versus independence, for example), you understand the differences. The difference between male and female leadership styles simply extends the base. The study on which the conclusions in this section are based was completed by Dr. Judith B. Rosener, professor at the University of California, Irvine.[20] Males, Rosener claims, tend to lead in the traditional way: by command and control. Their leadership is characterized by giving an order, explaining the reward for a job well done, and pretty much keeping their power and knowledge to themselves. It is an important kind of leadership needed, for example, if there is a fire. The command-and-control type of leader is likely to order everyone out with no questions asked.

Females, according to Rosener, tend to lead in nontraditional ways: by sharing information and power. Their leadership is characterized by

Are any obvious characteristics of women's talk or men's talk being exhibited here? Are characteristics of women's talk or men's talk easily perceivable? From a photograph?

inspiring good work by interacting with others, encouraging participation, and showing how group members' goals can be reached by meeting organizational goals. Notice that the female leadership style tends to be more rapport-oriented. It is a leadership style based on sharing knowledge, power, and responsibility.

Differences in Language

In her book *Gendered Lives,* Julia Wood provides one of the best explanations of differences in women's and men's talk. Here is a brief review of her conclusions for both.

Women's talk   Wood offered seven characteristics of **women's talk.** You will find all of these extensions of the characteristics discussed above. First, women believe that talk is the essence of relationships. For this reason, their talk reveals features that foster connections, support, closeness, and understanding. Second, a quest for equality is revealed in their language. You are more likely to hear women say, for example, "I see how you feel," or "You are not alone in how you feel," or "I've experienced the same kinds of things."[21]

CONSIDER THIS

What about gender sensitivity in the workplace? Read the following passage from J. K. Alberts, a writer on teasing and sexual harassment, and then answer the questions that follow.

> In sexual teasing, the injunctions offered are implied and are in direct opposition. When a man subjects a woman to a sexual tease, he is putting her in a situation that demands that she respond in a sexual manner (the primary negative injunction). The woman is aware that if she does not respond in a sexual way and thereby validate the perpetrator, she runs the risk of punishment, by continued harassment, increased work load, or repercussions on her promotions/retention. However, if she does, she knows that she will likely suffer loss of professional status and reputation. She also faces possible censure by her colleagues. So although the sexual tease demands by its nature that she respond sexually, at the same time, by virtue of the work context, it also demands that she *not* respond in a sexual way (the secondary injunction).
>
> All this is made worse by the tertiary injunction that prevents her from leaving the field—the fact that it occurs in a work context and she is in a powerless position. The woman is not in a position to call her harasser to task because she could be accused of not being able to take a joke or of misunderstanding the interaction which puts her in the wrong; she can be punished by virtue of her status, and she cannot leave the field because she is tied to it for economic reasons. Thus, the woman who suffers sexual teasing and harassment is effectively caught in a double bind from which there are limited opportunities for escape.
>
> Once the sexual teasing and harassment issue is examined as a communicative event and from the perspective of the double bind, it is easier to understand why it has continued to be perpetuated with little change in men's and women's interaction patterns.*

Questions

1. Do you think this is an example of something that actually happens in the workplace? Is it a serious problem?
2. Are there things that can be done, or are being done, to bring about change in this area?
3. If *you* were in this situation (as a *female*) what would you do? (Males, try answering this question, take the role of the female as you respond.)

*From J. K. Alberts, "Teasing and Sexual Harassment: Double-Bind Communication in the Workplace," in *Constructing and Reconstructing Gender: The Links Among Communication, Language, and Gender,* eds. Linda A. M. Perry, Lynn H. Turner, and Helen M. Sterk (pp. 185–196) (Albany, NY: State University of New York Press, 1992), p. 195.

TRY THIS

Have you discovered, in your interactions with the other sex, some distinctly feminine forms of expression and some distinctly masculine forms of expression? Over the next several days, keep a journal or log of these expressions. Do you use any of these expressions yourself?

Two other characteristics relate to women's concern for relationships. The third characteristic is related to the first two. Women's talk shows support for others. This is likely to be revealed in comments like "You must feel awful" or "I hear what you're saying." The fourth characteristic has to do with maintenance work—efforts to sustain conversation by inviting others to participate. Often, it is women who initiate conversation: "How was your day?" "Tell me about your class," "Did anything interesting happen?"[22] If you have ever wondered about why women think men don't talk, this may help explain it.

A fifth characteristic is responsiveness. Women tend to respond to what others say. If the response is verbal, it may be "That's interesting," or "Tell me more." If it is nonverbal, it may be a head nod, encouraging eye contact, or an inviting smile. Women want to care about others, to make them feel valued, and to include them.[23]

A sixth characteristic of women's talk is its personal, concrete style. Women include details, personal disclosures, anecdotes, and concrete reasoning in their conversation. These are features that relate to the characteristics above because they provide a personal tone and foster feelings of closeness by connecting women who talk with their receivers. This characteristic helps sustain interpersonal closeness.

The final feature of women's talk is tentativeness. For example, women may use verbal hedges, qualifiers, and tag questions. In the statement "I kind of feel like going" the words "kind of" hedge the statement. Another way to be tentative is to qualify. Women qualify by saying "I'm probably not the one to answer this question, but . . ." A third way to be tentative is to add a tag question: "That was a pretty good answer, wasn't it?" "We really should go out more, don't you think?" The goal in tentative language is to leave the door open for others to express their opinions and respond; it is the language of connectiveness.[24]

Men's talk Wood offers six characteristics of **men's talk.** Overall, the goals of men's talk are exerting control, preserving independence, and enhancing status. If you look back at the results of Rosener's leadership study, these characteristics are reflected there in the male leadership style. For men, conversation allows opportunities to prove themselves and negotiate prestige. Two qualities emerge from this. The first is that men use talk to establish and defend their ideas and personal status. The second is that when men want to offer comfort or support, they do it by respecting others' independence and avoiding communication they consider condescending.[25]

Wood's six characteristics build on these qualities. The first is that men speak to exhibit knowledge, skill, or ability. Disclosing personal feelings makes them appear weak or vulnerable. The second prominent feature is instrumentality. That is, men use talk to achieve goals. This is the resolution and problem-solving orientation referred to earlier.

The third feature of men's talk is conversational dominance. In most contexts, men dominate the conversation.[26] How do they do this? They talk more frequently; they talk for longer periods of time; they redirect conversations to their own topics; they interrupt; they challenge other speakers; they wrest the talk stage from others.[27]

The fourth feature is that men express themselves in absolute, assertive ways. Their talk tends to be forceful, direct, and authoritative. They seldom use tentative talk as revealed in the use of hedges, qualifiers, or tag questions.

The fifth feature is that compared with women, they communicate more abstractly. By speaking in general terms, they distance themselves from personal feelings and concrete experiences. Remember how Zhen responded to Avela about Jamal and Molly (see page 246). Zhen said, "I thought people only went to family counselors as a last resort." Here was an abstract statement.

The final feature of men's talk, as listed by Wood, was that it tends not to be highly responsive—especially not on the relationship level. Do you wonder why women become concerned about men's lack of interest in their relationship? Men offer minimal response cues such as "Yeah," or "Umhmmm," or "Sure," as noted in the third scenario between Zhen and Avela that begins the chapter.

Directly related to talk by men that is not highly responsive, men reveal less expressed sympathy, less understanding, and fewer self-disclosures. This follows from the rules that tend to govern men's talk. Sympathy is a sign of condescension; understanding may unveil feelings; revealing personal problems through self-disclosure makes one vulnerable.[28]

Differences in Nonverbal Communication

Many of the differences in nonverbal communication are extensions of some of the rules males and females use to govern their communication and some of the differences found in their verbal exchanges as well. For example, women use nonverbal signals to encourage others to converse; males use them to discourage others from speaking.[29] Suzanne may offer

Kevin direct eye contact to invite him into the conversation; Eric, in another situation, may give Monique no eye contact whatever when she talks. This may cause Monique to cease talking because she perceives Eric as uninterested.

The rules of interaction are important. Women follow a rule of responsiveness. Their nonverbal behavior indicates engagement with others, emotional involvement, and empathy. Men follow a rule of status and power. Thus, they use gestures and space to command attention. They use volume, too, to increase the strength of their ideas and positions.[30] These rules extend to their listening abilities as well. Women are taught to react, listen, and respond. Men are encouraged to assert themselves: the more forceful they are, the less they can listen.[31]

Besides the rules of interaction, there are social definitions, too, that define what nonverbal communication is likely to be revealed. For example, women often are defined as deferential, decorative, and relationship-centered. These social definitions are reinforced through nonverbal cues that emphasize their appearance, limits their space, and defines them as touchable. When the social definition of men is that they are independent, powerful, and in control, the corresponding nonverbal cues are likely to offer them larger territories, give them greater normative rights to invade others by entering their space, and license touching them.[32]

When women conform to the social definition described above, you are likely to observe them being soft-spoken, condensing space, yielding territory, and being facially responsive. You might say these behaviors "go with the territory." When men conform to the social definition described above, you are likely to observe them, likewise, commanding space, revealing volume, defending their turf, and adopting impassive facial expressions to keep their feelings camouflaged.

TRY THIS

From your own observations of male-female behavior, formulate at least three rules that men follow, and three separate and different rules that women follow, that seem to guide their communication and interaction behavior. One example of a rule for each might be the following. They are offered here as examples only.

Males: Males are independent.
Females: Females are relationship-oriented.

See if you can come up with three other rules for males and three other rules for females.

Reactions to Gender Talk

More important than the differences that characterize genders is the way people respond to the differences. There is no doubt there are differences in the responses. These differences create two problems. The first is that these differences are likely to reinforce gender stereotypes. For example, Wood suggests that "language reinforces social views of men as the standard and women as marginal and men and masculinity as more valuable than women and femininity."[33] Tannen supports this observation, but she offers several specific instances to support it.

1. Women are expected not to boast in public situations.[34] To be likable, they tend not to display their achievements in public. Men use self-aggrandizing information to achieve status. Women, thus, are systematically underestimated and are thought to be self-deprecating and insecure.[35] Tannen adds, "It is tempting to recommend that women learn to display their accomplishments in public to ensure that they receive the respect they have earned. Unfortunately," she adds, "women are judged by the standards of women's behavior."[36]

What differences between genders can you detect in what is going on here? Are these typical differences?

2. Linguistic strategies when used by women are seen as power-less, when used by men as powerful.[37]

3. Women who use tag questions and disclaimers are judged less intelligent and knowledgeable than men who use them.[38]

4. In contrast to men, women who do not give support for their arguments are judged less intelligent and knowledgeable.[39]

5. Women who apologize a lot are perceived to be in a one-down position.[40]

6. Male-female conversations are more like men's conversations than they are like women's. Both males and females make adjustments, but women make more.[41]

7. Women are more likely to phrase their ideas as questions, take up less time with their questions, and speak at a lower volume and higher pitch than men; this puts them at a disadvantage.[42]

8. Ways of talking that are considered feminine are not associated with leadership and authority.[43]

9. The words available to describe women and men are not the same words, and it is through language that images and attitudes are formed. Asymmetrical assumptions about men and women are passed on through our language.[44]

The second problem these differences create, of course, is the number of misunderstandings that are likely to occur. Gender talk often creates misunderstandings. Many of these misunderstandings occur simply because men and women rely on different sets of rules to guide their conversations, as noted previously. One rule, not mentioned thus far, is that men tend to follow a linear progression through a story without great detail. Women are more likely to relate their information to a larger context of people and events. They include the details to help listeners become more fully part of the situation described. Men find the female method of telling stories wandering and unfocused; women find the male method as devoid of interesting details.

▲▲▲ *Why Be Cautious in Applying These Generalizations?*

Several cautions need to be expressed with reference to the differences in gender communication. These have to do with (1) *variations,* (2) *separation of genders,* (3) *individual differences,* (4) *context,* (5) *generalizations,* and (6) *value judgments.*

Variations Gender differences in language use vary with time and place. Some features that distinguish male from female communicators in one study do not distinguish them in another study. This suggests that caution needs to be exercised in making generalizations.

CONSIDER THIS

Gender sensitivity is essential if interpersonal communication is to operate at its most effective levels. But what hope is there for serious change? Read what Nancy Hoar, a writer on gender communication, says about change in this area, and then answer the questions that follow.

> When measured in the context of a life span, social change comes slowly. I believe that one must play the game that's being played, even while working to change the rules of the game. I believe this because those who can play the game are more likely to change the rules than are those who cannot or will not play.
>
> In short, communicative style is not the only determiner of how women are perceived and treated, but it is a powerful influencer. Women should use communicative style as one important tool in achieving the social and professional status that they themselves want.*

Questions

1. Is this a plea for change, or is this support for the status quo? When people want quick, severe change, do they work within the system?
2. How do you think change can best be brought about?
3. Do you agree with Hoar's statement "those who can play the game are more likely to change the rules than those who cannot or will not play"?

*From Nancy Hoar, "Genderlect, Powerlect, and Politeness," in *Constructing and Reconstructing Gender: The Links Among Communication, Language, and Gender,"* eds. Linda A. M. Perry, Lynn H. Turner, and Helen M. Sterk (Albany, NY: State University of New York Press, 1992), pp. 127–136.

Separation of genders Culture is a general determinant of the nature and amount of fluctuation in the distinctions between male and female talk. That is, in some communities there is more separation of the genders; in others there is less. Even this, however, is a complex issue. One might think, for example, that "modernity" would be a factor. That is, "modern" males and females would show fewer distinctions in their language. But "modern" males and females in one study "were perfectly distinguishable on the basis of their language."[45]

Individual differences Just because one group of males or females reveals these differences does not mean that all males or females from that group do. It is easy to get caught in the trap of generalizing from the group to the individual.

Contexts Some contexts promote group differences, whereas others minimize them. Situations, for example, in which one sex may be operating in a context that is usually or predominantly occupied by the other sex may promote the differences. It could occur over lunch when a group of truck drivers, only one of whom is female, are conversing; or in a hospital hallway where a group of nurses, only one of whom is male, are discussing various duties. In groups where the mix of males and females is more equal, or where both sexes are normally represented equally, language differences may be less likely to occur.

Generalizations The differences outlined here represent generalizations. All are not true for everyone; but even more importantly, just because one difference occurs, or is true, does not mean the others necessarily occur, or are true.

Value judgment No value judgment is intended with respect to any single set of language choices. One is not necessarily better than another. One may be better for one individual in a specific context than another, of course, as with trying to clear an area in case of fire—an example used earlier. But a group of characteristics is just that: a group of characteristics. They are presented here for the purpose of enhancing understanding, fostering empathy, improving communication, and creating both awareness and discussion.

Building Gender Sensitivity Skills

Perhaps the most important idea in responding to the differences between males and females involves the same advice given to any two people who are different: understand and respect differences in how people communicate. Begin by suspending judgment based on your own perspectives. Try to consider more thoughtfully what others mean in their own terms.[46] More specifically, people have four ways of responding to differences in women's and men's conversation and personality styles. To use these ways in your interactions with the other gender will clearly reveal your own serious attempt at effective interpersonal communication.

CONSIDER THIS

This excerpt appeared in a newsletter entitled *World Goodwill* as the conclusion of the title article, "The Voice of Women." Read it, and then answer the questions that follow.

> The 'Voice of Woman' calls for a transformation of our society so that we move towards a world where women and the feminine principle are justly represented at all levels of life. Then women and men will both have the opportunity of full participation and the opportunity to give of their best . . . the women's movement . . . is emerging as a movement for equality, for life, for peace, for justice, for the earth. The new era depends upon the 'voice of woman' being heard and acted upon. This new era depends more than anything else upon the united action of women and men of goodwill and understanding in every part of the world, serving creatively together in equal partnership.*

Questions
1. Is such a transformation of our society likely?
2. What acts or changes are necessary to promote or bring about the new era?
3. If a new era does come to be, what are some of the things that will be different?
4. How do *you* personally feel about these kinds of changes? Are they important? Necessary?

*From "The Voice of Woman." 1988 *World Goodwill Newsletter* 1:1–3. As reprinted in Margaret Riley, "Gender in Communication: Within and Across Cultures," in *Constructing and Reconstructing Gender: The Links Among Communication, Language, and Gender,* eds. Linda A. M. Perry, Lynn H. Turner, and Helen M. Sterk (pp. 219–227) (Albany, NY: State University of New York Press, 1992), p. 226.

Learn about others' styles From such learning, you are more likely to communicate from a base of awareness, understanding, and sensitivity. Style differences are real, and they *do* make a difference. You can find out about others by asking them questions. You can learn, too, by listening and looking.

Override your automatic impulses Tannen makes it clear that the essential differences between men and women lie in deeply imbedded, enculturated differences that become habitual because of training, use, and reinforcement. When you become aware of your ways of talking and how effective you are (or can become), you can override your habits.[47] If it will help, ask others to help you change.

Avoid drawing conclusions about others based on personality or intentions Once you understand male/female style differences, you are likely to see little substance in such conclusions as "you're illogical," "you're insecure," "you're self-centered," or "you don't listen," "you put me down." To begin to believe that others have a *different way* of responding, listening, or showing how they care allows you to adjust to others without casting or taking blame.[48]

Adopt your own flexible style "The freest person," says Tannen, "is the one who can choose which strategies to use, not the one who must slavishly replay the same script over and over and over—as we all tend to do."[49] The more you know, the more you have practiced, the more flexible you become.

In the last section of her book, *He Says, She Says: Closing the Communication Gap Between the Sexes*, Lillian Glass says that the only way we will ever close the communication gap between the sexes "is through awareness, understanding, and compromise."[50]

▶ ## SUMMARY

In the first section on the importance of studying gender differences, five reasons why studying gender differences is important were discussed. First, it confirms that men and women communicate differently. Second, it offers one more piece of information that helps you understand others. Third, it is likely to bring increased empathy. Fourth, it is likely to improve communication. Fifth, and perhaps most important, it promotes sensitivity and concern between human beings.

Some of the major gender differences were discussed in the second section of the chapter. These included intimacy versus independence, topics of interest, lecturing versus listening, leadership styles, differences in language, differences in nonverbal communication, and reactions to gender talk.

Probably more important than the differences that characterize gender is the way people respond to those differences. Nine differences were mentioned, and they tend to reinforce gender stereotypes. The other problem discussed in this section was the misunderstandings that are likely to occur because men and women rely on different sets of rules to guide their conversations.

Several cautions were expressed with reference to differences in gender communication and our tendency to generalize from these differences. Six were listed. First, gender differences in language vary with time and place. Second, culture is a general determinant of the nature and amount of fluctuation in the distinctions between male and female talk. Third, just because one group of males or females reveals these differences does not mean that all males and females from that group reveal them. Fourth, some contexts promote group differences whereas others minimize them. Fifth, the differences outlined in this chapter represent generalization only; they are not true for everyone. Sixth and last, no value judgment is intended with respect to any single set of language choices.

Four suggestions were offered for improving gender communication skills: learning about each other's style, overriding automatic impulses, avoiding drawing conclusions about others, and adopting your own flexible style.

▶ ## KEY TERMS

gender communication	cross-talk	women's talk
intimacy	rapport-talk	men's talk
independence	report-talk	

▶ ## NOTES

1. Deborah Tannen, *You Just Don't Understand: Women and Men in Conversation.* Copyright © 1990 by Deborah Tannen, Ph.D. By Permission of William Morrow & Company, Inc., 74–95.
2. Joe Tanenbaum, *Male & Female Realities: Understanding the Opposite Sex* (Costa Mesa, CA: Tanenbaum Associates, 1990), 122.
3. Tannen, 49–73.
4. Tannen, 74–93.
5. Diana K. Ivy and Phil Backlund, *Exploring Gender Speak: Personal Effectiveness in Gender Communication* (New York: McGraw-Hill, 1994), 4.
6. Tannen. See Chapter 1, "Different Words, Different Worlds"; Chapter 3, "Rapport-talk and Report-talk"; Chapter 5, "Lecturing and Listening."
7. Tannen, 23–48.

8. "The Last Word on Gender Differences" (*Psychology Today* Essay), *Psychology Today* 27 (March/April 1994), 53.

9. Julia T. Wood, *Gendered Lives: Communication, Gender, and Culture* (Belmont, CA: Wadsworth, 1994), 89.

10. Wood, 89.

11. Tannen, 42.

12. John Gray, *Men Are From Mars, Women Are From Venus: A Practical Guide for Improving Communication and Getting What You Want in Your Relationships* (New York: HarperCollins, 1992), 16.

13. Gray, 18.

14. See Gray, 16.

15. Gray, 18.

16. Wood, 148.

17. A summary of the Maltz and Borker research is provided in Tannen, 43.

18. Tannen, 133.

19. Tannen, 146.

20. Judy B. Rosener, *International Women's Forum: Leadership Study* (1990). *Harvard Business Review*. The author requested and received a personal copy of this study.

21. Wood, 141–142.

22. Wood, 142.

23. Wood, 142.

24. Wood, 143.

25. Wood, 143.

26. Wood, 144.

27. Wood, 144.

28. Wood, 145.

29. Wood, 153.

30. Wood, 154.

31. Wood, 154.

32. Wood, 173.

33. Wood, 149.

34. Tannen, 224.

35. Tannen, 224.

36. Tannen, 224.

37. Tannen, 224.

38. Tannen, 228.

39. Tannen, 228.

40. Tannen, 232.

41. Tannen, 237.

42. Tannen, 239.

43. Tannen, 40.

44. Tannen, 243.

45. Anthony Mulac, Torborg Louisa Lundell, and James J. Bradac, "Male/Female Language Differences and Attributional Conse-

quences in a Public Speaking Situation: Toward an Explanation of the Gender-Linked Language Effect," *Communication Monographs* 53 (1986): 125.

46. Wood, 172.
47. Tannen, 295.
48. Tannen, 298.
49. Tannen, 295.
50. Lillian Glass, *He Says, She Says: Closing the Communication Gap Between the Sexes* (New York: G. P. Putnam's Sons, 1992), 229.

▶ ## FURTHER READING

Suzette Haden Elgin, *Genderspeak: Men, Women, and the Gentle Art of Verbal Self-Defense* (New York: John Wiley & Sons, Inc., 1993). Although Elgin does not uncover new insights in male and female differences, the strength of this book is in the true-to-life dialogues and scenarios she uses to illustrate her points. She covers differences in language, body language, conflict, complaints, sexual harassment, intimacy, and other topics.

Diana K. Ivy and Phil Backlund, *Exploring GenderSpeak: Personal Effectiveness in Gender Communication* (New York: McGraw-Hill, Inc., 1994). This textbook is both comprehensive and practical. The authors' "What If" boxes and practical examples as well as their relationship of gender to the media, marriage, the family, education, and the workplace make this a valuable addition to the gender literature.

Judy Cornelia Pearson, Lynn H. Turner, and William Todd-Mancillas, *Gender and Communication,* 2nd ed. (Dubuque, IA: Wm. C. Brown, 1991). The authors cover topics such as information processing, self-perceptions, images, language usage, nonverbal communication, self-disclosure, intimacy, public contexts, and mediated contexts. A well-researched textbook.

Joe Tanenbaum, *Male and Female Realities: Understanding the Opposite Sex* (Costa Mesa, CA: Tanenbaum Associates, 1990). Although designed for the trade-book market, this is a fine introduction to the whole area of gender differences. Tanenbaum is especially good at explaining biological, brain, and perceptual differences. He also has chapters on communication, emotion, and working together. Approximately 75 sources are cited.

Deborah Tannen, *You Just Don't Understand: Women and Men in Conversation* (New York: Ballantine Books, 1990). This has quickly become a classic in the field, partly because it introduced this area to the public, partly because of the time the book spent on the *New York Times* bestseller list, and partly because of the clarity of writing and organization. Tannen discusses asymmetries, rapport-talk versus report-talk, gossip, lecturing and listening, and dominance and control, among other topics.

Julia T. Wood, *Gendered Lives: Communication, Gender, and Culture* (Belmont, CA: Wadsworth Publishing Co., 1994). For her sources, for the topics she covers, for her writing style, and for the additional examples and anecdotes she includes, this is a superior textbook. Wood covers conceptual foundations, creating gendered identities, and gendered communication in practice. An easy-to-read, comprehensive textbook.

8

CHAPTER OBJECTIVES

After reading this chapter, you should be able to

▲ Relate communication to attitudes and values.
▲ Recognize the difference between attitudes and values.
▲ Explain the difference between instrumental and terminal values.
▲ Describe the components of attitudes.
▲ Explain the process of attitude change: its duration, resistance to it, selecting strategies in, and the ethics of interpersonal influence.
▲ Know the relationship between attitudes and behaviors.
▲ Explain some of the variables that determine which persuasive strategy is selected and describe the relationship of power to interpersonal influence.
▲ List and explain compliance-gaining strategies and give an example of each.
▲ Give an example of a compliance-resisting strategy.
▲ Discuss ways to improve skills in influencing others.

Conrad and Tina were discussing the value of the interpersonal communication class they were currently enrolled in. Conrad was convinced that it was all common sense. Tina was talking with him as they walked from class:

Tina: I know how you feel. So much of what we learn sounds like so much common sense.

Conrad: You're absolutely right. Why is such a course even necessary?

Tina: You realize that interpersonal communication makes up much of what we do every day?

Conrad: Sure, and we've been doing it for over twenty years.

Tina: But just because we've been doing it, Conrad, doesn't mean we're as effective or efficient as we could be.

Conrad: That's for sure.

Tina: I don't know how much work experience you have had, but I work for the local branch of the Department of Labor. If the experience of those who work there is a fair example, then it is clear to me that more people are common-senseless than full of common sense.

Conrad: I haven't had that much work experience.

Tina: If this course can emphasize the principles, concepts, and skills that can increase interpersonal effectiveness, my feeling is that it can make a significant contribution.

Conrad: But don't you think we will get better just with more practice alone?

Tina: Maybe. But it's probably more likely that we will simply reinforce our current habits.

Conrad: I suppose.

Tina: It makes sense. What this course will do, I think, is make our common sense into good sense. Just because it has to do with what we do everyday means that it could be one of the most valuable courses we take.

Conrad: Well, you certainly have given me a new way to view the course.

Tina: A lot of it has to do with attitude, doesn't it?

Conrad: You can say that again. Maybe I can do something about my attitude.

Tina: I didn't say that.

Conrad: No, I know where the responsibility lies. Hey, talk to you later. I have to go this way.

Tina: Talk to you later, Conrad. Take charge of your attitudes!

Zondra was the state sales representative for a large book company, and in her year of work with the company, she had been very successful—*lucky* and successful. Because of her success, she was in her supervisor's office, and they were discussing her future:

Monique: This past year you have been this company's outstanding state sales representative.

Zondra: Thank you. I think I've just been very lucky.

Monique: This company needs more people like you.

Zondra: Thank you.

Monique: You've probably heard that Paul, your regional representative, has been given editorial responsibilities in the home office here.

Zondra: Yes, I had heard that.

Monique: How would you feel about taking on some additional responsibilities?

Zondra: What do you mean?

Monique: How would you like to become the regional representative for your area?

Zondra: Would this mean giving up my state responsibilities?

Monique: Yes.

Zondra: I want you to know I have really enjoyed working at the state level.

Monique: You would still be able to maintain some of those contacts.

Zondra: Can you outline for me the additional responsibilities this would involve?

> *Monique:* Sure. Here is a booklet that details the changes. You don't have to make up your mind right now. Why don't you read the booklet, think about it, and talk to me next week?
>
> *Zondra:* Sounds like a plan. Thanks, Monique.

Christopher and Morella had been married for two years. In the beginning, they led an active social life, going out two and sometimes three times a weekend. But their social life has slowed down, and many hours now seem to be spent watching sports on television and perhaps going to a movie together once every couple of months or so. In this scene, Christopher is watching television, and Morella is trying to change things:

> *Morella:* Did you see that we have some new neighbors?
>
> *Christopher:* (watching football) Yep.
>
> *Morella:* They appear to be our age.
>
> *Christopher:* Yep.
>
> *Morella:* How about inviting them over for a cookout?
>
> *Christopher:* Could . . . I suppose.
>
> *Morella:* How about next weekend?
>
> *Christopher:* I may be working overtime next weekend.
>
> *Morella:* Okay, how about two weekends from now?
>
> *Christopher:* Well, let's wait and see.
>
> *Morella:* But if we want to do it two weekends from now, we should really invite them now.
>
> *Christopher:* Hmmmmmmm.
>
> *Morella:* Is it that you don't want to do anything but watch television?
>
> *Christopher:* That's not true . . . I work, too.
>
> *Morella:* You know what I mean. We have no social life lately.
>
> *Christopher:* Okay, okay. Let's invite them over.
>
> *Morella:* I'm going over to talk with them right now.

Edwin Weinstein, a writer on interpersonal competence, has said that the communicative ability to get others to do what we want them to do is likely to be the single most essential skill for participating in society.[1] As the above examples demonstrate, interpersonal persuasion can occur in a variety of contexts: (1) on campus, (2) at work, and (3) in relationships. The process of attempting to bring about change in other people's attitudes or behavior is known as persuasion. *Compliance gaining*—that is, getting a person to think or act in a specific way—is one form of persuasion. Researchers note that people "do not seem to possess this skill in equal measure. Some do it very well; others, terribly. Unfortunately," they add, "the consequences of not performing this communicative act successfully may be severe."[2] Although Conrad was just engaging in casual conversation, he may change his attitude and may gain in both knowledge and skills because of his talk with Tina. Because of her persuasive skills, Monique may acquire an excellent regional representative in Zondra. She was specific in what she wanted, offered information to clarify the change in responsibilities, gave Zondra time to think it over, and put the responsibility on her to come back and talk about it next week. In the final situation, Morella has taken the responsibility for trying to revive the social aspect of her relationship with Christopher.

Certainly, there are situations in which the consequences may be more severe. For example, Angela convinced her friend Tanya to seek psychological counseling on campus, which very likely prevented a suicide attempt by Tanya. Vaughn convinced Brent, one of his co-workers, to report the name of another co-worker, Eldon, to their supervisor. Because of evidence Brent had that Eldon was stealing company merchandise, Vaughn forestalled an investigation and additional suspicion that either he or Brent were guilty. In a third example, Stephanie chose to persuade Joelle that Dale was cheating on her. This caused Joelle to reconsider her plans to marry Dale. From these examples, it is clear that results can be severe.

What it boils down to is that inappropriate behavior in making requests of others or in responding to such requests (known as *compliance resistance*) may be attributed to incompetence.[3] Since you are likely to be judged—in *any* interpersonal situation—on your ability to make requests of others and to respond to them appropriately, it is important to develop and improve your skills in persuasion.

In this chapter, the relationship of communication to attitudes and values will be discussed at the outset. Why should you study attitudes and values in the first place? Attitudes and values will be discussed specifically in the second section of the chapter. What are they, and how do they relate to each other? In the third section on attitude change, four areas are discussed: the duration of attitude change, resistance to attitude change, selecting attitude-change strategies, and the ethics of interpersonal influence. This section ends with a short explanation of the relationship between attitudes and behaviors. Are they causally linked?

In the final half of the chapter, compliance gaining and resistance are discussed. In the section on compliance gaining, some general information is offered first. Specific strategies are discussed next, and the limitations of compliance-gaining research is discussed last. In the section on compliance resistance, compliance resistance strategies are discussed first; then, the section "Let's Be Realistic" explains some of the reasons people are resistant to change. The final section of the chapter offers suggestions for building skills in influencing others.

CONSIDER THIS

What are the expectations for a cross-cultural persuader? That is, how effective would you expect a person from one culture to be persuading someone from another culture? As you read this selection, notice what is involved in laying the foundation for such effectiveness. One would need to be first and foremost an intercultural person.

> The intercultural person is equipped with the capacity to function in more than one culture effectively. The intercultural person possesses cultural sensitivity, which is linked closely with the ability to show cultural empathy—not only to be able to step into another person's shoes but also to "imaginatively participate in the other's world view." A highly intercultural person thus possesses a third-culture perspective and the flexibility to accommodate the roles required by each cultural context, embodying the requisite attributes of an effective facilitator and catalyst.*

Questions
1. Do you think the expectations are too great? That is, considering these expectations, what are the chances for interpersonal-persuasive success in another culture?
2. Which of the suggestions in this piece would be relevant to interpersonal-persuasive success with *any* other person, not just a person from another culture?
3. Do you understand what the authors mean by a "third-culture perspective"? It is like having the ability to stand outside your own culture *and* the culture of the other person and observe what is going on—attempting to determine, from an objective point of view, what would be most effective. In interpersonal persuasion, do you think this is a realistic perspective?

*From William B. Gudykunst and Young Yun Kim, *Communicating With Strangers: An Approach to Intercultural Communication*, 2nd ed. (New York: McGraw-Hill, 1992), p. 253.

▲▲▲ *Communication and Attitudes and Values*

What have attitudes and values to do with interpersonal communication? First, speech communication is a form of behavior. Studying attitudes and values gives you insight into the *why* of human behavior. You can look at *what* is said by examining verbal communication, and you can study *how* it is being said by analyzing nonverbal components. Remember from the preceding chapter that the words you use are an indicator of what we are thinking; the nonverbals are an indicator of your emotional response to what you are thinking. But a deeper, more essential question is, *why* is it being said? And the answer to this question ties into the whole web of human experience that makes each of you unique.

Second, the roots of what people say lie in their attitudes and values. Thus, if you wish to touch people directly and deeply, you must do so by touching these roots. True, you cannot always know the exact nature of the roots. But, knowing that there *are* roots, and that the more you understand those roots the better you will be equipped to deal with them, will help you communicate with others in a direct and profound manner.

Third, such knowledge can aid you in interpersonal communication because it can guide you in probing for the roots. Suppose one day you hear a friend make a seemingly frivolous remark that expresses a positive attitude toward suicide. You know that your friend has been depressed and has suffered some small failures and rejections lately, so you have reason for concern. You may not want to pursue this attitude imme-

Can you guess what attitudes and values this young woman might be conveying? What are the cues you read when you try to discover the attitudes and values being conveyed?

diately, but you might start probing subtly. Has your friend had any direct experience involving suicide? The suicide of a friend or family member can have a powerful, lasting effect. How much does she value life? Does she value her own life? Does it appear that she has concrete reasons for living?

If you discover she has a weak value system supporting living, this is where you could concentrate future communications. Show her how valuable she is to you and to others. Emphasize the contribution she has to make, or how much others have to gain from her knowledge or expertise. What you want to do, in a sense, is to offer a positive value system to supplant her negative one.

What if your probing does not reveal a negative value system after all? What's left? You might find out if her remark was primarily an emotional response to a particular frustration: a low grade on a paper, a brush-off by an old friend, or being jilted by a relationship partner.

As you probe the emotional basis, you may discover a value system operating that you did not know about. The depression you detected at the outset is real, and your friend is experiencing an emotional response to a trying, complicated situation over which she has no control. Her father and mother are in the process of getting a divorce, and this situation is tearing your friend apart emotionally. At the moment she feels as though her only outlet is suicide; it is apparent that she needs serious counseling.

The value system operating here can be expressed succinctly: Your friend values family security (marriage, the traditional family). When these roots (values) are disturbed, attitude changes are likely to occur, or at least, attitudinal fluctuations.

What your probing has determined, then, is that your friend's emotional response (the attitude) is a result of values about her parents and her family (the value system). At that point, you can make your communication with her more specific and purposeful: try to show her that her parents' divorce need not destroy her, to let her know that she has a large group of concerned friends, and to encourage her to see a professional counselor.

Although this example is extended, it demonstrates how understanding these roots can make your communication more precise and purposeful. It adds a "depth" dimension to your communication that allows you to go beyond superficial, everyday interaction.

▲▲▲ *Attitudes and Values*

What exactly is an "attitude"? **Attitudes** *are general tendencies of people to act in a certain way under certain conditions.*[4] As such, they are intangible concepts. The tendency to feel despondent after getting back a paper with a low grade, the tendency to be concerned about your appearance when around members of the opposite sex, or the tendency to feel as though you are getting a bargain regardless of the type of product you buy during a sale would all be attitudes under this definition. More specifically, however, the word *attitude* is taken to mean *a tendency to evaluate a person, thing, or idea either favorably or unfavorably.*[5] The objects of your attitudes could be inanimate objects, living things, experiences, ideas, or events.

Sometimes people's attitudes are deduced from their behavior. For example, from the previous examples you might deduce that you have an unfavorable attitude toward getting low grades, feel favorably about looking good for members of the opposite sex, or feel favorably about getting bargains. Your behavior and communication habits are based, to a large extent, on your attitudes. But to properly understand and discuss attitudes, you must know about values because attitudes and values are closely interrelated. Because our real interest here is on attitudes and how attitudes can be changed, we will return to a fuller discussion of attitudes after an introduction to values.

Values

There are about as many definitions of **values** as there are writers on the subject. One helpful approach defines them as *matters of importance, as distinct from matters of fact.*[6] As matters of importance, values provide enduring standards or yardsticks that *guide your actions, attitudes, comparisons, evaluations, and even your justification of self and others.*[7] Because they *guide* your attitudes, they need to be considered first. It is their basic or fundamental nature that closely aligns them with your self-concept and puts them at the center of your personality structure. They form the roots for such strongly held beliefs as life, liberty, and the pursuit of happiness. And values most likely determine which clubs, groups, organizations, and associations you join: because they support the same values as you do.

Values can be organizing systems for attitudes. If you value honesty, for example, this value may provide guidelines for forming and developing attitudes. You may have favorable attitudes toward the police, controlling plagiarism, telling the truth, obeying traffic signs, following directions, and so on. Values are usually enduring because they relate to the way you conduct your life; they provide you with guidelines for your behavior. They influence your behavior—your communication—so that it is consistent with the achievement of your goals. The relationship of values and attitudes is shown in Figure 8.1.

Values can be classified as *instrumental* or *terminal*. According to Milton Rokeach, a well-known scholar of human values, **instrumental values** *are those that influence your daily decisions*—such as being ambitious, cheerful, honest, and polite. They provide the standards that you use on a daily basis. **Terminal values** *are goals that you strive for*. For example, you desire

Figure 8.1
The relationship of values (left) and attitudes (right).

Homemade clothes are better than store-bought clothes.
Food I fix myself is better than packaged convenience foods.
Furniture I make myself is better than any furniture I can buy.

I value self-reliance, industry, and personal creativity.

happiness, mature love, security, self-respect, and wisdom. Rokeach's list of instrumental and terminal values is provided in Table 8.1.[8]

One thing may have become obvious to you: You are likely to have a small number of values, whereas the number of attitudes you hold is many. Rokeach claims that the human values he lists are universal. Of course, the priority given to any single value depends on society and on the individual. But these are *the* values that serve as standards for behavior and judgment.

Attitudes

Attitudes exist internally. You derive them from different sources and hold them with different degrees of strength. Attitudes relate to things, people, and concepts. In general, you acquire them as a result of your experiences: you may have a favorable attitude toward animals because your parents allowed you to have pets as a child or toward reading because your parents read to you often. Peers, teachers, parents, and even television personalities shape our attitudes. The more experiences we have, the more varied our attitudes are likely to be. Each attitude has four characteristics: *direction, intensity, salience* (importance), and *differentiation*.

Direction An attitude's **direction** *may be favorable, unfavorable, or neutral* (no direction). In talking with others, it is often important to know the direction of their attitudes. If you are interested in persuading them, direction becomes vitally important. How you might begin, what words or arguments you choose, or how you structure your approach depends on whether the other person's attitude is favorable, unfavorable, or neutral.

Table 8.1
Rokeach's instrumental and terminal values

INSTRUMENTAL VALUES	TERMINAL VALUES
Ambitious	A comfortable life
Broadminded	An exciting life
Capable	A sense of accomplishment
Cheerful	A world at peace
Clean	A world of beauty
Courageous	Equality
Forgiving	Family security
Helpful	Freedom
Honest	Happiness
Imaginative	Inner harmony
Independent	Mature love
Intellectual	National security
Logical	Pleasure
Loving	Salvation
Obedient	Self-respect
Polite	Social recognition
Responsible	True friendship
Self-controlled	Wisdom

TRY THIS

Rank Rokeach's instrumental and terminal lists of values according to how *you* value them. Rank each list of 18 items separately. Give the lists to friends and have them rank the values. Compare your results. If there are differences, *why* did these differences occur?

When was the last time you wanted to convince someone of something? If, for example, you wanted to persuade a classmate to take a computer course with you, wouldn't it be helpful to know how the student felt about computers and their contribution to his or her career? To know how this classmate feels about computers would be to know the direction of his or her attitude.

Intensity The **intensity** *of an attitude is its strength.* If a person you wish to persuade holds a particular attitude with great intensity, there is little likelihood that you will change it. Intensity can vary from zero (absolutely none) to infinity (a person is willing to die for an attitude). Various people may hold attitudes in the same direction yet differ radically with respect to their intensity.

How might intensity be reflected in the example regarding computers? If you realized the student passionately hated computers, statistics, and mathematics, you might refrain from approaching him or her about taking a computer course—thinking, of course, that your efforts would have little result. The more intense an attitude, the more likely it is to produce consistent behavior.

Salience **Salience** *is the perceived importance of attitudes.* If you were an art student and hated computers, statistics, and mathematics, this attitude might not be as important—salient—for you as, perhaps, for a student in business administration. The more that things affect you directly—have a strong influence on your life—the more likely it is that attitudes regarding those things will be salient, even highly salient, for you. An attitude that is salient is less likely to change or be changed.

Differentiation **Differentiation** *is the complexity of attitudes.* This discussion of direction, intensity, and salience may have suggested that attitudes are solitary or isolated elements. Yet attitudes seldom exist alone. That is, they are part of an interrelated mix. *Attitudes with a large number of supporting beliefs are* **high in differentiation;** *those that are based on few beliefs are* **low in differentiation.**

You may believe that a teacher is good because he or she is knowledgeable, organized, concerned about students, prompt, efficient, prepared, and humorous. Your attitude toward this teacher would be high in differentiation because it is relatively complex. On the other hand, suppose you voted against a candidate in the last election simply because he or she supported the current administration. Your attitude toward that person, based on this one belief, would be relatively low in differentiation.

When you attempt to change an attitude, it is helpful to know the degree of differentiation of that attitude. The more complex it is, the more difficult it is to change. It should be pointed out, however, that some attitudes that appear simple—low in differentiation—may be very complex once they are explored in depth. In the example regarding the candidate who supported the current administration, your attitude could be very high in differentiation if you were really voting against the administration's stand on the economy, foreign affairs, education, concern for the poor, and exploration of outer space.

▲▲▲ *Attitude Change: For Better or Worse*

It is important when studying attitudes to realize that what you are studying may *not* be observable. In addition, what you are studying may be outside the grasp of scientific analysis. To make matters more difficult, our assumptions about human behavior—in whatever context—may be subject to error. The point is not to discourage study but to underscore the need to maintain an open mind. In this section I will discuss the likely duration of attitude change, the factors that affect the process of selecting influence strategies, and the ethics of interpersonal influence. This section concludes with a brief discussion of the relationship between attitudes and behavior.

The Duration of Attitude Change

The point of discussing attitudes is to provide a base for understanding attitude change in yourself and in others. What causes you to change your attitudes? Do you wake up one morning and say, "My attitude to-

TRY THIS

List all the clubs, groups, organizations, and associations to which you currently belong—either formally or informally. Now, place a large check beside those that have the same—or nearly the same—values as you do. Can you articulate one or two of the specific values that each club, group, organization, or association actually espouses?

If one of these organizations were to change its values, would you leave it? How much of a change would it take? How easily could you change to conform to this group? If you wanted to initiate a change in the group's values, could you do it? How would you go about it?

ward my family is poor. I think I'll replace it"? Not likely. You need time to realize the need for change and to make the change permanent.

You change your attitudes for a variety of reasons. Another person may *give you a reward for changing your behavior or punish you for not changing it*. Making a change under these circumstances is called **compliance.** You may comply for the moment but not really change your attitudes. This kind of change is frequently only temporary. For example, you know you will be punished if you get caught exceeding the speed limit. You may comply with the law, even if you object to it, when the threat of punishment is near—you see a police car—but the compliance is temporary if you speed up when the threat disappears.

You may change your attitudes because of **identification.** If someone you admire holds a particular opinion, you may *try to be like that person by adopting similar attitudes.* But when you are away from that person, your attitudes may change back to their original position. If you wanted to change another person's attitude through persuasion, one way to do it might be by using identification. You would try to present an honest, trustworthy, and credible image that the other person could identify with.

Internalization occurs when you *adopt an attitude because you are truly convinced by it.* If someone persuades you to quit smoking because it is harmful to your health, you may change your attitude toward smoking because you are truly convinced you will suffer if you do not. You may be inclined to change your attitude toward a pass-fail grading system if someone convinces you that prospective employers prefer job candidates who have taken courses for a letter grade. Changes such as these are likely to be long-lasting, since they are based on intellectual and emotional agreement and do not depend on the presence of arbitrary reward or punishment or on another person.[9]

Up to this point, I've been talking about the ways people deal with challenges to our existing attitudes and how they adjust their thinking to maintain and protect those attitudes. However, you actually do change attitudes at times. There are reasons. For example, you might be *coerced* to change. If you do something illegal, law enforcement authorities may force you to change. Your attitude toward freedom may result in continual excessive speeding. The authorities may coerce you by (1) giving you a warning, (2) taking away your driver's license, or (3) putting you in jail. Whether the result is a change in behavior only or a change in attitude, too, could be a product of how effectively the authorities convinced you that speeding is inappropriate and whether you internalized their arguments. You might change your behavior to change your attitudes. You might change your attitudes, too, because of more subtle coercion, or **propaganda.** An organization may get you to accept its doctrines through *"mass hypnosis, constant repetition, loaded language, the subtle use of social pressures, or the appeal to irrelevant loves, hates, and fears."*[10]

You might also change your attitudes because of **manipulation. A manipulator** may *exploit you, use you, or control you.*[11] This may be *blatant control,* as when a friend says, "If you have that attitude, you will no longer be my friend." Or it may be more *subtle,* as when advertisers try to change your attitude toward their product by suggesting it will make you happier and more popular.

The point is, there are many reasons for changing attitudes—some positive and some negative. You need to be aware of the forces at work on you. You also must try to avoid using coercion, propaganda, and manipulation in your interpersonal relations with other people. You should never use your knowledge of others for socially destructive behavior.

It may sound as if attitude change occurs rapidly or as the result of a single conversation. With compliance, this may well be the case. But it takes considerable time, and usually many interpersonal transactions, for important changes to occur. Ongoing interpersonal communication is vitally important in changing another person's attitude.

Resistance to Attitude Change

Why is changing attitudes difficult? Perhaps it would be helpful to know something about why they are resistant to change. *Attitudes are predispositions to respond,* as indicated previously. To be effective in influencing others, you need to overcome those listener attitudes that oppose your position and, at the same time, develop positive attitudes toward your

TRY THIS

When was the last time you changed one of your attitudes? Can you remember the reason why you changed it? Was the change caused by

▲ compliance?
▲ identification?
▲ internalization?
▲ coercion?
▲ manipulation?

Were you aware when the change occurred? Did you put up any resistance? What might have been the consequences had you not decided to change? Do you secretly wish that you had not changed?

position. Berko, Wolvin, and Curtis, writers on the business of communicating, summarize the research conclusions on attitudes.[12] As you read these conclusions, think of them as basic sources of resistance to change.

1. Attitudes that are developed early in life and have been held for long periods of time are more resistant to change.
2. Attitudes that have been successfully held and/or rewarded and reinforced are more difficult to change.
3. Attitudes that are of strong personal concern are difficult to change. Ego involvement means that someone has a personal stake in the attitude.
4. Attitudes that have been expressed publicly are more resistant to change. When people have gone on record in support of something, they are reluctant to change position.
5. Attitudes are more resistant to change if the attitude is seen as a central attitude related to other attitudes and beliefs.
6. Attitudes are more resistant to change if the change seems inconsistent with either a person's logic or a person's experience.
7. Attitudes are more resistant to change if the change is called for by a source of low credibility.
8. Attitudes may be more difficult to change if a strong fear appeal is used; that is, arguing for a change on the basis of strong threats or references to what might happen may backfire.

Selecting Strategies in Attitude Change

Writers on strategies realize that there is a difference between what you plan to do and what you actually do. The same is true when it comes to the variables that affect strategy choice. Charles Berger points out that several variables can affect which strategies persuaders (agents) select when they try to influence the behavior of others (targets).[13] Berger admits that these variables are relevant *only* to reasoned (well-thought-out) behavior, and the assumption here will be that those who are engaging in influencing others are engaging in reasoned behavior. Here is a brief look at seven variables.

Time allows agents to examine potential consequences, situational elements, relationship effects, the personality of the target, and other elements of the interaction. Without the luxury of time, there is greater possibility of error, ineffectiveness, and lack of success. For example, if a decision on a purchase must be made immediately, judgments about quality, other possible alternatives, or even time to discuss the merits of the purchase are less likely to be made.

Affecting another person significantly is often a slow process. If you want to be successful in changing attitudes or behavior, you usually must commit yourself to a long-term effort. Sometimes it may depend on how

If attitude change were going to take place here, on what basis would the change take place? Would the basis for change be the same no matter the direction of the persuasion that was taking place?

many different contacts with the target you are likely to have—the sheer number of times you meet increases the likelihood of change.

Degree of success *is how successful the strategy has proved in the past.* If it worked before, why not try it again? You all know people who lack behavioral flexibility and depend on the same strategic plan despite its high rate of failure. Failure, of course, should not preclude further use of a strategy. The key is flexibility and adaptability in the use of strategies.

Legitimacy *is an agent's right to use a particular strategy.* Is it an employee's right to demand a raise from an employer? Should a student stand up in class and tell a teacher that class members should not be expected to complete an assignment just made? Does a person have a right to tell a casual friend that his or her choice of a spouse is inappropriate?

Relational consequences *are the potential impact a strategy might have on the relationship of the agent and target.* If a persuader wants to maintain the relationship or improve it, potential consequences need to be considered. A newly married man was watching television and wanted the channel changed. He asked his wife, who was in another room, to change the channel. The wife replied, "Change it yourself." The husband never again asked his wife to change the television channel. His request was an attempt to establish a precedent for future behavior; she made it clear that she had the same intent. Their behavior had a long-range effect on the relationship—a relational consequence. She later confirmed that her response worked.

Intimacy *is closeness of a personal or private nature.* It is closely related to relational consequences. Sometimes you are less considerate of the people close to you than you are of others. It may be that their love is "guaranteed," even if you hurt them. Often, just because they are so close all the time, you do not think of them as being separate from yourself. Whatever the situation, intimacy needs to be a concern. If you are involved in an intimate relationship, you are likely to find that many (perhaps most) of the persuasive or influence situations that you find yourself in will in some way bear on your intimate relationship—if not now, perhaps some time in the future.

Personality *is the distinctive personal qualities of people considered collectively.* The personality of the agent will affect strategy selection. Assertive persuaders tend to use more direct strategies. Also, those agents who are cognitively complex—able to assess people and situations from several different perspectives—tend to select other-oriented strategies rather than self-oriented strategies. A cognitively complex person has a large number of attitudes that are high in differentiation. People like this tend to adjust their strategy to accommodate the other person—to say, for example, "You know, if you go to the library with me, you'll do better on tomorrow's test," rather than the self-oriented strategy, "Go to the library with me. I need company when I study."

Relative power *is the status of the agent compared with the status of the target.* **Power** *is the ability to affect the behavior of another person or group.*[14] Berger suggests that those agents with high power have a wider range of strategy choices, whereas those with low power tend to use less direct strategies. Let's look at the different kinds of power.

Think about whether or not you would change your behavior in these situations:

1. Your employer says you will get a raise if you would be willing to put in five more hours per week on weekends. (You currently do not work weekends and previously said you would not.)
2. Your girlfriend's (or boyfriend's) ex-relationship partner has come to you secretly and said, "You stop seeing [name of your relationship partner] or something dreadful is going to happen to one of you."
3. Your physician has told you that you must change your eating habits significantly or risk a life-threatening health problem in the next several years.

4. A celebrity whom you admire dresses in a distinctive and highly unusual manner, and you have an opportunity to purchase similar clothing for yourself.

5. You have been stopped by a state police officer for speeding, and she has chosen to give you a warning along with the comment, "If I ever catch you speeding in my jurisdiction again, I'll throw the book at you."

The question again is this: "In which situations would you make a change in your behavior?" Why? Why not? Power and influence go hand in hand. Powerful people control situations, but, as illustrated in these situations, power comes in many forms.[15]

In the first situation, *power occurs because the employer controls rewards.* This is called **reward power.** In the second instance, *you may respond to the ex-relationship partner out of fear.* This is called **coercive power.** This could be similar to your response to a mugger demanding your wallet or to a bully pushing in line in front of you saying, "You're *after* me, jerk!"

In the third situation, you might change your diet in response to your physician's suggestion. *When you respond because of a person who has special competence,* this is **expert power.** You are unlikely to question your physician's judgment, just as you would probably not question a lawyer, scientist, or engineer who was making a specific suggestion within his or her field of competence.

The fourth situation involves a response to a celebrity, but it could be *a response toward anyone who embodies moral or physical attributes that you admire.* This is known as **referent power.** Have you ever chosen to wear something just because you saw someone you admire wearing it? This kind of imitation is a form of interpersonal influence.

The final situation involves a response to a police officer. This is called **legitimate power**—*power sanctioned by law, custom, rights, or logic.* You comply *not* because the officer has a nice personality or fulfills her duty appropriately, but because she represents the powers of the state. You might question her fairness if she chose to give you the speeding ticket, just as you might question the fairness of an assignment made by a teacher, but you cannot question the officer's right to give you a ticket or your teacher's right to make assignments.

Power is just one variable in strategy selection, but the use of power requires communication, and that is why it is of concern to you. But in order for an agent to influence behavior through power, targets must associate the behavior requested with the power held by the agent (the same holds true for the variable labeled *legitimacy*). All power is based on targets' perceptions. For example, if I don't believe my boss is in a position to give me a raise or if I don't believe the ex-relationship partner is in a position to carry out the threat, appeals to those powers are unlikely to result in influence. Also, unless the agent associates the influence attempt with the power, the attempt may be unsuccessful. Why, for example, does a plainclothes police officer immediately flash a badge to back up a request? To associate the influence attempt with the power.

The Ethics of Interpersonal Influence

The process of influencing others is an ongoing, natural, and important part of your daily life. Because persuasion may have an impact on others, because it involves choices about communicative means and specific ends (things you want or desire from others), and because it can be judged by standards of right and wrong, it involves ethical issues.[16] Throughout this book I have stressed the transactional nature of communication: it involves people in relationships with one another. With this in mind, ethics in influencing others should emphasize "shared responsibility for the outcome of the transaction."[17] The point of this approach is to try "to achieve the best possible outcome for all the participants in [the] transaction."[18] How do persuaders do this? There are ten items mentioned in the prologue that will help achieve this goal. Two of the most essential items, according to Littlejohn and Jabusch, are openness and caring.[19]

Openness *is the honest and complete sharing of information.* The point here is that only when information is honest and complete can a target make the proper choices. An example of lack of honesty and completeness would be someone trying to sell a used car that had significant problems without informing the target of these problems.

Caring *is concern for the well-being of self and others.* As Littlejohn and Jabusch explain it, "It involves a feeling that what happens to others is as important as what happens to self. It is the spirit of good will."[20] Take, for example, the situation of trying to get a friend to go to a campus event when it is not in his or her best interests to do so. Consideration for the spirit of good will might cause the agent to back off when the target resists. In fact, if all the situational variables were known to begin with, a caring agent might decide not to engage in influencing the target in the first place.

The point is that influencing others involves a transactional relationship. Any change in attitude or behavior that occurs in that relationship results from joint decisions and actions. Since both parties are participating in the process, both should take responsibility for outcomes—shared responsibility. For this reason, both agent and target need as much information as possible, and they need to reveal a caring attitude about each other as well. In any influence situation, then, agents need to keep openness and caring in mind as guiding principles for their behavior, approaches, and strategies.

Attitudes and Behavior

It would be helpful if persuaders could know for certain that if they appealed to the right attitudes, the people being persuaded would change—that their behavior would be altered in the way the persuaders desired. It

CONSIDER THIS

There are ethical guidelines that govern interpersonal persuasion. Which of the following guidelines do you think are reasonable? Which do you think are unreasonable or difficult to follow?

1. Be candid and frank in sharing personal beliefs and feelings. Ideally, "we would like *no* to mean *no*; we would like a person who does not understand to say so, and a person who disagrees to express that disagreement directly."
2. In groups or cultures where interdependence is valued over individualism, keeping social relationships harmonious may be more ethical than speaking our minds.
3. Information should be communicated accurately, with minimal loss or distortion of intended meaning.
4. Intentional deception generally is unethical.
5. Verbal and nonverbal cues, words, and actions should be consistent in the meanings they communicate.
6. Usually it is unethical to block intentionally the communication process, such as cutting off persons before they have made their point, changing the subject when the other person obviously has more to say, or nonverbally distracting others from the intended subject.*

Questions
1. Which of these guidelines do you think are most often broken in interpersonal persuasion?
2. Do you think these suggestions, taken together, offer the foundation for a reasonable ethical standard? What guidelines are missing from "a reasonable ethical standard"?
3. Do you think ethical guidelines are even necessary in ordinary, everyday, interpersonal persuasion? Why or why not?

*From Richard L. Johannesen, *Ethics in Human Communication,* 3rd ed. (Prospect Heights, IL: Waveland Press, 1990), pp. 140–41. Johannesen has restated some of John Condon's views from John C. Condon, *Interpersonal Communication* (New York: Macmillan, 1977), Chapter 8.

would be helpful, but there is no information to support the relationship between attitudes and behavior. Charles U. Larson, a writer on persuasion for many years, says it this way: "Another problem is potentially more critical to any of the theories involving attitudes than these [the problems he had just discussed]: the inability of researchers regardless of their perspective, to demonstrate consistently attitude shift and subsequent behavioral change.[21]

The problem is that there is *no* cause-and-effect relationship between attitudes and behaviors. Why? Attitudes are not the only influences on behaviors. Not only do they interact with other attitudes in varied and unpredictable ways, but they do the same with a range of other variables as well.[22] They include the context in which the persuasion occurs, the subject of the communication, the credibility of the persuader, background information already known on the subject, other conflicting information already possessed, and one's own mental and physical character at the time of the communication. If nothing else, this problem helps to keep things in their proper perspective. Imagine what this world would be like if attitudes and behaviors *were* causally linked. Very likely, advertisers would be the first to have a field day.

▲▲▲ *Compliance Gaining*

Compliance gaining *is the process of getting others to do what you want.* Whether you are requesting another person to help with your homework, buy an encyclopedia, study more, or give you a promotion, compliance-gaining strategies play an important role in our interpersonal behavior. It is unlikely that a single day goes by during which you do not use one or more such strategies, and in most cases you use numerous ones over and over again. Learning how to use them will increase your chances for effectiveness and success in most interpersonal situations.

Most research in this area has been conducted within the last thirty years.[23] It is based on the principle that human experience involves interdependence: your goal outcomes (instrumental or terminal values) are dependent on others, just as others' goal outcomes are likely to be affected by your behavior. Thus, it is useful to develop a repertoire of strategies by which to solicit others' cooperation (compliance) in achieving goals.[24]

Some considerations need to be observed before compliance-gaining strategies are chosen. The way receivers or targets of messages perceive the situation plays an important part. Some factors of situation perception include potential personal benefits to be gained, potential apprehension, potential resistance, justification for making the request, degree of intimacy between interactants, dominance, authority, control of one person over the other, and the potential consequences of the behavior. The extent to which sources of messages can diminish any negative aspects of these perceptions—or reduce their effect—will enhance chances that compliance will be attained.

Can you identify the various compliance-gaining strategies that you use to get others to do what you want?

What these factors suggest is that receivers are not empty, inanimate vessels just waiting to be filled with your "choice" influence strategies! They may want to know what's in it for them. They may be apprehensive or nervous. They may be resistant to your persuasion. They may feel their rights are being threatened. They may think you have jeopardized your relationship with them. They may feel you have no authority to ask for a change, or they may sense that future consequences do not merit the request. The point is, as noted previously, some interdependence is operating that must be considered.

Once the receiver's perceptual base has been considered, other factors that affect the way an individual attempts to gain the compliance of another depends on how well the two people know each other—or their level of intimacy—and the power/status relationship between them.[25] Intimacy (closeness of a personal or private nature) will be discussed later. Finally, the size of the request will influence the response. That is, how much targets feel they are being asked to do—the degree of imposition—will be a factor.

In such complex situations, there are no guarantees. Because individuals, situations, and messages vary so much, it is better for those desiring compliance to have a variety of strategies at their command.

Strategies

Several lists of compliance-gaining strategies exist.[26] O'Hair and Cody provide one of the most succinct lists. Their seven global strategies are the essential ones that overtly ask for compliance to requests. A brief explanation of each strategy follows.

1. *Direct requests* contain no information in addition to the request. "Will you take me to the airport?" is a direct request.
2. *Exchange* strategies are those that compromise or negotiate for compliance. "I'll take out the garbage if you'll wash the dishes" is an exchange strategy.
3. *Distributive* tactics occur when one person attaches some negative consequences or lays "a guilt trip" on another person for noncompliance. "If you don't go with me, I'll never help you again" and "If you don't talk to him for me, you're *never* going to hear the end of this" are examples of distributive tactics.
4. *Face-maintenance* strategies use emotional appeals that cast the other person in a positive light—as having good qualities. "Since you get along with her so well, will you talk to her for me?" is a face-maintenance strategy.
5. *Supporting evidence* involves the use of reasoning and appeals to logic to gain compliance. "You can see from all these canceled checks that you are going to have to be more careful this month" uses the canceled checks as supporting evidence to gain compliance.
6. *Other-benefit* tactics are those that give receivers the impression that compliance will be in their best interests or will benefit them in some way. "I told her why this choice of a major would be the best one for her" is an other-benefit tactic.
7. *Referent influence* and *empathic understanding* are the final strategies grouped as a single item because of their similarity. In *referent influence*, sources appeal to the receiver's identification with them. "I know you'll like this movie because you like action and adventure just as much as I do" is an example of referent influence. In *empathic understanding*, sources appeal to the receiver's love and affection for them. "If you really loved me, you'd go to this movie with me" is an example of empathic understanding. Notice that both include the dependence on the relationship between the agent and the target.

Most individuals have their own ideas and perceptions about what strategies are most effective with which people. Many of these ideas and perceptions are based on either personal experience or the observations of others. Many, too, simply result from habit. It is probably best to use a variety of strategies, but whatever strategies are selected, careful analysis of the target and situation should occur first.

Limitations of Compliance-Gaining Research

Compliance-gaining research has its limitations (is anything perfect?)[27]. "Generally speaking, a request is a communicative act in which the agent attempts to get the target to perform an action at some time in the future, which the target would not have performed otherwise."[28] Given the enormous variety in types of requests and the enormous number of goals agents may have for making requests, one can begin to see some of the limitations of this type of research.

First, most of the studies deal with a single message and a single situation as their examples. The same results are not obtained when multiple messages are used. And, it is reasonable to conclude that the same results will not necessarily hold in different situations. Along these same lines, if behavior is a function of both the person and the situation, then researchers need to look at both person and situation functioning together. Let's say you wanted to borrow twenty dollars from a friend. You wouldn't just walk up to him and say, "May I borrow twenty dollars?"—that is, if you are really serious about getting it. You would probably greet him first and then engage him in small talk. From the greeting's response and the nature of the small talk, you would try to gauge your friend's mood. Also, you might try very subtly to find out whether your friend even had twenty dollars to lend you. If everything seemed favorable, you would then make the request; if it did not look favorable, you would not ask for the loan. You begin to realize the complexity of this issue when you consider the large number of individual difference variables versus the large number of situational variables. How would it ever be possible to catalog all the various interactions with all the possible results?

The second limitation involves the selection of strategies. Communicators act differently when asked to generate a spontaneous message than when asked to select a preformulated strategy. Individuals report that they tend to use more positive types of compliance-gaining strategies when selecting preformulated strategies than when spontaneously generating messages. Commenting on her research on the selection of communicative strategies, Ruth Anne Clark notes that

> *Message composition is a form of behavior in which individuals engage regularly. By contrast, asking an individual to select among strategies requires the person to reflect on his or her behavior in a way which might never occur naturally.*[29]

The third limitation has to do with the abstract level at which strategies are formulated by researchers. They need to pay attention to how strategies are actually implemented at the level of discourse. What kinds of things do people *actually* say in compliance-gaining situations? Can strategies be identified in actual use?

The final limitation of compliance-gaining research is the lack of attention to the fact that communicators have multiple goals. Think about it. When you are attempting to gain compliance, is this your *only* concern at that moment? Often, you are also concerned about self-presentation (how you are presenting yourself to others), relational impact (how you are affecting the relationship you have with others), and responding to reservations (how the target is reacting to your message thus far). Just take the example of borrowing twenty dollars from a friend cited above. This isn't your *only* concern—getting the money. First, you want to make sure your friend perceives you as both sincere and serious. Second, you do not want to offend your friend or jeopardize the relationship. Third, you want to be sensitive to any reluctance or reservations on the part of the friend. The job of making a request involves deciding when and how to be persuasive, when and how to be empathically sensitive, and when and how to push for compliance. In standard compliance-gaining experi-

CONSIDER THIS

Rather than offer specific differences in the way males and females control a conversation or try to influence others, a better approach, it seems, is to raise some questions. Think about these with respect to recent discussions you have had.

Did you display communication behaviors stereotypically connected to your sex and gender? Do you think that such dominant behaviors as interrupting and controlling the topic are necessarily male or masculine conversational devices? Is it "just like a woman" to wait for her turn at talk, rather than speak up and offer her input? Are the sexes somehow limited by such designations of "appropriate" behavior? What happens when the conversational expectations of women and men are violated? Consider the kind of condemnation a man who never speaks up might receive. What might be the response to a woman who interrupts others' comments and changes the topics, without the use of a disclaimer?*

Questions
1. Is sex typing that may accompany conversational style debilitating? How and why?
2. How does gender stereotyping get in the way of successful, effective gender communication?
3. How does answering the questions raised in this piece with respect to your own communication contribute to greater interpersonal effectiveness? Would it be better to just not raise these questions at all?

*From Diana K. Ivy and Phil Backlund, *Exploring GenderSpeak: Personal Effectiveness in Gender Communication* (New York: McGraw-Hill, 1994), p. 173.

ments, subjects work with a restricted set of strategies that focuses on the persuasive aspect of situations with minimal attention to possible interpersonal goals.[30]

The point here is not to try to frustrate your attempts at compliance gaining, nor is it to try to dissuade you from making such attempts. The point is simply to indicate the tremendous number of factors involved in the process. When you discover you haven't been successful, it is helpful to know that there are many potential explanations. These limitations should not *discourage* your attempts to influence others, but rather should *encourage* you to try again using a different approach, or the same approach at a different time, or a different combination of approaches.

▲▲▲ *Compliance Resistance*

The purpose of using compliance-gaining strategies is to achieve effective control, maintain relationships, and create change. Much of the research in compliance gaining has focused on the potential persuader—the influence agent—as the active element in interpersonal persuasion. Yet, the target of a compliance-gaining message has the option of resisting compliance. And, as researchers on **compliance resistance** point out, "the type of strategy selected by the target to resist the compliance-gaining attempt is just as important as the agent's strategy."[31]

It should be noted that the target's unwillingness to comply may frustrate the agent's need. Not only that, it is likely to imply (1) that the agent lacks power to effect certain changes or (2) that the agent has incorrectly assessed the situation. Such resistance, then, can result in rather serious relational consequences. For example, what if a person from whom you borrowed ten dollars said to you, "If you don't return that money, I am going to destroy your credit rating." Really? Could *this* person really affect your credit rating? With whom? However, not returning the ten dollars is likely to have a serious effect on *this* relationship for some time!

Unwillingness to comply also could indicate that the agent has incorrectly assessed the situation. A friend tries to get you to defend your choice of a political candidate in front of a group of people you happen to be talking to. It isn't that you can't defend your choice but that you would rather not do it in front of *this* group of people. A friend trying to get you to steal something from the company you work for might not realize how highly you value honesty or your commitment to *this* company. An intimate friend trying to get you to be more romantic might have underestimated the impact on you of news of a relative's death. Depending on the persistence of the compliance-gaining strategy, your resistance in any of these situations could affect the relationship you have with the agent(s). As you read the three situations described in this paragraph, did you think of ways you would resist these influence attempts? Researcher

Margaret McLaughlin and her colleagues have identified four basic compliance-resistance strategies: (1) identity management, (2) negotiation, (3) nonnegotiation, and (4) justifying.

Identity-management strategies *are indirect resistance in which the image of the agent, the target, or both is manipulated.* For example, if someone wanted to borrow a sweater from you, you might say, "I can't believe anybody would ask to borrow my brand new sweater that I've worn only once," or you might say, "I've never asked to borrow any of *your* clothes."

Identity managing is primarily a manipulative strategy. It should be used with greater discretion in intimate situations than in nonintimate situations. Caution is advised especially in intimate situations with long-term consequences. With nonintimates, identity managing is effective only if both parties are committed to some sort of future interaction.

Negotiation strategies *are, essentially, exchange strategies in which targets propose alternative behaviors to those suggested by the agent.* Related to negotiation strategies are empathic-understanding strategies, in which targets solicit discussion that will promote mutual accommodation. For example, a negotiation strategy would be used if you said, "I think ten dollars is too much to give; I'd be willing to give five, however." To show empathic understanding, you might say, "I'll tell you what—let's not decide that right now. Let's plan to talk more about it later today so we can come to some mutual agreement."

Negotiation strategies have high social desirability in all situations. In high-intimacy situations, negotiation is much more likely to be used—especially when the risk level is high and there could be long-term consequences. For example, relationship partners who had been dating for some time could decide to go somewhere with friends of one partner *if* the next time they go somewhere with friends of the other partner.

Nonnegotiation strategies *are straightforward, unapologetic tactics in which the target overtly declines to comply with the agent's request.* For example, "I'm sorry, no" or "That topic is not open to discussion" are nonnegotiation strategies. Nonnegotiation is less likely to be used in situations with long-term relational consequences, provided the relationship is highly intimate. In low-intimate situations there is greater likelihood that nonnegotiation strategies will be used.

Justifying strategies *are used when targets feel the need to justify or defend their unwillingness to comply because of the potential outcomes, whether positive or negative, to self or others.* "I told her that if I didn't go with her, I would get to use my father's car" is one example, or, on the negative side, "I explained that I didn't want to participate simply because everyone already knew me and would make fun of me."

Justifying strategies might be used in high-intimacy situations only when the consequences are short term. That is, you would not want to appear argumentative or self-serving to an intimate if the situation were of

If this were a compliance-resistance situation, what might be some of the reasons for resistance?

great consequence. With nonintimates, you would be less concerned about identity management and more likely to use justifying strategies.[32]

▲▲▲ *Let's Be Realistic*

Berko, Wolvin, and Curtis, writers previously referred to in this chapter, offer some tips that will help persuaders.[33] They say that people have been found to be resistant to change if

1. They have extreme attitudes on the matter being considered. If a person is a smoker, trying to change that person's mind toward accepting nonsmoking areas in your building is going to be more difficult than trying to influence those who are not smokers.
2. The source is held in low esteem. You must establish yourself or the organization you represent as being credible and interested in aiding the person to satisfy a need in a forthright way.
3. The suggestion or idea is contrary to their own experience. No matter how logical it is to you, if it doesn't fit into the other people's experience, you will have to find some way to show them that they may not have all the information necessary to make a decision.

4. It opposes their reference group. We identify with specific religious groups, political movements, or organizations. If the persuader goes against those groups, he or she will have a difficult time changing our loyalty affiliations.
5. It requires altering habits developed in early life. If you have believed all your life in a specific idea, belief, or way of doing things, it will be difficult to alter that belief.
6. They have gone on public record as favoring or opposing an idea, movement, or process. To change one's mind is often perceived as a

CONSIDER THIS

What would be the ideal circumstance for interpersonal persuasion to occur among friends, lovers, and spouses? Read what Tom Rusk, M.D., a clinical professor of psychiatry at the University of California, San Diego, says about this situation, and answer the questions that follow.

The power of hearing and being heard in a mutual context of respect, understanding, caring, and fairness will not only overcome typical gender differences; it can eventually wear down the much more powerful resistance to believing in one's own beauty and right to exist on this earth. To become champions of each other's self-acceptance is to take up the rewarding work of healing each other. As real intimacy grows from this work, the struggle over differences is increasingly replaced by the playful enjoyment of each other's inherent uniqueness and gifts.*

Questions
1. Is this statement too idealistic to be realistic? What are the chances that such an environment can be created and maintained between friends, lovers, or spouses?
2. What does Dr. Rusk mean by becoming "champions of each other's self-acceptance?"
3. If you felt compelled to establish such an atmosphere, where would you begin? How would you start? What would be the likely effect of establishing such an atmosphere with respect to interpersonal persuasion?

*From Tom Rusk (with Patrick Miller), *The Power of Ethical Persuasion: From Conflict to Partnership at Work and in Private Life* (New York: Viking (Penguin), 1993), p. 150.

sign of weakness. Once a person has signed a petition, declared support for a candidate or a party, or taken some action to allow others to know where he or she stands, it is difficult to convince that person to alter that stand.

Building Skills in Influencing Others

There are many situations in which you would like to make people think or act differently, would like to have an effect, or would like to persuade another person. There are situations, too, in which you have carefully selected a compliance-gaining strategy and used it only to be met by a compliance-resisting strategy that defeated you. What now?

To have an effect on others, you must first consider antecedent factors: What prior values and attitudes do they hold? Remember, too, that you are not the only influential factor. The strength of your message, the medium you use to convey your message, or the context in which the communication takes place can also have an effect. It is sometimes better to wait until circumstances are right before attempting persuasion. Internal processes such as perception, attention, and comprehension also may be important. Sometimes these elements are beyond your control.

In interpersonal situations, your personal credibility—the effect your character (competence, trustworthiness, and dynamism) has on the other person—will be highly important. But your effect on others depends on many other variables as well. If you are really interested in changing an attitude or behavior, being aware of these elements can help you improve the odds. The following are some additional specific suggestions for improving skills in influencing others.

Show that your proposal is approved by someone important to them This is the concept I earlier labeled as "referent influence."[34] Others have labeled it "bandwagon ethics." If others realize that people *they* consider important accept your ideas, your success will be more likely. Talking about friends, experts, or associates who already believe in what you are suggesting helps others put their present beliefs or actions in perspective.

Show that your proposal is consistent with their needs What are the personal needs of the people you hope to persuade? Abraham Maslow categorized seven types of human needs: needs related to physiology, safety, love, esteem, self-actualization, knowledge and understanding, and aesthetics. Think of these as a hierarchy: each level, beginning with basic physiological needs, must be taken care of before you go on to the next one. (See Figure 8.2.)

Figure 8.2
*Maslow's hierarchy of
needs.*[35]

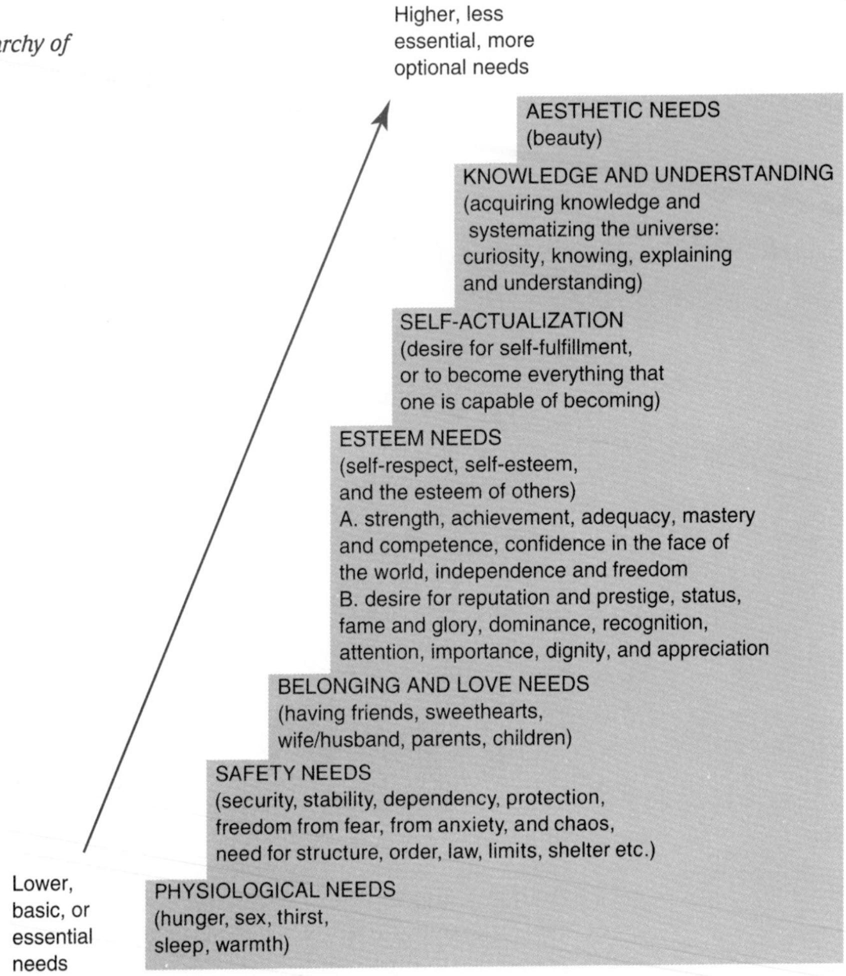

Higher, less
essential, more
optional needs

AESTHETIC NEEDS
(beauty)

KNOWLEDGE AND UNDERSTANDING
(acquiring knowledge and
 systematizing the universe:
curiosity, knowing, explaining
and understanding)

SELF-ACTUALIZATION
(desire for self-fulfillment,
or to become everything that
one is capable of becoming)

ESTEEM NEEDS
(self-respect, self-esteem,
and the esteem of others)
A. strength, achievement, adequacy, mastery
and competence, confidence in the face of
the world, independence and freedom
B. desire for reputation and prestige, status,
fame and glory, dominance, recognition,
attention, importance, dignity, and appreciation

BELONGING AND LOVE NEEDS
(having friends, sweethearts,
wife/husband, parents, children)

SAFETY NEEDS
(security, stability, dependency, protection,
freedom from fear, from anxiety, and chaos,
need for structure, order, law, limits, shelter etc.)

Lower,
basic, or
essential
needs

PHYSIOLOGICAL NEEDS
(hunger, sex, thirst,
sleep, warmth)

Actually, **Maslow's hierarchy of needs** is not as rigid as it sounds. Most people have these needs in about the order Maslow suggests, but there are exceptions. For example, there are people who seek esteem above all else, and there are people whose need to create takes precedence over any other need. Some people who have experienced long deprivation may be content for the rest of their lives with just having their most elemental needs satisfied. There are also some people who were so deprived of love in the earliest months of their lives that their need to give and receive love as adults is distorted.

Physiological needs. These are the most basic needs having to do with your survival. You need food, water, and sleep to survive. Unless these needs are satisfied, you cannot pay attention to anything else.

Safety needs. Once your physiological needs are satisfied, your next concern is safety. Your concern for safety in your environment is reflected in your need for shelter, clothing, and protection from heat and cold. You want to prevent any kind of threat; you resist changes that jeopardize your safety.

Belonging and love needs. Family and friends help you satisfy your need to love and to be loved. Your membership in groups fulfills a need to belong, to be accepted, and to have friends. Marriage and professional associations also satisfy this social need.

Esteem needs. You need to be respected by others. The need is related to your desire for status and a good reputation. If you seek recognition, aspire to leadership positions, or desire awards, compliments, or acknowledgment for your work, your esteem need is operating. Your need for self-esteem is an important part of this need.

Self-actualization needs. When your more basic needs are satisfied, you can move toward self-actualization. This is your need to be everything you can be, to develop yourself to your highest abilities.

The **need for knowledge and understanding.** You need to know and to understand in order to get along in society. For many people, knowledge and understanding are an important part of self-actualization. You need to inquire, learn, philosophize, experiment, and explain.

Aesthetic needs. Do you feel comfortable in a room where a picture on the wall is crooked? Many people find such a situation aesthetically displeasing, and they feel a need to remedy it. People have a wide range of aesthetic needs, but everyone needs to have things around them that they consider beautiful and orderly.

Exactly where your listeners are in their development along this hierarchy, and what they perceive to be the most pressing needs, will make a difference in how you approach them. If you want to persuade someone of something, you would do well to tie this to those needs most salient to your listener. If a person is hungry and desperately trying to feed a family, it is absurd to try to persuade that person to get a job on the grounds that it would be self-actualizing; the immediate need is for food. If you really want to change this individual's attitude toward working, you had better relate working to the most pressing needs.

Show that your proposal is consistent with alternative needs as well If appealing to one need does not work, perhaps appealing to another one will. Do not assume that satisfying one need is necessarily enough. New times mean new needs; people are always changing. You may have misperceived the other person's needs to begin with.

Know the power of fear in attitude change Your subconscious fears are constantly played upon by people who want you to change your attitudes. Advertisers, for example, try to convince you that social or professional success hinges on your buying their product. A teacher may say that your grade depends on the successful completion of a project; you complete the project because you fear failure. You may be persuaded to

TRY THIS

Try to persuade someone of something you are not convinced of. Spend some time—even several days if necessary—continuing your effort.

Notice the effects you have on your listener. Were you successful? Why or why not? What kind of listener needs did you appeal to in trying to persuade? Did you find some needs easier to work with than others? What happened to your attitudes?

carry a credit card out of fear of what would happen if you lost a large amount of cash.

Fear influences your attitudes and behavior. There is nothing new or wrong with that—a certain amount of fear is necessary and healthy in many situations. But if you arouse fear to get another person to accept your ideas, you should provide a means for removing the cause of the fear. Parents who persuade their children to wear boots in cold weather by saying they will get sick if they don't should make sure their children understand what they mean. That is, they need not suggest that pestilence and death will necessarily follow a few minutes with wet feet. And parents could say that the main point is not the boots themselves but that the children are likely to stay healthier if they keep warm and dry.

There is an element of manipulation in using the fear approach. Be aware when someone is trying to use it with you. It is a fairly low-level appeal and generally suggests a low evaluation of the person's intellectual powers. Still, a parent will use fear if necessary to keep a child from crossing a busy highway. You must decide for yourself if arousing fear as a means of persuasion has any place in mature communication.

Be persistent   Just because one strategy did not work does not mean persuasive attempts must end. The strategy might work in a different context or situation, for example. Also, a different strategy might be more effective. For example, Mark deTurck, in his research on the effects of noncompliance, found that when agents "were confronted with noncompliance from persuasive targets . . . they increased their preference for reward-oriented message strategies more than punishment-based appeals on subsequent persuasive requests."[36] More rewards in future messages maximized the chances of obtaining their goals while minimizing the chance of relational damage.

DeTurck also discovered that after targets' noncompliance with two compliance-gaining requests, agents turned to *threat* as their most preferred message strategy. Yet, previous research in compliance gaining indicates that threat is typically the least preferred strategy in any relational context.

Offer a reward or incentive How much incentive you need to offer to get a person to change an attitude depends upon the attitude, the listener, yourself, and the situation. There is no way this can be determined without knowledge of the variables that operate in a given case. Sometimes another person will go along with an idea if your reward is as simple as saying, "If you do it, I'll go with you." Sometimes it is not so simple. But generally our society operates on a system of rewards and incentives; people want something in return for something. That "something" may be as small as a word of praise at the right time, or it may be as elaborate as a large and expensive gift. The reward that works best depends wholly on the circumstances.

Think small Perhaps the most important suggestion for changing attitudes is to **think small:** to first try to change others in some small way that is consistent with their long-range goals.[37] Small changes are often more acceptable and create less conflict and defensiveness than big changes and may show results more quickly, making bigger changes easier later on. For example, if I asked you to contribute ten or fifteen dollars to my campaign, you might suggest I was asking for too much and give me nothing. But if I asked for fifty cents or a dollar, you might reach into your pocket immediately and contribute. It was the small request that got the response and that was successful.

This is not to suggest that only these suggestions will assist in your successful persuasion. Several others could be listed as well.

- ▲ Be specific; exclude all issues irrelevant to your case.
- ▲ Make any concessions you can. This shows you to be flexible and open to others.
- ▲ Show that times have changed, and demand a new approach.
- ▲ Show that what you are asking for is not so drastic.
- ▲ Allow the other person a graceful retreat. Make it easy for him or her to comply.
- ▲ Limit your use of highly emotional appeals. Like a high-pressure salesperson, these tend to repel, not attract.
- ▲ Show respect for their position; perhaps they will respect yours as well.

There is nothing simple about the process of influencing others. But knowing the importance of attitudes and values, the ways in which attitudes can be changed, the criteria for selecting various compliance strategies, and various ways to improve your skills in influencing others should help improve effectiveness and success.

► SUMMARY

This chapter began with a broad view of the connection between communication and attitudes and values. Next, the discussion was narrowed to focus just on attitudes and values. At that point, attitude change was introduced, and the subjects of duration of attitude change, resistance to attitude change, selecting strategies in attitude change, and the ethics of interpersonal influence were discussed. This section closed with a short discussion of the relationship of attitudes and behavior.

The second part of this chapter discussed compliance gaining and compliance resistance. In both cases, strategies were introduced to assist persuaders and persuadees. Sections on the limitations of research on compliance gaining and how to be realistic provided information that offered readers a realistic perspective of both processes: compliance gaining and compliance resistance. The chapter closed with seven specific suggestions on how to improve skills in influencing others. As noted in the last paragraph of the chapter, the process of influencing others is both difficult and complex. The next chapter discusses emotion, a subject that is closely related to influencing others.

► KEY TERMS

attitudes
values
instrumental values
terminal values
direction
intensity
salience
differentiation
high in differentiation
low in differentiation
compliance
identification
internalization
propaganda
manipulation

time
degree of success
legitimacy
relational consequences
intimacy
personality
relative power
power
reward power
coercive power
expert power
referent power
legitimate power
openness
caring

compliance gaining
compliance resistance
identity-management strategies
negotiation strategies
nonnegotiation strategies
justifying strategies
Maslow's hierarchy of needs
physiological needs
safety needs
belonging and love needs
esteem needs
self-actualization needs
need for knowledge and understanding
aesthetic needs
think small

► **NOTES**

1. Edwin A. Weinstein, "The Development of Interpersonal Competence," in *Handbook of Socialization Theory and Research*, eds. David A. Goslin and David C. Glass (New York: Rand McNally, 1969).
2. Karen Tracy, Robert T. Craig, Martin Smith, and Frances Spisak, "The Discourse of Requests: Assessment of a Compliance-Gaining Approach," *Human Communication Research* 10 (Summer 1984): 513.
3. William Labov and David Fanshel, *Therapeutic Discourse: Psychotherapy as Conversation* (New York: Academic Press, 1977), 94.
4. Robert F. Mager, *Developing Attitudes Toward Learning* (Palo Alto, CA: Fearon, 1968), 14.
5. Irving Sarnoff, "Psychoanalytic Theory and Social Attitudes," *Public Opinion Quarterly* 24 (1960): 261.
6. Gordon W. Allport, "Values and Our Youth," *Teachers College Record* 63 (1961): 211–19.
7. Milton Rokeach, *Beliefs, Attitudes and Values: A Theory of Organization and Change* (San Francisco: Jossey-Bass, 1968), 160.
8. See Milton Rokeach, *Value Survey* (Sunnyvale, CA: Halgren Tests, 1967).
9. Herbert C. Kelman, "Process of Opinion Change," *Public Opinion Quarterly* 25 (1961): 57–78.
10. Franklyn S. Haiman, "Democratic Ethics and the Hidden Persuaders," in *Readings in Speech*, ed. Haig A. Bosmajian (New York: Harper & Row, 1965), 196.
11. Everett L. Shostrom, *Man, the Manipulator* (New York: Abingdon Press, 1967), 15. Used by permission of Everett Shostrom.
12. Roy M. Berko, Andrew D. Wolvin, and Ray Curtis, *This Business of Communicating*, 4th ed., 344. Copyright © 1990 Wm. C. Brown Communications, Inc., Dubuque, IA. All rights reserved. Adapted by permission.
13. Charles R. Berger, "Social Power and Communication," in *Handbook of Communication*, eds. Mark L. Knapp and Gerald R. Miller (Beverly Hills, CA: Sage Publications, 1985), 486. Reprinted by permission.
14. James C. McCroskey, Virginia P. Richmond, and Robert A. Stewart, *One on One: The Foundations of Interpersonal Communication* (Englewood Cliffs, NJ: Prentice-Hall, 1986), 186.
15. John R. French and Bertram Raven, "The Bases of Social Power," in *Studies in Social Power* (Ann Arbor: University of Michigan Press, 1959).
16. Richard L. Johannesen, *Ethics in Human Communication*, 2d ed. (Prospect Heights, IL: Waveland Press, Inc., 1983).
17. Stephen W. Littlejohn and David M. Jabusch, *Persuasive Transactions* (Glenview, IL: Scott, Foresman, 1987), 16.

18. Littlejohn and Jabusch, 16.
19. I credit Littlejohn and Jabusch with the selection of the factors of openness and caring as essential to responsible interpersonal communication.
20. Littlejohn and Jabusch, 16.
21. Charles U. Larson, *Persuasion: Reception and Responsibility*, 6th ed. (Belmont, CA: Wadsworth Publishing Company, 1992), p. 69.
22. Larson, p. 69.
23. I am using as a beginning date the work by Gerald Marwell and David R. Schmitt, "Dimensions of Compliance-Gaining Behavior: An Empirical Analysis" *Sociometry* 30 (1967): 350–64. In their article, Marwell and Schmitt mention many of the preceding authors who provide lists or sets of strategies. Most date from about 1960. They mention B. F. Skinner, *Science and Human Behavior* (New York: Macmillan Publishing Company, 1953), who, they say, has "the most inclusive list of types of techniques" (Marwell and Schmitt, 354).
24. See Leslie A. Baxter, "An Investigation of Compliance-Gaining As Politeness," *Human Communication Research* 10 (Spring 1984): 427–56.
25. Karen Tracy, Robert T. Craig, Martin Smith, and Frances Spisak, "The Discourse of Requests: Assessment of a Compliance-Gaining Approach," *Human Communication Research* 10 (Summer 1984): 513–38.
26. The most often cited is the list of 16 strategies of Marwell and Schmitt, previously cited. Also see Gerald Miller, Frank Boster, Michael Roloff, and David Seibold, "Compliance-Gaining Message Strategies: A Typology and Some Findings Concerning Effects of Situational Differences," *Communication Monographs* 44 (March 1977): 37–51; William J. Schenck-Hamlin, Richard L. Wiseman, and G. N. Georgacarakos, "A Model of Properties of Compliance-Gaining Strategies," *Communication Quarterly* 30 (Spring 1982): 92–100. There are many other sources. See Erwin P. Bettinghaus and Michael J. Cody, *Persuasive Communication*, 4th ed. (New York: Holt, Rinehart and Winston, 1987), 185–87.
27. Tracy, Craig, Smith, and Spisak, 516–17.
28. Tracy, Craig, Smith, and Spisak, 514.
29. Ruth Anne Clark, "The Impact of Self Interest and Desire for Liking on the Selection of Communicative Strategies," *Communication Monographs* 46 (November 1979): 257–73.
30. Tracy, Craig, Smith, and Spisak, 516–18.
31. See Margaret L. McLaughlin, Michael J. Cody, and Carl S. Robey, "Situational Influences on the Selection of Strategies to Resist Compliance-Gaining Attempts," *Human Communication Research* 7 (Fall 1980): 14–36.
32. For more information on resisting compliance-gaining strategies, see McLaughlin, Cody, and Robey, as cited above.
33. Berko, Wolvin, and Curtis, 347–48.

34. Herbert C. Kelman, "Compliance, Identification, and Internalization: Three Processes of Attitude Change," *Journal of Conflict Resolution* 2 (1958): 51–60.
35. Data (for diagram) based on hierarchy of needs in "A Theory of Human Motivation" in *Motivation and Personality*, 2d ed., by Abraham H. Maslow. Copyright © 1970 by Abraham H. Maslow. By permission of Harper & Row, Publishers, Inc.
36. Mark A. deTurck, "A Transactional Analysis of Compliance-Gaining Behavior: Effects of Noncompliance, Relational Contexts, and Actor's Gender," *Human Communication Research* 12 (Fall 1985): 54–78.
37. A summary of the findings that support this generalization can be found in C. A. Kiesler, *The Psychology of Commitment* (New York: Academic Press, 1971), 14–17.

FURTHER READING

J. Kevin Barge, *Leadership: Communication Skills for Organizations and Groups* (New York: St. Martin's Press, 1994). Although the focus of this book is on leadership, much interpersonal influence is related to leadership. Barge offers two particularly relevant chapters: Chapter 7, "Exercising Social Influence," and Chapter 9, "Competent Leadership Communication." Both are relevant to anyone who engages in interpersonal influence.

Michael Z. Hackman and Craig E. Johnson, *Leadership: A Communication Perspective* (Prospect Heights, IL: Waveland Press, 1991). Hackman and Johnson discuss leadership and power, leadership and influence, and developing effective leadership communication. All relate to interpersonal influence. Their discussion of leaders as impression managers in the first chapter hits the target precisely.

James M. Kouzes and Barry Z. Posner, *Credibility: How Leaders Gain and Lose It, Why People Demand It* (San Francisco: Jossey-Bass Publishers, 1993). Credibility is essential to effective interpersonal influence. The authors discuss leadership as a relationship, discovering your self, appreciating constituents and their diversity, affirming shared values, serving a purpose, sustaining hope, and the struggle to be human. In the chapter titles alone, this looks like a textbook on interpersonal relations.

Charles U. Larson, *Persuasion: Reception and Responsibility*, 7th ed. (Belmont, CA: Wadsworth Publishing Co., 1995). In this thorough, well-written, and illustrated textbook, Larson treats many of the essential issues already examined in this book, such as ethics, language, culture, nonverbal messages, gender differences, and far more. Especially relevant to this chapter on interpersonal influence is his

Chapter 11, "Becoming a Persuader." This is a delightful book to read and use.

Roxane Salyer Lulofs, *Persuasion Contexts, People, and Messages* (Scottsdale, AZ: Gorsuch Scarisbrick, Publishers, 1991). Lulofs offers readers two chapters that have direct and immediate application to this chapter. In "The Process of Self-Persuasion," she shows how persuasion affects all other processes. In "Interpersonal Persuasion," she discusses tactics, strategies, and outcomes related to dyadic communication. This is over 400 pages of textbook material.

Tom Rusk (with Patrick Miller), *The Power of Ethical Persuasion: From Conflict to Partnership at Work and in Private Life* (New York: Viking [Penguin Books], 1993). This is a powerful, personal book. In the first part Rusk discusses why communication breaks down, feelings are facts, and the power of values. In the second, he divides his ideas into three phases: exploring the other person's viewpoint, explaining your viewpoint, and creating resolutions. In the third, he applies ethical persuasion to relationships, the workplace, families, and difficult people and situations. No sources are listed in the book.

9

Experiencing Emotion: Sharing Our Feelings

CHAPTER OBJECTIVES

After reading this chapter, you should be able to

▲ Explain the nature of emotions.
▲ Explain why it is important to understand emotions.
▲ Describe and briefly explain the three phases of recognizing emotions.
▲ Make specific suggestions for controlling emotions.
▲ Explain how to read another's emotions.
▲ Develop an approach for dealing with others' emotions.
▲ Explain several guidelines that can help you determine when it is appropriate to share your feelings with others.
▲ Make suggestions for clearly and vividly expressing your emotions.
▲ Explain how you can change your emotions.
▲ Describe and briefly explain the principles that serve as guidelines for improving skills in expressing feelings and emotions.

Gil is a 32-year-old postal clerk. His father was a workaholic insurance agent. Gil's father always worked late. When at home, he worked in his home office or sat in front of the television. As Gil grew up his interaction with his father consisted of his being yelled at, given orders, and being told how to act. Meaningful interaction never occurred. To his father, Gil was a nuisance and a distraction from his "important work." Now, as an adult, Gil is an angry, hateful man taking out his revenge on anyone who crosses him. At times he loses emotional control because someone says or does the wrong thing. Most of the time he keeps his anger inside himself; sometimes it pours out like an emotional avalanche.

Heidi loved her position in sales, and she loved the product line as well. But she had begun to dread getting up in the morning because of her anxiety about what was beginning to happen each day. Heidi's boss was driving her crazy. Even though Heidi was the company's highest-paid salesperson, her boss, Lana, would find something wrong with her work every day. It was as if Lana was going through her ritual check-off list until she could find something wrong with Heidi's work. Heidi dreaded the phone calls, conferences, and conversations because they always ended with her being wrong and Lana's being right. Even the sound of Lana's voice now filled Heidi with anger and fear. After one of these meetings, Heidi would notice her jaw clenching and her hands curling into fists. A visit to the doctor confirmed Heidi's emotional trauma. Her blood pressure and cholesterol were inching upward.

You have been pursuing the same academic goal since about the ninth grade. You are now a sophomore in college, and you have never deviated from your goal. But you have just completed two courses in a new area, and you are considering changing your major. It would be a radical change. The decision has been gnawing at you for some time, but now you know it has to be made. The pressure has made you highly anxious, distracted, agitated, on edge, and irritable. How are you going to explain this radical change to your parents? Is this the right decision for you? What if things don't go well, and you have to go back on your decision? Your emotions are driving you crazy.

Not to be aware of your emotions or to understand them is, according to one author, worse than being blind, deaf, or paralyzed.[1] Feelings are what make us human. Feelings are what draw people together. Feelings are what make life worth living. Feelings, too, when out of control, can be dangerous—even life-threatening, as in Gil's case. Gil is a time bomb just waiting to explode in a destructive way. Feelings can have physiological consequences, as in Heidi's case. And feelings, too, can be stirred powerfully as a result of the decisions you have to make—such as having to decide on a major.

Emotion is so basic to human existence that Charles Darwin suggested that some patterns of emotional expression are innate in both animals and humans—although the meaning of such expressions may vary from culture to culture. In this chapter the derivation of emotions will be examined first. What are they and where do they come from? Second, these questions will be answered: Why is it important to understand them? What difference does it make? The third section discusses recognition. How can you recognize your emotions? What is required for recognition to occur? The fourth part deals with control. Since emotions are powerful forces in influencing behavior, and since they can be triggered in an instant, as in Gil's case, you need to know how to control them. The final section examines the process of sharing emotions with others. Just because you experience them, does this mean you should share them? This section includes some practical ideas on how to share emotions successfully with others.

▲▲▲ *What Are Emotions?*

Often you describe people as too emotional or not emotional enough. You know some people who can hide their emotions very well, whereas others are like an open book, wearing their emotions on their sleeves for all

TRY THIS

Awareness is the first step in beginning to understand emotions. How do you feel inside when you experience the following emotions?

▲ affection ▲ disgust ▲ love
▲ anxiety ▲ elation ▲ pity
▲ apathy ▲ grief ▲ pride
▲ confidence ▲ hate ▲ reverence
▲ contentment ▲ inspiration ▲ serenity
▲ depression ▲ jealousy ▲ shame

Can you state how you feel in each case clearly and specifically? Can you recall specific situations in which you have felt any of these emotions? Does recalling specific situations help you state how you feel when you experience this emotion?

to see. **Emotions** *are felt tendencies toward stimuli.* Because emotions are feelings and feelings are emotions, I will use these terms interchangeably. You might wonder what a **felt tendency** is. *It is an internal physiological reaction to your experiences.*[2] Physiological cues probably contribute to the intensity of felt emotions. Emotions have the power to motivate us to action.

When you experience emotions, especially strong emotions, many bodily changes are likely to occur. Your heart rate increases, your blood pressure rises, your adrenaline secretions increase, your blood sugar level may increase, your digestive process may slow down, and your pupils may dilate. You may tremble or sweat. Tears may come. These are just a few of the physiological reactions that may occur. They provide some evidence that your physiological reactions probably contribute to the intensity of felt emotions. Notice how many physiological reactions can come into play at the same time. Here, for example, a woman describes what she felt in the presence of her father, who, she said, always seemed to get her angry: "I'm easily irritated and ready to snap. My face and mouth are tight, tense, and hard. My whole body is tense. My teeth are clenched and my muscles are rigid. I get a tight, knotted feeling in my stomach."

Feelings are always internal states, but you use overt behaviors as you communicate your feelings to others. You have many different ways to express your emotion to others.

Using nonverbal behaviors Your posture, gestures, and facial expressions are major clues. A young man who often felt depressed explained his nonverbal behaviors this way: "I feel heavy and sluggish. I am physically less responsive. My body seems to slow down." Body positioning and distance are additional nonverbal clues that indicate your emotional state. The young man describing his depression added, "I feel a certain distance from others; everyone seems far away. There is a sense of unrelatedness to others; I am out of contact, can't reach others. I feel as if I'm in a vacuum. I don't want to communicate with anyone. There is a sense of being deserted; my body wants to contract, draw closer to myself." In this case the internal states are profoundly felt.

Using verbal behaviors You use several ways of expressing your feelings verbally.[3] Sometimes you do it very briefly, saying just, "I feel guilty," "I'm furious," or "I'm afraid/sad/happy/confident/hopeful/confused/eager." Some people are limited to these single-word descriptions. The language they use to describe their feelings is impoverished, and they have difficulty going beyond a few basic feelings such as "good" or "bad," "happy" or "sad," "terrible" or "great."

Using descriptive phrases "I'm all mixed up inside" is a descriptive phrase. A student emerging from an examination was overheard saying, "I'm on top of the world." Another said, "That was the pits. I'm in the doghouse now!" After a lively class discussion, one student said, "I'm totally in the dark." About a perplexity in a relationship, a woman said, "That leaves me between a rock and a hard place." As long as the phrases are not too obscure, they can serve to effectively describe emotional states.

Describing what is happening To describe what is happening to you, you might say, "I feel as though he's always watching me." One student in a group said, "I feel like nobody here gives a damn." One in a relationship said, "I still feel that he cares about me." A third, also in a relationship, said, "I still feel she loves me." These are effective expressions because they are clear, specific, and vivid.

Describing what you'd like to do When you say something like "I just feel like crying my head off," you are describing what you'd like to do. After getting a flower from her roommate, the other roommate said, "Oh, I just feel like hugging her." A young woman getting ready for an exciting date said, "I just feel like singing at the top of my lungs!" A student frustrated by his grades said, "I feel like giving up." Although most of the time these expressions are clear, sometimes they can be confusing. For example, you cry from anger and fright as well as from great joy. You laugh nervously in fear, you laugh in uncomfortable situations to reduce tension; and you laugh, too, in happiness and pleasure. I remember once at an awards banquet noticing one mother with tears streaming down her face. I thought she was feeling bad and asked her if she would like some-

TRY THIS

Being able to state your emotions concretely is important to effective communication. Concreteness means being clear and specific instead of vague and general. Notice the difference between the following statements:

"Life isn't going too well."
"I'm really frustrated. I want to go to a movie with John, but I have one of my sinus headaches."

The first statement is so general that it could mean almost anything. The second is clear, specific, and concrete.

The following are general statements. Based on your own experiences, behaviors, and emotions, provide a concrete, clear, and specific statement to substitute for each of the following:

"I have a bad headache."
"People are bothering me."
"School is OK right now."
"I think I messed everything up with my mom yesterday."
"What you say stirs up a lot of feelings in me."

From Gerard Egan, *You and Me.* Copyright © 1977 by Wadsworth Publishing Co. Reprinted by permission of Brooks/Cole Publishing Company.

one to take her home. She said, "Oh no, I'm enjoying this so much! These are tears of joy!" The clear, specific, and vivid expression of emotions is essential to effective communication.

▲▲▲ How Emotions Are Aroused

There are a number of theories about how emotions are aroused. Not everyone agrees. Figure 9.1 presents one theory of what happens when an event occurs. Thoughts about the event are triggered, a chemical reaction (caused by the thoughts) is produced in the brain, the chemical reaction produces emotions, and the emotions create a physiological (body) reaction to the event. There is nothing mysterious or magical about the process. Emotions and thoughts can create further chemical reactions, and the circular process can continue building upon itself. This is sometimes what occurs when people become hysterical—out of control of their emotions. It is important to understand this process because of the role that thoughts play. If you can get control of your thoughts or change them, you can get control of your emotions or change them.

Changing thoughts is not easy, but there are numerous methods for doing so. First, you can get new information. You may think, for example, that a comment is unfair until you find out the context (more information) in which the comment was made. Second, you can reframe the information you have. A rainy day that prevents a picnic may be reframed as an opportunity to read a book that you have wanted to read. Third, you may agree to disagree. Rather than becoming emotional (upset) about a comment a person makes, you can simply accept it as disagreeable. Fourth, you can convince yourself that the event is unworthy of your concern—irrelevant or unimportant.

The point here is not to present all the possibilities for thought (stage two) intervention; rather, the point is to show that you are not at the mercy of your thoughts and thus your emotions. When you realize that your thoughts can trigger your emotions, and when you realize you can change your thoughts, it puts *you* in control of your emotions.

An understanding of your thoughts and how they relate to your emotions is important, but that does not excuse you from understanding your emotions as well. You need both, first because it provides you with a more holistic or balanced approach to human behavior and thus even

Figure 9.1
One theory about the relationship between emotion and physiological reactions. Thoughts are at the core of your behavior.

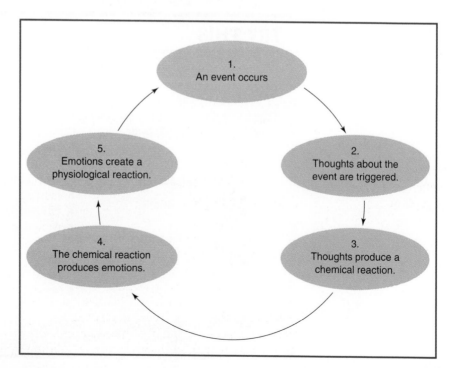

better control. Second, emotions are part of the human experience, and whether you think you are in control of them or not, they will occur. As part of human behavior, they demand your attention and understanding. Attention and understanding will increase your effectiveness as communicators.

▲▲▲ *Why Is It Important to Understand Emotions?*

Emotions are important because they affect both positively and negatively, your ability to communicate with others on all levels. Since feelings of competence and mastery over the environment are basic to survival, understanding your emotions and emotional responses adds to your competence—how suitable or fit you feel. When you control your emotions, you are in psychological control; when you control your emotional behavior and responses, you are in physical control.

Emotions are of fundamental importance to all living creatures. If you learn to understand them properly, it is likely that you can better control and share the emotions you experience. It should be clear that this may not always occur; just because you understand does not mean that control and sharing will follow. But understanding is certainly a first, and very important, step in the control and sharing process that follows.

TRY THIS

It is helpful to have different ways for expressing emotions. Try to express each of the following emotions (1) in a descriptive sentence, (2) by describing what's happening to you, and (3) by describing what you'd like to do. Be creative.

- ▲ ashamed, embarrassed
- ▲ feeling defeated
- ▲ confused
- ▲ guilty
- ▲ rejected
- ▲ repressed
- ▲ peaceful
- ▲ frustrated
- ▲ pressured

- ▲ capable, competent
- ▲ feeling bad about yourself
- ▲ satisfied
- ▲ misused, abused
- ▲ without energy
- ▲ distressed
- ▲ loving
- ▲ bored
- ▲ hopeful

From Gerard Egan, *You and Me.* Copyright © 1977 by Wadsworth Publishing Co. Reprinted by permission of Brooks/Cole Publishing Company.

Emotion Is Part of the Human Condition

Emotion and the expression of emotions are an essential part of the human condition. Because it underlies every communication exchange, emotion needs to be understood as an ingredient in understanding others and their messages.

Emotion Is an Element in Empathy

Empathy, discussed in Chapter 4, can be considered a process or encounter between individuals that aids in solving problems and mediating tensions between people.[4] Since emotion is a prime factor in achieving empathy, a clearer understanding of emotion is likely to add to the potential usefulness of **empathy**—*the projection of your own personality into that of another in order to understand and "feel" the other better.*

Emotion helps us in each of the four phases of empathy discussed in Chapter 4. Identification is essentially a "feeling" phase, in which you

What is it about this man's emotional expression that makes it distinctive and unique? What do you think he might be reacting to?

let another's feelings act on you. To incorporate their feelings into yourself, the second phase, you must try to feel as they do. Reverberation, the third phase of empathy, has you actually interact with the feelings experienced by the other. You achieve the fourth phase, detachment, if you have engaged successfully in the previous phases. You are likely to gain a more accurate picture if you have participated fully in what the other person is feeling.

Emotion Is an Aspect of Individual Uniqueness

However similar human beings are, there is something distinctive and unique about each one. One aspect of that uniqueness is the way each person has of experiencing and expressing emotions. If your goal is to understand what is individual and distinctive in people, then an understanding of emotion and the expression of emotions is essential.

Emotion Offers a Balance to Reason

In our culture, the traditional way to study a situation is to use reason. But if you want to understand another person in depth, you cannot rely on reason alone. A combination of the rational and emotional is needed to gain balance and thus a better understanding of human behavior and motivation.

Emotion Is a Means to Self-Understanding, Self-Control, and Security

An understanding of emotions offers an opportunity for appreciating, explaining, and analyzing yourself and your own inner experiences. Who are you? How do you experience yourself? With greater self-understanding comes the greater likelihood of control—the control of your emotional responses. With self-understanding and control, too, comes security. Once you are more proficient in your use of emotions, you know you have a reliable communication channel at your command. You can then direct your emotions better, and you are likely to become more spontaneous as well. Spontaneity results from your knowledge that you are in control. When you are more secure in your responses, you are then able to trust your own feelings and instincts. Thus, *anything* you can learn about the emotions, and emotional expression, will contribute to self-growth.

▲▲▲ How to Recognize Your Emotions

Recognition involves three phases: (1) awareness, (2) responsibility, and (3) investigation. They normally occur in this order. You cannot take responsibility for something of which you are unaware. Unless you take re-

CONSIDER THIS

Does emotionality have a gender component? An intercultural component? What is likely to be one of the major components that directly affects emotionality? Read the following passage and answer the questions that follow it.

> Masculine traits are typically attributes such as strength, assertiveness, competitiveness, and ambitiousness, whereas feminine traits are attributes such as affection, compassion, nurturance, and emotionality. Cross-cultural research shows that young girls are expected to be more nurturant than boys although there is considerable variation from country to country. [One researcher] . . . has measured the degree to which people of both sexes in a culture endorse masculine or feminine goals. Masculine cultures regard competition and assertiveness as important, whereas feminine cultures place more importance on nurturance and compassion.*

Questions
1. What do you project as the likely outcome of cultures typed as highly masculine? Would you be surprised to find out that people in countries considered very masculine show high levels of stress?
2. How would you type the United States: more masculine or more feminine? How can you tell?
3. What would you expect to be the likely outcome (cultural characteristics) of countries more feminine than masculine?
4. Which country (masculine or feminine) would you prefer, and why?

*Peter Andersen, "Explaining Intercultural Differences in Nonverbal Communication," in *Intercultural Communication: A Reader,* 6th ed., eds. Larry A. Samovar and Richard E. Porter (pp. 286–296) (Belmont, CA: Wadsworth, 1991), p. 291. (The nine countries with the highest masculinity scores, the most masculine being given first, are Japan, Austria, Venezuela, Italy, Switzerland, Mexico, Ireland, Great Britain, and Germany. The eight countries with the lowest masculinity scores, the least masculine first, are Sweden, Norway, The Netherlands, Denmark, Finland, Chile, Portugal, and Thailand.)

sponsibility, you are unlikely to do any investigation—why bother? Once you become aware of, take responsibility for, and investigate your emotions, there is a stronger likelihood that you will begin to experience more, express more, and understand more. There will be greater personal and emotional involvement as well as control.

A belief that one has no control over our environment can lead to giving up and eventually to death, even in previously healthy individuals.[5] Emotionally caused deaths sometimes occur in prison camps and in response to voodoo curses. Many cultures make no distinction between physical and mental diseases or between natural and supernatural causes. This is not to suggest that you will die without some understanding of the emotions! It is simply to point out the importance of the emotions to self-control and the relationship of self-control to good health.

Be Aware of Your Emotions

Before you share your emotions with others, you must be aware of them yourself. There are numerous ways to get in touch with your feelings:

▲ Notice the changes in your body. Because emotional reactions cause physiological changes, physiological changes can signal the presence of emotions.

▲ Monitor your nonverbal cues. Examine your facial expressions. Keep track of your vocal tone. As you talk, be responsive to your paralanguage. Notice your posture and gestures. Are the clues you notice fluid and natural, or are they rigid and tense?

▲ Recognize emotional expressions in your self-talk. How are you communicating with yourself? What messages are you receiving?

▲ Look at the verbal messages you send to others. "I hate you" is an obvious expression of anger, just as "I feel *so* bad" can signal unhappiness, boredom, fear, embarrassment, or even guilt.

Take Responsibility for Your Emotions

Awareness of emotions is important, but if you make excuses for your emotions, blame others for them, or otherwise escape responsibility for them, you are unlikely to increase your understanding of yourself or move closer to maturity. Maturity assumes responsibility. It means recognizing that others don't make you angry or happy, embarrassed or disgusted. Rather than saying, "You really make me mad," it means saying, "I feel angry when you say you'll stop by and then don't show up or call." *You* are responsible for the way you react. *You* are responsible for the emotions you feel. If you do not take responsibility for them, you will feel no need to change them if they are damaging or negative.

For example, Jeffrey found himself unable to smile or laugh easily. He was becoming less able to cope with his daily activities. It was almost as if he had lost the power to act or move. Finally, Jeffrey determined that he was "feeling fear" and that this fear concerned an upcoming major examination. The moment he realized the cause of his jumpiness and jitteriness, he was able to try to change. He created a schedule for daily study that would assure that he covered all the required material and that allowed for final, concentrated study just before the exam. Although Jeffrey's new study procedures did not eliminate all his concerns, he reduced his fear to a manageable and normal level of anxiety about the exam. He might have blamed his teacher; instead, Jeffrey took responsibility for his fear.

TRY THIS

It takes practice to know what you are feeling. It involves getting to know your body and the signals it gives to tell you what you are feeling. It also involves becoming familiar with the typical pattern of thoughts that go along with specific feelings for you.

To help you start this process, use the sample feeling chart below. When you want to know what you're feeling, look at the chart and select the word that best approximates how you feel at the moment.

Feeling Chart

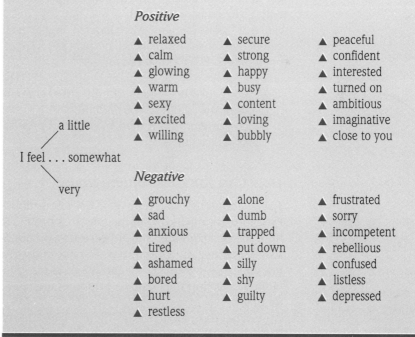

Positive

▲ relaxed	▲ secure	▲ peaceful
▲ calm	▲ strong	▲ confident
▲ glowing	▲ happy	▲ interested
▲ warm	▲ busy	▲ turned on
▲ sexy	▲ content	▲ ambitious
▲ excited	▲ loving	▲ imaginative
▲ willing	▲ bubbly	▲ close to you

a little
I feel . . . somewhat
very

Negative

▲ grouchy	▲ alone	▲ frustrated
▲ sad	▲ dumb	▲ sorry
▲ anxious	▲ trapped	▲ incompetent
▲ tired	▲ put down	▲ rebellious
▲ ashamed	▲ silly	▲ confused
▲ bored	▲ shy	▲ listless
▲ hurt	▲ guilty	▲ depressed
▲ restless		

Investigate Your Emotions

When you trace emotions to their roots, you may get surprising results. One thing you may find is that the emotions you express or reveal have their roots in personal problems or situations. I have a friend, for example, who appears hostile and spiteful. She seems to condemn almost everything. But if you listen long enough, you realize that much of her bitterness stems from the fact that she feels life has been unfair to her. She has an inferiority complex that manifests itself in excessive aggressiveness and a domineering attitude.

Another thing you may find is that the emotion being experienced is just one of a couple or several. Diane and Dave, for example, had had a great evening. Just after dinner, two friends of Diane, Vern and Donna, came over to their table. Diane and Dave had been involved in some self-disclosing, and Diane repeated a "juicy" anecdote to Vern and Donna. After Vern and Donna left, Dave became silent. Soon they left the restaurant. Dave was angry. His mouth was tight; his body was tense; he had a knotted feeling in his stomach. Dave's anger may have been justified, but had he expressed the *real* cause of his anger—the fact that he was embarrassed by the information Diane had revealed—it might have been easier for Diane to understand his reaction.

Anger often arises from other emotions. Ramon became angry at Maria because he was jealous of her relationship with José, her former boyfriend. Jealousy, not anger, was the root emotion. Deona became angry at her roommate, Athena, because she resented the time Athena spent with girlfriends down the hall and not with her. Resentment was the true cause of Deona's anger. Allen carried anger toward Sean. Once he investigated the cause, he realized he was envious of Sean's advantages and possessions. Envy caused his anger.

▲ Ask yourself, "Where did my anger come from?"
▲ Trace the origin of your emotion(s).
▲ Is your emotion rooted in personal problems, related situations, or other reactions?

How Can You Control Emotions?

Think about the last time you became emotional. What did you do? Probably, for most of you, the negative situations are easier to remember than the positive ones simply because you are likely to be more demonstrative in negative situations. For the most part, research on emotion has concentrated on the negative emotions (primarily anxiety and fear) while neglecting the positive emotions such as love, happiness, and contentment.[6]

What did you do the last time *you* became emotional? Sherrie yelled. Todd cursed. Rebecca felt like hitting. Gus threw something. Amanda broke something. Jonathan struck someone. Chances are that just before each of these people did what they did, they felt tense, wound up, maybe even nervous. Some people describe these feelings by saying, "I feel tied up in knots." Your physical response often is a way of releasing the body tension that strong emotions cause. One of the first ways of reducing this tension is to relax in some way. I don't want to assume that all emotional expression is negative; however, for the purposes of this section, let's assume you are dealing with the expression of strong negative emotions. Often, the negative expression is what causes problems. How can you control it? Learning to relax, learning self-control, and learning to read others' emotions are a few suggestions.

TRY THIS

The following is suggested as a relaxation technique:

1. Sit quietly in a comfortable position.
2. Close your eyes.
3. Beginning at your feet and progressing up to your face, deeply relax all your muscles. Keep them relaxed.
4. Breathe through your nose. Become aware of your breathing. As you breathe out, say the word *one* silently to yourself. Continue the pattern: breathe in . . . out, "one"; in . . . out, "one"; and so on. Breathe easily and naturally.
5. Continue for 10 to 20 minutes. You may open your eyes to check the time, but do not use an alarm. When you finish, sit quietly for several minutes, first with your eyes closed and later with your eyes opened. Do not stand up for a few minutes.
6. Do not worry about whether you are successful in achieving a deep level of relaxation. Maintain a passive attitude, and permit relaxation to occur at its own pace. When distracting thoughts occur, try to ignore them and return to repeating *one.* With practice, the response should come with little effort. Practice the technique once or twice daily but not within two hours after any meal, since the digestive processes seem to interfere with eliciting the relaxation response.

Learning to Relax

Stress is the body's response to environmental demands, positive or negative. It is an inevitable part of life, and one you must learn to cope with rather than try to avoid. In Chapter 11, stress management is discussed in relation to conflict. Here, relaxation is discussed in relation to emotional buildups. Taken together, these sections will help you cope with situations of high emotional intensity.

There are many ways to reduce tension, and these ways can be learned. Once you have learned relaxation skills, you can control emotional buildup in all areas of your life. Lisa learned one method in her public speaking class. Just before rising to give a speech, she would close her eyes, take a deep breath, exhale slowly and forcefully, and give herself a pep talk: "Okay, stay calm and relaxed now. This isn't a life-or-death situation. You can do it, and you can do it well."

TRY THIS

Think about a recent situation in which you became emotional. Imagine yourself experiencing the situation and the feelings again. Now, write down the emotion-producing statements (the negative labels) that you made. Look for all such labels. Were there statements or feelings that you made that

1. made you look bad?
2. provided proof that you were no good?
3. proved that things had to be *entirely* the way you wanted them to be?

Write down the negative statements you made. Now, write an alternative positive statement that disputes the negative one.

Negative Label
1. "She knows I hate going to parties with her friends. She did this purposely to spite me."
2. "She has no respect for my wishes."

Positive Alternative
1. "She knows I hate these parties, so she must have a reason for saying we'd go. Maybe this is something special."
2. "I'm the only one she likes to go out with, and I have asked her to go to parties with *my* friends."

Notice how we tend to jump to conclusions? Notice how inclined we are to place negative labels on situations? If the choice is fifty-fifty, why is it that we generally choose the negative viewpoint or perspective rather than the positive?

There are other methods, too. Monica uses yoga; Daniel uses meditation along with deep muscular relaxation. All these methods include breathing exercises, reduction of muscular tension, and a focus on internal bodily sensations.

Many situations escalate to an emotional outburst because of the buildup of tension. Relaxation along the way can help defuse the situation. The earlier a building-emotional situation can be detected, the sooner relaxation skills can be instituted.

Learning Self-Control

The most commonly heard excuse for becoming excessively emotional is that people are "out of control." In some cases, loss of control becomes an excuse for any actions that occur. Once "out of control," people claim they are no longer responsible for what they do. "Loss of control," for some, makes their behavior acceptable. I find it difficult to accept the fact that people *can't* control their behavior, easier to accept the fact they *don't* control their behavior. Perhaps it is just that it is easier to place blame for our behaviors than to accept responsibility for them. Self-control takes practice, but it can be learned if you accept responsibility for your own behavior.

Self-control *means revealing appropriate behavior.* You need to be spontaneous, expressive, and honest. But some people are so self-controlled they don't experience their feelings. You need to free your feelings, experience them, and express them when appropriate.

▲▲▲ *Reading Others' Emotions*

Because of the transactional nature of communication—the relationship that occurs between interacting partners—dyadic partners have an important and ongoing influence on each other. They do not operate independently. Thus, if you have learned to relax and have gained some self-control, this is likely to influence your relationship partner. Let's assume, for a moment, that you are calm and relaxed, but your partner has a potential emotional problem. How do you read his or her emotions?

According to the research, your most immediate source of information about a relationship partner's feelings is your own feelings.[7] Your own feelings can be easily observed and felt, they are important (since they *are* your own), and they are directly experienced. The second most immediate source of information about feelings is the partner's nonverbal emotional expression.[8] You judge emotion in others to a large extent on the basis of their nonverbal behavior; much of the overt behavior in emotion is learned in accordance with cultural norms and expectations. Facial expressions, gestures, posture, and tone of voice are important clues. Paralanguage, too, is an important clue. Nonverbal behavior is assumed to be a more direct and less-censored reflection of your underlying emotional feelings.[9] Verbal explanations are a third way to determine others' feelings. Although verbal behavior is often preempted by more immediate information about feelings, this is not always the case. Some people are especially sensitive to verbal disclosure and emotions. Often, this occurs when people are frank in their communication and engage in verbal sharing.[10]

CONSIDER THIS

Is the expression of emotions a problem that resides with senders or receivers or both? Much of it may reside with receivers and the way they associate certain ways of speaking with certain individuals. Read this passage by Deborah Tannen, and then answer the questions that follow.

> Ways of speaking do not *in and of themselves* communicate psychological states like authority, security, or confidence. We perceive them to connote those states because we associate certain ways of speaking with people we assume feel those emotions. Because Japanese adults learn to be indirect, they associate indirectness with maturity and power. Because middle-class European-American women are more likely to give orders and make requests in an indirect way, we associate indirectness with powerlessness and insecurity—emotions that women in our society are expected to have. And the situation is reinforced by the negative response people are likely to get if they do not speak in expected ways.*

Questions

1. How does this piece support the concept "meanings are in people," which was explained earlier in this book?
2. Do you have any examples from your own life that suggest that if you do not behave in expected ways you are likely to get a negative response?
3. Because we associate certain ways of speaking with people we assume feel those emotions, as Tannen explains, can you see how this would lead to problems in communication between people of different cultures? Between men and women?

*Deborah Tannen, *Talking From 9 to 5: How Women's and Men's Conversational Styles Affect Who Gets Heard, Who Gets Credit, and What Gets Done at Work* (New York: William Morrow and Company, Inc., 1994), p. 99.

In the following example, "A Case Study in Dealing with Others' Emotions," Penny, a student who is upset and angry with a grade she received, approached Dr. Williams, her teacher. Dr. Williams determined that the appropriate response was to calm Penny. Notice the number of different things Dr. Williams did in dealing with Penny.

▶ A Case Study in Dealing with Others' Emotions

Penny was furious. She had just gotten her paper back, and her grade was a "C." Penny had never received less than a "B" on her papers, so she followed her instructor to her office. On the way, she became more and more incensed. When she entered Dr. Williams's office, she exploded. But while she yelled, Dr. Williams remained calm. She responded to Penny's aggression with calmness. Dr. Williams's facial expression, her posture and gestures, and her tone of voice modeled calmness. Penny calmed down.

Dr. Williams did other things to help calm Penny. She encouraged her to talk. She allowed her to explain why she was upset. She even asked open-ended questions such as "What exactly upset you?" and "Why did this bother you so much" and "How do you suppose this happened?" In addition, Dr. Williams listened openly. She was paying close attention to what Penny was saying—and she showed it. She looked directly at Penny, nodded her head when appropriate, avoided interrupting, and even leaned toward Penny to show her concern and seriousness.

As Penny continued talking, Dr. Williams demonstrated that she understood what Penny was telling her. She used statements such as "I see what you mean," "I can understand that," and "I know how that must make you feel." She used the paraphrasing response discussed in Chapter 4 by restating the content of Penny's ideas. Dr. Williams would say back to Penny, in her own words, the essence of what Penny had said. In this way, she let Penny know that she was trying hard to stay with her and with what she was saying.

Dr. Williams also revealed empathy—the most effective way she had to communicate understanding to Penny. She concentrated more on what Penny was feeling than on what she was saying, and Dr. Williams let her understanding of Penny's feelings be known. To reveal empathy, Dr. Williams did several things:

1. She tried to put herself in Penny's place.
2. She asked herself what Penny was feeling and how strongly she was feeling it.
3. She tried to understand Penny's feelings.
4. She noticed what Penny said but also how she said it (tone, speed, loudness of words, breathing rate, stammering, sighing, gestures, posture, facial expressions).

Dr. Williams also helped calm Penny through reassurance. She tried several ways to reassure her. She told her, for example, "It's going to be okay," and "Let's work through this one step at a time."

She also said, "I'm really interested in helping you solve this problem." The purpose of reassurance is to reduce threat, arouse hope and optimism, clear up ambiguities, and make clear your willingness to help solve the problem. In addition to the words, Dr. Williams was warm and sincere when appropriate. Although she did not touch Penny, sometimes a touch, such as a hand on the other's shoulder, also provides reassurance.

The final thing Dr. Williams did to help calm Penny was to help her save face. She did not corner or humiliate Penny. She said that she would be willing to reread the paper, which was a concession on her part. In addition, she said she would be willing to change the grade *if* she found sufficient justification for it; this could be a compromise. In this way, Dr. Williams offered Penny at least part of what was being emotionally demanded. In doing this, Dr. Williams remained calm and self-controlled. She avoided comments that would be perceived as provoking, belittling, critical, threatening, or overly impatient.

▲▲▲ Sharing Emotions

Just because you experience an emotion does *not* mean you should or need to share it with others. Fortunately, there are some guidelines that you can use to determine when it is appropriate to share your feelings. In this section, how to decide whether to share your emotions will be discussed first, when to share them will be discussed next, and, finally, some specific methods for sharing emotions successfully will be offered.

Deciding Whether to Share Your Emotions

Maybe you have gotten to this point in this chapter still wondering *why* you should share your feelings, let alone when and how. Sharing is risky—even scary sometimes. But, in interpersonal communication, sharing emotions with others can help solve problems, resolve conflict, benefit your physical health, and increase intimacy with others. The questions raised in this section may help you decide whether or not to share your emotions with others.

Do you have problems that need to be solved? Interpersonal problems such as hurtful patterns of communication or unpleasant job conditions can often be alleviated when people share their feelings about them. If one or both partners in a relationship have problems that they are not talking about with each other, then their relationship is not a very full one. When problems are solved together, there is mutual investment in the relationship, and the relationship will grow stronger.

How easy is it for you to share your feelings with others? What determines whether or not you will share your feelings?

Do you have conflicts that need to be resolved? Conflicts such as disagreements over money, politics, religion, and the raising of children are easier to deal with when feelings are shared. The sharing of feelings does not provide the answers but sets up an atmosphere in which effective negotiation and compromise can occur. A common response is "I didn't know you felt that way! Now that I know, we can do something about it."

Are you impairing your physical health by holding in emotions? Expressing emotions can help you physically. Just as emotions are accompanied by physiological changes, the tension that occurs when you hold in emotions—especially strong emotions—also can have physiological results. One physician suggests that when there is no discharge of the energy buildup that results from getting emotional, some of the results include headaches, gastrointestinal disorders, respiratory disorders, skin disorders, genito-urinary disorders, arthritis, disabilities of the nervous system, and circulatory disorders.[11]

Are you involved in an intimate relationship that has the potential for greater closeness if you could express how you *really* feel on some issues? Expressing how you feel appropriately and on an ongoing basis with a relationship partner can bring you closer together.

Suppose that you have answered some (or all) of these four questions affirmatively. Suppose you do have problems to be solved, conflicts to be resolved, physical needs for emotional release, and needs for greater intimacy. Should you share your feelings? Since you cannot always open up to others indiscriminately, or easily, or without taking some responsibility for your actions, several factors may need to be taken into consideration. When is it appropriate to share your feelings? Questions like the following may help in deciding:

▲ *What do you want to achieve in this situation? Will expressing the emotion help achieve it?* I remember a snowy evening when our teenage daughter was driving a group of her friends to a concert. Fifteen minutes after the group had left, the mother of one of the other girls called our house to express her worries about driving in such weather. Of course we told her that we understood her worries and assured her that we would not have let our daughter drive on such a night if we hadn't felt sure she could handle it. But what purpose did the call serve? It was too late to cancel the outing—and I suspect that the mother hung up the phone just as worried as before, despite our reassurance. Had she thought through her response first, it would have been better for her *not* to share her feelings in this case.

▲ *Is this the appropriate person to share this with? Could you be misdirecting your emotion?* A student became enraged at what appeared to be a new policy imposed by his instructor and went immediately to the director of the course. After listening to the student, the director suggested that the student talk directly to the instructor. When the matter was finally clarified, it was simply a misunderstanding. Had the student gone to the instructor at once, there would have been no reason for getting upset.

▲ *Can you express your emotion honestly and responsibly, describing exactly what the emotion is and what you really want?* Bruce was having difficulty understanding Trina's behavior. One day she would talk about ending their relationship; the next day she seemed to really want to be with him. Finally, they had a long talk. Trina expressed her feelings honestly and responsibly when she said, "I'm confused by my feelings about you. Sometimes I feel that we are just too different and ought to call it off. But I also want you to know that I love you very much." Although expressing her confusion did not solve the problem, at least it helped Bruce understand her on-again, off-again behavior and laid the groundwork for open discussion of their differences.

▲ *Can you make certain that you express your feelings clearly? Can you provide brief reasons for feeling the way you do? Can you express the feeling directly rather than indirectly?* Jim had reached the point of not wanting to go home—he felt that his father was always "on his case." If it wasn't his messy room, it was the way he left the bathroom, or the chores he forgot to do. One evening at the family dinner table, Jim decided to speak up. He told his father that he felt he was coming down too hard on him for every little thing. Instead of stopping there, Jim got specific: "Dad, just in the five minutes before dinner you got after me for not returning a screwdriver to the workbench, not standing up straight, and not starting my homework the minute I got home from school." To his astonishment, his father admitted that he'd been too hard on him, wanting him to be "too perfect," and agreed to try to back off a little. The direct expression of feelings worked well for Jim.

▲ *Can you keep the feeling centered on specific circumstances rather than on things in general?* We all have ups and downs. *Can you focus on the "down" of the present moment only?* Joan was increasingly annoyed at finding hair in the bathroom sink after her husband, Zach, shaved in the morning. She had let him know before they were married that she would never be his household slave. When she told him how she felt about having to clean up after him every morning, she was careful *not* to mention the socks he dropped on the floor, the newspaper he forgot to put away, or the milk carton he left out on the counter. Joan focused on one specific circumstance only—and she chose the one that bothered her the most.

Sometimes it can help to talk your emotions over with someone else—a friend or a neutral party. This can help you understand what you are really emotional about and how to communicate it. It might be helpful to tell yourself first. Use *intra*personal communication. Sometimes, too, if the emotional reaction is very strong, it is a good idea to use some delaying tactics to give yourself time to understand your feelings. Count to ten. Put yourself in the other person's shoes. Walk around the block. Time provides perspective and, perhaps, a sense of humor.

In every discussion of sharing emotions with others, one question always seems to be brought up: Why is it that whenever your relationship partner becomes emotional, he or she always seems to take it out on you—first! If you think about this, however, you are the person your immediate relationship partner is around the most. Not only that, you are the person with whom he or she is probably most comfortable. In addition, you are the one from whom he or she is likely to get the most support and comfort. An advantage, too, is that two heads are often better than one. One relationship partner can calm the other, suggest possible alternatives for the other, and perhaps provide the only outlet that the relationship partner needs! Sometimes all you need is a listener—or a shoulder to cry on. Relationship partners are often excellent channels for emotional outlet. Think of it as a compliment—your relationship partner thought enough of you to come to you first!

Your emotions and their expression give you an opportunity to learn more about yourself. By looking honestly at how you feel and how you can best share your feelings with others, you can grow beyond immature reactions. Emotions are energy. Learning to channel them can provide great satisfaction and can turn problems into solutions.

Deciding When to Share Your Emotions

Because emotions are powerful, they have the potential for stirring people up. Thus, the time and place where they are shared is important. In general, the sooner you share your emotions the better. Research indicates that information that is more immediate has greater influence on understanding.[12] When sharing is immediate, the feelings are fresh, specific, and easier to identify;[13] thus, the results of immediate sharing are likely to be favorable. There will be less confusion, less difficulty trying to reconstruct the circumstances, and less misinformation.

On the other hand, it is probably best *not* to share emotions right away if you are

▲ rushed. Sometimes the emotion is so strong that you need time to think it over and get a little perspective on it.
▲ very disturbed. You may overstate your anger, saying or doing things that you'll regret later.
▲ too tired to exert the effort necessary to solve the problem.
▲ not ready to listen to what the other person has to say.

If you know that immediacy is best, but recognize that you can sometimes be too rushed, too disturbed, or too tired, this will help you determine when to share your emotions. Sharing is important, and you need to seek the best possible opportunity—soon—if you are to make the sharing pay rich dividends in increased understanding. The problem is that the issue of when to share your emotions is not a clear one. Sometimes it is better to do it at once; sometimes it is better to wait. You are the only person who can make that judgment.

Overcoming the Obstacles

Sometimes there are reasons for not wanting to or being able to share emotions. In some cases you may not feel as though you are in control of this decision. Thus, if you are aware of some of the obstacles to communicating your emotions, you may be able to face them, admit them, and perhaps overcome them. The obstacles, however, may be difficult.

Societal barriers *are those created by any community of related, interdependent individuals.* In our society, for example, many people frown on emotional expression, especially by men. Many males are closed and unexpressive. By being so, they reinforce the stereotypes of the strong and silent male. They do not cry, show fear, or feel sorry for themselves. Because of this image, many men are prevented from open, honest expression. As more women move into executive and management positions, they experience many of the same societal barriers.

Vulnerability barriers *are those created by comments that you think will open you to criticism or attack.* When people express their emotions, often they reveal an intimate and personal part of themselves. For example, one person hated her middle name. After much coaxing and cajoling, and after a great deal of honesty about how much she disliked the name, she finally revealed the name to a close friend. From then on, the friend teased her about the name and her distaste of it. From then on, too, the person who shared her name regretted ever telling this personal information. She revealed a part of herself and was hurt by an uncaring, thoughtless, insensitive person. She made herself vulnerable and then regretted it.

But opening oneself can just as easily bring trust and closeness. Had this "friend" been caring, sensitive, and thoughtful about the feelings this person had about her middle name and thus protected this information, the negative feelings might not have occurred. Instead, a warm feeling of trust and security could have been generated, and the bond of friendship could have been made stronger.

Denial barriers *are those created when you refuse to admit the truth.* Many people have learned that one way to deal with their emotions is to deny them. Because people in our society have judged emotionally expressive people as ineffective and insecure, emotions have come to represent their weaker side and thus a side to be repressed and hidden. To be effective, people (our society feels) need to be rational and logical. But to deny emotions is to deny part of your self—part of that which makes you human.

Communication barriers *are those created when you are unable to convey your thoughts and feelings to others in a meaningful and accurate manner.* One common problem for many who want to share their emotions is how to do it. You may have heard of people who cannot say "I love you," who only express their anger violently, or who cannot show appreciation. The purpose of the earlier parts of this chapter is to help you acquire awareness and understanding, gain control, and decide whether or not to share emotions. Now, the focus turns to sharing emotions successfully and improving skills for expressing them. In this progression of topics (and with the assistance of material from other chapters in this book), it is hoped that some of the communication barriers can be eliminated or at least effectively managed. Total control (or absolute accuracy) is unlikely; however, effectiveness results from awareness, understanding, desire (or motivation), and effective expression.

Sharing Your Emotions Successfully

Earlier in this chapter it was stated that the clear and vivid expression of emotions is essential to effective communication. Knowing *how* to be clear and vivid, however, is not all that simple. More than anything else, it requires practice. For example, look at the following pairs of sentences:

▲ You don't let me know how you feel about our relationship.
▲ When you don't let me know how you feel about our relationship, I get frustrated and insecure.

Can you identify the most common obstacles that prevent you from sharing your emotions with others?

▲ Since we had our fight, I haven't been able to say anything to you.

▲ Since we had our fight, I've said nothing to you because I've been hurt and confused.

Notice that the second statement in each of the pairs above includes a clear and specific emotional expression. The first is emotionally void. Sometimes people think they are expressing themselves emotionally, but they are not providing emotional content. I am not discussing paralanguage here, simply the words that people choose to use. For example, "I feel like going to the party" and "I feel we've been seeing too much of each other" are emotionally void statements. In the first of these sentences, the word "feel" is being used as a synonym for "want to": "I want to go to the party." In the second example, "feel" is being used as a synonym for "think": "I think we've been seeing too much of each other."

Emotive words *are those that express (are characterized by) an emotional state.*
Add an emotive word to each sentence below and notice the changes:

"I feel

alone	friendly
anxious	happy
curious	jealous
depressed	lonely
desperate	needy
disappointed	optimistic
eager	proud
excited	weary

and I want to go to the party."

or "I think we've been seeing too much of each other and I feel

afraid	glad	out of control
closed	hopeful	overcontrolled
concerned	hopeless	pessimistic
confined	hostile	pleased
contented	hurt	pressured
cut off from others	immobilized	proud
dependent	impatient	restrained
deprived	inhibited	secure
despondent	insecure	terrified
exhilarated	misunderstood	threatened

Consider the formula sentence: When you do or say "X," I feel "Y." "Y" is the emotive word.

The point of listing all these words is to demonstrate in how many directions the statement can go once the emotional term is added. Complete the statement using each word and sense the differences. Notice how clear and specific the statement becomes and how the emotional term adds to the communication.

A final point needs to be made in this discussion of the nature and expression of emotions. We have discussed their physiological nature as well as their nonverbal and verbal expression. Much of your reaction to an emotion, however, depends on how you label it. Think, for example, what a difference it makes when you label a person as a "friend" or as an "enemy." How you respond to that person depends on the label you have chosen. The same is true when you face emotional situations: you must remember that you control your emotional response, and you can label the situation in any way you choose. Labeling, then, can change your emotional viewpoint toward a situation, just the way you think about yourself has profound effects on all aspects of your lives. Many people are too ready to pin labels on themselves. The label becomes a self-fulfilling prophecy. If you perceive yourself as depressed, you will act depressed, others will respond to your depressing actions, and their responses will confirm the fact that you are, indeed, depressed. All of this *can* begin with the way you choose to label a situation. Saying "I am angry" will probably make you feel the physiological clues for anger. You may be able to change the situation by selecting a new label: "I am disappointed." The new word is likely to make you feel the physiological clues for disappointment—which are unlikely to be as strong as those of anger. The point is, *you* control the words you choose. With more care in your language choices, you exert more control over yourself *and* your environment.

The way you label situations becomes a powerful persuader. In an important experiment on shyness, subjects were asked how they would react in certain kinds of situations or with certain kinds of people. The researcher found that those who labeled themselves shy did not differ significantly in their reactions from those who said they were not shy. The difference was that those who labeled themselves shy blamed *themselves*: "I am reacting negatively because I am too shy; it's something I am—something I carry around wherever I go."[14] If these people could relabel these experiences and focus on external causes, they could work to change the situation.

An important element in emotional control and emotional sharing that has been discussed in this chapter needs further emphasis. Stressed throughout has been the fact that emotions occur within you, they are yours, and *you* control them. You not only cause them to occur but sometimes increase their intensity and prolong them. Then, having fanned the emotions yourself, you may even blame yourself because you have them. It's a curious process: you become emotional because you became emotional! The point is that the emotions are yours to control. And if you realize that you are in control, you can just as easily change your emotions—reduce their intensity—or create positive ones to replace those that are negative as you can create them in the first place.

Nobody can *make* you disappointed, or irritated. *You* do this to yourself. And if you do it, you can undo it. In their book *A New Guide to Rational Living*, Ellis and Harper say it best: "*You* create and control your feelings. You *can* change them."[15] To bring on this kind of change requires that you push yourself. When you feel afraid, angry, anxious, bored, defensive, disappointed, frustrated, guilty, hurt, inferior, jealous, lonely, rejected, repulsed, sad, shy, or suspicious—some of the most commonly experienced negative emotions—you should use these as cues that you need a shove! Change won't happen by itself. Tell yourself, "I can change this emotion from negative to positive or from negative to *less* negative." Think about it, then do it!

▲▲▲ *Legitimate Possession/Appropriate Expression*

It should be clear that you all experience a vast array of emotions. You have a legitimate right to possess them. However, there are conditions or circumstances that should limit or restrict your expression of them. This

CONSIDER THIS

Are women and men viewed in the same way when it comes to the expression of anger? Read the following selection from Andrea Wood, who was a weekly columnist for the *BGNEWS*, the student newspaper at Bowling Green State University.

> If a woman wishes to express anger or frustration, she is momentarily leaving the bounds of her esteemed place in society.
>
> She is supposed to clean the boat and maintain the harmony within, not rock it. She should be a mother, a peacemaker; level-headed and soothing. Women who assert themselves betray these assigned gender roles. They upset the order of our culture which, traditionally, states that women are to be subservient and lady-like.
>
> Men are encouraged to openly express anger as a symbol of their masculine assertiveness. In some situations, it may be viewed as an asset, as in the case of war, for example.
>
> But a woman who expresses frustration is immediately a target of ridicule.
>
> She may be labeled a nag, a bitch, a castrator, a manhater, neurotic or irrational. She has expressed a concern which would require change.*

Questions

1. Do you think Andrea has overstated the case for the purpose of effect (making an impression), or do you think hers is an accurate assessment?
2. Do you think that a woman who expresses a sense of power upsets the tradition of male dominance? Is the "power to complain" traditionally a man's work?
3. Could the anger expressed by a woman be a signal that she is giving so much of herself with nothing returned to grow on? Are there perhaps other explanations for what a woman's anger may represent?
4. With respect to the expression of anger in our society, do you think a related gender issue is involved?

*Andrea Wood, "Women Will Continue to be Angry," *The BG News,* (October 11, 1994), page 2.

does not mean that you do not have the freedom to express them; this means that you must be sensitive to others' feelings, to contexts, and to possible future effects of this expression. The point is that with freedom comes responsibility!

Examples of this will help explain the problem. Why would a person want to tell a friend who has spent hours getting ready for a date that he or she looks ugly just as he or she is about ready to walk out the door for the date—even if that is how the person legitimately feels? In another instance, why would a person want to tell a friend attending a close relative's funeral that his or her best friend was just in a serious accident? Wouldn't it be more appropriate to wait at least until the funeral was over? Why tell a person likely to die of cancer within the next several weeks of other serious problems in the family? There is a time and place for everything.

Just one other example—a personal one—that happened to my wife and me. When we came home one day, our future son-in-law came to greet us at the door with the news he had broken a living-room lamp. When the lamp was identified, both my wife and I had to withhold our true feelings. We had them, of course; this was our favorite lamp. But, it *was* broken. This *was* our future son-in-law. And there was no point in making him feel worse than he already did. Appropriate expression called for minimizing the event, suppressing our true feelings, and dismissing the situation as quickly as possible. Legitimate possession—appropriate expression.

You have a legitimate right to your feelings and emotions. Yet, living in a free society entails responsibilities, too. There are certain acceptable ways for acting or expressing those feelings and emotions. As much as you might love to yell "Fire!" in a crowded movie theater just to see the response, this is an inappropriate and unacceptable response—and could cause legal problems if someone was injured. Your actions have results; there *are* consequences. And you are not always able to observe them!

Often, the freedom to express yourself has ethical overtones. That is, what is right or wrong in situations is not always clear. In many cases, the guide you have to follow in situations is your own best judgment. *You* must decide, "Is this appropriate?" "Is this right?" Because there are so many contexts, so many circumstances, and so many different people with so many different values and ideas of what *is* right or what *is* wrong, often you are left with no other choice except to weigh all the variables of which you are aware and go with your best decision.

The point here is this: *because* you feel it does *not* mean you need to act on it *or* express it. In so many cases, it is what is left unsaid, unstated, and unexpressed that heals, binds, mends, or repairs. Communication that reveals every thought or emotion that you feel is *not* always best! One suggestion I heard about how to have a successful relationship had to do with learning what feelings need to be left unsaid—unexpressed. It appears to be excellent advice!

Those who feel total honesty is essential in relationships need to weigh their desire to reveal everything against the need to respect others' feelings. Total honesty can be a license to run roughshod over others and can threaten the existence or continuance of the relationship. The best guidance is common sense along with respect and support for the feelings of the other person.

CONSIDER THIS

How do you go about changing your emotions? Read the following selection, and answer the questions that follow.

Because conquering your hostility involves basic changes in your thoughts and actions, you must commit yourself to practicing over and over again new patterns of behavior. Lowering your hostility does not mean wiping out all your hostile attitudes, thoughts, and actions with one great eradication but gradually replacing this pattern of behavior with a healthier one. You will probably find lowering your high hostility levels hard work at first, but these small initial gains are important. Eventually these gains become cumulative. If you stay with these strategies, biological patterns of behavior you may have been born with will no longer rule you, any more than you will be controlled by your past.*

Questions
1. Do you think you can totally "conquer" your hostility?
2. What do you think is the biggest barrier to trying to get control over your hostility?
3. How much time do you think it takes to take charge of your hostile behavior?
4. Do the suggestions in this selection make sense to you? Why or why not?

*Redford Williams and Virginia Williams, *Anger Kills: Seventeen Strategies for Controlling the Hostility That Can Harm Your Health* (New York: HarperPerennial [A Division of HarperCollins Publishers], 1993), p. 62. The Williamses are a husband-and-wife writing team. Redford, a physician, is director of behavioral research at Duke University Medical Center, professor of psychiatry, and associate professor of medicine. Virginia holds a Ph.D. and is an historian and an author.

Building Skills for Expressing Emotions

Although expressions of emotions are important to the success of inter-personal transactions, they should not be an end in themselves. That is, you do not need to express *every* emotion. Yet, many people fear their emotions and live emotionally sterile impersonal lives as a result. This is the other side of the same coin. Notice how these positions are opposite ends of a continuum. (See Figure 9.2.)

Notice in the figure that responsible expression of feelings and emotions occupies the *middle* area of the continuum. It does *not* involve expressing all emotions, nor does it involve suppressing them totally. How often and how much to express are part of responsible assertiveness. Gerard Egan has suggested that the following principles can serve as guidelines: legitimacy, genuineness, constructiveness, immediacy, and control.[16]

Recognize the legitimacy of your emotions A basic, underlying principle that governs the expression of all emotions is their humanness. That is, because you are a human being, you have emotions, and it is legitimate to have and to express them. If you hesitate to express them because you feel they are barriers to interpersonal effectiveness, you undoubtedly question their legitimacy. It may be that you have not experienced the breadth, depth, or flavor they can add to relationships.

Let your emotions be genuine Emotions should be honest reflections of your mental state. Sometimes people hide behind manufactured reactions or repress emotions that should be expressed. Sometimes this results from trying to do what is "right" or what is "expected." Some people have little problem demonstrating negative emotions: anger, annoyance, exasperation, sorrow, misery, outrage, or hate. But these same people cannot (or do not) show joy, pleasure, delight, ecstasy, affection, or ela-tion. Others reveal the positive emotions but not the negative ones. This may be culturally induced behavior. Feelings and emotions, whether pos-itive or negative, are not good or bad. It is the way they are expressed that can be constructive or destructive.

Figure 9.2
The expression of all emotions and the suppression of emotions are at opposite ends of a continuum.

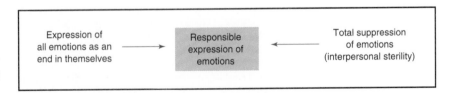

Expression of all emotions as an end in themselves ⟶ Responsible expression of emotions ⟵ Total suppression of emotions (interpersonal sterility)

Express your emotions constructively   Because of the power of emotions and the effect they can have, they can be used destructively in many ways. Some people, for example, save feelings up and then dump them all at once on another person in an emotional barrage. Others release them slowly (and sometimes painfully) over time in cynical or sarcastic ways to undermine another person's credibility or strength. Still another destructive use of emotions is for manipulation; for example: "If I act as if I'm hurt, they'll leave me alone," or "If I get angry and upset, I'll get my own way."

Constructive expression *means taking the responsibility for your emotions.* You need to be aware of them, admit them, investigate them, report them in a factual, objective manner, and integrate them with your other thoughts and feelings.[17] An example of the constructive expression of feelings would go something like this: "I'm feeling very defensive. I don't like to talk about my previous relationships. It just gets me upset and angry. Perhaps we could find something else to talk about."

Give immediacy to your expression of emotions   The timely expression of emotions allows you and others to deal with them while they are still manageable. To deal with them when they come up or soon afterward keeps them in the context in which they arose rather than having to reconstruct the context through explanation and description, like "Remember two days ago when we were talking about such and such, and you said. . . ." Reconstruction of past events is often vague and general, and sometimes the emotions being pinpointed get lost in the ambiguity of the description.

Another function of immediacy is **ventilation.** Expressing emotions immediately offers a channel for release and avoids saving them up and cashing them in all at once in a gigantic emotional avalanche. Most people are unprepared for such emotional outbursts. Immediacy supplies the readiness to explore various reactions and experiences as they occur— while they are clear and meaningful.

Exercise control over your emotions   Though you may be willing—even eager—to share your emotions, discipline is still required. Working through periods of intense emotions is not easy. An overall desire to explore the issues that give rise to the intensity is important.

Control has both positive and negative sides. Positively, control allows communication to continue in a supportive, open environment. Negatively, control can be used to punish, controlling the expression of emotions by repressing them, holding back cooperation, lapsing into silence, showing coldness, or offering cynicism. Control, here, means guiding and managing the expression of feelings. Even strong emotions, or the strong expression of emotions, can be controlled.[18] People who are in control do not give in to the strength of their emotions. Such people might respond to an intense situation in this way: "I really hate what you are saying. You are attacking some values that I care about very deeply. I want to blow up right now, but that isn't going to do either of us any good. I want to strike out at you for what you are saying—and yet I want to know why you are saying these things and why I am reacting so strongly."

There is nothing simple about the subject of emotions. But it is important to try to understand them because they are an essential part of daily life, an essential part of interpersonal communication. Communicating feelings is one of the most frequent sources of difficulty in relationships. You are likely to encounter opposition, conflict, and defensiveness as you deal with both emotions and attitudes. Some disagreement is always likely. And yet you should be able to stand up for your rights, defend your emotions, and effectively express your attitudes—in other words, to be assertive. Assertiveness will be discussed further in the next chapter.

▶ SUMMARY

The chapter began with an examination of emotions—felt tendencies toward stimuli. The ways emotions are expressed was explained. The second section discussed how emotions are aroused; then, five reasons were presented for why it is important to understand emotions. In the next section on recognizing emotions, the three phases of awareness, responsibility, and investigation were outlined. Learning to relax and learning self-control were important features of the section on how you can control emotions. In the section on reading others' emotions, a case study in dealing with others' emotions was presented. Next, guidelines were offered for deciding whether to share emotions, when to share emotions, and how to overcome obstacles to sharing. Techniques for successfully sharing emotions were discussed. After a section on legitimate possession and appropriate expression, five specific guidelines for improving skills for expressing emotions concluded the chapter.

▶ KEY TERMS

emotions	societal barriers	emotive words
felt tendency	vulnerability barriers	constructive expression
empathy	denial barriers	ventilation
self control	communication barriers	

▶ **NOTES**

1. David Viscott, *The Language of Feelings* (New York: Arbor House, 1976), p. 11.
2. David W. Johnson, *Reaching Out: Interpersonal Effectiveness and Self-Actualization,* 3d ed. (Englewood Cliffs, NJ: Prentice-Hall, 1986), 112.
3. These ways are described by Gerard Egan in *You & Me: The Skills of Communicating and Relating to Others* (Monterey, CA: Brooks/Cole, 1977), 87–88.
4. This definition comes from Robert L. Katz, *Empathy: Its Nature and Its Uses* (London: The Free Press of Glencoe, 1963), viii.
5. Philip G. Zimbardo and Floyd L. Ruch, *Psychology and Life,* 9th ed. (Glenview, IL: Scott, Foresman, 1975), 405.
6. Zimbardo and Ruch, 368.
7. Alan L. Sillars, Gary R. Pike, Tricia S. Jones, and Mary A. Murphy, "Communication and Understanding in Marriage," *Human Communication Research* 10 (Spring 1984): 342.
8. Sillars, Pike, Jones, and Murphy, 342.
9. See Mark L. Knapp, *Nonverbal Communication in Human Interaction,* 2d ed. (New York: Holt, Rinehart and Winston, 1978).
10. Sillars, Pike, Jones, and Murphy, 342.
11. Leo Madow, *Anger: How to Recognize and Cope with It* (New York: Charles Scribner's Sons, 1972), 71–85.
12. Sillars, Pike, Jones, and Murphy, 341.
13. Sillars, Pike, Jones, and Murphy, 341.
14. Philip G. Zimbardo, *Shyness: What It Is, What to Do About It* (New York: Harcourt Brace Jovanovich, 1977), 78.
15. Albert Ellis and Robert A. Harper, *A New Guide to Rational Living* (North Hollywood, CA: Wilshire Book Co., 1975), 211.
16. Gerard Egan, *Interpersonal Living: A Skills/Contract Approach to Human-Relations Training in Groups* (Monterey, CA: Brooks/Cole, 1976), 36–37.
17. John Powell, *Why Am I Afraid to Tell You Who I Am?* (Allen, TX: Argus Communications, 1969), 87–93.
18. Carol Tavris, *Anger: The Misunderstood Emotion* (New York: Simon and Schuster, 1982), 34.

▶ **FURTHER READING**

Robin Casarjian, *Forgiveness: A Bold Choice for a Peaceful Heart* (New York: Bantam Books, 1992). Casarjian is a psychologist and provides useful, personal examples throughout this book. Besides giving an excellent chapter on working with anger, the author assists readers with chapters on forgiving parents, spouse, children, and self. A readable book with reasonable suggestions.

Albert Ellis and Arthur Lange, *How to Keep People From Pushing Your Buttons* (New York: Carol Publishing Group [A Birch Lane Press Book], 1994). In this readable book by the author (Ellis) of Rational Emotive Behavior Therapy, the authors offer specific methods to help readers recognize irrational fears and beliefs. They offer straightforward skills to help them react more effectively so they can lead an active, alive, vigorous life. The button-pushers are bosses, colleagues, staff, kids, parents, friends, neighbors, and lovers.

Sidney B. Simon and Suzanne Simon, *Forgiveness: How to Make Peace With Your Past and Get on With Your Life* (New York: Warner Books, 1990). The Simons have written a practical book full of examples. They provide a dozen clarification strategies that will assist readers in building their self-esteem and getting their lives back in shape.

David Viscott, *Emotionally Free: Letting Go of the Past to Live in the Moment* (Chicago: Contemporary Books, 1992). Viscott explains how people can overcome self-limiting doubts, guilt, and anger so they can live a life of love, challenge, and creativity. Viscott helps readers build self-confidence, develop positive close relationships, and deal with difficult people. He offers a simple, step-by-step program for shedding emotional baggage and achieving personal happiness.

Redford Williams and Virginia Williams, *Anger Kills: Seventeen Strategies for Controlling the Hostility That Can Harm Your Health* (New York: HarperCollins Publishers [A HarperPerennial book], 1993). Redford Williams, an M.D., provides the research that connects anger to both heart disease and other life-threatening illnesses. The authors provide seventeen practical strategies that help readers translate scientific theory into meaningful action. They combine solid science with their own explorations into the nature of human relationships. A solid, readable book.

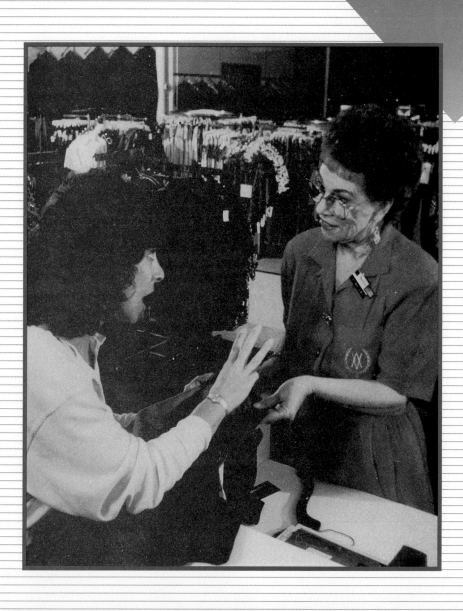

► CHAPTER OBJECTIVES

After reading this chapter, you should be able to

- ▲ Define assertiveness and explain the problems that result from *not* being assertive.
- ▲ Explain what it is that keeps people from being assertive.
- ▲ Distinguish between assertiveness, nonassertiveness, and aggression.
- ▲ Illustrate a negative cycle of self-doubt.
- ▲ Provide specific assertive, nonassertive, and aggressive responses to situations with which you are familiar.
- ▲ Define a script and the various levels of scripts
- ▲ Explain, illustrate, and construct a DESC script.
- ▲ Describe the ingredients of a personal development program designed for changing interpersonal behavior.
- ▲ Offer specific strategies for communicating with unresponsive people.
- ▲ Explain briefly each of your assertive rights.

▼ As Partha pulls his new sweater over his head, he realizes it is tighter than he prefers. It is all right, but a large size probably would be just right. As he takes the sweater off, he also notices a piece of yarn that has been pulled and broken. Of course, it can be tied so it won't make a hole. Partha decides to keep the sweater, even though the store where he bought it is within walking distance. He tells himself he doesn't want to face the hassle of returning it. Deep down, however, Partha doesn't feel comfortable taking things back after he has bought them. He just thinks to himself, "I'll be more careful next time."

Rosa and Cletus have been hanging out together for a year. During the last couple of months they have become very close. Cletus has told Rosa he loved her numerous times, but Rosa has not responded in the same way. Rosa, coming from a family whose members did not express their feelings out loud, and coming, too, out of a disastrous previous relationship, has been reluctant to return the sentiment. She knows she has the feelings; they have been there for several months. But she just can't bring herself to express them. She knows, too, that Cletus would love to hear her say "I love you." This just makes her feel more guilty about holding back.

Louise has worked as personnel manager at Midwest Envelope Company for three years, and she loves her job. One of the workers in her division has created several problems. Naomi does not get along with co-workers, takes excessive breaks, and has been taking company supplies home with her. The latter activity has been reported to Louise by several of her trusted confidantes. Unfortunately, Louise and Naomi have been friends since high school, and Naomi has been taking advantage of their friendship. Because of their friendship, Louise has been reluctant to bring Naomi's behavior to the attention of her supervisor.

Partha, Rosa, and Louise are each in a position where assertiveness is likely to bring positive results. Partha could get a sweater that fits and is free of flaws; Rosa could have a better relationship with Cletus; Louise is likely to lose a friend, but she could get rid of a marginal employee. In all three cases, through greater assertiveness, Partha, Rosa, and Louise could be operating with greater efficiency and effectiveness. They need to follow through on actions that they all know (deep down within themselves) they should be taking.

You've all had the experience of needing to assert yourselves with sales clerks, relationship partners, co-workers, teachers, doctors, and public employees. With friends and with strangers, as well as with children and with people much older than you are, the need for assertiveness is likely to occur often. How do you handle it? In this chapter, different ways of coping with situations that too often become awkward and leave you with bad feelings about yourself and other people are discussed. How do your attitudes, ideas, and values affect your choices? The information here will help you pinpoint your real feelings and improve your skills in direct, honest, and appropriate communication. After assertiveness is defined and discussed, assertiveness, nonassertiveness, and aggression are compared and contrasted. A section on changing negative scripts is followed by one on bringing about personal change and one on communicating with the unresponsive. The final section discusses building skills in assertiveness.

▲▲▲ *What Is Assertiveness?*

Assertiveness *is the ability to share the full range of your thoughts and emotions with confidence and skill.*[1] It means speaking and acting in a way that communicates who you *are* and what you *want*. You can be assertive without infringing on the rights of others and still feel comfortable about your behavior.[2]

According to psychologists Alberti and Emmons, people express their emotions situationally. That is, they have difficulty expressing themselves only in particular circumstances.[3] Most of the time they are fairly effective, but in certain circumstances or with specific people, they lack either the skill or the confidence necessary. Do you find it easy to express hate or anger but difficult to express affection? Do you reveal confidence and strength with friends as you explain how you plan to confront your boss, but fail to stand up for your rights in his or her presence? Effective interpersonal behavior involves identifying the times when assertive behavior would be useful and valuable and then being assertive at those times to the best of your ability.

The cycle in Figure 10.1 shows how assertive action and reaction contribute to and affirm your personal assertive power. Say, for example, that you no longer want to lend course material to a classmate who is depending on you entirely to pass a course he or she is not attending. You are attending class and working hard while this person is playing the role of a leech. You take action by refusing to lend your notes to this classmate. Then you assert yourself and express it in this way: "I don't feel right about giving you my notes. I don't mean to hurt you, but if you don't plan to attend class or do any of the other work yourself, you're going to have to find someone else to depend on in this class." If the classmate protests that you are not being fair, a responsible reaction might be: "Perhaps not in your eyes. However, I feel this action is right, and it will make me feel better about myself. I have never felt good about giving you all this material."

If this solves the problem, you can be assured that your own personal, assertive power will be reinforced. You have extricated yourself from a difficult, emotion-draining situation.

You have the right to be yourself and express yourself and to feel good about doing so as long as you do not hurt others in the process.[5] No matter how confident or successful you feel, there are still times in your life when you may hesitate to claim your rights, when you are anxious about your feelings, when you are unable to respond to anger, or when you feel powerless in your relations with power. But each of you has the right to be treated with respect. Each of you has the right to have and to express feelings, opinions, and wants; to be listened to and taken seriously by others; to set your own priorities; to be able to say "no" without feeling guilty; and to get what you pay for. These are some of your fundamental rights.[6]

You may wonder what's ineffective about *not* being assertive. Here are some of the problems that arise when you do not assert yourself:

1. You may end up with shoddy merchandise and service.
2. You bottle up your real feelings.
3. You are not doing anything to improve a bad situation.
4. You are cheating another person out of a chance to air the real issues.
5. You get involved in situations you would rather not be in.
6. You end up being a "yes" person—having to do all the work while others sit by and watch.
7. You run into communication barriers because nobody is willing to say what he or she *really* wants.

Figure 10.1
Cycle of assertiveness behavior.

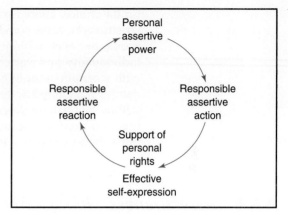

What, in any given situation, might make you hold back from asserting yourself? Here are a few possibilities:

1. Laziness.
2. Apathy.
3. Feelings of inadequacy.
4. Fear of being considered unworthy, unloved, or unacceptable.
5. Fear of hurting the other person or making him or her angry.
6. Fear of getting no reinforcement.
7. Not knowing how to accomplish your desired goal.
8. Feeling that if you don't do it, someone else will.

Acting in your own best interests is a matter of personal choice. Who knows better than you do what is best for you? The key to assertiveness *is* choice. Along with choice, of course, comes taking responsibility

Has something like this ever happened to you? Have things ever happened to keep you from being as assertive as you should be?

for the choice. There is rarely any one way that you *must* act in a particular situation. True, some situations have prescribed or "proper" ways of acting, but even within such guidelines, there is often great latitude for individuality and variety. For example, you know that you would act with a certain amount of deference if you were introduced to the president of the United States—that is a generally prescribed guideline—but within the realm of deference, you can still be yourself. The main point is that you need not be manipulated by circumstances or by people. You must choose for yourself how to act.

▲▲▲　*Assertiveness, Nonassertiveness, and Aggressiveness*

You have come to meet with an instructor to discuss a research paper you wrote and that she recently returned with a lower grade than you feel you deserved. She is a strict teacher, who scares you a little by her manner and approach. You put a great deal of time and effort into your paper and believe the grade is not justified. A girl you know wrote her paper the night before it was due and got an A; you spent the better part of a week on yours and received a low C. Your instructor begins the conversation with "Well, I'm glad we are going to have a chance to discuss your paper."

You have many different options in responding to this instructor. You might reply (1) "I'm sorry the paper didn't live up to your expectations. I really tried, but . . . you know . . . I guess I just didn't give the paper enough time . . ." or (2) "You have no right to give me a C on my paper! I worked harder than the girl down the hall and she got an A. Teachers are really unfair; they never give you credit for the work you do. If you don't change my grade, I'm going to see the dean" or (3) "I think you should know how hard I worked on this paper. I spent most of last week researching and writing. I really thought the paper deserved more than a C. Will you tell me your reasons for the grade? Then at least I would know how to approach the next assignment."

These three alternatives are oversimplified for the purposes of evaluation. You would, of course, have other options as well. You could discuss the grade and the reasons for it without becoming apologetic or defensive at the outset. Discussion that is free from apology or defensiveness is likely to create a positive climate and yield satisfying results as well. Discussion should be conducted in an atmosphere of strength and conviction. That is, you should not sacrifice your values or compromise your standards; you should be able to defend your work and support your overall effort. Discussion is a process of give-and-take that involves *mutual* compromise—not self-sacrifice, apology, or defensiveness. Effective discussion can and should take place in a climate of assertiveness.

Clearly, the (1) and (2) responses in this example are inadequate. In (1) you apologized and used the "excuse" technique. This nonassertive behavior is both dishonest and unfair. You did not really express your feelings, and you denied your teacher honest feedback to her evaluation of the paper. In (2) you showed little sensitivity to the instructor's feelings and used aggressive language that would probably put her off. Only in (3) could you save yourself and the instructor embarrassment, hurt, or awkwardness by a straightforward, assertive response.[7] Your initial response sets the tone for all the communication to follow.

Nonassertiveness

A person who is too politely restrained, tactful, diplomatic, modest, and self-denying—whose behavior falls at the extreme **nonassertive** end of the continuum—may be unable to make the choice to act. A nonassertive person says, in effect, that he or she will let someone else decide what will happen to him or her. You reveal a nonassertive style when you do the following things:

1. Never speak up in groups.
2. Always stick to the middle-of-the-road position or refrain from taking a stand.
3. Allow others to make decisions for you.
4. Pass by potential friendships because they seem like too much effort.
5. Always keep your voice low or avoid eye contact to keep from calling attention to yourself.
6. Verbally agree with others despite your real feelings.
7. Bring harm or inconvenience to yourself to avoid harming or inconveniencing others.
8. Procrastinate to avoid problems and to keep from making decisions.
9. Always consider yourself weaker and less capable than others.
10. Always escape responsibility with excuses and "good" reasons.

Nonassertiveness can cause the beginning of a **negative cycle.** In the example given above, if you go along with the teacher's evaluation without question or discussion, you may acquire a whole new set of doubts: "What is wrong with me? I am not cut out for college. I cannot compete. I'll never succeed." These doubts can lead to further and sometimes intensified inadequate behaviors. (See Figure 10.2.) You may come to think of yourself as wholly inadequate when, in fact, you may simply have misunderstood the assignment.

If you are nonassertive you deny yourself and fail to express your actual feelings. You leave it to someone else to decide what will happen to you, and you may *never* reach your desired goals. This places an unnatural and uncomfortable burden on your interpersonal communications. How do you know how others feel unless they are willing to tell you? Interpersonal communication should not be a game in which people must

Figure 10.2
Self-doubt may lead to further inadequate behavior.

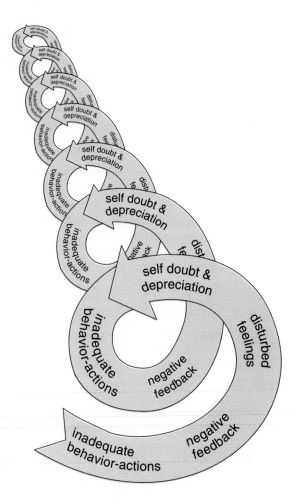

cleverly try to find out what the other person *really* thinks. Assertive behavior can help reduce game-playing and makes interpersonal communication more effective.

Aggressiveness

The **aggressive** style of response is essentially the complete opposite of the nonassertive style. If you are aggressive, you might

1. Interrupt others when they are speaking.
2. Try to impose your position on others.
3. Make decisions for others.
4. Use and abuse friendships.
5. Speak loudly and otherwise call attention to yourself.
6. Accuse, blame, and find fault with others without regard to their feelings.

7. Bring harm or cause inconvenience to others rather than bring harm or cause inconvenience to yourself.
8. Speak beside the issue, distort the facts, or misrepresent the truth to get your solutions accepted quickly.
9. Act as though you are stronger and more capable than others;
10. Accept responsibility and positions of authority for the purposes of manipulation or to give you a means of vehemently expressing yourself.

If you use aggressive behavior you try to accomplish your life goals at the expense of others. Although you may find that this behavior expresses your feelings, you may also hurt others in the process by making choices for them and by implying they are worth less than you are as people.

Assertiveness

The assertive style, in contrast, is self-enhancing because it shows a positive firmness. The assertive style is revealed when you

1. Allow others to complete their thoughts before you speak.
2. Stand up for the position that matches your feelings or the evidence.
3. Make your own decisions based on what you think is right.

Have you ever felt so aggressive with another person that you wanted to expres. your feelings in this way? Part of communicating effectively is exerting self-control.

4. Look to friendships as opportunities to learn more about yourself and others and to share ideas.
5. Spontaneously and naturally enter into conversations, using a moderate tone and volume of voice.
6. Try to understand the feelings of others before describing your own.
7. Try to avoid harm and inconvenience by talking out problems before they occur or by finding rational means for coping with unavoidable harm or inconvenience.
8. Face problems and decisions squarely.
9. Consider yourself strong and capable, but generally equal to most other people.
10. Face responsibility with respect to your situation, needs, and rights.

As a truly assertive person, you feel free to reveal yourself. You communicate in an open, direct, honest, and appropriate manner. You go after what you want and make things happen. Finally, you act in a way that you, yourself, can respect. You know that you cannot always win. You accept your limitations, but no matter what the situation, you always make a good try so that you will maintain your self-respect.[8]

People may not demonstrate the full range of their thoughts and emotions with confidence and skill in all situations. *Most people express*

TRY THIS

Make up an aggressive, an assertive, and a nonassertive response to each of the following questions and statements. This will help you become familiar with the differences between these response styles.

1. May I nominate you for president of our organization?
2. Would you carry in the things from the car?
3. Prepare a speech for us on why we should abolish grades.
4. Help me with my homework.
5. Could you take me downtown?
6. Would you babysit Saturday night while we go to the movie?
7. Go to the lecture and take notes for all of us.
8. Would you tell him for me?
9. We're all going. Aren't you going to join us?
10. Tell him he expects too much.

With which of the response styles do you feel most comfortable? Most uncomfortable? What additional information about these situations would help you determine a response style?

themselves well in most situations; this is called **general assertiveness. Situational assertiveness** *is expressed when people lack skill or confidence with certain people or in certain situations.* For example, some people have no difficulty expressing their anger or displeasure, but they have a hard time sharing affectionate feelings. Some communicate skillfully with friends but cannot communicate with strangers. Problems occur when people are nonassertive or aggressive too often—that is, when it becomes a habit for them to be one way or the other. Sometimes a situation calls for a certain response. The idea is to be assertive when you need to be—not to be controlled by your habits, the habits of others, or situations. Ineffective communicators are those who cannot choose for themselves how they will act. Effective choice making in situations is what determines effective communicators.

▲▲▲ *Changing Negative Scripts*

The word **script** is used in this context to mean *a rule-governed, habitual pattern of behavior.* Thomas Harris defines scripts as decisions about how life should be lived.[9] Muriel James and Dorothy Jongeward suggest that there are various levels of scripts: (1) **cultural,** *are dictated by society;* (2) **subcultural,** *defined by geographical location, ethnic background, religious beliefs, sex, education, age, and other common bonds;* (3) **family,** *the identifiable traditions and expectations for family members;* and (4) **psychological,** *people's compulsion to perform in a certain way, to live up to a specific identity, or to fulfill a destiny.*[10] In this section I will discuss psychological scripts: our ongoing program for our life drama, which dictates where we are going with our life and how we are going to get there.[11]

Scripts are shaped by past experiences. You are not always responsible for the scripts that govern your behavior. Your inability to swim, for example, may be a result of limited experience around the water. Your fear of dogs may result from an attack by a neighbor's dog when you were young. Past experiences—or the lack of past experiences—may be responsible for negative reactions in certain situations or unpleasant associations connected with specific circumstances. Behavior is shaped, in part, by experience. James and Jongeward label these "scripts with a curse."[12]

You may behave nonassertively because of inadequate or incomplete learning. But assertive behavior—or increased assertiveness—can be learned. You are not helpless. A history of nonassertive behavior does not sentence you to a similar future. But because of the time that the negative scripts have had to become well established, serious, concentrated work to reverse trends and establish new behaviors is necessary. You will need to set new goals and learn new styles of expression and response if you seriously want your style of communicating—your current scripts—to change.

CONSIDER THIS

Read the following selection with this question in mind: "How would these characteristics affect assertiveness?"

In the White Male System the center of focus is the self and work. In interactions, one person must be superior and others inferior. The center of focus in the Female System is relationships with others—including concern both for others and for self. Participants in an interaction can be equal, not necessarily superior or inferior. The purpose of communication in the White Male System frequently is to confuse, win, and remain superior. Negotiation is a way of manipulating others. The purpose of communication in the Female System is to bridge differences and promote understanding. Negotiation promotes clarification and an opportunity for as much goal attainment as possible for everyone.*

Questions

1. When people believe that one person must be superior and others inferior, is this likely to affect the degree or level of assertiveness displayed?
2. When participants in an interaction are equal, not necessarily superior or inferior, will the degree or level of assertiveness displayed be affected?
3. In presenting her research results, Schaef emphasizes that it is "important for both women *and* men to know and admit that the Female System exists and is good—not necessarily better, but good." Can you think of situations in which the Male System would be advantageous? In which the Female System would be advantageous?

*Richard L. Johannesen, *Ethics in Human Communication*, 3rd ed. (Prospect Heights, IL: Waveland Press, Inc., 1990), p. 131. Here, Johannesen summarizes research by Anne Wilson Schaef, *Women's Reality: An Emerging Female System in the White Male Society* (Minneapolis: Winston Press, 1981), pp. 99–145.

Positive expectations can aid your communication effectiveness. Have confidence in yourself. Be willing to experiment by striking up conversations with interesting people, getting help when you are confused, defending your rights, expressing your feelings and emotions when appropriate, and asking others to clarify or explain their feelings and emotions. Do not begin all at once, but realize that you *can* increase your assertive repertoire; you *can* become more confident; you *can* increase your skills as an interpersonal communicator.

Sharon and Gordon Bower have devised what they call a **DESC script** for use in planning your response in specific situations or for maintaining your rights.[13] DESC is short for Describe, Express, Specify, and Consequences. A DESC script forces you to state clearly what you want, and yet it permits freedom of response for the other person. A convenient way to think about it is in terms of "This is what I want. This is how I feel. This is when I want it. This is the result." In completing a DESC script, you should include the characters (you and the other person in the relationship), a plot (something that occurred that left you dissatisfied), a setting (the specific place and time of the occurrence), and a message (both the verbal and the nonverbal cues of the characters).

Describe   *Describe the situation or idea as objectively, clearly, and specifically as you can:* "I want Anita to date only me," "I want Daryl to stop ignoring me," or "I want Mom and Dad to give me more freedom." Specific and objective description allows you to explain the character, plot, setting, and message and to define your needs and goals as well.

Express   *Express how you are feeling and what you are thinking.* How do you feel about this situation? What feelings does this situation evoke in you? "I feel tense because I'm afraid I'm going to have to compete for Anita with some other guy," "I am irritated because Daryl doesn't notice me," or "I am upset because Mom and Dad treat me like a kid." The use of *I, me,* or *my* makes these personal, emotional statements.

Specify   *Specify a specific deadline for what you want.* In this way, there is a goal for action: "I would like Anita to let me know this weekend if she will date only me." "I want Daryl to talk to me after class this afternoon." "I would like to have Mom and Dad let me know before the next vacation whether I will have curfews when I'm home." Specifying is a two-way process, in which *freedom of response for the other person is permitted.* Others

TRY THIS

Plot some DESC scripts for several situations that you are involved in now. Notice how a DESC script clarifies situations and specifies exact behaviors for approaching those situations. The more general the situation or the behavior specified, the less useful the DESC script.

may find aspects of your behavior annoying. Compromise may be necessary. Assertive behavior often requires give-and-take.

Consequences *Consequences are the results of having your desires met or not met.* These can be phrased as if/then statements. "If I don't get a commitment from Anita this weekend, then I am going to find someone from whom I *can* get such a commitment." "If Daryl doesn't talk to me after class this afternoon, then I'm going to ask *him* some questions about class to encourage conversation." "If Mom and Dad do not drop my curfews, then I will have to negotiate with them during my next vacation period to get the curfews relaxed." Try to emphasize positive outcomes.

▲▲▲ *Bringing About Personal Change*

You need more than just an attitude and a DESC script to bring about change. You need specific ideas to aid you. Presented next is a brief program for personal development. If changing your interpersonal behavior is an important goal for you, then this program will help.

Here and now Live in the present. Try to forget your past, because most history will not be helpful. It is what is going on now that is important. Focus on what is and what could be. Avoid dwelling on harmful behaviors of the past. Use the past only if you can use a past success as a model for future behavior.

Look at behavior and not feelings. If you start changing behavior, feelings will start changing too. Begin to build a personal reserve of effective, positive behaviors on which you can depend—behaviors such as stating ideas concretely, expressing feelings openly and directly, persuading others convincingly, maintaining a firm position, expressing your wants and goals, and setting clear, reachable targets. Practice using them over and over so that they can become definite, clearly expressed, explicit scripts.

Responsibility Stop looking outside yourself for excuses for your behavior. When you find yourself saying, "If only he would . . ." or "Why does this always happen to me?" you are limiting the likelihood that "Maybe *I* can . . ." will occur. Even knock out the "maybe" so that possible behavior becomes probable. "I can" is more definite and assertive than "maybe I can."

What is required at this stage is an acceptance of what you need to do. What you do not need are excuses, self-pity, rationalization, and blaming: "This is a cruel world," "Such an undertaking is too much for me," "I'm not ready for this yet," or "It's my parents' fault." All this denial dams up your sense of responsibility for your behavior.

When you begin to take responsibility for your life, life becomes more meaningful. You will begin to fulfill your needs. Responsible behavior also involves awareness of the needs of others. Thus, as you begin to fulfill your own needs, this fulfillment embodies concern, consideration, and respect for the needs and feelings of others. Assertiveness is *not* a selfish one-way process.

Alternatives   If change is to occur, you need alternatives. Often it is self-doubt that limits you. Sometimes, however, it is simply your lack of imagination; you close out possibilities of change.

If you give your imagination free rein on a variety of different problems often enough, you will quickly discover that you are developing a facility for creating problem solving. Alternatives make assertiveness more likely, because assertive people are flexible, and flexibility requires choices. Action is more likely when you have many different possibilities for action.

Plan of action   Taking responsibility and having alternatives are not final points in an agenda of growth and development. You must be willing to take action, which may require compromise, readjustment of values, or a new lifestyle. To become more social, for example, may mean giving up some of the time you have had alone—some of the solitude you value. When friendships develop, commitments of time and energy are required to maintain those friendships. Are you willing to give up some of your independence to nurture a friendship?

After you have considered various alternatives and the consequences of each, you must choose which plan of action to pursue. The more alternatives you have, the easier this job will be, because many plans are a combination of various alternatives. Evaluation of plans involves judging them to see how well each one meets your needs. Seek a plan, or a combination of plans, with the most pluses and fewest minuses.

Commitment   However carefully mapped out, a plan of action will remain a dream unless there is some commitment to change. Is the change important to you? Do you want to put in the time, effort, and pain necessary to bring it about? How badly? Are there obstacles? Can you surmount them? Do you have sufficient involvement to overcome any barriers that confront you as well as any negative or hesitant attitudes that occur? Commitment to a plan of action must be more than "I'll *try* to do it" or I *might* do it." What is needed is "I *will* do it," "I am going to win," "I want to do this more than anything else." These are the attitudes of a person of commitment. Commitment must be 100 percent; why waste time and effort with a plan doomed to failure because of lack of commitment or self-doubt?

Success   Too often you may think of success in absolute terms—complete success or complete failure. Instead, you need to think of it in terms of constant effort, evaluation, and progress. Thus, you must design short-range goals—small steps—that can be accomplished. Each small success is a step toward a new success.

With respect to success, too, being assertive does *not* guarantee getting the results you seek. There are simply too many variables involved. Assertiveness is a positive, success-oriented, clear expression that is more likely to lead toward success than a nonassertive or aggressive response in most situations.

CONSIDER THIS

As you read this selection, think about how assertive you are likely to be when communicating with those from another culture. What are the barriers or restraints that must be overcome first?

> While avoiding anxiety is an important motivating factor in communication with people who are similar, it is critical in our communication with strangers. Intergroup anxiety is largely a function of our fear of negative consequences when we interact with people who are different. As our anxiety becomes high, our need for a sense of a common shared world and our need to sustain our self-conception become central. Having a sense of a common shared world and sustaining our self-concept are much more difficult when we communicate with strangers than when we communicate with people who are similar. High anxiety, therefore, leads us to avoid communicating with strangers.*

Questions

1. Can you cite any personal examples of times when you avoided communicating with a person from another culture (or a stranger) because of fear of negative consequences? What were the negative consequences you feared?

2. What methods would you suggest to those who have experienced a similar fear of negative consequences, to help them overcome the fear and open up new channels of communication with people from different cultures (or strangers)?

3. Is high anxiety likely to be a barrier to assertiveness in any interpersonal communication situation? Why or why not?

*William B. Gudykunst and Young Yun Kim, *Communicating With Strangers: An Approach to Intercultural Communication*, 2nd ed. (New York: McGraw-Hill, Inc., 1992), p. 191.

▲▲▲ *Communicating with the Unresponsive*

There are many reasons why people are noncommunicative. Usually, people fall somewhere on a continuum between "talks a lot" and "seldom talks."

Most people fall in the middle, but as noted previously, noncommunicativeness is likely to be situational.[14] What causes people not to want to talk? There are several likely causes:

1. **Shyness** *is characteristic of people who find discomfort, inhibition, and awkwardness in social situations.*[15] Such people are reluctant to talk, to make eye contact, to gesture, or to smile.
2. **Communication apprehension** *is "an individual's level of fear or anxiety associated with either real or anticipated communication with another person or persons."*[16]
3. *People with* **low willingness to communicate** *are those who withdraw from communicating with others, tell others they don't want to talk to them, avoid potential communication situations, and generally act shy.*[17] These are people who, in general, "are seen as neither task attractive nor credible and are rejected for leadership positions."[18]

What technique would you use if you were the one trying to communicate with this unresponsive individual?

From just these three characterizations—and there may be others—you can see how difficult it is to communicate with some unresponsive people. Unresponsiveness is not our problem; it is theirs, and it may be firmly entrenched as part of a personality style. It could be, of course, that trying to talk with them at all is inappropriate—an invasion of their privacy. This issue certainly needs to be investigated first. Here, I will assume that some communication is appropriate.

But, because unresponsiveness is their problem, we seldom have much control over the situation. If others do not want to talk, they won't. The decision is up to them. Difficult situations often require several different strategies: if one doesn't work, perhaps another will. There are no guarantees for success with any of them. But because guarantees do not exist does not mean we should not make an effort—when it is appropriate. The question is, how should the attempt be made?[19] Here are some strategies that may work:

1. Begin by establishing the proper attitude—an attitude of sensitivity to the communication of others. In the research on credibility, this attitude is also called sociability and it is described as friendliness, cheerfulness, goodnaturedness, warmth, and pleasantness.[20]

2. Strive to be a good listener. Aim to listen to the other person's messages entirely before speaking. In the conversation, allow opportunities for this person to enter the conversation. In addition, be sensitive to any cues that the other person may want to talk; stop immediately at such points, and allow this person to talk.

3. Make other people comfortable in communicating with you by revealing encouragement, support, openness, and honesty.

4. Closely related to number three is to be sympathetic, compassionate, and gentle. Sometimes people are reluctant to talk because they feel others do not sympathize with their ideas.

5. Because people are drawn to things they like, evaluate and praise highly, show preference for similarities, and emphasize things the other person likes. This conveys approval and invites communication.
    a. Recognize and appreciate the needs and desires of others. Try to demonstrate some actual appreciation for their needs and desires.
    b. Closely related, empathize with their ideas and feelings. Try to acknowledge their ideas and feelings in your own conversation.

6. Reveal relaxed composure. Try to come across as poised, relaxed, calm, cool, and controlled—but not too much. This is another com-

ponent of credibility.[21] Too much structure or control may turn others off; thus, relaxed composure is desirable.

7. Reveal immediacy through verbal closeness by using messages that encourage communication:
"I see what you mean . . ."
"Tell me more . . ."
"That is a good point . . ."
"I think so too . . ."
"That's a very important idea . . ."

8. Reveal immediacy through nonverbal messages such as these:
Space—reduce the physical distance between you and others.
Touch—when appropriate, it strongly communicates immediacy; when inappropriate, it is likely to be interpreted negatively.
Eye behavior—maintain appropriate eye contact: not too much, not too little.
Facial expression—the face, especially a smile, communicates attention, or lack of attention, and thus strong immediacy behavior.
Gestures and bodily movements—appear relaxed, keep an open body position, lean forward when communicating, and gesture positively.
Voice—express a high degree of vocal variety.
Scent—people respond positively to familiar, subtle scents.
Time—the more time we spend with others, the more immediacy we convey.

9. Understand, support, and use the principle of reciprocity. This principle suggests that "in communication situations there is a strong tendency for people to imitate the behavior of others with whom they communicate."[22] In other words,

> . . . communication patterns tend to be reciprocal—I do what you do and you do what I do. If one person smiles, or exhibits some other immediate behavior, it is increasingly likely the other person will engage in similar behavior.[23]

Despite these nine suggestions, communicators may not be successful in dealing with unresponsive communicators. Those who are unresponsive must *want* to talk, and any support or encouragement we can provide may not be enough to cause this to occur. That means neither that it will not work nor that we should not try; it just means we need to be realistic about our attempts and our chances for success.

The nine suggestions above are not mutually exclusive. One suggestion may work, or several together may be needed. Also, it may be more successful to encourage responsiveness over a period of time rather than in a single instance. Unresponsiveness is likely to be habitual—learned

CONSIDER THIS

Sometimes you will hear people talk about other assertive people as being manipulative, intimidating, or aggressive. Read the following piece on assertiveness, and answer the questions that follow.

> Assertiveness is not just an opportunity to manipulate others. It is a tool for making relationships more equal. It can help relationship partners avoid the one-down feeling that occurs when they don't express their true feelings. Equality does not mean getting your own way, getting back at the other person, or turning the other cheek. To practice assertiveness skills will help relationship partners develop more effective self-expression and healthier relationships.*

Questions

1. Can you see how assertive behavior can help foster equality in relationships?
2. Have you heard assertive people referred to as manipulative, intimidating, or aggressive? Why do you think this is so?
3. What suggestions would you make to an assertive person who seems to come across as manipulative, intimidating, or aggressive, that would help him or her become less so? That would help that person adjust his or her behavior to make a positive rather than a negative impression?

*Adapted from Robert E. Alberti and Michael L. Emmons, *Your Perfect Right: A Guide to Assertive Living*, 5th ed. (San Luis Obispo, CA: Impact Publishers, 1986), pp. 2–3.

over time. Thus, the supportive, nurturing, enduring climate must be in place, the specific strategies must be used over time, and patience and considerateness must be always expressed. What you are trying to do is replace one habit (unresponsiveness) with another (responsiveness). Because failure is likely, you must be patient as well as persevering.

Building Assertiveness Skills

Where do you begin? If you are serious about learning to assert yourself, you must understand your rights. Your rights as a human being are the framework upon which you build positive interpersonal relationships. If you often allow your rights to be violated, you will begin to find it difficult to express your individual self to others. Trust may give way to suspicion, compassion may evolve into cynicism, warmth and closeness may disappear, and love (if it exists at all) may acquire an acid bite. In his book *When I Say No, I Feel Guilty,* Manuel J. Smith talks about your humanness, about your responsibilities for yourself and your own well-being, and about what other people should be able to expect from you.[24] The advice that follows is drawn from Smith's discussion.

Take responsibility for yourself If you take responsibility for yourself, then you are in control of your own thinking, feeling, and behavior. When someone, for whatever reason, reduces your ability to be the judge of what you do, you are being manipulated, and your most basic right is in jeopardy.

When you can put this primary assertive right into practice, you will learn how to work out ways to judge your own behavior. Through trial and error, you will discover standards of behavior that fit your own personality and life-style. These standards need not be logical, consistent, or permanent; in fact, they may make no sense to others. But your own judgment is *your* guide. This means you take full responsibility for your own happiness and well-being. Your other rights are everyday applications of this prime right. They provide the foundation for assertive behavior.

Don't overapologize When you return merchandise, you are accustomed to explaining what went wrong with it. When you cannot go somewhere with a friend, you usually explain why you cannot go. But you may often tend to overexplain—to offer lengthy apologies when a brief one would do. While some word of explanation is both polite and helpful, people are hardly ever interested in long, involved excuses. When others demand your explanation to convince you that you are wrong, they are manipulating your behavior and feelings. No friendship should be based upon the requirement that you explain your behavior at every turn. In asserting this right, you should, of course, observe common courtesy. Not to give a reason when one would be helpful may be seen as a negative reaction, especially if you are accustomed to giving reasons and if others expect them from you. But it's best to be brief.

Don't try to rearrange someone else's life A friend may come to you wanting you to help him or her become healthy and happy. You may be compassionate, and you may give advice and counsel, but the person with the problems has the responsibility of solving them. Your best course in such situations is to assert who you are and the limits of what you're able to do. You should help the other person do the same. As much as you might wish good things for your friends, you really do not have the ability to create mental stability, well-being, or happiness for anyone else. You might temporarily be of some help, but real change requires hard work from the person who wants to change. The reality of the human condition is that everyone must learn to cope on his or her own.

Feel free to change your mind   A common view in our society is that people who change their minds are irresponsible, two-faced, scatter-brained, or unreliable. If you do change your mind, you are expected to justify your new choice or say that you were in error before. You may be afraid to vacillate because this can affect your credibility: "Don't trust him, he'll just turn around and change his mind!"

Human beings do, however, change their minds. You may make a decision about how to do something and no sooner get started than you find a better way. Goals and interests are constantly changing. Your choices may work for you in one situation, but there is no reason to believe they will work for you in another. To keep in touch with reality, and to promote your own well-being and happiness, you must believe that changing your mind is both healthy and normal.

Feel free to make mistakes   If you have a horror of making mistakes, you leave yourself open to manipulation every time you make one. You may feel compelled to retreat and not call attention to yourself for awhile. In that submissive posture, you are fair game for people who want to make you pay for your error or who want to put you down for it.

If you make an error of judgment, admit the mistake as soon as you realize it. Apologize to anybody who may have been hurt, do what you can to repair the damage, and then forget it. "It seemed like a good idea at the time" is often the most honest, simple explanation. You may well be genuinely sorry if others were hurt by your mistake; the important thing is not to feel subhuman for having made it. When you realize you've erred, simply show that you are responsible. In this way, you admit that you made the mistake, that it made trouble for the other person, and that, like everyone else, you make mistakes.

Learn to recognize unanswerable questions   Some questions are unanswerable. You may have heard some: "Didn't you know that would happen?" "Why didn't you remember to . . .?" "What would this world be like if everyone . . .?" What can you say to such questions? You do not need to have immediate answers for questions people ask you.

News reporters depend on the fact that most people are very uncomfortable leaving questions dangling and unanswered. Almost everyone will give *some* kind of answer, no matter how preposterous the question, but you should learn to see that questions in themselves do not demand answers. You need not be intimidated by inquiries.

You can recognize other people's attempts to manipulate you by phrases that begin with "What kind of a friend (or son or daughter) would . . .?" To deal with questions like this, you simply need to say, "I don't know." No one can know all the possible consequences of his or her own behavior. If someone else wants to know, let him or her speculate! This is not a defense or a manifestation of irresponsibility, but there *are* limits to how much you can know.

Feel free to say "I don't know" There are legitimate, answerable questions that you just do not have the answer to. Either you don't have the facts, you have not had time to think about them, or you do not have enough evidence to make a judgment. Whatever the case, the best response to questions like these is "I don't know." Sometimes others will try to commit you to a premature response or to force a quick answer to a question that is complex or confusing. It is better to say "I don't know" than to make the commitment. You should feel free to say you want more time to think about it.

Don't be overly dependent on the good will of others Everyone likes to be liked. Everyone needs to be liked. But although you need other people, they don't all need to be your brothers and sisters. No matter what you do, someone is not going to like it or is going to get his or her feelings hurt. If you feel that you must have other people's good will before dealing with them, you become open to manipulation.

Why do you suppose the smiling, friendly used-car dealer is such a stereotype? Because the assumption is that people will feel liked and will want to keep the dealer's good will by buying a car. There are many examples of the "I like you" smile used for manipulative purposes. Parents control children by withholding smiles, politicians win supporters with a broad grin, and advertisers generate sales by showing happy, smiling faces.

You are mistaken if you believe you must have the goodwill of anyone you relate with in order to deal with them. The next time you catch yourself thinking like this, think again. Do you really care whether this salesclerk (or whoever) likes you and the way you live your life? Would you accept this person's judgment on what you should or shouldn't have for lunch? Of course you wouldn't! So why let him or her judge *you*? You may have great difficulty saying "no" to someone if you assume that a relationship is impossible to maintain without 100 percent mutual agreement. You cannot always live in fear of hurting other people's feelings. Sometimes you may offend others. Such is life.

Feel free to be illogical Logic is not always the answer in dealing with wants, motivations, and feelings. Emotions occur in different degrees at different times. Logical reasoning may not help in understanding why you want what you want or in solving problems created by conflicting motivations.

Logic has its place, of course. You turn a paper in on time because you know that if you don't you will lose a grade. You fill up the gas tank when it's nearly empty because you know that if you don't, you could get stranded. But being logical works best when you are dealing with things you completely understand, and often solutions to problems lie outside these limits. In some cases you just have to guess, no matter how crude or inelegant the results. You must calculate the risks of the guesses. It is your right to be illogical at times. Human behavior is often illogical.

Feel free to say "I don't understand" You understand as a result of experience. But experience teaches that you do not always understand what another person means or wants. People may try to manipulate you by implying that you are expected to know something or to do something for them. You may not understand a teacher's explanation of a concept or a gas station attendant's directions. Rather than blame yourself automatically for not "getting" something, you should ask for clarification or restatement. How do you know the other person is being as clear as possible?

You can hardly be expected to always understand what other people's needs are. Sometimes when you don't guess correctly, people think you are irresponsible or ignorant. Often, this manipulation occurs after a conflict. People who believe they have been wronged may expect you to understand that they are displeased with your behavior, that you should know what behavior has displeased them, and that you should change so that they will no longer be hurt or angry. If you allow this manipulation, you end up blocked from what you want to do and often do something else to make up for wanting to do it in the first place. It is difficult enough trying to read your own mind without trying to perform this service for others.

Feel free to say "I don't care" If you set yourself up to be perfectly informed and concerned about all matters, you will be disappointed and frustrated. It can't be done. Some things will matter more to you, others less. You have the right to say that you do not care about certain things. You do not need perfect knowledge of what someone else has determined to be *the* important category. Some people may try to manipulate you into thinking you need to improve until you are perfect in all things.

The teacher who says "How can you call yourself a history major when you know nothing about medieval England?" and the athletic coach who says "How do you expect to run the 400m when you eat sugar instead of honey?" are trying to impose their standards on you. If you submit, you fall into the trap of being affected by someone else's arbitrary choice of what constitutes perfection. You end up apologizing for failing in your obligation to become perfect in all things. The only certain way to stop this manipulation is by asking yourself, "Am I satisfied with my own performance and with myself?" You should be free to make your own judgment about whether or not you wish to make a change.

Another writer in this field, Ronald B. Adler, has expanded Smith's list, giving specific tips on how to express one's needs and wants effectively.[25] His suggestions are discussed below.

Learn to make "I messages" When you are the one who is dissatisfied with a situation, you are the one with the problem. If your roommate is irritating you by leaving the room messy, *you* are the one dissatisfied, and it is your problem because your roommate will be content to go on as before. If your neighbors play loud music, *you* are the dissatisfied party if the loud music annoys you. If you are losing sleep because of unsatisfactory working conditions, it is *your* problem. When the circumstances prompting the dissatisfaction are troublesome primarily to you, leading you to want to speak up about them, then it is a problem *you* need to own—to take responsibility for.

Once you have identified a problem and declared ownership, then your statement of concern should contain the three elements discussed in Chapter 4. These three elements can be discovered by answering three questions:

1. *Behavior:* What is the behavior that presents the problem?
2. *Consequences:* What are the concrete, observable consequences of the problem?
3. *Feelings:* What feelings do you experience as a result of the problem?

Once these three questions are answered, the three parts can be framed as an "I message." You may want to refer back to the section on "I messages" at the end of Chapter 4. Developing and using them effectively is part of the feedback process. An "I message" simply starts with "I" and claims ownership: "I have a problem. When you (*behavior*), (*consequences*) happen, and I feel (*feelings*)." For example, with the messy roommate: "I have a problem. When you leave your clothes all over the room (behavior), I have to look at them, step over them, and even move them (consequences). I feel angry and get upset (feelings)." This formula works in all situations where *you* own the problem, where there are direct consequences, and where your feelings are involved. The order of the parts is

TRY THIS

Create "I messages" for the following relationship situations. In each case you are trying to get a relationship partner to

▲ Open up and communicate more.
▲ Take things (life) more seriously.
▲ Spend his or her money more wisely.
▲ Stop bringing up past (other) relationships.
▲ Show more love and respect for you.
▲ Be less possessive.
▲ Give you more freedom.
▲ Stop his or her drinking (or taking drugs).
▲ Spend more time with you.
▲ Understand *your* feelings about premarital sex.

not as important as their presence—they should all be present, but they can be offered in whatever order feels most comfortable.

Learn to repeat assertions In most cases, the "I have a problem" approach proves successful. But not always. There are times when it may not be clearly or accurately received. Or it may be clearly and accurately received and nothing may happen. Or what happens is not what you want to happen. All of these are less than satisfying responses. Since there is little likelihood that the problem will be resolved under these circumstances, the original assertion needs to be repeated. This should be done in a calm, genuine manner. Notice, for example, how Shirley gets Greg to set a time to talk about their relationship—which Greg has been avoiding:

> *Shirley:* You know, Greg, we need to set a time when we can talk about our relationship. When can we get together? [Assertion]
>
> *Greg:* Tomorrow I have that big calculus exam, and I just can't stop thinking about it right now.
>
> *Shirley:* I know—you really have to study for it. When can we get together? [Repeated assertion]

Greg:	Next week that history project is due, and I have plans to go home for the weekend.
Shirley:	It doesn't have to be this weekend, but we need to find a time when we can get together. [Repeated assertion]
Greg:	Hmmm, I don't know . . .
Shirley:	Since we won't be able to get together this weekend or next, how about the next weekend? [Repeated assertion]
Greg:	Well, I know Jim and Bill are going to want to do something . . .
Shirley:	Okay, but let's plan Saturday night just for us—no one else—and we are going to discuss our relationship. [Repeated assertion]
Greg:	All right. That sounds good.

Sometimes you may fail to make an assertive request a second or third time for fear of being seen as pushy and obnoxious. Although this is possible, it may be the only way to get your message across or to let the other person know how important it is to you. Even if the other person thinks less of you because of your persistence, sometimes this is necessary for self-respect.

Feel free to make requests   Requests are made to satisfy needs. For example, you ask your date to please arrive on time because you *need* to be at the concert promptly at eight or you won't be seated. You ask friends to go to the party with you because you *need* companionship. You ask an instructor for more information because you *need* to clear up some confusion. Requests and needs are not the same; requests are based on needs.

Sometimes it is best to state the need clearly before the request. Doing this helps others understand the importance of the request. Also, because the need is clarified, there is more chance that the request will be satisfied. For example, if a friend comes up to you at a party and says, "I am really feeling ill. Could you take me home?" you will be much more inclined to help out than if the request was, "Could you take me home right now?"—especially if you are having fun!

Another reason for stating the need before the request is that there may be better ways to solve the problem. If you can't suggest other alternatives, maybe someone else can. For example, if the friend is feeling ill, maybe an aspirin or a stomach remedy will take care of the problem. Maybe he or she simply needs to lie down for a bit. When my family and I were traveling around the world, we found that when we accompanied our requests for directions—which occurred often!—with the fact that we were new there (a need for help), we would get a totally different reaction than when we simply asked for directions. Sometimes the local residents responded by taking us on informal, informative sightseeing tours.

Feel free to say "no" Sometimes you get unreasonable, undesired, or unworkable requests. In such cases, you must bring yourself to say "no"—firmly and unequivocally. Of course it is easier to do this when the person doing the requesting has no personal importance to you. A waitress urges you to order a dessert you don't have room for. A door-to-door solicitor is seeking contributions to a cause you don't support. A coworker who does not repay his debts asks for five dollars for the weekend.

But it is not always easy to say "no" when your dignity or an important personal principle is threatened. Embarrassing others or breaking personal commitments could threaten your dignity. A group of friends invites you to join in on some gossip about an absent friend, or a party hostess asks you to take a drink when you abstain. Nonnegotiable principles might include breaking the law. A friend asks you to bring home some supplies free from the office, or you are asked to forge an instructor's signature so that a friend can drop a class without failing. What if a close friend asks you for a copy of a paper you've written—and you know that person is planning to use it as his or her own? It is difficult to stand by your guns when friends are urging you to compromise your principles. Peer pressure rears its ugly head!

Are you able to say "no" when you get unreasonable, undesired, or unworkable requests from others?

It is not easy to say "no," either, when the issues are unimportant but the people matter to you. Friends want you to join them for a study session at the library, and you don't feel like going. A neighbor asks you to help move some furniture, and you're just ready to leave the house to run some errands you've been postponing. An employer asks you to stay late to work on a noncritical project when you have already made other plans.

People often find it difficult to say "no." One reason for this difficulty is that they want to be accepted and approved of. Sometimes when you strive for this acceptance and approval you cause inconvenience to yourself, and you lose self-respect. Sometimes the problem is that you are trying to please more than one person at the same time, and they have conflicting needs. You may have seen this happening—for example, when you are out with a person, run into friends of his or hers, and notice a sudden behavior change. The person has been sincere, appreciative, and serious with you and suddenly becomes playful, callous, and obnoxious—trying to please the friends, not you. Trying to win acceptance and approval from everyone can be exhausting and discouraging.

Another reason some people find it difficult to say "no" is that they are trying to meet everyone's needs. This is their way of appearing perfect. To be perfect, they must do favors, lend money, run errands, and solve others' problems. These people are sometimes viewed as selfless martyrs but more often as suckers or doormats. People who constantly let others take advantage of them often begin to feel resentment and frustration, seldom expressed because it would detract from their "perfect" image. But the emotions often find an outlet in indirect aggression, such as criticism and gossip about those who make the demands of them.

The best way to say "no," especially to strangers or to people who don't mean anything to you personally, is directly and with no adornment. You are under no obligation to explain yourself, although you may choose to do so to keep from appearing curt or brutal. With friends, you may want to provide an explanation to let the other people know the reason behind your choice: "No, I really can't go—I have two tests tomorrow I have to study for." Explanations like this, framed in the first person, show that *you* accept responsibility for your refusal and are not blaming the refusal on someone else.

One other alternative to saying "no"—especially when you are faced with an undesirable request—is to withhold your decision until you have thought about the request. Who says you must respond at once? Of course, if this is simply a delaying tactic—a way to avoid assertiveness—then it would be better to say "no" and have the decision completed. But you are under no obligation to answer most requests immediately. Assertiveness does not require a quick reply. "Hmmm, I'd really like to think about it" is an acceptable response. You have the right to think it over. Just because you can think of no logical reason for saying "no" does not mean you must say "yes"—especially when you are caught off guard. Withhold your decision until you've had time to make sure that your eventual "no"—or "yes"—is a true expression of your thoughts and feelings.

Two final notes on assertiveness. If you plan to be assertive, you must plan and expect assertiveness—even conflict—in return. Life is a two-way street. If you are confronted, make sure you know what the other person is saying. Use paraphrasing to gain clarification if you are confused. Explore the confrontation nondefensively with the goal of mutual sharing, mutual discovery, and mutual growth. If a change in attitudes or values is requested, try experimenting with the new behavior. Just as you do not expect others to change suddenly, neither can you. Do not try to take care of the change all at once. Second, being assertive does not guarantee getting what you think is due you. It can be especially frustrating and discouraging when you summon up your courage and become assertive, only to be met with an equally assertive response. Assertiveness alone does not guarantee success.

Being assertive will help you communicate directly, honestly, and appropriately in dyadic communication situations. Assertiveness encourages good will and self-confidence and aids in pinpointing your real feelings. It is a means of self-expression and has the added advantage of making you feel good about yourself. Asserting yourself is how you get from here to there, from being an object or a pawn to being a human being with rights that should be recognized.

This freedom of positive expression will result in greater openness in the communication of genuine, positive feelings toward other people. Such open communication, combined with increased assertiveness, may make you more likely to encounter opposition, conflict, and defensiveness. Some disagreement is always likely. How to overcome the opposition, conflict, and defensiveness that stand in the way of successful interpersonal communication is the subject of the next chapter.

► **SUMMARY**

Assertiveness is the ability to share the full range of your thoughts and emotions with confidence and skill. After assertiveness, nonassertiveness, and aggression are compared, general assertiveness and situational assertiveness are discussed. In the section on changing negative scripts, DESC scripts are discussed, and then a method for bringing about personal change is presented. For communicating with the unresponsive, nine different strategies are suggested. In the final section of the chapter on improving skills in assertiveness, fifteen ideas are offered that will help you become more assertive. As noted at the end of the chapter, be-

TRY THIS

Practice assertive responses for each of the following situations:

1. Someone pushed in front of you in line.
2. You must tell someone you no longer wish to date him or her.
3. You are trying to study, and someone is making too much noise.
4. You are angry with your parents.
5. You must insist that your roommate does his or her fair share of the cleaning.
6. You must ask a friend to do a favor for you.
7. You have been served unsatisfactory food in a restaurant.
8. You want to express your love and affection to a special person.
9. A professor has made a statement that you consider untrue.
10. Someone you respect has expressed an opinion with which you strongly disagree.
11. A friend of yours is wearing a new outfit that you like.
12. A friend has made an unreasonable request of you.
13. A person is being blatantly unfair.
14. A friend has betrayed your confidence.
15. You want to ask a friend to lend you a few dollars.
16. Someone keeps kicking the back of your chair in a movie.
17. Someone interrupts you in the middle of an important conversation.
18. A friend has criticized you unjustly.

ing assertive helps you communicate directly, honestly, and appropriately.

► KEY TERMS

assertiveness
nonassertiveness
negative cycle
aggressiveness
general assertiveness
situational assertiveness
script

cultural scripts
subcultural scripts
family scripts
psychological scripts
DESC script
describe

express
specify
consequences
shyness
communication apprehension
low willingness to communicate

▶ NOTES

1. Ronald B. Adler, *Confidence in Communication: A Guide to Assertive and Social Skills* (New York: Holt, Rinehart and Winston, 1977), 6.

2. Lynn Z. Bloom, Karen Coburn, and Joan Pearlman, *The New Assertive Woman* (New York: Dell Publishing Co., 1975), 15.

3. Robert E. Alberti and Michael L. Emmons, *Stand Up, Speak Out, Talk Back! The Key to Self-Assertive Behavior* (New York: Pocket Books, 1975), 53.

4. Adapted from Beverly Byrum-Gaw, *It Depends: Appropriate Interpersonal Communication*, (1981), 200, by permission of Mayfield Publishing Company.

5. Robert E. Alberti and Michael L. Emmons, *Your Perfect Right: A Guide to Assertive Behavior* (San Luis Obispo, CA: Impact, 1974), 6.

6. Bloom, Coburn, and Pearlman, 11–12.

7. Gerard Egan, *Interpersonal Living: A Skills/Contract Approach to Human-Relations Training in Groups* (Monterey, CA: Brooks/Cole, 1976), 36–37.

8. Herbert Fensterheim and Jean Baer, *Don't Say Yes When You Want to Say No* (New York: Dell Publishing Co., 1975), 20.

9. Thomas A. Harris, *I'm OK!—You're OK: A Practical Guide to Transactional Analysis* (New York: Harper & Row, 1969), 45.

10. Muriel James and Dorothy Jongeward, *Born to Win: Transactional Analysis with Gestalt Experiments* (Reading, MA: Addison-Wesley Publishing Co., 1971), 69–79.

11. James and Jongeward, 69.

12. James and Jongeward, 81.

13. Sharon Anthony Bower and Gordon H. Bower, *Asserting Yourself* (Reading, MA: Addison-Wesley Publishing Co., 1976), 87–102.

14. Virginia P. Richmond and James C. McCroskey, *Communication: Apprehension, Avoidance, and Effectiveness*, 3d ed. (Scottsdale, AZ: Gorsuch Scarisbrick, Publishers, 1992), 25.

15. Richmond and McCroskey, 28.

16. Richmond and McCroskey, 41.

17. Richmond and McCroskey, 25.

18. Virginia P. Richmond and James C. McCroskey, "Willingness to Communicate and Dysfunctional Communication Processes." In Charles V. Roberts, Kittie W. Watson, and Larry L. Barker, eds., *Intrapersonal Communication Processes: Original Essays* (292–318). (New Orleans: SPECTRA Inc., Publishers, 1989), 314.

19. These suggestions were drawn from sections in Richmond and McCroskey (1992) entitled "Responsiveness" and "Versatility," 84–90.

20. James C. McCroskey and Thomas J. Young, "Ethos and Credibility: The Construct and Its Measurement After Three Decades," *Central States Speech Journal* 32 (Spring 1981): 24–34 (esp. 31–32).

21. McCroskey and Young, 31–32.
22. Richmond and McCroskey, 1992, 91.
23. Richmond and McCroskey, 1992, 91.
24. Manuel J. Smith, *When I Say No, I Feel Guilty*, 27–71. Copyright © 1975 by Manuel J. Smith. Used by permission of the Dial Press.
25. Ronald B. Adler, *Confidence in Communication: A Guide to Assertive and Social Skills* (New York: Holt, Rinehart and Winston, 1977), 219–245.

▶ ## FURTHER READING

Robert E. Alberti and Michael L. Emmons, *Your Perfect Right: A Guide to Assertive Living* (San Luis Obispo, CA: Impact Publishers, 1986). In this fifth edition of the book that popularized assertiveness training in 1970, the authors have totally revised and expanded the original material. In addition to basic information on assertiveness, chapters on assertive sexuality, goal setting, and on-the-job assertiveness are included. A classic book well worth reading.

J. Kevin Barge, *Leadership: Communication Skills for Organizations and Groups* (New York: St. Martin's Press, 1994). This book is listed here because many of the leadership skills discussed are those demonstrated by assertive people. They include communication skills, making sense of information, decision making, motivating followers, exercising social influence, and competent leadership communication. This is a well-written, comprehensive book full of specific guidelines and suggestions.

Sheila Murray Bethel, *Making A Difference: 12 Qualities That Make You A Leader* (New York: Berkley Books, 1990). Assertiveness skills and suggestions ooze from every chapter, direction, and example of this popular book. Writing in a personal, engaging manner, Bethel shows how to establish a mission, build trust, anticipate and master change, take risks, communicate effectively, and develop commitment.

Stephen R. Covey, *The Seven Habits of Highly Effective People: Restoring the Character Ethic* (New York: Simon and Schuster—A Fireside Book, 1989). In this readable, inspiring book, Covey discusses the habits of being proactive; beginning with the end in mind; putting first things first; thinking win/win; seeking first to understand, then to be understood; synergizing; and sharpening the saw. His is a holistic, integrated, principle-centered approach for living life with fairness, integrity, honesty, and human dignity. These foundations for proper assertiveness give readers the wisdom and power to take advantage of the opportunities that change creates.

Michael Z. Hackman and Craig E. Johnson, *Leadership: A Communication Perspective* (Prospect Heights, IL: Waveland Press, Inc., 1991). Hackman and Johnson discuss leadership and power, leadership and influence, and developing effective leadership communication. In this well-researched textbook, the authors offer specific strategies for effective leadership that apply to strong assertive skills as well.

Sally Helgesen, *The Female Advantage: Women's Ways of Leadership* (New York: Doubleday Currency, 1990). This book explores how women leaders make decisions, schedule their days, gather and disperse information, structure their companies, and hire and fire employees. Helgesen shows how women offer important leadership qualities and patterns such as communities where sharing information is key, and where the rules of hierarchy come undone in unexpected points of contact. This is an excellent book for those—male or female—who want to be more assertive.

Robert Moore and Douglas Gillette, *King, Warrior, Magician, Lover: Rediscovering the Archetypes of the Mature Masculine* (San Francisco: HarperSanFrancisco, 1990). Moore and Gillette offer a serious glimpse of the masculine psyche. Reading this book will help men understand their strengths and weaknesses. The authors make a case for the development of the "mature masculine" so that men no longer have to act out dominating, disempowering behavior toward others.

11

Overcoming Barriers: Coping with Conflict

CHAPTER OBJECTIVES

After reading this chapter, you should be able to

▲ Compare and contrast how society views conflict and how you view conflict, and explain what happens when people disagree.

▲ List and briefly identify the five elements that can cloud or destroy an atmosphere of acceptance.

▲ Explain the relationship between defensive-producing climates and supportive climates, and how this knowledge contributes to effective interpersonal communication.

▲ Describe Blake and Mouton's two-dimensional scheme for categorizing the ways in which people handle conflict.

▲ Compare and contrast the five styles of handling conflict.

▲ Understand the requirements of effective interpersonal communication in choosing appropriate conflict management strategies.

▲ Explain several possible stress management techniques and describe how you can personally adjust to stress.

▲ List and briefly explain the four main elements for managing stressful conflict situations.

▲ Explain briefly the four types of misunderstanding that are likely to escalate conflict.

▲ Construct, label, and explain a model of conflict management.

▼ Kimberly dreads hanging out with her boyfriend Duane because Duane is always late. He says he will be over at 7:30, and Kimberly can usually find him showing up about 8:15 or 8:30. Kimberly thinks of herself as a tolerant, flexible person, but this behavior really bothers her because it happens all the time. Duane knows how upset Kimberly gets, and he's always ready with an apology, but he doesn't seem to be willing to be there when he says he will be. The conflict continues, and it casts a shadow every time Kimberly and Duane decide to go out.

John is going to school full time. His wife, Carrie, works as a secretary to help put him through school. Because John's schedule is flexible, he tries to have dinner ready for Carrie when she comes home from work at 5:30. Conflict, however, occurs after the evening meal. John likes to get everything cleaned up before sitting down to study or watch television; Carrie wants to leave those chores until later. Because John likes to get everything cleaned up, often he finds himself in the kitchen alone after dinner. He thinks Carrie should at least help him out, since he prepared the meal. Every time John brings the issue up, they end up fighting.

Joy and Melinda have been colleagues for about a year. They get along only because they have to. Both are accountants; they serve on many of the same committees, and they are members of many of the same organizations. Their problem is simply that Joy tends to be a very hard worker, whereas Melinda is not. Joy often ends up doing much more work because she does her own, and she feels she has to do Melinda's work, too, when Melinda doesn't, so that the department, committee, or organization doesn't look bad. Melinda knows this, so she will not do her fair share, do a lousy job, or just quit early, knowing that Joy will pick up the loose ends. Joy has mentioned this problem to Melinda several times, but nothing seems to change.

Kimberly and Duane, John and Carrie, Joy and Melinda are all involved in conflict situations. These are common, everyday kinds of conflict—the kinds you experience often. With better understanding of their situations, Kimberly, John, and Joy could perhaps resolve their problems. Without resolution, it is likely that the problems will continue. It is likely, too, that they will withdraw some of the pleasure, happiness, and joy from the relationships they are in as well.

This chapter begins with an examination of how our society views conflict and how each person reacts to it personally. Next, some of the different ways of coping with conflict will be discussed, with suggestions for some skills to practice. Understanding the nature of conflict will help you facilitate cooperative behavior, resolve problems, and enhance your interpersonal relationships and contacts. You can't eliminate conflict, but you can start to look at it as something you can handle or lessen.

▲▲▲ *How Society Views Conflict*

Conflict is often considered undesirable in our society. You may believe that conflicts cause marriages to dissolve, employees to be fired, and demotions, demerits, demoralization, and divisiveness to occur. Certainly arguments, disagreements, and fights do force people apart and damage relationships. But more than likely, it is not the conflict itself that causes the break in these relationships, but the poor handling of the conflict.

Anger, one of the underlying causes of conflict, may be viewed as not "gentlemanly," "ladylike," "nice," or "mature." The mere mention of fighting is enough to make some people uncomfortable. They may talk of their "differences" or of their "silly arguments" but never of "fights," because they feel fighting implies a lack of maturity and self-control. (Fighting here means verbal and nonverbal quarreling, not physical battle.) Actually, not to admit to conflict or fighting implies a *lack* of maturity.

When you are on intimate terms with another person, your closeness may be characterized by quarreling and making up. You may try to live in harmony and agreement with another person, but this desire alone creates a need for conflict—just to establish and maintain *your* notion of harmony and agreement.[1] You also fight to resolve conflicts and to release frustration.

Our society has conditioned us to dislike personal aggressiveness. Well-liked people are described with such phrases as "She is very kind; she'll do anything for anyone" or "He doesn't have a nasty bone in his body" or "She wouldn't raise her voice to anyone." Think of people you know who are admired and the phrases people use to describe them. Nonaggressiveness is praised and admired.[2]

Our society's attitude toward nonaggressiveness may be responsible for the vicarious pleasure many people get from watching the violent acts of other people. Sports such as hockey, football, and boxing include elements of violence; violence also is prominent in the news, in movies, and on television. Although anger and aggressiveness are officially taboo, as a society we apparently admire and are fascinated by aggressive people. Our heroes and heroines are powerful, robust, forceful characters. There seems to be a difference between what we give lip service to and what we actually like. There is no doubt that conflict *can* be destructive. Whether it is harmful or helpful depends on how it is used.

TRY THIS

Can you think of specific people who fit the following phrases?

1. She really is kind.
2. Aren't they friendly?
3. They would do anything in the world for you.
4. He'd give you the shirt off his back.
5. She always has a smile on her face.
6. Isn't he sweet?
7. It wouldn't be a party without him.
8. She really is all heart.

Can you think of other phrases that emphasize nonaggressiveness?

▲▲▲ *How You View Conflict*

Healthy interpersonal communication is *not* conflict free. Conflict is a part of all your relationships with other people. It can be constructive or destructive, depending on how you manage it.[3] Conflict is often the constructive means you use to challenge established norms and practices, and at times it is the means through which you are your most creative and innovative. Conflict often motivates you to summon up your untapped abilities. Some of your most eloquent moments result spontaneously from situations that occur when you have been stopped from doing something or when you need to get your way. You should concentrate on managing interpersonal conflict to gain the maximum benefit for the relationship, discovering your own best style of handling it in the process.

Any time you get together with another person for more than a short while, conflicts may arise that are serious enough to destroy the relationship if you do not know how to handle them. There are no magic formulas for overcoming barriers and resolving breakdowns. But you can look at those breakdowns in a fresh way. The fact that you are unique and that you experience the world in a unique way is enough to generate conflict because conflict occurs when human differences or uniquenesses meet. Remember, too, that you selectively perceive; thus, what is a conflict to one person may not be a conflict to another person. In addition to being unique, each of you also is able to make choices. You can decide how to handle the disagreements you encounter.

It may seem discouraging to think that even in the very best of relationships there is going to be conflict and that, on top of that, there is no guarantee that the conflict can be resolved. *But you can change the way you deal with it.* First you need to confront your own feelings. To know what happens when you disagree is a useful starting point.

▲▲▲ *What Happens When People Disagree*

Conflict *is a situation in which you, your desires, or your intentions are in opposition to those of another person.* Opposition means incompatibility: if your desires predominate, the other person's will not.[4] If you want to go to one movie and your friend wants to go to another, a state of conflict results. If you feel you deserve an A and your instructor thinks a B is all you deserve, you are in conflict. If you believe that one interpretation of a poem is correct and your classmates think another one is more appropriate, you have another conflict situation. These are, of course, honest and unavoidable differences of opinion that lead to conflict. But there are also barriers and breakdowns in communication that create conflict and can be avoided.

CONSIDER THIS

Ritual opposition includes opposition that is an expected, automatic, built-in part of normal operations. Companies have their own distinctive culture, which is developed over time. Men and women are likely to respond differently to ritual opposition.

> Different companies tend to encourage more or less verbal opposition and argument. But within each company, there are people who are more or less given to the oppositional style. And in any conversation, those who are comfortable with open opposition have an advantage over those who do not. Regardless of which style is rewarded in a given company, it will be hard for those whose styles are different to do their best work.
>
> At work, women often take it personally when someone disagrees with them or openly argues.*

Questions

1. What is your feeling about ritual opposition? Should it be eliminated from the work place?
2. If ritual opposition were a common ritual among men, do you see how women could take it literally? Do you see how women could be offended by it?
3. Can you see any logic behind ritual opposition? That is, can you see any benefits to it? What happens when you are publicly challenged?

*From Deborah Tannen, *Talking From 9 to 5: How Women's and Men's Conversational Styles Affect Who Gets Heard, Who Gets Credit, and What Gets Done at Work* (New York: William Morrow and Company, 1994), pp. 59–60.

Communication Barriers and Breakdowns

An atmosphere of acceptance is essential to preventing breakdowns in communication. Technically, communication cannot break down. If you cannot *not* communicate, breakdowns cannot occur. The term *breakdown* is used here to refer to distortions and misinterpretations. Without acceptance, messages may not be received at all or may be distorted if they are received. Not receiving a message or distorting it causes conflicts. John Keltner identifies five elements that can cloud or destroy an atmosphere of acceptance: contrary attitudes, newly acquired contrary opinions, jumping to conclusions, low credibility, and hostility.[5]

What happens when people disagree? What is the likely outcome of this conflict situation? Are there ways in which such conflict situations can be resolved amicably?

Contrary attitudes   Your prejudices, biases, and predispositions affect the way you interact with and perceive others. This will become a barrier to communication unless you make a concerted attempt to be open-minded. One student's father saw a picture of her bearded professor and immediately decided that the professor was a left-wing, radical ex-hippie. Nothing the student could say would make him change his mind. She then realized that her father's contrary attitude resulted from his service as a Marine gunnery sergeant.

Newly acquired contrary opinions   Converts to a religious belief are generally thought to be stronger believers than those who have been brought up with the belief. The closer you are to the time when you acquired a new opinion, attitude, or belief, the more rigid you may be in defending it. And the more rigid you are, the less amenable you are to change. Conflict is most frustrating when neither person is willing to be flexible. As time passes, you may begin to be more receptive to contrary ideas, even though you may still firmly hold your original belief. If you are conscious of the effects of the passage of time on creating an atmosphere of acceptance, you will be more careful about your timing when you need to present a new and potentially controversial idea to someone.

For example, Darrell was in desperate search of a college major and a lifetime goal. But each semester, as a result of taking different classes, he had become a quick convert to another new course of study. Nobody could persuade him to step back, be objective, and weigh the alternatives. Darrell began as a music major, switched to education and then to business, and now was changing to his fourth major: speech communication. His best friend, Alicia, was trying to persuade him to remain a business major until he was more sure of his specific goals, but she was getting nowhere. Darrell had taken one speech communication course—a requirement—and was convinced he wanted to make that his major. No matter how much Alicia argued, Darrell was convinced *he* had the answer—and no one, including Alicia, was about to change his mind!

Jumping to conclusions The problem with jumping to conclusions is that it destroys the climate of acceptance. You make a decision before you have enough facts on which to base the judgment. When you do not really listen, review the facts, or try to examine all the messages you are receiving, you create an atmosphere that works against effective communication. Janet was absolutely convinced Robert was seeing someone else. She had called him twice and gotten no answer; he hadn't called her at the regular time; and Janet's best friend said she had seen him at the library with Ellen. What else could he be doing? When Janet and Robert met, Janet immediately became angry, upset, and nearly out of control.

TRY THIS

Every day you encounter many conflict situations. Of the following situations, which do you consider critically important? Which seem irrelevant to you?

1. Conflict with another person for control of your life.
2. Conflict over what you should eat.
3. Conflict about how you spend your money.
4. Conflict about how you relate to other people.
5. Conflict over how clean you keep your living area.
6. Conflict about how you spend your time.
7. Conflict over your lifetime goals.
8. Conflict over what you want to believe in.
9. Conflict over your use of tobacco, marijuana, alcohol, or drugs.
10. Conflict about how you think of your self (your self-respect, self-esteem, or ego).

Robert tried to calm her down. Once he was able to speak, he explained that he *had* called but gotten no answer. He said, "I was very concerned about that big chemistry test; Ellen is in the same class and was helping me study. Al was there, too. Now that it's over, we can celebrate!"

Low credibility Acceptance is affected if one person perceives another to be a person of low credibility. If you suspect someone of being unfair, biased, unreliable, hostile, or contradictory, you are not likely to hear what he or she says. This basic lack of acceptance creates a serious handicap to communication. Focusing on the content of the message and not on the person will help, but a climate of low credibility is difficult to overcome. Don told both Maurice and Virginia that Geography 253 was a lousy course and that they shouldn't take it. Both Maurice and Virginia argued with him, but he seemed to have the facts: incompetent teaching, terrible exams, and too much work. After Don left, Maurice and Virginia had a chance to talk. They reminded themselves that Don was a poor student who hated attending lectures, taking exams, or doing any work. He seldom went to class. Since Don had low credibility in this situation, they decided to enroll in the class anyway.

Hostility In the presence of outright hostility, it is hard to achieve an atmosphere of acceptance. Hostility begets hostility. When you become aware of hostility directed toward you, you are likely to respond with a potentially hostile posture—prepared, alert, and equipped for a self-defensive action. Hostility then intensifies, and communication is blocked. Joe and Sara were in a speech communication class together. As the term progressed, Joe began to like Sara less and less because, as it seemed to Joe, every time he wanted to say something, Sara would interrupt. At the end of the term Sara gave a persuasive speech promoting a petition to get a crosswalk at an important student crossing on campus. Asked why he wouldn't sign the petition, Joe said, "Why can't you just keep quiet for a while? You've interrupted me constantly all term." His response had nothing to do with her speech, but the presence of hostility made it hard for Sara to achieve an atmosphere of acceptance.

Defensive Communication

Any of these communication barriers and breakdowns can make other people defensive. Jack Gibb has examined defensive communication in detail, pointing out that **defensive behavior** *occurs when individuals perceive or anticipate threat.*[6] Defensiveness then leads to distortions in communication. People who feel defensive spend unnecessary time thinking about how they appear to others; how they may be seen more favorably; how they may win, dominate, impress, or escape punishment; or how they may avoid or mitigate (make less severe) a perceived or an anticipated attack. Such defensiveness creates defensiveness in others and provokes defensive listening.[7]

CONSIDER THIS

Why are conflicts likely to occur between people of different cultures? Could one reason for some of these conflicts be the posture or attitude Americans hold toward those of other cultures? Read the following passage, and answer the questions that follow.

> Most of the reasons why Americans overlook cultural differences are traceable to strong feelings of ethnocentrism [the emotional attitude that one's own race, nation, or culture is superior to all others] that influence how they send and receive messages. What makes ethnocentrism such a powerful and insidious force in communication is that it often exists invisibly (for example, we only study Western philosophers) and is usually invisible in its manifestations (for example, we approach problems with a Western orientation).*

Questions
1. How important are strong feelings of ethnocentrism likely to be in conflict situations? What is the likely effect?
2. Does sensitivity to cultural differences have to be present before any conflict gets negotiated or discussed?
3. In what way could colleges and universities help people reduce their ethnocentric behavior? Are they, for example, training students to do things "the American way"?

*From Susan A. Hellweg, Larry A. Samovar, and Lisa Skow, "Cultural Variations in Negotiation Styles," in *Intercultural Communication: A Reader,* 6th ed., ed. Larry A. Samovar and Richard E. Porter (pp. 185–192) (Belmont, CA: Wadsworth Publishing Company, 1991). This quotation begins the conclusion to this article on page 191.

If listeners listen defensively, they become less able to perceive accurately. The attitudes and values of other people are distorted, the efficiency of communication is lessened, and the chances for conflict increase. Gibb says that you must expect defensiveness if you engage in the following behaviors.[8]

1. **Judgmental behavior:** "You should not talk like that," or "Talking like that is bad."
2. **Controlling behavior:** "When you are in this house, you do it our way."

3. **Strategic behavior:** "A thoughtful person would have done it without being asked."
4. **Neutral behavior:** "Let's not get emotional, just give me the facts. Be objective, and you can solve this problem . . ."
5. **Superior behavior:** "As your father, I can tell you what *I* would do in such a situation . . ."
6. **Certain behavior:** "There is only one way to look at it; only one point of view that is acceptable . . ."

These defensive behaviors are important. When you get to the point where you are able to detect when you are using any of these defensive behaviors, you can take direct action. It's just like a thermostat: you set the temperature for what is a comfortable climate (your normal behavior); when the temperature drops (an event occurs), the furnace goes on (defensiveness is created); when things start heating up, the furnace goes off (you take direct action by using specific supportive behaviors to cool things off). (See Figure 11.1.)

The advantage of viewing defensiveness from Gibb's defensive behaviors is that he has provided six specific, parallel, and correlated **supportive behaviors** for each of the defense-producing behaviors given above.[9] This means that the extent to which you are able to detect yourself using one of his six defensive behaviors is the extent to which you can counter that behavior with an exact, parallel supportive behavior. The supportive behaviors are as follows:

Figure 11.1
Using supportive behaviors to combat defensive behaviors is similar to how a thermostat works to maintain a comfort zone.

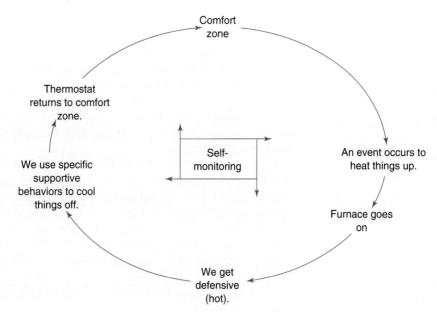

1. **Descriptive behavior:** "I am angry because you are cursing your mother." Or, to get the other person to describe, you might ask, "How would *you* describe the situation?"

2. **Problem-oriented behavior:** "I think we need to look at this idea together with no predetermined attitudes or solutions." Or, to get the other person to engage in problem solving, you might ask, "What are some solutions you can suggest for this problem?"

3. **Spontaneous behavior:** "I want to be open and flexible here." Or, to get the other person to engage in spontaneous behavior, you might say, "Okay, just be yourself—no tricks, deviousness, stratagems, or games now. Respond in a straightforward and honest way."

4. **Empathic behavior:** "I appreciate your feelings on this. Perhaps if you discuss it a bit more, I will understand your feelings even better." Or, to get the other person to engage in empathic behavior, you might say, "Try to see the problem as he or she does. How do you think he or she feels?"

5. **Equal behavior** (showing mutual trust and respect): "I think it is great that we can discuss problems from the same viewpoint." Or, to get the other person to engage in equal behavior, you might say, "Try to push aside your differences. Think about a real meeting of the minds on this."

6. **Provisional behavior:** "Since there doesn't seem to be any sure way to approach this situation, let's just try something, and if it doesn't work, we'll try something else." Or, to get the other person to engage in provisional behavior, you might say, "Maybe the best way is to come up with a list of possibilities, then pick what seems to be the best one and try it."

Having discussed a way of looking at defensive behavior and some coordinate supportive behaviors, let's look at an example. See Figure 11.1 again to follow the process here. Let's say that a friend's relationship partner was discovered dating other people, and the friend came to talk to you. This is the event that started to heat things up. Let's say, further, that you found yourself responding to your friend using "certain behavior" by saying things like "I'd drop him. I simply would not tolerate that kind of behavior."

Being sensitive to the friend's defensive reaction to your comment, and being a high self-monitor, you might realize this certain behavior was inappropriate. How to reduce the defensiveness? Using a supportive response—provisional behavior—you could quickly add, "Of course, there are other ways to approach this situation, too. Talking to him about what bothers you might help. If that doesn't work . . ." This kind of response—the use of the parallel supportive behavior—should return this defensive situation to the comfort zone.

Four chief requirements are necessary to defensive-reducing behaviors:

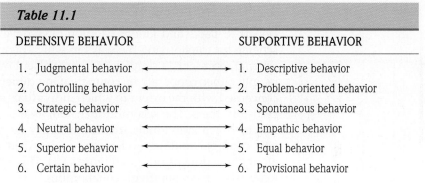

Table 11.1

DEFENSIVE BEHAVIOR	SUPPORTIVE BEHAVIOR
1. Judgmental behavior	1. Descriptive behavior
2. Controlling behavior	2. Problem-oriented behavior
3. Strategic behavior	3. Spontaneous behavior
4. Neutral behavior	4. Empathic behavior
5. Superior behavior	5. Equal behavior
6. Certain behavior	6. Provisional behavior

From this table, it should be clear that descriptive behavior is designed to help reduce defensiveness caused by judgmental behavior, problem-oriented behavior is designed to reduce defensiveness caused by controlling behavior, spontaneous behavior is designed to reduce defensiveness caused by strategic behavior, and so on. That is the purpose of this table: to show how the supportive behaviors are designed to be specific, directly linked, and parallel to the defensive behaviors.

1. *Sensitivity* to the other person, so you can detect the existence of a defensive reaction and the consequent need for supportive behavior.
2. *Self-monitoring,* or the ability to assess your own contribution to a defensive reaction, as in the example above.
3. *Familiarity* with the defensive behaviors and their specific, parallel, correlated supportive behaviors. See Table 11.1.
4. *Practice* using the behaviors. The more experience you have with them, the easier they will be to use.

Once again, this is what effective communication is all about. The more information you have, the more effective you become. The more alternative ways you have to behave, the more ways you have to choose from when situations call for them. As your behavioral repertoire increases, your flexibility and spontaneity in responding appropriately are likely to increase as well. The best part is that you are more likely to respond appropriately—at least, there is a greater chance for a successful outcome.

Is it worth learning and then practicing supportive behaviors? You can answer this question by answering a related one: How valuable and important is it to you to reduce defensiveness in those with whom you associate regularly? Do you just want to shoot from the hip with an occasional accurate shot, or do you want to respond with more precision and accuracy and greater assurance of success? Basically, that is the point of this discussion.

Styles of Handling Conflict

Robert R. Blake and Jane S. Mouton have developed a two-dimensional scheme for categorizing the ways in which people handle conflict.[10] This scheme represents a significant improvement over the simpler view that people either cooperate or compete. One dimension, cooperativeness, is concerned with the extent to which individuals attempt to satisfy the concerns of others. The second dimension, assertiveness, deals with the extent to which individuals attempt to satisfy their own concerns. Five specific conflict-handling modes can be identified in terms of their location along these dimensions (see Figure 11.2). These five modes are competing (assertive, uncooperative), collaborating (assertive, cooperative), avoiding (unassertive, uncooperative), accommodating (unassertive, cooperative), and compromising (intermediate in both cooperativeness and assertiveness). Much of the following discussion is based on the work of Kenneth W. Thomas and Ralph H. Kilmann.[11]

Competing *is used by individuals who desire to meet their own needs and concerns at the expense of others.* As Figure 11.2 indicates, it is the most assertive and least cooperative people who use this style, wielding what-

CONSIDER THIS

To what degree is "conflict for the sake of conflict" appropriate? Read the following passage and respond to the questions that follow.

> We believe tact to be of ethical importance because people have no right to injure the feelings of others unnecessarily. When a message might have been implemented in an effective way that would have spared the prestige and ego of a minority group but it did not, it falls short of being ethical.*

Questions
1. Should tastefulness and tact be included or excluded as a way to evaluate human communication?
2. Should some communicative tactics be judged inappropriate or unethical because they are too candid, obviously inappropriate, tasteless, or tactless in a given context?

*From Richard L. Johannesen, *Ethics in Human Communication,* 3rd ed. (Prospect Heights, IL: Waveland Press, Inc., 1990), p. 133. Johannesen is quoting from Winston L. Brembeck and William S. Howell, *Persuasion: A Means of Social Control,* 1st ed. (New York: Prentice-Hall, 1952), p. 462.

Figure 11.2
Styles of handling conflict.

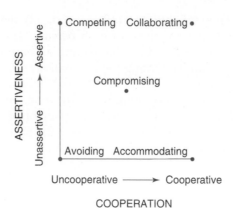

ever power is available to get the outcome they want. There is nothing wrong with power; it is how it is used that becomes important. One writer on negotiation suggests that power is a crucial variable in any negotiation situation.[12]

Collaborating *is maximum use of both cooperation and assertiveness to satisfy the needs of both parties.* Those using this style move through a series of important steps: (1) acknowledging that there is a conflict, (2) identify-

What supportive behaviors are likely to work to reduce this defensiveness?

ing and acknowledging each other's needs, (3) identifying alternative resolutions and consequences for each person, (4) selecting the alternative that meets the needs and concerns and accomplishes the goals of each party, and (5) implementing the alternatives selected and evaluating results.

Since collaborating requires more time, energy, and commitment than the other styles, an accurate assessment of the conflict situation is important. Do the needs and concerns of the parties involved warrant the use of this method? Are both parties committed to the resolution? If the answer to either question is "no," another method should probably be used.

Avoiding *is uncooperative and unassertive behavior by either or both parties.* There is no attempt to address the conflict or to discover or confront each other's needs and concerns. One or the other member evades the other, withdraws from the other, or leaves before a resolution is agreed upon.

Avoidance is not always negative—unless it becomes a permanent method for resolving conflicts. It can give people enough time to cool down if the conflict has become heated. It can provide time for more information to be accumulated. If an issue is relatively unimportant, avoidance may be a way to avoid conflict, but of course the problem here is "*Who* says it is unimportant?" Avoidance may also be helpful if there is not enough time to come to a solution or if the problem is a symptom of a more extensive problem that must be dealt with later. A final reason for choosing to avoid confronting the situation may be that others can resolve the conflict more effectively, efficiently, or easily.

Accommodating *is cooperative, unassertive behavior that places the other's needs and concerns above your own.* Accommodating is an appropriate method if one party is not as concerned as the other. For example, you are trying to decide with a friend where to go first. If you *really* don't care, it is easy to accommodate your friend's needs and concerns. Accommodating tends to build goodwill and leads to cooperative relationships, but it should not become one's only style of managing conflict. Although the method can promote harmony, avoid disruption, and reduce the power factor in a relationship, it can also mean that you are always suppressing your own needs and concerns, and always deferring to the other person, which is not a healthy situation.

Compromising *is using moderate amounts of cooperativeness and assertiveness in the search for a mutually acceptable solution.* Although the solution reached is mutually acceptable, it only partially satisfies each person's wants and needs. So, with respect to gaining a satisfying result, compromising is second to collaborating.

Compromise has an advantage if short-range solutions are sought for complex issues. Compromise works, too, when time is short. If the goals of both parties are moderately important but not worth the effort and time required by collaborating, compromise may be appropriate. It is also an effective backup strategy when collaboration breaks down.

You may have noticed from the discussion of each conflict-management style that there is nothing inherently right or wrong with any of them. Any of them may be appropriate or effective, depending on the situation or the people involved. You will need to assess situations and people carefully to determine which method is best. Consistently using the wrong approach can cause serious damage to a relationship. On the other hand, interpersonal communication can be enhanced if conflict is handled effectively. Effective interpersonal communication, then, requires flexibility—the ability to use whichever strategy is appropriate in the particular situation.

▲▲▲ *Stress Management: Personally Adjusting to Stress*

Stress *is a state of imbalance between demands made on you from outside sources and your capabilities to meet those demands.*[13] Often, it precedes and occurs concurrently with conflict. Stress, as you have seen, can be brought on by physical events, other people's behavior, social situations, our own behavior, feelings, thoughts, or anything that results in heightened bodily awareness. In many cases, when you experience pain, anger, fear, or depression, these emotions are a response to a stressful situation like conflict.

Sometimes, in highly stressful conflict situations, you must cope with the stress before you cope with the conflict. Relieving some of the intensity of the immediate emotional response will allow you to become more logical and tolerant in resolving the conflict. In this brief section, some of the ways in which you can control your physical reactions and your thoughts will be explained.

People respond differently to conflict, just as they respond differently to stress. Some people handle both better than others do. Individual differences are not as important as learning how to manage the stress you feel. The goal in stress management is self-control, particularly in the face of stressful events.

Stress reactions involve two major elements: (1) heightened physical arousal, as revealed by an increased heart rate, sweaty palms, rapid breathing, and muscular tension, and (2) anxious thoughts, such as thinking you are helpless or wanting to run away. Since your behavior and your emotions are controlled by the way you think, you must acquire skills to change those thoughts.

Are you able to adjust easily and comfortably to stressful situations? What do you do when you get upset?

Controlling the Physical Symptoms

Controlling the physical symptoms of stress requires relaxation. Sit in a comfortable position in a quiet place where there are no distractions. Close your eyes and pay no attention to the outside world. Concentrate only on your breathing. Slowly inhale and exhale. Now, with each exhaled breath, say "relax" gently and passively. Make it a relaxing experience. If you use this method to help you in conflict situations over a period of time, the word "relax" will become associated with a sense of physical calm; saying it in a stressful situation will help induce a sense of peace.

Another way to induce relaxation is through tension release. The theory here is that if you tense a set of muscles and then relax them, they will be more relaxed than before you tensed them. Practice with each muscle group separately. The ultimate goal, however, is to relax all muscle groups simultaneously to achieve total body relaxation. For each muscle group, in turn, tense the muscles and hold them tense for five seconds, then relax them. Repeat this tension-release sequence three times for each group of muscles. Next, tense all muscles together for five seconds, then release them. Now, take a low, deep breath and say "relax" softly and gently to yourself as you breathe out. Repeat this whole sequence three times.

You do not need to wait for special times to practice relaxing. If, during the course of your daily activities, you notice a tense muscle group, you can help relax this group by saying "relax" inwardly. Monitor your bodily tension. In some cases you can prepare yourself for stressful situations through relaxation *before* they occur. Practice will help you call up the relaxation response whenever needed.

For other ways to relax, do not overlook regular exercise. Yoga or aerobic exercise can be helpful. Personal fitness programs can be tied to these inner messages to "relax" for a complete relaxation response.

Controlling Your Thoughts

Controlling your thoughts is the second major element in stress management. Managing stress successfully requires flexibility in thinking. That is, you must consider alternative views. Your current view is causing the stress! You must also keep from attaching exaggerated importance to events. Everything seems life-threatening in a moment of panic; things dim in importance when viewed in retrospect.

Try to view conflict from a problem-solving approach: "Now, here is a new problem. How am I going to solve this one?" (A specific problem-solving approach will be discussed in the next section.) Too often, you may become stressed because you take things personally. When an adverse event occurs, you see it as a personal affront or as a threat to your ego. For example, when Christy told Paul she could not go to the concert with him, he felt she was letting him know she disliked him. This was a blow to Paul because he had never been turned down—rejected—before. Rather than dwell on that, however, he called Heather, she accepted his invitation, and he achieved his desired outcome—a date for the concert.

One effective strategy for stress management consists of talking to yourself. You become your own manager, and you guide your thoughts, feelings, and behavior in order to cope with *stressors*—that is, the events that result in behavioral outcomes called *stress reactions*. Phillip Le Gras suggests viewing the stress experience as a series of phases. Here, he presents the phases and some examples of coping statements:

1. *Preparing for a stressor.* What do I have to do? I can develop a plan to handle it. I have to think about this and not panic. Don't be negative. Think logically. Be rational. Don't worry. Maybe the tension I'm feeling is just eagerness to confront the situation.

2. *Confronting and handling a stressor.* I can do it. Stay relevant. I can psych myself up to handle this, I can meet the challenge. This tension is a cue to use my stress-management skills. Relax. I'm in control. Take a slow breath.

3. *Coping with the feeling of being overwhelmed.* I must concentrate on what I have to do right now. I can't eliminate my fear completely, but I can try to keep it under control. When the fear is overwhelming, I'll just pause for a minute.

4. *Reinforcing self-statements.* Well done. I did it! It worked. I wasn't successful this time, but I'm getting better. It almost worked. Next time I can do it. When I control my thoughts I control my fear.[14]

The purpose of such coping behavior is to become aware of and monitor your anxiety. In this way, you can help eliminate such self-defeating, negative statements as "I'm going to fail," or "I can't do this." Statements such as these are cues that you need to substitute positive, coping self-statements.

If the self-statements do not work, or if the stress reaction is exceptionally intense, then you may need to employ other techniques. Sometimes you can distract yourself by focusing on something outside the stressful experience—a pleasant memory, a sexual fantasy—or by doing mental arithmetic. Another technique is imaging. By manipulating mental images you can reinterpret, ignore, or change the context of the experience. For example, you can change the experience of unrequited love into a soap-opera fantasy or the experience of pain into a medieval torture by the rack. The point here is that love and pain are strongly subjective and personal, and when they cause you severe stress, you can mentally reconstruct the situation to ease the stress. In both these cases the technique of imaging helps to make your response more objective—to take it *outside* yourself. The more alternatives you have to aid you in stress reduction, the more likely you are to deal with it effectively. The following suggestion offers suggestions for approaching the conflict itself—successfully.

▲▲▲ *Coping with Conflict: A Successful Approach*

An approach has been designed for managing all stressful conflict situations that puts a high priority on creative coping and on maintaining self-esteem. How successfully you use these coping behaviors depends on your recognition of a conflict situation and on your ability to keep your wits about you as you put this approach into action. The four main elements of this approach are (1) gaining information, (2) organizing yourself, (3) striving for independence, and (4) anticipating conflict situations.[15]

Information: Get Enough of the Right Kind

In any communication setting, whether conflict laden or not, you act best when you are well informed. In a conflict situation, you need to find out all you can about the problem to assure yourself that you have more than one way to deal with it. The information you pick up may involve the na-

CONSIDER THIS

Cultural differences between people are likely to create misunderstandings and conflicts just because there are differences that the participants don't understand or don't respond to appropriately. Read the following example, and then answer the questions that follow.

> That Marcos and his friends have the health profession in common has not prevented misunderstandings. "When we first went out for meals together, my impulse was to pay for both of us," he says of another doctor, a Black woman who taught him not to leave his own behavior unexamined. "It wasn't that I thought she couldn't afford to pay; we were equally able to pick up the check. It was just that the cultural habit of paying for a woman was ingrained in my personality. But she misconstrued it. She felt I was trying to take care of her and put her down as a Black, a professional, and a woman. In order for our friendship to survive, she had to explain how she experiences things that I don't even think about."*

Questions
1. Do friendships across cultures require extra work? What kind?
2. It appears from the example above that one key to avoiding conflicts is "explaining." Would you agree with the statement that the greater the differences between people, the more explaining necessary? Explaining to themselves, to each other, and to their respective communities?

*From Letty Cottin Pogrebin, "The Same and Different: Crossing Boundaries of Color, Culture, Sexual Preference, Disability, and Age." In *Readings on Communicating With Strangers* (pp. 318–333), ed. William B. Gudykunst and Young Yun Kim (New York: McGraw-Hill, Inc., 1992). From p. 322.

ture of the communication itself, or it may involve the other person. Problems with information may develop in three major ways: through overload, through manipulation, and through ambiguity.

Communication overload If one person provides another person with more information than he or she can handle, a problem will arise.[16] This is called overload. The information I am referring to here has to do with the content of a communicator's message to a listener, not with general information about a conflict situation, as discussed above.

A human being can handle only so much information at one time. This has to do not only with the capability of the human brain to decipher material but also with the various ways in which emotions get bound to certain experiences. Often the root causes for conflict are closely tied to emotional response patterns. In such cases, as sure as conflicts are bound to come up, so are the emotions that go along with them. If you are having an emotionally involving experience, it is difficult to take on and fully comprehend a new "load" of information at the same time. Your senses are preoccupied. If someone else tries to share some vital news with you while your feelings are thus tied up, interpersonal conflicts may result. You may experience this when you try to listen to a classroom lecture just after you've heard some upsetting news. The intensity of the emotional experience overshadows any material the teacher can offer. You simply don't have room for any more information.

Manipulative communication Barriers to communication are likely to occur when a listener feels information is being offered with manipulative intent. You may have experienced manipulation at one time or another when you felt someone was using you or trying to control you. People manipulate other people for various reasons. In some cases, a person looks to others *for support*. Not trusting them to give it, he or she manipulates them to steer them in the right direction. Manipulation may also result *from love*. The problem is described by Everett Shostrom:

> We seem to assume that the more perfect we appear—the more flawless—the more we will be loved. Actually, the reverse is more apt to be true. The more willing we are to admit our weaknesses as human beings, the more lovable we are. Nevertheless, love is an achievement not easy to attain, and thus the alternative that the manipulator has is a desperate one—that of complete power over the other person, the power that makes him do what we want, feel what we want, think what we want, and which transforms him into a thing, our thing.[17]

Erich Fromm has said that the ultimate relationship between human beings is that of love—knowing a human being as he or she is and loving that person's ultimate essence.[18] Loving someone's "ultimate essence" is just the opposite of manipulation.

A third reason that manipulation occurs is *out of frustration with life*. People who feel overwhelmed may decide that since they cannot control everything, they will control nothing. They become passive manipulators. It should be clear, however, that passive manipulation can be a form of control. Passive manipulators may use various devices and tricks to accentuate their helplessness. They will try to get other people to make decisions for them and carry part of their burden, manipulating through their own feeling of powerlessness.

There are two other reasons why manipulation occurs that appear to be near opposites. People may deal with others ritualistically in an effort *to avoid intimacy or involvement*. An example of ritualistic communication is shown by the teacher who cannot deal with students in other than strictly teacher-student terms. The same type of ritualistic behavior might be seen in employer-employee and doctor-patient relationships.

Another reason people manipulate is *to gain the approval of others.* There are people who think they need to be approved of by everyone. They may be untruthful, trying to please everyone in their quest for acceptance. For example, a friend may tell you that everything you do is "great" just to keep you as a friend.

Ambiguous communication Ambiguous information may contribute to a conflict because ambiguity almost always leads to misunderstanding.[19] Ambiguity can result when not enough information is provided or when it is too general. If one of your friends tells you that everyone is going to the show tonight and that you should meet them downtown, you might easily misunderstand. Who is "everyone"? Where exactly should you meet them? What time? Also, the more abstract your language is, the more likely it is to be ambiguous and conflict-promoting.

Whenever you find yourself in a conflict situation, you should pay special attention to the kind of information you are exchanging with the other person: Is there enough? Is there too much? Is it manipulative? Is it ambiguous? It will be helpful to remember that every receiver of messages creates his or her own meaning for that communication based upon what he or she perceives. You can never know exactly which stimulus aroused meaning in someone else's head. The kinds of phenomena that can provoke meaning are limitless—there is no way anyone can control with certainty all the variables that will eliminate potential conflict situations.

Finally, remember that the message a receiver gets is the only one that counts in a conflict situation. The message that he or she acts upon may be quite different from the information that was sent. To discover precisely what message was received is useful in coping with conflict. You may need to ask the other person, "Now, what did you hear?" or "What is it that you understand?" or "What are you going to do?" As far as possible, you need to know how the other person understands the situation if you are to deal successfully with conflict.[20]

Organization: Sort Things Out

Think of a situation to which you had a powerful emotional response: fear, anger, grief, or passion. If you needed to cope with conflict at that time, you may have found your judgment was affected. To reestablish stability and a sense of right and wrong you need to organize yourself within yourself—you need to get yourself together.[21]

This is not to say you should avoid emotional experiences. Feelings of fear, anger, grief, and passion are healthy and normal and should not be repressed. But when in the throes of strong emotional experiences, you must remember that your senses are affected, that you cannot depend on

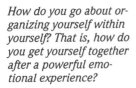

How do you go about organizing yourself within yourself? That is, how do you get yourself together after a powerful emotional experience?

your perceptions. This is why, for example, people are wise to make funeral arrangements *before* a person dies. In the emotional aftermath of the death of a loved one, decision making is difficult, and judgments are not as rational as they are at other times.

When perceptions are distorted, conflict is likely to escalate because of the misunderstandings exchanged. One such misunderstanding has been labeled by David W. Johnson as **mirror image.** In conflict, mirror image occurs *when both people think they are right, both think they were the one maligned, both think the other person is wrong, and both think they are the only one who wants a just solution.*[22]

Johnson labels a second perceptual distortion the **"mote-beam mechanism."** This occurs *when you are blind to the insensitive and mean things you do to others but clearly see all the vicious and underhanded things they do to you.* Johnson derives this label from Jesus' question in the Sermon on the Mount: "Why beholdest thou the mote [speck of sawdust] that is in thy brother's eye, but considerest not the beam [thick timber] that is in thine own eye?"

Another kind of misunderstanding occurs, according to Johnson, *when one person sees identical acts committed by both sides but considers those of the other person illegitimate, unfair, unjust, and unreasonable while viewing his or her own as legitimate, fair, just, and reasonable considering the circumstances.* For example, why should one person in a relationship be allowed to "play around" while the other must remain faithful? Why are rules "bent" for one person and not for the other? How can a father or mother make one set of rules for the oldest child and another for the others? This is known as the **double standard.**

In conflict situations, too, according to Johnson, thinking becomes **polarized.** Both individuals might come to have an oversimplified view of the conflict. In this uncomplicated view, *anything the other person does is bad and everything you do is good.* It is the oversimplification that distinguishes polarized thinking from mirror image and double standard. Obviously, when such misunderstandings are at work, it is difficult to organize our thinking.

When you are aware that you are not coping rationally, you would do well to seek help from others. It's a good idea to go to trusted friends for help in making decisions and carrying out plans. To recognize that you cannot make competent decisions until you have reorganized your thinking is not a weakness; it is realistic and mature.

To be organized within yourself is an awareness function. People who "have it together" are responsive, alive, and interested; they listen to themselves. The attitudes they express are based on firmly rooted values. An organized person takes time to think, to monitor, and to reevaluate before responding.

Independence: Be Your Own Person

Most conflict situations encountered on a daily basis are not the extremely taxing kind. The better you know yourself, the better you will be able to cope with daily conflict. The better organized you are, too, the more likely you are to be your own person—autonomous. You need to be free to act and to deal with conflict, and you must avoid being pushed into action before you are ready.[23]

The people best prepared to cope with conflict are appropriately spontaneous. They have the freedom to express their full range of potentials, to be the masters of their own lives, and not to be easily manipulated. Successful copers are open and responsive. They can appropriately assert their own independence without trying to stifle another person's. They show their independence by appropriately expressing their wants and needs instead of demanding them, by expressing their preferences instead of ordering, by expressing acceptance of each other rather than mere tolerance, and by being willing to surrender genuinely to another person's wishes when it is appropriate to do so rather than simply pretending to submit.[24]

It should be clear that uninhibited, uncaring, selfish independence is not being condoned. *Appropriate* spontaneity and expression are emphasized. That is, independence needs to be proper, fitting, and suitable. It needs to conform with accepted standards of manners or behavior. You might wonder how to learn what is appropriate. You learn it from parents, in church, through friends, by observation, in the groups to which you belong, and by reading authorities.

TRY THIS

It is human nature to blame others for conflict in which you find yourself. More often than not, however, a combination of factors, and your own personality, thoughts, or feelings, are part of the problem. Conduct a self-inventory by answering the following questions:

1. Do you consider your thoughts to be more important than those of others?
2. Are your feelings more positive than those of others?
3. Do you speak with authority?
4. Do you like to give orders to people?
5. Do you believe that your principles are superior to those of your society?
6. Do you believe in saying what you feel in dealing with other people?
7. Is your chief concern for your own individuality?
8. Do you admire forceful people more than cooperative ones?
9. Are you able to listen to others when you are annoyed by them?
10. Are you highly tolerant of other people's negative feelings?
11. Do you care for the people with whom you talk?

If you answered these questions honestly, and if your answers to the first eight questions were predominantly "yes," then it may be that your concern for yourself and for control engenders or aggravates much of the conflict in your life.

Paraphrased from a survey reprinted in Charles T. Brown and Paul W. Keller, *Monologue to Dialogue: An Exploration of Interpersonal Communication* (Englewood Cliffs, NJ: Prentice-Hall, 1979), pp. 260–263. Used by permission of Charles T. Brown, Western Michigan University.

Anticipation: Be Prepared for Conflict

Conflicts are more likely to become crises when they catch you totally unaware. Try to anticipate conflict situations. Try to control your emotional reactions before they escalate. Escalation can result in less control. If you are ready for conflict, and confident in your ability to deal with it, you'll be much less anxious if and when conflict develops.

By anticipating a conflict situation, you will be more likely to have some control over the context in which it occurs. Instead of focusing, for example, on whose fault the conflict is, you can try to get in touch with where you and the other person are, and attempt to work from there.

In addition, with some anticipation, you can take responsibility for your feelings and actions. You can plan, in advance, to say such things as "I am angry" instead of "You make me angry," or "I feel rejected" instead of "You are excluding me again," or "I am confused" instead of "You don't make sense." In this way, you own your feelings—you take full responsibility for them. You claim, "*I*" feel this way or "*I*" am this way. To do this rids you of the scapegoating you learn so well when you are young: "Billy made me do it." It is not only a move toward assertive behavior; it is a move toward maturity. And you convey your feelings to others, thereby creating trust in the process.

Finally, anticipation can cause you to be more aware. Resolving interpersonal conflict is easiest when you listen to the other person and respond to him or her with feedback. Conflict is likely to be reduced when you try to support and understand the other person.

Building Conflict Management Skills

The following ideas will aid in developing a constructive approach to dealing with conflict situations. Remember that there are no guaranteed solutions or sure-fire approaches. Remember, too, that not all conflicts can be resolved but that you can always choose how to handle them. This is an expansion of the collaborating style of conflict management.

Define the conflict[25]   How you view the cause, size, and type of conflict affects how you manage it. Thus, it is important to be as specific as possible when defining the conflict. If it is multifaceted (as many are), each part should be defined individually. If you know what events led up to the conflict and especially the specific event that triggered it, you may be able to anticipate and avoid future conflicts. You should learn to see the true size of a conflict: the smaller and more specific it is, the easier it will be to resolve. Am I concerned about your irresponsibility, or do I just want you to take out the trash? When a large, vague issue or principle is involved, the conflict is often escalated and enlarged. You can get very upset over how the system of higher education stifles individual initiative and growth, but that is a large, vague issue. To narrow the cause of the conflict, you might focus directly on a particular professor with whom you are having problems. Also, it is important to remove as much emotion as possible. You should strive for objectivity—a true representation of the conflict—rather than subjectivity—the conflict as it is attached to your feelings and emotions. Honesty is important as well. If the problem is not honestly defined from the beginning, no solution will resolve it.

CONSIDER THIS

What is the overall, guiding principle that aids people in facing conflict situations? Read the following passage, and answer the questions that follow.

> Probably the most important factor that will affect your ability to put the advice in this chapter into effect is to remember that you always have choices in conflict situations. Even when you feel that things are happening too fast or that you must deal with problems that arise suddenly, you still have choices as to how you act or react with respect to the other person. Your first response is not necessarily the best one. Slow down, think about the situation, and then respond to the other, using the skills discussed here. Learn from your mistakes, and move on. The only way you will develop conflict skills is to use them in conflict situations.*

Questions
1. Is it true that you always have choices? Aren't there some situations in which your emotions rule your actions?
2. Do you think you can gain an understanding of conflict and how to manage it by reading about it? Do you believe that much of your ability in conflict situations has to do with habits?

*From Roxane Salyer Lulofs, *Conflict: From Theory to Action* (Scottsdale, AZ: Gorsuch Scarisbrick, Publishers, 1994), p. 250.

View the conflict as a joint problem   There are two general ways of looking at a conflict—as a win-or-lose situation or as a joint problem: **win-win.** If you look at a conflict as a joint problem, there is a greater possibility for a creative solution that results in both parties' being satisfied. If you are having trouble with your English professor, you could easily turn the situation into a win-lose confrontation. You might say, "She thinks she's so great. I'm going to show her. I'll go to the department head. . . ." If you perceive the conflict as a joint problem, you might say, "Perhaps she has a point; maybe if I go in to see her, we could talk about this." The way you label a conflict partly determines the way you resolve it. A win-win attitude in conflicts suggests that there are creative alternatives and an infinite number of solutions for every problem. A win-win attitude also suggests that each party in the conflict assumes responsibility for his or her own behavior.

Defining conflict as a joint win-win problem means trying to discover the differences and similarities between yourself and the other person. There is always the question of not just how *you* define the problem but also of how the *other person* defines the problem and how the two definitions differ.

State the problem   You'll have a better chance of resolving a potential conflict quickly if you have a clear idea of what behavior is acceptable or unacceptable to you and if you express your position to the other person. When you say, "When you interrupt me when we are talking to other people, I feel put down and unimportant" or "Every time you publicly criticize the way I dress, I get angry with you," you explain specific behaviors that are unacceptable to you. And you can then discuss or change those behaviors.

When you focus on a specific bothersome behavior, you reveal what is going on inside you. You take responsibility for your feelings by using "I" language instead of "you" language. This lessens the likelihood of defensiveness by not placing the blame on the other person, as you would if you said "You insult me" or "You make me angry."

Check your perceptions   In any circumstances, it is easy to be misunderstood, misquoted, or misinterpreted. Especially in a conflict situation, you should always check to make certain your message has been received accurately. You should also make sure you understand the other person's responses by paraphrasing them before you answer. Because your emotions intensify in times of conflict, further hurt or resentment can occur quickly through distortions caused by expectations or predispositions. Empathic listening is critical. You can determine where you are in your conversation with another person through paraphrases and summaries.

Generate possible decisions   It is important, once you have shared what is bothering you, to consider how change can occur. You need not come up with all the decisions yourself. A joint, cooperative decision is more likely to work. Flexibility is important in this process. Julius Fast views flexibility as extremely valuable, calling it "an awareness of alternative solutions as well as the ability to discard one solution if it doesn't work and select another."[26] What is needed? What can the other person do? What can we do? What can be done together? These are realistic questions that should be raised. As you get possible answers to these questions, you should paraphrase and summarize them so that you are certain that both of you know what has been suggested and what alternatives exist.

Reach a mutually acceptable decision   When you have considered all the possible alternatives you and the other person could generate, you should decide which of them would be mutually acceptable.

When I was in graduate school, dinners became a problem because my wife worked. Conflict occurred because she was too tired to fix meals when she came home; I was in class. The alternatives were to fix meals early, order out, or have me prepare them. The mutually acceptable decision was for me to arrange my schedule to get home earlier to make dinner. It is important that we find an answer somewhat agreeable to everyone involved. But we could not stop there. We both needed to understand the possible outcomes of implementing the decision. What was likely to happen? We also had to understand the need for cooperative interaction. What was important, as we discussed the alternatives, was that my making dinner several nights a week involved me more in our relationship, allowed my wife some time to relax, and gave me a break from my studies. In what ways, for example, would a particular decision have required us to work together? When we came to a final agreement on how to settle our conflict, we made certain everyone fully understood what we agreed on by paraphrasing and summarizing the results. It was clear, then, that I would fix the evening meal Mondays, Wednesdays, and Fridays.

If you cannot reach an agreement you should stop. Plan another meeting. Try again later. Getting away from the problem for a while may generate new insights.

Implement and evaluate the decision   Before you put the proposed solution into effect, you should try to agree on how you will check it later to see if it solved the problem. Plan a meeting to evaluate progress. After you implement the decision, you'll want to find out if the results are mutually satisfying. If they aren't, you might have to go back to the beginning, possibly to your original definition of the conflict. You should have some way of knowing how to tell if the implemented decision worked well or did not work at all. If you have moved through the conflict successfully or are at least making progress, some gesture of appreciation might be appropriate from one (either!) party to the other.

It should be clear that these suggestions for coping with conflict are designed to provide a general framework (see Figure 11.3). No two conflict situations are identical; thus, no two ways of dealing with conflict will be exactly the same. Many of the decisions you face must be made instantaneously; how you cope is often a function of how quickly and accurately you are able to respond. However, successful coping may also result from slow, deliberate action. The discussion of ways to improve your skills in conflict management is not designed to make the situation more complex than necessary nor to prolong solutions unnecessarily. The point has been to set the tone or the appropriate frame of reference for decisions, whether quick or slow.

Conflict in interpersonal communication is an inevitable human experience. You are unique; the next person is unique; when these uniquenesses meet, conflict can occur. Conflict does not need to fracture friendships, dissolve marriages, or break up other interpersonal relationships. There is nothing inherently destructive, threatening, or mysterious about

Figure 11.3
Conflict management model.

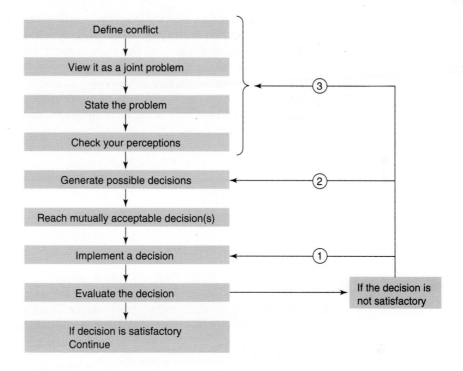

conflict. How well you handle it while maintaining your values and your self-esteem and, at the same time, protecting the values and self-esteem of other people, will help determine your effectiveness in interpersonal relationships.

▶ **SUMMARY**

Conflict is a situation in which you, your desires, or your intentions are in opposition to those of another person. This society often considers conflict undesirable, but interpersonal communication is *not* conflict free. Therefore, you must learn how to deal with it. The communication barriers and breakdowns associated with conflict include contrary attitudes, newly acquired contrary opinions, jumping to conclusions, low credibility, hostility, and defensive communication. Defensive behavior occurs when individuals perceive or anticipate threat. There are supportive behaviors designed to counter each of the six defensive behaviors.

The five conflict handling modes include competing, collaborating, avoiding, accommodating, and compromising. Because stress often accompanies conflict, specific ways to handle stress are discussed. The successful approach for coping with conflict includes getting enough information, sorting things out through organization, striving for independence, and being prepared for conflict. For improving your skills in conflict management, you are advised to define the conflict, view it as a joint problem, state it, check your perceptions, generate possible decisions, reach a mutually acceptable decision, and, finally, implement and evaluate the decision.

TRY THIS

A Guide to Keeping Conflicts Civil

Do you fight fairly? "Fighting dirty is often a way to avoid emotional intimacy, of keeping your distance," notes psychiatrist Mary Ann Bartusis, author of *Off To a Good Start*. "Or it can be a power play, a way of trying to 'win.' Or it can be a way of just dumping your emotions on somebody."

To learn whether or not you stay within the bounds of fair play, take this quiz designed by Bartusis. Do you

1. Refuse to stick to rules you made for handling fights?
2. Bring up old problems instead of sticking to the current issue?
3. Drag in references to in-laws, parents, children, etc.?
4. Call your partner names, such as "stupid"?
5. Yell at your partner?
6. Give your mate the silent treatment?
7. Leave the room to avoid conflict?
8. Use obscene language, knowing it offends your mate?
9. Quarrel under the influence of drugs or alcohol?
10. Try to physically intimidate your mate?
11. Deliberately push your partner's "buttons"?
12. Lie about facts or withhold information?
13. Refuse to listen attentively while preparing your own rebuttal instead?
14. Refuse to accept responsibility for your share of what went wrong?
15. Encourage friends and/or relatives to take sides?
16. Fight in public?
17. Refuse to make a sincere apology?
18. Hold a grudge? Seek revenge?
19. Confide in others about fights when you know your partner would not approve?
20. Keep fighting about the same problems over and over without seeking a true solution?

Scoring

Total the number of "no" answers:

> 16–20. Your fights help clear the air and come to a better understanding. Still, work to become a 20.
>
> 11–15. You're on your way to solving problems amicably. But you still have work to do.
>
> 5–10. You are struggling to handle conflict. Try honing relationship skills through a course in communication.
>
> 0–4. You might use fighting to avoid emotional intimacy. Take a relationships course or consider a counselor.

From *USA Today,* July 23, 1991, section D, page 4. Taken from Mary Ann Bartusis, *Off To a Good Start* (Donald I. Fine).

▶ # KEY TERMS

conflict	problem-oriented behavior	stress
defensive behavior	spontaneous behavior	communication overload
judgmental behavior	empathic behavior	manipulative communication
controlling behavior	equal behavior	ambiguous communication
strategic behavior	provisional behavior	mirror image
neutral behavior	competing	mote-beam mechanism
superior behavior	collaborating	double standard
certain behavior	avoiding	polarized
supportive behaviors	accommodating	win-win
descriptive behavior	compromising	

▶ # NOTES

1. George R. Bach and Peter Wyden, *The Intimate Enemy: How to Fight Fair in Love and Marriage* (New York: Avon Books, 1968), 25–26.
2. George R. Bach and Herb Goldberg, *Creative Aggression: The Art of Assertive Living* (New York: Avon Books, 1974), 82.
3. Robert J. Doolittle, "Conflicting Views of Conflict: An Analysis of the Basic Communication Textbooks," *Communication Education* 26 (March 1977): 121.

4. Kenneth E. Boulding, *Conflict and Defense* (New York: Harper & Row, 1962), 5.
5. Based on pp. 172–176 from *Elements of Interpersonal Communication* by John W. Keltner. Copyright © 1973 by Wadsworth Publishing Co. Used by permission of John W. Keltner.
6. Jack R. Gibb, "Defensive Communication," *Journal of Communication* 11:3 (1961): 141–148.
7. Gibb, 141.
8. Gibb, 147. Reprinted by permission.
9. Gibb, 147.
10. Robert R. Blake and Jane S. Mouton, *The Managerial Grid* (Houston: Gulf Publishing Co., 1964). See also Robert R. Blake and Jane S. Mouton, *The New Managerial Grid* (Houston: Gulf Publishing Co., 1978), 11.
11. Kenneth W. Thomas, "Conflict and Conflict Management," in *Handbook of Industrial and Organizational Psychology*, vol. II (Chicago: Rand McNally, 1976); Kenneth W. Thomas and Ralph H. Kilmann, *Thomas-Kilmann Conflict Mode Instrument* (Sterling Forest, Tuxedo, NY: Xicom, 1974). For an excellent interpretation of their work, see Martin B. Ross, "Coping with Conflict," in *The 1982 Annual Handbook for Facilitators, Trainers, and Consultants,* eds. J. William Pfeiffer and Leonard D. Goodstein (San Diego, CA: University Associates, 1982), 135–139. Table 11.1 is adapted by permission from this source.
12. See Herb Cohen, *You Can Negotiate Anything* (New York: Bantam Books, 1980), 49–113.
13. I am indebted to L. Phillip K. Le Gras, "Stress-Management Skills: Self-Modification for Personal Adjustment to Stress," in *The 1981 Annual Handbook for Group Facilitators,* eds. John E. Jones and J. William Pfeiffer (San Diego, CA: University Associates, 1981), 138–140, for his development of these ideas.
14. Le Gras, 139.
15. Julius Fast, *Creative Coping: A Guide to Positive Living* (New York: William Morrow and Co., Inc., 1976), 187–188.
16. W. Charles Redding, *Communication Within the Organization* (New York: Industrial Communication Council, 1972), 87.
17. From *Man, the Manipulator* by Everett Shostrom. Copyright © 1967 by Abingdon Press. Used by permission.
18. Erich Fromm, "Man Is Not a Thing," *Saturday Review* (March 16, 1957): 9–11.
19. Richard C. Huseman, James M. Lahiff, and John D. Hatfield, *Interpersonal Communications in Organizations: A Perceptual Approach* (Boston: Holbrook Press, 1976), 99.
20. Redding, 28, 30, and 37.
21. Fast, 187.

22. David W. Johnson, *Reaching Out: Interpersonal Effectiveness and Self-Actualization*, 4th ed. (Englewood Cliffs, NJ: Prentice-Hall, 1986), 212.
23. Shostrom, 50.
24. Shostrom, 53.
25. This approach is a variation of Dewey's problem solving method. See John Dewey, *How We Think* (Chicago: D. C. Heath, 1910).
26. Fast, 53.

▶ ## FURTHER READING

Kare Anderson, *Getting What You Want: How to Reach Agreement and Resolve Conflict Every Time* (New York: Penguin Group [A Plume Book], 1994). Although Anderson cites no sources in this book, the skills she offers for conflict resolution, negotiation, and persuasion are practical and realistic. A well-written book full of good advice.

Roger Fisher, Elizabeth Kopelman, and Andrea Kupfer Schneider, *Beyond Machiavelli: Tools for Coping With Conflict* (Cambridge, MA: Harvard University Press, 1994). The authors break conflict into manageable components and advance a process for problem solving. They argue that people need to move beyond one-shot "solutions" toward a constructive way for dealing with differences. This is a succinct, clear, and effective book.

Jeffrey A. Kottler, *Beyond Blame: A New Way of Resolving Conflicts in Relationships* (San Francisco: Jossey-Bass, 1994). Through examples, exercises, and explanations, Kottler helps readers confront the interactions that arouse their deepest fears, harness emotional pain to use as a force for constructive change, take responsibility without blaming, say no to guilt, and identify the positive functions of conflict. A useful and interesting presentation.

Roxane Salyer Lulofs, *Conflict: From Theory to Action* (Scottsdale, AZ: Gorsuch Scarisbrick, Publishers, 1994). In this well-written and well-researched textbook, Lulofs covers the nature of conflict, theoretical perspectives, effective behavior in conflict situations, and the introduction of third or multiple parties to conflict. Her case studies and application sections are excellent.

Howard Markman, Scott Stanley, and Susan L. Blumberg, *Fighting for Your Marriage: Positive Steps for Preventing Divorce and Preserving Love* (San Francisco: Jossey-Bass Publishers, 1994). Conflict in intimate relationships is as normal and essential as love. How people fight and resolve conflicts determines the difference between healthy, satisfying relationships and endless pain, frustration, and often divorce. The three parts of this book include handling conflict, dealing with core issues, and enhancement. A well-written, interesting, and important book.

Gini Graham Scott, *Resolving Conflict With Others and Within Yourself* (Oakland, CA: New Harbinger Publications, 1990). Scott bases her book on the rational-intuitive method for resolving conflict. The three parts of her book are clearing out the emotional closet, using your reason to understand and manage conflicts, and using your intuition to discover new possibilities. Although she cites no sources, her explanations and her resources appear strong and convincing.

12

Discovering Supportive Relationships: Finding Friendship

CHAPTER OBJECTIVES

After reading this chapter, you should be able to

▲ Define friendship.

▲ Distinguish between reciprocal, receptive, and associative friendships.

▲ Explain some of the myths about relationships.

▲ Identify some of the reasons why we seek friendship relationships.

▲ Discuss the characteristics of good conversationalists.

▲ List what are considered to be the qualities of friendship.

▲ Characterize the communication that goes on between friends.

▲ Explain the Johari Window, and compare and contrast each of the panes.

▲ Discuss some of the rules that are likely to govern friendship relationships.

▲ Describe ways to improve friendships.

Yitong and Samira met each other in high school. Because of similar backgrounds and interests, they hit it off immediately and began to hang out together. Because they both wanted to pursue a business degree, both decided to go to the same college, and they requested each other as roommates. They enrolled in many of the same classes, attended many of the same social events, and went to many of the same athletic contests together. Looking back on their college experience, both agree that it was great because they always had someone to talk with, to share with, and to be with. Yitong and Samira formed a lasting bond that exists to this day. Not only do they maintain contact via E-mail, they often arrange their travels so they can see each other. They consider themselves the very best of friends.

Kevin and Laura were in the same section of the basic speech course at their college. For the first interpersonal activity of the course, a dyadic encounter, the instructor assigned them to be a pair. Although they were awkward at first, as they began talking they realized they had a great deal in common. Even though Kevin thought the assignment was a little ridiculous, he began to look forward to the meetings with Laura. And Laura began to think of Kevin as more than just a way to complete an assignment. Their required meeting times of 20 minutes began to extend to an hour, and the final meeting lasted almost three hours as they spent an afternoon in a local mall. After the assignment was over, they worked together on the papers, they began seeing each other after class, and they went on several dates. As it turned out, a forced meeting because of an assignment resulted in a friendship that turned out to be satisfying and pleasurable for both Kevin and Laura.

Kathleen had worked in administration for a large real estate company, but because of a depressed market and company downsizing, she had recently been switched to another department as some employees were released and some moved to other positions within the company. In her new department she met Allison, an employee of the company for more than 15 years. Kathleen and Allison were now colleagues in the same office. Both were hard workers, were enthusiastic about the company, and played a major role in company activities. During their breaks, they would talk about their education and background. Kathleen had just emerged from a bitter divorce; Allison was happily married to an accountant and had two children, both in school. Allison became a close confidante to Kathleen, who needed support and encouragement. Also, because of her happy marriage, Allison was a positive role model. Allison often invited Kathleen over to have dinner and to participate in other family activities. Allison played a major role in stabilizing Kathleen after her divorce and in getting her back into serious dating.

Almost everyone, at some time in his or her life, has had a friend and because of this knows the value and importance of friendship. Notice that in all three cases above, although we cannot be certain about all the qualities these friends possessed or revealed, we can make certain assumptions. For example, from what we can tell, those involved in the friendship were honest and open. Each showed affection for the other. They told each other their secrets and problems. Each gave help when the other needed it. Not only were they trusting of each other, they were trustworthy. They shared time and activities with each other. Each treated the other with respect and valued the friendship. It appeared that the friends would be able to work through disagreements. Why is it possible to speculate about these three examples? Because these are, in general, things that people expect friends to do for them and, in return, expect to do for friends.[1]

"Having friends is one of the greatest pleasures humans have, and the ability to make and keep friends is an important skill."[2] Friends add something to our lives, and whatever this ingredient is, it stays with us throughout our lives. "Friends provide the support that we all need to convince ourselves that we are all right, that our ideas are not crazy, and that what is happening to us has happened to someone else. Friends are essential if we are to grow up sane."[3] Have you ever connected having friends with maintaining your sanity? Today, it seems, the number of friends people have may be a good measure of their social and personal success.[4] Despite this, "It is as normal to enjoy a close, small, intense set of friendships as it is to prefer to have lots of friends."[5]

The following discussion will explain the nature of friendship as well as why we form friendships. We will examine communication in friendship relationships as well as how to improve skills in friendship maintenance and repair.

▲▲▲ *The Nature of Friendship*

Friendships *are interpersonal relationships in which people voluntarily intertwine, enjoying others for their own sake and those others bringing them rewarding feelings about themselves.*

It should be clear, first, that people have freely chosen to be intertwined. Wright (1984), in his research, calls this the "voluntary interdependence" of friendship.[6] Second, Wright stresses the importance of enjoying people for their own sake rather than for the things they can do for you. Third, in Lea's research (1989), emphasis is placed on "self-referent rewards." That is, you pursue friendships for how they make you feel about yourself. If you think about these characteristics in reference to friendships you have had, you will discover their validity. When you do not enjoy others, or when they have no effect on you, you are likely to either not pursue a friendship or drop it. Another possibility is to handle the friendship differently.

There are three distinctly different types of friendship. No type is better than another because any one of them may serve your purposes at a given time. **Reciprocal friendship** *is that in which each individual shares equally in the relationship.* It is the kind most often described when you think of close friends. These are friends who are loyal, generous, self-sacrificing, and mutually affectionate. It is based on equality—equal sharing, equal giving and receiving of rewards and benefits. If you think about it, there is a limit to how many reciprocal friendships one can have, simply because there is a limit to the time and energy you can devote to friendships.

A receptive friendship *is one in which one person is always the primary giver and one is always the primary receiver.* It depends on a difference in status. It is like the friendships that develop between teacher and student, doctor and patient, lawyer and client, employer and employee, mentor and mentee. In receptive friendships there is an imbalance in giving and receiving. The imbalance is positive because both giver and receiver gain something from the relationship. Again, if you think about it, there is some limit to how many receptive friendships one can have, simply because they require time and energy. Often, students develop receptive friendships with teachers they like.

Associative friendships *are those in which the giving or receiving that occurs is minimal, and the association between friends is superficial rather than intense.* They are transitory. These are like those you have with co-work-

CONSIDER THIS

According to Barry L. Duncan and Joseph W. Rock, in "Saving Relationships: The Power of the Unpredictable," some people operate under various relationship myths, beliefs, and feelings about relationships for which there is no evidence. The authors think the following are *myths*: traditional stories of unknown authorship:

Myth #1: What people say is very important and has a big impact on what they do. Words often fall short of accurately depicting someone's intentions and we can't really guess at times what someone else really means. In the long term, behavior is what gives evidence of our true intentions.

Myth #2: People can and should understand and explain their own and others' motives. Behavior is the result of a tremendous number of interacting influences: biological, psychological, interpersonal, situational. We never get answers to "why," only plausible-sounding guesses. Knowing "why" seldom produces a solution. *Understanding* a behavior pattern and changing it are often completely different. Consider *what* is happening now between you and your partner and *how* that pattern can be changed.

Myth #3: In close relationships being completely open and honest is critical if the relationship is to work. If the person with whom you are communicating is unable or unwilling to respond honestly and openly, honesty and openness may well be a bad idea at times. Being open with someone who will use the information to manipulate you or gain power over you is like playing poker and showing your cards before you bet. An open and honest expression must be interpreted as such by the receiver of the message for it to be truly open and honest. Openness is not the only way, and, in some situations, not the best way.

Myth #4: A good relationship is one in which both people give unselfishly. Unselfish giving is not a prerequisite for a good relationship. In fact, attempts to do so usually create more problems than they solve. Giving is an important part of any relationship. However, all of us expect something back; it helps to let the other person know what that is. Balance is also important. Rather than expecting to meet all of each other's needs, stay in practice at meeting some of your own. It adds stability to a relationship and reduces the risk of resentment. Complete selfishness certainly does not lend itself to healthy relationships, but it turns out that neither does utter unselfishness.

Myth #5: In any situation there is only one reality or one truth. Reality is entirely dependent on who is observing and describing it, especially in complex situations such as interactions in relationships.

When two people have very different stories to tell about the same situation, it does not mean that one is lying, although each partner usually believes that about the other. Rather, each is describing reality from his or her frame of reference. A lot of time usually is wasted trying to convince your partner that you are right. This time could be better spent trying to understand the other's point of view and using that understanding to change your own behavior in a way that will help the relationship.*

Questions
1. Do you believe in the aphorism "Actions speak louder than words?"
2. Have you ever operated under the assumption that being in a relationship with someone else requires or demands complete honesty and openness? Do you see the possible problems with this belief?
3. Can an exact balance between selfishness and unselfishness in a relationship be set? What are the factors that help determine what balance works best?
4. Have you ever said, "I was there. I saw it with my own eyes. I know exactly what happened"? What is meant by the phrase "Perceived reality is negotiable." Is it accurate?

*From Barry L. Duncan and Joseph W. Rock, "Saving Relationships: The Power of the Unpredictable," *Psychology Today*, 26 (January/February, 1993), pp. 46–51, 86 and 95. The information on "Relationship Myths" appears on p. 49.

What does having a friend mean to you? Does having a friend mean different things depending on the friend? On the situation?

ers, neighbors, classmates, or store employees. In associative friendships there is no special loyalty or trust. They are like friendly relationships rather than true friendships. There is no limit to the number of associative friendships that are likely to occur.

As you saw in the earlier chapters of this book, a great deal of personal growth is possible within friendships. As you become wiser in the ways of human beings, more sensitive to yourself and more perceptive about others, you become more careful about the kinds of friendships you begin. The more you know about the types of personalities with whom you should or should not become involved, the more likely you are to choose friends with whom a relationship will last a long time.

Often people view the art of acquiring and holding friends as a passive process. They feel fortunate when they find a friend and are happy when that friendship lasts, but they do not realize that friendship involves commitment, giving, and energy. Often people are too lazy to make friendships work. These people never discover what friendships can be and do, and the mutual needs that can be fulfilled. Andrew Greeley, in *The Friendship Game,* calls friendship "the most pleasurable and most difficult of specifically human activities."[8]

In forming and maintaining relationships, all your interpersonal skills come into play. Friendship involves making choices that are not always based on logic. A chemistry occurs between good friends. Sometimes an instant rapport is deceptive and dangerous; you learn to distinguish this from what is authentic. The skills described here for forming and maintaining relationships assume that you know someone with whom friendship seems likely, and you wish to proceed. The purpose of this chapter is to help you think more clearly about the problems and challenges of friendship, especially close friendships.

Why You Form Friendships[9]

A **friendship relationship** *is one marked by very close association, contact, or familiarity.* Usually a warm friendship has developed as a result of a long association, but this is not always the case. Sometimes friendship develops suddenly. Friendship relationships are very personal or private, and they are often characterized by different types of communication.

There is no doubt that many factors govern the nature, development, maintenance, and dissolution of friendship relationships. As bases for friendship relationships, Mark Knapp lists personality and background factors, situational and developmental factors, cultural guidelines, emotional considerations, self-fulfillment, self-surrender, and commitment.[10] Many of these factors have been discussed elsewhere in this book.

People seek friendship relationships for many reasons. These reasons may operate singly or in conjunction with each other. Many overlap. In some situations, with some people, one of these reasons may sustain a relationship, whereas in others, several are likely to operate. The more needs that are fulfilled in a relationship, the more solid the foundation upon which the relationship rests. You seek friendship relationships to fulfill six basic needs: for enjoyment, security, affection, self-esteem, freedom, and equality.[11] They are not necessarily ranked here in order of importance.

Enjoyment is an important, perhaps *the* most important, need that friendships fulfill. Simply put, friends enjoy each other's company. The "what do you want to do" syndrome ("I don't know, what do *you* want to do?") often occurs because neither friend really cares. Just enjoying being together is enough; *doing* something (anything!) is secondary.

Enjoyment often is attained through play. Play has important value in relationships:[12]

1. It offers evidence to the parties that their relationship is one of synchrony (working together), closeness, and perhaps intimacy.
2. It moderates conflict and tension, allowing the parties to manage sensitive or conflictual issues without fear of jeopardizing the underlying relational stability.
3. It offers a low-risk communication strategy that allows parties to undertake a variety of actions that might otherwise prove embarrassing.
4. It is a creative outlet for individual expression.
5. It enhances the communication between parties.
6. It promotes relational intimacy in addition to merely reflecting it.

Because play is so important, Table 12.1 is included. This table, derived from research by Baxter (1992) on play,[13] is designed to provide some examples of how people play. There is no suggestion that these are ideal or preferred styles of play. If nothing else, however, they may give you suggestions—in addition to your own creative imagination—for how to play effectively. They may even confirm that the play you already engage in is normal, healthy, and natural.

Security is one need that friendship can fulfill. The primary concern here is the psychological security to be gained from the absence of threat. The nature of the threat differs. It may be being single in a society that prizes relationships. It may be the threat of no commitment, since making a commitment to another person is one of the most important events in most people's lives. Security is gained from situations in which there is much ego-supportive communication and a healthy amount of predictiveness. Maslow lists it as the second most basic need humans have, second only to satisfying such needs as hunger, sex, thirst, sleep, warmth, and shelter.

Affection relates to a sense of belonging. This could encompass sexual gratification, but does not need to. Affection suggests a moderate feel-

Table 12.1
Types of Play

1. When we're in a crazy or excited mood, or when we're greeting each other sometimes, we'll waltz up and down the halls or wherever.
2. We have named our mutual friends after Walt Disney characters and we update each other about funny things they do that are "in character" (e.g., a friend of ours we named "Sleepy" who falls asleep in class a lot).
3. We give each other a bad time about meeting our "daily quotas of stupidity."
4. We impersonate our most disliked TV characters when we're with each other.
5. When we're in full elevators, we talk loudly about inappropriate things and watch people's reactions.
6. We imagine the past and act out scenarios (e.g., pretending we're in medieval England).
7. We have winking competitions to see who can wink at the other one first. The person who gets in three good winks is the winner.
8. We have this whole vocabulary of nonsense words we use when we talk to each other that we acquired gradually over time based on various funny or strange experiences we've had together.
9. We make jokes about each other's physical features.
10. We throw pillows at each other, which sometimes develops into full-blown pillow fights.
11. In describing our days to each other, we "nominate" someone we both know as our candidate for "Twilight Zone finalist" and tell what stupid or bizarre thing the person did.
12. We always say "blye" instead of "bye" to each other since the time when one of us was drunk and mispronounced "bye."
13. When friends are around, we'll pretend to argue so they will freak out and think something's wrong.
14. We go to the grocery store, usually late at night, to do what we call our "sugar shopping." We buy the sweetest, richest thing we can locate and take it home to have our "sugar fix."
15. We steal something that belongs to the other so that the other person will try to get it back.
16. We have story competitions in which we make up stories that don't make any sense. One of us starts and we take turns building on each other. The loser is the one who can't think of anything.

From Leslie A. Baxter, "Forms and Functions of Intimate Play in Personal Relationships," *Human Communication Research* 18 (March 1992): 336–363.

ing toward or emotional attachment to another person. When you feel tender attachment for others or pleasure in being with them, you are experiencing affection. As discussed in Chapter 8, Abraham Maslow labels this "belonging and love needs," placing this need among the basic or essential needs after "physiological" and "safety" needs.

Self-esteem is felt when you are recognized or appreciated by others. Sometimes being with someone enhances your status. Also, if other people attribute a joint identity to your relationship with another person, this may also increase your self-esteem. Self-esteem is affected because such a high premium is often placed on dating and "going steady." Maslow

CONSIDER THIS

Did you ever think that the way males and females view what is right and what is wrong could be different? Just because one is a male and one is a female? Read the following and answer the questions.

> An *ethic of justice,* according to Gilligan,* characterizes the male moral voice. Rooted in a desire for individual autonomy and independence, the ethic of justice centers on the balance of competing rights and claims of one's self and others. This male moral voice is rule-centered and embodies a logic of equality and fairness. Everyone should be treated the same. In contrast, an *ethic of care* characterizes the female moral voice. Rooted in the primacy of relationships and the interdependence of self and others, compassion and nurturance are standards that help resolve conflicting responsibilities to all concerned, including self. This female moral voice considers the needs both of self and others, not just the survival of one's self or not just avoidance of hurting others. Ideally no one should be hurt. While justice and fairness are important, moral decisions must make allowances for differences in needs.†

Questions
1. Do you agree with Gilligan's characterizations?
2. Can you see how these two voices can potentially be complimentary—that is, how the two voices could complement and reinforce each other?
3. Have you any examples from your own or others' experience that would confirm or deny the existence of these two moral voices?

*Carol Gilligan, *In a Different Voice: Psychological Theory and Women's Development* (Cambridge, MA: Harvard University Press, 1982), pp. 19, 73–74, 127, 143, 149, 156–165, and 174.

†From Richard L. Joannesen, *Ethics in Human Communication,* 3rd ed. (Prospect Heights, IL: Waveland Press, Inc., 1990), p. 130. Johannesen cites Gilligan as his source.

places self-esteem needs only one step higher than affection—as slightly less essential and more optional.

Freedom is another reason for friendship. You may think of friendship situations as just the reverse: restrictive, confining, and limiting. This is one area that needs to be negotiated in most friendships. In some areas, for example, you may want self-reliance and independence; in other areas

TRY THIS

To begin to make the contacts that may result in friendship, try practicing the following characteristics of good conversationalists:

1. Spend less time talking about yourself and more time inviting others to converse.
2. Steer away from disagreement.
3. Avoid dogmatic statements.
4. Strive for an attentive, accepting, and gently interpretative manner.
5. Deliberately summarize what others say.
6. Reveal attentive references to past points.
7. Extend invitations to others to expand on their views in an unthreatening way.
8. Stress interest in the other person.
9. Give others reassurances of their worth.
10. At all points, emphasize that you are listening carefully and not just standing (or sitting) there uninvolved.

From John Daly, "Competent Conversation." Paper delivered to the Iowa Ideas Forum, University of Iowa, February 1990.

you may want dependency and reliance. You may want independence in going around with whomever you want but reliance on a set of friends when it comes to going out and doing things together. You then negotiate, sometimes subtly, for freedom of movement for yourself and for control of your social calendar.

Another area of freedom often negotiated is how much the friends will be together. Suppose one person in a friendship enjoys what you might label a "smothering" relationship, whereas you want more openness and less togetherness. Can openness be negotiated? Is flexibility possible? You may end up weighing your reasons for maintaining this friendship against your need for freedom. People need *self*-fulfillment, and this is best realized when they are not too limited or restrained by their relationships with others. David Viscott, a psychiatrist, expresses it this way:

No relationship can provide everything needed for the complete experience of being yourself. Many important answers must come from ourselves, not from another person. The role of another person in our search for ourselves will at times be little more than that of a friendly, accepting bystander. The greatest burdens in our lives will clearly fall upon our own shoulders, not on our relationship with another person.[14]

Equality is difficult to define and is also linked with all the other needs. I have discussed this in Chapter 1, where I labeled equality between people as a symmetrical relationship and inequality as a complementary one. There may be times when you need to be superior, times when you need to be subordinate, and times when you need to be equal. These needs may even change, so that in a situation where you were previously superior or dominant, you now want to be equal or subordinate. The point is that there are needs in relationships for equality; sometimes these are negotiated. Relationships tend to be stronger when people's needs for equality and inequality are met.

TRY THIS

To find whether you have the basis for a fruitful and productive friendship, ask yourself the following questions. If you can answer yes to most of the questions, it is likely that the friendship will grow and develop; if not, it is likely to become troublesome.

1. Are you willing to risk—to overcome fear of the unknown?
2. Are you attracted to the other person?
3. Do you share values and goals with the other person?
4. Do you have some of the same interests, commitments, and expectations?
5. Are you willing to be open and honest? To acknowledge your part in the relationship? To respond to the other person authentically?
6. Can you count on each other to be responsible and reliable?
7. Can you play together—let yourselves go and have fun without feeling embarrassed or ill at ease?
8. Does the relationship enable you to see yourself more clearly?
9. Does the relationship allow you to remain open to other kinds of relationships with other people?
10. Does the relationship feel good?

If you answered no to many of these questions, then you should probably either get out of the relationship or begin at once looking for ways to improve it. Neither solution will be painless, but the longer you wait, the harder it will get.

Communication in Friendship Relationships

The communication that occurs in friendship situations can be affected by all the preceding factors. It is often personal and unique—highly idiosyncratic (peculiar to the constitution and temperament of the individuals involved).

The communication that goes on between friends represents a special case of exchanged discourse that has had limited attention from researchers.[15] Among the kinds of communication that characterize friendship relationships, Mark Knapp lists self-disclosure, constructive discourse, forms of expressions, commitment, nonverbal messages, private jargon and meanings, and shared experiences as being the most important.[16] Each of these will be discussed in the following sections.

Self-disclosure   Self-disclosure by friends contributes to the growth of relationships. Personal self-disclosures increase as relationships progress. Most disclosures prompt disclosures by others. Sometimes this does not occur immediately; however, it usually balances out over the duration of relationships. (See Figure 12.1.) It should be noted, too, that *perceived disclosure and perceived reciprocity of disclosure may be more important than what actually takes place.*

In one study of close relationships, Gerald Phillips found that disclosure was *not* an essential feature. What was essential was *regularity*—that is, your frequency of contact with another person is likely to be more important than the amount or kind of disclosure that occurs.[18] Phillips lists several kinds of contact; essentially, anything that brings you and your friend together regularly becomes important.

Figure 12.1[17]
Notice how the level of intimacy of a relationship affects both the breadth and the depth of self-disclosure in that relationship. This figure also shows how breadth and depth of self-disclosure differ between you and a stranger, an acquaintance, and a close friend.

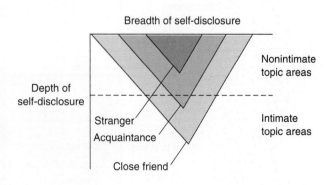

The Johari Window: A View of Self-Disclosure in Relationships

Joseph Luft and Harrington Ingham created a diagram that looks at the self-disclosure process as a function of the relationships in which you find yourself. They called it the **Johari Window** (Joseph + Harrington).[19] (See Figure 12.2.)

The Johari Window identifies four kinds of information about yourself that affect your communication. Think of the whole diagram as representing your total self as you relate to other human beings. Remember that for every person you relate with, a new window can be drawn. The panes of the window change in size according to your awareness, and the awareness of others, of your behavior, feelings, and motivations. The size will also vary for different people because your behavior, feelings, and motivations are actually different with them. Every relationship you have can be described by a Johari Window, and no two will be alike.

The open pane The size of the **open pane** reveals the amount of risk you take in relationships. As relationships become deeper, the open pane gets bigger, reflecting your willingness to be known. This pane comprises all aspects of yourself known to you *and* others. It includes such things as your sex, the color of your eyes, and whether you are standing up or sitting down at the moment. It may also include things you know and don't mind admitting about yourself, such as the fact that you are

Figure 12.2
The Johari Window identifies different kinds of information about yourself.

	Information known to self	Information not known to self
Information known to others	1 Open	2 Blind
Information not known to others	3 Hidden	4 Unknown

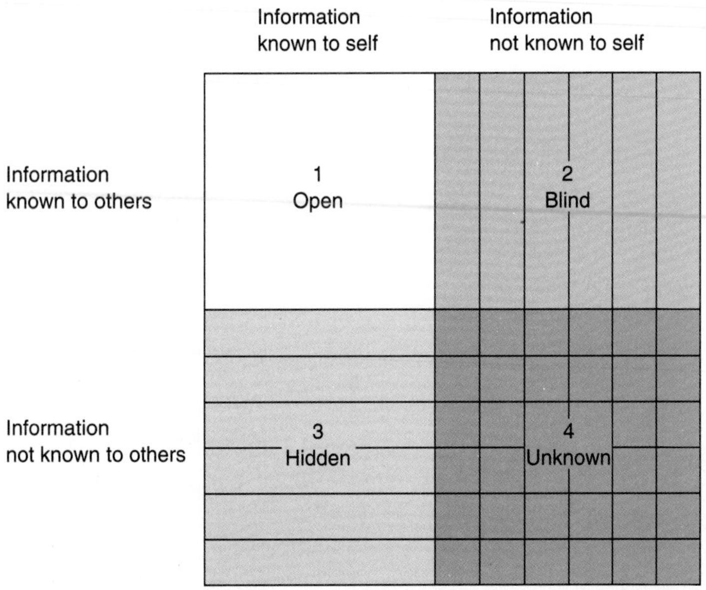

married or a teacher or happy or depressed. Information included in this pane provides the substance for the biggest part of your communications with others.

The blind pane   The **blind pane** consists of all the things about yourself that other people perceive but that are not known to you. For example, you may see yourself as open and friendly, but you may come across to others as reserved and somewhat cold. You may think of yourself as genuinely humorous; others may think your humor has an acid bite. On the other hand, the blind pane may contain some good qualities you don't realize you have. For example, you may be very aware of your own insecurities; others may see you as confident and self-assured. The more you learn about the qualities in your blind pane, the more you will be able to control the impressions you make on others, understand their reactions to you, and learn to grow beyond them. Growth requires such discovery of things unknown to you, but known to others.

The hidden pane   In the **hidden pane,** you are the one who exercises control. This pane is made up of all those behaviors, feelings, and motivations that you prefer not to disclose to someone else. These things could be events that occurred during your childhood that you do not want known. They could include the fact that you failed biology in high school, that you like soap operas, that you eat peanut butter at every meal. They could concern other people besides you, and they need not be things you are ashamed of or think are wrong. Everyone is entitled to secrets. There are certain things that can remain private and personal and need never be disclosed. These things remain in the hidden pane: things unknown to others but known to you.

The unknown pane   The **unknown pane** is made up of everything unknown to you and to others. No matter how much you grow and discover and learn about yourself, thus shrinking the size of this pane, it can never completely disappear. You can never know all there is to know about yourself. This pane represents everything about yourself that you and other people have never explored. This pane includes all your untapped resources and potentials, everything that currently lies dormant. It is through interpersonal communication that you can reduce the size of this pane; without communicating with others, much of your potential will remain unrealized.

The interdependence of the panes   The four panes of the Johari Window are interdependent, that is, a change in the size of one pane will affect all the others. For example, if through talking with a friend you discover something about yourself you never knew before (something that existed in the blind pane), this would enlarge the open pane and reduce the size

TRY THIS

Plot a Johari Window for the following encounters in your life, as specifically as you can:

1. Your roommate (if you have one)
2. Your best friend
3. Someone you recently met for the first time
4. The teacher of this course
5. One of your parents
6. Someone you know who does not know you (and has not spoken to you)

Note that Johari Window represents a relationship between you and this other person. The relative size of the various panes of the window depends on the amount of self-disclosure that has occurred between you.

of the blind one. Your discovery could be of something crucial to your relationship, like the fact that Sam doesn't care about you as much as you thought he did.

It can be rewarding and satisfying to add to your open pane, whether by revealing or by discovering things about yourself. It can also be painful; enlarging the open pane involves some risk. You need to use discretion here, as inappropriate disclosure can be damaging whether you are giving it or receiving it. Be sure you are ready to cope with the consequences before you try to empty your hidden and blind panes into your open pane.

Generally, though, the more you reveal yourself to others so that they can know you better, the more you will learn about yourself. And the more truth about yourself you are willing to accept from others, the more accurate your self-concept will be. This increased knowledge of self can result in greater self-acceptance. After all, if your friend is not shocked by your C average, perhaps you can accept it too. A Johari Window representing a close relationship between two people in which there is a great deal of free and honest exchange has a very large open pane. (See Figure 12.3.)

Sidney Jourard, a researcher, has concluded that humans spend an incredible amount of energy trying to avoid becoming known by other human beings.[20] Jourard contends that when we permit ourselves to be known, we expose ourselves to a lover's balm, but also to a hater's

Figure 12.3
This window describes a relationship with a great deal of free and honest exchange.

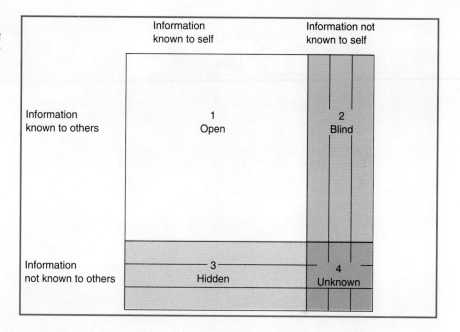

bombs! When haters know you, they know just where to plant their bombs for maximum effect. But acts of avoidance keep us from healthy human relationships. According to Jourard, allowing yourself to be known to at least one other person who is important to you and whose opinions and judgment you value and respect highly is one characteristic of a healthy personality. It is risky, but it is important.

Constructive discourse   Not only does disclosure occur more regularly in positive relationships, but there are more positive disclosures than negative ones. For example, just the fact that Mike and Yvonne share ideas about anything and everything means that there are likely to be more positive disclosures than negative ones. When subjects come up, they discuss them. Sometimes their discussions lead to "heavy" topics, but more often "light" topics are the substance of their sharing.

Mike and Yvonne recognize the value and purpose of constructive discourse. Their attitudes toward it are positive. They know, for example, that conflict is a natural part of all human relationships, that not all conflicts can be resolved, that the feelings of the other person must be taken into account because the relationship is more important than the conflict, and that the good of all concerned is of more value than a personal victory.[21]

Forms of expressions   In strong friendship relationships, participants often use supportive forms of expression—especially when relationships

Why is more self-disclosure likely to occur in situations like this? What are the factors that tend to promote increased self-disclosure?

begin. **Absolute statements** such as "You are the most energetic person I've ever seen" often appear early but are not as prominent as relationships develop and more rationality takes over. Also, as relationships begin, forms of expression like "You're the greatest" or "I think you're fantastic" tend to be *repeated* over and over. Participants also use the *present tense* in friendship relationships: "We can see more of each other," or "I want to be your friend forever." There is a tendency toward hyperbole at the outset of most new relationships; perhaps this tendency is what helps relationships get off the ground.

Forms of address also change as relationships become closer. The more intimate you feel toward someone else, the less formal will be the form of address you use with them. You are introduced to a Mr. Richardson at a party. As you talk with him, you say, "I'm sorry, I didn't catch your name." He replies, "Howard." In talking to others you discover that his friends call him "Rich." Later, after much self-disclosure and considerable intimacy, you hear that his grandmother used to call him "Butch," and because this is a family (intimate) name, you adopt it for "Mr. Richardson." If you become his relationship partner or spouse, you may sometimes switch and call him "Honey" or "Sweetheart" for variety and as the mood dictates.

Notice the stages through which the changes in forms of address occurred. "Mr. Richardson" is a formal form of address. "Howard" is ambiguous formal—ambiguous because it is capable of being understood in two possible senses: first, as informal if you do not know other alternative names, and second, as formal because this is Mr. Richardson's formal first name. "Rich" is informal. And "Butch," "Honey," and "Sweetheart" are used to show affection.[22]

Commitment   No satisfying relationship can exist for long without commitment. This is just as important in friendships as in family relationships. In his study, Phillips found there was a possessive element in most relationships.[23] This is revealed in a relationship when a third party intervenes. A third party often functions as an irritant, altering the relationship to accommodate the real or possible displacement of affection.[24]

A commitment is an obligation or pledge. In a relationship, this commitment is not revealed through possessiveness alone; loyalty is another aspect of commitment. Loyalty involves faithfulness to the other person—steadfast affection, firm in adherence to promises that are (or have been) made, or firm in observance of duty. Loyalty between partners means dependability—each partner can depend on the other.

A related aspect of commitment is constancy, or the word we have used for constancy, **regularity.** Phillips found that "in order to keep relationships going, constant talk and contact was imperative."[25] I prefer the word *regular* to *constant*, but the idea is the same. Behaviors tend to lose their value over time; that is, behavior that is immediate (now!) is vibrant and meaningful. Thus, to keep a relationship going, readjustments and continued negotiation are necessary. Relationships come apart when communication patterns become stereotypical. New behaviors need to be developed, or old behaviors need to be examined with new eyes.[26] This requires commitment—a commitment to the friendship.

Commitment also involves willingness to follow the *rules* of friendship. The strongest rules are rather simple: friends hold conversations, they do not disclose confidences to other people, they refrain from public criticism, and they repay debts and favors. In high-quality friendships, additional rules include showing emotional support, revealing trust, and confiding in one another.[27] There may well be other rules, too, such as making the other person happy when you're together, offering to help out in time of need, standing up for the other person in his or her absence, or sharing your successes. The point here is not to outline all the potential rules but to indicate that commitment to a relationship means abiding by certain rules. Some of these may be formally laid out and discussed; some may be informal and discovered only when broken; others may be thought of as "that's what friends do!"

Commitment boils down to one essential question: How much do you care? People who want a friendship realize that friendships require time and energy. They require reciprocation. Whatever you expect to receive, you must be willing to give.

Nonverbal messages Nonverbal messages become more important as relationships continue. For a moment look back at Figure 12.1. If the figure were relabeled on the left side "Areas of touch" and at the top "Amount of touch," the figure would reveal that you touch strangers nonintimately and occasionally touch acquaintances intimately, such as the goodbye kiss or the friendly pat on the shoulder. Only with close friends is touch intimate—especially with respect to areas and amounts. With strangers and acquaintances, you rely on widely understood and stereotyped touching. Intimacy brings about the use of a broad spectrum of nonverbal communication, including touch.[28]

The nonverbal messages exchanged among friends are likely to vary dramatically from pair to pair. Some people tend to be "touchers"; others do not touch as much. The nonverbal messages exchanged among

CONSIDER THIS

Patrick, age 42, a restaurant designer, is frustrated with his live-in girlfriend Jennifer, age 36, who is an artist. He loves her and thinks about marrying her, but is unsure because they fight so much of the time. "Whenever I say something constructive to try to help her," Patrick says, "Jen reacts as though I am attacking her. Then when I explain myself, she gets more upset. I have no idea what to do. I feel frustrated because I really want to support her. I love her but when she overreacts to everything I do, I become mean and defensive. I don't know how long I can take it."*

Questions
1. What is missing in Patrick and Jennifer's relationship?
2. Would knowledge about how men and women are different help them?
3. Would a greater understanding of interpersonal communication help them? In what ways?
4. If you were serving as a counselor or advisor to Patrick and Jennifer, what would you recommend?

*From John Gray, *Men, Women and Relationships: Making Peace With the Opposite Sex* (Hillsboro, OR: Beyond Words Publishing, Inc., 1993), p. 5.

intimates are associated with greater liking, warmth, and affection than those used with strangers or close acquaintances. Also, they are likely to occur more frequently.[29] Touches, for example, are likely to be greater in number, in length, and in number of places.

Eye contact among friends occurs more frequently than with strangers or acquaintances. Eye contact is likely to be held longer as well. Mutual eye gazing signals that communication channels are open, psychologically reduces the physical distance, and is a useful method for gaining visual feedback.

Many other nonverbal behaviors increase as well. Friends are likely to nod more, lean toward each other more, maintain open arms and body, and direct the body orientation toward the other. Positive facial expressions of happiness, interest, joy, and amusement are likely to predominate over negative facial expressions.[30] Vocal characteristics may also reveal friendship. Friends may use a lower vocal pitch, softer voice, slower rate of speech, and somewhat slurred enunciation.[31]

Private jargon and meanings Friends often develop interpersonal jargon (terminology characteristic of only that pair) that reflects private symbols and private meanings. Certain common words and phrases come to have special meanings for them. Have you ever winked, smiled, or glanced at a close friend when one of "your" words or phrases was used publicly? These words and phrases come to be considered private possessions.

This can occur nonverbally as well. Have you ever shared a "special look" with a friend? The mutual eye gazing referred to in the previous section may provide opportunities for such exchanges—private worlds being shared in public situations through private means.

Shared experiences Over time, friends establish a relationship that is a unique enterprise with its own characteristic talk. In a sense, friends develop a unique cultural identity. A **cultural identity** *is the distinguishing pattern of shared behaviors that includes thoughts, emotions, speech, and actions by which a relationship can be identified.*

TRY THIS

Think of a friendship that has been worthwhile and meaningful for you. In what ways has it required discipline, concentration, and patience? Have you noticed times during the development and maintenance of the friendship when you or the other person showed supreme concern? Think of some specific examples. Would you say that you have shown deep love for each other in this friendship? In what ways?

A cultural identity evolves; it cannot be forced. However, the more friends communicate, establish understandings, and share experiences, the sooner a cultural identity can be identified. The greater the shared expectations, experiences, and assumptions—and the more easily these can be pinpointed by both parties—the clearer, or more precise, the cultural identity.

So what? What is the value of a cultural identity? There are numerous values. Here are some: First, if necessary, a cultural identity makes it clear to the participants that a distinct relationship exists. Second, it helps define the relationship. The kind of relationship, depth of commitment, or level of intimacy can be determined once a definition of the relationship is discovered. Third, if the relationship is good, a cultural identity provides a positive history on which the participants can build. If the relationship is weak, it may offer ideas for change, growth, or progress. Also, the cultural identity may offer the suggestion that the relationship should be terminated. Fourth, it lets outsiders know that some mutual commitment has been made. Others may begin to treat the two of you as one—as members of the same relationship. This can be especially important where intervening third parties are involved.

Building Friendship Skills

The following suggestions will assist you in maintaining or repairing your friendships. These are not new ideas; as a matter of fact, they are quite ordinary and consist of common sense. Too often, however, they are not thought about or applied, and many friendships falter and die because one or the other partner overlooks the obvious requirements of friendships. It still boils down to one thing, as mentioned previously in this chapter: how much do you really care?

Friends share information Friends involve themselves in an active search for information about their partners. There is a need for friends to reveal their attitudes and beliefs, their importance, and their extent.[32] What is it partners need to learn about their partners? How open are they to others' views? How tolerant are they? What are their passions and flat spots? What are their dogmas and assumptions? What are their views about life? What are their attitudes toward other people? What kinds of relationships to others do they have? What kinds of expressions of feelings do they manifest? What are their views on how others should be treated?[33]

Friends self-disclose Because we have discussed self-disclosure in Chapter 3, we will avoid further discussion here except to list the skills

What are some of the ways you have for improving your friendships?

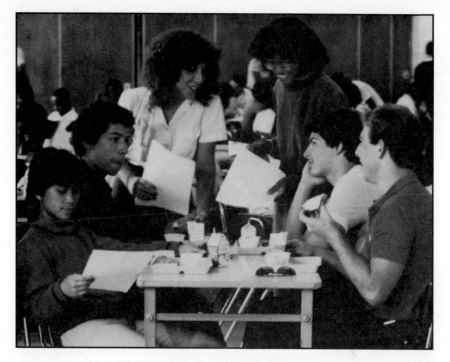

mentioned there: build trust, share your feelings, take a chance, don't manipulate, watch your timing, and clarify, clarify. At the end of that section, the characteristics of clear self-disclosure messages were listed. Clear self-disclosure messages are mutually relevant, personally owned, source specific, based on a clear causal connection with your feelings or perceptions, and behavior specific. The point is that friends need to communicate with each other about their personality and get their partner to do the same—sharing views, opinions, preferences, needs, and attitudes.[34]

Friends spend time together Joint activity is fun, but it serves as an accepted, social, signaling response as well. It indicates to both partners, and to the world, that the partners are friends. As friendships grow, "Not only will the partners do more together and spend a higher percentage of their time in one another's company, they will also tend to do different things together."[35] "Pairs of people who do not diversify their interactions are quietly strangling the relationship in these early stages."[36]

Friends make more than a 50–50 commitment Many people believe that if they put in a 50 percent commitment to the friendship, and their partner does the same, that level of commitment will make the relationship work. Not true! The truth is that relationships take far more commitment than that from *both* partners. Some say 100 percent from each; some even say 110 percent! The point is that when both partners are willing to give something more than 60 or 70 percent of the commitment, the relationship absorbs the extra effort, and the friendship soars! That's what makes some friendships so full of energy and vitality. That is often why one relationship falls, slides, or decays whereas another almost takes on a life of its own.

Friends have conflicts   You could almost say that when people get together there will be conflict; thus, to say that friends have conflicts is a simple extension of this premise. I overheard one partner of a friendship say, "If fighting is a criterion for a good friendship, then we will be friends forever!" Conflict is healthy—as is clearly pointed out in Chapter 11. Partners must learn to deal with conflicts. That is why the information on conflict resolution in that chapter is so important. No matter what your own style for dealing with conflicts is, and no matter what your partner's style for dealing with conflicts is, when partners get together, a new style must be developed: a negotiated style. When partners learn how to deal with the small conflicts and the little arguments, then when the big ones occur—as they surely will—there is far greater likelihood that the partners will be able to deal with them.

Friends have tolerance   When different people get together, differences become known. Sometimes this happens at once; sometimes it takes time. This skill is closely aligned with the first one, "Friends share information." When you ask for information, you are likely to get as much that does not conform with your own attitudes, beliefs, and values as that which does. At least the potential is there.

One thing people need to recognize is that no matter how long they look, and no matter how many friends they go through, they will never find someone else like themselves—some people would even say as perfect, flawless, sound, impeccable, and ideal as they are! It is as important in pursuing friendship as in pursuing more intimate relationships that people should never go into them thinking they are going to change the other person. And that is precisely where tolerance comes in. Often, too, it is the little flaws, blemishes, and defects that are the biggest irritants. Tolerance may come down to simply knowing when to keep your mouth shut. Some friendships may depend more on what is left unsaid than on what is communicated!

Friends must provide freedom   Partners need to remember that even though sharing information, self-disclosing, spending time together, and making a commitment—all features that take time—are important, partners have separate personalities, and each needs space to grow. Being alone and admitting that you need separateness does *not* mean a lack of commitment to or lack of caring in the friendship. Friendships must have opportunities for partners to develop in the way they find suitable or *not* to develop at all. Even if one partner chooses to live a less effective inter-

CONSIDER THIS

Roger Fisher and Scott Brown, in their book *Getting Together: Building Better Relationships As We Negotiate** have created a strategy for negotiating with strangers. What would be the strengths and weaknesses of using a strategy such as this when one is interacting with people from other cultures?

An Unconditionally Constructive Strategy

Do only those things that are both good for the relationship and good for us, whether or not they reciprocate.

1. *Rationality.* Even if they are acting emotionally, *balance emotions with reason.*
2. *Understanding.* Even if they misunderstand us, *try to understand them.*
3. *Communication.* Even if they are not listening, *consult them before deciding on matters that affect them.*
4. *Reliability.* Even if they are trying to deceive us, neither trust them nor deceive them; *be reliable.*
5. *Noncoercive modes of influence.* Even if they are trying to coerce us, neither yield to that coercion nor try to coerce them; *be open to persuasion and try to persuade them.*
6. *Acceptance.* Even if they reject us and our concerns as unworthy of their consideration, *accept them as worthy of our consideration, care about them, and be open to learning from them.*[†]

Questions

1. How well would these guidelines work when one is forming interpersonal relationships with people from other cultures? What are the strengths and what are the weaknesses?
2. In what situations are the above guidelines likely to work best? In what situations are they less likely to be effective?
3. Can any set of rules govern the formation of interpersonal relationships? Why or why not?

*Roger Fisher and Scott Brown, *Getting Together: Building Better Relationships As We Negotiate* (Boston: Houghton Mifflin, 1988), pp. 24–39.

†From Roger and Scott Brown, "A Strategy for Building Better Relationships As We Negotiate," in William B. Gudykunst and Young Yun Kim, *Readings on Communicating With Strangers* (New York: McGraw-Hill, Inc., 1992), pp. 393–398. The information here can be found on p. 398.

personal life than he or she is capable of living, that choice must be respected by the other partner. This, indeed, is what *respect* for another person in a friendship means.

Friends have a sense of humor This doesn't require extensive discussion, but friendship is more likely to last when partners have fun together. Partners should not take things too seriously. They need to be themselves. They need to have fun. They need to let the child in them be free to play. Many of the trials, agonies, stresses, sorrows, and difficulties that occur in friendships can be placed in the proper perspective if partners can demonstrate their sense of humor.

Friends assume goodwill Because it is impossible to know another person's real, deep, true intentions at all times, you do not need to assume the intentions are negative. It is better for you, for your partner, and for the friendship to assume that your partner is in it freely, that he or she *wants* to be there, and that he or she *wants* to make a go of it. If you assume your partner is just as willing as you are to make a go of the friendship, you will also assume that he or she is just as willing as you are to work to make the relationship effective. This can free you from much unnecessary worry—worry like "Am I giving more than I'm getting?" You need to assume reciprocity!

What is even more important is assuming goodwill. It means you can turn all of your worry, suspicions, and doubt about your partner into showing support and revealing encouragement. When you start to help each other to get the most out of the friendship as possible, then your successes and the other person's successes will benefit the friendship—both of you! You both gain.

I have included this chapter on friends because it is within such relationships that so much of our interpersonal communication occurs. Your success in these relationships depends largely on how much you care about succeeding. It is based on your attitude. No support can occur if you do not care—if you do not commit yourself to these relationships.

As friendships continue they sometimes develop into intimacy. At other times, intimate relationships develop separately from friendships. This chapter serves as a useful foundation for the next one on intimacy.

▶ ## SUMMARY

Friendships are interpersonal relationships in which people voluntarily intertwine, enjoying others for their own sake while those others bring them rewarding feelings about themselves. The three types of friendship are reciprocal, receptive, and associative. You form friendships for enjoyment, security, affection, self-esteem, freedom, and equality. Among the kinds of communication that characterize friendship relationships, self-disclosure, constructive discourse, forms of expressions, commitment, nonverbal messages, private jargon and meanings, and shared experiences are discussed. To improve friendships, you must share information, self-disclose, spend time together, make more than a 50–50 commitment, have conflicts, have tolerance, provide freedom, have a sense of humor, and assume goodwill. Essentially, strong friendships boil down to one thing—how much do you really care?

▶ **KEY TERMS**

friendships	Johari Window	unknown pane
reciprocal friendship	open pane	absolute statements
receptive friendship	blind pane	regularity
associative friendship	hidden pane	cultural identity
friendship relationship		

▶ **NOTES**

1. Steve Duck, *Understanding Relationships* (New York: The Guilford Press, 1991), 7.
2. Gerald M. Phillips and H. Lloyd Goodall, Jr., *Loving & Living: Improve Your Friendships and Marriage* (Englewood Cliffs, NJ: Prentice-Hall [A Spectrum Book], 1983), 59.
3. Phillips and Goodall, 59.
4. Duck, 23.
5. Duck, 40.
6. P. H. Wright, "Self Referent Motivation and the Intrinsic Quality of Friendship," *Journal of Social and Personal Relationships* 1 (1984): 114–130.
7. M. Lea, "Factors Underlying Friendship: An Analysis of Responses on the Acquaintance Description Form in Relation to Wright's Friendship Model," *Journal of Social and Personal Relationships* 6 (1989): 275–292.
8. Andrew M. Greeley, *The Friendship Game* (Garden City, NY: Doubleday, 1971), 15; see also 25–32, 46–56, 74–83, and 135.

9. For more information on intimate communication, see Gerald M. Phillips and Nancy J. Metzger, *Intimate Communication* (Boston: Allyn and Bacon, 1975), and Murray David, *Intimate Relations* (New York: The Free Press, 1973).

10. Mark Knapp, *Interpersonal Communication and Human Relationships* (Boston: Allyn and Bacon, 1984), 189–202.

11. Knapp, 1984, 197–199. Also see Robert E. Eubanks, "Relationships: The Manifestations of Humanness," in *Human Communication: The Process of Relating,* eds. George A. Borden and John D. Stone (Menlo Park, CA: Cummings Publishings Co., 1976), 185–190.

12. Leslie A. Baxter, "Forms and Functions of Intimate Play in Personal Relationships," *Human Communication Research* 18 (1992): 336–363.

13. Baxter, 353.

14. David Viscott, *How to Live with Another Person* (New York: Arbor House, 1974), 155.

15. Gerald M. Phillips, "Rhetoric and Its Alternatives as Bases for Examination of Intimate Communication," *Communication Quarterly* 24 (1976): 11.

16. Mark Knapp, *Social Intercourse: From Greeting to Goodbye* (Boston: Allyn and Bacon, 1978), 174–175.

17. Adapted with permission from Irwin Altman and W. W. Haythorn, "Interpersonal Exchange in Isolation," Figure 3, *Sociometry* 28 (1965): 422.

18. Phillips, 21.

19. Adapted from *Group Processes: An Introduction to Group Dynamics* by Joseph Luft, by permission of Mayfield Publishing Co. Copyright © 1984, 1970, and 1963 by Joseph Luft. See also Luft, *Of Human Interaction* (Palo Alto, CA: National Press Books, 1969).

20. Sidney M. Jourard, *The Transparent Self* (New York: D. Van Nostrand Co., 1971), p. 6.

21. Knapp, 1984, 216.

22. Knapp, 1984, 228–231.

23. Phillips, 21.

24. Phillips, 21.

25. Phillips, 21.

26. Phillips, 21.

27. See M. Argyle and M. Henderson, *The Anatomy of Relationships* (London: Methuen, 1985).

28. Knapp, 1984, 234.

29. Knapp, 1984, 234.

30. Albert Mehrabian, *Nonverbal Communication* (Chicago: Aldine Publishing Co., 1972).

31. Joel R. Davitz, *The Communication of Emotional Meaning* (New York: McGraw-Hill, 1964), 63.

32. Duck, 67.

33. Duck, 67–68.
34. Duck, 71–85.
35. Duck, 87.
36. Duck, 87.

▶ ## FURTHER READING

Rosemary Blieszner and Rebecca G. Adams, *Adult Friendship* (Newbury Park, CA: SAGE [Sage Series on Close Relationships], 1992). Blieszner and Adams offer a theoretical framework that includes both sociological and psychological perspectives on friendship. They use their model to synthesize the research, identify research gaps, scrutinize research methods, and produce a map to guide future research. They also cover historical conceptions, internal structure, and the phases of friendship. For the serious student.

Steve Duck, *Human Relationships,* 2nd ed. (Newbury Park, CA: SAGE Publications, 1992). Duck addresses such topics as attraction, love, friendship, and experiences with shyness, jealousy, and loneliness. He considers how and why relationships are established, sustained, and break down. He looks at how people's health and well-being are affected by the nature of the relationships in which they are embedded. An excellent book with terrific examples.

John Gray, *Men, Women and Relationships: Making Peace with the Opposite Sex,* 2nd ed. (Hillsboro, OR: Beyond Words Publishing, Inc., 1993). Gray has written a practical book that, although not research-based, is full of examples on building relationships, differences between men and women, symptoms of stress, finding balance, the art of fulfilling relationships, how to give and receive emotional support, and the secret of complementary natures.

Ruthellen Josselson, *The Space Between Us: Exploring the Dimensions of Human Relationships* (San Francisco: Jossey-Bass, 1992). Josselson presents a positive view of the human connections that make us whole. Integrating psychological theories with rich experience, she draws conclusions about the nature and types of relationships and explains eight basic dimensions of relatedness. In addition to describing how men and women differ in their approaches to relationships, Josselson describes the environments we create in which relationships flourish.

Anne Maydan Nicotera, ed., *Interpersonal Communication In Friend and Mate Relationships* (Albany, NY: State University of New York, 1993). It is important for students to have an opportunity to see how theories are generated in the area of friendship relationships. The contributors to this book explore the kind of information exchanged in the process of initiating, developing, and maintaining relationships. Not only do they assess past research, but they suggest future directions as well. This is a scholarly book for serious students.

William K. Rawlins, *Friendship Matters: Communication, Dialectics, and the Life Course* (New York: Aldine De Gruyter, 1992). Rawlins states his thesis in the introduction: "I develop a broad conceptual perspective for tracing and probing the varieties, tensions, and functions of friendship over the life course" (p. 2). This is a heavily documented (from a program of theoretical and empirical research spanning 12 years—about 500 sources), illustrative (based on more than 100 interviews), reflective examination of middle-class Americans' experiences.

Julia T. Wood, *Relational Communication: Continuity and Change in Personal Relationships* (Belmont, CA: Wadsworth Publishing Company, 1995). Wood offers a sophisticated and comprehensive integration of current theory and research on communication in relationships. She emphasizes communication as the primary process through which individuals develop, create, and sustain intimate relationships over time. She explores the ways in which gender, culture, and social context affect communication in personal interactions. A well-written, well-researched, well-presented effort.

13

▶ CHAPTER OBJECTIVES

After reading this chapter, you should be able to

- ▲ Define intimate relationships and briefly explain each element of the definition.
- ▲ List and briefly describe some of the factors in others that affect how we feel about them.
- ▲ Identify the six stages of relationship development.
- ▲ Define small talk and explain its functions.
- ▲ Explain the verbal and nonverbal cues that reveal that integrating has occurred.
- ▲ Explain how intimate relationships can be maintained and nurtured.
- ▲ List and explain briefly the four characteristics of relational change.
- ▲ Explain the causes of relationship disintegration.
- ▲ List and describe briefly each of the five stages of relational disintegration.
- ▲ Describe four specific ways to improve intimacy skills.

▼ Dallas and Tanya fell madly in love soon after they were introduced by Tanya's friends, who had said to her, "You are just going to *love* this guy!" They met in a local coffee house, and the relationship just seemed to take off. Tanya loved Dallas's innocent humor and charm. Dallas was passionately drawn to Tanya, and he was determined to be with her because of the warmth, confidence, and self-esteem he experienced when they were together. Dallas worked as produce manager at the local supermarket while completing his M.B.A. Tanya was a receptionist in an orthopedic surgeon's office and was taking courses to complete her college degree. Although they had difficulty finding large amounts of time to be together, the time they had became high quality. They talked of their lifetime goals, important values, and essential interests as well as their background experiences and family life. They knew they had much in common, but they did not want to move too quickly, and both wanted to complete school and get their degrees before planning a wedding and starting a family. For Dallas and Tanya, knowing they had each other, knowing they were working for someone in particular, and knowing they now had specific mutual goals to strive for made their schoolwork more enjoyable and worthwhile.

Sara met Wonsang while they waited for pizza orders to be placed. Both were drivers for Pizza World and worked part time in the evenings, delivering pizza around campus and to the local community to help pay for school. Until meeting Sara, Wonsang had been very lonely. Because they loved talking to each other, they arranged their schedules so as to work the same nights. Sometimes they had hours to talk; other nights they had no time at all. Both of Wonsang's parents were naturalized citizens, and both lived in a distant city. Wonsang had grown up in the United States, and he loved kids. Sara had a child, Simon, from a previous relationship, and Wonsang loved spending time with Simon on weekends. Sara was impressed by how good Wonsang was with Simon and by how much Simon liked him. She believed every boy should have a father figure in his life, and if Wonsang was to be one for Simon, his lack of machismo and his willingness to help her out with domestic chores made him a better male image than many other men she knew.

Bethany and Jamie met in a ninth-grade social studies class. Both had turned in career notebooks on the medical profession. Bethany wanted to specialize in pediatrics; Jamie wanted to go into internal medicine, like her mother. Since both were studying to be doctors, many of their math and science classes throughout high school turned out to be the same. They decided to do their undergraduate work at the same university as well, and they created similar class schedules. Bethany and Jamie not only had the same professional interests but joined the same sorority, both played volleyball for their college, and dated men who liked each other. Bethany and Jamie became intimate friends, sharing their deepest thoughts and feelings and becoming each other's strongest supporting friend. Neither had ever known another person for whom they had such strong feelings. Even their boyfriends recognized the bond between them.

Intimate relationships—those that reveal personal and private closeness—provide much of the structure of our society. Marriage may be the best example, as an institution in which intimacy is maintained over a period of time, but people in a wide variety of relationships experience intimacy that is never formalized, much as in the relationship between Bethany and Jamie. Intimacy contributes to personal needs by offering protection from loneliness, just as Wonsang was lonely until he found Sara. Intimate relationships also offer warmth, confidence, selfesteem, and love. These were precisely Dallas's feelings when he was with Tanya.

Obviously, not all dyadic relationships develop into intimacy. But intimacy is central to everyone's growth and fulfillment. One does not need marriage to achieve intimacy. It can occur in friendships as well as in romantic relationships, and, also in male-to-male or female-to-female relationships. No matter the type of relationship involved, the same factors in others have the same effects on how we feel about them, the same stages of relationship development and disintegration occur, the relationships are maintained and nurtured in much the same way, the same characteristics of relational change occur, and the same ways to improve intimacy skills apply.

And what are you likely to gain from intimacy? Most intimate relationships are deeply personal. Only with an intimate partner can you be and experience yourself. Intimate relationships are emotionally gratifying. Only with an intimate partner can you express and share the range of emotions. They are mutually rewarding. Healthy relationships offer each partner gratification, affection, joy, and understanding. In intimate relationships both partners can candidly express themselves and not be rejected, share their tremendous joys and horrendous sorrows, and be spontaneous without concern for how they talk or how they will be received. How wonderful to be accepted despite weaknesses!

In this chapter, I will first discuss the nature of intimacy and some of the reasons people form intimate relationships. We will then look at the course of relationship development, at relational maintenance, and the promotion of relational growth. After examining relational change and the causes of disintegration, I will describe the stages of relationship disintegration and what happens when a relationship has been terminated. Finally, there is a brief section on building intimacy skills.

▲▲▲ *What Is Intimacy?*

When Stan began picking up Pete each day on his way to work, he had no idea how close they would soon become. During their half-hour ride together every morning, they first found themselves talking about their work, since that was what they seemed to have most in common. The discussion quickly moved to their backgrounds and families and then to their goals and aspirations. Although they were of different religions and political parties, they minimized these differences because they enjoyed each other's company. Besides, their differences seemed to add a unique dimension to their discussions: each approached life and its problems from a somewhat different perspective. They began calling each other in the evenings, and soon their families got together for barbecues and croquet. Stan and Pete shared an intimacy from which both gained benefits.

Alan Sillars and Michael Scott have defined **intimate relationships** as those *"in which there is repeated interaction, high self-disclosure, high interdependence (i.e., mutual influence), and high emotional involvement."*[1] This definition assumes an important connection between the two individuals, and it emphasizes those elements distinctive to intimate and ongoing re-

CONSIDER THIS

There are well-established differences in the way males and females view intimacy. Read Julia Wood's explanation, noting that I have condensed it to fit the space, and answer the questions that follow it.

> Perhaps the two most basic principles of a feminine standpoint on relationships are that intimacy is understood as a continuous process, and personal communication is regarded as the primary dynamic that sustains connections with others. . . . Because women are generally taught to build and nurture relationships, they typically understand close connections as fluid processes. Thus, even when commitment is secure, women tend to see partners and relationships as continuously evolving in large and small ways. . . .
>
> Two linchpins of a masculine orientation toward close relationships are a view of intimacy as an event that is resolved at some point, and a focus on activities as the heart of closeness. Unlike women in general, many men tend to see intimacy as something that is established at one time and then stays more or less in place. . . . Thus, when a commitment is made, some men regard it as a given that does not need ongoing comment.*

Questions

1. Knowing that these differences exist, how should a man and a woman approach a common, desired relationship in such a way that the differences in viewpoint can be minimized?
2. When women see talking deeply and closely as the centerpiece of a relationship, and men see activities as the way to create and express closeness, is it easy to see why misunderstandings in relationships occur? Are misunderstandings necessary?
3. Since problems in relationships are likely to arise not because either the male or the female style of relating is bad, but because partners don't understand each other's ways of expressing and creating closeness, are there prerequisites or priorities that can be established that would help foster understanding?

*From Julia T. Wood, *Relational Communication: Continuity and Change in Personal Relationships* (Belmont, CA: Wadsworth Publishing Group, 1995), pp. 245–246. Wood supports these conclusions with numerous sources that I have left out. Also, these are not contiguous paragraphs; more information is provided that I have not included here.

lationships. In this section I will briefly examine each element of the Sillars and Scott definition.

Repeated Interaction and High Self-Disclosure

The first two elements that help define intimate relationships suggest that intimates share a great deal of common experience. This is likely to increase their mutual understanding. Because of increased mutual understanding, those in intimate relationships are more likely to predict their partner's attitudes accurately, possess greater attitude similarity, predict the other's word choice in hypothetical conversations, possess specialized codes for communicating, and reveal greater efficiency in communication than nonintimates.

Repeated interactions and self-disclosure will cause communication between intimates to become more individualized. As couples become more intimate, this helps reduce any erroneous perceptions that may have resulted from reliance on cultural and social stereotypes earlier in the relationship. For example, one may have assumed that a partner was highly reliant on a close, tight-knit family (a cultural stereotype), but closer acquaintance shows that he or she is really quite independent. Or the assumption that a partner prefers quiet evenings at home rather than partying (a social stereotype) may be negated as one finds that he or she enjoys an active social life.

One interesting negative aspect of these first two elements is that having a great deal of information about someone *can* be misleading! For example, familiarity increases our confidence in our understanding of others. This confidence may lead us to take too much for granted. Individuals tend to overestimate how much they and their relationship partners know about each other, and therefore tend to seek less information. For example, if I think I *knew* that you would want to be with your family on *all* holidays or that you would *never* want to go to loud parties, I may never ask you about these matters.

Many examples of such overestimations exist. One partner, for example, knows that the other supports causes that promote minorities and the underprivileged and assumes (without gaining further information) that this partner also supports a political candidate who espouses these causes. In another example, one partner knows the other likes to hike and explore the outdoors and assumes he or she also likes camping.

Another negative aspect, according to Sillars and Scott, is that repeated interactions and high self-disclosure may lead to the entrenchment of existing impressions. Familiarity leads individuals to believe their partners are constants—never changing. When new behavior occurs, they tend to view it as a continuation of previous behavior. This means that when individuals undergo personal changes, misperceptions may occur between intimate partners. The point is that the more we know, the more difficult it may be to accept new information. Relational change, as you will see in a later section in this chapter, is always difficult.

Interdependence

Each person's behavior in a relationship is partly a response to the other relationship partner. Interdependence is high in most intimate relationships because of the negotiation that occurs. Intimate partners, for example, negotiate unique modes of conduct, specialized communication codes, and even a joint identity.

The negative aspect of interdependence is that as it grows, you may reach a point where you feel you know *why* the partner behaves the way he or she does. You think you know the underlying traits, attitudes, intentions, or perceptions that cause the behavior. In fact, however, the partner could be exhibiting a new behavior that has no roots in the traits, attitudes, intentions, or perceptions with which you are familiar! For example, suddenly at a party, one partner becomes animated, engaging in friendly put-downs of others and telling jokes, whereas she has previously tended to be a wallflower. It may be that unbeknownst to her partner, she is suddenly trying to be more outgoing, assertive, and fun-loving. And this is her debut!

This negative aspect is reinforced in conflict situations. When the reason for a behavior appears ambiguous, it is all too easy to blame the other person for the conflict. Also, when relationship patterns are involved in interdependent situations, partners may overlook many of the effects of their own behavior on others. For example, Sharon and Robb had agreed not to discuss politics because Sharon had been brought up in a rock-solid Democratic household, whereas Robb's background was die-hard Republican. After a news broadcast, Sharon made a negative comment about what one news analyst said about the local Democratic candidate. Robb made no comment but discussed the news analyst's comment with co-workers the next day, and he told Sharon about the discussion at dinner that night. Sharon became upset, since she thought they had agreed *not* to discuss politics. Robb thought Sharon was taking it all too seriously—getting upset because of a conversation he reported—but he blamed her for starting the conflict. Sharon thought it was Robb who was taking it too seriously by talking to his co-workers. At this point, their mutual distress was having an effect on each other, and the political issue had receded into the background. The actual reason for the conflict was ambiguous; thus, it was easy for each to blame the other!

Emotional Involvement

Sillars and Scott state that "emotions are felt most strongly and expressed most spontaneously between intimates."[2] These researchers cite evidence to support the claims that conflicts between intimates have greater potential to become physically emotional, that even milder forms of negative behavior occur more often, that relationship partners are less polite and interrupt each other more, show more disapproval of one another, communicate less positively, and use more emotional and abrasive conflict-resolutions strategies.

There are three concerns with respect to emotionality between intimates. First, it tends to bias the interpretation of messages. Intimates presume greater agreement than actually exists and greater disagreement than actually exists. Sillars and Scott say, in addition, "We suspect that there may be an equal though less well-documented tendency for intimates to distort, by contrast, the meaning and affective intent of messages exchanged during emotionally involving conflicts."[3] In other words, when you get into a conflict with an intimate, the chances of misinterpretation are high.

The second concern suggests that intimates focus heavily on the negative and more dramatic actions of their partner and give less consideration to a partner's less noticeable behavior or to their own behavior. In other words, emotional expressions capture your attention just like a blinking neon light in a neighborhood of lights of many colors and sizes. Thus, when a partner becomes highly emotional, you pay greater attention to the emotional presentation.

The third concern is that emotionality tends to short circuit any cognitive response. For example, in situations of high stress "individuals experience a drop-off in their ability to engage in complex integrated thought."[4] This drop-off results in less desire to pursue further information, failure to discriminate between items of information and points of view, and inability to see the difference between stereotypic and retaliatory responses and the perception of only one side of issues. Emotionality simply clouds issues and makes rational thinking and analysis difficult. Essentially, this supports the cliche "My mind is made up; don't confuse me with the facts."

The point of the foregoing is not only to define intimacy but also to point out some of the concerns and problems with intimacy. The four elements that clearly define intimate relationships are the same elements that can lead to relationship myopia (shortsightedness). Those who are entering an intimate relationship for the first time are especially prone to looking at the relationship through rose-colored glasses, in a way that makes everything look terrific. That is not necessarily bad; it is just unre-

CONSIDER THIS

There is something called a Cultural Narrative that helps guide couples in what is considered acceptable behavior with respect to relationship development. Read the following information, and then answer the questions that follow.

> The Cultural Narrative is the sum of society's messages about how people are supposed to do things. In our time, the Cultural Narrative about couples begins with a very simple story. A couple consists of a man and a woman who meet, fall in love, and remain together for life. They solve all their problems, keep their love alive, live independently of their families, encourage each other's personal development, have healthy and happy children, and endure as partners and friends.*

Questions
1. Is this an acceptable Cultural Narrative for *you?* Why or why not?
2. Do you know of a Cultural Narrative from another culture? In what ways does it differ from the one above?
3. Do you think it is necessary to determine the existence of a Cultural Narrative from a person with whom you hope to establish a serious relationship? Why or why not?
4. What is the likelihood that a Cultural Narrative will be different for two people from the "same" culture? What are the likely consequences for people who do not accept or who do not fit the Cultural Narrative that is put forth, promoted, or imposed on them by their society? By the other person?

*From Barry Dym and Michael L. Glenn, *Couples: Exploring and Understanding the Cycles of Intimate Relationships* (New York: HarperCollins Publishers, 1993), p. 39.

alistic. This discussion of potential problems is not meant to appear pessimistic but rather to serve as a challenge to potential relationship partners. The point is that we need to seek a balance; the same elements that define intimacy can lead to the destruction of intimacy.

What is it that attracts you to another person? What are the cues you use to indicate that you are attracted to another person? Is it clear to you that these two are attracted to each other?

▲▲▲ *Formation of Intimate Relationships*

Why do you form intimate relationships with others? What is it about others that attracts you to them? This section will focus on some of the factors in others that affect how you feel about them. These include competence, attractiveness, similarity, liking, and self-disclosure.

You Are Attracted to Competent but "Human" People

There is no doubt that you like people who are qualified, fit, and able. Surrounding yourself with such people makes you feel qualified, fit, and able, and sometimes you think that by association their skills may rub off on you. But not all the associations are necessarily positive. Their competency may well make you look poor by comparison! Also, they may make you feel uncomfortable because they appear too unapproachable, perfect, and unlike you. Thus, when you think others are too competent, you are more attracted to them when they also appear human—capable of failing,

TRY THIS

Before you begin this section, do your own survey of the top five characteristics others look for in a mate. While you are asking, find out the five least desirable characteristics as well. Tell others that you are involved in a psychological study. What you are likely to discover is that the most preferred characteristics are those that anyone with a sense of caring, commitment, and self-esteem could easily fulfill!

or revealing some imperfections, of blundering now and then. You are attracted by competence, but you don't especially like perfection!

There are ways for you to be proactive (act first) in getting others attracted to you. In Table 13.1 I have included more than 20 suggestions for getting people to like you and to feel positively toward you.

You Are Attracted to Physically Attractive People

I think most of you would like to believe that people's personality, character, integrity, sincerity, and honesty are the qualities that attract you to them. And indeed, if relationships continue, these traits are often responsible for that continuance, and the physical attraction that first may have brought you together recedes in importance. Initially, however, physical attractiveness is likely to be the *most* important factor that draws people together. No matter how old, no matter how committed to a current relationship partner, no matter how convinced you are that personality features are important, you can still be affected by a pretty face, a nice body, or a handsome profile. "Physical appearance is one of the most powerful determinants of attraction," says Don E. Hamachek, summarizing the research on this subject in his book on interpersonal relationships.[5]

One reason you are attracted to attractive people is probably that an attractive person seems to enhance your own credibility—it makes *you* look and feel good to be able to attract people with good looks, and others may think more highly of you because of it! Second, research suggests that people associate positive traits with good looks. Karen Dion and her colleagues found that good-looking people are generally thought to be more sensitive, kind, interesting, strong, poised, modest, sociable, outgoing, and exciting.[6] But Hamachek cautions that "attractive physical features may open doors but apparently, it takes more than physical beauty to keep them open."[7]

Table 13.1
A typology of affinity-seeking strategies

HOW TO GET PEOPLE TO LIKE US AND FEEL POSITIVELY TOWARD US

Altruism. Be of help to other.

Assume control. Appear "in control," look like a leader, like one who takes charge.

Be comfortable. Present yourself as comfortable and relaxed when with others.

Concede control. Allow other to assume control over relational activities.

Conversational rule keeping. Follow the cultural rules for polite, cooperative conversation with other.

Dynamism. Appear active, enthusiastic, and dynamic.

Elicit other's disclosures. Stimulate and encourage other to talk about himself or herself: reinforce disclosures and contributions of other.

Facilitate enjoyment. Ensure that activities with other are enjoyable and positive.

Inclusion of other. Include other in your social activities and groupings.

Listening. Listen to other attentively and actively.

Nonverbal immediacy. Communicate interest in other.

Openness. Engage in self-disclosure with other.

Optimism. Appear optimistic and positive rather than pessimistic and negative.

Personal autonomy. Appear to other as an independent and freethinking individual.

Physical attractiveness. Appear to other as physically attractive as possible.

Present interesting self. Appear to other as an interesting person to get to know.

Reward association. Appear as one who is able to reward other for associating with you.

Self-concept confirmation. Show respect for other and help other to feel positively about himself or herself.

Self-inclusion. Arrange circumstances so that you and other come into frequent contact.

Sensitivity. Communicate warmth and empathy to other.

Similarity. Demonstrate that you share significant attitudes and values with other.

Supportiveness. Communicate supportiveness in other's interpersonal interactions.

Trustworthiness. Appear to other as honest and reliable.

Adapted from Robert A. Bell and John A. Daly, "The Affinity-Seeking Function of Communication," *Communication Monographs* (June 1984): 92–115. Copyright by the Speech Communication Association. Reprinted by permission of the publisher and author.

You Are Attracted to People Who Are Similar to You

The essential element here is that the similarity occurs on **core issues**. Core issues are mutually important issues as opposed to trivial ones. For example, agreement on a favorite movie or brand of toothpaste would probably not be as important as agreement about vegetarianism, religion, politics, money, the family, and so on.

Why is similarity so important? First, when someone who is important to you agrees with you, it provides reinforcement for your own feelings. Second, when there is agreement on major issues, it helps avoid many of the needless, daily little hassles. For example, if both partners agree that being on time is important, the little annoyances of lateness are likely to be avoided. Third, similarity reduces the chances that you will have to change in any way. Change is difficult, especially on core issues.

It is useful to note that you do not like *all* people who are similar to you. When those with similar backgrounds and attitudes behave in strange or socially offensive ways, you tend to dislike them. Your dislike of them keeps them at arm's length and preserves and protects your self-image. Dislike of them also reduces the disturbing anxiety that you may have more in common with them than you may want to admit!

You Are Sometimes Attracted to Opposites

You often hear that opposites attract; indeed, if they complement each other, they *do* attract because one partner's needs and characteristics help the other become more complete and well-rounded. But if the two are opposite on core issues or core personality traits, then their opposition may keep them at a distance. A dynamic, assertive individual may not get along with a low-energy, nonassertive individual. An orderly, neat person may find it difficult living with an unkempt, sloppy person. A deeply religious person may have trouble with an individual who is not at all religious.

The other side of this opposites coin is positive, however. One individual might be a person who makes quick, snap decisions and drives himself or herself very hard. The other may take his or her time making decisions and thus have a tempering, rational, calming effect on the partner. One person draws out the other, while the other is slow and relaxed. This could occur as well when one partner is dependent and emotionally needy and the other is highly nurturing and giving, or when one is dominant and the other is submissive.

You Are Attracted to People Who Like You

Don't you experience a warm feeling when you hear that someone likes you? Hamachek considers this to be one of the most powerful influences in attraction. "Knowing that a person likes us, or even loves us, may be enough to start a relationship, but it is seldom enough, it seems, to keep a relationship going."[8]

You may not be attracted to someone who likes you, though, if you think they may have ulterior motives for doing so. Think of the anonymous telephone caller who begins by inquiring how you are. It sounds like a friend calling, which immediately makes you want to respond. When you begin to suspect that the other person is after a sale, a donation, or some other favor, you may be less inclined to respond. Also, if the praise or feedback you are getting differs radically from your own estimation of what is appropriate, you may dislike those who like you. If somebody thinks you are beautiful, and you know you have only average looks, or if someone says you are brilliant and you know you are of average intelligence, you may feel an urge to pull away—to doubt the other's motives, to be suspicious, to remain skeptical and alert for hidden causes.

You Are Attracted to People Who Disclose Themselves to You

For you to tell me something personal about yourself involves risk. But that risk indicates the presence of trust and an atmosphere of good will. That trust and good will are likely to cause me to trust you and to self-disclose in return. A cycle of mutual trust and reciprocity has begun, which tends to increase attractiveness. Reciprocity and mutuality are necessary for a strong, enduring attraction to occur. Those unwilling to say much about themselves are likely to find few people attracted to them.

As we saw in Chapter 3, there are some guidelines for appropriate self-disclosure. To jump into deep self-revelations too early in a relationship can reflect immaturity, insecurity, and phoniness. Timing is important. Also, people who disclose too much may be perceived as boring.

▲▲▲ Stages of Relationship Development

Mark Knapp has identified five stages of relationship development.[9] I have included one additional stage suggested by writer Julia T. Wood.[10] These six stages of relationship development are initiating, experimenting, intensifying, integrating, revising, and bonding. These stages are not always discrete or clearly separated. These stages and the five stages of relationship disintegration (which will be discussed later) are presented in Table 13.2 along with some representative dialogue.

Initiating

The **initiating** stage may take as little as fifteen seconds and includes all those processes that occur as people first come together. You are at a party and see a stranger for the first time. You assess the person's attractiveness. You decide whether or not you want to initiate communication. You try to determine whether the person is likely to be accepting: Is the person alone? In a group? Is he or she occupied? In a hurry? Next, you probably search for an appropriate opening line: "What brings you here?" "Do you know the host?" "Would you like a drink?" "Did you happen to hear on the evening news about . . . ?"

In the initiating stage, often your goal is simply to present others with an attractive package—yourself. You try to come across as pleasant,

Table 13.2
Stages of relationship development and disintegration

	STAGE	REPRESENTATIVE DIALOGUE
Relationship Development	Initiating	"Hi, how's it going?" "Fine, how about you?"
	Experimenting	"You like movies?" "Yes very much."
	Intensifying	"I really love you." "I love you, too."
	Integrating	"What is mine is yours." "And what is mine is yours too."
	Revising	"We need to spend more time together." "You're right . . . let's try."
	Bonding	"Would you marry me?" "Oh, yes, yes, yes!"
Relationship Disintegration	Differentiating	"I do not like your friends." "I don't like yours either."
	Circumscribing	"How did work go today?" "Did you get the mail?"
	Stagnating	"I have nothing to say to you." "And I have nothing to say to you either."
	Avoiding	"I have too many things to do. I have no time to talk." "I'm not around when you are free anyway."
	Terminating	"As far as I'm concerned, our relationship is history." "That goes for me, too."

Adapted from Mark L. Knapp, *Interpersonal Communication and Human Relationships.* Copyright © 1984 by Allyn and Bacon. Used with permission. The stage of "Revising" is excerpted from Julia T. Wood, *Human Communication: A Symbolic Interactionist Perspective.* Copyright © 1982 by Holt, Rinehart and Winston. Reprinted by permission of the publisher.

warm, friendly, empathetic, and socially adept. In a sense, all you are doing is trying to present an attractive first impression that will open channels of communication for more contact and talk.

Experimenting

The goal of **experimenting** is to explore the unknown. Once initiation has occurred, you want to find out who this stranger is and what you have in common. This is the stage of **small talk**, in which some rather standard information is collected in an informal, unstructured, and relaxed manner.

You are not conducting an interview but engaging in comfortable give-and-take. Answers that are given are often expanded upon as mutual self-disclosure takes place. Examples and illustrations are used to fill in details and to make the experimentation stage interesting and enjoyable.

Small talk, Knapp suggests, often fulfills important and sufficient functions in relationships:

> (1) It is a useful process for uncovering integrating topics and openings for more penetrating conversation. (2) It can be an audition for a future friendship or a way of increasing the scope of a current relationship. (3) It provides a safe procedure for indicating who we are and how another can come to know us better (reduction of uncertainty). (4) It allows us to maintain a sense of community with our fellow human beings.[11]

Thus small talk is *not* necessarily a waste of time, as most people believe. Experimenting is a rewarding stage because communication at this point is usually pleasant, relaxed, casual, and uncritical. There are few commitments, and acquisition of information is usually interesting and unthreatening. Small talk, then, is the beginning of the disclosure process. If the small talk goes well, the relationship may proceed to the intensifying stage.

Many of my students want guidance at this stage—that is, they want some suggestions about what kind of information to discover. Of course, it would be inappropriate to begin grilling a person after just meeting him or her. Such behavior would be likely to end any potential relationship right there! But a variety of questions can be naturally and comfortably worked into conversations during the experimenting stage. You might want to try one or more of the following:

- ▲ What is your name?
- ▲ What do you do (like to do)?
- ▲ Where are you from (do you live)?
- ▲ What are your hobbies?
- ▲ What do you do for fun?
- ▲ What do you do for relaxation?
- ▲ Do you enjoy traveling?
- ▲ Are you a sports fan?
- ▲ Who is your favorite author?
- ▲ What kind of movies do you like to go to?
- ▲ Do you enjoy classical music (jazz, rock)?
- ▲ Who are your heroes (heroines)?
- ▲ Are you active in politics?
- ▲ What is your religion? Do you attend services regularly?

What would lead you to believe this couple is in the experimenting stage of relationship development? What goes on during the experimenting stage?

▲ What would you like to be doing five years from now?

The point of all this may be to gain breadth, to pass the time, or even to prevent the relationship from developing further. You can maintain relationships at this level, and we often do. In fact, most relationships do not go beyond this stage.

It should be noted that some people consistently connect with others on a rather shallow level. They enjoy pleasant experiences and light conversation for a while and may be very impressed with each other's physical appearance. But they never bond more deeply. Their relationships are very different from those who choose to deepen their commitment, trust more, and bond more strongly. Many intelligent, educated people prefer the lighter style. A particular relationship may be only one of many valuable things in their personal life. Some people find relationships expendable. This may be especially true of those who have been wounded deeply. Such a wound may create a lasting preference for lighter, less risky involvement.

Intensifying

When the **intensifying** stage is reached, an acquaintance has become a close friend. This includes greater commitment to the relationship, an increase in self-disclosure, and a willingness to make yourself vulnerable. You may wonder what signs indicate that the intensifying stage has been reached. Knapp offers six verbal cues:

> (1) Forms of address become more informal—first name, nickname, or some term of endearment. (2) Use of the first personal plural becomes more common—"We should do this" or "Let's do this." (3) Private symbols begin to develop, sometimes in the form of special slang or jargon, sometimes using conventional language forms that have understood, private meanings. (4) Verbal shortcuts built on a backlog of accumulated and shared assumptions, expectations, interests, knowledge, interactions, and experiences appear more often; one may request that a newspaper be passed by simply saying, "paper." (5) More direct expressions of commitment may appear—"We really have a good thing going" or "I don't know who I'd talk to if you weren't around." Sometimes such expressions receive an echo—"I really like you a lot." "I really like you, too." (6) Increasingly, one's partner will act as a helper in the daily process of understanding what you're all about—"In other words, you mean you're . . ." or "But yesterday, you said you were. . . ."[12]

More reliance on nonverbal communication also occurs. Sometimes couples will replace talk with a touch or a gesture. To emphasize their commitment, individuals may allow their possessions and space to become more accessible to the other, and they may coordinate the clothes they wear to emphasize their growing relationship. In a sense, they are beginning to declare, publicly, a partnership.

Integrating

The **integrating** stage represents greater commitment. The two individuals begin to blend, fuse, and coalesce. An important aspect of this stage (important because it reverses when relationships disintegrate) is that the "I," "me," and "mine" that frequent the communication of individuals becomes "we," "us," and "ours"—signifying sharing and mutuality. The relationship takes on a uniqueness that distinguishes itself from other relationships and from partners acting alone. Partners now share in perceptions, outlooks, and decisions. Rules, roles, definitions, and strategies are secured and tested at this stage.

Because individuals are so enthusiastic about each other in this stage, some distortion occurs. Optimism and euphoria sometimes cause partners to see what they want to see. Much as Sandy hates fishing, for example, she loves Paul so much that she takes fishing trips with him in order that they can be together and get to know each other better. Raymond dislikes Christa's smoking, but he overlooks it because he knows how difficult it would be for her to give it up.

Once again, Knapp provides the verbal and nonverbal cues that reveal that integrating has occurred.

> (1) Attitudes, opinions, interests, and tastes that clearly distinguish the pair from others are vigorously cultivated—"We have something special; we are unique." (2) Social circles merge and others begin to treat the two individuals as a common package—one present, one letter, one invitation. (3) Intimacy "trophies" are exchanged so each can "wear" the other's identity—pictures, pins, rings. (4) Similarities in manner, dress, and verbal behavior may also accentuate the oneness. (5) Actual physical penetration of various body parts contributes to the perceived unification. (6) Sometimes common property is designated—"our song," a joint bank account, or authoring a book together. (7) Empathic processes seem to peak so that explanation and prediction of behavior are much easier. (8) Body rhythms and routines achieve heightened synchrony. (9) Sometimes the love of a third person or object will serve as glue for the relationship—"Love me, love my rhinos."[13]

Revising

Julia T. Wood adds another stage, **revising**, at this point. She suggests that after the intensity and infatuation of the integration stage, "individuals need time to think over what has happened, to get back in touch with themselves, and to consider the desirability of continuing the relationship."[14]

It is at this stage, after a rather emotional integrating stage, that rationality takes over. This is a highly intrapersonal stage because much of the assessment takes place as self-talk. "Can I learn to like fishing?" "Can I tolerate her smoking?" "Is he too dependent on me?" You may compare this relationship with others or this relationship partner with others. You may also consider other alternatives available to you. Are there other (better?) prospects?

Another set of considerations involves the kinds of changes likely to take place. Will I have to change to accommodate Bill's assertiveness, Lisa's intelligence, Steve's athletic ability, Tanya's attractiveness, Vince's generosity, or Cherie's orderliness and efficiency? Often, you compare yourself with your partner. Am I willing to modify my values, attitudes, or behaviors? Who am I becoming because of this relationship, and do I like it? The revising stage allows you time to take stock. If you are unhappy, you may end the relationship at this stage. If not, you may pursue it.

If you have decided to pursue a relationship, you may conclude that revisions or modifications are necessary. These revisions are usually negotiated in this stage as a result of requests from the partner. "I wish you

TRY THIS

What kinds of questions would you ask if you were to do a fairly complete assessment of your relationship at the revising stage? Here are some questions; perhaps you can think of others.

1. Do you listen to and empathize with each other?
2. Do you give each other encouragement and support?
3. Do you play together?
4. Do you express your feelings openly and freely?
5. Do you ask each other for things you are not getting?
6. Do you accept and work through your differences?
7. Do you identify, define, and solve problems together?
8. Do you work together well as a team?
9. Do you share opinions, thoughts, and ideas without becoming defensive?
10. Overall, are you satisfied with the relationship?

would spend more time with me." "Maybe you could just try golf." "Your swearing is really obnoxious." "I wish you wouldn't watch so much TV." Such requests require some modification of behavior to make continuance of the relationship attractive and possible.

There is no doubt that this stage can breed anxiety, tension, and defensiveness. Accepting constructive criticism—even from a loved one—is difficult. Trying to change may be even more challenging. Changing is tough. How would *you* like to be asked to change your manner of dress, drinking habits, friends, language, or the way you deal with others? Such requests are normal at this stage, and such negotiation is often necessary to lay the proper foundation for the next stage. Establishing the proper atmosphere in the revising stage requires listening skills and maintaining a supportive climate. Anxiety, tension, and defensiveness can be reduced by sensitive, empathic, supportive communication between partners. Success at this stage is likely to lead to bonding.

Bonding

The main difference between this stage and all the others is that the others are processes; **bonding** is both an event *and* a process. Bonding is a commitment to the revised relationship. A bonding ceremony may be public or private. If it's public, such as marriage or going steady, the rela-

What are the main characteristics of the bonding stage of relationship development?

tionship gains social or institutional support because the couple can rely on laws, policies, or precedents for guidance. If private, the couple must rely on each other to keep the relationship intact. Bonding is simply the contract for the union of the two individuals.

Features of the bonding event are that it is voluntary, for an indefinite period (who knows how long it will last?), and under special rules. The voluntary commitment can be a powerful new force in the relationship. Individuals have new freedom to interact and discuss without worrying that trivial concerns will break up the relationship. They can be themselves more.

The indefinite period of commitment causes a hardening of the relationship to occur. Partners cannot leave each other as easily. There is likely to be a change in the language used between partners as they become more relaxed and informal. The contract itself may be a frequent topic of conversation.

Special rules refer to the social and institutional, formal and informal guidelines that assist partners who are going steady, engaged, or married. No longer are partners as free to see former boyfriends and girlfriends. There may be some restrictions on partners' freedom to see their former group of friends—perhaps even other family members. The partners spend more time together. Generally, individuals in a relationship

TRY THIS

One of the problems with relationships is that people seldom discuss—within the relationship itself—matters that relate to the relationship. Allow some time in your current relationship to sit down and talk. The following questions are designed to give you something to talk about:

What is an intimate relationship? What does it ask of me? Of you?

What are our expectations of this relationship? Of each other?

Does our relationship mean exclusivity? What kinds of freedom will be provided? Is it us, only us, and no one else but us?

Does our relationship mean long evenings talking and laughing together?

Does our relationship mean sharing a closeness both physically and psychologically?

Does our relationship mean having sex? Living together? Having gourmet meals?

Where do the two of us want to be—with respect to this relationship—in six months? One year? Five years? Ten years?

support each other in the presence of others. Decisions are now made jointly. When a decision that affects both partners or the relationship must be made, each individual must consult the other and not behave as though the other does not exist. And when and where individuals in relationships go—and their freedom to go—is usually negotiated. One partner usually knows where the other is. All of this because bonding has occurred! New rules cause new adjustments that result in new behaviors!

Bonding is a process, too. Once a commitment has been made, the relationship will continue to evolve. To think of bonding as just an event may lead people to believe that evolution stops. Those who have bonded recognize the need to view what happens next as relationship maintenance, negotiation, adjustment, and readjustment. To suggest that the development of a relationship ends here—with the possible exception of disintegration or dissolution—is to deny the rewards, excitement, challenges, and interest that relationship partners who have moved to this stage can and often do experience. Indeed, I believe that this stage, at most times, may be equated with peak communication—"complete emotional and personal communication."[15] Some may believe that this correlation with peak communication is too zealous or enthusiastic, but at least it should be viewed as a goal or as a realistic possibility.

CONSIDER THIS

Do the traditional concepts and principles of rhetoric for public influence apply equally well to intimate and interpersonal communication? Richard Johannesen, citing Harold Barrett, describes some "subtly violent" verbal and nonverbal techniques that are ethically objectionable in interpersonal communication. Read them, and see if you agree.

> *Scapegoating* involves blaming others for faults or problems that primarily are our own. *Unnecessarily critical condemnation* of others, as a kind of rhetorical assault, leads to guilt feelings and eventual weakening of the persuasive powers of the person criticized. *Coercion* through threats against weaker persons is rhetorical bullying. *Restriction of freedom to choose* could be achieved by withholding information necessary to make a decision or by not revealing a relevant personal feeling. *Lying or deceiving* (as opposed to harmless fibbing) can intentionally or unintentionally cause others personal distress or painful emotional injury. *Violating a trust* harms or destroys relationships.*

Questions
1. Do you think these techniques offer useful guidelines?
2. Can you think of others that could be added to this list?
3. Which of these do you think are most common? Which are most objectionable?
4. If you were in a relationship where some of these techniques were being used, what could you do about it?

*From Richard L. Johannesen, *Ethics in Human Communication*, 3rd ed. (Prospect Heights, IL: Waveland Press, Inc., 1990), pp. 143–144.

▲▲▲ *Maintaining and Nurturing Intimate Relationships*

The chances of two people sharing the same blueprint for a relationship are rather slim. But the chances decrease dramatically when there is no communication. Without communication, frustration is likely to result, and both partners may give up whatever ideals they brought to the relationship, either settling for a mediocre relationship or allowing whatever relationship existed to disintegrate.

But let's assume for the moment that intimacy is desired and achieved. How do people maintain it? What are the keys to sustaining interest? We will examine communication, sharing activities, constant effort, and protecting individuality.

Communication

Intimacy involves talking together. Without talk, relationships become stalemated, partners become walled off from each other, and any exchanges that do take place become superficial, unable to touch the deep, real concerns of the participants.

Why is communication essential? Often, relationships are thought to be stable, static, fixed entities. However, this is far from true. A relationship is a dynamic, fluid, constantly changing mixture that reflects the changes in the relationship partners and in their life situations. Without communication, these changes may not be understood, may cause surprise or even shock, and may lead to deterioration rather than growth of the relationship.

Changes in relationships cause inevitable and constant difficulties. Partners must adjust and face the obstacles together. How they do this is unique to each relationship and often cannot be predicted. But with open communication at a deep, meaningful level, the chances for adjustment improve, and the chances for relational growth improve as well. Relationship partners who stubbornly resist change and growth may find growing dissatisfaction in their relationship with concurrent problems and crises and likely disintegration.

Sharing Activities

Intimacy involves both talking *and* doing together. Talking and doing enhance each other. Activities offer opportunities to see into each other. You not only get a better look at your relationship partner but can approve of what you see as well. Earlier this benefit of relationships was labeled ego building—contributing to the positive development of self. You want your partner to accept that part of the self you expose. The sharing of activities can bring people very close.

Some shared activities are rituals. A **ritual** is a patterned interaction that is predictable. Because ritual behavior is governed by rules (either given or negotiated), it is also recognizable by other members of the culture and repeatable at other times and places. Anniversaries, honeymoons, and birthdays are rituals, as well as such holidays as Thanksgiving, Christmas, Valentine's Day, Passover, and Easter. But rituals also can include the once-a-week lunch dates, the Friday afternoon happy hour with partner and friends, the weekly dinner out, or the nightly walk around the block. Rituals affirm the value partners place on spending

TRY THIS

Tensions develop from time to time in any relationship. Healthy relationship partners take the time to study the tensions that exist, explore some of their underlying dynamics, and take some steps toward resolving them constructively. This is accomplished together as the partners share ideas, insights, and suggestions. Take time out with your partner to air, clarify, and possibly resolve any discomforts, frustrations, hurts, or irritations (however slight). Find a comfortable, quiet place, and the two of you *each* complete the following sentences:

> One of the ways I sometimes hurt you is . . .
> One of the ways I sometimes make you angry is . . .
> One of the ways I sometimes frustrate you is . . .
> One of the ways I sometimes make it difficult for you to love me is . . .
> One of the ways I sometimes make it difficult for you to give me what
>   I want is . . .

Listen as your partner completes the sentences. Feel free to discuss and expand on responses that are given. This is a time for sharing. Change the sentence stems, as necessary, to make them apply directly to your relationship and your relationship needs.

Nathaniel Branden, "*If You Could Hear What I Cannot Say*": *Learning to Communicate with the Ones You Love* (New York: Bantam Books, 1983), p. 162. Copyright © 1983 by Nathanial Branden, Published by Bantam Books.

time together, and they serve to anchor the bond and promote relational growth. They are a great means for sharing activities.

Constant Effort

Andrew Greeley has said, "Intimacy . . . is always difficult, and when it stops being difficult it stops being intimacy."[16] Not only is intimacy difficult to achieve, it is difficult to sustain. It requires both work and patience. The ideal relationship is sometimes described as a 50–50 effort. But with this ratio, if either partner decides to let the relationship slide, intimacy will suffer. The best guidance, if you want intimacy badly enough, is for *each* partner to give the relationship 100 percent of his or her effort, and the relationship will absorb the extra energy. When Eric and Linda were in school, they found increasing tensions between them. When they talked about it, they realized they had let the pressures of school eclipse the importance of their relationship with each other. Although school was important to both of them, they decided to set aside a specific amount of time each week just for themselves. Soon they found their relationship once again growing pleasurable. Such decisions are not easy. They must take into account the age of the relationship partners, their goals, and the nature of their relationship.

Protecting Individuality

Talking about marriage in *The Prophet*, Kahlil Gibran says, "But let there be spaces in your togetherness, and let the winds of the heavens dance between you." Gibran continues in this way.

> *Love one another, but make not a bond of love:*
> *Let it rather be a moving sea between the shores of your souls.*
> *Fill each other's cup but drink not from one cup.*
> *Give one another of your bread but eat not from the same loaf.*
> *Sing and dance together and be joyous, but let each one of you be alone,*
> *Even as the strings of a lute are alone though they quiver with the same music.*[17]

Intimacy must not destroy individuality, but too much individuality can destroy intimacy. A useful way to view **dependence, independence,** and **interdependence** in a relationship is in terms of an A, H, and M frame, as illustrated in Figure 13.1.[18] The **A frame** represents dependence. Absorption in the other is so strong that if one partner lets go, the other falls. In the reverse situation, shown in the **H frame**, there is strong individual identity, a great deal of self-sufficiency, and no couple identity. If one partner lets go, the other hardly feels it. Finally, in the **M frame**, there is interdependence, a combination of dependence and independence. If one partner lets go, the other feels a loss but recovers balance. There is meaningful couple identity without sacrifice of individual identity.

Although partners must give themselves to the relationship and to each other, they must also exist as individuals. When people grow together as a couple, they must be free to grow as individuals as well—the M frame. Whose responsibility is this? Partners need to guard each other's personal need for individual freedom to grow and yet protect interdependence. This underscores the reasons why constant communication is essential, because with growth comes change. When intimacy becomes oppressive, partners need to back off before coming back together for more intense involvement or perhaps for a newly redefined level of involvement.

Figure 13.1
Levels of dependence in relationships.

A FRAME

DEPENDENCE

If one lets go, the other falls.

No individual identity

Self absorbed in the other

Strong couple identity

H FRAME

INDEPENDENCE

If one lets go, the other hardly feels a thing.

Strong individual identity

Self-sufficient

No couple identity

M FRAME

INTERDEPENDENCE

If one lets go, the other feels a loss but recovers balance.

Healthy individual identity

Self relates meaning-fully to the other

Meaningful couple identity

▲▲▲ *Relational Change*

The development and maintenance of relationships always involves change. Richard Conville, a researcher of interpersonal communication, has speculated about change. He claims that change in any part of the relationship is likely to affect the whole relationship. Conville identifies four characteristics of relational change: (1) predictability, (2) uniqueness, (3) obliqueness, and (4) exchange.[19] These characteristics affect partners whether the relationship is developing, being maintained, or disintegrating.

Predictability

Predictability refers to the nature and order of change. Conville suggests that relational change that alters the relationship itself follows a predictable course. Once change begins, certain other stages of change must follow. After three years of living with John, Diane realized that her romanticized world was not what she really wanted. As a result, Diane lost a clear picture of the future. Her relationship with John became ambiguous. No clear definition of the relationship seemed possible because of her new perspective. Because normal humans cannot exist long without anchors in the future and anchors, as well, in significant others, Diane struggled for stability. She finally found it in her own values. This, according to Conville, is a predictable course of events.

Changes in relationships create new concerns not previously faced. Thus, the way partners evaluate and assess change, like Diane's and John's need to evaluate and assess her changed view, needs to change as well. Part of predictability is also the struggle necessary to obtain stability within the relationship. Diane and John faced a new situation. This potential change in their relationship may make it stronger or weaker, but whatever happens, it will be different because of the change, and Diane and John will evaluate the relationship differently both now and in the future.

Uniqueness

Because relational change is unique to each couple, there are no sure-fire guaranteed methods for dealing appropriately with it. Whenever change occurs, partners are forced to fight for survival. Whether it involves a change in jobs or geographical location, the death of a parent, a divorce, a religious conversion, or a risk-laden journey, individuals seldom can rely on past experiences for guidelines on how to respond. People are severely jolted, forced to rely on their own resources, and faced with the need for an intense struggle. In many cases, it is just such a struggle—partners working together in a battle for the survival of the relationship—that brings individuals closer together and cements the bond. But *how* the partners deal with the change, and how that cementing occurs (if it does), is likely to be unique.

Obliqueness

One meaning of *oblique* is "indirect" or "not straightforward." Conville suggests that when partners are in the midst of relational change, they cannot see what is happening. Their awareness of the change is indirect—not straightforward. Partners may be aware that some change is occurring, but it is only upon reflection—looking back—that the individuals may be able to understand the true nature of the change and its effect on them.

Moving closer to a partner's parents may be a good example of obliqueness. Such a move is likely to have profound effects on a relationship. These effects may occur so rapidly that it is impossible to digest them all: more meals with the relatives, more coordination of plans, more visits, more exchange of gifts, more interference with personal plans, less time together for the relationship couple, etc. Nothing can be done about it. However, after a move away from this situation, both partners are able to look back on the situation and understand its effect. They use the experience as a basis for sharing stories and advice with others. But at the actual time of the experience, their only thoughts may be how to change the situation.

Of course, a situation does not have to be *past* before partners can look at it objectively. Sometimes, when the emotional attachments are low, or when there is low differentiation in the attitudes toward the situation, partners might be able to adjust to situations to face them with equanimity. Sometimes, it takes both time and distance from a situation to achieve the objectivity and calm rationality required to deal appropriately with it.

Exchange

Change also involves exchange. Conville claims it is "the exchange of certain present securities for certain future securities."[20] Take the case of Don and Mary Ann. Their present securities include spending time together, having a "traditional" DINK (double-income-no-kids) relationship with a "traditional" division of labor, and the security of experiencing no change. Mary Ann is considering accepting a promotion to supervisor. Possible future securities include increased income, one partner (the wife) having a higher-status position, and the likelihood of acquiring a new group of friends (her new colleagues). Would these individuals risk exchanging their present securities for these future securities?

Sometimes, individuals choose to maintain a relationship because present securities are better than what they see as *no* securities. For example, having a guaranteed date, transportation, companionship, and a group of friends may seem much better than having none of these securities at all, or trying to build a new relationship with someone else. "It's not the best relationship or the ideal person," one may say, "but it is better than none at all!" When change occurs, you must assess your relationship in terms of exchange. Is the exchange of securities worth the risk?

▲▲▲ Marriage and Commitment

What keeps couples together? In her book *Lasting Love*, Judy C. Pearson, a communication specialist, poses this question. Here I will list some of her discoveries from one and a half hour interviews each with 34 couples. Each of her discoveries will be cast as things you can expect if you want longevity and happiness.

1. *Expect the relationship to last.* Go into the marriage as if for a lifetime. Pretend there is no way out, and expect to work out all problems rather than escape them.[21]
2. *Expect to communicate.* It is the most fundamental and important aspect of marriage. It is largely through communication that marriages are satisfying.[22]

TRY THIS

Seven Kinds of Love

Love has at least seven definitions. To say that you "love" another person could mean any of seven different things, or it could bring together a variety of definitions. What do *you* mean when you say you "love" someone else? Can you think of a kind of love *not* represented by these definitions? If you were to arrange these seven definitions in order from the beginning stages of a relationship to the end stages, in what order would they likely appear?

Storgic—based on parental affection. This is seen in parents' expression of strong affection for their children.

Manic—based on excessive and persistent enthusiasm for another. Often this is seen during infatuation, in which the other person becomes an obsession.

Philos—based on the Greek word meaning "loving," this form combines the meaning of loving, liking, and having a predilection for. It means tender affection. It is seen when people have an unselfish love and are ready to serve.

Pragmatic—based on activity, this is an active, diligent, busy kind of love. Often it is seen in long-term relationships where love has become a day-to-day, active love reflected in ordinary, daily, affectionate behaviors.

Erotic— based on sexual desire. This is love prompted by sexual feelings and desires. It is amorous and may be characterized by a preoccupation with sex. (Often, when people think of love, this erotic kind of love is the only association they may make. Too often, love is connected with the sexual alone.)

Agape—based on God's love for people, or Christian love. (It is said that both Buddha and Gandhi practiced and preached agape love, too.) This is seen in the Christian sense of brotherhood or in people's spontaneous and altruistic love for others.

Ludus—based on the Latin word *ludicrus,* meaning "sportive," which is from the Latin word *ludere,* meaning "to play." This is a playful kind of love that causes enjoyment and laughter. It is that kind of love often demonstrated between small children who are playmates.

    3. *Expect to engage in relationship work.* Because none of us remains the same, relationships are dynamic social processes in constant flux. Communication helps us understand and deal with change.[23]

    4. *Expect to maintain a flexible, versatile, adaptable approach.* There is no single formula for success. The variables that can be credited for the

CONSIDER THIS

Do the experts know what factors predict marital satisfaction? They know that some features don't make a difference. For example, a recent survey by the Consumers Union determined that age, education, religion, and health are not strong predictors of marital happiness. Similarly, where someone lived, whether they were a man or a woman, and their income do not predict satisfaction.

From Judy C. Pearson, *Lasting Love: What Keeps Couples Together* (Dubuque, IA: Wm. C. Brown Co., 1992), pp. 10–11.

longevity and happiness of one couple may be anathema [anything greatly detested] for another.[24]

5. *Expect to negotiate the power relationship.* Although marriages in which power is shared or split are mostly highly related to marital satisfaction, with the husband-dominated pattern second choice, and the woman dominated pattern a distant third choice, this is an issue that needs to be discussed.[25]

6. *Expect to positively reinforce and confirm each other.* Although this may not always be evident to outsiders, most partners interpret their spouse's behavior as positive.[26]

7. *Expect to manage conflicts.* Although most happy couples prefer talking it out, conflict resolution takes on a variety of forms in happy marriages.[27] Long-married couples argue gracefully.[28]

8. *Expect to keep your expectations reasonable.* Happy couples fare better with respect to both longevity and happiness when they have lowered expectations for the relationship.[29]

9. *Expect to face serious problems.* Stress, disruptions, disquieting influences, and hardships are inevitable. Nobody said life would be easy.[30]

10. *Expect to develop and maintain social networks.* Although friends and extended family members are always valuable, they become increasingly important during times of stress.[31]

11. *Expect to love yourself and each other.* Partners who exhibit respect and acceptance of themselves reveal understanding, empathic, and supportive behaviors of others. "Loving couples accept each other as they are."[32] Acceptance is best shown by appreciating the other's idiosyncrasies.

12. *Expect to determine your own reality.* Happy couples see themselves as extraordinary; they do not take their cues from the rest of the world. They are their own judges of effectiveness, success, and happiness.[33]

13. *Expect to take a positive, optimistic view of things.* This may sound strange, but long-term, happily married couples "view their partner, their marriage, and other events as highly positive."[34] Success seems to mean putting a positive interpretation on events. Happy couples tend to be happy in general—this includes a sense of certainty, acceptance, and affirmation.[35]

14. *Expect to avoid negative sentiment.* This does not mean avoiding all negative issues. But, long-term happy couples tend to avoid negative words and actions. Also, they seldom have a negative bias towards messages sent by their partner.[36]

15. *Expect to maintain good physical and psychological health.* Satisfied couples do. Happily married couples tend to look younger than their years because of their good physical and psychological health.[37]

16. *Expect to maintain your own identity.* Although when you get married you become one, happy couples "find their way to a space between commitment and suffocation."[38]

17. *Expect a happy sex life.* "Satisfaction with sexuality makes happy relationships."[39] Also, it is likely that the better partners get along, the better their sex life is likely to be. It is through talk that couples teach each other about their sexual needs, preferences, fantasies, and desires.[40]

18. *Expect to be persistent.* Happy partners refuse to let go of their marriage or to give up. Commit yourself to your spouse, as a person, and you will have "significantly fewer problems making decisions and setting goals . . . , fewer conflicts over relatives, fewer disagreements about personal care, and less dissatisfaction with the expression of affection."[41]

19. *Expect to give more than 50–50.* Happy partners give more than they take. "If you go for sixty, and I think most of us do, then you know, you come out about 50–50."[42]

20. *Expect your history together as a couple to dictate appropriateness.* Because every couple has its own history, what is appropriate for one is not appropriate for another. Thus, one must be sensitive to one's own history together to help determine behavior.[43]

All of these expectations are important, but what they prove is that one cannot predict success; one simply must be ready for it. Overall, if one has a good sense of self, a good sense of others, a good sense of what life is all about, and a good sense of humor, one is likely to have a good relationship as well.

Figure 13.2
How much energy do you have to give to a relationship? When you are preoccupied with yourself, or preoccupied with a task (your work), the relationship is likely to suffer.

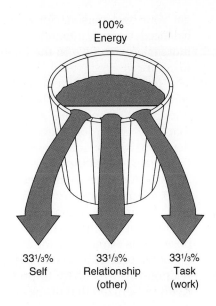

100%
Energy

33¹/₃%
Self

33¹/₃%
Relationship
(other)

33¹/₃%
Task
(work)

▲▲▲ *Why Relationships Disintegrate*

Disintegration can be caused by either partner, both partners, or neither partner. Either partner may decide to go a separate way, to take on a new partner, or to go it alone while the other wants to continue the relationship. Both partners may come to an agreement that separation would be best. Or both partners may want to continue, but other situations may intervene that cause disintegration. The partners, for example, become unavoidably separated by distance, or one partner who had free time takes on a job, or the lifestyles of the partners change. Although neither wants the change in intimacy, it happens nonetheless. Outside threats will sometimes strengthen relationships and at other times weaken them or tear them apart.

One way to view disintegration is with respect to your total *energy bucket*. Think of yourself as having a bucket 100 percent full of energy. You can distribute that energy in any way you choose. (See Figure 13.2.) Now, what happens to the energy distribution when you become preoccupied with yourself? When you have a massive inferiority complex? When you feel unloved or unworthy? Some of the energy shifts to yourself, and you have less available to give to the relationship.

The same thing (a shift in energy) occurs when you become preoccupied with a task. Less energy remains for the relationship. Once you get your own personal problems solved, and once your work can be a balanced, normal, integrated part of your life, then you are likely to have more energy to give to the relationship, and disintegration is less likely to occur.

Sometimes partners need to weigh the costs versus the rewards of continuing the relationship. It may be that disintegration is the best thing. For example, Phil and Sam, partners in a small business, realized that they were doing everything together. Phil wanted his independence, partly to free himself to seek new business contacts. Alice and Paul realized that they were both being smothered by their relationship. They decided they both needed more distance to give them a chance to think about themselves, each other, and the relationship.

An important consideration for people embarking on an intimate relationship for the first time is the restriction that intimacy tends to impose. Chris wondered, for example, how willing she should be to give up other potential relationships. She quickly discovered that her new relationship was likely to prevent her from making other new friends. Keith recognized that his new relationship was preventing him from exploring different types of relationships with different people. He wanted freedom to experiment and explore.

Each relationship is different. What may be benefits for some may be burdens for others. It is impossible to offer specific guidelines for couples, but those who are experiencing some waning interest in a relationship might want to discuss the benefits of staying together or breaking up. In many cases, such discussions offer lessons that can be used later. Gene learned from one such discussion that every time a relationship reached intimacy, he lost interest in it. With that knowledge, he began to approach intimate situations differently. Table 13.3 is Michael Cody's list of the causes that can precipitate disintegration of a relationship—or what he calls relational disengagements.

Relationships disintegrate for many different reasons. John and Tracey had formed a relationship just when their previous intimate relationships had terminated. But both had formed new support groups, and they now felt that their needs for each other had virtually ceased. Dan and Sandy had established an intimate relationship in high school. Dan went to work for his father in an independent insurance company, and Sandy went on to college. In Sandy's junior year, it became clear to her that her attitudes had become incompatible with Dan's, that her intellectual interests and abilities had outdistanced Dan's, and that her major goals had changed. Their relationship had begun to wobble and was now coming unglued.

Table 13.3
Causes precipitating relational disengagements

1. I realized that he/she had too many faults (personality and otherwise).
2. I felt his/her personality was incompatible with mine.
3. I felt that she/he was too demanding.
4. The partner behaved in ways that embarrassed me.
5. Generally, the partner's behaviors and/or personality was more to blame for the breakup than anything else.
6. I realized she/he was unwilling to make enough contributions to the relationship.
7. I felt that he/she no longer behaved towards me, as romantically as she/he once did.
8. I felt that he/she took me for granted.
9. I felt that he/she wasn't willing to compromise for the good of the relationship.
10. I simply felt that the relationship was beginning to constrain me, and I felt a lack of freedom.
11. Although I still cared for the partner, I wanted to start dating other people.
12. While this relationship was a good one, I started to get bored with it.
13. The partner made too many contributions, and I started to feel suffocated.
14. I felt that she/he was becoming too possessive of me.
15. Although I still liked the partner, I felt that the romance had gone out of the relationship.
16. I was primarily interested in having a good time and not with maintaining a relationship.
17. I felt that he/she was too dependent on me.
18. The two of us simply developed different interests and had less in common.
19. I realized that I couldn't trust him/her.
20. One of us moved away and we couldn't see each other very much.
21. Most of my friends (or all of them) didn't like him/her (most of his/her friends didn't like me), causing problems that detracted from the relationship.
22. Generally, the relationship itself didn't seem right and the faults of the relationship could not be blamed on any one person in the relationship.
23. My parents didn't approve of him/her (or her/his parents didn't approve of me).
24. The partner showed too much physical affection (or was too aggressive).

From Michael J. Cody, "A Typology of Disengagement Strategies," *Communication Monographs* 49 (September 1982): 162. Reprinted by permission of the Speech Communication Association and the author.

▲▲▲ *Stages of Relational Disintegration*

There is no inevitability in relational disintegration. That is, just because a relationship begins to disintegrate does not mean there is no turning back. Knowing the stages and what *can* happen helps couples become aware of

If this couple is experiencing relational disintegrations, which stage are they likely to be in? What could either member of this relationship do to attempt to reverse the disintegration?

a problem. Entering the first stage of disintegration may be enough to create the awareness of a need for renewal. In such cases, couples may

▲ confront problems   ▲ explore changes
▲ renegotiate roles   ▲ revise their world
▲ get back in touch   ▲ redefine their relationship
▲ institute new rituals   ▲ recommit themselves
▲ renegotiate rules   ▲ get outside help

We need not assume that when something interferes with an intimate relationship, disintegration will follow. What really determines the effect of the interference is **commitment:** *the obligation partners feel toward each other and the relationship.* Relationship strength is often directly related to commitment strength. How much do partners care? When the commitment is very strong, many obstacles can be overcome and the process of disintegration can be reversed. Partners need not allow themselves to be victims of disintegration or victims of negative influences. They *can* fight back if they use the strategies suggested for maintaining intimacy and those at the end of this chapter on improving intimacy skills. Even if disintegration has begun, it should be clear that at *any* stage, partners may decide to reverse the process by using the renewal strategies listed above.

Knapp suggests that there are five stages of disintegration: differentiating, circumscribing, stagnating, avoiding, and terminating.[44]

Differentiating

Since this is the first stage of disintegration, it is simply a signal that problems are occurring. **Differentiating** partners make clear the differences they see in each other. Instead of focusing on the other and on the relationship, individuals begin to focus on themselves. How are *they* different? Perhaps the best sign of this change in focus is the change in language. The "we," "us," and "our" that once became a signal that integrating was occurring revert to the "I," "me," and "mine" used before the relationship began. Shared possessions, shared friendships, and shared times become less important. Conversations focus on the awareness of differences.

Circumscribing

The point of **circumscribing** is to control areas of discussion and restrict communication to safe areas. This means fewer interactions, less depth in the subjects discussed, and shorter communications. Partners avoid risky topics, topics related to basic values or hidden secrets, or topics that require extended discussion. A whole new set of ground rules comes into play, prescribing what interaction topics are acceptable and unacceptable.

Couples avoid inappropriate discussion with comments like "I'd rather not talk about that," "Let's call discussion of *that* off limits," or "*That* is none of your business," or with silence. Sometimes, to avoid a discussion, one partner will simply change the topic.

Stagnating

Stagnation means no motion or activity. As the disintegration progresses, partners decide that total silence in each other's presence is better than oral communication. Most areas and topics are closed off from discussion, even the superficial. Participants just mark time now until the end. When they have to talk they treat each other as strangers. Any discussion of the relationship is off limits. Knapp characterizes communication at this stage, when it occurs, as "more stylized, difficult, rigid, hesitant, awkward, and narrow."[45] The main theme characterizing this stage, according to him, can be phrased "There is little sense bringing anything up because I know what will happen, and it won't be particularly pleasant."

You may wonder why anyone would delay at the stagnating stage. There may be several reasons. Individuals may be gaining rewards outside their relationship—at work, in their primary family, or with another relationship partner. Some may simply be avoiding the eventual pain of termination or even be hoping to revive the relationship. Some, too, may enjoy giving back the pain they think they have already suffered—an eye for an eye!

Avoiding

Avoiding is a transition stage between stagnation and terminating the relationship. In avoidance, however, individuals attempt to remove themselves from the same physical environment. Participants seek to avoid face-to-face or voice-to-voice interaction of any kind. "I don't want to see you" and "I want to avoid communicating with you" are the messages being sent at this stage. Unfriendliness and antagonism may accompany these messages.

If the parents are unable to avoid one another, each will act as if the other is not present. They remove themselves from any interactions. They may inject negative evaluations of the other when possible. They seldom offer any rewards to the other like congratulations for getting a raise or a "Good luck" when the other is facing a difficult situation. These tactics tend to lower the other's self-concept and perhaps lead him or her to question "Am *I* still all right?" "Am *I* still lovable?"

Terminating

Often the **terminating** stage is not a stage at all but only the end or an announcement of final separation. Individuals settle their final joint concerns such as property, custody of children and pets, or the last phone bill. Also, they construct necessary psychological barriers to create distance: "It was bound to happen sooner or later," "It will be better for both of us," or "We were never *really* meant for each other." These make any final grieving—if it occurs—easier.

Termination dialogue is characterized by messages that create distance and disassociation. But these messages are likely to vary with the kind of relationship being dissolved and how the final dissolution takes place. Was there a lengthy commitment? What was the relative status between the partners? What kind of relationship was it? What kind of future relationship was desired? How was the dialogue conducted? By telephone? By letter? Face-to-face?

When Terminating Is Over

As anyone who has been part of a serious relationship knows, sometimes terminating is *never* over. The relationship remains in your consciousness forever—sometimes with good and sometimes with bad residual effects. But relationships change you. You are a different person because of them. They may alter your values, attitudes, and behaviors as well as your future plans, needs, and expectations. You may reassess yourself, and you may alter the criteria you use to judge potential relationship partners or relationships. You may decide to wait until you are more mature, more secure, or more prepared. You may choose never to enter a relationship again. You may choose to avoid people who are neurotic, nervous, smothering, mothering, domineering, or untrustworthy. Whatever the case, terminated relationships provide an enduring point of comparison for all future relationships.

Building Intimacy Skills

The concept of intimacy demands several things of relationship partners. Success in intimacy often results from a union of differences. The following sections describe how couples can use these differences to enhance their relationships.

Accept each other's differences For a satisfying relationship, partners must learn to accept each other's differences. One of the joys of intimacy is learning to receive and to know fully a person different from yourself. Too often these differences are allowed to drive people apart because one partner is unwilling to allow the other to be himself or herself.

Another problem is competition. Sometimes, you may reject your partner's differences and begin to compete with him or her. This happened in the beginning of my own relationship with my wife. Once we talked about it, we both realized that a strength for one of us—either one of us—was a strength for both of us. Although competition may be friendly at first, it can become critical and destructive.

See differences as a chance for intimacy Differences can provide a great opportunity for intimacy. One of the biggest contributions you can make to the development of trust and respect in a relationship is to understand the other as a unique human being. Frank had recently been overlooked for a promotion. He was feeling depressed, but he didn't feel he could talk to his good friend Jim about it. Frank and Jim were opposites. Jim was very assertive, outgoing, and buoyant. He seemed to sail through his

CONSIDER THIS

Many theories have been proposed to explain the rising number of divorces in our society. What is your explanation? Read through the following explanation of some of the possible culprits, and then answer the questions that follow.

> Some social scientists point to our society's shift from a family farm economy to factories, which undercut the importance of family, as the core of the problem. Others have blamed changes in law that make divorce easier, or women's emerging financial independence, which enables wives to leave bad marriages more easily. Some experts point to our society's increasing levels of violence, the psychological abuses of contempt and hostility that often precede divorce may be considered a low-level form of violence.*

Questions

1. Do you believe that there is a weakening of the social threads that keep marriages intact?
2. Why do some marriages last despite these pressures?
3. If you are currently married or you are planning to marry, how do you avoid falling on the bad side of the statistics?

*From John Gottman (with Nan Silver) *Why Marriages Succeed or Fail: What You Can Learn from the Breakthrough Research to Make Your Marriage Last* (New York: Simon & Schuster, 1994), p. 21.

life without problems. Frank was unassuming and rather shy. How could he expect a person like Jim to understand how he was feeling? When he finally decided to talk to Jim, he found Jim not only supportive but helpful in suggesting some options. Sharing his feelings with someone very different from himself gave him a new perspective on his problems—and served to strengthen their friendship.

See differences as complementary A good relationship rests on the formula "One plus one equals three." This simply means that the whole is greater than the sum of the parts. Each person in an intimate relationship is a unique human being who brings his or her uniqueness to the relationship. When you add the strength of one partner to the strength of the other, the result is a sum that could not be achieved by either acting separately: hence three instead of two in the formula.

"*You are about to experience something rare in your life, Stan—rejection.*"

Drawing by Korenz; © 1988 The New Yorker Magazine, Inc.

Sometimes it is the differences that keep the intimacy relationship strong. One partner is a socially quiet person and the other is an outgoing person. The socially quiet person helps contain the excesses of the other,

Joy and happiness can result when partners cannot only see but can celebrate each other's differences.

CONSIDER THIS

I must be ready to accept you as you are. If either of us comes to the relationship without this determination of mutual honesty and openness, there can be no friendship, no growth; rather there can be only a subject-object kind of thing that is typified by adolescent bickering, pouting, jealousy, anger and accusations.

John Powell, *Why Am I Afraid to Tell You Who I Am?* (Allen, TX: Argus Communications, 1969), p. 63.

while the outgoing person helps draw out and encourage the other. Robin is easily depressed and Andy is lighthearted. He helps her with her down moods, much as Jim helped Frank in the previous example:

> Depressed again, she sits in her dormitory room wondering how she can make it through the evening. Then she hears his Suzuki coming down the street and her sadness begins to lift.
>
> When she meets him at the door, she says: "I'm really down tonight." Not letting it faze him, he invites her to hop on and off they go for an evening of mirth that has her laughing as she walks back into her dorm room. How she loves him; like no one else he has brought happiness into her life.[47]

It is Robin's and Andy's differences that make their relationship strong because they add dimensions not present in their relationships with others.

See communication as essential Lack of communication in a relationship may indicate general withdrawal, unwillingness to engage in self-disclosure, and reduced supportiveness—all indicators that the relationship may be disintegrating. But communication in itself does not guarantee intimacy. If we are using communication to deceive our partner or simply evaluate him or her, the relationship may be faltering.

Good communication allows us to manage relationships to the mutual satisfaction of both partners. Whether the relationship is to be changed or dissolved, communication is essential to such negotiation.

Honesty is the most important element. Can partners express their needs, dissatisfactions, fears, and unfulfilled ambitions? Can partners look honestly at themselves, at each other, and at the relationship? Flexibility is also important. Can partners bend and change? Can they remain open to the other's feelings and to alternative points of view? Tentativeness is important too. Can partners phrase their ideas so they do not become absolutes? Can they look at decisions so they are not permanent, absolute, or final? Refraining from judgments is essential as well. Can partners keep from an "I'm right and you're wrong" frame of mind? Can they avoid name calling, labeling, and other biased approaches so that true discussion and sharing can take place?

▶ SUMMARY

In this chapter I have discussed the nature and meaning of intimate relationships. I have also discussed some of the nourishing ways of relating that can lead to the development and maintenance of such relationships. As the book began, I showed how personal strength and security are built on self-esteem and self-acceptance. But it is clear from this chapter that self-esteem and self-acceptance can best be nourished within intimate relationships. The ultimate in human interaction is intimate one-to-one relating, but what occurs in intimate relationships often results from what occurred previously within the family. Ironically, the base for self-esteem and self-acceptance established in intimate relationships is then likely to be played out in the families we create. Communication within families is likely to encourage further growth and change. Family communication is considered next.

▶ KEY TERMS

intimate relationships
core issues
initiating
experimenting
small talk
intensifying
integrating
revising
bonding
ritual
dependence
independence

interdependence
A Frame
H Frame
M Frame
predictability
uniqueness
obliqueness
exchange
storgic
manic
philos

pragmatic
erotic
agape
ludus
energy bucket
commitment
differentiating
circumscribing
stagnating
avoiding
terminating

▶ **NOTES**

1. Alan J. Sillars and Michael D. Scott, "Interpersonal Perception Between Intimates: An Integrative Review," *Human Communication Research* 10 (Fall 1983): 154. See Sillars and Scott, 153–176, for a summary of the research findings on intimate relationships.
2. Sillars and Scott, 162. They claim that several sources affirm this everyday observation.
3. Sillars and Scott, 163.
4. Sillars and Scott, 164.
5. The factors described in this section have been selected and discussed by Don E. Hamachek in *Encounters with Others: Interpersonal Relationships and You* (New York: Holt, Rinehart and Winston, 1982), 52–70.
6. Karen Dion, Ellen Berschied, and Elaine Walster, "What is Beautiful is Good," *Journal of Personality and Social Psychology* 24(1972): 285–290.
7. Hamachek, 59.
8. Hamachek, 65.
9. Mark L. Knapp, *Interpersonal Communication and Human Relationships* (Boston: Allyn and Bacon, 1984), 35–39.
10. Julia T. Wood, *Human Communication: A Symbolic Interactionist Perspective* (New York: Holt, Rinehart and Winston, 1982), 178–180.
11. Knapp, 36.
12. Knapp, 37.
13. Knapp, 38.
14. Wood, 178–179.
15. John Powell, *Why Am I Afraid to Tell You Who I Am?* (Allen, TX: Tabor Publishing, 1969), 62.
16. Andrew Greeley, *Sexual Intimacy* (Chicago: Thomas More Press, 1973), 26.
17. Kahlil Gibran, *The Prophet* (New York: Alfred A. Knopf, 1975), 15–16.
18. From John F. Crosby, *Illusion and Disillusionment*, 3d ed. (Belmont, CA: Wadsworth Publishing Co., 1985), 49.
19. I am indebted to Richard L. Conville for the ideas in this section. See Richard L. Conville, "Second-Order Development in Interpersonal Communication," *Human Communication Research* 9 (Spring 1983): 195–207.
20. Conville, 205.
21. Judy C. Pearson, *Lasting Love: What Keeps Couples Together* (Dubuque, IA: Wm. C. Brown Co., 1992), 2.
22. Pearson, 7.
23. Pearson, 8.
24. Pearson, 20–21 and 50.
25. Pearson, 21–26.

26. Pearson, 27.
27. Pearson, 28.
28. Pearson, 150.
29. Pearson, 32.
30. Pearson, 37.
31. Pearson, 50.
32. Pearson, 54.
33. Pearson, 73–74.
34. Pearson, 76–77.
35. Pearson, 77.
36. Pearson, 83.
37. Pearson, 84–85.
38. Pearson, 88.
39. Pearson, 127.
40. Pearson, 140.
41. Pearson, 162–163.
42. Pearson, 164–165.
43. Pearson, 116.
44. Knapp, 40–44.
45. Knapp, 42.
46. Charles M. Sell, *Achieving the Impossible: Intimate Marriage* (New York: Ballantine Books, 1982), 46.
47. Sell, 49–50.

▶ **FURTHER READING**

John Bradshaw, *Creating Love: The Next Stage of Growth* (New York: Bantam Books, 1992). In this easy-to-read, 374-page paperback, Bradshaw discusses the bafflement of love, the possibility of love, and creating love. He reveals the difficulties, alerts you to the decisions, and makes clear the requirements. Bradshaw provides hope and a new direction.

Rodney M. Cate and Sally A. Lloyd, *Courtship* (Newbury Park, CA: SAGE Publications, 1992). Cate and Lloyd discuss the importance of courtship, the history of courtship, models of courtship, factors predicting premarital relationship stability, courtships in crisis, and future perspectives on courtship. This is a research-oriented book for the serious student.

Barry Dym and Michael L. Glenn, *Couples: Exploring and Understanding the Cycles of Intimate Relationships* (New York: HarperCollins, 1993). Dym and Glenn chart the stages of a couple's journey together. Their stages, labeled expansion and promise, contraction, and resolution, offer couples a map. In-depth examples and accessible suggestions guide couples and individuals in how to manage their own periods of turmoil and transition. Original, engaging, and thoughtful.

Larry Glanz and Robert H. Phillips, *How to Start A Romantic Encounter: Where to Go to Find Love and What to Say When You Find It* (Garden City Park, NY: Avery Publishing Group, 1994). This is a how-to-do-it book for beginners that provides you with the important basics. Not only do Glanz and Phillips tell you where to go to make contacts, they tell you what to say to begin conversations. Their first part discusses enhancing your own assets; the second suggests new and unusual places to find people. Practical and full of sensible, down-to-earth advice for the novice.

Lori H. Gordon, *Passage to Intimacy* (New York: Simon & Schuster (a Fireside Book), 1993). Gordon begins by introducing the relationship road map. In her second section she discusses the arts of talking, listening, mind reading, anger, and fighting fair. In "Making the Invisible Visible," her third section, she looks at emotional roots, arriving at maturity, and taking charge. The final two sections are on pleasuring and putting it all together. Here are the key elements and basic tools that make up her 16-week PAIRS (Practical Application of Intimate Relationship Skills) program.

John Gottman, *Why Marriages Succeed or Fail: What You Can Learn from the Breakthrough Research to Make Your Marriage Last* (New York: Simon & Schuster, 1994). This book is based on Gottman's two-decade study of 2000 married couples. Here, he provides the tools that will make marriages last, and he makes suggestions for avoiding the most serious threats to lasting marriages: criticism, contempt, defensiveness, and stonewalling. With his self-tests, readers can determine their own strengths and weaknesses. Useful and full of interesting examples.

Susan S. Hendrick and Clyde Hendrick, *Romantic Love* (Newbury Park, CA: SAGE Publications, 1992). The authors examine love in close relationships, a brief history of love, contemporary research on love, love styles, the practice of love in everyday life, and love, in a broader context. Interesting, well-researched, and well-presented for the serious student.

Kathleen Wall and Gary Ferguson, *Lights of Passage: Rituals and Rites of Passage for the Problems and Pleasures of Modern Life* (San Francisco: HarperSanFrancisco, 1994). Wall and Ferguson provide a hopeful, enriching, and practical guide to reinventing the rituals and ceremonies needed to guide you through the different relationship stages. Although they include chapters on work and career, friendship, the family, midlife passage, and the last half of life, the book is listed here for its chapter "Ritual and Your Intimate Relationships." Interesting examples, practical advice, and a unique approach.

Ann Weber and John H. Harvey, eds. *Perspectives on Close Relationships* (Boston: Allyn and Bacon, 1994). This is an excellent compilation of academic articles on relationships. It covers such topics as how to study relationships, interpersonal attraction, communication, emotions, attachment, love, commitment, resource allocation, sexuality, jealousy, betrayal, physical abuse, and many more. This would make a fine textbook for an advanced interpersonal course focusing on relationships.

14

Experiencing Growth and Change: Communicating with Family

► CHAPTER OBJECTIVES

After reading this chapter, you should be able to

- ▲ Explain the three relational definitions that may affect family communication.
- ▲ Relate assumed or assigned roles to family communication.
- ▲ Identify communication barriers likely to occur in families.
- ▲ Explain the problems associated with appropriate rules, restricted freedom, emotional buildups, possessiveness, and double standards.
- ▲ Describe the difference between healthy rules and toxic rules.
- ▲ Describe the six-stage system for maintaining family relationships and for acquiring good arguing skills.
- ▲ Explain the importance of surveying in maintaining family relationships.
- ▲ List and explain the 11 skills for improving family communication.
- ▲ List ways for developing family unity.

▼ Carrié Ann grew up in a large family, the only girl among five boys. When she was seven, her mother underwent the first of numerous hospitalizations for mental illness. With her mother out of the home, Carrie Ann was pressed into service as a surrogate mother. She prepared the meals for her father and brothers, did the wash, cleaned the house, and performed all the tasks her mother was unable to do. She functioned in this role until she left for college. This experience in her family of origin groomed Carrie Ann to be a caretaker. She found meaning in taking care of others. The extent to which she was shaped by this role was demonstrated by the man she chose to marry as well as by her chosen career in nursing. Both involved caretaking.

Florin's immediate, original family was small. She had just two brothers. But her extended family was large, and she had stopped counting cousins at over 20. All family members lived in the neighborhood, and everyone supported everyone else. When there was trouble of any kind, people came out of the woodwork to show support. Florin was a rarity among members of her extended family because she liked school, did well, and went on to college because of her outstanding high school grades. Only one other member of her extended family had gone to college, and he had flunked out after two semesters. Florin's goal was to become a politician so that she could have a significant, noticeable influence on the lives she cared so much about. She majored in political science, took an active part in student government, and worked in the campaigns of local politicians. Throughout her schooling, her family stood by her—proud, strong, and supportive. She graduated summa cum laude as the president of her college class, and the first people she thanked in her valedictory address were the members of her family.

Tony's mother was a divorceé and family law attorney, and his father was a high school English teacher. Tony's older sister, Elissa, graduated from college, went on to graduate school in dentistry, and was currently beginning her practice in orthodontics. Because neither of Tony's parents had been home much during his upbringing, he and Elissa had become close even though she was more than six years older. Elissa had a strong influence on Tony, and when he had problems or concerns, he would take them to her rather than to either of his busy parents, both of whom would bring volumes of work home from the office. Because of his family, Tony learned to be independent. He read and studied for hours in the privacy of his bedroom, he shunned athletics and other physical activities, and he had several close friends whom he enjoyed being with on his own time.

Carrie Ann, Florin, and Tony each grew up in a different kind of family climate. These family climates had profound and lasting effects on their lives—the kind of people they were and the kind of people they would become. In this chapter, the special needs and demands of communicating interpersonally in the family will be discussed. You all have certain conceptions and expectations for your family. What are they based on? What are your values in this important area? Although Carrie Ann, Florin, and Tony could not change their pasts, they could influence their futures and the kinds of families they would establish.

There is no doubt about the influence of such concepts, discussed earlier, perception, self-disclosure, listening, and verbal and nonverbal communication on interaction within the family. You need some additional skills, however, to gain the most from interactions within the family. Many of these are extensions of ideas already mentioned; they are discussed here again because of their particular relevance to communication within the family.

▲▲▲ Family

"The greatest happiness and the deepest satisfaction in life, the most intense enthusiasm and the most profound inner peace," says Sven Wahlroos in *Family Communication*, "all come from being a member of a loving family."[1] The reverse is also true: some of the greatest pain can come from family relationships. You choose your friends, but you do not choose your family. You can move in and out of relationships with most people, but it is often more difficult with family members. Your choices and your freedom are more limited within family relationships. Family relationships present unique problems and unique satisfactions in interpersonal communication.

Relational Definitions[2]

One way to begin thinking about family communication is by looking at relationship types. This examination offers an overall perspective and some basic understandings. Mary Anne Fitzpatrick and her colleagues, researchers on relationships, have identified three relational definitions: traditionals, independents, and separates.[3] As you will see, when each is identified, these may have a strong effect on the nature and amount of communication that occurs within the family.

Traditionals have conventional ideas about marital roles. That means, for example, that they expect the male to be dominant and the female to be submissive. Even within dominant and submissive roles, a willingness to deal with conflict accompanied by a lack of assertiveness may still indicate expectations of equality. That is, it should be clear that holding traditional values about male and female roles does not mean that each individual is not valued equally in the relationship. Also, traditionals tend to expect more intimacy from their spouses. This involves inclusion, affection, depth, and possibly more similarity and involvement.

Independents are less conventional in their beliefs. With respect to sharing, they occupy a central position between traditionals and separates, sharing more than separates and less than traditionals. Like traditionals, they are expressive in their communication and perceive themselves to be high self-disclosers. Independents expect relational messages to involve a desire for increased intimacy, though not as much inclusion and similarity as traditionals expect. In addition, they expect a lack of formality and an emphasis on equality.

Separates have a lower expectation for intimacy than other couples. They tend to share less, express less positive feelings, and perceive less self-disclosure than the other relational types. Because they tend to avoid conflict and expect less intimacy, they may expect less emotional arousal as well. Because they hold conventional ideologies, they may expect the male to be more dominant. Because often they are committed to two opposing ideologies—traditionalism and uncertainty—they may express ambivalence with respect to relational values. This is likely to be revealed in less certainty and rigidity concerning relational expectations; thus, there are likely to be discrepancies between expectations set and expectations met. But because of ambivalence, these discrepancies are likely to have less relational impact on separates than on traditionals and independents.

It is important to point out there are mixed types as well. Research is not complete on mixed types; however, separates and traditionals tend to openly express affection to one another. Although competitive, they attempt to compromise when gaining compliance from their spouses. Also, they are quite energetic when attempting to persuade one another. Relational messages of dominance and intimacy (particularly affection) are important to all mixed types.

The point of this discussion is not to pigeonhole others with exact labels and behavior expectations. The point is to begin to try to understand why others behave as they do so that you can understand how and why you communicate as you do within your family units. One style isn't right and another wrong. In many cases, people are defined relationally because of personality, the models to which they have been exposed (their own families), personal preferences, and the other person in the relationship. But, as previously explained, their relational definition will affect the nature and amount of their communication.

The Familiar Question: Who Am I?

A useful way to begin to think about communicating with your family is to think about the various family roles you may have assumed or been assigned. "Sister" or "daughter" are some obvious roles, but for most of you things are more complicated than that. There are other influences that decide your role. Whether you are male or female may have determined whether you mowed the lawn or did the dishes, carried out the garbage or cleaned the house, were given freedom in dating or were more controlled—just to cite some obvious examples. Your sex may have affected how you were perceived: forthright, aggressive, athletic, awkward, friendly, or mischievous.

Physical and mental attributes also affect the role you may have assumed or been assigned. The physically biggest child in a family may be perceived as the clumsiest or may be given the most responsibility. The smartest may have had "success" in school drilled into him or her since kindergarten. Family members may peg a highly emotional child as the family troublemaker, the one who starts arguments. These qualities (and many more) determine our roles to a great extent. Because they tend to be constantly reinforced, they come to be the roles with which you feel most comfortable.

Communication Barriers in the Family

Although the emphasis here is on the family in which you grew up, because of its importance in establishing many of your patterns of communication, some of these things will operate in the family you may form for yourself later on. You will be establishing another pattern of roles in that family. These roles will be based in part on what your growing-up experience was.

Family roles provide a subtle but continuing influence on your life. One of the first communication barriers that may develop out of family

TRY THIS

Take a moment to identify your family's cast of characters. Using your own definition for each of the roles listed, identify the family member who played the role in your original family, and whether or not the role continues today in adulthood. As you assign roles, remember three things: (1) Not every family has players for all the roles. (2) There may be roles played in your family not included in this list. (3) Some family members play more than one role.

Family Role	Family Member	Role Continues (yes or no)
Caretaker	_____	_____
Hero	_____	_____
Scapegoat	_____	_____
Lost Child	_____	_____
Mascot	_____	_____
Perfectionist	_____	_____
Persecutor	_____	_____
Rescuer	_____	_____
Abuser	_____	_____
Victim	_____	_____
Dunce	_____	_____
Bully	_____	_____
Odd Person Out	_____	_____
Guru	_____	_____
Critic	_____	_____
Angel	_____	_____
Other	_____	_____

*From William Blevins, *Your Family, Your Self: How to Analyze Your Family System to Understand Yourself, and Achieve More Satisfying Relationships With Your Loved Ones* (Oakland, CA: New Harbinger Publications, 1993), pp. 51–52.

roles is the tendency within the family to see a family member *only* in one role. This does not allow for growth or change. Despite the fact that you may have become outgoing or more independent, family members may still treat you as if you are shy or dependent. You may become a corporation president, but family members may still perceive you as a helpless kid sister. This not only may limit your own possibilities for change but may cause breakdowns in communication resulting from misperceptions and false assumptions. It has the potential to drive you away from your family.

There is a related communication problem, the assumption that no matter *what* you actually say, the other members of your family will understand you. Though family members often communicate with each other very efficiently by means of a kind of communication shorthand, sometimes you come to depend too much on this system of signals and implied meanings. An example of this is the son who agreed with his father that whenever he wanted to use the family car, he would make arrangements with him in advance. The son used the car, and the father accused him of violating the agreement. The son insisted he had told him: "You saw me washing and waxing the car, and you know I never do that unless I'm planning to use it." Your meaning is not always as clear as you might think, even within your own family.

In the family relationship, much **mutual "picture taking"** goes on. That is, members are often involved in forming mental pictures of how others are feeling, reacting, or thinking. As Virginia Satir, a leader in the field of family therapy, states in *Peoplemaking:* "The people involved may not share their pictures, the meanings they give the pictures, nor the feelings the pictures arouse."[4] Those involved guess at meaning and then assume those guesses are facts. This guessing procedure results in a great many unnecessary family communication barriers.

You simply cannot assume that another person always knows what you mean, even if you have grown up with that person. The reason this assumption causes special problems in the family is that people who share such a close relationship feel they *should* be able to read each other's minds. Everyone is supposed to know how everyone else feels—no one needs to say or show what he or she feels. Serious misunderstandings can result when this doesn't work. Think of a time when you felt *very strongly* that the family should take a specific vacation, make a certain purchase, or eat at a certain restaurant. Did you reveal this strong feeling to other family members? Just because you felt it does not mean you showed it to others. You are not as transparent to others as you are to yourself.

This extends to your policy of criticizing and complimenting other family members, too. Whether you're aware of it or not, you look to your families for reinforcement and rewards. You may not voice praise or gratitude, because you expect family members to know your feelings without spelling them out. But your message doesn't always get through, and it should. A pat on the back is not only welcomed but needed from time to time. Not surprisingly, family members are often less inclined to hold back criticisms of each other. When the free and heavy flow of criticism gets to be too much, family relationships may turn into nothing more than opportunities for negative exchanges, and estrangement and resentment result. Wahlroos even goes so far as to say that "the main reason for . . . discord [in families] is simply that the consciously felt love and the good intentions harbored by the family members are not *communicated* in such a way that they are recognized."[5]

It should be acknowledged, too, that not all family relationships are conducted by healthy people in healthy situations. What is offered in this chapter is an ideal scenario. It may be that some families have to work very hard just to create a climate for communication. "Making contact," as Satir calls it, can be a major accomplishment in family situations involving child abuse, alcoholism, or other serious problems. In some such situations, professional counseling is needed to facilitate communication among family members.

Other Behaviors That May Cause Problems

Such behaviors as inappropriate rules, restricting the freedoms of others, allowing emotional buildups, possessiveness, and double standards can cause problems in family relationships as well.

Inappropriate rules *are those that do not accomplish goals for the common good of the family and generate unhealthy behavior patterns.*[6] Obviously, **appropriate rules** accomplish goals for the common good of the family and generate healthy behavior patterns. People are rule makers and rule followers. The family is a rule-governed system. Rules in families make it possible for family members to live without getting in each other's way or violating other's rights. The appropriateness and logic of the rules affects both family and individual health. For example, in our household, rules governed the privacy of one's bedroom; protection from intrusion when using the bathroom; calling when plans changed, especially when it infringed on the common dinner time; length of time phone lines could be tied up; the process of taking phone messages for other family members; and even where family members sat around the table. "Individuals who grow up in a family regulated by appropriate rules tend to be physically, spiritually, and emotionally healthier than those who live in families with unhealthy and rigid rules."[7]

Rules can be overt or covert. An **overt rule** is openly communicated to family members. Usually such rules have high visibility, and they are reinforced by rewards and punishments. For example, in our household, overt rules governed who cleaned the dishes after meals, how family members were expected to interact with each other, how members were to behave in certain situations (like church or the grocery store), and what was or was not permissible behavior (foul language was never permissible).

What behaviors could possibly have caused problems here? What are the likely outcomes of this situation?

Covert rules are neither clear nor openly communicated. Covert rules might govern which parent you would ask if you needed more money, which you would ask if you had a personal question or problem, or which you would ask if you wanted permission to do something. An example of a covert rule in our household occurs in our family room. When Dad is in the room, he gets the recliner. This has never been specifically stated, and everyone feels comfortable using the chair when Dad isn't present. Even when people are told they can remain in the chair, they will move from "Dad's chair" when Dad enters the room.

Rules can be flexible or rigid. **Flexible rules** can be relaxed or even changed to meet the demands of unusual circumstances. For example, we would relax curfews for our children for a prom or for a special ball game. Special concerts, visits by relatives, or community activities might set aside the rule prohibiting social activities on school nights. Flexible rules are important to the needs and development of family members. As children get older and grow more responsible, flexible rules are altered to reflect those changes. Flexible rules promote the health of families and tend to cause a lower level of stress and anxiety among members.

Rigid rules focus on strict obedience regardless of the situation. They must be followed without deviation. For example, in one home, children must turn off television precisely at 9 P.M. In another, curfews are never to be broken under any circumstances. In yet another, "Dad's word is the final word on everything." "In more dysfunctional families, the letter of the law takes precedence over individual needs."[8]

What are healthy rules?[9] There are nine characteristics of healthy family rules.

Healthy Rules:
   1. Are attainable. They can realistically be carried out and are consistent with reality.
   2. Promote openness. Family members should feel free to discuss almost any issue with frankness and candor. Of course, discretion and good sense must govern openness.
   3. Confirm a person's inherent worth and dignity. Such rules do not put family members down or make them feel unworthy.
   4. Foster feelings of unconditional acceptance and love. They require accountability, but in a manner that reinforces the child's basic sense of being loved, even if the parent is sometimes angry.
   5. Benefit all family members. They are not designed merely for the well-being of the parents or other particular family members.
   6. Permit family members to be different from one another. They don't violate a member's uniqueness or potential for growth and change.
   7. Recognize the equal worth of each family member. Even though family members all have different roles, responsibilities, limits of freedom, and amounts of authority, they still must be recognized as having equal worth and dignity as human beings.
   8. Are learning tools, enabling family members to discover appropriate, functional, and acceptable behaviors. For instance, rules about brushing one's teeth or taking a bath enable children to learn important lessons about personal hygiene.
   9. Embrace basic freedoms that are the birthright of every human being. These freedoms include a person's right to have his or her own perceptions, feelings, thoughts, desires, and beliefs.

   Restricted freedom *means less opportunity to behave at any moment just as you please.* Living with others may affect the time you may study, eat, sleep, dress, or even use the bathroom. When freedoms are restricted, interpersonal stress results. For example, one parent may have just come home after a harried day of decision making at work. It may be later than usual. As he or she comes in the door, a new set of decisions may have to be faced: homework that is not finished, television-related requests, civic or community events, invitations from friends, requests for use of the car, and on and on. Such demands and responsibilities are part of family membership, but they can also cause stress. Often they carry with them unstated assumptions and understandings: to be a "good father" you

CONSIDER THIS

Most family functioning is regulated by rules. **Toxic rules** are those that produce "dis-ease" among family members. They destabilize the balance of the family, increase family dysfunction, and impede family relationships. Read the following information about toxic rules, and answer the questions that follow.

> Over the past decade, a number of professionals with an expertise in family therapy have explored the negative consequences of toxic rules, especially in codependent families.* Eight particular rules have been isolated that are characteristic of severely dysfunctional families.†

1. Don't talk about problems.
2. Don't express feelings.
3. Don't communicate directly.
4. Don't have realistic expectations.
5. Don't be selfish.
6. Do as I say, not as I do.
7. It's not okay to play.
8. Don't rock the boat.‡

Questions
1. From your own experience, can you see how these toxic rules are likely to create dysfunction?
2. Can you add any other toxic rules that are not mentioned here?
3. If you were in a family that used toxic rules, what procedure might you use to help family members recognize the rules being used?
4. Are the rules that you experienced in your original family ones that you would like to live by, or are they rules that you are likely to rebel against? Can you see how the rules of your original family are likely to have a profound effect on how you live your adult life?

*See J. Bradshaw, *Bradshaw on the Family* (Deerfield Beach, FL: Health Communications, 1988); J. A. Kitchens, *Understanding and Treating Codependence* (Englewood Cliffs, NJ: Prentice-Hall, 1991); and S. Wegscheider, *Another Chance: Hope and Health for the Alcoholic Family* (Palo Alto, CA: Science and Behavior Books, 1981).

†See R. Subby and J. Friel, "Codependency—A Paradoxical Dependency." *Codependency: An Emerging Issue.* Pompano Beach, FL: Health Communications, 1984).

‡From William Blevins, *Your Family, Your Self: How to Analyze Your Family System to Understand Yourself, and Achieve More Satisfying Relationships With Your Loved Ones* (Oakland, CA: New Harbinger Publications, Inc., 1993), p. 99.

should help Tim with his homework, or to be "good neighbors" you should go over to the Joneses' open house tonight, or to be "good parents" or "good citizens" you should go to the school board meeting tonight. As well as assumptions and understandings, sometimes such decisions also carry emotional freight. This can occur when one spouse makes an informal commitment to something, and the other spouse makes a decision that does not correspond with or counters the other. One spouse, for example, may decide to go golfing or bowling when the other believes that that time should be spent with the children.

It may take a while for someone who has been used to living alone to become "we" oriented. It takes a while to learn how to share one's space, time, and physical objects with another person, to be able to say, in response to an invitation, "I can't tell you whether or not we can come; I'll have to check with . . . " or "I'll have to check our calendar." With the relinquishment of certain freedoms, tension and stress must be accommodated.

Emotional buildups *are stored-up thoughts and feelings.* To the words, phrases, and situations that you are involved in, you add emotional associations. Sometimes the emotional link is already so strong that all another person has to do is refer to it, like saying "I saw Fred today" to activate the emotional avalanche "I thought we agreed that you were never going to see him again!" The more intimate the relationship, the more likely emotional buildups are to occur. Questions such as "Have you studied?" "Have you practiced?" "Can I use the car?" or "Can I borrow your tools?" are likely to have powerful linkages because of many shared past experiences. Think of all the shared recollections that are likely in such situations: times when studying or practicing was not given a first or even a high priority, or times when the car was left dirty or out of gas, or still other times when tools were lost or misplaced. When these shared experiences have occurred, a question that looks like a simple request for information is no longer perceived as one. Emotional linkages will affect the way the question is asked, the way it is perceived, and the behavior that is likely to follow.

Possessiveness in family relationships occurs *when members feel they have a right to control or influence the behaviors of one another.* This is a normal feeling that grows out of the interpretation of family situations by members belonging to the family. You hear it said, "That's my girl . . . " or "As long as you live in this house, you aren't going to do that." Or people may make statements like "He's my husband" or "He's my son." There are expectations that accompany these statements and feelings—expectations that imply control.

Parents are known to say such things as "If you really cared about us you would . . . " or "If you loved us, you wouldn't act that way." Although it is natural to want to please those you love, it is when others' expectations include changes in behavior that control and possessiveness are demonstrated.

Double standards also can cause problems among family members. Double standards emerge when *parents expect their children to follow rules or perform rituals from which they, as parents, are exempt.* Parents often follow a "do as I say, not as I do" philosophy. The rules may have to do with lying, stealing, or, on a smaller scale, interrupting others or talking with one's mouth full. Rituals may prescribe proper eating habits, going to church, or other daily or weekly occurrences. Often there is a distinct gap between what the parents do and what they expect of their children.

A double standard may also be operative between other segments of the family. For example, there may be a stiff requirement that one child must keep a bedroom neat because it is visible to everyone, including guests, whereas the other children, whose bedrooms are in another part of the house, do not have the same requirement. It may occur, too, over the way chores are assigned or over who must fill in when someone is not present. The cry "it's not fair" is a common one in some households. Some parents stress to their children that things are *not* equal: life is not equal for all. Different privileges may be considered appropriate for male and female children. A teenage boy, for example, may be allowed to travel alone some distance from home, whereas a teenage girl may be more restricted. The point here is not whether double standards operate, or whether they are good or bad, but simply that they can become points of conflict within a family.

Maintaining Family Relationships

Most people want to maintain or improve their family relationships. Aware, open people, or those who want to become more aware and open, can utilize the following system. This system provides the knowledge, understanding, and equipment that will enable people to make conscious, deliberate use of the process of interaction in family situations. It is from such interaction in meaningful situations that change and growth can occur. If a family already has established a foundation of mutual affection and shared interests, then acquiring good arguing skills will give them a much better chance of having healthy, satisfying interactions that are likely to continue into the future.[10]

Stage 1: Seek information   Although this stage appears obvious, it is not. If you have been offended by someone else's actions, you may charge into the situation without investigating how the other person feels, trying to get even without sufficient knowledge or a solid foundation on which to base your response. You may tend to "shoot from the hip" because it is easier, because you let your emotions take over, or because that is your problem-solving style.

Seeking information is a continual, rational process that requires time and commitment. It requires that you step back from the immediate situation occasionally and answer some crucial questions. Although these

TRY THIS

On what issues do members of your family have strong emotional linkages? Are they attached to such issues as these?

▲ religion
▲ politics
▲ sex
▲ studying
▲ your use of time
▲ how seriously you take school
▲ what you wear
▲ your friends

▲ how late you stay up
▲ how much television you watch
▲ what you read
▲ where you go
▲ what you eat
▲ how late you stay up
▲ your appearance

How do you face these issues when you know strong emotional linkages are present? Can you avoid emotional explosions over them? Is avoidance one of the techniques you use? Is it easier to talk to some family members about them than others? Do you think complete avoidance contributes to a healthy interpersonal relationship? Is it likely that emotional linkages will change on some of the issues above? Is so, what may contribute to the change?

questions should be answered with respect to the immediate situation, answers will not be as difficult to discover if the process has indeed been ongoing:

1. Who am I in this family?
2. How do I relate to others?
3. How do they relate to me?
4. How do we communicate?
5. How do we normally resolve problems?

Seeking information *means being aware of and sensitive to what is occurring around you.* Keep your eyes and ears open all the time. Then, when problems arise, they occur in an already established matrix of information and knowledge.

You may be asking, "But how do I keep my emotions in check?" First, if emotions are intense, it might be wise to put off any discussion of the immediate problem until after a brief cooling-off period (20 to 30 minutes). Second, it is important to understand that emotional involvement is a natural, normal part of family problem solving. Emotions lie at the heart of everything you think and do. Third, they are an integral part of the information-seeking stage, and another set of questions needs to be asked:

CONSIDER THIS

Is there a relationship between gender and power in family units? Read the following explanation, and answer the questions that follow.

> Couples in more traditional sex role relationships would be expected to have less open conflict and negotiation because the roles, rules, and norms are more clearly established in the relationships—the power matrix in the relationship is laid down by the conventions and normative prescriptions of appropriate husband-wife behavior.* On the other hand, couples in marriages where partners have little commitment to traditional sex roles will be more likely to engage in open conflict, negotiation, and bargaining with the partner. The roles, rules, and norms of this marriage, along with the distribution of power, need to be defined and renegotiated with changes in the relationships and/or the environment.†

Questions

1. Are traditional sex roles in families acceptable to you, or do you have little commitment to traditional sex roles?
2. Would you expect that people who see their marriages as both equitable (the level of rewards and the relative gains between partners are equal) and equal (each partner gets what he or she contributes, but the contributions are very different) tend to be more satisfied with their marriages and expect their marriages to last longer? Or would you expect that traditional expectations would produce greater satisfaction?
3. How would you go about defining and negotiating roles, rules, norms, and the distribution of power with a potential marriage partner? Given a choice between accepting tradition, or having to engage in conflict, negotiation, and bargaining, what would be your choice?
4. If you perceived injustice and inequality in roles, rules, norms, and the distribution of power in your original family, how would you go about influencing change? Or would you?

*See J. Scanzoni and G. L. Fox, "Sex Roles, Families and Society: The Seventies and Beyond," *Journal of Marriage and the Family,* 42 (1980): 743–756.
†From Patricia Noller and Mary Anne Fitzpatrick, *Communication in Family Relationships* (Englewood Cliffs, NJ: Prentice-Hall, 1993), p. 128.

Here is a family making conscious, deliberate use of the process of interaction to foster change and growth. What are the likely benefits?

1. What are my feelings on this issue?
2. How intense are they?
3. What are the other's feelings on the issue?
4. How intense are they?
5. How will our feelings interact?
6. How are feelings likely to affect those involved? To affect others—even those not directly involved with the problem now?

The final aspect of Stage 1 has been labeled by psychologist John Gottman as **mind-reading strategies,**[11] *attempts to put the pieces of the puzzle together.* This may entail methodical, consistent detective work. It may mean taking the position of an outsider—someone outside the immediate situation—and trying to respond as an objective bystander would. Or you may gain such a picture as the result of the "aha!" experience—the meaning suddenly occurs to you. Whatever process you use, you must try to lay the foundation for later stages by trying to understand as much about the feelings, opinions, and motives of the other person as possible—guessing, anticipating, perceiving, and observing—and combining these with all other interacting ingredients.

Stage 2: Share meanings No situation has exactly the same meaning for each of the people involved. If two or more people do not sit down and organize the data and identify (together) the various thoughts and feelings that bear on the problem, they are likely to continue to act unilaterally.

Sharing meanings is a give-and-take process of *open, trusting, honest interaction between people.* It allows underlying wishes, guilts, and jealousies to be brought to the surface. It helps clarify options and evaluate their appropriateness and workability.

In his article "Avoiding Couple Karate," Anthony Brandt provides an example of the benefits of sharing meaning:

> The happily married couples come to all agreements fairly readily, either through one partner giving in to the other without resentment or through compromise:
>
> "We spent all of Christmas at your mother's last year. This time let's spend it at my mother's."
>
> "Yeah, you're right, that's not fair. How about 50–50 this year?"[12]

Perhaps the biggest barrier to sharing meaning is the tendency to blame. Hating to be found wrong, you may blame another for your difficulty and simply not listen to the other's side of the discussion. Or you may place all the blame on yourself, no matter what the situation, and begin the sharing in a one-down position. The best sharing is equal, allows give-and-take, deals with the facts, has both parties taking responsibility, and strives for mutual growth and understanding.

One warning regarding open communication within the family is necessary. There are sometimes collusions (secret agreements), years old, that when revealed can create more problems and emotional responses rather than helping. The best advice here is that communication channels be opened gradually, with lower levels of self-disclosure before any "heavy" revelations of emotional "stashes."

Stage 3: State alternatives In 1910, in his book *How We Think,* and as part of the plan he labeled "reflective thinking," John Dewey called for the "cultivation of a variety of alternative suggestions."[13] Once again, the need to **state alternatives** may seem too obvious a stage of problem solving to deserve mention. But think about how open and receptive you are to various other ways of proceeding when you think *you* have the answer, the right method, or the only way. People tend to see the world through self-prescribed lenses.

In this stage, the partners make conscious and deliberate efforts to discover and evaluate all possible alternatives. This can be an opportunity to be speculative and adventuresome. Alternatives do not need to be polished proposals; they can be merely suppositions and guesses.

Stage 4: Select solutions   From the mixture developed in Stage 3, partners need to weigh the advantages of the alternatives suggested, as well as the strengths and weaknesses of possible combinations of those alternatives, and **select solutions**. Often, it is a combination that best satisfies both parties.

Looking back to the discussion of styles of handling conflict in Chapter 11, it is clear that there are really five basic ways in which decisions are made in families, and that these can be identified in terms of the dimensions of assertiveness and cooperation. A family member who is highly assertive and uncooperative uses a competing style of problem solving characterized by power, persuasion, and coercion. If another family member wants to prevent conflict or avert a potential blowup, he or she may assume an avoiding style despite its weaknesses. Sometimes a problem is just not worth getting upset over or spending time on. But when avoiding becomes the only way to achieve peace, the family members lose mutuality, and the avoiding person loses a voice in problem solving.

The highly cooperative and nonassertive person seeks to satisfy the other person(s) at all costs. This accommodating style may be appropriate for short-range, unimportant, unemotional issues. Some people can build relationships based on accommodation because, as we saw in Chapter 11, it can build goodwill, promote harmony, avoid disruption, and reduce the power factor in a relationship. Its major weakness is that it depends on a high degree of nonassertiveness in one of the members. Mutuality—the coming together of people on a near or equal footing—requires some degree of assertiveness by all parties.

The middle position on both dimensions is compromising, whereby people give in or agree even though they may not be pleased or satisfied with the decision.

Collaborating is the method that involves the highest degree of both assertiveness and cooperation. In collaboration, respect is shown for everyone, and the solution will be based on what is appropriate and constructive for the family as a whole. In solving problems, it is not necessary for all parties to agree. They could agree to disagree. They could agree to allow all those involved to do as they wish. Collaboration is based on every family member's appreciation of and respect for one another's uniqueness and for the preservation of the family relationship as a whole.

Stage 5: Start implementation   Selecting the solution is of little value if no effort is made to put it into practice: to **start implementation.** Sharing meaning is important at this stage, too, to make certain both sides perceive the same solution and the same methods of implementation. How often have you found yourself saying, "Yes, I remember what we agreed upon, but I thought we were going to do it this way." Feelings and reactions need to be controlled. Judgment about the final outcome needs to be suspended until the solution is tried.

The most important ingredient you can contribute to starting the implementation process is personal responsibility. You should feel responsible for helping the agreed-upon solution work. You should feel responsible because you care about others. You should feel responsible, too, because of a commitment to the relationship. You also should feel responsible because of your human need to learn and grow. But you can feel responsible for implementing the decision only if you have had input into it and agree with it. Indeed, that is what collaboration is all about.

Stage 6: Survey results   There are no guarantees that solutions will work when they are implemented. Surveying the results of Stage 5 may be a continuation of Stage 1: seeking information. You need to **survey results** by monitoring the process, asking such questions as these:

1. Is the solution working?
2. Is everyone pleased with the results?
3. Are there changes that need to, or can, be made to improve effectiveness or pleasure?

Surveying also is a continual process of sharing meaning. In many cases, several different solutions will be going on at the same time. To make certain the relationship is continuing as expected, communication between participants must be a regular feature. One family member may think things are all right while the other is playing the silent role. Many people have well-entrenched habits of assuming they know what the other person means, thinks, feels, or intends. Surveying should involve adapting to each other under the new conditions, altering circumstances as needed, and gaining renewed balance or stability in the relationship. Although surveying results is a final stage in the problem-solving system, it is also an integral part of the ongoing process of interaction. It never really ends.

This six-stage program can be useful for problem solving if your commitment to maintaining and improving family relationships is strong, and if you want to grow closer to the other members. Putting it into effect takes work and practice. Do not let occasional failures deter you. Gradually, sometimes laboriously, you will find yourself altering old ways and shifting from former habits. Eventually, perhaps even unknowingly, the process will become second nature.

Building Family Communication Skills

In his book *Breaking Free of Addictive Family Relationships: Healing Your Own Inner Child* (1991), Barry K. Weinhold, a licensed psychologist, author of 12 books, professor of education at the University of Colorado,

CONSIDER THIS

It is easy to believe that all families tend to be the same. Unless you have actually experienced a family from another culture, you may not be aware of how extensive the differences are likely to be. Read the following dialogue from a Mexican American household, and answer the questions that follow.

"You are going out so soon? At what time will you be back, *hijo?*" the mother asks as she approaches her son and fixes the collar of his shirt. She touches his cheek with the palm of her hand while looking at him with love and pride. Manuel, a 6-foot-tall, 25-year-old man, checks the rest of his attire, then embraces his mother and kisses her farewell on the cheek.

"I will be back soon, no later than 11," he replies. "Jenny and I are going to the movies. And, yes, *Mami,* I left the money for the rent on your night table, where Cristina left the money for the food."

As he departs, his sister Cristina enters the apartment. "Have fun, Manuel," she says and turns around to kiss her mother on the cheek. "*Hola, Mami.* What are we having for supper? Is Dad still at work? Where is Uncle Beto? Is Grandma asleep?" She sits on a couch.

"Cristina," the mother says without answering any of her questions, "when are you going to get married to Joe? He is four years older than you; you are 22, and you will be graduating from college this year. We will help you get started and help you along. Joe is a good, hardworking young man."*

Questions

1. How does this dialogue differ from what might take place in an Anglo-American family? Could the interdependence of family members in the Mexican American household versus the independence of family members in the Anglo- (or Euro-) American household account for some of the differences?
2. Is sharing time in conversation a valued form of interaction in most Anglo-American households?
3. Do touch, affection, and greeting rituals play an important role in most Anglo-American households?
4. Is there likely to be some effect on family members with respect to how household communication is conducted? What might the effects be? Could one effect be how quickly family members are likely to leave the home—that is, how soon they are likely to become independent from the family?

*From Margarita Gangotena, "The Rhetoric of *La Familia* among Mexican Americans," in *Our Voices: Essays in Culture, Ethnicity, and Communication—An Intercultural Anthology,* ed. Alberto Gonzalez, Marsha Houston, and Victoria Chen (pp. 69–80) (Los Angeles, CA: Roxbury Publishing Company, 1994), p. 69.

and co-founder of the Colorado Institute for Conflict Resolution and Creative Leadership, lists 11 characteristics of a dysfunctional family. He says, "as many as 97 out of 100 families may be dysfunctional and addictive in some major areas."[14] To improve skills would mean turning his dysfunctions into functions—positive features. Here I have listed them as skills. Healthy families:

Maintain flexibility in the rules established There must be rules, of course, but a rigid and compulsive set of rules that everyone has to follow perfectly so as not to get into trouble becomes militaristic, restrictive, inhibiting, and unnecessarily annoying in families. Flexibility is an important key to proper family functioning.

Maintain flexibility in the roles given Often, it is easier to function when prescribed roles are set and all members perform their roles as dictated. This is easy because expectations and behaviors are predictable and seldom spontaneous. But just as rules can be stifling, so can roles. First, people feel better if they can be part of the process of deciding on roles. Second, there should be opportunities for change and even flexibility within the system.

Maintain open communication Family members learn trust by being trusted. Strive to keep family secrets to a minimum. Closeness and security often are built by sharing things that happen with all members of the family. Excluding members and keeping and telling secrets not only create distrust but generate jealousy, envy, and conflict.

Create positive humor People who laugh together stay together. Dysfunctional families are serious and burdened. The humor that exists is often sarcastic, snide, cynical, or rude. People are made fun of, or children become the butt of jokes. Often, positive humor is not planned; it is spontaneous and arises naturally from daily activities, interactions, and occurrences.

Allow for personal privacy, and establish clear personal boundaries Family members need their own personal space, their own clothing, and their own personal belongings. A study I once saw suggested that family happiness was correlated with the number of bathrooms in the home. The more bathrooms, the more satisfaction family members expressed with the family. It makes sense, since bathrooms provide places for personal privacy.

Establish family traditions When families can celebrate birthdays and holidays together, or when they can share a common meal, or when they can travel and have experiences together, they construct a sense of loyalty through common experiences and values. These rich, meaningful, positive experiences help members relate to the family in positive ways and make it unnecessary to develop a false sense of loyalty that is used to control family members and keep them dependent on the family.

Develop a healthy view of others   The family is part of a societal matrix of units that are interdependent. An attitude of resistance to outsiders, a "we versus them" attitude, can create distrust, contempt, and an unhealthy outlook. A healthy, happy, balanced home life can help foster a healthy, happy, balanced view of others.

Allow members to express their feelings no matter how strong   Think about it: where do family members feel secure, comfortable, and self-confident enough to express their innermost (strongest) feelings? Home is a natural place for this. When compulsive and addictive behaviors are used to suppress or avoid strong feelings, this is unnatural and creates confusion, hostility, and perhaps conflict. It is unhealthy. When people live together, strong feelings will be felt. They need a supportive and encouraging atmosphere to promote effective psychological health. This means that strong feelings need a convenient and available communication channel. Supportive families offer this.

Permit conflict   Like strong feelings, conflict will occur. With an understanding of how to manage conflict properly, one does not need to be fearful of it. It should not be denied or ignored. Conflict can improve the

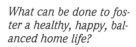

What can be done to foster a healthy, happy, balanced home life?

What are some of the ways the family you grew up in developed family unity?

quality of the family, stimulate member involvement in family problems and decisions, and build cohesion (loyalty) within the family unit.

View change as positive   The healthy family is a dynamic unit. This means that it is always growing, developing, changing, and progressing. This is one reason why communication within the family is so important—it helps everyone stay in touch with the changes. Talk about it. The family of today is *not* the family of tomorrow or the next day. If it is, it is stagnant, uninteresting, and unwilling to try new things.

Develop family unity   Many of the suggestions already made will assist in developing family unity, especially those under "establish family traditions." Here are some other suggestions: don't show favoritism, treat all members with respect, keep everyone involved and active in family decision making, make everyone feel secure and protected, listen to each other, do things as a family unit, and learn things together. These are the

CONSIDER THIS

The right to life, the right to liberty, and the right to property are granted to individuals by the United States Constitution. Are there times when individual rights conflict with family rights? Read the following passage, and answer the questions that follow.

> The courts continue to deny marriage rights to homosexual couples. Although the Supreme Court has not spoken on this issue, several states have, including Washington in 1974, where the state court ruled that same-sex marriages were distinct from other monogamous unions because of the impossibility of reproduction.* That impossibility, though, has not deterred thousands of gay and lesbian couples from establishing exclusive, permanent, committed relationships, characterized by common residence, financial interdependence, and mutual support. These relationships so resemble marriages that it may be difficult for the courts to persist in denying marriage rights.†

Questions
1. Do the courts have an obligation to protect the individual's right to select any non–blood relative as a marriage partner?
2. To what extent do you think it is right for gays and lesbians to be able to marry and establish the same foundation for a family unit as non-gays and non-lesbians?
3. With the exception of reproductive possibilities, as noted in the passage above, what are likely to be the differences between gay and lesbian family units and the family units established by non-gays and non-lesbians?

*See W. Wadlington and M. G. Paulsen, eds. *Domestic Relations* (New York: Foundation Press, 1978), p. 38.
†From Laurie P. Arliss, *Contemporary Family Communication: Messages and Meanings* (New York: St. Martin's Press, Inc., 1993), pp. 211–212.

kinds of things that help prevent fragmentation, isolation, stagnation, and lack of protection. Also, when all members are part of important family decisions, members will not feel that it is necessary to get support by creating alliances with other family members.

SUMMARY

Family relationships present unique problems and unique satisfactions in interpersonal communication. The chapter began by providing an overall perspective and basic understandings with three relational definitions. It was noted, too, that how you see your own role in the family may have a great deal to do with your comfort in a family unit. The family provides some unique communication barriers, which require acknowledgment. Rules, restricted freedom, emotional buildups, possessiveness, and double standards are other behaviors that can cause problems. To maintain family relationships requires following a six-stage plan. Also, improving skills in family communication means turning dysfunctions into functions. A successful family life can provide happiness, satisfaction, enthusiasm, and inner peace.

KEY TERMS

traditionals	flexible rules	seeking information
independents	rigid rules	mind-reading strategies
separates	toxic rules	sharing meanings
mutual "picture taking"	restricted freedom	state alternatives
appropriate rules	emotional buildups	select solutions
overt rules	possessiveness	start implementation
covert rules	double standards	survey results

NOTES

1. Sven Wahlroos, *Family Communication: A Guide to Emotional Health* (New York: New American Library, 1974), xi.
2. This summary is based on the work of Douglas L. Kelley and Judee K. Burgoon, "Understanding Marital Satisfaction and Couple Type as Functions of Relational Expectations," *Human Communication Research* (September 1991): 40–69. See especially pages 47–48.
3. See Mary Ann Fitzpatrick, "A Typological Approach to Communication in Relationships," in *Communication Yearbook 1*, ed. Brent Rubin (New Brunswick, NJ: Transaction Press, 1977), 263–275, and Mary Ann Fitzpatrick, "A Typological Approach to Marital Interaction: Recent Theory and Research," in *Advances in Experimental Social Psychology*, vol. 18, ed. L. Berkowitz (New York: Academic Press, 1984), 1–47.

4. Virginia Satir, *Peoplemaking* (Palo Alto, CA: Science and Behavior Books, 1972), 51–56.
5. Wahlroos, xii.
6. I am indebted to William Blevins for the ideas in this section. See William Blevins, *Your Family, Your Self: How to Analyze Your Family System to Understand Yourself, and Achieve More Satisfying Relationships with Your Loved Ones* (Oakland, CA: New Harbinger Publications, 1993), 89–108.
7. Blevins, 90.
8. Blevins, 97.
9. Healthy rules have been discussed by J. A. Kitchens, *Understanding and Treating Codependence* (Englewood Cliffs, NJ: Prentice-Hall, 1991), and J. Bradshaw, *Bradshaw On: The Family* (Deerfield Beach, FL: Health Communications, 1988). They are summarized here by Blevins, 97–98.
10. Anthony Brandt, "Avoiding Couple Karate: Lessons in the Marital Arts," *Psychology Today* 16 (October 1982): 38. Brandt's conclusion is based on the work of John M. Gottman, *Marital Interaction: Experimental Investigations* (Orlando, FL: Academic Press, 1979).
11. Brandt, 41.
12. Brandt, 41–42. Reprinted by permission of the author.
13. John Dewey, *How We Think* (Boston: D.C. Heath & Co., 1910), 36.
14. Barry K. Weinhold, *Breaking Free of Addictive Family Relationships: Healing Your Own Inner Child* (Walpole, NH: Stillpoint Publishing, 1991), 6.

▶ ## FURTHER READING

Laurie P. Arliss, *Contemporary Family Communication: Messages and Meanings* (New York: St. Martin's Press, 1993). Arliss reflects the recent interdisciplinary flavor of family research but emphasizes the fact that family relationships are created, perpetuated, and coped with through communication. In "Appreciating Diversity" she provides a view of the family in our culture. In "Negotiating Realities" she examines communication between family members. In "Living with Expectations" she discusses communication about the family. A well-written, thoroughly researched textbook.

William Blevins, *Your Family, Your Self: How to Analyze Your Family System to Understand Yourself, and Achieve More Satisfying Relationships with Your Loved Ones* (Oakland, CA: New Harbinger Publications, Inc., 1993). This is a how-to book designed to help readers claim their own identity and personal destiny by reconnecting with their ancestral heritage—their family. It is a guide for those who want to discover themselves by exploring their family of origin. It is practical, well-written, and fun.

Carolyn Foster, *The Family Patterns Workbook: Breaking Free from Your Past and Creating a Life of Your Own* (New York: Jeremy P. Tarcher/Perigee Books, 1993). In concrete, practical, and inspirational exercises, Foster shows how writing can reveal the connection between past events and present problems. She offers strategies for assessing your family's dynamics and for making healthy changes in how early patterns play out in your life.

Lynn Lott and Riki Intner, *The Family That Works Together . . . Turning Family Chores from Drudgery to Fun* (Rocklin, CA: Prima Publishing, 1995). Lott and Intner offer a practical guide that leads readers step by step through the process of changing the way the family operates. This method encourages family members to experience a sense of belonging, contribution, and fair play. Basically, this is a delightful book about team effort.

Patricia Noller and Mary Anne Fitzpatrick, *Communication in Family Relationships* (Englewood Cliffs, NJ: Prentice-Hall, 1993). The authors have divided this book into six parts: (1) Centrality of Communication in the Family, (2) Theory and Methods in the Study of the Family, (3) Basic Family Processes, (4) Communication in Family Subsystems, (5) Communication in Different Types of Families, and (6) Seeking Help. A comprehensive, thoroughly-researched, solid textbook.

Virginia Satir, *The New Peoplemaking* (Mountain View, CA: Science and Behavior Books, Inc., 1988). This is a classic book on family life. Satir provides basic ideas for helping families discover the causes of some of their problems and offers creative ways of working through them. This is a clear and comprehensive treatment of family living—a workbook designed to enhance self-awareness, to stimulate partner conversation, and to induce new levels of family communication.

Barry K. Weinhold, *Breaking Free of Addictive Family Relationships* (Walpole, NH: Stillpoint Publishing, 1991). Based on his work as a psychologist and professor of education at the University of Colorado, Weinhold makes readers aware of dysfunctional and addictive attitudes and behavior patterns learned during childhood. Weinhold alerts readers to feelings and behaviors, offers activities that help identify your own, and teaches a new process for healing. A well-written, solid book full of excellent examples and sources for further information.

Credits

Unless otherwise acknowledged, all photographs are the property of Scott, Foresman and Company. Page abbreviations are as follows: (T) top, (C) center, (B) bottom, (L) left, (R) right.

10: Paula M. Lerner/The Picture Cube; **17:** Paul Fortin/Stock Boston; **20:** Joel Gordon Photography; **22:** Tim Barnwell/Stock Boston; **37:** Tim Barnwell/Stock Boston; **44:** Steve Goldberg/Monkmeyer Press Photo Service; **53:** Kopstein/Monkmeyer Press Photo Service; **63:** Michael Siluk/The Image Works; **66B:** Elizabeth Crews/Stock Boston; **79:** Gale Zucker/Stock Boston; **84:** George Bellerose/Stock Boston; **95:** Spencer Grant/Photo Researchers; **102:** Rhoda Sidney/The Image Works; **118:** Joel Gordon Photography; **128:** W. Hill, Jr./The Image Works; **140:** Ann McQueen/Stock Boston; **149:** Robert Brenner/PhotoEdit; **160:** Joel Gordon Photography; **176:** Spencer Grant/Stock Boston; **179:** Mike Mazzaschi/Stock Boston; **188:** Joel Gordon Photography; **198:** Roberta Herschenson/Photo Researchers; **204:** Judy Gelles/Stock Boston; **211:** Jim Whitmer/Stock Boston; **218:** Tim Barnwell/Stock Boston; **231:** Susan Rosenberg/Photo Researchers; **244:** Joel Gordon Photography; **250:** Laima Druskis/Stock Boston; **255:** Steve Goldberg/Monkmeyer Press Photo Service; **256:** Alan Carey/The Image Works; **261:** Zimbel/Monkmeyer Press Photo Service; **271:** Bob Daemmrich/The Image Works; **277:** Spencer Grant/Stock Boston; **287:** Susan Lapides 1990/Design Conceptions; **293:** Paul Fortin/Stock Boston; **299:** Laima Druskis/Stock Boston; **311:** Robert Daniel Ullmann/Design Conceptions; **319:** 1991/Joel Gordon Photography; **331:** Rick Winsor/Woodfin Camp & Associates; **336:** Michael Grezy/Stock Boston; **347:** Bob Daemmrich/The Image Works; **355:** Goodwin/Monkmeyer Press Photo Service; **363:** E. Williamson/The Picture Cube; **374:** Brady/Monkmeyer Press Photo Service; **381:** Farley Andrews/The Picture Cube; **387:** Bob Daemmrich/The Image Works; **395:** Lynn Jaeger Weinstein/Woodfin Camp & Associates; **398:** Bob Kramer/The Picture Cube; **404:** Owen Franken/Stock Boston; **417:** Jean-Claude LeJeune/Stock Boston; **422:** The Picture Cube; **434:** Judy Canty/Stock Boston; **439:** Richard Hutchings; **447:** Alan Carey/The Image Works; **455:** P. Grecco/Stock Boston; **461:** Spencer Grant/Stock Boston; **465:** Joel Gordon Photography; **480:** Bachmann/The Image Works; **484:** Drawing by Korenz; (c)1988 The New Yorker Magazine, Inc.; **485, 491:** Joel Gordon Photography; **499:** H.Gans/The Image Works; **505:** Dean Abramson/Stock Boston; **512:** Joel Gordon Photography; **513:** Jean-Claude LeJeune